Micha

Woodbridge Lane.

Sedchester.

Shaftesbury.

Dorset

MAKERS OF THE
HARPSICHORD AND CLAVICHORD
1440–1840

MAKERS OF THE HARPSICHORD AND CLAVICHORD 1440–1840

DONALD H. BOALCH
M.A., F.S.A.
Fellow of Corpus Christi College, Oxford

SECOND EDITION

OXFORD
AT THE CLARENDON PRESS
1974

Oxford University Press, Ely House, London W. 1

GLASGOW NEW YORK TORONTO MELBOURNE WELLINGTON
CAPE TOWN IBADAN NAIROBI DAR ES SALAAM LUSAKA ADDIS ABABA
DELHI BOMBAY CALCUTTA MADRAS KARACHI LAHORE DACCA
KUALA LUMPUR SINGAPORE HONG KONG TOKYO

ISBN 0 19 816123 9

First edition published by George Ronald, London, 1956

Printed in Great Britain
at the University Press, Oxford
by Vivian Ridler
Printer to the University

MEMORIAE PERVIRENTI

RAIMONDI RUSSELL

INDAGATORIS ASSIDUI

COOPERATORIS LIBERALIS

AMICI FIDELIS

ANNO MCMLXIV MELITAE MORTUI

HAEC EDITIO

DEDICATUR

PREFACE

DURING the seventeen years which have elapsed since the original edition of this book, interest in early musical instruments has increased to a remarkable degree. One result of this is that early harpsichords and clavichords which had lain neglected for decades in attics or barns have been brought out into the light of day once more.

This has rendered a revised and enlarged edition of this book essential, since the first edition, besides being unobtainable new, includes many errors and is blemished by many omissions.

As in that edition, my descriptions of instruments vary widely in their detail, since I have seen only few of them myself and have, therefore, had to rely on published catalogues or letters from informants.

My sources are given in abbreviated form in square brackets, and a key to them is provided in the bibliography at the end of the book. When the number of manuals of an instrument is not specified, the instrument should be presumed to have one manual. 'Surviving instruments' means instruments surviving, or presumed to have survived, into the twentieth century. In descriptions of the compass, the lowest note is given first. The geographical and chronological conspectus indicates the chief centres of instrument-making.

Inscriptions on instruments are reproduced here in italic letters, whatever the style of the original. Plain dates, e.g. 1650–1720, indicate a maker's life-span; dates given after *fl.* mean that a maker is known to have been alive in those years.

As to the numbering of surviving instruments, I have as far as possible, in order to avoid confusion, retained the number used in the first edition, fresh instruments being given numbers such as '7a', '7b', or '01'. In one or two instances, however, such as Longman and Broderip, there was no practical alternative to a complete recasting and renumbering of the list; when this was necessary I have added the first-edition number in a second column.

In the alphabetical arrangement of makers' names, diacritical marks such as the umlaut and the superscript '°' are disregarded. Also, when several members of a family are given, their names are arranged sometimes alphabetically and sometimes chronologically.

The years which have passed since the first edition have seen the publication of many excellent illustrations, both in colour and in half-tone, of early keyboard instruments and of individual parts of them. It is not proposed to add to their number here, but rather to reproduce makers' signatures and roses and the like.

As with the original edition, I am indebted to many correspondents who have given me information, all of whom will, I hope, take this paragraph as an expression of my sincere thanks. Special acknowledgement should, however, be made to the following: Derek Adlam (Goudhurst, Kent); Mme la Comtesse de Chambure (Paris); Hugh Gough (New York); Professor Gustav Leonhardt (Amsterdam); Sibyl Marcuse (Oxford); Charles Mould (Oxford); Alfred Reeve (Maidenhead); Otto Rindlisbacher (Zürich), and Dr. J. H. van der Meer (Nuremberg).

Most particularly I am grateful to Edwin M. Ripin (New York) who has contributed much valuable information and read through the entire work in manuscript.

Any corrections or additions will now, as before, be gratefully welcomed from users of the book.

D. H. BOALCH

Oxford
October 1972

CONTENTS

LIST OF ILLUSTRATIONS

LIST OF ABBREVIATIONS USED TO INDICATE TYPES OF INSTRUMENT

Cc	Clavicytherium (upright harpsichord)
Cd	Clavichord
Co	Claviorganum (combination of harpsichord and organ)
Gpf	Grand pianoforte
H	Harpsichord
Kb	Keyboard
Ot	Ottavino (small virginal, rectangular, 4′ pitch), or polygonal ottavino (small virginal having five or more sides, 4′ pitch)
Pol. V	Pentagonal or polygonal virginal
S	Spinet (wing-shaped or 'leg-of-mutton')
V	Virginal (oblong)

THE CHIEF COLLECTIONS CONTAINING EARLY KEYBOARD INSTRUMENTS, AND THEIR CATALOGUES

Note. When more than one catalogue of a collection has been published, I have usually given only the best. A number of private collections, now dispersed or made over to public collections, have been included. Wherever possible I have given the date of their dispersal. A few temporary exhibitions, and their catalogues, have also been recorded.

ÅBO. Historical Museum (Turun Kaupungin Historiallinen Museo).

ÅBO AKADEMI. Sibeliusmuseum.

AMBRAS COLLECTION.
See: Vienna. Kunsthistorisches Museum.

AMSTERDAM. Rijksmuseum.
The collection of J. C. Boers was added in 1899.
See: *ZIM*, Vol. 1, 1900, p. 30.
The instruments are now (1971) all housed in the Gemeentemuseum at The Hague, except a Ruckers (?) virginal (no. 111).

ANN ARBOR, Michigan. Michigan University.
Albert A. Stanley, *Catalogue of the Stearns collection of musical instruments*, 2nd edition. Ann Arbor, University of Michigan, 1921.

ANTWERP. Musée du Steen.
P. Génard, *Catalogue du Musée d'Antiquités d'Anvers*, 4e édition. Anvers, 1894. In the 1950s this became a maritime museum, and the instruments were transferred to the Vleeshuis.

ANTWERP. Vleeshuis.
Contains instruments from the Musée d'Antiquités which superseded the Musée du Steen, Antwerp. In 1966 the instruments in the Conservatoire were deposited on loan in the Vleeshuis. The relevant catalogues are: Vleeshuis Museum, Antwerp. *Catalogus: V, Muziekinstrumenten* [1956], and *Catalogus: V bis, Muziekinstrumenten* [1967]. (*See also*: J. Lambrechts-Douillez. *Collections of musical instruments in Antwerp*. In: *Hin*. The Rubenshuis and the Plantin Moretus Museum also contain instruments.

ASHMOLEAN MUSEUM.
See under: Oxford.

BARCELONA. Museo de Música (Avenida República Argentina I).

BARROW COLLECTION.
See: Llandudno. William Barrow Collection.

BASEL. Historisches Museum.
Karl Nef, *Historisches Museum, Basel. Katalog no. 4, Musikinstrumente*. Basel, 1906.

BELLE SKINNER COLLECTION.
Now part of the Yale Collection. (*See under*: New Haven, Conn.)

BENTON FLETCHER COLLECTION.
See: London. Benton Fletcher Collection.

BERLINER MUSIKINSTRUMENTEN-SAMMLUNG (Institut für Musikforschung).
Founded 1888 in the Alte Bauakademie, Schinkelplatz; later in the Hochschule für Musik; later in the Palais Kreutz; dispersed during 1939–45 and considerably damaged; reassembled in the Schloß Charlottenburg; now (1971) in the former Joachimsthal Gymnasium in the Bundesallee.

The collection incorporates those of Paul de Wit at Leipzig (1888–91) and the first of César Snoeck at Ghent (1905). Catalogues: Curt Sachs, *Sammlung alter Musikinstrumente bei der Staatlichen Hochschule für Musik zu Berlin. Beschreibender Katalog* (Berlin, Julius Bard, 1922), which superseded Oskar Fleischer's *Führer durch die Sammlung der Königlichen Hochschule für Musik in Berlin* (Berlin, 1882), and was succeeded by *Führer durch das Musikinstrumenten-Museum, Abt. III des Staatl. Instituts für Deutsche Musikforschung* (1939), and by Alfred Berner, *Die Berliner Musikinstrumenten-Sammlung: Einführung mit historischen und technischen Erläuterungen* (Berlin, 1952). In 1965 was published Irmgard Otto's *Musikinstrumenten-Museum Berlin: Ausstellungsverzeichnis mit Personen- und Sachregistern*.

This collection is referred to simply as 'Berlin Collection' in my text.

BODDINGTON COLLECTION.
See: Manchester. Boddington Collection.

BOERS COLLECTION.
See: Amsterdam. Rijksmuseum.

BOLOGNA. Liceo Musicale [*now* Conservatorio Musicale 'G. B. Martini'].
Raccolta di antichi strumenti armonici . . . Bologna, 1880. (The collection was transferred from the Liceo to the Museo Civico.)

BOLOGNA. Museo Civico.

BOOMKAMP COLLECTION.
See under: Bussum.

BOSTON, Mass. Museum of Fine Arts.
Nicholas Bessaraboff, *Ancient European musical instruments: an organological study of the musical instruments in the Leslie Lindsay Mason Collection at the Museum of Fine Arts* . . . Boston, Harvard University Press, 1941. Reissued, 1964.—Contains the greater part of the

BOSTON, Mass. Museum of Fine Arts (*cont.*):
Galpin Collection formerly at Hatfield Broad Oak, Essex; see also an article with illustrations in *Museum of Fine Arts Bulletin*, Boston, Mass., 1917.

BOUSQUET COLLECTION.
See: Paris. De Bousquet Collection.

BRESLAU. Schlesisches Museum für Kunstgewerbe und Altertümer.
Peter Epstein and Ernst Scheyer, *Führer und Katalog zur Sammlung alter Musikinstrumente*. Breslau, Verlag des Museums, 1932.

BRICQUEVILLE COLLECTION.
See: Versailles. Bricqueville Collection.

BROADWOOD COLLECTION.
See: London. Broadwood Collection.

BROWNSEA ISLAND, Dorset. Van Raalte Collection.
Dispersed in 1927. Part was sold by auction; the remainder is now the collection of Lord Howard de Walden, Dean Castle, Kilmarnock.

BRUGES. Hôtel de Gruuthuuse.

BRUNSWICK. Städtisches Museum.
Hans Schröder, *Verzeichnis der Sammlung alter Musikinstrumente* . . . Braunschweig, Appelhans, 1928.

BRUSSELS. Conservatoire Royal de Musique.
Victor Mahillon, *Catalogue descriptif et analytique du Musée Instrumentale* . . . 2ᵉ édition. Gand, 1893–1922. 4 v.—Incorporates some of the collection A. Tolbecque, Paris, and most of that of Correr in Venice.

BUDAPEST. National Museum of Hungary.
György Gábry, *Old Musical instruments*. Budapest, Corvina Press, 1969.—A selection of instruments in the Museum described and illustrated. Contains 1 virginal, 2 harpsichords, and 2 clavichords, all unsigned.

BUSSUM, near Amsterdam. C. v. L. Boomkamp Collection of Musical Instruments.
C. v. L. Boomkamp and J. H. van der Meer, The Carel van Leeuwen Boomkamp Collection of musical instruments. *Descriptive catalogue*. Amsterdam, Frits Knuf, 1971.
This collection does not yet contain any early stringed keyboard instruments.

CHICAGO. George F. Harding Collection.

CHRISTIANIA.
See: Oslo.

CLAUDIUS COLLECTION.
See: Copenhagen. Carl Claudius Collection.

COLOGNE. Heyer Collection.
See: Leipzig. Heyer Collection.

COLT CLAVIER COLLECTION, Bethersden, Kent.
The Colt Clavier Collection, Silver Jubilee 1944–1969: *List*. Bethersden, 1969 (contains four early harpsichords).

COOPER UNION.
See under: New York.

COPENHAGEN. Carl Claudius Collection.
Carl Claudius, *Carl Claudius' Samling af gamle Musikinstrumenter*. København, Levin & Munksgaard, 1931.

COPENHAGEN. Musikhistorisk Museum.
Angul Hammerich, *Beskrivende illustreret katalog . . . København*, Hos Nielsen & Lydiche, 1909. (German edition: *Beschreibender Katalog* . . . Kopenhagen, 1911.—*Supplement zum Katalog* . . . Kopenhagen, 1960 [reproduction of typescript].)

CORRER COLLECTION.
See: Venice. Correr Collection.

CROSBY BROWN COLLECTION.
See: New York. Metropolitan Museum of Art. Crosby Brown Collection.

DEAN CASTLE COLLECTION, Kilmarnock.
See under: Howard de Walden.

DE BOUSQUET COLLECTION.
See: Paris. De Bousquet Collection.

DONALDSON COLLECTION.
See: London. Royal College of Music. Donaldson Collection.

DUBLIN. National Museum.
Many of the keyboard instruments in this collection receive mention in W. H. Grattan-Flood, 'Dublin harpsichord and pianoforte makers' (In: *Journal of the Royal Society of Antiquaries of Ireland*, Vol. 39, Dublin, 1909, pp. 137–45).

DUNDEE. Museum. W. A. Simpson Collection.

EDINBURGH UNIVERSITY. The Russell Collection of Early Keyboard Instruments.
Sidney Newman and Peter Williams, *The Russell Collection and other early keyboard instruments in Saint Cecilia's Hall, Edinburgh*. Edinburgh University Press, 1968. (This collection contains the whole of Raymond Russell's private collection, except for four instruments which were retained by his mother, Mrs. Maud Russell: (1) Kirkman harpsichord no. 4; (2) Kirkman harpsichord no. 49; (3) Taskin harpsichord no. 01; (4) Hass clavichord no. 19, and a small number of others.)

EISENACH. Bachmuseum.
Curt Sachs, *Verzeichnis* . . ., Leipzig, 1918. (Neue Bachgesellschaft, Jhg. 19, Heft I.) No harpsichords or clavichords have been added since this collection was compiled, which is therefore as useful for the present purpose as: Friedrich Breidert and Conrad Freyse, *Verzeichnis der Sammlung alter Musikinstrumente im Bachhaus zu Eisenach, herausgegeben von der Neuen Bachgesellschaft*. Leipzig, Breitkopf und Härtel, 1939; 4th edition, 1964.

ERLANGEN. Rück Collection.
See under: Nuremberg. Germanisches Nationalmuseum.

FIALA–AHLGRIMM COLLECTION.
See: Vienna. Sammlung Fiala–Ahlgrimm.

FLORENCE. Conservatorio di Musica 'Luigi Cherubini'.
L. Bargagna, *Gli strumenti musicali raccolti nel Museo del R. Istituto 'L. Cherubini' a Firenze*. Firenze, 1911.

Vinicio Gai, *Gli strumenti musicali della corte Medicea e il Museo del Conservatorio 'Luigi Cherubini' di Firenze*. Firenze, Licosa, 1969.

FLORENCE. Kraus Collection.
Alexander Kraus, the Younger, *Catalogo della collezione etnografico-musicale Kraus in Firenze. Sezione strumenti musicali.* Firenze, Tipografia di Salvadore Landi, 1901.—This collection was absorbed by the Heyer Collection (then at Cologne, now at Leipzig) in 1908.

FORSYTH COLLECTION.
See under: Manchester.

FRANKFURT AM MAIN. Historisches Museum.
Peter Epstein, *Katalog der Musikinstrumente im Historischen Museum der Stadt Frankfurt am Main.* Frankfurt, 1927.

FRANZ FERDINAND COLLECTION.
See: Vienna. Sammlung des Erzherzogs Franz Ferdinand von Österreich-Este.

FRISMUTH COLLECTION.
See: Philadelphia. University of Pennsylvania. Frismuth Collection.

GALLINI COLLECTION.
See under: Milan.

GALPIN COLLECTION.
The greater part of this collection, originally assembled by Canon F. W. Galpin at Hatfield Broad Oak, Essex, was sold to the Boston Museum of Fine Arts, Mass., during the First World War; most of the remaining instruments were sold by auction in London, 1946.

William Lynd, *Ancient musical instruments . . . as illustrated by typical examples in the Galpin Collection* . . . London, 1897; most of the instruments are also illustrated in F. W. Galpin, *Old English instruments of music*, 3rd edition. London, Methuen, 1932. *See also above*: Boston, Mass., Museum of Fine Arts.

GERMANISCHES NATIONALMUSEUM.
See under: Nuremberg.

GHENT
Two collections were formed at Ghent by C. C. Snoeck:
(1) C. C. Snoeck, *Catalogue de la collection d'instruments de musique anciens ou curieux formée par C. C. Snoeck.* Gand, Vuylsteke, 1894. Incorporated in the Berlin Collection in 1902.

(2) C. C. Snoeck, *Catalogue de la collection d'instruments de musique flamands et néerlandais de C. C. Snoeck.* Gand, 1903. Bought by the Belgian Government in 1909 and added to the Brussels Conservatoire Collection.

A number of Snoeck instruments also went to St. Petersburg. Among these there was only one keyboard instrument, an Italian spinet.

GORGA COLLECTION.
See: Rome. Museo Strumenti Musicali.

GOTHENBURG. Museum.
Otto Thulin, *Historiska Avdelningen, Göteborgs Museum. Musikinstrument* [Gothenburg, Elanders Boktryckeri, 1931].

HAGUE. Gemeente-Museum.
The nucleus of the instrument-collection consists of the Scheurleer Collection, assembled between 1885 and 1927. Nearly as many instruments again have been added since. A complete catalogue is being prepared under the editorship of Dr. Clemens von Gleich, of which Vol. II will cover keyboard instruments (Publisher: Frits Knuf, Amsterdam).

Dirk Balfoort, *Gemeente-Museum's-Gravenhage. II De Muziekhistorische Afdeeling* (*verz. D. F. Scheurleer*) . . . [The Hague], 1935.

HALLE. Händel-Haus.
Konrad Sasse, *Katalog zu der Sammlungen des Händel-Hauses in Halle: 5. Teil, Musikinstrumentensammlung, Besaitete Tasteninstrumente.* Halle an der Saale, 1966.

HAMBURG. Museum für Hamburgische Geschichte.
Hans Schröder, *Verzeichnis der Sammlung alter Musikinstrumente* . . . Hamburg, 1930.

HAMBURG. Museum für Kunst und Gewerbe.

HAMMER COLLECTION.
See: Stockholm. Museum Christian Hammer.

HARDING COLLECTION.
See: Chicago. George F. Harding Collection.

HATFIELD BROAD OAK, ESSEX.
See: Galpin Collection.

HOLYOKE, Mass. Belle Skinner Collection.
William Skinner, *The Belle Skinner Collection of musical instruments. Catalog* . . . Holyoke [Philadelphia printed], 1933.

Later incorporated in the Yale Collection (*see under*: New Haven, Conn.).

HORNIMAN MUSEUM.
See: London. Horniman Museum.

HOWARD DE WALDEN COLLECTION.
The collection of Lord Howard de Walden at Dean Castle, Kilmarnock, Ayrshire, which formed at one time part of the van Raalte Collection, Brownsea Island, Dorset, and was dispersed in 1927; it contained no signed instruments.

HUNGARIAN NATIONAL MUSEUM.
See under: Budapest.

KRAUS COLLECTION.
See: Florence. Kraus Collection.

LEIPZIG. Heyer Collection.
Georg Kinsky, *Musikhistorisches Museum von Wilhelm Heyer . . . Katalog: Erster Band: Besaitete Tasteninstrumente* . . . Cöln, Wilhelm Heyer (Kommissions-Verlag von Breitkopf & Härtel in Leipzig), 1910.

The collection was presented to Leipzig by H. Hinrichsen in 1926. It was originally housed in the Musikhistorisches Museum Wilhelm Heyer, Cologne, but became in 1927 part of the Musikinstrumenten-Sammlung of Leipzig University noted below.

LEIPZIG. Sammlung Paul de Wit.
Paul de Wit, *Perlen aus der Instrumentensammlung Paul de Wit.* Leipzig, 1892.

This collection was absorbed in 1905 into the Heyer Collection, then at Cologne. The Berlin Collection had bought, in 1888 and 1891, two collections made by de Wit. Some of the de Wit instruments have disappeared altogether (see for instance Loth (Johann) below, p. 107).

LEIPZIG. Universität. Musikwissenschaftliches Institut. Musikinstrumenten-Sammlung.

Contains the Heyer Collection (see above).

Paul Rubardt, *Führer durch das Musikinstrumentenmuseum der Karl-Marx Universität Leipzig*. Leipzig, 1964.

LENINGRAD. Institute for Scientific Research on the Theatre and Music.

(Gosudarstvennyĭ Nauchno-Issledovatel'skii Institut Teatra i Muzyki.) The collection of instruments at the Hermitage (see *Ginz*) has been moved to this Institute. There is no collection at the Leningrad Conservatoire.

LÉRY COLLECTION.

See: Paris. Léry Collection.

LINZ. Museum Francisco-Carolinum.

Führer durch das Museum . . . Herausgegeben von der Museums-Verwaltung. 3. Auflage. Linz, 1910.

LINZ. Oberösterreichisches Landesmuseum. Musikinstrumentensammlung.

Othmar Wessely, *Die Musikinstrumentensammlung d. Oberöst. Landesmus.* Linz [1952].

LISBON. Conservatorio Nacional.

Michel'Angelo Lambertini, *Primeiro núcleo de um museu instrumental em Lisboa: catálogo sumário*, Lisboa, 1914, records some of the instruments in the collection, which has, however, grown considerably since that date.

A general account of the Museu Instrumental, with illustrations of three of the keyboard Instruments, is in: *Boletim do Conservatório Nacional*. Vol. I, no. 1, [Lisbon], 1946/7.

LIVERPOOL. Rushworth & Dreaper Collection.

Rushworth & Dreaper Ltd., *The Rushworth & Dreaper collection of antique musical instruments and historical manuscripts*. Liverpool, [*c.* 1925].

LLANDUDNO, North Wales. William Barrow Collection.

Most of the instruments are listed in: William Barrow, *Instruments of the masters* (In: *The Listener*, London, 12 January 1939, p. 100).

LONDON. Benton Fletcher Collection.

Benton Fletcher, *Early music at Devonshire House* (In: *The Listener*, London, 1938, pp. 713–14) gives an illustrated description.

Its pre-war home, Devonshire House, Bloomsbury, was destroyed in an air raid in 1940, but the most important instruments had been sent to safety. They are now reassembled at Fenton House, Hampstead.

Raymond Russell, *Catalogue of the Benton Fletcher collection of early keyboard instruments at Fenton House, Hampstead*. London, Country Life Ltd., for the National Trust, 1957.

LONDON. Broadwood Collection.

John Broadwood & Sons, *Collection of antique instruments at John Broadwood & Sons, Ltd.*, [then in] *Conduit Street, Bond Street, London*. London, [1903].— Now in Hanover Street.

LONDON. Captain J. Lane's Collection, Wanstead, Essex, near London.

Dispersed after World War II.

LONDON. Horniman Museum.

Jean Jenkins, *Musical instruments . . . Horniman Museum*. London, 1958 (2nd edition. London, 1970).

LONDON. Music Loan Exhibition, Fishmongers' Hall, 1904.

[Illustrated catalogue.] London, Novello, 1909.

LONDON. Raymond Russell Collection.

After Russell's death in 1964 most of his instruments went to Edinburgh University (q.v.).

LONDON. Royal College of Music Collection (including the Donaldson and Hipkins collections).

Sir George Donaldson, *Catalogue of the musical instruments and objects forming the Donaldson Museum . . . the Royal College of Music* [London, 1899].—Not reliable.

LONDON. Victoria and Albert Museum.

Carl Engel, *A descriptive catalogue of the musical instruments in the South Kensington Museum*. 2nd edition. London, Chapman & Hall, 1874.

Raymond Russell, *Catalogue of musical instruments* (*Victoria and Albert Museum*): Vol. I: *Keyboard instruments*. London, Her Majesty's Stationery Office, 1968.

Many of the instruments in this collection are illustrated and described in Philip James, *Early keyboard instruments*, London, Peter Davies, 1930; and the Museum issued a *Picture book of keyboard musical instruments*, London, 1929, which was superseded in 1959 by *Early keyboard instruments*, by Raymond Russell (Small picture book no. 48).

LOUP COLLECTION.

See: Paris. Loup Collection.

LUCERNE. Schumacher Collection.

Heinrich Schumacher, *Katalog zu der Ausstellung von Muzikinstrumenten früherer Zeiten*. Luzern, 1888.— *See also*: Franz August Göhlinger. *Geschichte des Klavichords*. Basel, Birkhäuser, 1910, p. 68. This collection was offered for sale in 1909, but apparently was finally dispersed in 1923.

MANCHESTER. Boddington Collection.

J. Kendrick Pyne, *Catalogue of musical instruments principally illustrative of the history of the piano-forte, the property of Henry Boddington* [formerly of J. K. Pyne]. Manchester, 1888. J. K. Pyne (1852–1938) was city organist at Manchester. H. Boddington lived at Pownall Hall, Wilmslow, Ches. The collection was dispersed about 1900.

MANCHESTER. Forsyth Collection.

(Messrs. Forsyth Bros., Ltd., 126/8 Deansgate, Manchester.)

MANCHESTER. Henry Watson Collection.

Henry Watson, *The Royal Manchester College of Music. Catalogue of the Henry Watson collection of musical instruments*. Manchester, 1906.

Divided between the Central Library, Manchester, and the R. Manchester College of Music; some instruments were destroyed in World War II.

MEYER COLLECTION.

See: Paris. André Meyer Collection.

MICHIGAN UNIVERSITY.

See: Ann Arbor, Michigan.

MILAN. Conservatorio di Musica.
Eugenio de' Guarinoni, *Gli strumenti musicali nel museo del Conservatorio* . . . Milano, [1908].

MILAN. Museo Civico, Gallini Collection.
Natale Gallini, *Mostra di antichi strumenti musicali della collezione N. Gallini.* Milano, 1953. Pp. 43; 32 plates. 190 instruments in all, 10 of them keyboard instruments.

Natale Gallini, *Civico Museo di Antichi Strumenti Musicali: catalogo descrittivo.* Milano, Comune di Milano, 1958. Pp. 128; 77 plates.

Natale and Franco Gallini. *Museo degli Strumenti Musicali (Comune di Milano): Catalogo.* [Milan], Castello Sforzesco, 1963.

MODENA. Museo Civico.
A short description of the collection of instruments appeared in Luigi Francesco Valdrighi, *Nomocheliurgografia* . . . Modena, Società Tipografica, 1884. *See also* the catalogue of the Italian section of the Vienna Exhibition, 1892 (*Internationale Ausstellung für Musik- und Theaterwesen, Wien, 1892. Fach-Katalog der Musik-historischen Abtheilung des Königreiches Italien.* Wien, 1892, pp. 293–4).

MUNICH. Bayerisches Nationalmuseum.
K. A. Bierdimpfl, *Die Sammlung der Musikinstrumente des Bayerischen Nationalmuseums.* München, 1883. This collection was severely damaged during World War II.

MUNICH. Deutsches Museum von Meisterwerken der Naturwissenschaft und Technik.
Führer durch die Sammlungen. Leipzig, [1907].

NAPLES. Conservatorio di Musica 'S. Pietro a Majella', Museo Storico Musicale.
Ettore Santagata, *Il Museo Storico Musicale di 'S. Pietro a Majella'*, Napoli, Francesco Giannini & Figli, 1930.

NEUPERT COLLECTION.
See under: Nuremberg. Germanisches Nationalmuseum.

NEW HAVEN, Conn. Yale University. Collection of Musical Instruments.
Morris Steinert presented part of his collection to Yale University in 1900. (*See below*: Steinert Collection.) The Albert Steinert Collection is now (1972) also on long-term loan to the Yale Collection. The Belle Skinner Collection was incorporated in that of Yale about 1960; its catalogue is noted above under Holyoke, Mass.

Sibyl Marcuse, *Check-list of Western instruments.* (*Yale Univ. School of Music.*) *Part I: Keyboard instruments.* New Haven, 1958. (This includes some Cooper Union instruments which were later (1960) given to the Smithsonian Institution.)

An exhibition of selected instruments in the Yale Collection was held in the University Art Gallery, February–March 1960. Catalogue by Sibyl Marcuse: *Musical Instruments at Yale*, 1960.

Richard Rephann, *Checklist, Yale Collection of musical instruments.* New Haven, 1968.

NEW YORK. Cooper Union.
The instruments were on loan to the Yale Collection in 1957. In 1960 they were given to the Smithsonian Institution, Washington.

NEW YORK. Metropolitan Museum of Art.
The Crosby Brown Collection of musical instruments . . . Catalog of keyboard instruments. (*Metropolitan Museum of Art Handbook no. 13.*) New York, Metropolitan Museum of Art, 1903.

Emanuel Winternitz, *Keyboard instruments in the Metropolitan Museum of Art: a picture book.* New York, M.M.A., 1961.

NEW YORK. Morris Steinert Collection.
See: Steinert Collection.

NUREMBERG. Germanisches Nationalmuseum. Damaged during World War II. Later incorporated the Neupert (1968) and the Rück (1962) collections.

NUREMBERG. Neupert Collection.
Führer durch das Musikhistorische Museum Neupert in Nürnberg. J. C. Neupert, 1938.

Its Nuremberg home having been destroyed in World War II, this collection was temporarily housed at Bamberg. In 1968 it was acquired by the Germanisches Nationalmuseum, Nuremberg.

A number of the instruments are illustrated, not only in the guide noted above, but also in: Hanns Neupert, *Das Cembalo.* 2. Aufl. Kassel, Bärenreiter-Verlag, 1951; Hanns Neupert, *Vom Musikstab zum modernen Klavier.* 3. Aufl. Berlin, Krause, 1952; and in *Katalog der internationalen Ausstellung 'Musik im Leben der Völker'*, von Kathi Meyer. Frankfurt/Main, 1927.

A check-list of the Collection, by J. H. van der Meer, was issued in the *Anzeiger des Germanischen Nationalmuseums*, 1969 (?), pp. 255–66.

NUREMBERG. Rück Collection.
At one time partly housed in the University of Erlangen. A number of the instruments are described in Tobias Norlind, *Systematik der Saiteninstrumente* (*Musikhistorisches Museum, Stockholm*). 2. *Geschichte des Klaviers.* Hannover, Albert Küster, 1939. The Rück Collection was later incorporated in the Germanisches Nationalmuseum, Nuremberg.

NYDAHL COLLECTION.
See under: Stockholm.

OSLO. Musik-Konservatoriet.
Kristiania, 1904.

OSLO. Norsk Folkemuseum, Bygdøy.
Harry Fett, *Norsk Folkemuseum, Særudstilling nr. 2. Musikinstrumenter.*

OXFORD. Ashmolean Museum.
Thurston Dart, 'The instruments in the Ashmolean Museum'. (In: *GSJ*, Vol. 7, 1954.)

David D. Boyden, *Catalogue of the Hill Collection of musical instruments in the Ashmolean Museum, Oxford.* London, Oxford University Press, 1969.

OXFORD. Taphouse Collection.
On loan to the Music School of Oxford University, this collection now consists of three instruments, the greater part of it having been sold at Sotheby's on 7 June 1905.

PARIS. André Meyer Collection. 148 Bd. Malesherbes, 8ᵉ.
See: *Hin*, plates 31–4.

PARIS. Conservatoire de Musique.
Gustave Chouquet, *Catalogue descriptif et raisonné* . . . Nouvelle édition. Paris, Didot, 1884; also: Léon Pillaut, *Ier supplément au catalogue de 1884*. Paris, 1894; *2e supplément*. Paris, 1899; *3e supplément*. Paris, 1903.

PARIS. De Bousquet Collection.
This collection, formed by Mme de Bousquet, was for the most part dispersed at her death in 1955, a few instruments, including the Ruckers harpsichord no. 21, being retained by her great-grandson M. Maurice le Roux.

PARIS. Léry Collection.
Catalogue des anciens instruments de musique . . . composant l'ancienne collection de M. le Baron de Léry. Paris, 1910. [Sale catalogue.]
The collection, which contained 491 items, was sold by auction in Paris in 1910.

PARIS. Loup Collection.
Collection d'instruments de musique. Paris, 1888. Its 296 instruments were sold by auction in Paris in 1888.

PARIS. Savoye Collection I.
Catalogue des instruments de musique . . . des XVe, XVIe, XVIIe et XVIIIe siècles. Paris, 1882. This, the 'Old Savoye Collection', containing 214 instruments, was sold by auction on 15 May 1882.

PARIS. Savoye Collection II.
René Savoye, 'Catalogue des instruments de musique de la collection Savoye. Liste numérique et désignation des instruments'. MS., [1910]. A copy of this unpublished catalogue, which contains 756 items, was in the Heyer Collection, Leipzig.

PARIS. Savoye Collection III.
Léon Savoye, *Catalogue des anciens instruments de musique*. Clavecins et orgues . . . [Sale catalogue, Hôtel Drouot, Paris, 13 June 1924.]

PARIS. Tolbecque Collection.
The collection of A. Tolbecque, eventually added to the Brussels Conservatoire.

PHILADELPHIA. Pennsylvania University Museum.
The Frismuth Collection of Musical Instruments.

POZNAŃ. Muzeum Wielkopolskie.

PRAGUE. National Museum.
Führer durch die Sammlungen des Museums des Königreiches Böhmen, in Prag. Prag, 1897.

PROVIDENCE, R.I. Rhode Island School of Design.
Albert Steinert Collection (a portion of the collection of Morris Steinert. *See below*: Steinert Collection). On long-term loan to the Yale University Collection.

RENAIX. Régibo Collection.
Abel Régibo, *Catalogue d'une . . . bibliothèque musicale et d'une collection d'antiquités*. Renaix, 1897. Pp. 89–95 deal with the instruments, which numbered 117.
The collection, which contained a number of harpsichords and virginals by the Ruckers and other Flemish makers, was sold by auction in September 1897.

RINGVE MUSEUM.
See: Trondheim. Ringve Museum.

ROME. Gorga Collection.
Mostly now in the Museo Strumenti Musicali, Rome, though inaccessible for some years.

ROME. Museo Strumenti Musicali.
Piazza S. Croce in Gerusalemme, 9a. Now contains most of the instruments formerly in the collection of Commendatore Evan Gorga. A catalogue is in preparation (1971).

ROTHSCHILD COLLECTION.
See: Vienna. Sammlung des Baron Nathaniel von Rothschild.

RÜCK COLLECTION.
See: Nuremberg. Germanisches Nationalmuseum, in which it was incorporated.

RUSHWORTH & DREAPER COLLECTION.
See under: Liverpool.

RUSSELL COLLECTION.
See under: Edinburgh.

SABATHIL COLLECTION.
See under: Vancouver.

SALZBURG. Museum Carolino-Augusteum.
Karl Geiringer, *Alte Musikinstrumente . . . Führer und beschreibendes Verzeichnis* . . . Leipzig, Breitkopf und Härtel, 1932.
John H. van der Meer, *Die Kielklaviere im Salzburger Museum Carolino-Augusteum*. (In: *Jahresschrift. Salzburger Museum Carolino-Augusteum*, Vol. 12/13, 1966/7, pp. 84–96.)

SAVOYE COLLECTION.
See: Paris. Savoye Collection.

SCHUMACHER COLLECTION.
See LUCERNE. Schumacher Collection.

SIBELIUSMUSEUM, Åbo.
See under: Åbo Akademi.

SMITHSONIAN INSTITUTION.
See: Washington. Smithsonian Institution.

SNOECK COLLECTION.
See: Ghent. Snoeck Collection.

STEARNS COLLECTION.
See under: Ann Arbor, Michigan University.

STEINERT COLLECTION.
Morris Steinert printed a catalogue of his New York collection of harpsichords and clavichords, entitled: *The Morris Steinert Collection of keyed and stringed instruments* (New York, C. F. Tretbar, 1893). The collection was shewn at the World's Fair in Chicago, 1893, and a part of it presented to Yale University (*see* New Haven). Steinert's sons were bequeathed the remainder, of which a number are in the Albert Steinert collection in the Rhode Island School of Design, Providence (q.v.), while others were sold, four of these being bought by the Belle Skinner Collection which is now at Yale.
The various Steinert catalogues are described in Sibyl Marcuse's *Check-list* . . . (*see above* under New Haven). The chief are: (1) Morris Steinert. *The Morris Steinert collection of keyed and stringed instruments* . . . New York, Charles F. Tretbar, 1893; and (2) Theodore

Booth Willson. *Historical catalogue of the Morris Steinert collection of musical instruments.* New Haven, Yale University, 1913.

STOCKHOLM. Museum Christian Hammer.
Katalog der . . . Kunst-Sammlung des Museums Christian-Hammer . . . Serie II . . . Die Sammlung der Musikinstrumente. Köln, 1893.
The Collection, which contained 210 items, was sold by auction at Cologne in 1893.

STOCKHOLM. Musikhistoriska Museet.
Johannes Svanberg, *Musikhistoriska Museets i Stockholm — Instrumentsamling. År 1902.* Stockholm, 1902.
Tobias Norlind, *Systematik der Saiteninstrumente . . . 2. Geschichte des Klaviers.* Hannover, Albert Küster, 1939, is almost a catalogue of the keyboard section of this collection.

STOCKHOLM. Nordiska Museet.

STOCKHOLM. Nydahl Collection.
Private collection of Captain Nydahl. No catalogue.

STUTTGART. Württembergisches Landesgewerbemuseum.
Hanns H. Josten, *Die Sammlung der Musikinstrumente* . . . Stuttgart, 1928.

TAPHOUSE COLLECTION.
See: Oxford. Taphouse Collection.

TOLBECQUE COLLECTION.
See: Brussels. Conservatoire Royal de Musique.

TORONTO. Royal Ontario Museum.
(A catalogue of early keyboard instruments has been announced as imminent.)

TRONDHEIM. Ringve Museum.

TURKU.
See: Åbo.

VANCOUVER. Sabathil Collection.
This collection has been dispersed.

VAN RAALTE COLLECTION.
See: Brownsea Island.

VENICE. Correr Collection.
Elenco degli strumenti musicali antichi da arco, fiato, pizzico e tasto, posseduti dal Nob. Conte Pietro Correr . . . [Venice, 1872]. Also, a catalogue by Fürstenau was published in *Monatshefte für Musikwissenschaft*, Vol. 6, 1874, pp. 105–7.
The greater part of this collection, which contained 121 instruments of the sixteenth and seventeenth centuries, was acquired by the Brussels Conservatoire; a few instruments passed into the Museo Civico at Venice.

VERSAILLES. Bricqueville Collection.
Eugène de Bricqueville. *Catalogue sommaire de la collection d'instruments de musique anciens* . . . Versailles, Cerf, 1893.
I have not been able to discover when this collection was dispersed.

VIENNA. Gesellschaft der Musikfreunde.
Gebäude und Kunstsammlungen der Gesellschaft der Musikfreunde in Wien und ihres Conservatoriums. Wien, 1872. Pp. 12–20: 'Musikalische Instrumente'. A descriptive article by E. Mandiczewski appeared in the *Jubiläums-Festschrift* of the Society (*Geschichte der K. K. Gesellschaft der Musikfreunde, Zusatzband.* Wien, 1912).
The early instruments are now in the Kunsthistorisches Museum, Vienna.

VIENNA. Kunsthistorisches Museum.
Julius Schlosser, *Die Sammlung alter Musikinstrumente. Beschreibendes Verzeichnis.* Wien, Kunstverlag Anton Schroll, 1920.
Victor Luithlen. *Katalog der Sammlung alter Musikinstrumente. I. Teil: Saitenklaviere.* Wien, Kunsthistorisches Museum, 1966.
Contains the famous Ambras Collection, also some instruments bought from E. Fiala.

VIENNA. Sammlung des Baron Nathaniel von Rothschild.
A list of its 117 instruments appears in: *Internationale Ausstellung für Musik- und Theaterwesen, Wien, 1892. Fach-Katalog der Musikhistorischen Abtheilung von Deutschland und Österreich-Ungarn.* Wien, 1892, pp. 181–8.
I have not been able to discover when this collection was dispersed.

VIENNA. Sammlung des Erzherzogs Franz Ferdinand von Österreich-Este.
A catalogue appears in the *Fach-Katalog* mentioned in the previous entry, pp. 83–8. The greater part, if not all, of this collection reached the Kunsthistorisches Museum, Vienna.

VIENNA. Sammlung Fiala–Ahlgrimm.
Some of the instruments are described and illustrated in *HaasBM*.

WASHINGTON. Smithsonian Institution, U.S. National Museum.
Frances Densmore, *Handbook of the collection of musical instruments in the United States National Museum* (Smithsonian Institution Bulletin 136). Washington, U.S. Government Printing Office, 1927.
Check-list of keyboard instruments at the Smithsonian Institution. Prepared by the Division of Musical Instruments. Washington, 1967. (Includes the extensive Worch keyboard collection, which was not recorded in Densmore, and the former Cooper Union instruments, which were given in 1960.)
Cynthia A. Hoover, *Harpsichords and clavichords.* [Illustrations of selected instruments in the Smithsonian Institution.] Washington, Smithsonian Institution Press, 1969.

WATSON COLLECTION.
See: Manchester. Henry Watson Collection.

WIT COLLECTION.
See: Leipzig. Sammlung Paul de Wit.

WORCH COLLECTION.
Now in the Smithsonian Institution, Washington.

WÜRTTEMBERGISCHES LANDESGEWERBEMUSEUM.
See under: Stuttgart.

YALE UNIVERSITY
See under: New Haven, Conn.

THE MAKERS

THE MAKERS

A, C. *See*: ASTON, Cawton.

A, D. *See*: D, A.

A, F. Messrs. Hubbard & Dowd, of Boston, Mass., had (1950) a harpsichord bearing upon the top and bottom keys the inscription: *FA 1677*. The instrument is Italian in style, of cypress in a red painted case. Compass C/E–C, 4 octaves with short octave; 2×8′ stops in movable slides.

A, I. A clavichord in the Kunsthistorisches Museum, Vienna, bears the initials *IA* on the nameboard. These refer presumably not to the maker but to a previous owner Ignaz Assmayer (1790–1862), Hofkapellmeister, who was a friend of Schubert's. It had belonged earlier to two other Hofkapellmeister: Josef Eybler (1765–1846) and Adalbert Gyrowetz (1763–1850). Presented by the violin maker Gabriel Lemböck in 1873. (Ges. d. Musikfreunde nr. 4.) [*Luith*, p. 8.]

A, T. The lowest key on an anonymous spinet which belonged to Raymond Russell bears the initials *T.A.*

ADAM, Abel, of Turin. Maker of virginals and harpsichords. Dates ascertained, 1657–1714.

Surviving Instruments

(1) 1657. Ottavino. Yale University. Inscribed: *Abel Adam MDCLVII*. Compass C/E–C. Boxwood naturals; painted case. (Previous owners: 1949, E. M. W. Paul, London; 1952, Mrs. A. Dana, Princeton; 1954, Mrs. Gregory Smith, Washington, who presented it to Yale.) Restored by Alari.

(2) 1663. Spinet (Ottavino?). Recorded by *Va*.

(3) 1693. Ottavino. Berlin Collection (formerly in the Snoeck Collection). Inscribed: *Abel Adam fecit Tavrini 1693*. Compass C/E–C; rose; 79×47 cm.

(4) 1712. Ottavino. Leipzig, Heyer Collection. Inscribed: *Abel Adam fecit Tavrini* 1712. Compass G/C–C, 4½ octaves; 93×57 cm. Instrument and inscription illustrated in *Ks*.

(5) 1714. Small harpsichord. Old Savoye Collection (sold by auction, 1882).

ADAM, Alexander. A Scottish virginal maker, *fl.* 1659 [*GD* (1928), s.v. *Virginal*].

ADLUNG, Jakob. Organist and maker of clavichords; 1699–1762. Born at Bindersleben near Erfurt on 14 January 1699, son of David Adlung, who was school attendant (*Schuldiener*) and organist there, his mother being Dorothea Elisabetha, *née* Meuerin, of Tondorf.

In 1711 he went to the Andreasschule in Erfurt as a choral pupil; he also played the violin and had lessons on the clavichord and the kettledrum. He went to Jena in 1723, when Johann Nikolaus Bach (q.v.) was organist there. J. N. Bach gave Adlung permission to practise on the organ, which he did in his spare time after attending general lectures and doing some writing on musical subjects. Hiller thinks well of his writing, but politely disapproves of his manner of playing—'den Geschmack im Vortrage könnte man vielleicht etwas anders bey ihm wünschen.'

In 1727 Adlung became organist at the Predigerkirche in Erfurt in succession to Buttstedt, a post which he held till his death. In 1732 he married Beata Elisabetha Ritter, of Grosswannsleben near Magdeburg, by whom he had one daughter, Sophia Elisabetha.

He gave instruction in keyboard playing and in languages, and lectured on various subjects. Teaching must have taken up a good deal of his time, for between 1728 and 1762 he instructed 218 people in playing and 248 in languages. He says that he started making clavichords as an alternative to studying, but exactly when this was we do not know. 'He had so little inclination for further study', writes Hiller, 'that he preferred to pick up his plane and devote himself to clavichord-making.' He made 16 of them, and sold them all except one, but was very careful to distinguish himself from the professional instrument maker:

> I have never been responsible [he writes] for bad work, since there are for this purpose instrument makers who have to earn their bread by it; I have never wished to become such as they, and when I have found such clavichords anywhere I have thought that I should have employed my time on other things to better purpose. However, it has been done without detriment to my main work, in my space time; partly for physical exercise and the preservation of my health. They are mostly veneered ['fourniret', perhaps 'inlaid'] all round; the keys are faced with ivory and black ebony, and reach from FF to d with 3 strokes [i.e. 5 octaves minus 3 notes].

He goes on to relate proudly that he applied stops which gave 6 varieties of tone—less discerning in this than some of his contemporaries who realized that the clavichord is not really suited for stops. In the lowest 20 notes he used covered strings; in the rest, brass.

However, on Sunday, 21 October 1736, the great Erfurt fire destroyed his house, his stock of rare woods, and most of his music and furniture; and what was not burnt was looted. This nearly broke his heart, and he never had the same enthusiasm afterwards. Amongst his losses in the great fire were 3 works which he had written at Jena, *Eine vollständige Anweisung zum Generalbasse*, *Eine Anweisung zur Fantasie und zu den Fugen*, and *Eine Anweisung zur italienischen Tabulatur*. He had also written a work on Latin grammar called *Parallelismus latinae linguae*.

He died at Erfurt on 5 July 1762.

Adlung is known to us today chiefly through his *Musica mechanica organoedi*, published in 1768, which is a work of great interest to students of the history of the organ and other keyboard instruments. He started it in Jena at the age of 27, and added to it constantly throughout the rest of his life. Albrecht prepared it for the press after its author's death (J. F. Agricola adding some footnotes), which will partly account for the lack of arrangement in many parts. Its prolixity, however, must be a reflection of the author himself and of his time and environment. At any rate the book was a success—'die Besitzer dieses Werks haben dabei sehr viel gewonnen.'

Adlung does not seem to have occupied himself much with composition. The Berlin Library has a manuscript (not autograph) of an organ arrangement by him of the chorale *Herr Jesu Christ der Einig*.

[*Adl, AdlG, Hil, Eit, Ge.*]

ADRIANO, *of Rome. See*: HADRIANUS, *of Rome.*

AELBRECHTS, Jacob. Harpsichord and clavichord maker of Antwerp. Earliest date ascertained, 1542; he died before 26 September 1585.

On 28 March 1558 he entered the Guild of St. Luke as a harpsichord maker [*St*].

AELBRECHTS, Lucas. Harpsichord maker of Antwerp, *fl.* 1588, in which year he entered the Guild of St. Luke. He was probably the son of Jacob [*St*], and seems to have made lutes as well as keyboard instruments [*Lü*].

AERTSZ, Jan. Harpsichord maker in Amsterdam, *fl.* 1594 when his son by his wife Cathalyna *née* Sarvaes was baptized in the Oude Kerk [*Curtis*, p. 47].

ALAND, James. *See*: SLADE, Benjamin.

ALARI, Giannantonio, of Rome. Harpsichord maker, *fl.* 1700 [*Va*]. Restored instrument no. 1 under Adam (q.v.), his name being on the back of the nameboard.

ALBANA, Orazio, of Rome. Harpsichord maker; dates ascertained, 1628–45.

Surviving Harpsichords

(01) An undoubtedly spurious inscription in *FrancI* reads: *Horatius Albana Romanus 1589* (on a 'spinetta').

(1) 1628. Bologna, Museo Civico. Inscribed: *Horatius Albana Romanus F MDCXXVIII.*

(2) 1633. Washington, Smithsonian Institution. Inscribed: *Horatius Albana F. Anno MDCXXXIII.* $2 \times 8'$ registers; 4 octaves with short octave. Boxwood naturals. Elaborately painted case, with ornate gilt stucco stand.

(3) 1645. Miami, Vizcaya Dade County Museum. Inscribed: *Horatius Albana F anno Dni MDCXXXXV.* A conflation, probably by Franciolini who lists it in *FrancI*, of the action of a harpsichord having $2 \times 8'$ stops and 5 split keys with the outer case from another instrument, the angle of whose tail was slightly less acute. [Inspected by *Rip.*] Boxwood naturals; black sharps; now 4 octaves with short octave; geometric rose.

Prof. (p. 292) mistakenly observes that Albana was 'the first to make 4-octave harpsichords—much earlier than Trasontino'.

ALBANI, Andrea. Harpsichord maker, probably in Florence, early in the seventeenth century. He is mentioned by G. B. Doni, writing *c.* 1640:

> Alcuni [cembali enarmonici] fabbricò già Andrea Albani cembalaro a' dì nostri molto reputato. [*Trattato sopra il genere enarmonico.* In: *Lyra barberina*, Florentiae, 1763, Vol. I, p. 307.]

ALBANI, Nicolo, ? of Venice. Spinet maker; *fl.* 1579 [*Va*].

ALBRICI, Vincenzo. Italian harpsichord maker who lived before 1681, in which year a Dresden inventory records a 'Clavicimbul. Mitt 2 Registern, und von Cipressenholz, mitt einem Eltenbeinern Clavir, bis in Contra G . . .' by him [*Drechsel*, p. 31].

ALDIGERIO, of Ferrara, *fl.* 1549. Made clavichords [*Va*].

ALESSANDRO *di Modena. See*: PASI, Alessandro.

ALESSANDRO DAGLI ORGANI, of Mantua [?], *fl.* 1540. Made organs and harpsichords [*Va*].

ALLERY, Thomas Charles Auguste d'. *See*: DALLERY, Thomas Charles Auguste.

ALLIAMET, François [Allaumet]. Parisian spinet maker. Dates ascertained, 1587–94. In 1594 he took Pierre Moulle as apprentice [*Verlet, Laborde*].

ALVISE, Giacomo. Horn maker of Padua, *fl.* 1595. That he also concerned himself with the harpsichord is shewn by a letter written by him with the date 3 March 1595, preserved in the Este records:

> I have let Messer Alessandro see and hear . . . one of my quill [*da penna*] instruments of new invention, that with two unisons [*due mani di corde*] forms three changes of sound [*GD* (1928), s.v. Stops (Harpsichord)—taken from *Va*].

ANDRESSI, Giovanni Bartolomeo. *FrancI* lists a 'cimbalone' [large harpsichord] inscribed: *Io. Bartolomeo Andressi F.A.* 1769 *Napoli.*

ANGEL, Jürgen Hinrichsen. Danish eighteenth-century clavichord maker, perhaps of Flensburg.

Surviving Clavichords

(1) Skien, Norway, Fylkesmuseum for Telemark og Grenland. Signed on right corner of soundboard: *Jürgen Hinrichsen Angel in F. . .nsburg*; 5 octaves F–F, with octave strings in bass. Ivory naturals, ebony sharps. Flowers painted on soundboard, and a scene with musicians playing inside lid.

ANJO, Miguel [Manuel]. *See*: LEO, Manuel Anjos.

ANNIBALE, *of Milan. See*: ROSSI, Annibale.

ANNIBALE, *of Rome.* Harpsichord maker at Rome, *fl.* 1655 [*Va*].

ANTEGNATO, Antonio. An ottavino inscribed *Antonius Antegnatius fecit Breccia* [*sic*] 1583 on the nameboard was owned by Steingraeber. In an outer case.

ANTEGNATO, Giovanni Francesco [Joannes Franciscus Briscianus; *probably = also* Franciscus Brixiensis]. Harpsichord and virginal maker in Brescia, *fl.* 1533–83. (The date 1533 is obtained from *Lan*, p. 143.)

Surviving Instruments

(1) 1537. London, Victoria and Albert Museum. Polygonal virginal, inscribed: *A.D. Opus Joannis Francisci*

Antegnati Brixiani MDXXXVII; 4½ octaves C/E–F with short octave (original compass F–F lacking bottom F sharp and G sharp). Arcaded pearwood naturals, ebony sharps; case of limewood, painted. Inside the lid is painted a device of clasped hands, with the motto: *Amoris vulnus idem qui sanat fecit* ('He dealt the wound of love who heals it'). Purchased from the Bardini Collection, 1899. Illustrated in *RussellV&A*.

(2) 1544. Milan. Museo Teatrale alla Scala. A 'spinetta' [? polygonal virginal] inscribed *Johannis Francisci Brisciani, 1544*. It has 50 keys. Above the keys the legend: *Virtu' beltà et confort' in Dio rapir dei suoni et canti al cui desio* [Catalogue (1940), p. 308]. This is doubtless the instrument with the same date and motto reported to me as being in the Parma Conservatory.

(3) 1564. Dublin Museum. Harpsichord, which also bears the signature of Dominicus Pisaurensis (q.v.) who worked on it in 1590. It has 1×8′, 1×4′ stops.

(4) 1569. London, Victoria and Albert Museum. Polygonal virginal signed *Marci Iadrae MDLXVIII* on the jackrail, but having under the soundboard an inscription concluding with *Francisci* [sic] *Brixiensis fecit 1569*, indicating probably that Antegnato made it for Jadra but was late in finishing it. Full details and illustration see *RussellV&A*.

(5) 1583. Berlin Collection. Signed: *Antonius Antegnatius Brescia 1583*.

(6) Undated. Rome, in private ownership. Signed. Four roses in soundboard.

(7) Undated. A polygonal virginal by this maker was shewn at the Internationale Ausstellung 'Musik im Leben der Völker', Frankfurt, 1927 [*Frankf, 1927*, p. 148, where the inscription is quoted as: *Joann Francisii* [sic] *Brixiani*].

ANTES, John. Made harpsichords and other stringed keyboard instruments at Bethlehem, Pa., in the 1760s [*Armstr*, p. 17].

ANTONI, Joannes. *See*: Joannes, Antoni.

ANTONIUS, *Bononiensis* or Antonio of Bologna. *See*: Brenzi, Antonio.

ANTONIUS, *Patavinus* or Antonio of Padua. Virginal maker, *fl.* 1550. The Brussels Conservatoire has a virginal by him with this date (inscription *Antoni Patavini opus MDXXXXX*, compass C/E–F, 4½ octaves without bottom G sharp and top D sharp), which was shewn at the International Inventions Exhibition, London, in 1885. *See also*: Franciscus Patavinus.

ANTUNES, Joachim José. Portuguese harpsichord maker; dates ascertained, 1758–89.

Surviving Harpsichords

(1) 1758. Lisbon Conservatoire. Inscription on nameboard: *Joach. José Ant^es^*. Date on bottom key. Compass 4 octaves and a 3rd, C–E.

(2) 1789. Ibidem. Inscription on bottom and top key: *Antunes 1789*. Compass 5 octaves and a 3rd, F–A. Painted soundboard. Formerly belonged to the Conte de Castel Branco.

ARGANO, Paolo. Restorer and perhaps maker. In 1808 he repaired an anonymous ottavino virginal which later reached the Heyer Collection, Leipzig. Inscription: *Paolo Argano l'accomodato l'anno 1808*. Round the inside of the case runs the inscription: *Omnia dat Dominus Non Habet Ergo Minus*. Compass 2 octaves and a 6th, G–E, without bottom G sharp and top D sharp. Dimensions 37×21 cm. Depicted in *Ks*.

ARGENT, Humphrey, of Cambridge, *fl.* 1789–91. Organ builder and keyboard-instrument maker. A spinet by him was sold at Sotheby's on 7 June 1963. He is recorded as an organ builder in Bailey's Directory for 1791 (Guildhall Library). The same spinet (on nameboard *Humphrey Argent fecit Cambridge 1789*) was at Sotheby's again on 3 April 1964. 5 octaves E–F; buff, pedal; 6′ 8″×2′ 7″; lid swell, apparently original. Bjarne B. Dahl, of Sunnyvale, Calif., when restoring the instrument in 1970, found an inscription *Thomas Hattersley, shoemaker, Cambridge*, who presumably supplied the leather for the plectra (? and perhaps even voiced the spinet).

ARGIROPOULOS, Isaac [Isac Argyropulo], of Milan. Organ builder, organist, and harpsichordist. Galeazzo Maria, Duke of Sforza, described him in 1472 as 'nostro Cortesano et Sonatore de gravacymbolo' [F. Malaguzzi Valeri, *La corte di Ludovico il Moro*, Vol. IV, Milano, 1923, p. 194]. Argiropoulos may have made harpsichords also, but I have found no authority for *Prof.*'s statement (p. 291) that he had a factory ('fabbrica') for harpsichords in Milan *c.* 1474.

He was commended as an organist, together with 'Domenico the Venetian' and Daniel Stack, by Pope Leo X [*Bed*, p. 34].

ARKEL, Rijk van. The Gemeentemuseum at The Hague has a travelling spinet, folding in 3 sections; date ascribed: 1768 (no inscription visible). Rose; ivory naturals. It is (1966) on loan from the Rijksmuseum, Amsterdam.

ARNAULT, Henri, *of Zwolle* [Henricus Arnault de Zuuolis]. Was familiar with the details of the design of clavichords, harpsichords, and other instruments. He is a very important and early authority on the early history of keyboard instruments; it seemed pardonable, therefore, to record him here, even though it is most unlikely that he ever made an instrument with his own hands.

He was born at Zwolle, probably soon after 1400. In his youth he studied at Paris University under Johannes Fusoris, becoming a Master of Medicine. Entering the service of Philip the Good, Duke of Burgundy, as a physician and astronomer, he lived for a period at Dijon.

He passed into the service of Louis XI and died in Paris on 6 September 1466, having been stricken by the plague which ravaged the city severely in that year.

Jean de Roye refers to him as 'Maistre Arnoult . . . qui estoit fort homme de bien, saige et plaisant'.

While at Dijon Arnault constructed astronomical instruments, for one of which the record of payment is preserved. That he devoted some time also to the designing of musical instruments, amongst them the clavichord and harpsichord, seems likely, for about the year 1440 he wrote (as observer rather than inventor) a Latin treatise giving a detailed description of the design and working of the clavichord, lute, organ, *clavisimbalum*, and *dulce melos*, with a note on the harp, accompanied by excellent diagrams shewing their layout, and by some less satisfactory sketches of various types of action employed in the stringed keyboard instruments of his day.

The passages dealing with the *clavisimbalum* and the *dulce melos* are especially interesting, although unfortunately obscure in parts. The *clavisimbalum* has the wing-like shape of a harpsichord, and Arnault offers us a choice of 4 actions for use in it. In the first 3 the string appears to be plucked by a plectrum of metal, and a form of escape mechanism is implied (though the jacks, *forpices*, are quite different from those familiar to us in the classical period) and their elaborateness brings to mind the action of a clavicytherium [*Box*]. We have here the earliest description of the harpsichord. In the fourth the string is struck by a rebounding hammer, being in fact a simple form of pianoforte action, which was to disappear, and then be rediscovered about three centuries later.

Elsewhere in the manuscript there is a brief reference to another plucking medium, quill, which was soon to oust the metal plectra with which Arnault was most familiar.

But the fourth ('pianoforte') action was associated *par excellence* with the *dulce melos*, in its developed form with keyboard, a rectangular instrument identified by the late F. W. Galpin with the *échiquier* or *chekker* thus suggesting a solution to a long-standing problem.

Arnault's treatise (Bibl. Nat., Paris, MS. Latin 7295) was published in facsimile, with a transcription, French translation, and commentary, by F. Le Cerf and E. F. Labande under the title: *Instruments de musique du XVe siècle. Les traités d'Henri-Arnaut de Zwolle et de divers anonymes* . . . (Paris, Auguste Picard, 1932), from which most of the biographical details given above are derived and which should be consulted for further information. Arnault's drawing of a harpsichord is reproduced in *Jur*, p. 20 also, and in colour in *Brag 1967*.

ASARD, John. A mis-reading by Rimbault of *IOHANNES [H]A[W]ARD*, name of the well-known harpsichord maker. *See below*: HAWARD; also *Ri*, p. 401 and *J*, p. 120.

ASHE, John. Harpsichord maker in Cope Street, Dublin, in 1788 [*Teahan*].

ASIOLI, Quirino, of Fazzano [?], *fl.* in the eighteenth century. Maker of harpsichords and organs [*Va*].

ASSALONE, Gaspare. Ostensibly a clavichord maker, *fl.* 1732 in Rome.

Surviving Clavichords

(1) 1732. Barcelona Conservatoire. Signed: *Gaspare Assalone fecit Romae Anno MDCCXXXII.* Compass C/E–B, short octave. Painting of Adam and Eve on the lid. Projecting keyboard. Appears in *FrancI* (as no. 16), and has the same improbably bent keys as the fakes listed as nos. 2 and 3 under Trasuntino, q.v.

ASSEMANI. Name, found in Paris, of an Italian harpsichord maker; dates unknown [*GL*]. (Unless it is in fact the Parisian restorer Asseman of recent times.)

ASTON, Cawton, of London. Spinet maker, apprenticed to John Player for 8 years from 1693. Freeman of the Joiners' Company 1705 [*Join*]. In 1730 he lived at the Prince's Arms, New Queen Street [*J*].

Surviving Spinets

(01) 1709. Inscribed on wrestplank: *Aston & Barton Londini FF* and on one of the jacks: *1709*. From the Ligonier Museum, Ligonier, Pa., it passed in 1966 to E. M. Ripin.

(1) 1726. Inscribed: *Cawton Aston Londini fecit no. 268 A.D. 1726*. Compass 5 octaves G–G. Skunktail sharps. Width 5′ 10″.

(2?) *Undated.* A spinet owned by Peter C. Barnes, Whalley Range, has the initials *CA* on the bottom key and might be ascribable to Aston. The late eighteenth-century stand includes a pedal which works a kind of nag's-head swell. Compass G/B–D, 4½ octaves. Former owners: the Earl of Newborough, Bodvean, N. Wales; M. Goldstone, Bakewell, from whom the present owner bought it in 1971. Presumably the instrument offered for sale at Sotheby's, 21 December 1972.

AUBÉ, Antoine. Parisian harpsichord maker, *fl.* 1758. Only son of Pierre Aubé, an organ builder [*Hubb, Verlet*].

AUGUSTIN, Johann Gottfried, 1762–1806. Organ builder at Bautzen; also made pianos and clavichords [*Biehle*, p. 48].

AUTERBON, L. *See*: LAUTERBON.

B, C. An undated Italian spinet, seventeenth century, in the Berlin Collection bears the initials *C.B.*, perhaps those of the maker [*Sa*, p. 59]. *See also*: BRACKLEY, Charles.

B, F. *See*: F, B. F.

B, G. B. *See*: BONI, Giovanni Battista.

B, I. M. A gebunden clavichord dated 1705 in the Folkemuseum, Oslo, is signed with these initials. Four octaves C–C. White naturals.

BACCHUS, Andrew. *See*: BACKERS, Americus.

BACH, Johann Michael, 1648–9. Son of Heinrich Bach. Born at Arnstadt on 9 August 1648. A second cousin of J. S. Bach, he became organist at Gehren near Arnstadt in 1673. He married in 1675, and his youngest daughter became the wife of J. S. Bach.

He also composed, and was interested in constructing instruments, particularly clavichords (according to *Fé*), of which he supplied several to Councillor Wentzing of Arnstadt in 1686. He died at Gehren in May 1694. *See* further *Eit*.

BACH, Johann Nikolaus, 1669–1753. Maker of organs and other keyboard instruments. He was born at Eisenach on 10 October 1669, his father being Johann Christoph Bach, organist at Eisenach. In 1695 he became City- and University-organist at Jena. He married in 1697 Anna Amalia Baurath of Jena, and after her death in 1713, Anna Sibylla Lange of Isserstadt [*Ge*]. He had in all ten children. His contemporaries regarded him as a clever composer of suites [*Fé*]. In his spare time he was very active as a maker of organs and keyboard instruments, and was widely known as a repairer and restorer. *Adl*, II. 108, gives an account of a new (and it would seem, rather cumbersome) method of changing the registration on a harpsichord by means of shifting the keyboard, invented by J. N. Bach. Spitta (*J. S. Bach*, 2 vols., Leipzig, 1873–80, I. 137), refers to this invention without criticism.

Adlung commends his *Lautenklavier*—a gut-strung harpsichord invented probably by J. C. Fleischer of Hamburg, and designed to imitate the tone of a lute [*Adl*]. J. N. B. made them with 2 and even 3 keyboards; the latter he sold for about 60 thalers. *AdlG* (p. 665 n.) mentions a push–pull keyboard coupler on a J. N. Bach harpsichord. J. N. Bach died at Jena on 4 November 1753 at the age of 84 [*Gö*].

BACKERS, Americus. Harpsichord and pianoforte maker. Dates ascertained, 1763–81.

He was a Dutchman who (according to *Ri*, p. 131) was employed in the Silbermann workshop for a time. He must have come over to England by 1763, for he was a resident in Jermyn Street, London, under the name of Andrew Backus (sometimes Bacchus!), from 1763 until 1778, which latter may be the date of his death [*RBJ*].

John Hitchcock's spinet number 2012 is signed: *Backus No. 8*. Backers may thus have worked for Hitchcock before he set up on his own account.

It was Backers who, with the assistance of his apprentice Robert Stodart and John Broadwood, invented the 'English' pianoforte action, as Henry Fowler Broadwood tells us in his comments on the ms. notes of his father, James Shudi Broadwood. These notes (privately printed in 1838) give 1776 as the date of Backers's invention: but the same author, writing in the *Gentleman's Magazine* (1812) dates it 1772 and the grand pianoforte of this year by Backers (Edinburgh University Collection) incorporates it. Broadwood began producing grand pianos with this action about 1784; no. 103, dated 1788, is still in existence.

Burney (II. 147) writes with approval of 'the *pianofortes* of Backers'; but the reference to him in Abraham Rees's *Cyclopaedia* (1819) as a 'harpsichord maker of the second rank' does not do him justice.

Surviving Harpsichords

(1) 1766. In the possession of Lord Hylton. Two manuals; inscribed: *Americus Backers Londini fecit 1766*. 2×8′, 1×4′, lute. Lid swell operated by a pedal which originally brought on the 4′ stop. Gilt rose embodying musical trophy but without initials. Five-octave compass. Belonged at one time to Tenducci, the celebrated castrato (born *c.* 1736). Repaired by George Stuart Semple in 1876 and by Hugh Gough in 1948.

BADER, Hans Heinrich [*also* Baders]. Came from Unna in Westphalia, organ builder in the seventeenth century. In the contract dated 1639 for building an organ at Zutphen he is described as a harpsichord maker also [*GL*; see also *Vente*, p. 149].

BADER, Peter Daniel [Boder]. Maker of organs, harpsichords, and virginals. Dates ascertained, 1600–7 [*Vannes*].

A German resident in Antwerp, he entered the Guild of St. Luke as an organ and harpsichord maker in 1600. His contract to build an organ in the St. Jacobskerk, Antwerp, survives [*St*, who reproduces Bader's signature in facsimile, *Daniell Bader*].

In 1769 a lute bearing his name was auctioned in London [*Lü*].

Surviving Instruments

(1) Undated. Brussels Conservatoire. A virginal of 4-octave compass, 155×48 cm. The initials in the rose are *PDB*. (The catalogue gives his surname as 'Boder'.) Formerly in the Régibo Collection, Renaix, and afterwards in that of Snoeck.

BAETHMANN, W. H. A clavichord in the Goethehaus, Frankfurt/Main, is inscribed: *W. H. Baethmann Hoforgelbauer in Hannover 1799 f.* (F–F, 5 octaves, octave strings in bass).

BAFFO, Giovanni Antonio, of Venice. Celebrated maker of harpsichords and virginals, dates ascertained, 1570–81. The lute and harp maker mentioned by *Lü* as Antonio Baffo may be the same man. (The date 1523, if correct, points to another maker of the same name.) *See table 1.*

A harpsichord by Baffo was amongst the instruments of Ferdinand de' Medici entrusted to the care of Cristofori in 1716 [*Pu*].

BAGNINIUS, Jacobus, of Lucca. Virginal maker; *fl.* 1613.

Surviving Instruments

(1) 1613. Copenhagen. Claudius Collection. An ottavino virginal signed: *Jacobus Bagninius fecit Lucensis Anno 1613*. Compass 4 octaves C–C with short octave. Rose in the soundboard. 84×46 cm. Illustrated in the Catalogue, p. 61. A dubious instrument.

BAILLON, Pierre. French harpsichord and organ maker, music engraver, and organist in Paris. Died 1681. In 1659 he married Jeanne Leviez. He seems to have started his career as an organ builder. As a harpsichord maker he may well have been a pupil of one of the Denis family (q.v.). He was a friend of and collaborator with Nicolas Lebègue, organist and composer.

He died on 20 October 1681. The inventory of the contents of his house includes a number of harpsichords, spinets, and clavichords [*see* N. Dufourcq in *Hin*, pp. 196–200; also *Verlet*].

BALBASTRE, Claude. Organist. *Ge* credits him with the original invention of *peau de buffle*: 'verfertiget durch Mr. Taskin'. Burney described his Ruckers harpsichord which he saw in Paris.

BAN, J. M. de DE. *See*: DEDEBAN, Jean Marie.

BAN, Jan Albert [Bannius], *c.* 1597 to 1644. Archbishop of Haarlem. According to *Bl* [also *VdS*, I. 61] he made an *archicymbalum*, whose virtues were set forth in his *Zangh-bloemzel, dat is, staeltjes van den zinroerenden zangh* . . . (Amsterdam, P. Matthysz voor L. Elzevier), but which won very little interest.

BANKS, Benjamin. Harpsichord, spinet, and pianoforte maker; *fl.* at Salisbury, Wilts. in 1768. An advertisement in the *Salisbury Journal* for 26 September 1768 reads: 'To be Sold, A Neat Second-Hand Harpsichord consisting of two Unisons, a Lute and Harp Stops: Enquire of Benjamin Banks, Musical Instrument-maker, (at his Music-Shop, in Catherine-Street, Sarum;) by whom Harpsichords, Piano Fortes, and Spinnets, are made, tuned, and carefully repaired . . .'

BARBERINA, *Sieur. See*: BARBERINI, Jacques.

BARBERINI, Jacques. Harpsichord and pianoforte maker; *fl.* 1770–91. Between 1783 and 1791 he lived in the rue de la Verrerie, Paris, where he also stocked English pianofortes of the best makers. In 1783 he entered the Guild of Parisian harpsichord makers [*Pi*].

G. Cucuel (*Bulletin de la Société française de musicologie*, Vol. 3) says he was an Italian maker who lived in the rue Chenoise, Grenoble, in 1770.

Vallas, pp. 355, 378, refers to a 'Sieur Barbarina' who made harpsichords and pianofortes at Lyons, *fl.* 1770; almost certainly the same man as Barberini.

TABLE 1. *Surviving Instruments by BAFFO (or purporting to be by him)*

No.	Date	Type	Kbs.	Signature	Owner/Remarks
1	1523	H	1		In 1910 [*Ks*, p. 211] and probably 1930 [*J*, p. 115] in the Vienna Museum f. Kunst und Industrie. Disappeared in World War II.
2	1570	Pol. V	1	*Joannes Antonius Baffo Venetus MDLXX*	Paris, Hôtel de Cluny. Geometrical rose. C–F originally C/E–F, 4½ octaves with short octave. Projecting keyboard. Both the instrument and the case have been shortened, perhaps by about 10″.
3	1574	H	1	*Ioanes Antonius Baffo Venetus MDLXXIIII*	London, Victoria and Albert Museum. C–F, 4 octaves and a 4th. Illustrated at *J*, p. 114, *V&A*, *MIWA*, and *Russell 1959*.
4	1574	H	1		Nyack, New York. Private ownership (1951). Formerly owned by A. Motta, Geneva [*MarcP*].
5	1578	H	1		Paris Conservatoire (formerly Savoye Collection I).
5a	1579	H	1		Referred to by *Hubb 1965*, without giving the location.
[5aa]	1580	H	1		Leipzig, Heyer Collection. *See Ks*, p. 96.
5b	158–	H	1		Loynel d'Estrie, Paris (?), in 1969 [*ClavHist*]; 54 keys; 2×8′ stops.
6	1581	V	1	*Joannes Antonius Baffo Venetus F. MDLXXXI*	Liverpool, Rushworth and Dreaper Collection; (Catalogue reads 'Ballo'). Originally C/E–F, now (1972) C–F chromatic. Rough and possibly spurious. Restored by Dolmetsch in 1895. Rose very crude. *Pesario* written on back of nameboard [*Barnes*]. Decorated by Alma Tadema.
[7]	1581	H	1	*Johannes Antonius Baffo Venetus F MDLXXXI*	Nuremberg, Germanisches Nationalmuseum, Neupert Collection. 2×8′ stops. G–C, 4 octaves and a 4th. A late seventeenth-century instrument, the inscription being devised by Franciolini.
[8]	1581	H	1	*Johannes Antonius Baffo Venetus F MDLXXXI*	Washington, Smithsonian Institution.—A spurious instrument.
[8a]	1581	H	1	*Ioannes Antonius Baffo Venetus F. MDLXXXI*	Stockholm, Nydahl Collection. Inscribed: *Proprieta di Enrico Broccardi Schelmi* on back of nameboard. G–C, 4½ octaves. Dubious instrument.
[9]	1581	H	2		Basel, Hist. Mus. 2×8′ stops and a 4′ added later.
[10]	n.d.	V	1	[Not signed by Baffo]	London, Benton Fletcher Collection, Fenton House. No reason for this attribution.
11	15..	H			Privately owned in France [*ChamP*].

BARBI, Michele. Venetian maker of polygonal virginals, *fl.* 1758. One by him was shewn by L. Savoye at the Paris Exhibition, 1900. The catalogue entry reads: 'Epinette portative de Michel Barbi, 1758, M. L. Savoye, à Sevran' [*Par. 1900*, p. 109].

Daniel Fryklund's collection at Hälsingborg contains a dulcimer by Barbi of Venice dated 1748 (formerly in the Bricqueville Collection and shewn at the Paris Exhibition in 1900).

BARBIER. Harpsichord maker, referred to in passing by *Cor* (p. 84). Antoine Barbier was the expert for the inventory of Jean Denis (II) in 1686 [*MC*]. He had been made Juré of the Community in 1667.

BARBIERI, *of Modena.* Harpsichord maker in the nineteenth century according to *Va*, who must surely be wrong here. Giovanni Barbieri of Modena made barrel-organs, and well before the nineteenth century [*MarcP*].

BARTELS, Julius Heinrich. Clavichord maker, lived in the Mühlengasse, Cologne, in 1797, according to a directory for that year [*Ks*].

BARTOLI, A. *FrancII* records a 'spinetta a tavolino' inscribed: *A. Bartoli 1777* (item 7). Deansboro (N.Y.) Musical Museum has a harpsichord by him allegedly made for Ercole II, Duke of Ferrara (former owner: C. Albert Jacob, Jr.).

BARTON, Thomas. Maker of spinets and harpsichords. Son of Thomas and Mary Barton of Hoxton in the parish of St. Leonard Shoreditch; baptized 1 January 1685 [*Parish Reg.*]. Apprenticed for 7 years to Stephen Keene (whose no. 5a bears his initials) from 1 August 1699; freeman of the Joiners' Company, August 1706 [*Join*]. Master of John Ladyman (q.v.).

He was dead by 1735 [*Join*]. His son William was made free of the Joiners' Company by patrimony, 6 March 1743/4. He lived at 'The Crown, near the South Seas House', Bishopsgate Street, London. In 1726 he designed an upright harpsichord, which he advertised in the press [*J*]. *See table 2.*

A spinet by Thomas Barton belonging to Messrs. J. G. Morley was repaired by Messrs. Robert Morley, Bromley, in 1958 and later sold. One of the Bartons—presumably

TABLE 2. *Surviving Instruments by Thomas BARTON*

No.	Date	Type	Kbs.	Signature	Owner/Remarks
01	1709	H	1	*Tho. Barton Londini fecit*	Dr. Mirrey, Redhill, who bought it at Sotheby's on 12 March 1970 from C. Mould, who had bought it at auction at Purton, near Swindon, 15 October 1969. 2×8′ stops; D/G–D 5 octaves; broken bass octave with 2 split sharps. Signed and dated on 2 of the jacks.
1	1714	S	1		Cirencester, C. A. Legg (1941).
2	1719	S	1	*Thomas Barton Londini fecit 1719*	Berwick-on-Tweed, C. Brackenbury. (Shewn by G. Williamson at International Inventions Exhibition, London, 1885.) Black naturals; ivory sharps inlaid with ebony.
3	1720	S	1	*Thomas Barton Londini fecit 1720*	Invergordon. Captain A. F. Matheson, R.N. 36 naturals (black) and 25 sharps (white). Calligraphy of the date suspicious.
4	1725	S	1	*Thomas Barton Londini Fecit 1725*	Sotheby's 31 July 1953; withdrawn.
4a	1727	S	1	*Thomas Barton MDCCXXVII Londini Fecit*	Sotheby's 11 March 1960. G–G. Skunktail sharps.
[5	1730	S	1		Same instrument as no. 7 below.]
6	1730	S	1		Shewn by Wm. Dale at International Inventions Exhibition, 1885.
7	1730	S	1		Washington, Smithsonian Institution. Previously New York, Cooper Union. 5 octaves G–G. White naturals, inlaid sharps. Given originally by Adam Norrie, who bought it from Steinert.
8	1731	S	1		Michaelstowe, Roger Yates.
9	1740	S	1		Reported as having once been in the Taphouse Collection, Oxford. $4\frac{1}{2}$ octaves G–D. Black naturals. 5′ 4″×23″.
10	n.d.	S	1		Aix-en-Provence, W. Dobson.

Thomas—worked with Cawton Aston (q.v.) for a time; and it is probably Thomas Barton to whom the composer John Baptist Grano refers in his journal written in the Marshalsea Prison from May 1728 to September 1729, being confined there for debt [Bodleian Lib., MS. Rawlinson D. 34]. Grano records on Wednesday, 9 October 1728: 'John Anthony, the Tauny Moor I teach brought me an old spinnet which I intend to put in order and divert myself with'; but on 1 April 1729, after teaching one of his pupils, he 'sent him away with my spinnet to Mr. Barton to have it repaired'. Two days later the pupil 'brought home my spinnet from Barton's who told him it was not worth repairing for he would not give half a crown for it' [*Byrne*].

BARTON, William. English harpsichord maker, *fl.* 1730, in which year he took out a patent, numbered 525,

to improve the Use of Harpsichords, Spinnetts, and Musical Instruments used in most Families of the Nobility and Gentry of this our Kingdom, he hath after four Years Application and Study, and with great Expence, invented Pens of Silver, Brass, Steel, and other Sorts of Metall, which will improve the Tone of the said Instruments, and last many Yeares without Amendment, Crow and Raven Quills, of which they are now made, requiring frequent Charge and Trouble in repairing . . . the said new-invented pens have been highly approved of by several gentlemen and professors who have seen the same . . .

Like many devices in the history of keyboard instruments, these metal plectra were a rediscovery. (William may possibly have been the son of Thomas Barton.)

BAS. Spinet maker, of Lyons, *fl.* 1786.

Surviving Instruments

(1) 1786. Musée Granet, Aix-en-Provence. Spinet in mahogany case with 3 legs in Louis Seize style. Inscription on soundboard: *Fait par Bas à Lyon 1786*.

BAS, Jean. Harpsichord maker of Marseilles, *fl.* 1737–81 [*Hirt*]. A harpsichord by him from the Château d'Osny, with a case in *vernis Martin* richly painted, was sold by auction for fr. 6,500 at the Hôtel Drouot, Paris, in 1902. [*ZI*, 1901/2, p. 539.] It is now (1971) owned by C. Mercier-Ythier, Paris. Signed: *Jean Bas fecit Ano 1737* on the name-batten and *Fait a Marseille* [sic] *par Jean Bas 1737* round a 'rose' painted on the soundboard. Five octaves F–F.

BAS, Louis. Harpsichord maker of Marseilles, perhaps son of the foregoing, *fl.* 1778–86. A harpsichord of the above date by Bas, restored by Martel in 1831, C/E–F, was in de Bricqueville's collection [*Pi*]. A harpsichord of the same date, converted into a piano, was for sale in New York in August 1949—possibly the same instrument. A wing-shaped spinet, signed: *Fait par Bas à Marseille, 1783*, E–F, 5 octaves and 1 note, now at Cannes ('Au Bonheur du Jour') may well be by this maker. Another such spinet by him, signed: *Louis Bas à Lyon, 1786* is in the Musée Granet, Aix-en-Provence.

BASSI, G. In the auction catalogue of the Anderson Gallery, New York, October 1938 (no. 4409): 'an Italian spinet by G. Bassi dated 1772' is listed [*MarcP*].

BASSILICHI, Luigi. Harpsichord maker in the Via Larga, Florence, in 1695, in which year he is recorded as paying a matriculation fee to his Guild. His father's name was Gaetano B. and his grandfather's Giovanni B. [*Pu*].

BASTIANO, *of Verona.* Lived in the fifteenth and sixteenth centuries. He is said to have made lutes, viols, lyres, flutes, horns, monochords, psalteries, harps, and harpsichords [*Lü, Gö*].

BATES & CO., of London, eighteenth century. May have made harpsichords, seeing that Houston & Co., who took over their business, made spinets and harpsichords as well as pianos.

BATI, Antonio, of Arezzo, *c.* 1691. Made virginals and harpsichords, also theorboes of moderate workmanship [*Lü*].

FranclI records a 'spinetta a tavolino' inscribed *Antonius Bati me fecit in Arezzo 1691* (item 9).

BATOV, Ivan Andreevich, born 1767. Maker of violins, etc., also of harpsichords and fortepianos, St. Petersburg [*Moos* II. 645] and elsewhere in Russia. *See further Vannes*. He had been apprenticed to a Moscow maker called Vladimirov.

BATTAGLIA, Francesco. Eighteenth-century stringed instrument maker in Milan. A painted spinet (with bent side) in the Gallini Collection, Milan, inscribed *F.B.F. Mediolani 1735* is probably by him. Compass 3 octaves and 7 notes; parchment rose (formerly in the Castello Sforzesco). Illustrated in *Pag*, p. 61.

BAUDIN, François. He was apprenticed soon after 1623 to Jean Marie Galland, the Parisian harpsichord maker [*Verlet*].

BAUDIN, J. Was apprenticed to Jean Galland on 1 August 1723, which implies that he was born about 1708. Later settled in England.

Rimbault possessed in 1860 a spinet by Baudin (pictured in *Ri*, p. 69). It had belonged formerly to Simon Fraser, Lord Lovat; and afterwards passed into the possession of T. W. Taphouse of Oxford, who shewed it at the International Inventions Exhibition, London, in 1885. It was bought in that year by William Dale; and was in 1950 the property of Mrs. Jarvis of Newbury.

Inscription on the back of the nameboard: *Josephus Baudin Londini fecit 1723*. Compass 4½ octaves. Rose in soundboard. Walnut case; ebony naturals, and ivory-inlaid sharps in the Hitchcock style. Restored by Arnold Dolmetsch in 1894.

ClP (p. 71) gives the name as Boudin.

BAUDIN, Robert. Was apprenticed to Claude Lesclan (q.v.) in 1632 [*Hubb*]. He was still alive in 1646 [*Laborde*].

BAUER, *Hofrat*, of Berlin. Built in 1768 a transposing harpsichord called a *Royal crescendo* [*Ri*, p. 207; *Fi* gives the date as 1786]. But he was not a true harpsichord maker.

BAUMGARTNER, Abraham. Lived in Berne. According to an advertisement of 1756 he made harpsichords, clavicytheria, and clavichords [*Rindl*].

BAUMGARTNER, Johann. Clavichord maker, *fl.* 1683 at Bozen (Bolzano, Austrian Tirol). The National Museum in Prague has a clavichord by him inscribed: *Erzeuger Johann Baumgartner, Bozen 1683.* Black naturals, white sharps. Compass C–F; 134 × 42 cm.

BAYR, Antoni. *Fl.* as an organ builder in Munich in 1781. He also made clavichords, of which one survives in the Hotel Poste, Poschiavo, Switzerland, inscribed on a label inside the tuning-hammer box to the left of the keyboard: *Antoni Bayr Burgerlicher Orgl und Instrumentmacher in München fecit d. 15 Merz 1781* [*Rindl*].

BECK. Spinet maker in England in 1741. He may have been a forebear of the London pianoforte maker Frederick Beck, whose ascertained dates according to *J* are 1774–94. They are unlikely to have been the same man, although Taskin owed 'Mr. Beck in London' money in 1777 [*Hubb 1965*, p. 295].

Surviving Spinets

(1) 1741. Lavenham, Alec Hodsdon (1948). In mahogany. Compass 4 octaves and a 6th, G–E. Ivory naturals; skunktail sharps. Dimensions 6′ 0″ × 2′ 6″.

BEEST, Martin van der. *See*: BIEST, Marten van der.

BELAMY, Pol *or* **Paul** (I). Parisian instrument maker, apprenticed to Claude Denis (q.v.). *Fl.* 1571–91 [*Les*; *Laborde*].

BELAMY, Paul (II). Parisian maker of harpsichords and other instruments; perhaps nephew of Paul I. Died 1612 [*Verlet*].

BELISONIUS, Paul, of Pavia, a priest. Dates ascertained, 1522–39. He was considered an expert in quilling harpsichords with vulture's or raven's feathers. A reference to him by Teseo Albonesio (*Introductio in chaldaicam linguam*, Pavia, 1539) is quoted by *Va*.

BELLOT, Pierre (I). Parisian harpsichord maker; born about 1675, died between 1732 and 1747. He had 2 sons, Louis Charles and Pierre, both harpsichord makers. A 'clavecin de Bellot le père' was advertised for sale, 5 November 1761 [*Bq*].

Surviving Harpsichords

(1) 1729. Chartres, The Archbishop's Palace. By *Le Père Bellot.* 1 ml, G–C, 4½ octaves; 2 × 8′ stops.

BELLOT, Pierre (II). Son of I, harpsichord maker. In 1747 he was living in the rue des Boucheries [*Verlet*].

BELLOT, Louis Charles. Parisian harpsichord maker, second son of Pierre I. Worked between 1717 and 1759 [*Verlet*].

In 1732 he is said to have devised a harpsichord bridge which would give exactly the same speaking-length to each pair of unison strings, his object being a greater uniformity of tone. On 18 September 1752 and 7 April 1753 he provided spinets for use at the Opéra [*Pi*, p. 90].

Cor (p. 84) refers to the 'petits clavecins à deux cordes de Bellot'.

Surviving Harpsichords

(1) 1742. New York, Metropolitan Museum of Art. Two manuals. Compass 4 octaves and a 6th, G–E. Rose with maker's name: *Louis Bellot*; 2 × 8′, 1 × 4′ stops. Length 8′ 2″. *Lois* [sic] *Bellot* inscribed on the batten between the keyboards.

BENARD, Louis. Parisian harpsichord maker. Dates ascertained, 1776–89. Between 1776 and 1778 he entered the Guild of Instrument Makers [*Pi*].

BENISMIS, Doanusa. A little pentagonal virginal in cypress wood formerly owned by Captain Lane, of Wanstead, but now (1972) by the 'Friends of Historic Essex' is housed at Ingatestone Hall; its nameboard is inscribed: *Doanusa Benismis.* It has an outer case and stand in one piece, painted, the inside being unpainted. On the bottom inside is written: *Questa spinetta fu* [?] *1560 del Duca d'Urbino.* A further inscription, partly erased, suggests that it was repaired in 1615.

Doanusa Benismis is an almost incredible name. Moreover, the appearance of the nameboard suggests that it is not original, although it looks old.

It is possible that the present name represents a misreading of the signature *Franciscus Bonafinis*, a spinet maker (*fl.* 1585) one of whose instruments is preserved in the New York Metropolitan Museum of Art.

BENTI, Antonio. *FrancI* lists a 'spinetta' inscribed: *Antonius Bentes Brexia anno Domini 1580* (item 21).

BENTI, Matteo, of Brescia, born 1580, latest date ascertained 1653 [*Vannes*]. Lute maker. Also made violins and (according to *Lü* and *Gö*) virginals.

BERCHTHOLD ZU SONNENBURG, Joseph von, early owner, not a maker. He lived at Salzburg and St. Gilgen and married Marianne ('Nannerl'), Mozart's sister, in 1784. He died in 1801.

He owned an undated clavichord now in the Museum Carolino-Augusteum, Salzburg, bundfrei, F–F, 5 octaves. Inscription (almost illegible) on soundboard: *Joseph von Berch-thold zu Sonnenburg* [?]. The instrument dates from the end of the eighteenth century.

BERERA, Joannes Antonius [Berero], of Trento, *fl.* 1745–61. Maker of harpsichords and other instruments.

A study by C. Lunelli entitled 'Giovanni Antonio Berera: costruttore di strumenti musicali, incisore e violinista del settecento' appeared in *Studi trentini di scienze storiche . . .*, 1969.

Surviving Instruments

(1) 1761. Berlin Collection. Harpsichord, C/E–F, 4½ octaves (with short octave). Inscription: *Joannes Antonius Berera faciebat Tridenti. A. MDCCLXI.* Two fixed 8′ registers. Rose. 89 × 195 cm. Exhibited at the Allgemeine Musikausstellung, Berlin, 1898. Lid lost in World War II.

(There is also a psaltery by him, dated 1745, in the New York Metropolitan Museum of Art.)

BERETONI, Rinaldo. *FrancI* lists a 'spinetta' inscribed: *Rinardo* [sic] *Beretoni fecit anno 1738* (item 24). *See also below*: CARCASSI, Giovanni.

BERGER, Giovanni Domenico [? Birger], of Milan. Virginal maker, *fl.* 1746.

Surviving Virginals

(1) 1746. Toulouse, Musée Paul-Dupuy. Inscription: *Iouanes Dominicus Berger* [? Birger] *fecit Mediolani 1746.* Dimensions 73×37 cm.

(2) Undated. Rome, Palazzo Venezia.

BERGER, Joseph-Antoine, 1719–77. Organist at Grenoble Cathedral. He invented a mechanism for producing a *crescendo* on the harpsichord and spinet by means of a genouillère, and, submitting it to the *Académie des Sciences* at Paris in 1762, received a certificate of merit from them. But the invention did not become popular, and no trace of it survives. Perhaps the plans and parts were stolen by Frick, the German who worked for him in 1765 and ran off with his plans for a keyed harp [*Pi*, p. 92]. G. Cucuel (in *Bulletin de la Société française de musicologie*, Vol. 2) gives his first name as *Joseph* and says that he built a *clavecin organisé* which was played in Grenoble in 1764.

In 1762 a proposal for subscriptions towards the application of his *crescendo* pedal to the instruments of subscribers appeared in the *Mercure de France*. He is mentioned in Diderot's *Encyclopédie*, s.v. 'Epinette'. *Les Annonces*, Paris, 1765, contains a paragraph on his 'pneumo-corde' [*Hubb*].

BERNERI, Giorgio, of Trento. *Fl.* 1594 at Rome as a maker of virginals [*Va*]. An ottavino in the Toledo (Ohio) Museum of Art is inscribed in ink: *Giorgio da Trento figliolo di Antonio B*[?]*urneri da edad* [?] . . . [next line illegible] *Anno* . . . Front of wrestplank inscribed: *Giorgius Berneri Tridenirus* [sic] *fecit Romae AD MDLXXXXIV.* E flat to C, 2 octaves plus a 6th.

Is he the maker of the triangular virginals, compass C–E, dated 1608, at the Collegio Romano, Rome? [*GL*].

BERTARINI, Giambattista, of Pesaro. Harpsichord maker; dates ascertained, 1554–95 [*Va*].

The Museo Bardini, Florence, has a harpsichord by him inscribed: *Joannes Baptista Bertarinus Pisauren. fecit Romae Anno S. MDLXXVII.* Four octaves C–C including short octave; 2×8′ stops; rose; but the inscription is probably spurious.

BERTI, Niccolò. Florentine harpsichord maker, *fl.* 1693–6. Son of Pier Francesco Berti, he paid a matriculation fee to his Guild in 1696, when he was residing near the church of S. Giovannino [*Pu*; *Gai*, p. 12].

An undated harpsichord by him was shewn at the International Inventions Exhibition, London, 1885 by F. Smallfield. The Exhibition catalogue gives a repair date: *1864*. But a Berti harpsichord in the U.S.A. has a repair date: *1764*. It is probably the same instrument.

FrancI lists a harpsichord inscribed: *Nicolaus Bertius Florentinus 1682* (item 9); *FrancIII* lists one dated 1681.

BERTIN, Daniel, of Memel. Organ Builder, *fl. c.* 1757. Albert Jacquot (*Dictionnaire pratique . . . des instruments . . .*, Paris, 1886) writes that he 'inventa le clavecin d'amour vers 1757; les cordes étaient du double plus longues que celles du clavecin ordinaire.' The invention was presumably a copy of the so-called 'cembal d'amour' invented by Silbermann in 1721.

BERTOLOTTI, Alexander, of Venice. Virginal and harpsichord maker [*Va*]. Dates ascertained, 1585–6.

Surviving Instruments

(1) 1585. Brussels Conservatoire. Claviorganum inscribed *Alexander Bortolotti MDLXXXV.* The harpsichord compass is G/B–C, 4 octaves and 3 notes; 2×8′ registers, but formerly 1×8′, 1×4′ [*Hubb 1965*, p. 29]. (*See further*: *GSJ*, 1967, p. 51; 1968, p. 179.) Formerly in the Correr Collection, Venice. (The catalogue gives the name as 'Bertolotti'.)

(2) 1586. Edinburgh University (formerly Raymond Russell). Polygonal virginal. Nameboard inscribed: *Alexander Bertolotti MDLXXXVI.* Compass C/E–F. Illustrated in *RussColl. See also*: *GSJ*, 1967, p. 52.

It is impossible to decide whether Bertolotti or Bortolotti is the correct form of the name. The inscriptions on both instruments are finely written, clearly by the same man, presumably a professional scribe. We should assume that either the *o* or the *e* is simply a scribe's error.

The organ part of instrument 1 is nearly a century later, by a German maker. Inscribed *Theodorus Wilhelmus Sigismundus Agathe Saxoniensis* [then some uncertain words] *1677* [? 1657—then more illegible words]—i.e. Gottlob W. S. Gut [*GSJ*, 1967, p. 50].

BETTON, William. Maker of stringed keyboard instruments in London, *fl.* 1538–53 [*Russell 1959*, p. 65].

BIAGIO, Stefano di. *See*: BONISSIMO, Stefano.

BIDERMAN, Samuel. Born at Ulm in 1540; died at Augsburg in 1622. Organ builder and spinet maker, best known for his automatic spinets—ottavinos with a clockwork mechanism which may be used or turned off at will. (The action of one of these instruments is photographed in A. Protz, *Mechanische Musikinstrumente*, Kassel, Bärenreiter-Verlag [1943], p. 56.) After his death Biderman's work was continued by his sons, Samuel the Younger (1600–at least 1653) and Daniel (1603–63).

Surviving Instruments by the Biderman Family

(1) Undated. Nuremberg, Germanisches Nationalmuseum, Rück Collection. Automatic spinet.

(1a) 1606. Harburg, Fürstlich Oettingen-Wallenstein'sche Bibliothek. Ottavino virginal inscribed: *Ioannes Bidermann MDCVI* on jackrail. Restored in 1960 by Fritz Thomas, Munich.

(2) 1627. Leningrad, Institute for Scientific Research on the Theatre and Music. Ottavino virginal, signed: *Samuel Biderman Augusta* [sic] *1627.* Compass F–F, 3 octaves; 37 keys. Rose.

(3) 1651. Breslau. Schlesisches Museum. Automatic spinet; compass C–C with short octave. Forty-five keys. It plays 6 tunes, listed on a MS. label, presumably original:

Beschreibung dieses Instrumentes, was es vor Stück von sich selbsten spielet.

Zum Ersten einen lustigen Aufzug, so durch die Trompeter (:Alss Jr Kay: May: in Nürrenberg den Einzug gehalten:) geblasen ist worden.

Anderen, einen Polnischen Tanz und repetiret ihn zweimal.
Dritten, Noch ein andren Polnischen Tanz und repetieret ihn auch zweimal.
Vierten, Lobet Gott unsern Herren in seinem Heiligthum, und repetiret zwei gesetze.
Fünften, Ess stehen für Gottes Throne:/:und repetiret zwei gesetze.
Sechsten, Allein Gott in der Höhe sei [Ehr'], und danken vor seine Gnade, repetiret zwei gesetze.
Nochmals mag ein Jeder, der nur schlagen kann, auf diesem Instrument aufspielen alle diejenigen Stück, die man sonsten auf andern Instrumenten zu Spielen pfleget.

(4) Undated. Vienna. Kunsthistorisches Museum. Automatic spinet; second half of the sixteenth century. Compass C–C, 4 octaves. Contains 4 labels inscribed: *Samuel Biderman, Instrumentmacher in Augsburg.* It plays 6 pieces, which are transcribed in Schlosser's catalogue. Some, if not all, of them are different pieces from those played by the Breslau instrument.

This instrument was taken over from the Ambras Collection in 1880.

(5) Undated. Uppsala. An automatic spinet, not playable.

(6) Undated. A spinet in a case, signed *Samuel Biderman Augusta* [sic], was in the Old Savoye Collection, Paris. Compass 2 octaves and 8 notes.

(6a) Undated. Paris, Mr. Tagger (1971). Perhaps the same instrument as no. 6.

(7) Undated. Leningrad, Institute for Scientific Research on the Theatre and Music. Automatic spinet, anonymous; perhaps by Bidermann. E–C 3 octaves and a 6th, 45 keys; uninitialled rose.

BIDERMANN, Johann, *fl.* 1606. A toy rectangular virginal in the Fürstlich Oettingen-Wallenstein'sche Bibliothek und Kunstsammlungen at Schloss Harburg, near Donauwörth, is signed: *Joannes Biderman MDCVI.*

It is quite possible that this maker was related to Samuel Biderman: Donauwörth is not far from Augsburg [*VdM*].

BIEST, Marten van der, of Antwerp. Harpsichord maker. Dates ascertained, 1557–84.

In 1557 he entered the Guild of St. Luke as a harpsichord maker. In 1575 he was a witness to the marriage of Hans Ruckers the Elder (q.v.) at the O. L. Vrouwe Kerk: 'Hans Ruckaerts—Naenken Cnaeps—Solemnisatum 25 junii a° 75 Testes Merten Van der Byest, Adam Boest' [*St*].

Shortly before 1587 he moved to Amsterdam, where he was enrolled as a citizen on 25 May 1587 [*Curtis*, p. 47].

Surviving Instruments

(1) 1580. Nuremberg, Germanisches Nationalmuseum. A double virginal with ottavino on the right having a compass of 4 octaves C–C. Inscription on jackrail: *Martinus Vander Biest m[e]f[ecit] 1580.* (See further *RGI*, pp. 71–3, in a paper by J. H. van der Meer.) Said to have been made for Alessandro Farnese. It is illustrated in *Po* (pl. 14).

An anonymous painting of the Dutch school, in the Gemeente-Museum, The Hague, shews a virginal bearing on the jackrail the inscription: *Martin van der Biest 1584.*

BIRGER, Giovanni Domenico. *See*: BERGER, Giovanni Domenico.

BLACKARD, Jasper. *See*: BLANCKART, Jasper.

BLAHA, V. von. *Fl.* 1765 in Prague; built claviorgana, and invented a new stop for harpsichords [*Abhandlungen über Klaviersaiteninstrumente*, 1843].

BLANCHE, François Yacinthe, of Estavayer, Switzerland (canton of Fribourg). Harpsichord maker. From 1758 to 1761 he worked in Fribourg and 1762–3 in Yverdon [*Rindl*].

BLANCHES, François. Harpsichord maker at Lyons in the eighteenth or late seventeenth century, according to *Vallas*, p. 379.

BLANCHET. A family of harpsichord makers resident in Paris in the eighteenth century. (See *Verlet* for an account in greater detail.)

(1) **Nicolas Blanchet,** Parisian harpsichord maker, 1660–1731. A native of Rheims, he set up in Paris shortly before 1686 [*Hardouin 1957*, p. 10], in the rue des Fossés St. Germain. (He is not to be confused with his son Nicolas Pierre Blanchet, who was priest of the parish church of St. Merry, Paris, in 1752 and lived in the rue St. Martin in that parish in 1789 [*Bouv.*].) His name appears on one harpsichord (see list of instruments in table 3) together with that of his younger son:

(2) **François-Etienne Blanchet** (I) [*often called* Etienne Blanchet]. Born *c.* 1695 and died in 1761. The approximate date of his birth is indicated by the birth of one of his daughters, Elizabeth Antoinette, in 1729, at which time Blanchet was living in the rue de la Verrerie in the parish of Saint Merry, Paris. The house belonged to his second wife, Elizabeth; he moved into it soon after his marriage to her in 1727. He was still residing in the same street in 1752, when Elizabeth Antoinette was married to the organist and composer Armand-Louis Couperin (1727–89), a cousin of François Couperin-le-Grand [*Bouv*].

A document of 1741 refers to 'François-Etienne Blanchet et Paul Villars, maîtres luthiers, faiseurs d'instruments de musique et jurés en charge de leur communauté' [*Loub*, p. 174], who had brought an action against certain persons, not members of the Guild of Instrument Makers, who were producing instruments (Villars was a maker of woodwind instruments. See *Pi*, p. 99).

About 1756 Blanchet was maker to the King of France. Pascal Taskin was apprenticed to him, and later succeeded to his business [*J*, p. 135]. (An impeccable source for this is Taskin's own trade-card, pasted on to Taskin harpsichord no. 2.) A harpsichord made by Blanchet in 1749 is mentioned in an inventory dated 1794 [*Br*, p. 101].

Besides making and repairing instruments, Blanchet did a good deal of extending (*mettre à grand ravalement*) of the early Flemish harpsichords, especially those from the Ruckers workshops, and his work clearly had a wide reputation. In fact he made the 'Ruckers' no. 89, q.v. The *Dictionnaire portatif des arts et métiers* (Yverdon, 1767, Vol. 2, p. 7) refers to him:—'C'est dans cet art d'aggrandir les clavecins des Ruckers que feu Blanchet a réussi incomparablement bien . . . Un clavecin de Ruckers ou de Couchet, artistement coupé & enlargi, avec des sauteraux, régistres et claviers de Blanchet, devient aujourd'hui un instrument très-précieux.'

The name of Blanchet's son was also:

(3) **François-Etienne Blanchet** (II), *c.* 1730–66. Pascal Taskin (I) married his widow, but she bore him no children. François-Etienne Blanchet II inherited from his father the title *Facteur du Roi*.

(4) **Armand François Nicolas Blanchet,** 1763–1818. Son of François-Etienne II, was born in Paris. He learnt harpsichord making from his father's former apprentice Pascal Taskin. Highly skilled in tuning, he was tuner to the King of France.

In 1795, and in 1801 when he published his *Méthode abregée pour accorder le clavecin et le piano,* he was living at 167 rue de la Verrerie, which appears to have been the house bequeathed to Taskin by François-Etienne Blanchet.

He died in Paris on 18 April 1818 [*Fé*], and his son **Nicolas** succeeded to his business, by then devoted entirely to pianoforte making.

Tree of **Blanchet** and **Taskin**

(Harpsichord makers are in **bold** type)

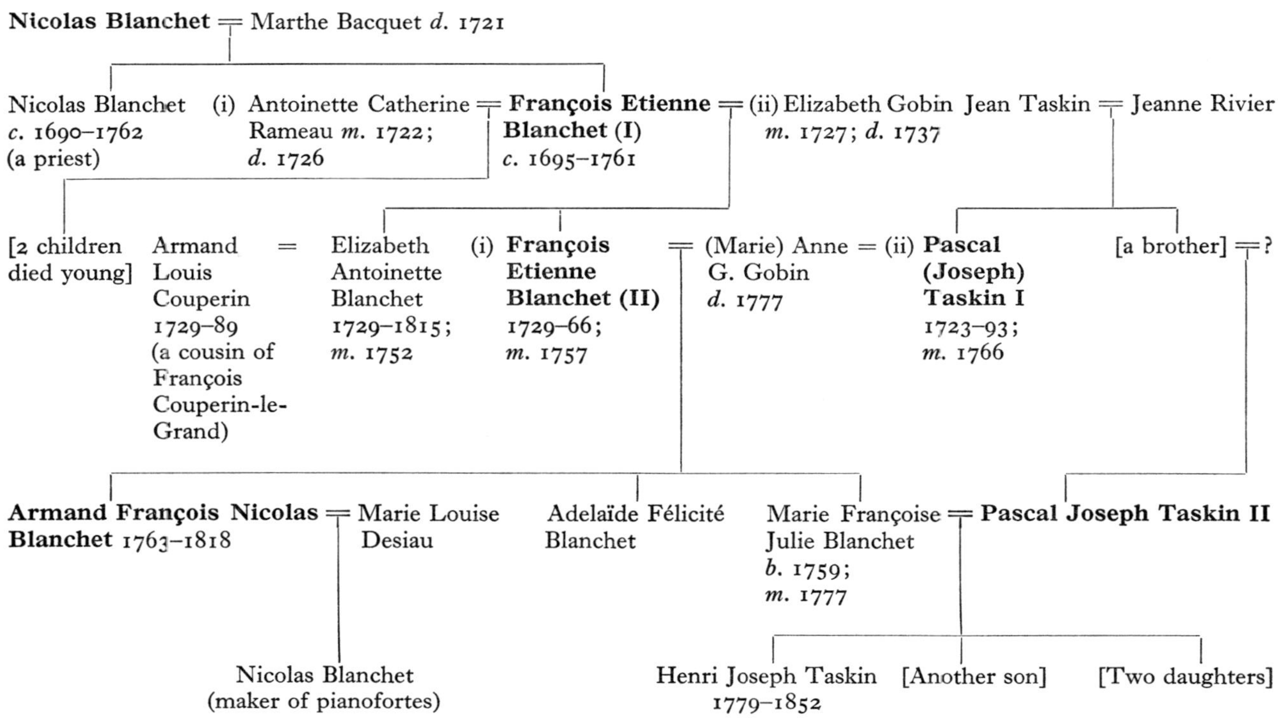

TABLE 3. *Surviving Instruments by the BLANCHET Family*

No.	Date	Type	Kbs.	Signature	Owner/Remarks
01	1693	H	2		Paris, private ownership. Pedalboard (30 notes) missing.
02	1698	S	1		In private ownership in France.
03	1710	S	1		Angers (Maine-et-Loire), Conservatoire.
04	1725	H	2	*Andreas Ruckers me fecit Antverpiae*	Recorded as Ruckers instrument no. 89 s.v. Ruckers, but actually a Blanchet. See *VdMRuck*, p. 10.
1	1730	H	2	*N. et François Blanchet 1730* [round the rose]	Framingham, Mass., Charles Fisher (formerly Raymond Russell). *NB* rose.
2		H	2		Paris, Huguette Dreyfus (formerly Raymond Russell, who sold it at Sotheby's on 29 June 1956 to the Pelham Galleries, London). Illustrated on plates 12 and 13 of *Hof*. Compass 5 octaves; *NB* rose. The numerals *1744* pencilled on the jack-rail do not record the year of construction, which must have been before 1731.

TABLE 3 (*cont.*):

No.	Date	Type	Kbs.	Signature	Owner/Remarks
2a	1733	H			Thoiry, Comte de la Panouse (1969). Made by François Blanchet. See *ClavHist*, s.v. 'Hemsch'. Has its original strings (1970) [*Chambure*].
3	—	H	2	*François Blanchet Paris* [round the rose]	Paris, Mme Oury. F–C, 4½ octaves; 2×8′, 1×4′. *FB* rose.
3a	1746	H	2		Versailles, Palais. Compass 5 octaves; 2×8′, 1×4′. Found by Harold Priest, 1961.
4(?)	[1709]	S	1	*Blanchet*	Hever Castle, Kent. The inscription, giving the date as 1709 and the maker's name as *Blanchet*, is suspicious. The maker would be Nicolas Blanchet, if the date is right. (This is perhaps the 'virginale de François [*sic*] Blanchet' in the Savoye Collection III, sold in Paris on 13 June 1924, though it is not likely.)
5	17..	H	2	*François Blanchet, Paris*	Versailles Museum. Five octaves.

BLANCKART, Jasper. Maker of virginals. Dates ascertained, 1566–82 [*J*]. He came over from Flanders to London in 1566 and worked for William Treasorer (q.v.). Afterwards he set up on his own account. He lived in Aldgate [*J*].

BLANKENBURG, Quirijn Gerbrandt van. Born at Gouda in 1654; died at The Hague about 1740. Primarily theorist, organist, and composer. Studied at Leyden University. In 1708 he rebuilt a Ruckers harpsichord. The process is described on p. 145 of his book *Elementa musica, of nieuw licht tot het welverstaan van de musiec en de bascontinuo* (The Hague, L. Berkoske, 1739). For further details of his life see *GD*.

BLASSER, Thomas. Harpsichord maker in London, *fl.* 1744. Some aspects of the instrument below suggest that he may have worked at some time for Shudi. (He must have served his apprenticeship outside London, as he does not appear in *Join.*)

Surviving Harpsichords

(1) 1744. Goudhurst, Kent, Messrs. Adlam and Burnett, who bought it at Sotheby's on 13 March 1972 from the Countess of Dysart, who had kept it at Strobo Castle, Peebles. Two manuals. Inscription on nameboard: *Thomas Blasser fecit Londini 1744*; restorer's label on underside of soundboard: *Restored by Arnold Dolmetsch and W. Nearn (12 Windmill Street) London Sept. 1895.* F–F, 5 octaves without lowest F sharp; 2×8′ (one of them dog-leg), 4′ (with a pedal added later), lute, buff (added later). Five handstops. No rose. A typical English instrument and a very early example of the use of mahogany for the case (the key-surround and inside of case veneered with burr walnut with boxwood inlay).

BLOMSTEEN, Marten, of Antwerp. Harpsichord maker. Dates ascertained, 1535–62.

The contract whereby he took Ghijsbrecht van Sammelt into his workshop as assistant in 1535 is quoted by *St*. In 1540 he was received into the Guild of St. Luke as harpsichord maker. He married Pauline, daughter of the organ builder Antonius Moors in 1562 [*St*].

BLOMSTEEN, Christoffel, of Antwerp. Harpsichord maker, son of Marten B. Dates ascertained, 1550–8, in which latter he entered the Guild of St. Luke as harpsichord maker [*St*]. *Hirt* gives his latest known date as 1580.

BLOUNT, Edward. *See* BLUNT, Edward.

BLUME, Heinrich Julius, of Brunswick, *fl.* 1804. His name appears as an *Instrumentenmacher* together with that of Lemme. He probably made harpsichords and clavichords [*SB*, p. 48].

BLUMER, Samuel. London maker of harpsichords, spinets, and clavicytheria. Dates ascertained, 1749–88. He was probably a member of an old-established family of this name in Schwanden, Glarus, Switzerland, and was driven by economic conditions to seek a livelihood elsewhere, like other joiners such as his fellow citizen Burkat Shudi, for whom he worked at some time before about 1745.

A bill-head bearing his name states that he was 'harpsichord and spinet maker, in Great Poulteney Street near Golden Square, London. NB. late Foreman to Mr. Shudi'. This document is a receipt for £63 paid for a clavicytherium or upright harpsichord on 22 August 1753 [*Da*, p. 51].

His trade card between 1749 and 1755, on which he is depicted tuning a harpsichord in the presence of a lady and gentleman is reproduced by *J* (p. 129), where an advertisement from *The World* of 12 January 1788 is quoted, offering a 'capital double-keyed Harpsichord, one of Blumer's best make and cost 46 guineas'.

Blumer lived in Great Pulteney Street from 1749 to 1755 [*RBJ*].

Is it possible that before working for Shudi, Blumer worked for John Hitchcock and was the 'Sam' who signed 4 surviving instruments of this maker?

BLUNT, Edward. Born about 1678; died before December 1718. Apprenticed to Stephen Keene for 7 years from 5 September 1693; freeman of the Joiners' Company December 1700 [*Join*]. (His father, Edward B., recorded as a 'citizen and weaver' of London, may possibly have made instruments also.) *J*, p. 65, refers to 2 spinets labelled 'Blunt', made in 1664 and 1703 respectively, both of them signed *Thos. Hitchcock* on jack or key. *See below*: HITCHCOCK; also *Musical Times*, 1890, p. 719.

Surviving Spinets

(1) An undated spinet signed *Edwardus Blunt* belongs (1965) to M. D. Corke, Bury St. Edmunds. (It was repaired by Messrs. Robert Morley of Bromley.)

(2) The Boston Museum of Fine Arts has a spinet whose top key is inscribed: *E.B. 1700*. G/B–D, 4½ octaves with short octave; 2 split keys.

BLUNTE, Thomas, of London. Virginal maker, *fl.* 1594. [Parish records of St. Giles, Cripplegate.]

BLYTH, Samuel, of Salem, Mass. Painter, organist, and maker of musical instruments. He was baptized in 1744 and died in 1795. On 7 February 1786 he charged Mrs. Margaret Barton 'to making a spinnett for her daughter £18.0.0.'.

Surviving Instruments

(1) Salem, Mass., Essex Institute. Spinet signed on nameboard: *Samuel Blyth Salem Massachusetts Fecit*. It appears to be undated and is assigned by the Institute to the period 1785–90. (*J*, p. 112, gives its date as 1789; the catalogue of the 1902 Chickering Exhibition, Boston, as 1786; and *Michel*, p. 129, as 1784.)

[(2) New York, Metropolitan Museum of Art—a mistake for Clemm, q.v.]

BOCCALARI, Giovanni Nataje. Harpsichord maker at Naples in 1717.

Surviving Harpsichords

(1) 1699. Amsterdam, G. Leonhardt. One manual; $2 \times 8'$ registers; C–E, 4 octaves and a 3rd.

(2) 1717, Basel. Schola Cantorum Basiliensis. Otto Lobeck Collection; $2 \times 8'$ stops, and buff. Compass C–C, 4 octaves. Inscription on back of nameboard: *Giovanni Natale Boccalari Napoli alli 22 de Maio 1717*.

BOCK, Christoph, *fl.* 1804. Maker of keyboard instruments in Vienna, where he was 'tuner of keyboard instruments in both of the Court Theatres'.

The Kunsthistorisches Museum, Vienna, has a spinet by him inscribed *Christoph Bock, Clavierstimer beider K.K. Hoftheater fecit año 1804 in Wien* on the back of the nameboard. C–F, 4 octaves and a 4th. The only plucked keyboard instrument of Viennese provenance extant, it was transferred to the Museum from the Court furniture-store. See *Luith*, p. 23.

BODE, Johann Friedrich, of Berlin, *fl.* 1798. Made clavichords and pianofortes [*Ge*].

BODECHTEL, Johann Jacob. Maker of organs and stringed keyboard instruments in Nuremberg in the eighteenth century.

Surviving Instruments

(1) London, Alexander Helman. Gebunden clavichord undated *c.* 1750. Compass 4½ octaves C to F; fine tone. Probably the same instrument as that bought by Messrs. Morley at Puttick & Simpson's, 18 June 1931.

BODER, Daniel. *See*: BADER, Daniel.

BODY, Thomas. Virginal maker in London. Dates ascertained, 1647–62. Came to London from Handborough, Oxon.; in 1647 apprentice to Joseph Boddy, presumably a relative, joiner; free of the Joiners Company, 1656 [*Join*].

Surviving Instruments

(1) Typical seventeenth-century English virginal with painted case and vaulted lid. Jackrail inscribed: *Thomas Body Londini Fecit 1662*. Two gilded roses. Boxwood naturals.

Acquired in August 1967 by William Lee of York, the instrument apparently having been since its making in the possession of the family of the previous owner, the late Sir Mark Millbank, Bt., of Barningham Park, Richmond, Yorks. Now (May 1969) owned by Roger Warner, Burford.

BOGAERDE, Ghijsbrecht van den. Harpsichord maker of Antwerp; dates ascertained, 1557–9.

He was born at Ghent, son of Joos v. d. B., and entered the Guild of St. Luke, Antwerp, in 1557 [*St*].

He also made lutes and zithers [*Lü*].

BOHAK, Johann. Clavichord maker, probably Bohemian, *fl.* 1794. In an article in the *Musical Times* (April 1930) Philip James illustrated a 5-octave clavichord by this maker and adduced evidence connecting it with Haydn. It is dated 1794. Its compass is F–F, and it has a double-pinned bridge and its original tangent rail. Illustrated by *Walter*, 272, where several pages are devoted to its history. It appears to have passed, on Haydn's death, to the well-known Fanny Elssler (1810–84), daughter of Haydn's servant and copyist Johann Elssler; then to the Esterházy horn-players Anton and Michael Prinster; then in 1831 to Demetrius Lichtenthal of Eisenstadt; then to Anton Richter the Esterházy singer (d. 1854); then to his son, the conductor Hans Richter, from whom it passed in 1911 to Miss Chapman and later to the Royal College of Music, London.

BOHR, Christoph H., of Dresden. *Fl.* 1713, the date of a 2-manual spinet by him in the Heyer Collection, whose catalogue (*Ks*) records it as anonymous (*Fla*].

BOLCIONE, Vicentio. *Fl.* 1608–12 at Florence as a maker of harpsichords, organs, and other instruments [*VM*, Vol. 5, 1889, pp. 552 ff.].

BOLCIONI, Stefano. Harpsichord maker; dates ascertained 1627(?)–41. He was living in the Via dei Servi, Florence, in 1634, in which year his name appears on the matriculation books of his Guild there. His father's name was Vincenzo B. [*Pu*]. The epithet *Pratensis*, which follows his name in the inscription mentioned below, may indicate that he was a native of Prato, 11 miles north-west of Florence.

Va (p. 279) notes a Stefano Folcione, spinet maker of Prato *fl.* 1641, and a Stephanus Colciunnius [?], spinet maker of Prato, *fl.* 1629. Both of these are presumably Stefano Bolcioni.

FrancI lists a 'spinetta' inscribed: *Stefanus Bolcionius Pratensis 1629.*

Surviving Instruments with a Stefano Bolcioni signature

(1) 1627. Edinburgh University (formerly Raymond Russell). Harpsichord with 3 manuals. Inscribed on back of nameboard: *Stefanus Bolcionius Pratensis F. A.D. MDCXXVII F.* An elaborate fraud.

(2) 1629. In *FrancI* (item 31). Pol. V, inscribed: *Stefanus Bolcionius Pratensis 1629.* Inscription dubious.

(3) 1631. Providence, R.I., Rhode Island School of Design. Harpsichord, 1-manual; 2×8′ stops. Inscribed: *F. Stefanus Bolcionius Pratensis MDCXXXI F.* Compass C/E–F. Repaired in 1921 by Adolf Wihan.

BOLCIONI, Antonio. Son of Stefano, Florentine harpsichord maker; dates ascertained, 1663–4. In 1663 his name appears on the matriculation books of his Guild in Florence: 'Faciente far bottega di strumentaio, riconosce suo padre.' In the following year he is recorded as working for Bartolomeo Pini (q.v.) [*Pu*].

BOLCIONI, Janus. A polygonal virginal in Leipzig University in 1935, on loan from the Kunstgewerbemuseum there, is said to be inscribed by Janus Colcionus of Prato. I suspect that he is a member of the Bolcioni family.

BOMBINI, of Modena and Rome. *Fl.* in the sixteenth century (a harpsichord by him was in Modena in 1598). *Va* (p. 129) quotes from a wardrobe inventory of the house of Este (eighteenth century): 'Un cembalo piccolo, con tastatura di bussolo e legno nero, con due registri, opera dell'abb. [= Abate] Bombini danneggiato e con una bruciatura nel davanti, in controcassa di piella con serratura e senza chiave. Cosi e stato restituito da casa Marsciani a di Maggio 1771.'

BONAFINIS, Francesco. Italian virginal maker, *fl.* 1585–7.

Surviving Instruments

(1) 1587. New York, Metropolitan Museum of Art. A polygonal virginal in a rectangular case. Inscribed on name-batten: *Franciscus Bonafinis MDLXXXV*, but on its back, in a crude hand: *Factum anno 1587.* The 2 dates would seem to indicate that, for some unusual reason, the instrument was begun in 1585 and completed 2 years later.

A further inscription in a neater hand, also on the back of the name-batten, reads: *Post spacium centum triginta duo añorum Restauratum à me N: N: anno 1717.* I have not been able to identify this restorer (who may not necessarily of course have been Italian).

Compass 3 octaves and a 6th, C–A. Illustrated in the museum catalogue. Inscriptions illustrated below, plates 20–1. *See also*: Benismis.

BONDBOUGH, John. *See*: Pringle, Archibald.

BONETTI, Pietro. A spurious ottavino at the Smithsonian Institution, Washington (until 1960 in the Cooper Union, New York), is inscribed on the nameboard: *Petrus Bonettus faciebat anno domini 1531.*

BONGIORNO. Harpsichord maker of Rome. A harpsichord with 2×8′ registers by him dated 1656 (?), is owned by W. Dobson, Aix-en-Provence [*GL*].

BONI, Gioseffe [Buoni], of Cortona. Harpsichord maker. A harpsichord inscribed *Giuseppe Buoni da Cortona faceva MDCLXXXI* was in the collection of Prince Ferdinand of Tuscany in 1700. It had 2×8′, 1×4′ stops; 45 keys; no rose [*Gai*, p. 12].

This maker was presumably related to the next maker. *FrancII* records a 'spinetta di viaggio' with the astonishing inscription: *Joseph Bonos et Cortona.*

Surviving Instruments

(1) 1693. Paterson, N.J., Harry A. Joelson, acquired from Dean Brown of New York. Harpsichord signed (on a key): *1693 Gioseff*[*e*] *Buoni Corton*[*a*]; one of the jacks initialled: *GBC 1693.* At one time restored by Alec Hodsdon.

BONI, Giovanni Battista, of Cortona. Harpsichord maker; dates ascertained: 1617–75 [*Va*]. He is recorded in Pinaroti's MS. *Polyanthea technica* as 'Giuseppe De Bonis, detto il Certina o Cortina' [*Vds*, Vol. 6, p. 514].

An Italian harpsichord in private ownership in Vienna may be by this maker as the bottom key is signed in ink: *1638 GB.* 2×8′ stops; compass G/B–C, 4½ octaves. Boxwood naturals. Dimensions 241×87·5 cm. Restored by Peter Kukelka in 1969. Initials *CPC* (? of an earlier owner) cut in left side of case.

Surviving Instruments

(1) 1617. Smithsonian Institution, Washington (given by the Cooper Union, New York). Polygonal virginal. Inscription on jackrail: *Joannes Batt. Boni da Cortona fecit anno 1617.* C/E–F, 4½ octaves. Split keys: lowest F sharp, G sharp, D sharp, then G sharp and D sharp throughout. Boxwood naturals, black sharps. Lid painted, with coat of arms in centre. Rose. Illustrated in *Wash 1969.*

(2) 1619. Brussels Conservatoire. Harpsichord inscribed *Gio Battista Boni Cortenesi 1619.* C/E–C, 4 octaves; bottom 2 sharps divided. Formerly in the Correr Collection, Venice [*Mah*, III. 169].

(3) Undated. The collection of Lyonel d'Estries in France contains a harpsichord signed *G.B.B. fecit* which may well be by this maker. It has 2×8′ stops.

BONISSIMO

(1) **Giannantonio.** Referred to as 'Zaneantonio dai manachordi' and 'Joane Antonio maistro da manachordi'. Harpsichord and clavichord maker of Modena; *fl.* 1485 [*Va*; *MarcP*].

(2) **Stefano** [Stefano di Giannantonio, Stefano di Biagio] son of (1). Of Venice, maker of harpsichords and clavichords. Dates ascertained, 1506–15; also referred to as 'maistro d'arpicordi' [*Va*; *MarcP*].

BONNOT, Joseph [Josef Bonau]. *Fl.* 1665 at Avignon as maker of harpsichords and other instruments. In June 1665 he signed (using the form Josef Bonau) a contract to make a double harpsichord with 2×8′ and 1×4′ stops, a compass of 50 keys, and apparently a push–pull coupler, for the nobleman Jean de Roland [F. Lesure in *GSJ*, Vol. 6, 1953, p. 106].

BONOMEN, Giovanni-Baptista. *See*: JOHANNES BAPTISTA, *Bononiensis.*

BONONIENSIS, Antonius. *See*: ANTONIUS, *Bononiensis.*

BONONIENSIS, Hieronymus. *See*: HIERONYMUS, *Bononiensis.*

BONTAN, Pierre. *See*: TOURNAN, Bertrand.

BONTEMPS, Nicolas. Dates ascertained, 1506–23. Clavichord maker who lived at Lyons as a 'faiseur d'instruments' and 'de manichordions'. [*Cou*; see also *Mah.* III. 169, and *Pi*, p. 63.] *Va* provides his earliest date (1506) and M. Dalbanne of Lyons his latest.

BORDEGATUS, Antonius. Italian virginal maker in the seventeenth century.

Surviving Instruments

(1) 1703. Padua, Museo Civico. Polygonal virginal, signed: *Antonius Bordegatus Fecit MDCCIII.* Rose without monogram. Compass 3 octaves C/E to C.

BORTOLO PADOVANO. *See*: CRISTOFORI, Bartolommeo.

BORTOLOTTI, Alexander. *See*: BERTOLOTTI, Alexander.

BORTOLUS. Virginal maker in the seventeenth century, probably Italian. A polygonal virginal in Heinrich Schumacher's collection, Lucerne (1910), bore the inscription: *Bortolus fecit anno 16.. Quintilius Cap[ezzo renovavit] et ornavit Sensis* [?] [*Gö*].

The Old Music Store, Deansboro, New York, had (March 1957) a lavishly decorated single harpsichord inscribed: *Her II Fer Dux IIII CRI*, presumably recording ownership by Ercole d'Este II, Duke of Ferrara (b. 1508, succeeded 1534, d. 1559). It is signed *Bortolus fecit* on the back of the nameboard and has been assigned to the 1540s. It is now (1971) owned by C. F. Maikoffske, Naples, and is perhaps instrument no. 551 in *Kraus.* (It seems therefore that *16..* in the inscription on the Schumacher virginal is a misreading for *15..*)

BOS, Hans [Bossus]. Dates ascertained, 1543–72. Well-known organ builder of Antwerp, who also made harpsichords. He entered the Guild of St. Luke, Antwerp, in 1558 as an organ builder [*St*].

In 1543 he lived in the parish of St. Joris, and married Jeanne Oden of the parish of O. L. Vrouw. Various entries in official books relating to Bos's activities as organ builder and tuner are quoted by *St.* In two documents of 1550 and 1572 he is described as 'harpsichord maker' (*clavesimbelmaker*) [*Po*].

Pr (p. 16) mentions him as an outstanding maker of harpsichords and symphonies, most of them tuned a third lower than those in Germany: 'der vortreffliche Instrumentmacher zu Antorff Johannes Bossus . . .'

A virginal by him is in the Monasterio de Santa Clara, Tordesillas, Spain. Compass C/E–C. Typical Antwerp instrument, with sea-horse paper. Inscribed on jackrail: *[H]uius instrumenti factor est Iohannes Bossus factor org.* The date 1570 was ascribed to it in the catalogue when it was shewn in the Toledo 1958 exhibition ('Carlos V y su ambiente: exposición homenoje en el IV centenario de su muerte'); when E. M. Ripin saw the instrument in 1969 he could find no date on it. (*Russell 1959*, p. 116, mentions it, but calls it a harpsichord and slightly misquotes the inscription; he gives no date.)

BOSSART, Emanuel. Organ builder in Berne, born 1729 (?). Also made spinets, of which he advertised one in 1755 [*Rindl*].

BOTTISANGO, Giulio Cesare [? *or* Bottifango]. Died at Rome 1626. Amateur maker of wind and other instruments. He made a harpsichord ['Clavicymbel'] and bequeathed it to the Jesuit College at Rome [*Wa*].

BOUDIN, Joseph. *CIP* (p. 71) gives this form in mistake for Baudin, q.v.

BOURDET, Jacques (I). *c.* 1660–1737, when an inventory [*MC*, pp. 91, 758, 2 March 1757] lists instruments in his possession, his tools having apparently already been taken over by his son Jacques Guillaume. He entered the guild of harpsichord makers in 1678 and became *juré* in 1689 [*Hubb 1965*, p. 92].

Either the father or the son attended the Goermans marriage in 1730—probably the father.

For further details see *Verlet* and *Hubb 1965*.

BOURDET, Jacques (II). Parisian harpsichord maker, son of Jacques Guillaume's first marriage. Born before 1711; died before 1764 [*Verlet*].

BOURDET, Jacques Guillaume. Parisian harpsichord maker, *fl.* 1736–50, in which year he made certain repairs to the harpsichord at the *Opéra* [*Pi*, p. 90]. In 1736 he became instrument maker to the Queen. See further *Verlet.*

BOUSSU, Jacques. Parisian harpsichord maker, *fl.* 1706 [*Verlet*].

BOUTON, Jacques. Harpsichord maker in Paris; *fl.* 1627 as 'Maître Faiseur d'espinettes du Roy' [*Laborde*].

BRACKLEY, Charles. Spinet maker in London, born *c.* 1688. Apprenticed to Stephen Keene for 7 years from 2 November 1703; by 1719 had been taken into partnership by him. Freeman of the Joiners' Company, January 1711. One of his instruments is illustrated in *DEF* (II. 374); undated; inscribed: *Carolus Brackley Londini Fecit.* (Property of Capt. N. R. Colville.) For a spinet initialled by him during his apprenticeship see Keene, instrument no. 5b.

BRADSHAW, Albion. Mr. Morley, South Kensington, had in 1964 for repair a seventeenth-century spinet inscribed: *Albion Bradshaw Londini Fecit.* Black naturals, white sharps. G–E 4 octaves plus 6th. Walnut case.

Bradshaw was apprenticed to Thomas Watts for 8 years from 18 March 1701; freeman of the Joiners' Company, January 1712.

BRÄUTIGAM, Johannes. *See*: BRUYDEGOM, Johannes.

BREBOS, Jan *or* **Hans.** Flemish builder of organs and harpsichords, son of the celebrated organ builder Gillis Brebos (d. 1584). Dates ascertained, 1567–1609, the latter being the year of his death.

In 1567 he became the pupil of Peter van Geelaer [*Bu*], and in the following year is recorded as announcing his intention of going to Copenhagen [quoted in *St*].

In 1592 he went to Toledo to build a monumental organ. The documents relating to this are quoted in *VdS* (VIII. 246–52).

He repaired the Queen's harpsichord at Valladolid [ibid., p. 254].

Other undertakings of his were the organ in the Royal Chapel of the Alcazar, a claviorganum for the Count de Nieve, an organ in Madrid, 2 regals for the Escorial [ibid., p. 255].

He was buried in the church of St. Martin, Madrid, in 1609. His will is quoted in *VdS* (VIII. 255–8).

BREITENBACH. *Adl* (II. 110) writes: 'Es ist mir aber auch ein Breitenbachisches Clavessin mit 2 Clavieren vorgekommen, das dreychöricht war.' He goes on to describe the instrument (1×4′, 1×8′, 1×16′, coupler) in detail. The 4′ and 16′ registers worked on the lower keyboard; the 8′ on the upper. Breitenbach probably refers to the town in Thuringia, 30 miles south of Erfurt, called Gross-Breitenbach, where several makers worked. J. H. Harrass (q.v.) was probably the man whom Adlung had in mind.

BRELIN, Niels *or* **Nicholas,** 1690–1753, of Sweden. Studied instrument making abroad. Became Pastor at Volstadt near Carlstadt. In 1741 he invented a clavicytherium, with 8 variations of tone controlled by pedals. This is described and illustrated in the *Svenska Vetenskaps Akademiens Handlingar*, Stockholm, 1741. *Nor* (p. 140) reproduces the illustrations and gives further sources of information about Brelin.

He also published in 1739 in the journal mentioned above an article entitled 'At oka clawers och Cymbalers godhet', in which he sets forth a new jack mechanism and method of improving the upper registers of the harpsichord by providing sympathetic strings. This article, translated into German, appeared in *Marp*, II. 322. See also *Ge* (1814).

BREMERS, Mathias, of Brussels. Eighteenth-century harpsichord and pianoforte maker. In 1785 he, with Ermel *père* and *fils* (q.v.) and 2 anonymous makers, laid a successful petition for an import duty on incoming harpsichords and other keyboard instruments, for the protection of local makers [*VdS*, II. 121].

BRENZI, Antonio, *of Bologna* (otherwise Antonius Bononiensis). Maker of musical instruments including (though not primarily) keyboard instruments at Bologna, *fl.* 1592–1628. Winternitz (*Musical Instruments of the Western World*, 1966) illustrates a lira da gamba, now in the Leipzig Collection, signed: *Antonius Brensius Bonon. 1592.* Also a viola survives bearing an authentic printed label reading: *Ant. Brenzi Bologna Año 1628.*

Surviving Keyboard Instruments

(1) Lisbon Conservatoire. Polygonal virginal signed on the soundboard: *Antonius Bononiensis fecit anno 1592.* Rose; C/E–F, 4½ octaves. Geometrical rose. Shewn at the International Inventions Exhibition, London, in 1885. We should, however, be cautious about this instrument since it figures as no. 44 in *FrancI.*

BRESCIANO. *See*: TRAERI, Domenico.

BRESSANO, Carlo, of Bologna. Virginal maker, *fl.* 1772 [*Va*].

BRETON, Jacques le. *See*: LE BRETON, Jacques.

BRIDGE, Richard, of London. Spinet-maker, *fl.* 1753. The Forsyth Collection, Manchester, has a 5-octave G–G spinet inscribed: *Ricardus Bridge London Fecit MDCCLIII.* Case profusely inlaid. Skunktail sharps.

He is probably the organ builder Richard Bridge or Bridges, pupil of Renatus Harris II; *fl.* London 1729–30 [*GD*, 5th edition, V. 384].

BRISCIANO, Giovanni Francesco. *See*: ANTEGNATO, Giovanni Francesco.

BRISSART, Jehan. Known to have been working in Paris as a harpsichord maker (*épinetier*), 1578–1607, first in the parish of St. Merry and later in the rue Montorgueil; friend of Pol Belamy and Médéric Lorillart (q.v.) [*Les*].

BRITSEN. Family of harpsichord makers in Antwerp in the seventeenth century. We know of:

(1) **Joris** I. Dates ascertained, 1613–56. In 1613 he was accepted by the Guild of St. Luke as a pupil of M. Ykens ('Joris Britsen by Melsen Ykens, antyckensnyder' [*Ro*, I. 498], 'Joris Britsen by Melchior Yckens, antycksnyder' [*Ro*, I. 500]).

(2) **Joris** II, probably son of Joris I. Entered the Guild of St. Luke as a harpsichord maker, in 1655–6.

(3) **Joris** III [called *The Younger*]. Received into the Guild as a master's son, 1658–9.

(4) **Alexander,** received into the Guild in 1717.

Several instruments have survived bearing the name of Joris Britsen. It is impossible to ascribe them with certainty to any one of the 3 makers of that name.

Surviving Joris Britsen Instruments

(1) 1675. Location unknown. (See *VdS*, VIII. 458–9.) Harpsichord, single-manual, signed: *Georgius Britsen Antverpiae 1675.*

(2) 1676. Virginal. Brussels Conservatoire, no. 2923. Formerly in the Régibo Collection (1897 catalogue, no. 22?), then in the Snoeck Collection (1903 catalogue, no. 408). See also *VdS*, VIII. 458–9.

(3) 1681. Location unknown. Double-manual harpsichord. Compass 4 octaves and 1 note; length 200 cm. Formerly in the Régibo Collection (1897 catalogue no. 7).

(4) 1681. Brussels no. 631. Virginal. Dimensions 76×47 cm. Shewn at the International Inventions Exhibition, London, 1885. Inscriptions: *Georgius Britsen me fecit Antverpiae*; also: *Sic transit gloria mundi* and *Acta virum probant*. There are also lutes bearing the name of Britsen [*Lü*].

BRIXIENSIS, Franciscus. *See*: ANTEGNATO, Giovanni Francesco.

BROADWOOD, John, 1732–1812. Founder of the firm of John Broadwood & Sons, pianoforte makers. He was born at Cockburnspath in Scotland, and died in London.

Broadwood, who was by trade a joiner, came to London in his twenties and was employed in 1761 by Shudi (q.v.) in his harpsichord workshop (*Gazetteer and Daily Advertiser*, London, 14 January 1767). In 1769 he married Shudi's daughter Barbara, and in the following year was taken into partnership by his father-in-law. After the latter's death in 1773 the partnership was continued with Shudi's son (named Burkat, like his father), and although Broadwood was now the senior partner his name still appears second in the harpsichord nameboard inscriptions (after 1780, however, his Christian name appears in full, Johannes). The latest surviving harpsichord which is known to bear both their names is dated 1791; but, according to Hipkins, Broadwood carried on the direction of the firm alone from 1782 onwards, although Burkat Shudi Junior survived until 1803.

In 1795 Broadwood took his son James Shudi Broadwood into partnership, making the firm John Broadwood and Son (by this time devoted wholly to the pianoforte); and when another son, Thomas, entered the partnership in 1807, it became John Broadwood and Sons.

BROCK, Hermann Willen. *See* WILLENBROCK, Hermann.

BRODERIP, Francis Fane. *See*: LONGMAN AND BRODERIP.

BROEDLER. Organ builder and clavichord maker from Vaihingen a.d. Enz, *fl.* 1809.

Surviving Clavichords

(1) 1809. Nuremberg, Germanisches Nationalmuseum, Rück Collection. Signed: *Orgelmacher Broedler aus Vaihingen a. d. Enz. 1809.*

BROMAN, Olof. Clavichord maker at Ronneby (Blekinge); born *c.* 1712, died or was dead in 1760.

Surviving Instruments

(1) 1758. Clavichord. Kulturhistoriska Museet, Lund. Signed: *Olof Broman Runneby* [sic] *1758.*

(2) 1736 (or 1756). Clavichord; 4 octaves plus 1 note; in Nordiska Museet, Stockholm.

(3) 1750. Harpsichord, 2 manuals. Musikhistoriska Museet, Stockholm. F–F, 5 octaves; 3×8′, 1×4′ stops. Length 3·60 m.

BROSY.

(1) **Peter Friedrich** of Schwäbisch-Hall. In the middle of the eighteenth century the only organ (and probably harpsichord) maker in Basel. Baptized 14 January 1700 [*RindlKlav*]. In 1745 he obtained citizenship. Died in 1764.

Surviving Instruments

(1) 1755. Schweizerisches Landesmuseum, Zürich. Spinet, signed on wrestplank: *Brosy in Basel 1755.* See *RindlKlav*, p. 32, for details and illustration.

(2) **Johann Jacob** born about 1750 in Basel, son of Peter Friedrich. After his father's death he was trained, from the age of 15, in the same craft by a foreign master, probably J. H. Silbermann, at the cost of the state and some musicians, 'because there had to be someone to look after the organs and harpsichords' (weil doch die allhiesigen Orgeln und Clavessins jemand zur Unterhaltung derselben nötig haben). Latest date ascertained, 1815 [*RindlKlav*, *Hirt*]. He also made pianos.

Surviving Instruments

(1) 1775. Basel, Historisches Museum. Spinet, very much in the Silbermann style. Inscription on a label: *Johann Jacob Brosy, Instrument und Orgelmacher in Basel 1775.* Compass F–F, 5 octaves. Walnut. Five legs. Rose similar to J. H. Silbermann's.

(2) 1790. Passed through the workshop of Messrs. Sabathil, Vancouver, 1971.

BROWNE, Thomas [Broun]. Organ builder, of Cambridge; *fl.* 1508. He probably made virginals as well, for his dealings with Robert Colyns 'wyerseller' are recorded. (See further *MA*, 1910–11, p. 179.)

BRUCK, Mathias. Clavichord maker, lived in the Katzenbauch (now Katzenbug), Cologne, in 1797, according to a directory for that year [*Ks*].

BRUNELLI, Antonio. Italian virginal maker, *fl.* 1798.

The Heyer Collection, Leipzig, has an ottavino by him, inscribed on the soundboard: *Antonio Brunelli fecce 1798.* Compass C–C, 3 octaves. Boxwood naturals, ebony sharps. 59·5×29·5 cm. Inscription reproduced at *Ks* (p. 214).

BRUNER, Frederick. Harpsichord maker at Tyler's Court, Westminster, 1790. [Westminster Poll Book.] [*Byrne.*]

BRUNETO *dalli Organi*, of Verona. Known particularly for his organ building, *fl.* 1556. A polygonal virginal by him in the Milan Conservatoire is reported to me as inscribed: *Bruneto dalli Organi veronese—fece l'anno 1556. Adi 18 Luglio* [18 July 1556]. Dimensions 156×51 cm. His name seems to appear again on a polygonal virginal of 1532 in the Institute for Scientific Research on the Theatre and Music, Leningrad. *See below*: TRASONTINO, Giovanni Francesco *and* FLORIANO, Benedetto.

Surviving Instruments

(1) 1556. Milan. Details above.

(2) 1558. Copenhagen. Musikhistorisk Museum. Pol. V, inscribed on lower jack-guide (inside the instrument):

Brunetto [d]al[li] Organi Veronēsis 1558. Rose, without initials. Sold by J. G. Steingraeber to the Museum in 1932.

(3) 1564. Germanisches Nationalmuseum, Rück Collection. Pol. V, inscribed on the jack-guide: *Bruneti Veronēsis MDLXIIII 23 Marzo*. On a front-board it is also inscribed: *Benedicti Floriani MDLXVIIII*, and a restorer's inscription: *Fu restaurato da me Carlo Piaža / Año 1749*.

BRUYDEGOM, Johannes. Maker of keyboard instruments. Born at Stargard in Pomerania in 1704 or 1705. On 22 October 1747 he married Catharina Barbara van Asten from Stolberg. By 1743 he had settled in The Hague. Marpurg refers to him under the name Bräutigam in the 11 December 1762 issue of his *Kritische Briefe* as 'ein braver Clavier-macher im Haag'. References to harpsichords by him appear in wills of 1780 and 1786. See further *Curtis*, pp. 47–8.

BUCA, Isabella, *fl.* 1612, of Naples and Rome. Was concerned with the making of harpsichords [*Va*]. Her husband was Francesco della Nona (q.v.).

BUCHHOLZ, Fryderyk. An 'épinette' signed *Fryderyk Buchholz w Warszawie* is reported to me as being in the Piotrków Museum. Whether it is indeed a spinet or virginal, or only a square piano, I have not been able to verify.

BUGGIANO. A pentagonal virginal in the Berlin Collection is inscribed: *Per Buggiano, e che non si presti mai a Nissuno Spinetta costruita l'Anno 1618, e acquistata dalla casa N . . . l'An . . .* On the nameboard the date 1706.

BUGNON, Aimé. Organist at Chalon-sur-Sâone. Built in 1535 an 'orgue-épinette' [*Nor*, p. 144]. For fuller details see *Fleury*.

BÜHLER, Johann Michael. Instrument maker at Vaihingen an der Enz in Württemberg *c.* 1791. He worked with Späth and Schmahl (q.v.) at Regensburg, and devised a pianoforte with 2 keyboards. Later he sold bundfrei clavichords for 30 florins [*Ge* (1814)].

BUL, Nikolaas. The last harpsichord maker entered on the books of the Guild of St. Luke, Antwerp, 1793. *Gö* thinks it possible that he may be identical with the next maker, though it is unlikely that he is.

BULL, Johann Peter. Harpsichord maker in Antwerp. According to the *Musikalischer Almanach* of 1782 he was born in Germany. Dates ascertained, 1772–89. He was trained in the workshop of J. D. Dülcken (q.v.) and receives favourable mention in *BurnG* (I. 47)—'a good workman . . . who sells his double harpsichords for a hundred ducats each . . .'

It is pleasant to speculate upon a relationship between this maker and the English composer John Bull (*c.* 1562–1628), who was organist at the Cathedral in Antwerp from 1617 until his death there 11 years later.

Surviving Instruments

(1) 1776. Brussels Conservatoire. Harpsichord, inscribed: *Joannes Petrus Bull me fecit Antwerpiae anno 1776*. Rose. Formerly in the Mahillon Collection.

(2) 1778. Watertown, Mass., R. K. Lee. Two manuals; 4 rows of jacks; double-tongued dogleg 8′, 4′, lower-manual 8′; genouillère.

(3) 1779. Antwerp, Museum Vleeshuis. Harpsichord. Inscribed: *Joannes Petrus Bull me fecit Antwerpiae anno 1779*. Three rows of jacks.

(4) 1789. Brussels Conservatoire, Snoeck Collection. Harpsichord; 2 manuals; 5 octaves F–F; 3 registers. Inscribed: *Joannes Petrus Bull me fecit Antwerpiae anno 1789*. Formerly in Régibo's Collection, Renaix.

BULYOWSKY DE DULYCZ, Michael. Presumably Polish, *c.* 1700, an organist, made a transposing harpsichord. Friedrich Suppig's *Calculus musicus* (in *Labyrinthus musicus*, MS., 1722, in Paris Conservatoire) mentions the 'gantz neuen fünffachen Transponier-Clavier des Hoch- und Weltberühmten Michaelis Bulyowsky de Dulycz' and refers to the maker as 'Hoforganist'.

BUNCE, F., of Oxford. Though hardly a professional maker, he placed this notice in *Jackson's Oxford Journal* (22 and 29 October 1785): 'F. Bunce, late apprentice to Mr. Cross begs leave to acquaint the ladies and gentlemen of Oxford and its vicinity that he teaches, tunes and keeps in repair harpsichords, spinnets and pianofortes. All orders directed to Mr. Bunce at Mrs. Bird's Ship Lane will be thankfully received and due attention paid to them' [*Byrne*].

BUONFIGLIUOLI, Pierfrancesco. Florentine harpsichord maker, *fl.* 1660. [*Va* gives his *floruit* as 1653, but I do not know on what grounds.]

Surviving Instruments

(1) 1660. Harpsichord, single-manual; compass C/E–C, 4 octaves. Signed: *Pierfrancesco Buonfigliuoli*, and on bottom key: *P.B. 1660* [followed by an ornament]. Rustic scene painted on inside of lid. Formerly owned by Alec Hodsdon [?], Lavenham. Restored by Michael Thomas, 1958. Present (1970) owner: Forsyth Brothers Ltd., Deansgate, Manchester.

BUONI, Gioseffe. *See*: Boni, Gioseffe.

BURCKHARD, Christian. Harpsichord maker of Swallow Street, St. James's, London. Died some time between 1772 and 1792. He was a cousin of Jacob Kirkman, who bequeathed £40 to his son, likewise called Christian Burckhard [*Kirkman's will*].

BURR, Henry. Organ and harpsichord maker, lived in Great Queen Street, Lincoln's Inn Fields, London, in 1763 [*Un*].

He was born in London about 1716, apprenticed to Richard Coombes 6 October 1731, and became free of the Joiners' Company 5 July 1743.

BURR, J. His signature appears on keys in the Mahoon instrument no. 2a, q.v.

BUSCORNI, Nicolao, of Rome, *fl.* 1624. Harpsichord maker [*Va*].

BUSSY, Johann Heinrich Sury de. An early owner, not a maker. A clavichord bearing his name is in the Richard-Wagner-Museum, Tribschen/Lucerne; owner's date: 1723. See further *RindlKlav*, p. 218.

BYARD, Mary. An early owner, not a maker. See instrument no. 5 s.vv. James and Thomas White.

C. A. *See*: ASTON, Cawton.

C. B. *See*: B, C.

C. G. *See*: G, C.

C, I. N. Edward McElwee, of Hagerstown, Md., possesses a harpsichord having an *INC* rose. It has 1 × 8′, and 1 × 4′ registers, and a double curve to the bent side. The case and stand are of oak. In this instrument a Flemish soundboard with its floral decoration and rose would appear to have been enclosed in its present oaken case in England or Germany *c.* 1700. *Hubb* says that it has an inscription recording its maker as *Cousseneers* (or some such spelling) in Cologne, and that Challis would not believe this inscription. Neither Hubbard nor Dowd, who worked on it *chez* Challis, found any trace of English workmanship on it; they believe it was made in Cologne (? Cousseneers = Cuisinier). (A harpsichord (1 × 8′, 1 × 4′) formerly in the Berlin Collection, formerly in the Snoeck Collection, Ghent, has a rose shewing the harping angel and the letters *INC*. In the catalogue Sachs simply comments '? Couchet in Antwerpen'. Both Jean Couchet and P. E. Jean Couchet normally used the initials *IC* in their roses, and there is no known member of the Couchet family with the initials *I.N.* Sachs's guess must be erroneous.)

C. R. *See*: R, C.

CAAVELLA, Alfonso. An early owner, not a maker. *See*: D, A.

CAGNOLATI, Filippo, of Reggio nell'Emilia. Harpsichord maker; *fl.* 1655 [*Va*].

CAMPI, Niccolò. *Francl* lists a harpsichord inscribed: *Niccolo Campi 1632 Florenza.* This is presumably the instrument owned by the Hon. George A. Drew, Toronto, and illustrated at *Alb*, p. 23.

CAMUS, Felicianus Fidelis. The outer case only of a harpsichord dated 1806 made by Camus is in the museum at Aix-en-Provence [*GL*].

CANCELLIERI, Virgilio, of Rome. Harpsichord maker in the seventeenth century [*Va*].

CAPEZZO. *See*: BORTOLUS.

CAPILUTO, Giulio, of Mantua. Virginal maker, *fl.* 1545 [*Va*].

CARCASSI, Giovanni. Probably of Florence, dates ascertained 1688–98; maker of virginals. (1688 is supplied by *Hirt.*)

Surviving Polygonal Virginals

(1) 1698. Stockholm. Musikhistoriska Museet. Inscribed on top and bottom keys: *Joannes Carcassi Fecit Anno Domini MDCLXXXXVIII*, and on the jackrail: *In cilmbalis* [*sic*] *bene sonatibus* [*sic*]. The bottom key also bears the legend *Rinaldo Beretoni fecit 1744*, and the top *Di Propietà* [*sic*] *di Leopoldo Franciolini di Firenze.* 3½ octaves. Brown naturals, black sharps. Restored in 1899 by Robert Berg of Stockholm. Formerly in the Claudius Collection.

CARDINALI, Matteo. Maker of keyboard instruments at Aquileia in 1659. The Gallini Collection in Milan has a polygonal virginal by him signed on the nameboard: *Matthaei Cardinalis Aquileiae MDCLIX.* Compass 4 octaves and 1 note. Illustrated in *Gall.*

CAREST. *See*: KAREST.

CARGNONUS. Italian seventeenth-century harpsichord maker. *Hubb 1965* records a harpsichord by him with 2 × 8′ stops, in outer case, dated 1689 (p. 38, table 6), as being in the possession of Alain Vian, Paris, in 1957.

CARMO, M. de S., of Oporto. Clavichord maker, *fl.* 1796.

Surviving Clavichords

(1) 1796. Lisbon Conservatoire. Inscription: *M. de S. Carm*[o] *senior o fez na rua dirt*[a] *de St*[o] *Ildefonso da Cid*[a] *do Porto. ã. 1796.*

CARPEL, Nicolas van. Harpsichord maker. Born at Antwerp. Died at Amsterdam in 1637 [*Cl*, p. 34]. By 1634 he was living in Amsterdam, where he married. In the same year he entered an agreement to study with Lucas van Huffel (q.v.) for 2 years to learn 'het hantwerck ende de conste van clavecimbel maeken gelijckerwijs de Rückersz 't selve zijn exercerende' [*Curtis*, p. 48].

CARRETTI, Giovanni Domenico, of Piedmont, blind harpsichord maker. On 14 February 1786 he was presented to the Académie de Lyon as the maker of 'un instrument nouveau à l'instar d'un clavecin ou d'un pianoforte' [*Vallas*, p. 490].

CARTON, Jean Louis, *fl.* Paris 1769. Master harpsichord maker [*Hubb*].

CASINI, Giammaria, of Florence, *fl.* 1675. Harpsichord maker [*Va*].

CASPARINI, Eugen, 1623–1706. From Sorau in Lower Lusatia, organ builder, mostly at Dresden. Also built claviorgana during his time in Venice (*c.* 1656–9). [*VdMZeiss*, p. 155; *LunCas.*]

CASSINEAU. *Fl.* 1770 of the rue des Prouvaires près Saint-Eustache, Paris, 'fait, vend, achete et loue toutes sortes d'instruments, violons, basses de violes, pardessus, guitares, clavecins, mandolines, contrebasses, vielles et autres instruments' [*Pi*, p. 110].

CASSUS, Jesses. The very uncertain reading of a signature on a harpsichord formerly owned by Robert Johnson of Los Angeles and previously by Dr. Robert B. Haas of Los Angeles; now at the University of Arizona. The signature, which is on the wrestplank and is normally invisible, presumably relates to a repairer. The instrument has a compass of 4 octaves plus, A to F, 2×8′ stops, lute, boxwood naturals with 4 scorings, and a drawer under the keyboard. Nameboard decorated with gilt paper embossed with the coat of arms of one of the royal houses of England. Two roses in soundboard. The decoration on the nameboard and round the roses suggests English workmanship of the middle of the seventeenth century.

CASTEEL, Henrique van. A harpsichord nameboard, reported to me as in the Brussels Conservatoire, is inscribed: *Henricus van Casteel fecit Bruxellis 1778*. A *cravo de martelos* (a grand pianoforte with a Cristofori-derived action) in the Lisbon Conservatoire, having a compass of 4 octaves and 2 notes (C–D) is inscribed: *Henrique van Casteel 1763*.

CASTIGLIONI, Luigi, dates unknown. His name appears as restorer on the jack of an anonymous harpsichord [*Ks*, p. 89 n.].

CASTLEMAN, George. *See*: SLADE, Benjamin.

CAVALLETTI, Stefano. A polygonal virginal on which the boy Verdi learnt to play (1821) is in the Museo Teatrale alla Scala, Milan. On the lid is an inscription stating that Stefano Cavalletti restored it in 1825. (Illustrated in the catalogue (1940), p. 28.) C/E–F, 4 octaves with short octave plus 1 note.

CELESTINI, Giovanni, of Venice. Harpsichord and virginal maker; *fl.* 1583–1610. *J* (p. 101) quotes the *Daily Journal* of 16 May 1724, announcing the sale of some instruments belonging to William Corbett including 'two fine-toned Cyprus [i.e. cypress] spinnets, one of Celestini and the other of Donatus Undeus'.

A painting once owned by Alfred Cortot shews a boy purporting to be the young Mozart seated at a harpsichord signed: *Joannes Celestini Veneti MDLXXXIII*. (The painting, done in 1770, was formerly attributed to Cignaroli, but is ascribed by *Clem*, who reproduces it, to Saverio della Rosa.) *See table 4*.

CELLINI, Giovanni, of Florence. Born *c.* 1460; died 1527 or 1528 in Pest. He was primarily an architect, but turned his hand to many crafts. His famous son Benvenuto writes of him in his *Memoirs*:[1] 'My father made wonderful organs with wooden pipes, and harpsichords the best and finest that had ever been seen, as well as viols, lutes, and harps, all of them beautifully and excellently fashioned.' Unfortunately no Cellini instrument seems to have survived, so that we cannot verify Benvenuto's high estimate of his father's skill.

CELSON, Ephraim. Harpsichord maker in London in the eighteenth century. *J* (p. 65) quotes from an announcement in the *Public Ledger*, London, 2 October 1778:

To be sold by Christie & Ansell . . . (Earl Ferrers decd. effects) . . . A remarkable fine toned Harpsichord by EPHRAIM CELSON . . . it contains a double Bass [presumably a 16′ register], two Unisons and an Octave, the Welch harp [probably the buffstop], Piano Forte [i.e. a piano action as well as the harpsichord action][2] and Celestial Harp [a device which removed the dampers from the strings].

CENTAMIN, Petrus, of Venice. Virginal maker, *fl.* 1711.

Surviving Virginals

(1) 1711. Munich, Deutsches Museum. 4½ octaves. Split sharps. Signature on jackrail: *Petrus Centamin faciebat in Venetia Calle de Carbon No 277[1] Anno 1711*.

CESTINETTI. *See*: NIGETTI, Francesco.

CEULEN, Hans van. *See*: HANS VAN CUELEN.

CHAPPELLE, François. Instrument maker at Soissons, *fl.* 1739, in which year he rebuilt the Hans Ruckers virginal no. 8. (See *Russell 1959*, pl. 27, and *RG.I*, p. 80.)

CHARRON, *Sieur*.

Le Sieur Charron, organiste et facteur d'orgues chez les RR. PP. Cordeliers de Saint-Bonaventure [Lyons], a fait depuis peu un clavessin d'un mécanisme nouveau et de son invention...; l'on y fait forte, piano et crescendo avec un seul clavier, et sans les secours des plumes... [Petites affiches, 12 July 1769; quoted in *Vallas*, p. 355].

CHEERDINCK, Artus. *See*: GHEERDINCK, Artus.

CHEW. *See*: CREW.

CHIANEI, Giovanni, of Venice. Harpsichord maker. Dates ascertained, 1766–71.

Surviving Instruments

(1) 1766. Halle, Händelhaus. Inscribed: *Joannis Chianei Veneti opus anno MDCCLXVI*. Four octaves C/E–C with short octave; 2×4′ stops only.

(2) Germanisches Nationalmuseum, Neupert Collection. 1771. Of similar type, and with similar inscription apart from the date.

CHILD, Francis. Harpsichord maker, *fl.* 1749 in London. His name appears in a Westminster poll book [*J*].

CHIQUELIER, Christophe (I). Parisian harpsichord maker, born *c.* 1661, died 1748; lived in the rue Tiquetonne all his life. Married a widow in 1703. Appointed keeper of the King's Instruments in 1728. He also made other instruments: a viol by him is in the Paris Conservatoire [*Verlet*]. He was said to have constructed a harpsichord with 21 notes to the octave [*ClP*, p. 59].

CHIQUELIER, Christophe (II). Parisian harpsichord maker, 1715–92. Keeper of instruments to the royal family. He lived in the rue St. Honoré, and later at Versailles. In 1770 he procured for Pascal Taskin the succession to his post and retired in 1792 [*Verlet*].

[1] Benvenuto Cellini, *Memoirs* [translated by Anne Macdonell] (adapted). London, J. M. Dent, 1907, p. 8.

[2] Robert Stodart took out a patent for a combined harpsichord and piano in 1777, though J. S. Broadwood (*Gentleman's Magazine*, London, 1812) says that Backers made such an instrument as early as 1772.

CHIUSOLE. *Fl. c.* 1775 in the Trentino; made harpsichords, spinets, and clavichords [*MarcP*].

CHRISTENSEN, M. Clavichord maker at Copenhagen, *fl.* 1759.

Surviving Clavichords

(1) 1759. Frederiksborg, Hillerød. Signed on the soundboard: *M. Christensen fecit / Hafniae 1759.* No rose. Bundfrei; trichord in bass. A handle at the front raises an extra set of tangents and keeps them pressed against the strings. This *Veränderung* is called by *Hirt* (p. 122, no. 16) a *Pantaleonzug*. (The extra tangents are on the *right* of the normal ones.) Given to the Museum in 1916 by Count Wedell-Neergaard, of Svenstrup manor, Borup, Denmark [*Müller*].

CHRISTOPH. Austrian clavichord maker, date unknown though probably eighteenth century [*Fi*, p. 26]. A harpsichord at the Rhode Island School of Design, Providence, R.I., is inscribed *Christoph Fecit London 1789* but is probably an early 'revival' instrument, whose maker knew nothing about harpsichords. It has 2×16′ registers and 1×8′.

TABLE 4. *Surviving CELESTINI Instruments*

No.	Date	Type	Kbs.	Signature	Owner/Remarks
1	1587	H	1	*Joannis Celestini Veneti MDLXXXVII*	Bournemouth, F. R. Greenen (formerly in Highcliffe Castle). Compass C–F, 4½ octaves with short octave. Naturals lettered.
1a	1589	Pol. V	1	*Joannis Celestini Veneti MDLXXXIX*	The Hague, Gemeente-Museum (formerly René Clemencic, Vienna, and earlier in the Correr Collection, Venice). In rectangular outer case, the keyboard partially protruding. C/F–F, 4 octaves and a 5th. Arcaded naturals; ivory buttons on sharps. Illustrated in *Clem*, pp. 36–7. Bought from the dealer W. A. Seidler, Spiegelgasse 3.
2	1593	Pol. V	1	*Joannis Celestini Veneti MDXCIII*	London, Royal College of Music. C/E–F, 4½ octaves with short octave. Rose [*J*, p. 101].
3	1594	Pol. V	1	*Joannis Celestini Veneti MDXCIV*	Hamburg, Museum f. Kunst u. Gewerbe. Sent away during World War II; now housed in the Museum für Kunsthandwerk, Dresden.
3a	1595	H	1		Berkeley, Calif. [*GL*].
4	1596	H	1	*Joannis Celestini Veneti MDXCVI*	Toronto, Royal Ontario Museum. 2×8′ stops; 4½ octaves C–F with short octave.
5	1605	H	1	*Joannis Celestini Veneti MDCV*	The Hague, Gemeente-Museum. 2×8′ stops. Very wide, the octave span being wider than normal. Morley's label on jackrail. Rose-hole but no rose. Painting on outer lid dated 1620.
6	1608	Pol. V	1	*Joannis Celestini Veneti MDCVIII*	Vienna, Kunsthist. Museum. Formerly in Schloss Catajo. See *Luith*, p. 20.
7	1608	Pol. V (?)	1	*Joañis Celestini Veneti MDCVIII*	Hamburg, Museum f. Kunst u. Gewerbe. Sent away during World War II; now in the Eastern Zone.
8	1610	Pol. V	1	*Joanes Celestini Venetus MDCX*	Brussels Conservatoire. 4 octaves plus a 4th. Described on the instrument itself as an *arci-spineta*. Formerly in the Correr Collection.
9	—	H	1	*Celestini* [on nameboard]	Lafayette, Calif., R. M. Rosenberg. Now 2×8′ stops but originally 1×8′. Compass C/E–C, 4 octaves. Elaborate rose resembling that in no. 8. Signature lettering resembles that in no. 1a. Wrestplank-face has string-gauges: 4, 2, 5, 7, 8, 9. Acquired in Italy by present owner in 1960. Restored by Kaufman in Brussels, 1961, and outer case added.

CHRISTOPHORI, B. *See*: Cristofori, Bartolommeo.

CICERONE, Giovanni, of Rome. Harpsichord maker; *fl.* eighteenth century [*Va*; *VdS*, VI. 514].

CIGULARI, Agnolo. Florentine harpsichord maker, *fl.* 1669 [*Pu*].

CLARELLI, Geronimo [Hieronymus Clarellus Vicentinus], of Vicenza. Harpsichord maker, *fl.* 1695. A small harpsichord by him was sold at Sotheby's on 11 February 1938. Four octaves. 2×8′ stops, boxwood naturals, enclosed in painted case; inscribed: *Hieronymi Clarelli Vicentini 1695*. It belonged to Alfred du Cros, and was shewn at the Crystal Palace in 1900; 2′ 5″×5′ 9″.

CLARK, Andrew. Eighteenth-century harpsichord maker in the parish of St. James, Piccadilly, *fl.* 1767, before which he had at some time been apprenticed to Shudi and had worked for him for over 9 years. He figures in an affidavit sworn on 12 January 1767 concerning the work of Shudi's nephew, Joshua, q.v.

CLAUDE [*surname unreadable*]. *Fl.* 1699 as a harpsichord maker at Carpentras, near Avignon. A 2-manual harpsichord in private ownership in France is signed: *Claude . . . à Carpentras, 1699*. It has 2×8′, 1×4′ stops (4′ dogleg), and a compass C/G–C, 4 octaves.

CLAUDIUS, C. Scandinavian clavichord maker of the seventeenth or early eighteenth century.

Surviving Clavichords

(1) *Undated*. Copenhagen. Musikhistorisk Museum. Gebunden; 4 octaves C/E–C with short octave.

CLEMENTI, Muzio. Born at Rome in 1752, died at Evesham in 1832, celebrated pianist, teacher, and composer. About the age of 50 he took to instrument making and founded the firm of Clementi & Co., makers of pianofortes, which later became Collard & Collard, in its turn taken over by Messrs. Chappell & Co., Ltd. For the various metamorphoses of these firms see *H&S*.

The only evidence that the firm made harpsichords is a passage in *Hi* (p. 92): 'A harpsichord was made by Clementi . . . as late as 1802.' It seems likely that this instrument was made for Clementi to sell, rather than by him—which applies also to the large number of wind instruments bearing his name which survive.

CLEMM, Johann Gottlob [Klemm]. Organ builder and spinet maker, 1690–1762. Born 12 May 1690 near Dresden. Emigrated to America via Rotterdam, reaching Philadelphia on 18 September 1733. He settled near there working at his craft, and occasionally making stringed keyboard instruments besides organs, until 1745 or 1746. Later he moved to New York and, in 1757, to Bethlehem, Pa., where he died on 5 May 1762.

David Tannenberg (q.v.) was an apprentice of his. For fuller details see *Armstr.*

Surviving Instruments

(1) 1739. New York, Metropolitan Museum of Art. Spinet, inscribed: *Johannes Clemm fecit Philadelphia 1739*. Compass F–C, 4½ octaves.

CLOYS, Bartholomew. *Fl.* in London 1623; made 'Klavierautomaten'. See Kinsky in *ZfM*, Vol. 4 (1921–2).

COCCINIS. *See*: Coninus.

COENEN, Johannes Josephus, *fl.* 1735. Organist at the Cathedral of Roermond, an amateur maker of instruments, like Adlung (q.v.) who was his contemporary.

A 2-manual harpsichord with a virginal built into the bent side, made at Roermond in 1735, is preserved in the Plantin Museum at Antwerp. Inscription: *Joannes Josephus Coenen presbyta et organista cathedralis me fecit Ruraemondae Ao 1735*. The 2 roses (1 destroyed in World War II) were dated 1734—a year earlier.

COLCIONUS, Janus. *See*: Bolcioni, Janus.

COLCIUNNIUS, Stephanus. *See*: Bolcioni, Stefano.

COLESSE. *See*: Collesse, *L'Ainé*.

COLLESS, I. H. A French eighteenth-century double harpsichord belonging to E. M. Ripin (Forest Hills, N.Y.) bears, on one of the diagonal braces running from the bentside liner to the lower edge of the spine, an inscription. The brace has been at some time rudely reduced in width, and the inscription mutilated in the process. It would seem to read: *Per I. H. Colless / a Lion 1739*, but this reading is only tentative.

COLLESSE, Jacques. Musician and harpsichord maker of Lyons. Born 1716 or 1717; latest date ascertained, 1768. Son of Jacques Collesse, organist at Nantes Cathedral; married Mlle Argaud at Saint-Pierre on 20 January 1740, when he was 23 years of age [*Vallas*].

COLLESSE, ***L'Ainé*** [Colesse]. Dates ascertained, 1763–70. He settled in Lyons about 1766 as a maker of organs and harpsichords, residing at first with his brother Joseph, but seems not to have remained long [*Vallas*].

Surviving Harpsichords

(1) 1768. Château de Terrebasse (Isère), M. Louis de Varax. Inscribed on the rose: *Colesse â Lyon 1768*. Two manuals. (Although not certain, it seems probable that Colesse l'Ainé was responsible for this instrument.)

COLLESSE, Joseph. Brother of Collesse l'Ainé, musician and harpsichord maker of Lyons. Dates ascertained, 1768 to his death in 1776 [*Vallas*, p. 377].

Surviving Harpsichords

(01) Privately owned in France. Two-manual harpsichord signed: *J. Collesse à Lion, 1768*. Five octaves and 1 note E–F [*ChamP*].

(1) 1777. Paris Conservatoire. Owned by the Comtesse H. de Chambure. Two manuals; E–F, 5 octaves plus. Inscribed on soundboard: *Commencé par Ioseph Collesse Fini par Jean Franky 1777*.

(2?) Michael M. Koerner, Toronto, has (1971) a 2-manual harpsichord which he bought at auction at Parke Bernet's in 1956 and which had at one time belonged to Mrs. Armour, Chicago. It has 2×8′, 1×4′ and buffstops and a push–pull coupler. Compass F–F, 5 octaves. Painted rose without initials. Painting inside lid signed 'M. Lebart' [?] and dated 1778. Frank Hubbard who, with William Dowd, restored the instrument, puts its date at about 1760 and is disposed to attribute it to Joseph Collesse on the grounds of its similarity to the Paris instrument above.

COLOMBO, Vincenzo. Italian harpsichord maker. Date unknown to me.

COLONNA, Antonio. Organ and harpsichord maker of Bologna, *fl.* 1635. His portrait in oils is preserved in the Liceo Musicale, Bologna. His son Giovanni Paolo instructed Buononcini.

COLONNA, Fabio, called *Linceo*. Born at Naples *c.* 1580, one of the founders of the Accademia dei Lincei in Rome.

He designed an enharmonic harpsichord having 8 manuals, called the 'Sambuca Lincea' and described, with a drawing, in his *La sambuca lincea overo dell'instrumento musico perfetto*, Napoli, Vitale, 1618.

(The ancient Greek instrument σαμβύκη was a kind of triangular psaltery, having 4 strings and a shrill tone. Cf. Curts Sachs, *Real-Lexicon der Musikinstrumente*, Berlin, Bard, 1913, p. 329.)

COLYNS, Michiel, of Antwerp. Dates ascertained, 1631–2 to 1667–8.

In 1631–2 he entered the Guild of St. Luke as *Clavesingelstelder* (harpsichord tuner). He must have been able to undertake repairs, though there is no record of his having become a harpsichord maker. In 1636 he was organist of the Church of St. Andries. He was buried in Antwerp Cathedral [*St*].

COMPENIUS, Ludwig. Born *c.* 1603, died 1671, son of Heinrich Compenius junior. Organ builder, chiefly of Erfurt, but also made harpsichords. [A. Schering, *Musikgeschichte Leipzigs*, II. 111.]

CONINUS, Joseph Max, of Bologna. Ostensibly a virginal maker, *fl.* 1657.

The Deutsches Museum, Munich, has an ottavino inscribed with this name, and dated 1657. The inscription, strange and suspicious, is reported to me as: *Joseph Mae de Coninus Bononiensis opus MDCLVII.* In fact 'Coninus' is a mere conjecture, the word being illegible. It might be Couinus. The whole inscription smacks of Franciolini; indeed *FrancII* records a harpsichord inscribed: *Ioseph Mae de Coccinis Bononiensis Opus MDCCVI D.O.D.*

CONRAD, Johann Gottlieb, of Berlin. Eighteenth-century clavichord maker. A clavichord by him is in the Berlin Collection. A maker of this name is mentioned for 1804 and 1806 [C. Sachs, in *ZI*, Vol. 32, 1912, p. 1088].

COOLY, John. Apprenticed to Gabriel Townsend 1647; free of the Joiners' Company 1656 [*Join*].

COPIJN de Holanda. Harpsichord and virginal maker originating from the Low Countries who established himself in Lisbon and *fl.* 1523–53 at the court of Juan III.

CORDELIER, *priest*, of Avignon. Made a harpsichord in 1768. A nameboard, on a 2-manual harpsichord in private ownership in Paris but not related to it, reads: *Fait par le P. Ma. Cordelier a Avignon L'an 1768.*

CORTONA. Harpsichord maker at Rome in the seventeenth century [*Va*].

Amongst the instruments of Ferdinand de' Medici entrusted to the care of Cristofori in 1716 was 'Un' cimbalo piccolo opã del Cortona di Roma' [*Pu*]. A harpsichord by him dated 1678 was shewn at the Paris Exhibition of 1889; painted white, with flowers; seascape on lid [*ErnstP*].

COSTANZA, Orlando. *See* Guarracino, Honofrio.

COSTON, Francis. Harpsichord maker of Brownlow Street, Drury Lane, London. Dates ascertained, *c.* 1700–38 [*J*]. He was paid 5 gns. in 1728 for repairs to the Duke of Chandos's harpsichords at Cannons [*Chandos*, p. 132]. He sold up his stock in 1738.

An early eighteenth-century harpsichord, formerly in the Boddington Collection, Manchester, was attributed to him. (Two manuals; compass 5 octaves F–F. Oak case inlaid with satin-wood. No pedals. 2×8′, 1×4′, buff. Ivory naturals.) It was shewn by the Dowager Lady Heathcote at the International Inventions Exhibition, London, 1885. A 2-manual harpsichord by Coston was restored some time ago by Messrs. Morley of South Kensington—perhaps the same instrument.

COUCHET. Family of harpsichord makers in Antwerp in the seventeenth century. Their relationship is complex. See Lambrechts-Douillez in *GSJ*, Vol. 22, p. 99.

(1) **Jan** [Joannes, Jean, *or* Jan the Elder]. Born *c.* 1611, died 1655. He was a grandson of Hans Ruckers the Elder and nephew of Hans the Younger (Jean Ruckers) *pace St*, p. 33, and *Po*, p. 48; in Hans the Younger's workshop he was employed for 16 years.

In 1642 he entered the Guild of St. Luke. Between 1646 and 1653 the official records mention him frequently as repairing and tuning the organ in the O.L.V. Kerk at Antwerp. The composer Chambonnières had a harpsichord by him, and expressed himself as extremely pleased with it.

E. M. Ripin, in *GSJ*, Vol. 21, suggested that iconographic evidence shewed that contrasting double harpsichords existed in Flanders at least as early as in France, and proposed that the distinction to which Delabarre referred in 1648 was the invention of the manual coupler.

Constantijn Huygens's letter to H. Dumont of 6 April 1655 [*St*, p. 35] would seem to say merely that in his opinion no one builds double harpsichords as good as Couchet's.

A definite innovation by Couchet (although Gaspard Duarte claimed to have made it) was a harpsichord scaled to sound a tone above normal pitch. See Ripin in *RG.I*, pp. 19–20, where Couchet's letter of 1648 to Constantijn Huygens claiming credit for this is reproduced, transcribed, and translated.

He died at the end of March or beginning of April 1655, and was buried in the O.L.V. Kerk on 4 April [*St*, p. 38]; 2 days later his death was alluded to by Constantin Huygens in a letter [*St*, p. 35], where he is called 'le célèbre Couchet'.

A number of Couchet harpsichords were among those advertised for sale in Paris in the second half of the eighteenth century, as recorded in *Bq*:

Clavecin de Jean Couchet [22 July 1754].

Clavecin de Couchet 25 louis [24 February 1755].

Clavecin de Jean Couchet. d'Anvers, ayant 5 tons de plus que les clav. à grands rav. et dont toutes les cordes basses sont en argent doré, 1000 livres. Il en a coûté 3000. [10 September 1772. A Kirkman harpsichord had been offered two years earlier for 1200 livres.]

Clavecin de Couchet refait à neuf et mis à grand rav. par P. Taskin, avecd es peintures précieuses et mécaniques au pied pour varier le jeu de 10 à 12 manières (décès de M. Demarville, receveur général des finances, rue du Sentier) [1782].

(2) **Peter Jan** [Petrus Jan the Younger; P. E. Jean] son of (1), whose business he carried on. Dates ascertained, 1655–6 to 1680. He entered the Guild of St. Luke as the son of Jan Couchet the Elder in 1655–6; the entries in the Guild's books call him 'Jan Couchiet' and again 'Joannes Couchet' [*St*, p. 38]. (Both *J* and *Po* mistakenly give 1696 as the date of his admission to the Guild.) His instruments, however, seem to have been signed 'P. E. Joannes Couchet' or 'Petrus Joannes Couchet'. (It has been questioned whether Jan the Younger and Peter E. Jean were indeed the same person. I think it most likely that they were.)

St quotes from the catalogue of the Nicolaas Seelhof sale, The Hague, 1759:

Nr. 113. Een staertstuk van den vermaerden P. E. Johannis Couchet, Antverpiae, 1662, met 3 registers en 1 register Spinet, dubbel clavier, boven tot D en beneden tot contra E.

Nr. 117. Een dito staertstuk van P. E. Joannis Couchet, zoon van Jan Couchet, Antverpiae, met 2 registers unison, lang clavier.

—the keyboard having been lengthened ('mis en ravalement') according to the common eighteenth-century practice.

(3) **Joseph** [Jan, Joannes Josephus], son of (1). He entered the Guild of St. Luke in 1666–7 [*St*], and was still alive in 1681 [*Vlam*, p. 101].

(4) **Abraham** [Maria Abraham]. Son of (1). He entered the Guild in 1666–7 as both painter and harpsichord maker [*St*].

Sachs thought that a harpsichord formerly in the Berlin Collection having an *INC* rose was perhaps a Couchet. But see below, I, N.C.

The 2 types of rose known to have been used by the Couchet family are:

(1) The body of the harping angel is turned towards her right; her head is half turned towards her left. One of her feet reaches the surround of the rose. Large figure: small wings.

(2) The body and head of the angel face to the front. Wings bigger than in type (1). Neither foot reaches the surround. Small figure: large wings.

These are not, however, reliable criteria for assigning instruments to a particular member of the family, for although the surviving instruments by Jan the Elder all carry, as far as I have been able to ascertain, rose no. 1, yet instrument no. 6 (which cannot have been the work of this maker, who died in 1655) also carries the same type of rose.

As the table of instruments shews, the first type of rose is found in 6 instruments, while the second type is found in 1. A rose of this second type, divorced from its instrument, was discovered at Toledo in Spain [*VdS*, VIII. 432].

See table 5.

TABLE 5. *Surviving COUCHET Instruments*

No.	Date	Type	Kbs.	Signature	Type of Rose	Owner/Remarks
1	1645	H	1	*Joannes Couchet*	1	Edinburgh University (formerly Raymond Russell; earlier Messrs. Legg, Cirencester. Illustrated in *RussColl.* Compass 4 octaves. Sea-horse paper with colours reversed (i.e. white on black). *See* Barnes in *RG.I*, pp. 35–6.
2	1646	H	2	*Johannes Couchet fecit Antverpiae*	1	Brussels Conservatoire (presented by de Sorlus). B–F, 4½ octaves. Date on soundboard. Originally a transposing instrument. See *MeeùsCouch* for a detailed and illustrated account.
	1650			[See nos. 8 and 9 below.]		
3	1651	H	2	*Joannes Couchet*	1	Formerly Régibo [*VdS*, VIII. 431].
4	1669	H	2	*Petrus Joannes Couchet me fecit Antverpiae*	2	The Hague, Gemeente-Museum. (Formerly Boers Collection.) Date on soundboard; 2×8′, 1×4′, lute. Originally a 1-manual instrument.
5	1679	H	1	*Joseph Johannes Couchet*	?	Formerly Morris Steinert Collection; present location unknown. 4 octaves; 2×8′, 1×4′. Painting by Van Kessell. Inscription recorded in Steinert Catalogue (Chicago version).

TABLE 5 (*cont.*):

No.	Date	Type	Kbs.	Signature	Type of Rose	Owner/Remarks
6	1680	H	2		1	New York, E. M. Ripin (formerly Miss S. Marcuse, formerly Karl Freund (sold in New York at Freund sale in 1925)). 3×8′, 1×4′; all quill except one 8′ which has plectra of *peau de buffle*. Stops worked by genouillères: the first takes off all registers except the *peau de buffle*; the second takes off the 4′; the third takes off the lower-manual 8′; the fourth pushes the upper manual inward, coupling it to the lower manual; the fifth takes off the *peau de buffle*; the sixth raises the *peau de buffle* jacks, to leave 1 set of 8′ strings undamped and possibly lighten the touch. The instrument was enlarged in 1758 by Blanchet (q.v.), whose signature appears on the lowest key of the upper manual, and rebuilt in 1781 by Taskin (q.v.), who added the genouillères. Soundboard dated 1680.
[7]		H	2		1	The instrument was recorded here in the first edition in error. It was in fact made in 1764 by Pascal Taskin, q.v., and *not* by Couchet.
8	[*c.* 1650]	H	2	*Joannes Couchet fecit Antverpiae*		New York, Metropolitan Museum of Art. For a detailed and illustrated account see *Rip-Couch.* Originally had 1 manual and 1×8′, 1×4′ stops. Illustrated also in *Wint 1966.*
9	1650	V	1	*Joannes Couchet*	2	Formerly in Régibo Collection. Bought by Vleeshuis Museum, Antwerp, in 1967 (March). Restored by Hubert Bédard, Paris, who gives a detailed account of the process in *RG.I*, pp. 41–3. Compass 5 octaves. Length 1·75 m.
10		H	2	?	?	Edinburgh (in 1956). Listed in *GD5*.
11		H	?	?	?	London. *Cl* (p. 37) refers to one in London. But he may have been thinking of no. 6.
12		H	2	*Non nisi mota cano*	?	Stockholm, Nydahl Collection. *IC* rose; 5 octaves F–F. Not a Couchet but probably French, about mid seventeenth century. F–F, 5 octaves.

COUSHETTE. Variant spelling of COUCHET (q.v.) in Burney's article 'Harpsichord' in Rees's *Cyclopaedia.*

COUTURE. *See*: LA COUTURE.

COWTES. 'One Cowtes, of London', who mended Princess Mary's instruments during the reign of Henry VIII, was presumably a maker of virginals as well as other instruments [*Ga*].

CRAMOR, Thomas. 'Virginal maker' was buried on 15 May 1598 in the parish of St. Mary Woolnoth, London [*Byrne*].

CRANG, John, of Devonshire and London, organ builder. Dates ascertained, 1745–92, when he died. Also made harpsichords, spinets, and claviorgana.

His spinets, and to a lesser degree his harpsichords, are commended in the preface to John Arnold's *Compleat Psalmody* (5th edition, London, 1761):

> The spinnet comes next of course, it being of the Harpsichord kind, but is much more convenient for a small Room; for it being smaller will therefore stand in less Compass; of which Mr. Hitchcock's and Mr. Crang's are said to be the best. Mr. Hitchcock and Mr. Crang also make very good Harpsichords; Mr. Crang likewise builds Organs of all kinds.

Crang appears as an organ builder in *Un* (1763), where he is described as 'resident in Great Queen-Street, Lincoln's-Inn-fields'. At another time he was living in Wych Street. He died near Maidstone in January 1792 [*Sum*, p. 173].

He became a partner with Hancock, q.v. The firm turned to piano making, and patented an action in 1790.

Surviving Instruments

(1) 1745. Formerly at Nettlefold Castle. Claviorganum. Shewn by Kelly & Co. at the International Inventions Exhibition, London, 1885. The organ part was discarded about 1953 by John Osborn, piano tuner, of London.

Offered at Christie's on 18 July 1957, but bought in. Inscription: *This organ and harpsichord were a present from Beeston Long Esq., to his sister Mrs. Drake* and *Crang Londini 1745*. (Beeston Long of Carshalton Park, Surrey, was born 1710 and died 1735.) Sold at Sotheby's on 9 May 1958; buyer Greville, and price £380. Two manuals, F–F, 5 octaves without low F sharp, lute; arcaded keys; mahogany case; length 8′ 6″. White naturals; skunktail sharps. Four brass handbooks. Brass rose. Now (1972) owned by Dr. R. Mirrey, Redhill, Surrey.

(2) 1758. Victoria and Albert Museum. Spinet, signed: *Crang Londini fecit, 1758*. Compass 5 octaves G–G. Marquetry of walnut and other woods. Motto inlaid in foreboard: *Musica Laborum Dulce Levamen*, with trophy of instruments.

CREHORE, Benjamin. Born at Milton, Massachusetts, where he died 1819. According to Hipkins he was the first to make pianos in Boston, about 1798–1800. He also made violins and probably harpsichords. According to *Cl*, probably in error for the Blythe instrument, there is a spinet by him in Salem, Mass. A square piano by him is in the New York Metropolitan Museum of Art, and another (lent by Mrs. Alexander Steinert) in Boston Public Library, Mass. Bequeathed by Miss C. A. R. Adams. Illustrated in *V&A*, *MIWA* and in *Russell V&A*.

CRESCHI, Antonio, of Pisa. ? Harpsichord maker. To an eighteenth-century harpsichord, 2×8′ stops, in private ownership in New York, is attached a slip of wood bearing this name, but it may never have been an integral part of the instrument.

CRESCI. Family harpsichord-making firm at Leghorn; dates ascertained, 1760–78. Three members are known—Alessandro, Federigo, and Roberto, but their relationship has not been discovered.

Surviving Cresci Harpsichords

(1) 1760. Hurley, Michael Thomas, who plays it on the record Oryx 1725. Stops 2×8′, 1×4′.

(2) 1778. Nuremberg, Germanisches Nationalmuseum (Rück Collection). Inscribed: *Roberto, e Federigo Cresci in Livorno l'anno 1778* on the foreboard and *1778 Sotto la Protezione / dello Spiritossanto* [*sic*] *Roberto & Federigo Cresci Fecero* on the bottom board. (Formerly owned by Klinkerfuss.)

CREW. Harpsichord maker at Worcester, *fl.* 1769 [*Byrne*].

CRICCA.

(1) **Alfonso,** *called* Paliarino, of Ferrara; *fl.* 1591 as maker of organs and other keyboard instruments [*Lü*].

(2) **Hippolito,** *also called* Paliarino, of Ferrara, apparently brother of (1), *fl.* 1598. Maker of organs and other keyboard instruments. In a letter of December 1598 he signs himself 'Hippolito Cricca detto Paliarino' [Luigi Francesco Valdrighi, *Musurgiana*, Modena, 1879, p. 26].

A letter to his patron the Duke of Modena, dated 31 December 1598, contains this list of materials needed for instrument making:

> Asse tre di Tio [tiglio] per far tastadure per lo Instromento Pian e Forte che si fa di nuovo et per altri che e in camera.
> Avoglio per far tutti li Pironj alle Violle del Concerto.
> Asse IV una di cipresso per far il fondo de sudetto Instrumento.
> Colla Tudesca e Caravella per detto bisogno.
> Ebano, per detto bisogno.
> Fillo d'ottone.
> Buxe per coprire dette tastadure

It seems probable that the 'Instromento Pian e Forte' above was a 2-register harpsichord with movable jack-slides.

CRINETUS, Franciscus Poggio. *See*: Poggio, Franciscus, *Crinetus*.

CRISTOFORI, Bartolommeo [Bortolo Padovano], 1655–1731. Son of Francesco Cristofori, was born at Padua on 4 May 1655, his parents being of humble origin.

He was not slow in winning recognition as a harpsichord maker, the earliest recorded, and likewise surviving, one being dated 1690 [*Gai*, p. 10], instrument no. 01 in Table 6 being highly suspect. When the Grand Duke Ferdinand de' Medici visited Padua on his way to Venice in 1687, Cristofori's instruments were so much admired by him that their maker was persuaded to move to the Court at Florence, where we find trace of him in August 1690 and afterwards.

On a visit to Florence in 1709 Scipione Maffei, the writer and archaeologist, became acquainted with Cristofori and with his invention, the *gravicembalo col piano e forte*.[1] Two years later he published an account of it in the *Giornale dei Letterati d'Italia*. König's translation of Maffei's article into German appeared 14 years afterwards.[2]

In 1713 Ferdinand died, but Cristofori remained at the Court, to receive 3 years later from the Grand Duke Cosimo III the curatorship of the collection of instruments left by Ferdinand.[3]

On 27 January 1731 Cristofori died at Florence. His work on instruments was carried on by his assistant Giovanni Ferrini, while in the following year Pietro Mazzetti was made curator of the Court collection.

[1] The much-discussed question of the invention of the pianoforte is not our concern here. There were several claimants early in the eighteenth century, but the origins of the pianoforte go back much further. A Flemish instrument dated 1610 in the Savoye Collection II, Paris, had a hammer action; not to mention the actions described about 1440 by Henri Arnault (q.v.), all of them percussive and one of them the archetype of the modern pianoforte mechanism. However, it was not until Cristofori that the pianoforte was established, and M. Fabbri (*Chigiana*, Vol. 21, 1964, pp. 162–72) has shewn that Cristofori was working on a hammer action as early as 1698.

[2] *MatCM*, II. 335–43.

[3] The inventory of this collection is quoted *in extenso* by *Pu*.

Cristofori is called 'Bortolo Padovano' by *Sac* (quoted by *Kirk*, p. 176).

Ks points out (p. 219) that the violin maker Bartolommeo Cristofori must be another person, since he is mentioned in 1680 as a 13-year-old pupil of Niccolō Amati, that is to say he was 12 years younger than the pianoforte maker. A cello by him, dated 1716, was sold at Puttick & Simpson's, 18 October 1934. Moreover a number of surviving documents suggest that the pianoforte maker confined himself to keyboard instruments.

A portrait of him, discovered by Professor Schünemann of Berlin and described in *ZfM*, Vol. 16 (1934), was formerly in the Staatliches Institut für Musikforschung, Berlin, but was destroyed in World War II. It is reproduced in *Fla* (1953), p. 256. *Ks* reproduces two documents with his signature.

TABLE 6. *Surviving Plucked Instruments by CRISTOFORI*

No.	Date	Type	Kbs.	Signature	Owner/Remarks
01(?)	1689	H	1	*Bartolomeo Cristofori 1689*	*FrancII* (item 12). Suspect.
02	1690	H	2		Neuilly sur Seine, the Comtesse de Chambure.
1	1693	S	1	*Bartholomaeus Christophori Patavinus / Faciebat Florentiae / MDCXCIII*	Leipzig, Heyer Collection. A unique spinet with 2 strings to each note, illustrated at *Ks*, p. 71. Made for Prince Ferdinand de' Medici; 4 octaves plus, C–D; 184 × 73 cm. Original bill, still extant, reproduced at *Ks*, p. 217.
2	1702	H	3	*Bartolomeo Cristofori fecit Firenze MDCCII* [on nameboard]	Munich, Deutsches Museum. 1 × 16′, 1 × 8′, 1 × 4′; 4½ octaves. Originally 2 × 8′, 1 × 4′. Compass C–F, 4½ octaves. On underside of soundboard inscribed: *Repariert 1906 / G. Steingraeber, Hofpianofortefabrikant / München*; also *Alle Steingraeber / Gretl Steingraeber / 5. Nov. 1906.* 3 geometrical roses. Undoubtedly an Italian instrument, but the third manual and 16′ stop probably fitted by Franciolini, who also renewed most of the paintwork. Given to the Museum in 1907 by Georg Steingraeber.
2a	1702	H	3	*Bartolomeo Cristofori fece in Firenze Anno 1702*	Michigan University, Stearns Collection. Unauthentic.
3	1703	H	3	*Bartholomaeo Christofori Patavinus fecit Florentiae 1703*	Neupert Collection, Germanisches Nationalmuseum. 5 octaves F to F. Lowest kb: 2 × 8′; middle kb: 1 × 8′, 1 × 4′; top kb: 1 × 4′. Illustrated in Neupert, *Das Cembalo* (1933). Not genuine.
4	1722	H	1	*Bartholomaeus de Christophoris Patavinus faciebat Florentiae MDCCXXII*	Leipzig, Heyer Collection. 2 × 8′. C–C, 4 octaves 24 × 33 cm. Illustrated. *Ks*, p. 101.
5	1726	H	1	[As no. 4, except date] *MDCCXXVI*	Leipzig, Heyer Collection. 1 × 4′, 1 × 8′, 1 × 16′. C–C, 4 octaves. Illustrated at *Ks*, p. 101; inscribed at *Ks*, p. 218.
6	1726	H	2		Was in the Kraus Collection, Florence. Called *archicembalo*, but was not enharmonic. Dubious instrument.
7	n.d.	H	1		Leipzig, Heyer Collection. 1 × 8′, 1 × 4′. F to F, 5 octaves without bottom F sharp and G sharp; 246 × 80 cm. Attributed to Cristofori by Kraus and *Ks*, who depicts it at p. 103. Said to have been found in the monastery of San Niccolò at Prato. Dubious instrument.

CROSS. Worked for Jacob Kirkman (q.v.) in 1769. A single-manual Kirkman harpsichord of that year bears Cross's signature on the back of the nameboard, and on the top key.

CROTONE. Mentioned by *Prof* (p. 272)—probably a corruption of Cortona, q.v.

CRUDELI, Giuseppe, of Lucca. Virginal maker, *fl.* 1781. Probably related to the organ builder Federigo Crudeli (*fl.* 1820).

Surviving Instruments

(1) 1781. Leipzig, Heyer Collection. An ottavino inscribed: *Jn Lucca Giuseppe Crudeli Fece sua prima Opera il 1781.* Rose. Compass C–C, 4 octaves with short octave. Boxwood naturals, ebony-faced sharps; 85×49 cm. Illustrated at *Ks*, p. 77. Inscription reproduced by *Ks*, p. 218.

CUELEN, Hans van. *See*: HANS VAN CUELEN.

CUISINIER [Cuisinié]. Dates ascertained, 1708–34. French harpsichord maker. He also experimented with a *clavecin-vielle,* which worked on the same principle as the *Nürnbergisch Geigenwerck* [*Pi*, p. 90].

CULLIFORD, Thomas. Maker of spinets, harpsichords, and pianofortes. Dates ascertained: 1750–1800 [*J*]. Addresses: Fountain Court, Cheapside; 112, Cheapside; 172, Strand, London.

He worked for John Hitchcock, and (1795–7) with Rolfe and Barrow [*H&S*]. (A square piano at Cirencester is signed: *Culliford & Barrow, 172 Strand.*) This firm succeeded Culliford, Rolfe & Barrow [*H&S*]. (In 1785 it was called simply 'Culliford and Co.'—see instruments 13–14 under Longman and Broderip.)

He supplied instruments to Longman and Broderip, who sold them with their names on the nameboard. Culliford signed these instruments in some other part, e.g. under the soundboard. *See under*: LONGMAN AND BRODERIP for details of these.

Surviving Instruments

(1) *See below under*: LONGMAN AND BRODERIP, no. 11a.

(2) [Date not known.] A harpsichord reported to be in the possession of Hector McCurrach (1951).

(3?) *N.d.* Spinet, sold by Norman Wilkinson at Sotheby's, 6 July 1934, to Messrs. Morley. Compass 5 octaves; length 6′ 0″. Perhaps by Culliford.

CUNTZ, Lucas. Organ builder in Nuremberg in the seventeenth century. In 1619 he made a claviorganum for Lucas Friedrich Behaim, using for the stringed part of this instrument a German polygonal virginal of which the lid, bearing a painting of the complete claviorganum, is in the Germanisches Nationalmuseum at Nuremberg [*VdM Salzb*, p. 88].

D, A. A gebunden clavichord in the Heyer Collection (no. 2), formerly in the Kraus Collection (no. 529), bears on the floor of the case under the keyboard a much-faded inscription: *AD / 1562* (Kraus gives '1502'), and on the top key: *D : Tim° 1690*—presumably a repairer's mark. The *AD* may, however, simply stand for 'Anno Domini'. A printed label on the back of the nameboard shows that the instrument was repaired by Luigi Landi in Siena in 1836. Parchment rose. Illustrated in *Ks*. (The name *Alfo[n]so Caavella* on the outside of the case presumably records the first owner.)

D, A. Mrs. Currie, Edinburgh, has (1958) a spinet with a rose: *AD 1750.* Compass 6 octaves plus 2 notes F–G; 7′ 3″×2′ 9″×9½″. Largely oaken case lacquered red. It can hardly be by Delin with this compass [*ThomasW*].

D. E. *See*: E, D.

D. F. *See*: F, D., *also* D, E.

D, H. *See*: H, D.

DADDI, Lorenzo. *See*: DOTTI, Lorenzo.

DAGONEAU [*also* Dagneau]. Surgeon at Malines, *fl.* 1773. He turned to harpsichord making [*Cl*, pp. 7, 39].

DALLERY, Thomas Charles Auguste. Born at Amiens 4 September 1754, died Jouy-en-Josas (Seine-et-Oise) 1 June 1835.

Son of Charles Dallery the organ-builder, he made harps, claviorgana, and organs, being entrusted with the building of an organ for Amiens Cathedral, which was, however, never realized owing to the Revolution [*Fé*, who has a long article].

DANAYS. Clavichord maker, *fl.* 1838 [*Va*]. Apparently a mistake by *Va.*

DANGEVILLE. 'Facteur d'orgues et de clavecin de Paris' in 1774 [*Hubb*].

DANIS, Joseph, of Treviso. Virginal maker, *fl.* 1570. A polygonal virginal preserved in the Royal Manchester College of Music until World War II, when it was destroyed, is said by the Catalogue of the Henry Watson Collection (1906) to have borne the inscription: *Joseph Danis fecit in Trevisus Anno 1570.* Boxwood naturals, black sharps; projecting keyboard; 3 octaves. Exterior painted with scroll work on a greenish ground; inside the lid was painted the figure of Saint Joseph. The instrument appears in one of Franciolini's catalogues.

DARGILLIÈRES, Antoine. Parisian organ builder, organist and organ builder to the King; earliest date known, 1540; died 1572. He may well have made harpsichords also [*Verlet*; see also *Laborde*].

DARGILLIÈRES, Jean. Parisian organ and harpsichord maker. *Fl.* 1563–8. His godmother was Jean Dugué's wife [*Verdet, Laborde*]. *Cor.* (p. 84) refers to him in passing.

DASTENET. Harpsichord maker, probably seventeenth-century French. *Cor* (p. 84) refers to him in passing.

DAULPHIN, Jean (I). Parisian maker of spinets and other instruments, mid sixteenth century [*Verlet*].

DAULPHIN, Jean (II). Parisian spinet-maker, perhaps son of I. Dates ascertained 1553–71 [*Verlet*].

DAULPHIN, Maria. Parisian maker of instruments, probably including spinets. Perhaps another son of Jean I [*Verlet*].

DAVIDSON, John. Scottish virginal maker, *fl.* 1652 [*GD*, 1928, s.v. Virginal].

DAVIES, James, of Tottenham Court Road, London. Organ builder. In 1792 he patented a combined harpsichord and pianoforte, the action of each having its own keyboard [Patent no. 1887, dated 6 June 1792].

DAWSON, Gilbert. Perhaps an eighteenth-century repairer [and maker?] of spinets. *See*: KEENE, Stephen.

DEACONS, William [Deakens, Deecken, Deckens, Diaken]. Harpsichord maker, born *c.* 1600 and presumably in England, who worked in the Low Countries. In 1627 he exhibited an automatic claviorganum at the Mary Magdalen fair in Utrecht. This instrument was held by Pieter Pampus (q.v.) to infringe his 6-year patent of 18 February 1626, and he sued Deacons, with what result we do not know.

About 1634 Deacons was living in Leyden, and by 1640 in Haarlem. In 1645 he settled in Bergen-op-Zoom, but 2 years later he appears to have been living in Dordrecht [*GSJ*, no. 11, 1958, pp. 63 seq.; *TVNM*, Vol. 4, 1894, pp. 54 f.; *Curtis*, p. 48].

His signature (spelt 'William Deakens') is reproduced on p. 65 of the *GSJ* paper.

DEBBONIS, Franciscus. Seventeenth-century harpsichord maker of Cortona who worked in Rome. A harpsichord inscribed behind the nameboard: *Franciscus Debbonis Cortonensis fecit Romae 1678* is privately owned in France. The front of the nameboard is inscribed: *Luigi de Carli*—presumably an early owner. C–E, 4 octaves and 2 notes; 2×8′, 1×4′.

DECKENS, Willem. *See*: DEACONS, William.

DECKERS, Henry. Harpsichord maker at Gorinchem, Low Countries. Dates ascertained, 1625–9 [*Curtis*].

DECKERT, Georg Nikolaus. German harpsichord maker, 1772–1844 [*Ks*, Vol. 2, p. 660].

DECKERT, Johann Nicolaus. Father of Georg Nikolaus, 1733–1826. Born at Grossbreitenbach near Arnstadt. (*Hirt* gives his dates as 1772–1844.) About 1800 he made clavichords and harpsichords, as well as square pianos and lutes [*Fé*]. His clavichords fetched prices between 5 and 7 louis d'or [*Gö*].

Surviving Clavichords

(1) Undated. Leipzig, Heyer Collection. Bundfrei, C–G, 4½ octaves. Inscription on soundboard: *Deckert in Breitenbach*. Made towards the end of the eighteenth century. Inscription reproduced at *Ks*, p. 218.

(2) Undated. Belonged to Carl Engel in 1879. Inscription on soundboard: *J. N. Deckert, Gross-Breitenbach bei Arnstadt*. About 1800.

(3) Undated (?). Michael Thomas, Hurley, owned in 1966 a large Deckert clavichord which was probably a different instrument from nos. 1 and 2.

DEDEBAN, Jean Marie. Parisian harpsichord maker; dates ascertained 1774–91. The Corcoran Gallery of Art, Washington, D.C., has a 2-manual harpsichord by him dated 1770 (*not* 1710) on the soundboard, which is also inscribed (round the *ID* rose) + *Jean* + *Marie-De-De-Ban* in yellow paint. The inscription *1770 Jean Marie DeDeBan 1770* on the nameboard is probably a modern addition. Originally 2×8′, 1×4′, buff, push–pull coupler; now 3×8′, 1×4′, 2×buff, genouillères. Restored by J. Scott Odell, 1970. The paintings on the case were at one time attributed to Boucher.

Dedeban was an expert for the inventory on the death of Treyer (L'Empereur) in 1778 [*MC*]. See further *Verlet* and *Laborde*.

DEELEY, William. English spinet maker, flourished *c.* 1700.

Surviving Instruments

(1) Undated. Messrs. Morley of South Kensington had (May 1946) a small undated spinet in an oak case.

(2) Undated. Messrs. Moss Harris, London, had (1949) a spinet, also in oak, formerly at Hurstmonceaux. Compass 4¼ octaves. Inscription on jackrail: *William Deeley fecit*. Dimensions, 5′×1′ 9″. Illustrated in *Antiques*, New York, June 1950, p. 423 in an advertisement of Messrs. Frank Partridge & Sons, where the name is given as 'Dealey'.

DEFIELD, Paul. Virginal maker born at Louvain who fled to England from religious persecution in 1568 and worked for L. Theeuwes (q.v.) in London. He had left Theeuwes by 1571 and is last mentioned in 1582/3. His name, which must originally have been Vandervelde or something like it, appears as Pawyl Fandevell, Polle Fyeld, and Pawle Defield [C. van den Borren, *Les Musiciens belges en Angleterre . . .*, p. 137].

DE L . . . *See*: L . . ., de.

DE LA BARRE, P. de C. *See*: LA BARRE, Pierre de Chabanceau, *Sieur de la Barre*.

DE LA BORDE, Jean Baptiste. *See*: LA BORDE, Jean Baptiste de.

DE LA COUTURE. *See*: LA COUTURE, DE.

DE LAINE. *See*: LAINE, D.

DE LALANDE. *See*: LALANDE, DE.

DELAVIGNE, Philibert, of Paris. A wood-turner. He made harpsichords and certain other instruments, but in 1723 and 1741 these were confiscated, as he was not a member of the Guild of Instrument Makers [*Loub*, p. 176; *Verlet*].

DELIN, Albert. Harpsichord maker living at Tournai, Belgium; dates ascertained, 1750–70. *See table 7, also* D, A.

TABLE 7. *Surviving Instruments by Albert DELIN*

No.	Date	Type	Kbs.	Signature	Owner/Remarks
1	1750	H	1	*Albertus Delin me fecit Tornaci 1750*	Berlin Collection. C–C, 4 octaves; *AD* rose; 2×8′, and divided buffstop.
2	1750	S	1	*A. Delin me fecit Tornaci 1750*	Brussels Conservatoire (Snoeck Collection). *AD* rose. Described at *VdS*, I. 193.
3	1751	Cc	1	*Albertus Delin me fecit Tornaci 1751*	Brussels Conservatoire.
4	1752	Cc	1	*Albertus Delin me fecit Tornaci 1752*	Berlin Collection. G–E, 4 octaves and a 6th. Divided buffstop.
5	1756	S	1	*Albertus Delin me fecit Tornaci 1756*	Seen by *VdS* (I. 194 n.) in 1863. Seen again in an antique dealer's shop in Brussels in 1951.
6	1763	S	1		Antwerp Conservatoire. *AR* rose; C–F, 4½ octaves; black naturals.
7	1763	S	1		Formerly in Régibo Collection; sale catalogue (1897) reads: 'épinette triangulaire d'Albert Delin, 1763. Longueur 157 cm'.
8	1765	S	1	*Albertus Delin me fecit Tornaci 1765*	Berlin Collection (formerly Snoeck Collection).
9	1766	H	?	?	Formerly Snoeck Collection. C–D, 4 octaves and 1 note. Black sharps.
9a	1768	H	1	*Albertus Delin me fecit Tornaci 1768*	Paris, Jean Martinod (1971). *AD* rose; 2×8′ stops; G–E, 4 octaves and a 6th. Very little restored. Bought from Jacques Vian. Kenneth Gilbert (1973).
10	1768	S	1	*Albertus Delin me fecit Tornaci 1768*	Antwerp, the late J. A. Stellfeld.
11	1770	S	1	*Albertus Delin me fecit Tornaci 1770*	Brussels Conservatoire. C–E, 4 octaves and a 3rd. Presented by F. A. Gevaert.
12	1770	H	?	?	Formerly Snoeck Collection.
13	?	Cc	1	[None]	The Hague, Gemeente-Museum. *AD* rose; 2×8′ stops (no buff). Black naturals. Illustrated in *Russell 1959*.
14	?	H	2	?	Formerly Régibo Collection. Sale catalogue (1897) reads: 'Clavecin d'Albert Delin, 2 claviers dont l'un est supprimé. 4 octaves. Longueur 190 cm.'.
15	?	H	1		Privately owned in France. 2×8′.

DELINEAU, Joseph Cassella. A harpsichord in a collection offered anonymously in France (1953) has an inscription reported to me as: *Joseph Cassella Delineau, Terre Cujani 1793*, and on the desk *Di Cituy Alphion Rhebanas . . . Conditorare . . . 1793*. I will not attempt to interpret.

DE L'ISLE, Blondel. *See*: L'ISLE, Blondel de.

DELITZ. Born in Danzig. In 1765 he was a noted maker of organs and keyboard instruments. He invented a harpsichord with a wind register and other innovations. Wagner of Dresden improved on this and called his result the 'clavecin royal', giving it out as his own invention.

Delitz was a pupil of Hildebrand, after whose death he continued to build organs and keyboard instruments in Danzig and Thorn [*Gö*].

DELLA VALLE, Pietro. *See*: VALLE, Pietro della.

DEL MELA, Domenico. *See*: MELA, Domenico del.

DELOEUVRE, Honoré, of Lyons. 'Faiseur d'espinettes' [i.e. harpsichords and virginals]; dates ascertained, 1523–57 [*Lyons Archives*]. (According to *Va* he died in 1550.)

DELOEUVRE, Pierre, of Lyons. 'Faiseur d'espinettes', *fl.* 1551 [*Lyons Archives*].

DE LYEN, Pieter. *See*: LYEN, Pieter de.

DEMACHY, P. *See*: MACHY, Pierre Antoine de.

DENIS. A family of organ builders and harpsichord makers who flourished in Paris from the sixteenth to the eighteenth centuries. For further details of places of residence and family relationships see *Verlet*, from which a good deal of the following information is derived. See also *Hubb 1965 passim.*

DENIS, Robert (I). Organ and harpsichord maker; 1520–between August 1588 and April 1589. He worked in the parish of Saint-Merri from 1544, the date of the birth of his eldest son Claude.

DENIS, Claude. Harpsichord maker and dealer in instruments, 27 May 1544–87. Son of Robert I. From 1580 he lived in the parish of Saint-Gervais (rue de la Planche-Mibraye). He married a sister of Paul Belamy (q.v.) in 1570, and took Paul as an apprentice 1571–6.

DENIS, Jean (I). Maker of harpsichords and other instruments; 23 March 1549–after 1634. Second son of Robert I. Apprenticed to the organ builder Gabriel Dargillières, q.v. In 1601 he was elected *juré* of the Guild. All his 3 sons were harpsichord makers. It may well be this Jean Denis whom *Mer* mentions, together with Jacquart, as one of the best harpsichord makers of his day.

DENIS, Robert (II). Harpsichord maker and dealer in instruments; born after 1550, died 1589. Youngest son of Robert I, he worked with Dargillières (q.v.).

DENIS, Thomas. Maker of instruments, probably including harpsichords; born 1585, died before 1634. Eldest son of Jean I. In 1615 he was elected *juré* of the Guild.

DENIS, Jean (II). Organist, harpsichord maker, and writer on tuning; *c.* 1600–January 1672. Second son of Jean I. He became *juré* of the Guild in 1647. In 1650 the second edition of his *Traité de l'accord de l'espinette . . .* was issued; in it he calls the harpsichord the 'plus bel Instrument du monde, et le plus parfaict'. He went to Nancy in 1653, where he restored the Duchesse de Lorraine's harpsichord. See also *Hubb 1965*, pp. 122–3.

Surviving Spinets

(1) 1667. Varzy (Nièvre), Musée Municipal.

DENIS, Pierre (I). Maker of instruments, almost certainly including harpsichords; *c.* 1600–after 1664. Youngest son of Jean I. In 1632 he qualified as 'maître faiseur et maître joueur d'instruments de musique' [*MC*]. He was *juré* of the Guild in 1662.

DENIS, Jean (III). Organist and harpsichord maker; *c.* 1630–December 1685. Eldest son of Jean II. In 1682 he obtained 8 votes in the election of a *juré* of the Guild, but was not elected. A harpsichord by him dated 1658 was in one of the Savoie Collections.

DENIS, Louis. Organist and maker of instruments, almost certainly including harpsichords; 16 November 1635–after 4 June 1710. Second son of Jean II, he bore the title in 1666 of 'maître faiseur d'instruments ordinaire du Roy'. In 1689 his daughter married the organist Louis Marchant. Besides his Paris house he had a property at Cormeilles which he bought in 1683.

A harpsichord privately owned in France (formerly in Le Cerf's collection) is signed underneath the soundboard: *Fait par Louis Denis à Paris, 1658.* Two manuals, *BS* [*sic*] rose (? = B. Stehlin).

DENIS, Philippe. Organist, instrument maker, and record-keeper of the King's buildings; *c.* 1615–2 January 1705. Youngest son of Jean II. Accepted by the Guild in 1637, and *juré* in 1669. An ottavino made by him in Paris and dated 1677 is privately owned in France.

DENIS, Pierre (II). Maker of instruments including harpsichords; *fl.* 1705. Son of Philippe.

Surviving Instruments

(1) 1672. Ottavino. Paris Conservatoire.

(2) 1674. Harpsichord. The late F. Le Cerf, Paris. (Was in the hands of C. Saloman, Paris, in 1923.)

(3) 1691. Harpsichord. *Ravalé* in 1763. Owned in 1905 by the 'Couperin' Concert Group.

(4) ?. Harpsichord. Private ownership in Paris (1953).

Condensed Tree of the Denis Family of Organ Builders and Harpsichord Makers. (Only the makers of instruments are recorded in this tree)

Robert (I) (1520–89)
- **Claude** (1544–87)
- **Jean** (I) (1549–after 1634)
  - **Thomas** (1585–1634)
  - **Jean** (II) (1600–72) [Author of the *Traité de l'accord . . .*]
    - **Jean** (III) (*c.* 1630–85)
    - **Louis** (1635–?1718)
    - **Philippe** (d. 1705)
      - **Pierre** (II) (1675–after 1705)
  - **Pierre** (I) (*c.* 1600–after 1664)
- **Robert** (II) (After 1550–89)

DESPONT, Antoine (I), **Luc,** *and* **Robert.** Three brothers who were harpsichord makers in Paris in the seventeenth century, as also were Antoine (II) (b. 1573), Jean, Philippe (I), and Robert—all sons of Antoine I, and Louis and Philippe (II), sons of Luc; also a Pierre Despont [*Hubb 1965*, p. 92, based on *MC*]; further details of the family are given in *Verlet.*

DES RUISSEAUX, Gilbert. French seventeenth-century harpsichord maker. Apprenticed to Michel Richard in 1670 [*Hubb 1965*, p. 101]. The 2-manual harpsichord mentioned by de Bricqueville as belonging to the Société de Musique d'Autrefois is now in the possession of Mme de Chambure, Paris. Illustrated in *Connaissance des Arts*, Paris, 15 August 1954.

DES RUISSEAUX, Louis. French seventeenth-century harpsichord maker, presumably related to the foregoing. A harpsichord by him dated 1658 was in one of the Savoye collections.

DE TAEGHS, V. de. *See*: TAEGHS, Vincentius de.

DETERPIGNY, Jacques. Born in the diocese of Noyon, France. Went to Grenoble where he married in 1779 and set up as a maker of organs, harpsichords, and spinets [*Fleury*].

DE VRIES, Dirck. *See*: VRIES, Dirck de.

DIAKEN, W. *See*: DEACONS, William.

DIEPENRIJCK, Lodewijk van. Was received into the Guild of St. Luke, Antwerp, as a harpsichord maker in 1558, and was still alive in 1589. He also made lutes [*Bu*, *Lü*].

DIERCKX, Jan [*also* Diericxsen]. Harpsichord maker of Antwerp. Born 1531; entered the Guild of St. Luke in 1557. In 1574 he is referred to in a legal document as 'Mter Jan Diericxen clavesingelmaker' [*St*].

DIEREN, Willem van. Harpsichord maker in Amsterdam. The *Amsterdamse courant* of 3 May 1757 contains: 'Willem van Dieren, clavecimbaal-maker en stemmeester, adverteerd, dat hy is gaan woonen in de derde Weterings-dwars-straat . . . Amsterdam.' He was dead by 1782 [*Curtis*, p. 48].

DILKEN. *See*: DULCKEN.

DIVISS, Procopius [Diwisch], 1696–1765. Preacher at Znojmo (Znaim) in Moravia. About 1730 he invented a keyboard instrument called 'orchestrion', 'goldne Dionys', or 'Denis d'or'. It had 790 strings and 130 variations of tone, and imitated the tone of nearly all wind and stringed instruments. Its dimensions were 150 cm long by 60 to 90 cm wide.

He may have made a harpsichord or so as well [*Gö*; Bluethner and Gretschel, *Der Pianofortebau*, Leipzig, 1909, p. 9].

DOBBS, Thomas. Harpsichord and pianoforte maker in New York, *fl.* 1756 [*Hirt*]. He arrived from London in 1785 [*Hin*, p. 180]. *Hirt* gives his name as Dodds and his *floruit* as 1756.

DOHAUSEN, Claus, of Brunswick, *fl.* 1635. Son of Claus Dohausen; maker of clavichords and other instruments. He learnt instrument making for 4 years from Gottfried Fritzsch, organ builder, of Hamburg, apparently finishing his training in 1635 [*SB*, p. 48].

DOHNAL, Joseph. *See*: G, C.

DOMENICO DEL MELA DA GAGLIANO. *See*: MELA, Domenico del.

DOMENICO, Giovanni, *of Venice*. The same maker as Dominicus Pisaurensis, q.v.

DOMENICUS *Venetus*. *See*: DOMINICUS PISAURENSIS.

DOMINICUS *Pisaurensis*. 'Domenico of Pesaro', maker of harpsichords, virginals, and clavichords in the sixteenth century. Instruments bearing Dominicus's name are found as far apart in date as 1533 and 1600; these would, if genuine, imply more than one maker of this name.

Born at Pesaro, he was well known as an instrument maker at Venice by 1548 when the theorist Zarlino had a harpsichord made by him with an enharmonic keyboard ('il quale fece Maestro Dominico Pesarese fabricatore eccelente di simili instrumenti; nel quale non solamente li semituoni maggiori sono diuisi in due parti, ma anche tutti li minori', Gioseffe Zarlino, *Institutioni harmoniche* . . ., Venetia, 1558, p. 140). Doctor Burney saw this instrument in Florence in 1770, and says that it was afterwards sent to England; but no trace of it has survived.

In an inventory of musical instruments of King Philip II of Spain there is an entry: 'Cinco vihuelas de arco de maderna blanco, con unos quadros samblados de taraçea de mano de Dominico entres caxas no. 59', which was thought by *Lü* to refer to this maker; but this is, to say the least, doubtful [*Ks*, p. 224].

Numerous instruments signed *Dominicus Pisaurensis*, ranging in date from 1533 to 1600, have survived or are presumed to have survived, and several signed: *Domenicus Venetus*. *See table 8*.

A harpsichord in the Dublin Museum is signed by Domenico in 1590. He was considered to have been the maker until another inscription was found on it suggesting that it was made by Francesco da Brescia in 1564.

A 2-manual harpsichord in the Claudius Collection, Copenhagen, decorated in rococo style and inscribed *Dominicus Pisaurensis* without date, is regarded by the catalogue as unauthentic.

The Medici collection of which Cristofori (q.v.) was in charge contained 4 instruments by Domenico: a harpsichord, a claviorganum, an ottavino, and a clavichord [*Pu*, p. 101]. In 1693 Cristofori repaired a harpsichord and a virginal by Domenico [Ferdinando Casaglia, *Per le onoranze a Bartolommeo Cristofori* . . ., Firenze, 1876, pp. 24, 27].

DOMOS. *See*: Douwes, Klaas.

DONAT, Johann Jakob, of Leipzig, *fl.* 1700. Organ builder and maker of keyboard instruments. He belonged to a family of organ builders, branches of which were spread over Saxony during the seventeenth and eighteenth centuries. Christoph Donat, who built the organ in the Leipzig Stadtkirche in 1667, was probably an earlier member of the same family as J. J. [*Ks*, p. 225].

A gebunden clavichord in the Heyer Collection, Leipzig, bears on the underside of the lowest key: *Lipsiae Factum â Johanno* [sic] *Jacobo Donato Organopaeo* [sic] / *Mense Septembri Ao. 1700* [*Ks*, p. 36]. Compass, C–C, 4 octaves, 33 pairs of strings; 123 × 34·5 cm.

DONIS, Joseph. *See* DANIS, Joseph.

TABLE 8. *Surviving Instruments by, or Attributed to, DOMINICUS PISAURENSIS, alias DOMENICUS VENETUS*

No.	Date	Type	Kbs.	Signature	Owner/Remarks
1	1533	H	1	*Dominicus Pisaurensis MDXXXIII*	Leipzig, Heyer Collection. 1×8′ register. Compass C–F, 4 octaves and 4th with short octave. Rose in soundboard. Inscription reproduced at *Ks*, p. 222; 1·85 m. long×81 cm. broad.
1a	1540	Pol. V	1	*Dominicus Pisaurensis MDXXXX*	Rück Collection, Germanisches Nationalmuseum.
2	1543	H	1	*Dominicus Pisaurensis MDXXXXIII*	Paris Conservatoire (formerly Kraus Collection). No outer case. C/E–C, probably quint pitch, not octave (*pace Russell 1959*, p. 36). *Gö* refers to Dominicus harpsichords in the Kraus Collection.
3	1543	Cl	1	*Dominicus Pisaurensis MDXXXXIII*	Leipzig, Heyer Collection. Gebunden. 22 pairs of strings; 45 keys. Compass 4 octaves C–C with short octave. Dimensions 1·31 m. broad×43 cm. deep. This is the earliest dated clavichord in existence, those purporting to be by Alessandro Trasontino (q.v.) being fakes.
4	1546	H	1	*Dominicus Pesaur. 1546*	Vienna Kunsthist. Museum, lent by Ges. Mus. Freunde. 2×8′ registers.
?5	1547	Cl	1	[Unsigned; attributed to this maker]	Paris Conservatoire. Gebunden. Trapeze-shaped. A curious instrument. Shewn in the Historical Collection of the Paris Exhibition in 1889, being then the property of M. Thibout *fils* [*Hi*, p. 59].
6	1548	Pol. V	1	*Dominicus Pisaurensis MDXXXXVIII*	Brussels Conservatoire (formerly Correr). 4 octaves with short octave. Rose.
7	1553	H	1		Paris Conservatoire. C–D, 4 octaves plus 1 note. Later buffstop. Has an outer case.
7a	1556	Pol. V	1	*Domenicus Venetus fecit MDLVI*	Yale University, Belle Skinner Collection. C–C with short octave. Jack bears letters *IB*.
7b	1560	Pol. V	1	*Dominicus Venetus 1560*	*FrancI* (item 34).
8	1561	Pol. V	1		New York, Metropolitan Museum of Art. *Shortridge* (p. 107) gives date as '1548' in error. 4 octaves; rose.
8a	1564	Pol. V	1		Haslemere, Dolmetsch Collection. Bought by Arnold Dolmetsch in Italy. Restored by the firm in 1958. Dated *1564*.
8b	1566	Pol. V	1		Nuremberg, Germanisches Nationalmuseum, Rück Collection. C–F, 4½ octaves. Illustrated in *Nor*.
9	1575	Pol. V	1	*Dominicus Pisaurensis MDLXXV*	The Hague, Gemeente-Museum. Inscribed on nameboard. Probably the instrument sold by auction in London in 1901 [*ZIM*, II. 408].
10	1590	H	1		Dublin Museum; formerly London, Victoria and Albert Museum, in 1888. See *HiMi* (p. 47). 2×8′, 1×4′ registers. *Ks* (p. 224) doubts the authenticity of this instrument.
10a	1590	H	2	*Domenico da Pesaro fecit anno 1590*	Lucerne, in the former Schumacher Collection.

TABLE 8 (*cont.*):

No.	Date	Type	Kbs.	Signature	Owner/Remarks
11	1600	H	2	*Dominicus Pisaurensis fecit Anno Domini 1600*	Sold by Alfred du Cros, 1938; bought by H. M. Clark. Sold at Sotheby's on 11 February 1938. 4 octaves. 3 registers, boxwood naturals, sharps with ivory studs at the back. Shewn at the Crystal Palace, 1900. Dimensions 2′ 9″×6′ 11″.
11a	1622	H	1	*Dominicus Pisaurensis fecit 1622*	Recorded in *FrancI* (item 5) and *FrancII* (item 4).
12	n.d.	Pol. V	1	*Dominicus Pisaurensis*	Berlin Collection. Compass 4 octaves with short octave. Rose. Inscription on back of nameboard: *Di Jacopo Dinucci* | *Di S. Pietro a Marcigliano.*
13	n.d.	H	1	*Dominicus Pisaurensis*	Brussels Conservatoire. Compass 4½ octaves.
14	n.d.	Pol. V	1		Formerly in the Correr Collection, Venice [*Ks*, II. 663].
15	n.d.	Pol. V	1		Boston, Museum of Fine Arts. Attributed to this maker.
[16]	n.d.	H	2	*Dominicus Pisaurensis*	Copenhagen, Claudius Collection. Not authentic.

DONNER, Johann Jakob Heinrich. German harpsichord maker, who worked in London for some years. His name appears in the list of subscribers to Sheraton's *Cabinet-maker* [*J*]. Donner was born at Hamburg on 16 December 1760 and died there on 12 June 1802. From *c.* 1780 to *c.* 1795 he lived in London; 1796–8 he was instrument maker in the firm of Donner & Schultz in Hamburg [*Schultze*].

DONZELAGUE. Family of instrument makers at Aix-en-Provence and Lyons in the seventeenth and eighteenth centuries:

(1) **François,** maker of instruments, including harpsichords, at Aix-en-Provence.

(2) **Pierre,** elder son of 1; dates ascertained, 1688–1731. Besides making harpsichords he played the cello and bass viol, and sang.

Born at Aix-en-Provence, he had moved to Lyons by 1688; married at the parish church of Saint-Nizier, 5 or 6 June 1691. In 1719 he acquired Lyons citizenship. 'Des clavecins à grand clavier de Donzelague' were sold in 1750; this may have been the liquidation of his workshop. (His younger brother Martin François had a long career as an artist.)

A 1754 issue of the *Zürcher Wochenblatt* contains this advertisement: '1 fürtrefliches Clavecin mit 3 Registern und 2 Clavieren, deren jedes 61 Claves hat, verfertigt von dem berühmten Meister Donzelhage, in Lion; es hat einen sowol überaus angenehmen als starken Thon, und ist in allen Absichten in gänzlich vollkommenem Stand, auch mit dazugehörigem sauber verarbeiteten Fuss versehen' [*Rindl*].

Surviving Harpsichords

(1) 1716. Seen by Claude Dalbanne, Director of the Musée Historique de Lyon, in 1937. Inscription on nameboard: *Donzelague à Lyon 1716.* A 2-manual instrument but the keyboards missing. Paintings *in tempera* of tulips, pinks, and birds on the soundboard.

DOPPO. Harpsichord maker in Florence at some time before 1665, if we may rely on *Wald*'s transcription from the Innsbruck inventory (1665) of the Archduke Siegmund Franz of Austria: 'Ein anders Instrument mit 3 Registern mit einem weissen Futtral, so der *Doppo* von Florenz gemacht, ist von Cypress.'

DORT, Cornelis van. Amsterdam harpsichord maker. Born 1673 or 1674. In the *Amsterdamse courant* of 6 October 1694 he advertised 'various harpsichords with 2 to 3 manuals . . .'. His latest ascertained date is 1703, when he married Machteld Herwegh [*Curtis*, p. 48].

DOTTI, Lorenzo, of Empoli. Virginal maker; born 1686 in Siena. [*Va*, who quotes a signature on an ottavino: *Lorenzo Daddi* [sic] *Hempolese fece in Sienna 1686.*] This instrument is now (1972) in the Museo Nazionale degli Strumenti Musicali, Rome [*ChamP*].

DOUVÉ, Michel. Parisian master harpsichord maker in 1661. He married in 1643 [*Hubb 1965*, p. 92].

DOUWES, Klaas [= Nicolas]. Called *Domos* by Marpurg and Lustig; theorist and amateur clavichord maker, was born at Leeuwarden in 1668 or 1669. He became a schoolmaster and organist at the school at Tzum (Friesland), as we learn from the title-page of his work, *Grondig onderzoek van de toonen der muzyk,* which appeared in 1699. On p. 104 of this he refers to a device in the construction of pedal-clavichords which he says was employed by no one else but himself.

This little volume, of which a second edition appeared in 1722 and a third in 1773, contains much interesting information on various instruments including the clavichord and harpsichord. It gives detailed instructions in clavichord design, including pedal-clavichords, together with virginal scaling and string gauges; and contains terse but relevant observations on the harpsichord, e.g. 'The pleasantness of the tone depends on the soundboard being of the correct thinness, and on the soundboard bars lying in the right place.' ('De aangenaamheit van 't geluidt bestaat daar in, dat de sangbodem behoorlijk dun is, ende dat de spalken onder de sangbodem op de regte plaats leggen', p. 105.)

He died before 1722 [*Eit, Fé*].

DOWNING, George. Harpsichord maker, 243 Strand, London. Dates ascertained, 1763–83 [*J*].

DRIEL, Abraham von. Became a citizen of Hamburg in 1710. He made lutes, and probably keyboard instruments as well [*Lü*].

DUBOIS, Henry. Was apprenticed to Jean Jacquet, harpsichord maker of rue Beaubourg, Paris, on 14 February 1658 [*Hubb*].

DUBOIS, Pierre. Parisian harpsichord maker. Dates ascertained: 1778–98 or 1799. Entered the Guild of Instrument makers in 1778. Was living then, and in *an VII* (1798–9), in the rue St. Honoré 'vis a vis Les ecurij du roij (as inscribed on the underside of a harpsichord 're-fait [by him] . . . 1780'.—See below, Ruckers no. 138).

DUBUC, Nicolas. Harpsichord maker in Paris. Born 1638 or 1639 [*Laborde*].

See also: SELLIER, Jean.

DUBUT GUISSIÈRE, Charles Philippe. Parisian harpsichord maker in 1729 [*Hubb*].

DUCASTEL, Augustin Hippolyte. Parisian harpsichord maker, born *c.* 1698. Latest date ascertained, 1734. *Verlet* gives further details.

DU FOUR, Claude [Gondard]. Harpsichord maker at Lyons; born 1628 or 1629, died 1709. The Lyons archives record him as 'Me. faisseur de clavecins, mort le 8 juillet 1709, à 80 ans'. 'Claude Gondart dit du Four' became master on 17 August 1680, according to documents apparently overlooked by *Verlet*. An edict of the King dated March 1700 referred to him as:

faiseur de clavecins demeurant en cette Ville [Lyons] place Bellecour, maison de Mr. Bay, pour satisfaire au susdit edict [an *édit somptuaire* of 1700], a déclaré qu'il a dans son domicille scauoir douze vieux clavessins et six neuf, dont la roze et les émoulures sont dorées, quatre autre clavessins dont les frises qui sont autour et au dedans sont peintes sur papier doré et les émoulures sont dorées; un pied d'un vieux clavessin de boys doré . . .

Cor (p. 84) mentions him in passing. A 'clavecin de Dufour' was advertised on 27 August 1753 [*Bq*].

See also: GONDARD.

Surviving Instruments

(1) 1674. Paris, Collection Samy Chalom. Harpsichord. Apparently has 2 manuals; painted case. Signed: *Claude du Four / An 1674*. Illustrated in *Connaissance des arts*, Paris, 15 August 1954.

(2) 167 . . . Spinet. Owned by Louis-Daniel Perret, Lutry (Switzerland)

DUGUÉ, Pierre. *Fl.* at Paris in the sixteenth century; organist, and afterwards maker of instruments including probably the harpsichord [*Les*, p. 15].

According to Norbert Dufourcq's *Le clavecin* (Paris, 1949, p. 16) there was a Parisian harpsichord maker called Dugué in the seventeenth century. *Verlet* calls him 'an organist and instrument maker'.

DUKERN. The inventory of the greffier Duxout (9 April 1756; 91, 930) refers to a 'clavecin de Dukern . . . 800 livres'. But this may be an error for Ruckers or Dulcken.

DULCKEN. A family of distinguished harpsichord makers:

(1) **Antoine.** Died 1763. Maker of instruments including harpsichords at Antwerp. The scope of his work is indicated by his widow's words: 'Nous avons eu de tout tems et nous y avons encore des ouvriers en toutes sortes d'instruments' [*VdS*, I. 197–205].

(2) **Johan Daniel.** Dates ascertained 1736–69. Son of (1). Born at Maastricht, but left there for Antwerp before 1741. He made keyboard instruments of high reputation. J. P. Bull (q.v.) was trained in his shop. By 1764 he had moved to Brussels, where he died after 1769. Some lutes survive bearing his name [*Lü*]. *BurnG* (I. 48) refers to him as the master of Bull, and says that 'the harpsichord maker of the greatest eminence after them [i.e. the Ruckers] was J. Dan. Dulcken; he was a Hessian. At present there is . . . Bull.' See further *VdS*, I. 197–205. (Burney was in error in calling him a Hessian.)

(3) **Johan Lodewijk** *the Elder*. Son of Johan Daniel. Baptized 15 April 1736 in Maastricht. He had moved to Amsterdam by 1756, when he married Catrina Koning. His son Jan [Johan] Lodewijk the younger was baptized at Amsterdam in 1761, and it seems likely that father and son remained in that town, the son learning the craft of instrument-making from his father, until 1781 when the son went to Munich. The father may or may not have remained in Amsterdam.

(4) **Johan Lodewijk** *the Younger*. Son of (3). Baptized in Amsterdam on 9 August 1761. (*Ge*, and others following him, mistakenly regard him as the son of Johan Daniel.) In 1781 the Elector of Bavaria summoned him to become 'mechanischer Hofklaviermacher' in Munich, where in 1799 he married the pianist Sophie Lebrun and turned to piano-making. He was still living there in 1835 [*Curtis*, p. 49].

(5) **Louis.** A Louis Dulcken was making pianos in Paris during the period at any rate 1783–93. *Verlet* records him there from 1780 to 1791, though her entry is not very clear. A single-manual harpsichord in the Gemeente-Museum at The Hague, signed *Louis Dulcken 1793* was originally a grand piano in the Viennese style. (It was presented by Albert Hess; the date of its conversion is not known.)

A list, compiled in 1795, of instruments belonging to victims of the Terror, contains 'un clavecin, par Ludovicus Dulcken, avec pupitre' [*Br*].

See table 9.

TABLE 9. *Surviving Instruments by Johan Daniel DULCKEN*

No.	Date	Type	Kbs.	Signature	Owner/Remarks
1	[17—]	H	1	*Joannes Daniel Dulcken me fecit Antwerpiae 1689* [spurious]	Nuremberg, Germanisches Nationalmuseum, Neupert Collection. *IDD* rose; 5 octaves, F–F. Date, occurring on the jackrail and nameboard is spurious. The instrument is clearly eighteenth century and was presumably made by the well-known J. D. Dulcken about 1750. See Van der Meer's paper in *RG.I*, p. 69.
[2]					Same instrument as 5 below.
[2a]	*c.* 1740	H	2		Rouen, private ownership. Originally 1-manual, the 2nd being added later.
[2b]	1744			*Joannes Daniel Dulcken me fecit Antwerpiae anno 1744*	Brussels Conservatoire. Nameboard from a harpsichord.
3	1745	H	2	*Ioannes Daniel Dulcken me fecit Antwerpiae Ao. 1745*	Washington, Smithsonian Institution. Compass, 5 octaves; 2×8′, 1×4′ registers, with lute. Illustrated in *Wash 1969*.
4	1745	H	2	*Joannes Daniel Dulcken Faecit Antwerpiae 1745*	Vienna, Kunsthist. Museum (lent by Mus. f. Angewandte Kunst). F–F, 5 octaves; 2×8′, 1×4′ stops. Rose with initials [*Luith*, pp. 14–15].
4a	1745	H	1	*Joannes Daniel Dulcken me faecit Antverpiae*	Liège, Jacques Bernard (1969). About 1880 it was bought in Antwerp by Armand van Zuylen; it passed to Albert van Zuylen, of Liège, who owned it until 1964. Inscription on nameboard; 2×8′ stops. One row of jacks (beechen) not original. Gilded lead rose with initials: *JD*. Present compass (*ravalé*) A–E, 4½ octaves. Dimensions 224·3×83·5×25·3 cm. [*Nev*].
5	1747	H	1	*Joannes Daniel Dulcken fecit Antwerpiae anno 1747*	Antwerp Conservatoire. 5 octaves F–F. 2×8′, 1×4′. Formerly in Snoeck Collection.
6	1755	H	2		Formerly Régibo Collection. 5 octaves; 3 registers. Length 258 cm.
6a	1755	H	2	*Joannes Daniel Duckin me fecit Antverpiae anno 1755*	Brussels, Robert Kohner (1970). F–F, 5 octaves; 2×8′, 1×4′ (1 row dogleg). *IDD* gilded rose. Ebony naturals; white sharps. Bought recently in Krainem near Brussels from Mrs. Capart, who inherited it from her mother Mrs. Vaes, who had owned it for a considerable time. Restored in 1898 by de Vestibule who was then working for the Brussels Conservatoire Collection, and more recently by Hubert Bédard, Paris [*Nev*]. Perhaps = no. 6.
7	1755	H	1	*Johannes Daniel Dulcken me fecit Antwerpiae 1755*	Brussels Conservatoire.
8	1755	H	1	*Johannes Daniel Dulcken me fecit Antwerpiae 1755*	Antwerp, M. Roose (1953). 2×8′, 1×4′.
9	1764	H	1	*Joannes Daniel Dulcken me fecit Bruxellis anno 1764*	Berlin Collection. F–F, 5 octaves; 2×8′, 1×4′ registers.
10	1769	H	1	*Johannes Daniel Dulcken me fecit Bruxellis anno 1769.*	Brussels Conservatoire. *IDD* rose.

TABLE 9 (*cont.*):

No.	Date	Type	Kbs.	Signature	Owner/Remarks
11	n.d.	H	2		Brussels Conservatoire, no. 1605. No legend or date. *IDD* rose. Painting on lid signed by C. Bigée.
12	n.d.	H	1		Seale, Farnham, R. B. Bibby (1966), who bought it from Bristol Museum at Christie's, 29 November 1962. *IDD* rose; 2×8′, 1×4′, buff. Restorer's number 2685 on main 8′ register-lever. Two handstops above keyboard. Painted case. Presented by Mrs. K. H. Rees-Mogg in 1944 to Bristol Museum.
13	n.d.	H	1		Berlin Collection. *IDD* rose.
14	n.d.	H	1		Formerly Régibo Collection. Sale catalogue (1897) reads: 'Grand clavecin de Dulcken, 1 clavier, 4 octaves et une quarte, 3 régistres. Longueur, 220 cm.'
15	n.d.	H	[1]		Formerly Régibo Collection. Sale catalogue (1897) reads: 'Grand clavecin de Dulcken.'

DULYCZ, Michael Bulyowsky de. *See*: BULYOWSKY DE DULYCZ, Michael.

DUMONT, Jean. Eighteenth-century French harpsichord maker. Louis XVI (born 1754, guillotined 1793) had 3 harpsichords by him [*MarcP*].

DUMONT, Nicolas. Parisian harpsichord maker, *fl.* 1673–97. He was married in 1673 [*MC*], and was received into the Guild of Instrument Makers in 1675 [*Verlet*]. A 1680 harpsichord by him was offered for sale on 7 May 1782 [*Bq*]. *Cor* (p. 84) refers to him in passing. The inventory of Stehlin (died 1774) includes a harpsichord made by him in 1695.

Surviving Instruments

(1) 1697. Paris Conservatoire. Harpsichord inscribed: *Nicolas Dumont à Paris 1697* and (on the wrestplank) *Refait par Pascal Taskin à Paris, 1789*. Two manuals; 5 octaves F–F, though the original compass was less. *N.-D* rose; 2×8′, 1×4′, *jeu de buffle*. Jacks early, but leathered by Tomasini in the nineteenth century. *Genouillères* added by Taskin, doubtless in 1789. For a discussion of the instrument see *Hubb 1965*, p. 114.

E, D. A 2-manual harpsichord, almost certainly French and dating from the late seventeenth or early eighteenth century, is owned by M. J. Vollant, Grignan, France. Push-pull coupler; 2×8′, 1×4′ stops; B–C, with bottom D sharp split. Rose having winged figure with D to the left and E (or possibly F—there has been slight damage) to the right. Jacks modern, with delrin plectra. The instrument is in excellent order and is regularly used. [Information from John Ritchie, Blewbury.]

EAST, Peter. *See* JOYCE, George.

EDELMANN, Gottfried Ludwig. Maker of keyboard instruments (including harpsichords, spinets, and pianofortes) and organist; born at Strasbourg on 24 January 1753, the second son of Caspar Samuel Edelmann, a joiner. (His elder brother Johann Friedrich, the composer (born 1749) moved to Paris and was guillotined there in 1794.) [R. Benton, in *MQ*, April 1964.] 'Une épinette à grand rav[alement] de Edelmann, à Strasbourg, laquelle se replie en deux et se met dans une caisse' was advertised for sale, 16 October 1775 [*Bq*].

EESBROECK, Jan van. Born at Mariakerck, son of Josse van Eesbroeck. Received the citizenship of Antwerp on 9 December 1583. He was primarily a lute maker, but apparently also made harpsichords [*Lü*].

ELSCHE, Jakob van den [*also* van Elsen]. Harpsichord maker in Antwerp. Dates ascertained, 1710–72. He entered the Guild of St. Luke in 1717. In 1767 he was commissioned to repair the harpsichord in the cathedral, used for choir training, and sometimes for services [*Bu*].

BurnG (I. 48), commenting on the Antwerp harpsichord makers in 1772, writes of him: 'The work too of Van den Elsche, a Flamand, has a considerable share of merit.'

Surviving Harpsichords

(1) 1710. Berlin Collection. Two manuals, F–G, 5 octaves plus 2 notes; 3×8′, 1×4′, of which two 8′ work on 1 string. Rose. The nameboard is missing. According to Snoeck (*Catalogue*, 1894, p. 48) it was inscribed: *Jacobus van den Elsche me fecit Antwerpiae anno 1710. Johannes Heinemann refecit ao 1790.*

(2) 1767. Antwerp Conservatoire (lent 1966 to the Vleeshuis). Two manuals; F–F, 5 octaves. Inscription: *Iacobus van den Elsche me fecit Antverpiae Ao 1763*, above the keyboards; 2×8′, 1×4′ stops.

The Brussels Conservatoire has a nameboard inscribed: *Jacobus van den Elsschen me fecit Antwerpiae 1715.*

ELSNER. Carpenter in Grottkau, Prussia, in the first half of the eighteenth century. He made harpsichords and other musical instruments. Father of Joseph Elsner the composer (1766–1854) [*Fé*, *Eit*].

ELST, Aert, *or* **Arnold van der,** of Antwerp. Harpsichord maker; dates ascertained, 1576–9 [*St*].

ELWICK, Joseph. Recorded as a harpsichord maker at 53 Long Acre, London in 1788 [*Byrne*].

ELWICK, Joshua. Maker of harpsichords, resident 1790–7 in Long Acre, on the corner of Phoenix Alley, London [*RB.A*].

He is mentioned as a harpsichord maker in J. Doane's *Musical Directory* (London, 1794) [L. G. Langwill, *Two Rare Eighteenth Century London Directories*. In: *Music and Letters*. London, January 1949].

EMERY. *See*: LORILLART, Médéric.

ENGLAND, George. Organ builder and harpsichord maker, *fl.* in London 1763 [Langwill].

ÉRARD, Sébastien [Erhard], 1752–1831. Maker of harpsichords and pianofortes, and founder of the firm of Érard.

He was born on 5 April 1752 at Strasbourg, of German stock. In 1768 he went to Paris and started work under a harpsichord maker there. After a few years his ingenuity found expression in a mechanical harpsichord which was noticed in 1776 by the Abbé Roussier.

In the following year he made the first pianoforte (a square) to be made in France, at the château of the Duchesse de Villeroi. Soon afterwards he was joined by his brother Jean-Baptiste, and set up in the rue de Bourbon, Paris. From this time onwards his attention turned more and more to piano-making. In 1796 he was in London, where he remained for 10 years; after which he returned to Paris and made his first grand piano.

For further details see the long article in *Fé* (vol. 3); also *GD*, and *Ks*, p. 226.

The firm of Érard has made a number of harpsichords since the revival.

An anonymous portrait of Sébastien Érard was shewn at the International Inventions Exhibition, 1885 (Catalogue, p. 63).

Surviving Harpsichords of the Classical Period

(1) 1779. Two manuals; 4 registers, 3 quilled and 1 leathered. Knee-levers and pedals. Shewn by Mme Érard at the Exhibition of Ancient Musical Instruments, South Kensington Museum, 1872. For some years at Hever Castle, Kent. Bought by M. Thomas, Hurley, in 1969 [*Rip*]. Acquired by the Paris Conservatoire, 1973.

(2) A harpsichord by him dated 1791 was formerly at Lemberg [*Vienna Exhibition Catalogue*, 1892].

ERHART, A. F. Clavichord maker at Strasbourg in 1679 [*Hirt*]. Perhaps an ancestor of Sébastien Érard.

ERMEL, J. J., of Mons. Maker of harpsichords, pianofortes, and organized pianofortes. Dates ascertained, 1780–5.

In 1780 he sold a harpsichord with a 'jeu de buffle formant le piano'. In or before 1785 he sold another 'ayant 2 jeux de bufle formant le piano'; and in 1785 a 'clavessin dit forte piano' and others [*VdS*, II. 121].

He joined with Bremers (q.v.) in petitioning for an increased import duty on keyboard instruments for the protection of native makers, 1785 [ibid.].

ERMEL, Eugène. Son of the preceding, also of Mons, where he worked with his father [*VdS*, II. 121]. *Fl.* 1779; made organs and pianos as well as harpsichords. He laid claim to an invention of *crescendo* and *diminuendo* on the harpsichord [*Cl*, p. 40].

ESTAMPROY, Gregory. *Fl.* 1526 in London as a maker of stringed keyboard instruments [*Russell 1959*, p. 65].

EULER, Leonhardt. The celebrated mathematician (1707–83) is said by the eighteenth-century scientist John Robison (1739–1805) to have invented a variety of clavichord (a variant of Silbermann's *cembal d'amour*) [*RipScot*, p. 488].

EVERBROEK, Gommaar van. Harpsichord maker at Antwerp. Died 1655–6 [*St*, p. 49].

EVERRATT, Henry, of London. Virginal maker, *fl.* 1664. [Parish records of St. Giles Cripplegate.]

EYLENSTEIN, Johann Friedrich. Born at Weimar 11 May 1705. In 1724 he became a pupil of Joseph Heinrich Ruppert, a violin maker at Erfurt. By 1731 he had taken over Ruppert's position and was Court instrument maker of Weimar. As well as keyboard instruments he made violins, lutes, mandolins, and other instruments [*Eit*, *Ge*, *Lü*].

F, A. *See*: A, F.

F, B. F. *See*: BATTAGLIA, Francesco.

F, D. A 2-manual seventeenth-century harpsichord, probably French but made in the Flemish style, and bearing apparently the maker's initials *DF*, is owned by C. Mercier-Ythier, Paris. *See also*: E, D.

F, F. *See*: FABER, Franciscus.

F, J. A harpsichord in private ownership in Paris has (1953) a rose bearing the initials: *J. F.*

FABER, Daniel Tobias. Organist at Crailsheim in 1725; made a bundfrei clavichord at that time. *Wa*'s words are: Faber 'hat ein Clavichordium erfunden, so durchgehends Bundfrey ist . . .' (he is quoting from the *Coburgischer Zeitungs-Extract* for 1725). This much-cited passage has been interpreted as signifying that bundfrei clavichords were not known before this time, which of course is a mistake, for instance the clavichord pictured in Mersenne (1636) is bundfrei apart from the 5 topmost notes. The first volume of Bach's *Forty-eight*, published in 1722 demands a bundfrei instrument. But it is true that until the eighteenth century bundfrei clavichords were the exception rather than the rule.

(*Note*: The piece of evidence most frequently adduced to refute Faber's claim to being the inventor of the bundfrei clavichord is the Grüneberg instrument in Manchester. This is dated 17.0—the third digit being illegible—and has been assigned to the year 1700; but it must be many decades later than this. *See below, under*: GRÜNEBERG.)

FABER, Franciscus, of Senigallia. The Rück Collection in the Germanisches Nationalmuseum, Nuremberg, has a harpsichord of 1631 by him. Inscription: *Franciscus Faber Semnogalliensis fecit Anno Domini MDCXXXI.* It was originally an enharmonic instrument having 19 keys to the octave but was changed to its present compass probably towards the end of the seventeenth century [*VdM*].

Pro Musica, Annapolis, Md., had an undated harpsichord by him in 1967. W. Zuckermann had in 1968 an Italian harpsichord, C–C bass short octave, 2×8′ stops, boxwood keys. The top and bottom keys bore the initials *FF*, and it may well have been by Faber. Sold in 1969 to a private buyer in New York [*Zuck*].

FABER, Wolfgang. Organist at Munich *c.* 1560, he also made organs, harpsichords, flutes, lutes, and other instruments [*Lü*].

FABRIZIUS, Wolfgang. *See*: FABER, Wolfgang.

FABY, P. Born in Bologna. Settled as instrument maker in France. Dates ascertained, 1677–91.

Surviving Instruments

(1) 1677. Paris, Conservatoire. Harpsichord. Made for Count Hercole Pepoli, godson of Louis XIV. Compass, 4 octaves minus 1 note. Low F sharp and G sharp split.

(2) 1691. Ibid. Another, on loan from the Louvre. Inscribed: *P. Faby de Bononia Ord. Min. Obs. opus.* Compass B–C, 4 octaves plus; short octave. Bottom C sharp and D sharp split. 2×8′ stops.

(3) 1684. Trondheim, Ringve Museum. Spinet by Faby, inscribed on nameboard: *P. Faby Bononiensis opus Anno Dom. MDCLXXXIV.* Three octaves F–C. Parchment geometrical rose. Previous owners: Duce d'Aosta; Evan Gorga, Rome; Mrs. Victoria Bachke, founder of the Ringve Museum.

(4) Undated. Paris, Collection André Meyer. A small virginal in a silk-covered outer case, illustrated in *Hin* (pl. 31), is signed by Faby. It has 26 notes.

FAHRHOFF. A clavichord in the Museum Blumenstein, Solothurn, has an almost illegible signature which might be read: *Fahrhoff Nr. 4.*

FAINI, Francesco. Florentine harpsichord maker, *fl.* 1791 [*Fab*, p. 171].

FAIRN, Alexander. English harpsichord maker, *fl.* 1793. His name appears in the list of subscribers to Sheraton's *Cabinet maker* [*J*].

FALCONER. *See*: FALKENER.

FALCONI, Giuseppe, of Florence. Maker of keyboard instruments, living in the Via dei Calzolai in 1689, in which year he paid a matriculation fee to his Guild. His father's name was Jacopo [*Pu*].

FALCONI, of Florence. Maker of keyboard instruments, *fl.* 1765. Probably a descendant of the foregoing.

A clavichord by him dated 1765 in the Van Raalte Collection, Brownsea Island, Dorset, was sold in 1927. The catalogue describes it as bundfrei, with ivory naturals and mother-of-pearl sharps. Short octave. Compass, 2 octaves [?]. Paper rose, and case covered with paper.

FALKENER, Robert [*also* Falconer, Falkner, Ffalknor]. Harpsichord maker of Salisbury Court, Fleet Street. Dates ascertained, 1760–73. *J* (p. 67 n.) quotes a reference to 'the famous Falconer' as maker of a 'curious Ton'd, double key'd, new harpsichord, just imported in Capt. *Millard* from London', in the *Boston Gazette* of 27 June 1763.

His name appears in *Un* as a harpsichord maker.

The Robert Ffalknor against whom Jakob Kirkman brought an action in 1771 for exposing 'to sale a certain Harpsichord for a large sum of money to wit the Sum of £27. 6*s.* as and for a harpsichord made by the said Jacob' (see *J*, p. 43 n.) was this Falkener; as also was the Robert Falkener who wrote *Instructions for playing the harpsichord. Wherein is fully explained the mystery of thoroughbass . . . to which is added exact rules for tuning the harpsichord, with all the different-siz'd wires used in that instrument . . .* London, 1774. (This is the second edition; the first was published in 1762, but no copy seems to have survived. The author was a German who settled in England in the middle of the eighteenth century. *Ge* and *Fé* give his Christian name as Rudolph. It would seem that he exchanged Rudolph for Robert after his arrival in England.)

Harpsichords no. 56 and 42a of Kirkman bear on the underside of the soundboard Falkener's signature. Since, however, they have Kirkman nameboards they appear below as Kirkman instruments.

FANDEVELL, Pawyl. *See*: Defield.

FANI, Luigi (?). *Ks* (p. 64) lists an ottavino in the Heyer Collection, Leipzig, on whose topmost jack is the barely legible inscription: *Luigi / Fani*[?] / *16 / 35.* On the same key is a repairer's note: *Aprile / 1769 / rest:*

FARINI. Florentine harpsichord maker who experimented *c.* 1620 with the substitution of gut strings for metal [*Ch*]. Cf. Hildebrand.

FARNABY, Nicholas, of London. Maker of virginals. Dates ascertained, 1587–1630, the latter being the year of his death [Registers, St. Olave Jewry, London]. He was probably related to Giles Farnaby the composer (d. 1640) and his father Thomas (d. 1594), both of whom appear in the books of the Joiners' Company as 'Citizen and Joiner' [information supplied by John Boston]. Two apprentices of his, John Haslupp and Henry Walker, are mentioned in *Join.*

Nicholas Farnaby's son, also called Nicholas, is recorded as a virginal maker, during his father's lifetime [Ibid.].

FAULKNER, Robert. *See*: FALKENER, Robert.

FEDERIGI, Agostino. Virginal maker in Pisa in the eighteenth century.

Surviving Instruments

(1) 1767. Virginal; 4′ pitch, inscribed: *Agostinus Federigius fecit in Pisis Anno 1767*. Paris, André Meyer Collection, 1970. Listed in *FrancI* (no. 23).

(2) 1786. Virginal (?), inscribed: *Agostinus Federigus fecit in Pisis 1786* [*FrancI*, no. 26].

FEIGENSER, Johann Christian. An anonymous clavichord in Købstadmuseet 'Den Gamle By', Aarhus, Denmark, bears the inscription: *Joh. Christ. Feigenser / Reparirt 1778 und in / Cammerton gebracht*, followed by a record of repair in 1909. Bundfrei; F–F, 5 octaves; the 2 lowest octaves have a third string (octave) to each note.

Presented to the Museum in 1908 by Jens Ølsgaard, 'alterdegn' at Aarhus Cathedral. His father had bought it by auction in Faarup before 1885 [*Müller*].

FENTON. English spinet maker, *c.* 1700 [*Ri*, pp. 69, 85].

FERCHUR, Jean. Harpsichord maker in Paris, of German origin, died 30 January 1729 leaving a minor son Pierre. He acted as expert for the inventories of de Machy (1726) and Blanchet (1726) [*MC*]. *Cor* (p. 84) refers to him in passing under the name of 'Verjure'. See further *Verlet*.

FERDENANT, Zacharias [Ferdinand]. In 1684 he worked, apparently in Amsterdam, as an 'orgel ende clavesimbel maker'. He was then about 60 years of age [*Curtis*, p. 49].

FERMANNI, Pietro. Spinet maker, presumably Italian. The Deutsches Museum, Munich has an ottavino by him signed on the jackrail: *Pietrus Fermanni fecit A.D. 1750*. Three octaves.

FERNANDEZ, Diego, of Madrid. Designed in collaboration with the singer Farinelli a harpsichord for Queen Maria Barbara of Spain (daughter of John V of Portugal and queen of Ferdinand VI of Spain), who died in 1758. It was bequeathed to Farinelli by the Queen and became one of his favourite instruments [*Sac*, p. 47, cited by *Kirk*].

FEROCI.

(1) **Michele,** Florentine harpsichord maker, living in the Via dei Calzolai in 1680, in which year he paid a matriculation fee to his Guild. His father's name was Giuseppe F. [*Pu*].

(2) **Agostino,** Italian spinet maker, *fl.* 1705, son of (1). A spinet in the Stuttgart Collection is inscribed: *Agostinus Feroci Filius Micheaele* [sic] *Fecit Ao 1705*. Josten's monograph gives no further details of the instrument.

FERREIRA, Jacintho. Clavichord maker at Lisbon, *fl.* 1783.

Surviving Clavichords

(1) 1783. Lisbon Conservatoire. Inscribed almost illegibly: *Jacintho Ferreira Lisboa 1783 fecit*. Compass 4 octaves and 2 notes. For full details see *Dod*, pp. 67–72 in the German text.

FERRINI, Giovanni, of Florence. Harpsichord maker, *fl.* 1699(?)–1755. He was a pupil of Cristofori, and carried on his work after his death in 1731 [*Sac*, cited by *Kirk*, who records that Farinelli had a pianoforte by him].

Surviving Instruments

(1) 1699. Stuttgart, Württembergisches Museum. Harpsichord. Compass $4\frac{1}{2}$ octaves G–C; $2 \times 8'$. Suspect. Perhaps = *FrancI*, item 46.

(1a) 1731. Pistoia, Don G. Pineschi. A 'cembalo traverso'; $2 \times 8'$ stops; compass C–C, 4 octaves.

[(?2) 1751. Chicago, Harding Museum. Clavichord. Compass $3\frac{5}{8}$ octaves. This instrument is reported to me as not authentic.]

Note: The nameboard of a harpsichord in the Metropolitan Museum of Art, New York, bears an inscription stating that it was made by Zenti (q.v.) and restored by Ferrini in 1755 (see Catalogue, p. 66).

FESSEL, Johann Heinrich Ernst. Maker of clavichords and other keyboard instruments. Born at Wernigerode, 17 April 1764; latest date ascertained, 1796.

In 1785 he was working with Horn at Dresden and receiving instruction in instrument-making; after which in 1791 he set up on his own. His clavichords which had the 'double soundboard' were said to possess a good strong tone [*Ge*, *Gö*].

FEYRING, Philip [Feuring], 1730–67. Maker of harpsichords, spinets, and other instruments including organs. Born at Arfeld, Germany, 5 September 1730, he emigrated to Philadelphia in his youth and soon gained a good reputation for his instruments. He died in 1767. See further *Armstr*, p. 28.

FFALKNOR, Robert. *See*: Falkener, Robert.

FISSOT. Restored in 1762 a harpsichord which belonged to the late Paul Brunold, who ascribed it erroneously to Vater (q.v.).

FITELER, Jean. Organ builder in Paris; *fl.* 1650. He probably made harpsichords also [*Laborde*].

FLEISCHER. Surname of a family of instrument makers at Hamburg in the seventeenth and eighteenth centuries.

(1) **Hans Christoph** [Johann Christoffer I), born 1638, still alive 1688. Was baptized in the S. Petri Kirche on 28 May 1638 as the son of Christoffer Fleischer. He received Hamburg citizenship on 12 April 1672, and married in 1675 Sophia Margaretha Zaego, who 1676–89 bore him 9 children (but by 1694 was married to Johann Middelburg the organ and clavichord builder). His sister Catherina married (7 September 1669) Joachim Tielke the lute maker (1641–1719) who was god-father to one or more of his children [*Hbg*].

Although chiefly known as a lute maker, Hans Christoph is said to have made keyboard instruments; a double-bass by him was sold at The Hague in 1759 [*Lü*].

(2) **Johann Christoph** [Johann Christoffer II], born 1676, still alive 1724. Eldest son of Hans Christoph, was baptized in the S. Petri Kirche on 4 July 1676. He received

Hamburg citizenship on 12 June 1705, and between 1706 and 1710 three children of his were baptized there [*Hbg*].

In 1708 he was in serious conflict with the Guild of Joiners, who considered his work an encroachment upon their rights. He made lutes and viols, but specialized in keyboard instruments, and invented in 1718 a 'Lauten-clavecin', which was a gut-strung harpsichord with 2×8′ registers, and a 'Theorbenflügel', which had 2 gut-strung registers and 1 of metal.

Wa calls him (p. 248) a 'very well known and experienced artist in the making of all kinds of musical instruments, but especially stringed and keyboard instruments', and says that his harpsichords cost 60, 70, 100, and up to 1,000 talers.

MatNO mentions him and his brother, together with Middelburg (q.v.), as makers of good clavichords.

J. C. Fleischer restored the Ruckers instrument no. 35a, q.v.

(3) **Carl Conrad,** born 1680, still alive 1721 but had died by 1738. Another son of Hans Christoph, he was baptized 13 November 1680 in the S. Petri Kirche as his fourth child. He received Hamburg citizenship on 3 January 1716. Four daughters and 1 son of his were baptized between 1712 and 1721 [*Hbg*]. The year of his death is given in *Vannes* as 1737.

Surviving FLEISCHER Instruments

(1) 1710; harpsichord; by Johann Christoph F. Berlin Collection. Registers: 1×8′, 1×4′, buff; round tail; rose. An obscure ink inscription on the wrestplank seems to indicate that Fleischer made the instrument in 1710 and restored it in 1724: *Johan Christoph Fleischer auxit Ano 1710. Restituit Ano 1724 Hamburgi.* On the underside of the soundboard: *Anno 1724 reparavit* and *Soli Deo Gloria.* (For '*auxit*' meaning simply 'made', cf. J. C. Heinrich no. 1.) The instrument formerly belonged to H. Sobotka, New York, and passed after his death in 1970 to Berlin.

(2) 1720; harpsichord, by Carl Conrad F. Barcelona, Museo de Música. Inscribed: *Carl Conradt Fleischer me fecit in Hamburg 1720.* Single manual. G–C 4 octaves and a 4th. Geometrical rose sunk in soundboard.

(3) 1727; clavichord, signed: *Johan Christoph Fleischer auxit Hamb. Año 1727.* Gebunden C–C, 4 octaves; 15 notes have additional 4′ strings. Size 147·7×43·1 cm.

The FLEISCHER Family, Instrument Makers at Hamburg

Christoffer Fleischer

? Tobias F. *fl.* 1683

Joachim Tielke = Catherina F.
lutemaker

(1) **Hans Christoph** Fleischer = Sophia Margaretha Zaego = (2) Johann Middelburg, *m.* by 1694; organ builder and clavichord maker
b. 1638, *m.* 1675, still alive 1688; lute maker, also made other instruments

Johann Christoph Fleischer = ?
b. 1676, still alive 1724; maker of instruments, incl. harpsichords
at least 3 children

Carl Conrad Fleischer = ?
b. 1680, still alive 1721; organ builder and harpsichord maker
at least 5 children

7 more children

FLEUROT. French maker of *épinettes* in Val d'Ajol, in the Vosges, eighteenth century [*Pi*]. An *épinette* by him was lot 489 in the de Léry sale in Paris in 1910.

FLORANO, Gianpietro, of Rome. Harpsichord maker, *fl.* 1624 [*Va*].

FLORIANO, Benedetto [*also* Floriani], of Venice. Virginal and harpsichord maker. Dates ascertained: 1568–72. (*Hirt* gives 1558 as his earliest known date.) *See also*: BRUNETO *dalli Organi.*

Philip James conjectures that a polygonal virginal in the Victoria and Albert Museum known as Queen Elizabeth's virginal may be the work of this maker.

Surviving Instruments

(01) 1562. Milan, Museo Civico. Polygonal virginal inscribed: *Fecit B*[ctus] *Floriani MDLXII.* Illustrated in *Gall* and in *Pag* (pp. 52–3).

(1) 1568. Florence Conservatoire. Polygonal virginal, inscribed: *Benedicti Floriani MDLXVIII.* C/E–F, 4½ octaves. Rose without monogram; 50 keys.

(2) 1571. Leipzig, Heyer Collection. Polygonal virginal. C–F, 4 octaves and a 4th. Inscribed: *Benedicti Floriani MDLXXI* (illustrated in *Ks*). Dimensions 156×50 cm.

(3) 1572. Paris, Conservatoire des Arts et Métiers. Harpsichord. See *Ks*, p. 229.

(4) 1572(?). Polygonal virginal. Sold at Puttick and Simpson's, 12 May 1909. Ivory naturals, ebony sharps. Gilded rose. Catalogue gives date as '1752' which may be an error for 1572.

FODINI, Michael. *See*: TODINI, Michael.

FOGIOLO. *See under*: TRASONTINO, Giovanni Francesco.

FOLCIONE, Steffano. *See*: BOLCIONI, Stefano.

FOLLON, Nicolas. Organ builder, and very probably harpsichord maker, in Paris; *fl.* 1532 [*Laborde*].

FONTANA, Nicola. Harpsichord maker at Reggio nell'Emilia; *fl.* 1573.

Surviving Instruments

(01) 1571. Budapest, National Museum. Harpsichord, signed: *Nicolo Fontana da Reggio Lepidi, 1571* [*ChamP*].

(1) 1573. Marseilles, Dr. J. Cain. Polygonal virginal, inscribed: *Nicolaus Fontana ex Regio Lepido M.D.LXXIII.* C–F, 4½ octaves with short octave; boxwood naturals. (Formerly belonged to M. Legouix, Paris.)

FORCHHEIM, Johann Wilhelm. German maker of stringed keyboard instruments, *fl.* before 1681, in which year a Dresden inventory records an 'Instrument, welches einfach bezogen, und Eckicht, von Cipressen Holz . . .' made by him [*Drechsel*, p. 496].

FORKEL, Johann Nikolaus. 1747–1818. Musician, writer on music and composer. The son of a cobbler, he was born on 22 February 1749 at Meeder bei Coburg and died 20 March 1818 at Göttingen where he had spent the greater part of his life. He was an early champion of the music of J. S. Bach, of whom he wrote a biography published in 1802 (reprinted by Kassel, Bärenreiter-Verlag, 1932: *Über J. S. Bachs Leben, Kunst und Kunstwerke*).

His love of the clavichord is exemplified in his essay *Von der wahren Güte der Clavichorde* (MS. in Deutsche Staatsbibliothek, Berlin), and it was doubtless his friendship with the Göttingen family of clavichord makers, the Krämers (q.v.) that caused him to try his hand at clavichord making on an amateur basis. [See *Ernst 1961*; also *MGG*, Vol. 4, cols. 514–20.]

FOUCAULT. According to the *Almanach Dauphin* of 1777 a harpsichord maker of this name was living in the rue Plâtrière, Paris [*Hubb*].

FOURNAFORIS, of Lyons. Harpsichord maker, *fl.* 1791. A harpsichord existed in the last years of the nineteenth century signed *Fournaforis Lyon 1791*.

FOURNAN, Bertrand. A mis-reading of Tournan, q.v.

FRANCESCO *da Brescia. See*: ANTEGNATO, Giovanni Francesco.

FRANCISCUS *Brixiensis. See*: ANTEGNATO, Giovanni Francesco.

FRANCISCUS *Patavinus* 'Francesco of Padua', also called *Il Hongaro* ('the Hungarian'). Harpsichord and virginal maker who worked, at any rate for a time, in Venice. Dates ascertained, 1527–62. Possibly the brother of Antonius Patavinus (q.v.).

(*FrancII* lists a 'spinettina' bearing an inscription given as: *Ionnes* [sic] *Patavini decti* [sic] *Hongari MDXXXX.* One supposes that Franciolini had mixed up the Patavinuses when he was composing this inscription.)

The inventory of the Raymond Fugger Collection in Augsburg, dated 1566 and sent 10 years later to Albrecht V of Bavaria, records 4 harpsichords by Franciscus Patavinus made in Venice. (The inventory is quoted *in extenso* in Sandberger's introduction to vol. 5 of *Denkmäler der Tonkunst in Bayern*, Leipzig, 1904, pp. l–li.)

A harpsichord by him dated 1562 was in the collection of Prince Ferdinand of Tuscany in 1700 [*Gai*, p. 13]; 2×8′, 1×4′ stops; 4 roses.

Surviving Instruments

(1) 1527. Brussels, Conservatoire. A polygonal virginal inscribed: *Francisci Patavini dicti hongari MDXXVII.* The lid bears the legend: *Io da le piaghe mie forma ricevo.* Compass 4 octaves C–C with short octave.

(1a?) 1540. *FrancII*, item 14, lists an instrument dated 1540 by this maker.

(2) 1561. Munich, Deutsches Museum. Harpsichord. Inscription (on the nameboard, now lost) said to have read: *Francisci Patavini Dicti Ongaro 1561.* Four octaves; 1×8′, 1×4′ registers. Side stops.

FRANCK, Ludwig, of Lübeck. He was born about 1700 and died on 9 April 1763. He received the citizenship of the town as instrument maker on 16 June 1724 and became cathedral organist in the following year.

In 1729 he married Catherina Dorothea Raggen. His son Ludwig died in 1752.

Franck seems to have devoted most of his attention to making organs and clavichords; but he also repaired lutes and harpsichords.

Surviving Instruments

(1) 1749. Bygdöy, Oslo, Norsk Folkemuseum. Clavichord signed: *Ludewick Frank in Lübeck fecit 1749*; 4 octaves C–C; white naturals.

(2) 1751 (? or 1754). Museum at Langeland (an island south of Funen). Clavichord signed on soundboard: *Ludewick Franck in Lübeck fecit Ao 1751* (? or *1754*); 4 octaves plus C–D. Triple-strung in bass; bundfrei. Belonged at one time to S. C. Ørsted at Rudkøbing, Langeland, father of the Danish physician Hans C. Ørsted (1772–1851).

(3) 1756. Lübeck Museum (in 1910). Clavichord [*Gö*, p. 81].

FRANCO, Giovanni Francesco. Harpsichord maker, *fl.* 1757; probably of Turin [*Ks*].

Surviving Instruments

(1) 1757. Leipzig, Heyer Collection. Harpsichord, 3×8′ stops. Inscription on lowest key: *Gio. Francesco Franco Fecit 1757 / nel mese di Novembre.* Compass C–F, 4 octaves and a 5th. Naturals ebony, sharps ivory-laid; 175×90 cm. Pictured at *Ks*, p. 106; inscription reproduced at *Ks*, p. 222. For many years in the possession of a family in Turin.

FRANKY, Jean. Worked on harpsichords in Lyons in 1775, when he finished an incompleted harpsichord by Joseph Collesse (q.v.).

FRELICH, Matthäus, of Gurk. *Fl.* 1550 at Innsbruck as a maker of harpsichords and virginals [*Senn*, p. 53; *VdMDeu*].

FREUDENTHALER, Wilhelm. Made harpsichords in Paris towards the end of the nineteenth century, and subsequently pianos [*Verlet*].

FREY, Carl Heinrich. An early owner, not a maker. A clavichord bearing his name and the date 1765 is in the Historisches Museum, Basel. See further *RindlKlav*, p. 218.

FREY, Michael, of Leipzig. Clavichord maker, *fl.* 1535 [*Kü*, p. 19].

FRICK. A German who worked for Berger (q.v.) in 1765 [*Enc*(*Did*) s.v. Epinette].

FRICKER. *See*: HILL, H.

FRIEDERICI [*originally* Friderici]. Surname of a family who made keyboard instruments of all kinds, resident in Germany, whither they moved from Austria (South Tyrol) early in the eighteenth century. (The name is Italianized from the German 'Friederichs'.)

(1) **Christian Ernst** (1709–80, born at Meerane, Saxony, 8 March 1709, died at Gera 4 May 1780. He was a pupil of Gottfried Silbermann at Freiburg [*Ks*]. In 1737 he moved to Gera, and 8 years later invented the *Pyramidenflügel*, 3 examples of which survive, one in the Brussels Conservatoire, another (illustrated and described in *ZI*, Vol. 21, 1900–1) at the Goethehaus, Frankfurt, both dated 1745; a third, dated 1750, is in the Neupert Collection, Germanisches Nationalmuseum.

C. P. E. Bach wrote to Forkel (10 November 1773) that he preferred Friederici's clavichords to those by Fritz and Hass because of their workmanship (*Tractament*), and because they had no octave strings in the bass, which he hated. [Letter in the Preussische Staatsbibliothek, quoted by C. H. Bitter in *C. P. E. Bach und W. F. Bach . . .*, 1868.] At his death C. P. E. Bach possessed two Friederici clavichords, one of which must be the 'vortrefflicher dieser Art' referred to by Gerber.

In book IV of *Dichtung und Wahrheit* Goethe mentions the harpsichord in his parents' house, by 'Frederici in Gera whose instruments are famous far and wide'. Likewise Mozart's home contained Friederici instruments, for he wrote (9 October 1777): 'Wenn Du mit Herrn Stein

TABLE 10. *Surviving FRIEDERICI Instruments*

No.	Date	Type	Kbs.	Signature	Owner/Remarks
Christian Ernst Friederici (1709–80)					
1	1772	Cd	1	*Fait par C. E. Friederici a Gera en Voigtland 1772*	Vienna, Historisches Museum. Bundfrei, 4 octaves and a fifth; black naturals, white sharps. This instrument apparently belonged to Mozart and later to Liszt.
Christian Gottlob Friederici (1750–1805)					
2		Cd	1	*C. G. Friederici* [on lid of tuning-hammer box]	Leipzig, Heyer Collection. Bundfrei, undated, 5 octaves F–F. *Ks* (p. 50) assigns it to the last quarter of the eighteenth century.
3	1791	Cd	1	*The maker of this Clavichorde is Christian Gottlob Frederic, Counsellor of the Chamber of . . .* [illegible] *at Gera, Saxony, in the month of March and year of Grace 1791*	Auctioned at Bethlehem, Va., 19 June 1873. Later owned by Mary Eyre of Bethlehem and her niece Rosalie Tiers of Philadelphia. [*Transactions. Moravian Historical Society*, Vol. 1 (1888), p. 217.]

Tree of the FRIEDERICI Family

Johann FRIEDERICI (Deputy-Mayor of Meerane) = Eva Maria Salzbrenner

- Christian Ernst (1709–80)
- Christian Gottfried (1714–77) = Christiane Dorothee Steinbeeck (1717–70)
  - Christian Gottlob (1750–1805) = Christiane W. Fürbringer (1756–1840)
    - Christian Ernst Wilhelm (1782–1872)
      - Ernst Ludwig (1806–83) presumably son of C. E. W.
    - 6 other children

On the Friederici family see further *ZI*, Vols. 24, 25 (1903–5), articles by Emil Fischer based on source material; also Christian Gottlob's autobiography, which appeared in the *Lobensteinischer Gemeinnützziger Intelligenzblatt*, 16 January 1802.

[i.e. Johann Andreas Stein, q.v.] sprichst, so musst Du alle Gelegenheit vermeiden, von unseren Instrumenten von Gera eine Meldung zu machen, denn er ist eifersüchtig mit dem Friederici' (If you speak with Herr Stein, you must avoid all occasion of mentioning our instruments from Gera, for he is jealous of Friederici).

Gerber says that Friederici built 50 organs, the one at Chemnitz costing 3,000 talers. 'His clavichords', he continues, 'and pianofortes in the shape of clavichords [i.e. square pianos] which he called *Fortbiens* are famed and scattered over half the world.'

In 1770, according to *Ge*, Friederici published an *Avertissement von seiner Invention, eine Bebung auf den Klavecin anzubringen* ('Notice of his invention for introducing a vibrato on the harpsichord')—probably in a musical periodical, for I have not been able to trace a copy.

Agricola, in a note to *Adl*, Vol. 2, p. 139, states that Friederici also made *Lautenklavecymbels*.

(2) **Christian Gottfried** (1714–77). Born at Meerane, 21 March 1714, died at Gera, 6 March 1777; brother of (1), with whom he worked at instrument-making. Moved to Gera in 1744. He married Christiane Dorothee Steinbeeck (1717–70) [*Ks*, *Gö*].

(3) **Christian Gottlob** (1750–1805) a son of (2); was born at Gera 23 August 1750, and died there 21 January 1805. From 1769 to 1774 he studied law at Leipzig University, then returned to Gera and worked at instrument-making with his uncle Christian Ernst (1), whose business he took over in 1780. In the following year he married Christiane Wilhelmine Fürbringer (1756–1840), who bore him 7 children.

In 1786 he attained the title of 'Fürst. Reuss. Lobensteinischer Kammerrat'. According to the Kantor Gruner's statement in 1793, his clavichords were equal in quality to those of his uncle.

In 1798 he put a notice in the *Reichsanzeiger* that '. . . er Clavichorde mit der monochordischen Abteilung, desgleichen auch neu erfundene Sordin-Fortepianos mit 6 Veränderungen anfertige, deren Intonation der Flöte und Oboe zur Taüschung ähnlich sei'.

(4) **Christian Ernst Wilhelm** (1782–1872) eldest son of (3), was born near Liebschwitz, 19 April 1782. After schooling he trained in his father's workshops as an instrument maker, and from there went on to Dresden and Berlin.

In 1803 he came back to Gera, and took over his father's business when he died.

The account-books of the firm make it clear that he made mostly pianos. Less frequently he sold clavichords for 25–40 talers. Between 1803 and 1872 he made a great number of instruments ('more than 1000 instruments', says *Gö*).

He died on 3 February 1872.

(5) **Ernst Ludwig** (1806–83) presumably son of (4), born 27 November 1806, carried on his father's business. In 1883 he died, the last keyboard instrument maker in Gera bearing the name of Friederici.

See table 10.

(*Note*: *Michel*, p. 134 shews a clavichord-like instrument with the caption 'Frederica Square Piano, Gera, Germany about 1773; bichord clavichord'. It is perhaps worth recording, for the benefit of all baffled readers of this caption, that the instrument was originally a square piano. Apparently the action had disappeared, and a botcher in Germany put an inefficient plucking action in it and sold it as a Friederici spinet. Finally, a clavichord action was put in it, and it went to America [*Rindl*].)

FRIQUE. *See*: FRICK.

FRITSCH, Gottfried. 'Organ and clavichord maker in Hamburg'—a mistake of Schroeter's for Barthold Fritz (q.v.).

FRITZ, Barthold [Bartholomaeus Fritze], 1697–1766. Maker of clavichords and organs. He was born, the son of a miller, at Holle, 20 miles south-west of Brunswick, to which town he moved, being granted citizenship there on 12 July 1720. In 1729 he restored the organ at the Moravian Church in Brunswick. Apparently he was taxed at a reduced rate, having married a widow of the town.

It seems that in 1755 he and Tölleke were the only instrument makers in Brunswick [*SB*]. During the following year his 'Anweisung wie man Claviere, Clavecins, und Orgeln, nach einer mechanischen Art, in allen zwölf Tonen gleich rein stimmen könne, das aus solchen allen sowohl dur als moll wohlklingend zu spielen sey . . .' (dedicated to C. P. E. Bach) was published by J. G. I. Breitkopf in Leipzig. It went through 5 editions between 1756 and 1829, and a Dutch translation appeared in Amsterdam.

According to *Ge* he made 'more than 500' clavichords, some of which were exported as far afield as Archangel. *Schub* speaks highly of his clavichords.

Like a number of other German makers such as Hass and Horn, he strengthened the bass register in his clavichords by adding a third string, tuned an octave higher. *Ge* praises this expedient, 'Sie haben vor andern eine vorzügliche Stärke im Bass', but C. P. E. Bach regarded it as intolerable. [Letter to Forkel, 10 November 1773, quoted by C. H. Bitter in *C. P. E. Bach und W. F. Bach*' . . . (1868).]

Fritz had an inventive turn of mind, which found expression in such pursuits, apart from instrument-making, as constructing musical clocks, mechanical singing-birds, special weavers' looms, and even a horizontal windmill—reminding us of his contemporary in England, John Joseph Merlin (q.v.).

Fritz died on 17 July 1766 at the age of 70 years, and was buried in the churchyard of St. Ulrici, Brunswick.

A portrait of him by J. C. Eberling is reproduced at *SB*, p. 4.

Surviving Clavichords

(1) 1747. Berlin Collection. Inscribed: . . . *Fritz fecit Braunschweig 1747*. C–F, $4\frac{1}{2}$ octaves, with 13 octave strings in the bass. Advertised in Liepmanssohn's catalogue, no. 237. Dimensions 152×43 cm.

(2) 1751. London, Victoria and Albert Museum (formerly Carl Engel). F–A, $5\frac{1}{3}$ octaves, with octave strings in the bass. Dimensions 5′ $10\frac{1}{2}$″×1′ $10\frac{1}{2}$″. Illustrated in *J*, p. 95 and *V&A*, *MIWA* and *Russell V&A*.

(3) Date not ascertained. Brunswick, Grotrian-Steinweg [*SB*, p. 49].

(4) Date not ascertained. Bochum, private ownership.

FUCHS, Johann Anton. Maker of organs and stringed keyboard instruments at Innsbruck, *fl.* 1781.

Surviving Clavichords

(1) 1781. A 5-octave clavichord by him signed: *Joh. Antoni Fuchss* [sic] / *Orgl und Clavier* / *Macher zu Insbruck*/ *1781* survives at Tione di Trento, N. Italy [*Lun*, pp. 48–9 (illustrated)].

(2) 1781. Nuremberg, Germanisches Nationalmuseum, Rück Collection. Signed: *Joh. Antoni: Fuchs* / *Orgl und Clavier Macher* / *zu Insbruck 1781.*

FÜSSEL, Johann. German maker of stringed keyboard instruments, *fl.* before 1681, when a Dresden inventory records an 'Instrument, welches einfach bezogen, undt Eckicht, mitt einem Lauten Zuge . . .' made by him [*Drechsel*, p. 496].

FYELD, Polle. *See*: DEFIELD.

G. B. B. *See*: BONI, Giovanni Battista.

G, C. A clavichord in the Fiala-Ahlgrimm Collection, Vienna, bears a pencilled date *1789* and the initials *C. G.* On the soundboard is a label: *Reparirt 1827* / *Joseph Dohnal* / *bürgerl. Instrumentenmacher* / *wohnt an der neuen Wienn in der Gart-/ner-Gasse im eigenen Haus beym Meer-/sturm No. 176* / *in Wien.* Six octaves F–F. Much restored, front guide pins having been fitted; 162 × 54 cm.

G, C. A Flemish harpsichord of the seventeenth century in the Berlin Collection (2 manuals, push-coupler, 2 × 8′, 2 × 4′, size 81 × 219 cm.) has a rose with harping angel and the initials *C. G.* in it [*Sa*, p. 65].

G, I. *See*: GELLINGER, Israel.

G, Z. *See*: Z, G.

GABRECHT. Made harpsichords in Königsberg in the second half of the sixteenth century [*Pa*].

GAI, of Paris. Harpsichord maker in the second half of the eighteenth century [*Pa*].

GAIRAUD, of Nantes, where about 1735 he was making violins and also harpsichords. In 1737 he married Margarethe Destains. He was still alive in 1770 [*Lü*].

GALLAND, Jean, of Paris. Harpsichord maker, *juré comptable* of the Guild, 1744–5; died 1760. Father-in-law of the maker Robert Richard (q.v.). He resided in the rue des Petits Champs St. Honoré. The notice of the sale of his stock which appeared 19 June 1760 contains this passage: 'Clavecins organisés et brisés (après le décès de Galland, facteur de clavecins, beau-père du mécanicien et facteur Richard) . . .' [*Bq*, p. 11]. His widow maintained the shop until 1779 [*Pi*]. *Cor* in a passing reference on p. 84, spells his name 'Galand'.

GAND, Mattia di. *See*: MATTHIAS, *of Ghent.*

GANER, Christopher. Harpsichord, spinet, and piano maker of Leipzig and later London (22 Broad Street, Golden Square; afterwards 47, 48, and 49 in the same street). Earliest and latest dates known, 1774–1811 [*J*; *H&S*].

Letters of denization were granted on 11 February, 1792 to Ganer 'formerly of Leipzig . . . but now of Broad Street, Carnaby Market, in the parish of St. James's Westminster . . . grand pianoforte maker' [*HuD*, XXVII].

The shell of a harpsichord by him, dated 1781, is in the possession of John Challis, Detroit (1953). No spinets seem to have survived, although a few handsome square pianos from Ganer's workshop are still to be seen.

He is recorded as a pianoforte maker in J. Doane's *Musical Directory* (London, 1794) [L. G. Langwill, in *Music and Letters*, London, 1949].

Note. There was sold at Christie's on 14 March 1792 'an organized pianoforte with harp stop, pedal, etc., by Ganer in an elegant inlaid case with leather cover'.

GANSEN, Wolf. It appears from the inventory of instruments at the court of Eberhard III, taken at Stuttgart in 1589, that Wolf Gansen made harpsichords, spinets etc. '1 Instrument von Wolf Gansen an ein ander Instrument vertaucht worden, welches auch zu den Täntzen gebraucht wird' [*WVS*, Vol. 21, 1912, pp. 133–7].

GARBUTT, Thomas. Harpsichord maker living in King Street, Golden Square, London, from March 1770 until 1776 [*RB.J*].

A certain J. Garbutt (piano maker, *fl.* 1793) was probably his son [*J*].

GARNIER, Sébastien. Harpsichord maker in Paris in the middle of the eighteenth century.

Surviving Harpsichords

(1) 1747. Flemish in style; 2 manuals with push–pull coupler; 2 × 8′, 1 × 4′. Inscribed *Sebastien Garnier 1747* on the top key and *Garnier Luthier* on underside of soundboard. Case in lime, veneered, except the straight side, which is beech, as also is the wrestplank. Present (November 1971) owner, Michael Thomas, Hurley.

GASPARRINI, Francesco Antonio. Italian harpsichord maker, *fl.* 1762.

Surviving Harpsichords

(1) 1762. New York, Barnard College (formerly Joline Collection). The inscription, which reads *Opus Fracisci Antony Gasparrini a Monte Carotto 2e July 1762* is suspicious.

GATEAUX, Pierre. Parisian harpsichord maker, *fl.* 1780–8. Admitted to the Corporation in 1780 and the Guild in 1783; lived in 1783 in the rue Guérin-Boisseau and in 1788 in the rue de la Harpe [*Verlet*; *Pi*].

GAUD, Matthias. *See*: MATTHIAS, of Ghent.

GEBEL, Georg. Organist and composer, born at Breslau in 1685. He became organist of the Church of St. Christopher in that town in 1713.

His autobiography, quoted in *MatGE* (pp. 405 f.), reveals an inventive disposition. He devised (he tells us) a clavichord with quarter-tones; also a clavichord with pedal keyboard all in one case, similar, no doubt, to the instrument depicted in *Reynv*; and finally a harpsichord of 6-octave compass, C–C, with pedal keyboard in one case. References to this latter type of instrument are not common; some are: *Halle 1764*, p. 363; *Türk 1802*, p. 2; *Adl*, p. 528; *AdlG*, note *m* to § 248. According to some, it was for a pedal harpsichord that Bach's *Aria variata alla maniera italiana*, possibly his Trios, the Aria in F, and a few other pieces of the Weimar period were composed. (*See also*: NEUBAUER below.)

For details of the compositions of Georg Gebel, and of his son of the same name, see *Eit*, IV. 186.

GEERDINX, Harmanus [Geerdings]. Harpsichord maker in Amsterdam, presumably related to Artus Gheerdinck, q.v. Dates ascertained, 1659–74. See *Curtis*, p. 50, for further details.

GEIB, John Lawrence. Maker of harpsichords, pianofortes, and organs. Born on 27 February 1744 at Standerheim; died on 30 October 1818 at Newark, N.J. [*New York evening post*, 31 October 1818].

It is not known when he came to England, but on 20 August 1779 he married Rebecca Shrimpton in London. For a time he lived in the Old Bailey, then in Tottenham Court Road (1786). In 1792 when he was living in Southampton Row [or Place] he patented 'a new musical instrument, the end and intention of which is to play the pianoforte, clavichord or spinett, with two sets of keys, to which either of these three instruments may be joined together . . .' [Patent no. 1866]. On 11 February in the same year letters of denization were granted to Geib 'formerly of Standerheim in the Upper Palatinate of the Rhine . . . now of Southampton Place, in the parish of St. Pancras . . . organ builder' [*HuD*, Vol. 27].

He was in Shudi's employ for a time, and also worked for Longman & Broderip. Signatures on some of his early pianos shew that he worked with Goldsworth; he was later in partnership with Lenkfeld for a period. He patented a new piano action in 1786, and a combined piano and clavichord in 1792.

On 24 July 1797 he emigrated to America [*SmithM*; see also *Antiques*, Vol. 16, p. 12]. There is no evidence that he made any harpsichords in America. He died at Newark, N.J., and was buried in St. Paul's churchyard, New York City (*SmithM*]. See further *John Geib and his seven children*, by Alger C. Gildersleeve, Far Rockaway N.Y., 1945.

GEISSINGER, of Rothenburg. Keyboard instrument maker. The Rück Collection in the Germanisches Nationalmuseum, Nuremberg, contains a clavichord by him dated 1782 or 1788 [*GL*]. *See also*: SCHNELL, Johann JAKOB.

GELLINGER, Israel. Organ, harpsichord, and clavichord maker; dates ascertained, 1639–77. Born at Strasbourg, he moved in 1639 to Frankfurt am Main, where he became organist at St. Katherina's 10 years later. On 23 April 1653 he received the citizenship of Frankfurt, entering the Joiners' Guild there as an instrument maker 2 months afterwards. He married 4 times.

In 1672 his son Andreas became organist at the Barfüsser Kirche. In 1716 an organ builder named Israel Gellinger, presumably a descendant of this one, received the citizenship of Frankfurt [*Ks*].

Surviving Instruments

(1) 1670. Namur, Musée Hôtel de Croix. Clavichord. Rose; 4 octaves, without lowest C sharp. Gebunden except for lowest C–A. Date on soundboard. Monogram *IG* enclosed in a heart is incised in the right-hand corner of the soundboard.

(2) 1677. Leipzig University, Heyer Collection. Ottavino. Signed on floor of case: *Fecit in francoforti* [sic] *am Meijn 1677 Ißrael Gellinger* and on the wrestplank: *Frankfurt am Majn 1677 israel Gellinger*. On the wrestplank an *IG* monogram enclosed in a heart is branded.

(3?) Formerly Van der Straeten. Rose. In decoration and style similar to no. 1. Monogram with *IGF* (? *Israel Gellinger fecit*) and a hammer enclosed in a broken circle. See *VdS*, VIII. 303, where the monograms of instruments 1 and 3 are reproduced.

GENOVESE. *Va* lists an Italian harpsichord maker of Genoa known simply as 'Il Genovese'.

GEORGE, *Meister*. An inventory drawn up in 1613 for Moritz, Landgrave of Hesse, includes mention of 2 small virginals [*Instrument*] made by Meister George [Anthony C. Baines, in *GSJ*, IV, June 1951, p. 34].

GÉRARD, Jean. Parisian harpsichord maker, living in the place Cambray in 1769 [*Pi*].

GERBER, Heinrich Nicolas, 1702–75. Court organist at Sondershausen, father of the lexicographer, and amateur clavichord maker.

He was born at Wenigen-Ehrich on 6 September 1702.

In 1724 he went to Leipzig to study under J. S. Bach, but was so shy (his son tells us) that he could not muster the courage to approach the great man until at last he

> told his desire to a friend, called Wilde . . . who introduced him to Bach. Bach took to Gerber at once as a Schwarzburger, and thereafter always addressed him as 'fellow countryman'. He undertook to give him lessons as he desired, and asked at once whether he had worked hard at fugue-playing. During the first lesson he put his *Inventions* before him. After he had worked through these to Bach's satisfaction there followed a number of suites, and then *das Temperirte Klavier* [i.e. the first book of the '48']. Bach played this last volume through to him with his unequalled skill three times . . . [and Gerber] counted among his happiest hours those in which Bach, on the pretext of having no inclination to give a lesson, sat down at one of his excellent instruments and so transformed these hours into minutes . . .

In 1727 Gerber returned to his father in the country and began to marshal the knowledge collected at Leipzig. He also started to make a small organ of 12 stops with pedals, with the help of a joiner.

Next year he became organist at Heringen, and 3 years after that at Sondershausen.

In 1742, according to his son, he began work, again with the help of a joiner, on a clavichord 'almost in the shape of a pyramid, with two manuals and a pedal keyboard, and 10 variations of tone'.

H. N. Gerber also gave music lessons, and produced a number of compositions, which his son lists in his *Historisch-biographisches Lexicon.*

GERBER, William. Harpsichord maker who flourished in England in 1775, probably a German by birth who, like a number of German instrument makers in the eighteenth century, came over to England.

A harpsichord by him, dated 1775, bears the number 115 [*J*].

GERLACH, Johann Christian. Maker of clavichords and harpsichords. On 24 January 1744 he was granted the freedom of the city of Hamburg, where he was still living about 1790 [*Ge, Lü*].

A clavichord in the Hamburg eighteenth-century style in the Ringve Museum, Trondheim, bears on the soundboard a maker's signature which we must probably regard as illegible. It might conceivably be interpreted *Johan Gerlach Artifex / Anno 1778*; but this must be conceded to be little more than guesswork.

GERMAIN. *See*: GOERMANS.

GERMAN, Erich. The Musikhistorisk Museet, Stockholm, has a clavichord by this maker dated at Stockholm, 1736. Gebunden, A–D, with octave strings in the bass. Inscription: *Erich German me fecit Holmia A^o 1736.*

GERONIMO. *See*: ZENTI, Girolamo.

GERONIMO, *of Bologna. See*: HIERONYMUS *Bononiensis.*

GERONIMO, *of Florence.* The 'Geronimo da Firenze' mentioned by *Prof* (p. 272) is probably a mistake for Geronimo da Bologna.

GERSTENBERG, Johann David, 1716–96. Builder of organs and other keyboard instruments at Geringswalde in Saxony. His name was properly Gerstenberger, having been born on 2 May 1716 to Hanss Gerstenberger of Hilmsdorf and his wife Susanne. He died on 24 December 1796 [*Ks*].

Surviving Stringed Instruments

(1) 1760. Leipzig, Heyer Collection. A bundfrei clavichord, 2 manuals (i.e. 2 clavichords, one above the other) and pedal keyboard. Compass of manuals, 4 octaves and a 3rd, C–E; of pedals, 2 octaves, C–C. Stringing of manuals, 2×8′; of pedals, 2×8′, 2×16′. Inscription: *Johann David Gerstenberg, Orgelbauer zu Geringswalda, hat uns gemacht, 1760* [*Ks*]. Length of lower case, 225 cm.; depth, 49 cm., with pedal 95 cm. The 2 clavichords are 159 cm. long, and 42·5 cm. deep. Instrument and inscription depicted in *Ks* and *Russell 1959*.

GESE [Geza], *of Halberstadt.* Eighteenth-century maker of 'Claviere'—doubtless primarily clavichords, *fl.* 1752 [*Musikalischer Almanach*, 1782].

GESSINGER, Georg Martin. Clavichord maker at Rothenburg, 1717–91.

Surviving Clavichords

(1) Nuremberg, Germanisches Nationalmuseum (Rück Collection) signed: *Georg Martin Gessinger / Orgel [und] Instrumenten / macher in Rotenburg / ob der Tauber 1780.*

GHEERDINCK, Artus [Geerdincx]. Maker of harpsichords, etc. in Amsterdam. Born 1564 [*Curtis*]; died June 1624 [*GL*]. The Germanisches Nationalmuseum, Nuremberg, has a virginal by him inscribed *Artus Gheerdinck me fecit anno 1605* on the jackrail. Compass 4 octaves C/E–C; illustrated in the 1938 Neupert Collection catalogue. This is almost certainly the virginal which in 1910 was in the collection of Heinrich Schumacher, Lucerne, mentioned in *Gö*, who, however, misread the name as 'Artus C. Heerdinck'.

Francl lists a 'cimbalo', 1-manual inscribed: *Altus Gheerdinck me fecit anno 1603.* This may well be the obviously Italian polygonal virginal now in the Smithsonian Institution (formerly at Yale, previously Morris Steinert's) whose jackrail (bearing the clumsily lettered inscription) appears not to be native to the instrument [*MarcY*, pp. 5–6, where it is described in detail].

GHEERDINCK, Harmanus. Of Amsterdam, undoubtedly related to the preceding maker though the relationship is not known; harpsichord maker. Earliest date ascertained 1644 [*GL*]; latest date ascertained 1674 [*Curtis*].

GHERARDI, of Parma. Makers of virginals and harpsichords.

1. **Antonio,** *fl.* 1823.
2. **Giambattista.**
3. **Camillo.**
4. **Giuseppe.**

[*Va.*]

GHERARDO, of Padua [*Prof*, p. 272]. Probably a member of the preceding family.

GHERARDO, Giacomo, *of Bologna. Francl* lists a harpsichord inscribed: *Giacumus Gherardus 1663 Bononiae.*

GHERLA, of Ferrara. *Fl.* sixteenth to seventeenth centuries as harpsichord maker [*Va*]. A harpsichord by him was in Modena in 1598.

GIACOMO, *da Modena. See*: JACOBUS, *of Modena.*

GIANNANTONIO, *called* Il Veneto, of Venice, virginal maker who flourished in the seventeenth century [*Va*].

GIANNANTONIO, *di Biagio. See*: BONISSIMO, Giannantonio.

GIANNINI, Gaetano. Italian virginal maker, *fl.* 1628.

Surviving Instruments

(1) 1628. Lisbon Conservatoire. Ottavino. Inscription on nameboard: *Gaetanus Giannini faciebat Anno 1628.* Compass 3 octaves and a minor 3rd, E–G. Rose without monogram. Painted case bearing the arms of a noble family. Size 75×32 cm. Projecting keyboard.

GIANNINI, Marco. *Francl* (item 27) lists a 'spinetta' inscribed: *Marcus Gianninus faciebat Florentiae anno 1570.*

GIBSON, William, of Dublin. Dates ascertained, 1764–died 1790, was primarily a guitar maker, but also interested himself in the harpsichord. From 1766 to 1774 he was on College Green, whence he moved to 6 Grafton Street (1774–90), where he was in partnership (1775–8) with Robert Woffington (q.v.) who may have been the Woffington elected organist of St. Mary's in 1773.

In 1778 the firm dissolved, but in 1784 Gibson's address is still given as 6 Grafton St. [*Dubl. 1784*]. [*Fld, MA, H&S.*]

GIGLI, Giovanni. A harpsichord in Paris (1972) is inscribed: *Joanes Giglius fecit Romae Anno Domini 1610.* 2×8′ stops. C–C, 4 octaves with short octave. Boxwood naturals. In outer case. This instrument appears in *FrancI* (item 15) and *FrancII* (item 5, the date here being given as 1510).

GIJSEN, Coenradus. From Elberfeld—the German form of his surname is not certain—entered into a contract in 1628 with Pieter Pampus (q.v.) by which Pampus was to teach him to make automatic harpsichords (*Curtis*].

GILCHRIST, Doug'ld. Harpsichord maker, presumably Scottish, who flourished in 1793. He subscribed to Sheraton's *Cabinet-maker* [*J*].

GILL, George, *fl.* at London, 1641. He is described in *La* (111) as 'Musical Instrument Maker', which probably includes virginals and harpsichords.

GILLESPY, Samuel. Harpsichord maker of Brownlow Street, St. Giles in the Fields, London. Dates ascertained 1769–74 [*J*].

On 28 December 1774 he patented 'my New-Constructed Principle of Putting on the Quills to Strike the Strings of a Harpsichord with a Peddle and Swell, which raises the Top, brings on the Tone, and Swells a new Celestial Stop, at the same time Preserving the Instrument compleat' [Patent no. 1092]. (The Celestial tone is produced by 'heads of taned [*sic*] leather, buff leather, kid leather, cloth and wood'.)

GIOBERNARDI, Bartolomeo. *See*: JOBERNARDI, Bartolomeo.

GIOVACINO. *See*: GUARRACINO, Honofrio.

GIOVAN-MARCO, *di Ferrara.* Maker of harpsichords at Ferrara. Dates ascertained, 1522–50 [*Va*].

GIOVANNI. *Va* lists a Fra' Giovanni of Metz, clavichord maker, flourishing in 1506.

GIOVANNI, *da Udine.* Harpsichord maker of Udine and Venice, *fl.* 1473 [*Va*].

GIOVANNINI, Giuliano. Italian harpsichord maker, probably of the seventeenth century. A single-manual (2×8′) harpsichord, undated, by him was in the collection of Prince Ferdinand of Tuscany in 1700 [*Gai*, p. 12].

GIROLAMO. Virginal maker of Rome, *fl.* 1655 [*Va*]. *See*: ZENTI, Girolamo.

GIUSEPPE, *d'Organe.* A polygonal virginal in the Museo Civico, Padua, is inscribed: *Giuseppe d'Organe. Anno MDXXII.* Compass 4 octaves, C/E to C. Rose without monogram. Assigned to the eighteenth century by the catalogue.

GIUSTI, Giovanni Battista, of Lucca. Maker of harpsichords and lutes, *fl.* 1676–93. A number of instruments bear his name spuriously. See table 11 for surviving instruments ascribed to him; also Addenda.

GLANVILLE, George. Harpsichord maker in Westminster in 1749. His name appears in a Westminster pollbook [*J*].

GLEICHMANN, Johann Georg, 1685–1770. Born at Stelzen, near Hildburghausen in Saxe-Meiningen. At the age of 13 he built himself a clavichord without any instruction. Working along the lines of Hans Hayden's *Geigenwerk*, he invented in 1709 his *Klaviergamba*, and was imitated later by Michael Pachelbel of Hamburg and Hohlfeld of Berlin.

In 1706 he was appointed organist at Schalkau near Coburg and in 1717 organist at Ilmenau, not far away, where he later became a town councillor [*Wa, Ko, Eit, Adl.II*, pp. 126, 138].

Ge states that in his day (1790) one of Gleichmann's instruments was in Sondershausen.

GLEINIGER, Theophile Gottlieb [Gleinicher]. Born 1766 at Hermsdorf (Lower Saxony); died 1823 at Bern, where he had settled in 1756 as a keyboard instrument maker. In the *Berner Adressbuch* of 1810 he is recorded as 'facteur de clavecins et forte-pianos' [*Hirt*, p. 472].

GLISS, Johann. Nuremberg organ builder in the first half of the eighteenth century. He built an organ for the Lutheran church in that town in 1737–8; and must have made clavichords as well, for he is presumably the maker referred to by *Schub* (pp. 207–8) in his description of the dying Löffelloth, who played the 'Glisiches Clavichord' which stood by his death-bed.

GLONNER, Joseph. Clavichord and harpsichord maker to the Court at Munich. Dates ascertained, 1753–72. He built there in 1756 a 3-manual clavichord ('ein dreifaches Clavicord') for the Electress of Bavaria at a price of 60 florins. He also supplied harpsichords to the Court, e.g.:

1753. '3 neue doppelte fligen' [2-manual harpsichords], 200 florins.

1757. '2 Churfürstliche Kammerflügen' [harpsichords, presumably single-manual], 60 florins.

[K. A. Bierdimpffl, *Die Sammlung der Musik-Instrumente im Baierischen Nationalmuseum*, München, 1883, pp. 54, 56.]

GLÜCK. An undated clavichord in the Deutsches Museum, Munich, is said to bear the inscription (not normally visible): *Glück, Friedberg*, which may refer to the maker. The compass is 4½ octaves. It had a pedal keyboard. But the 'pedalboard is now [1950] missing, but the trackers are still hanging down from the pedal box'—*Jeans 1950*, where the instrument is assigned to the early eighteenth century.

GODELART, Pierre Jacques. Harpmaker living in the rue du Faubourg-Saint-Germain, Paris; dates ascertained, 1783–9. Also made harpsichords [*Pi*, p. 133 n.]. Admitted to the Guild in 1781 [*Verlet*].

TABLE 11. *Surviving Instruments by or Attributed to Giovanni Battista GIUSTI*

No.	Previous no.	Date	Type	Kbs.	Signature	Owner/Remarks
1	—	1580	H	1	*Joannes Antonius Baffo Venetus. F. MDLXXX*	Leipzig University, Heyer Collection no. 79. Spurious.
[2]	1	1667	H	1		Halle, Händel-Haus. (Neupert Catalogue (1938), no. 52.) Inscription on jackrail; 2×8′ stops; C–C with short octaves. See no. 7 below.
3(?)	—	1673	H	1	*Jonnes* [sic] *Baptista Giusti Lucensis faciebat anno 1673*	*FrancII* records such an instrument.
4	2	1676	H	1	*Joannes Baptista Giusti Lucensis 1676*	Leipzig, Heyer Collection. 2×8′, 1×4′. Boxwood naturals, ebony sharps. Owner's inscription on jackrail: *Presidentus della Republicha 1681*. Illustrated at *Ks*, p. 92, inscription at *Ks*, p. 228. Dimensions 238×95 cm.
5(?)	—	1676	H	1	*Joannes Batista Giusti Lucensis 1676*	*FrancIII* (no item no.).
6(?)	—	1677	H	1	*Joannes Baptista Giusti Lucensis faciebat anno domini 1677*	*FrancI*, item A42.
7	1	1677	H	1	*Johannes Baptista Giusti Lucen. faciebat 1677*	Halle, Händel-Haus. *Sasse* (p. 41). Same instrument as [2] above.
8	—	1677	H	1		Flensburg, Städtisches Museum.
9(?)	—	1679	Sp	1	*Joannes Baptisti Giusti Lucensis faciebat 1679*	*FrancI*, item A17.
9a	—	1679	H	1		Bologna, L. F. Tagliavini. 2×8′, 1×4′ stops [*ChamP*].
10	3	1681	H	1	*Joannes Baptista Giusti Lucensis faciebat 1681*	Nuremberg, Germanisches Nationalmuseum (formerly no. 51 in Neupert's 1938 catalogue). At one time (e.g. 1953) housed in the Händel-Haus, Halle. Compass 4 octaves with short octave, C–C; 2×8′ stops.
11	—	1681	H	1	*GBG fecit 1681*	Washington, private ownership. Inscription on jackrail; also *1681* on bottom key. 'False inner-outer' case; 2×8′ stops; E–D nearly 5 octaves (originally C/E–C, 4 octaves).
12	4	1693	H	1	*Joannes Baptista Giusti Lucensis faciebat anno 1693*	Michigan University. Compass 4½ octaves.
[13]	5	1700	H	1		A 'ghost' instrument which never existed. My first edition recorded it as 'Bamberg, Neupert Museum (not in catalogue)'.
14(?)	6	n.d.	H	1	—	Leipzig University, Heyer Collection, no. 81. Unsigned, but attributed by *Ks* to Giusti. G–F, 4 octaves and a 7th; 2×8′ stops. Illustrated at *Ks*, p. 105.

GOERMANS [*also* Germain]. Surname of a family of instrument makers and musicians, of Flemish origin but resident in Paris in the second half of the eighteenth century.

(1) **Jean, the Elder,** harpsichord maker. Born 1703 in 'Galdere, near the Brandenburg frontier'; was admitted as master harpsichord maker in Paris before 1730, when he was living in the rue St. Denis. He died 18 February 1777, at which time he was resident in the rue Férou [*Pi*].

Br (p. 201) mentions an undated harpsichord by him. *Bq* (p. 9) records the sale of a harpsichord by a 'Germain', perhaps this member of the family.

(2) **Jacques,** son of (1). Maker of harpsichords, harps, and pianos. Accepted as Master, 1766. Dates ascertained, 1740–89 (the year of his death), during which period, according to *Pi*, he resided in the rue des Fossés, Saint-Germain-des-Prés, though *Bq* (p. 15) quotes a 'sieur Goermans, marchand de clavecins et de harpes, rue de Limoges' in 1778.

In 1781 he designed a harpsichord which was described in the *Almanach Musical* of the following year as having 21 keys to the octave.

He was one of the many eighteenth-century makers who made harpsichords based on the pieces of earlier Flemish instruments. See *Hubb 1965*, p. 55.

For further details see *Hardouin 1957*, pp. 21–5, and *Verlet*.

See table 12 for Goermans instruments.

TABLE 12. *Surviving Instruments by the GOERMANS (Germain) Family*

No.	Date	Type	Kbs.	Signature	Owner/Remarks
Jean, *the Elder*					
01	1738	H	1	*Joannes Gormans* [sic]	Stockholm, Musikhistoriskmuseet. G–C, 3½ octaves; 2×8′, 1×4′ registers.
1	1748	H	2	*Joannes Gormans* [sic]	Haverford, Pa., private ownership (formerly in Boston, Mass.). 2×8′, 1×4′ stops; push–pull coupler. Signature round an *IG* rose. This may well be the Goermans now (1972) owned by Frederic Cunningham, Haverford, Pa.
2	1754	H	2	*Joannes Goermans me fecit Parisiis 1754*	New York, Metropolitan Museum of Art. Converted into a piano. Pewter rose in Ruckers style with initials: *IG*. Inside of lid has chinoiserie in black and gold depicting a 2-ml. harpsichord, recorder, viol da bracchia, viol da gamba, bagpipe, with their performers. Tray stand with cabriole legs. Depicted in *Bulletin of the Metr. Mus. Art, N.Y.* Vol. 4, number 10 (June 1946), and in *Wint 1966*. (Given in 1944 by Mrs. Susan Dwight Bliss.)
3	1768	H	2	*Johannes Goermans 1768*	Formerly in Savoye Collection III, Paris. (Sale catalogue, 13 June 1924.)
3a	1768	H	2		Sold in Paris after World War II. Perhaps = no. 3.
3b	?	Ot	1		In Lisbon in 1971 [*MarcP*].
Jacques					
[4]	1735	H	2		Is perhaps no. 6 below, the painted date having been altered at some time.
5	1774	H	2		Paris, M. Bouquet. F–F, 5 octaves. 2×8′, 1×4′ strings, 4 rows of jacks. *IG* rose.
6	1785(?)	H	2	*Jacques Germain 1785(?)*	A label John Challis removed shewed it was restored by Salomon in 1925. In 1972 owned by E. McElwee of Hagerstown, Md., who acquired it from Challis in 1952. Challis had bought it in 1950 from the heirs of Leander Sherman, who had bought it in Paris about 1930. When Challis acquired the instrument it bore 2 dates: *1735* in red paint on the soundboard and *1785* carved into the rose. Feeling that the *3* of the *1735* had probably been an *8* once, he restored it as an *8*. The painted decoration on the instrument is, however, in the 'genre pittoresque' style (which began about 1735 and was already out of fashion by 1750), probably that of Jacques de Lajoue (1687–1761). It is thus possible, perhaps indeed probable, that it was made in 1735, as recorded in the first edition.

Jean *GOERMANS, the Elder* (1703–77) = Jeanne-Lucie Delbourse *m.* 1730; *d.* 1783

- Jean, *the Younger* (harpsichordist, *b. c.* 1735; *d.* 1795)
- (a Bernardine monk)
- Jacques (maker of harpsichords, etc., *d.* 1789)
  - a son
  - a daughter
- Marie-Thérèse-Victoire (*b.* 1749; *m.* 1773, J.-L. Hermes, harpsichord maker, foreman to her father)
- 3 other daughters, 1 of whom, Jeanne-Thérèse, became a friend of La Pouplinière, 1753–66 [*Cuc*].

GOLDSWORTH. *See*: Geib, John.

GOMPAERTS, William, of Antwerp. Harpsichord maker; dates ascertained, 1560–1610.

Received into the Guild of St. Luke as harpsichord maker. A son is recorded as born to him on 7 November 1580. He seems to have been closely connected, perhaps related, to the Ruckers family [*St*]. He also made harps and lutes [*Lü*].

GONDARD, Claude. *See*: Dufour, Claude.

GOODMAN, William [*also* Goodale]. Virginal maker at Chester in the reign of Queen Elizabeth I [*Bos*].

GOSSET, of Rheims, *fl.* 1776. He made a clavicytherium [*Hubb* based on the *Mercure de France*, September 1776.] A harpsichord (? 2-manual) by him is owned (1971) by Mme Fayolle of Toulouse [*GL*].

GOTTHEIMER, Christian Gottlieb. German clavichord maker of the eighteenth century. A photograph taken in America *c.* 1905 shews Arnold Dolmetsch playing a Gottheimer clavichord of 5 octaves, with 3 roses.

GOUJON, Jean Claude. French harpsichord maker of the eighteenth century. An 'épinette de Goujon' was advertised for sale on 14 January 1760; and, on 12 January of the following year, another '5 pieds de long sur 2 de large, grand raval[ement]. prix 12 louis' [*Bq*].

Cor (p. 84) refers to him in passing.

A harpsichord in the Paris Conservatoire Collection purporting to be by Hans Ruckers (no. 4) was found, when opened up for repair, to have the pencilled signature of Goujon inside [*RG.I*, p. 81]. It may be Goujon who made the 3 rows of jacks dated 1749.

Surviving Instruments

(01) 1743. Paris Conservatoire. Wing-shaped spinet, inscribed *Jean Goujon à Paris, 1743,* and *ravalé et mis en bauff l'année 1789 par l'Abbé Tapray.*

(1) 1749(?). Paris Conservatoire, Harpsichord, 2-manual. It is ostensibly a Ruckers instrument *ravalé*, but should really be regarded as by Goujon, although details of it are given below s.v. Ruckers, instrument no. 4.

(2) 1758. Paris Conservatoire (acquired 1971). Spinet signed: *Jean Goujon, 1758.*

GOZZINI, Joseph Maria [Goccini, Gozzino]. Harpsichord maker, of Italian origin. Dates ascertained, 1725–6. The Carl Claudius Collection at Copenhagen has an octagonal spinet (bichord, and therefore properly a harpsichord) by him inscribed on the nameboard: *Joseph Maria Gozzini Fecit Anno MDCCXXVI*; 2×8′ stops, 2 manuals. Four octaves C–C with short octave. Illustrated in the catalogue. The shape is a longish rectangle with the corners cut off.

The iconographical collection at the Brussels Conservatoire has a photograph of a Gozzini harpsichord dated 1725 painted by Cavazzoni.

GRABALOS, Jozé. Clavichord maker at Tarazona in the eighteenth century. A 6-octave (F–F) clavichord in the Museo de Música, Barcelona, was signed by him.

GRÄBNER. Makers of organs, harpsichords, and other instruments at Dresden in the seventeenth and eighteenth centuries:

(*a*) **Johann Christian,** maker of organs and other instruments; dates ascertained 1678–1704. In 1692 he built the organ in the church of St. John at Dresden [*Fé*].

(*b*) **Johann Heinrich,** *the Elder*, brother of (*a*); 1665–1739. Kurfürstl. Sächs. and Kgl. Polnisch. Hoforgelmacher. Also made harpsichords, and clavichords [*Wa*, p. 287]. Organist at the Frauenkirche, Dresden, 1696 onwards. *Ks* (Vol. 2, p. 657) suggests that he was a pupil of G. Silbermann.

(*c*) **Johann Heinrich,** *the Younger*, son of (*b*); *c.* 1700–*c.* 1777. Became Court organ and harpsichord maker.

(*d*) **Johann Gottfried,** eldest son of (*c*). Born Dresden 1736. Like his father he became Court organ and harpsichord maker. Died 1808 [*Hirt*]. From 1786 onwards he made pianofortes with his brother Johann Wilhelm, and, after his death, with his half-brother Karl August [*Hirt*].

(*e*) **Johann Wilhelm,** another son of (*c*). Born 1737; died 1798 [*Hirt*].

(*f*) **Karl August,** third son of (*c*), to whom he was born in 1749 by his second wife. After his father's death he left his brothers and set up a firm of his own, which produced keyboard instruments of high quality [*Fé*]. Latest date ascertained, 1796 [*Hirt*].

(*g*) **Ernst Gottlob,** 1734–59, son of (*c*) by his first marriage. Organ and instrument maker [*Hirt*].

Surviving GRÄBNER Harpsichords

Johann Heinrich, *the Elder*

(1) 1722. Two manuals. Inscribed: *Johann Heinrich Graebner, Kgl. Hof-Orgelmacher und Organist an der*

Frauenkirche me fecit Dresden 1722. E–E, 5 octaves; 2×8′, 1×4′ stops. Used by Mozart in Prague, 1787. Shewn at the Centenary Exhibition of the Prague Conservatoire, 1911. Now in Villa Bertramka, Prague; illustrated in *Hirt*, p. 34. See Kinsky in *Acta musicologica*, Vol. 12, 1940.

Johann Heinrich, *the Elder* or *the Younger*

(1a) 1739. In Schloss Pillnitz, near Dresden; 2 manuals. Inscribed: *Johann Heinrich Gräbner Orgel und Instrumentenmacher Dreszden* [sic] *Anno 1739* [*Thoene*, p. 98 n.].

Johann Heinrich, *the Younger*

(2) 1744. Heyer Collection, Leipzig University. Two manuals. Inscribed: *Johann Heinrich Gräbner fecit in Dreszden 1744.* In his catalogue (Vol. 1, 1910) *Ks* attributed it to G. Silbermann; but later repairs revealed inside the instrument the signature of Gräbner (Vol. 2, p. 657); 4′ on upper manual, 8′ and 16′ on lower; originally 2×8′, 1×4′ [*Ernst 1955*, p. 73].

Karl August

(3) 1775. Harpsichord at Brunswick [*Hirt*]. 2×8′ stops.

(4) 1782. Rück Collection, Germanisches Nationalmuseum, Nuremberg; 2 manuals; illustrated *Nor*, p. 128. Inscription (not visible): *Carl August Gräbner Instrumenten macher in Dresden anno 1782* (on the front face of the wrestplank, behind the nameboard).

GRAET, Willem. *Fl.* 1663–82 as a harpsichord maker at Warmond near Leiden [*Curtis*, p. 50].

GRAUWELS, Johannes. *See*: GROUWELS, Johannes.

GRAY, Robert and William. Makers of harpsichords, pianos, and organs at '72 Queen Ann [*sic*] Street East', London, in 1793. Their trade card is reproduced in *J*, pl. xlix. A harpsichord by them is in the Castle Museum, York.

GREGORI, Nicolas de. Richard Luckett, Cambridge, has a single Italian harpsichord. C/E to C, 4 octaves, 2×8′ stops, probably made between 1650 and 1680. It bears the highly suspicious inscription: *Nicolae de Gregorij fecitti Anno Domini 1740.*

GREGORIO, Ælpidio. An Italian harpsichord belonging to John Barnes of Edinburgh bears the very curious inscription: *Opus Aelpidij Gregorj a S. Aelpidio 1736.* An owner's name appears under the music desk: *Giov. Baptista . . . Maestro di Cappella . . . 1816.* Compass C/E–E, 4⅓ octaves plus, without top E flat; 48 keys; 2×8′, buff. Painted case; size: 6′ 3″×2′ 8″. (The '3' in the date is not clear, it could be a '2'.)

Francl lists a harpsichord inscribed: *1691 Elpidius Gregori e Selfidio fecit*; also another (I. 45): *Opus Elpidii Gregorii et Sancta Elpidis Caefani Quarta Katena Areminis 1779.* All these inscriptions invite the gravest suspicions, particularly the last, with its extraordinary Latin gibberish. *Hubb 1965* (p. 37) cites a fourth harpsichord, dated 1697, without giving its location.

GREINER, Johann Karl. Born at Wetzlar in 1753; died 8 October 1798. Probably a harpsichord maker first and foremost, he is chiefly remembered for an instrument imitating Hans Hayden's *Geigenwerk* [*Ko, Gö*].

GRENOT, Pierre. Dates ascertained, 1778–89. Harpsichord maker living in the rue du Moulin-Neuf, Paris, 1778–83, and in the rue de la Calandre, 1788–9. In 1778 he entered the Guild of Instrument Makers [*Pi*].

GRIMALDI, Carlo, of Messina. Lutemaker, *fl.* 1697. Also made harpsichords [*Vannes, Hirt*]. The Rück Collection in the Germanisches Nationalmuseum, Nuremberg has a harpsichord signed: *Carolus Grimaldi fecit + Messane, 1697.*

GROU, Damien. Maker and player of the harpsichord at Lyons in the parish of Sainte-Croix (though perhaps a native of Paris); dates ascertained, 1723–65[?]. A daughter of his was baptized at Sainte-Croix on 28 June 1724.

The Lyons directories, 1716–65, record a Grou who was a teacher of the mandolin and made instruments—perhaps the same man [*Vallas*].

The viol *Faîte à Lyon Par Grou de Paris 1753* [*Bq*, p. 8] may have been by this maker.

GROUWELS, Johannes [Grauwels]. Maker of virginals and harpsichords. Master of the Guild of St. Luke, Antwerp, 1579 [*Bu*]. He is recorded as becoming a citizen of Middelburg in 1593 [*Curtis*, p. 50].

Surviving Instruments

(1) Undated. Brussels Conservatoire, Snoeck Collection. A virginal, *c.* 1580. Inscription on jackrail: *Johannes Grouwels fecit.* The inside of the lid has a painting which the Snoeck catalogue attributes to Peter Brueghel the Elder. Compass, 3 octaves and a 6th, with short octave. Size 153×45 cm.

GROUWELS, Lodewijck [Ludovicus Grouuelus]. Probably son of the above. *Fl.* at Middelburg, near Flushing, in 1593 [*Curtis*, p. 51]. The Metropolitan Museum of Art, New York, has a double virginal by him (i.e. a virginal and an ottavino virginal in one case). Arnold Dolmetsch made an ottavino to replace the original, which had been lost. The instrument belonged earlier to C. M. Holdich of Islington, who shewed it at the South Kensington Museum in 1872. On the jackrail is inscribed: *Ludouicus Grouuelus me fecit 1600.* Illustrated in *Wint 1961.*

GRÜNEBERG, Johann Wilhelm, of Alt-Brandenburg. Dates ascertained, 1776–96. Maker of organs, pianos, and other keyboard instruments. In 1796 he erected an organ in the church of St. Catherine at Magdeburg [*Fé*].

The Royal Manchester College of Music has a bundfrei clavichord by him inscribed: *Fabriert von Johann Wilhelm Grüneberg in Alt Brandenburg 17.0* [indistinct; probably 1780]. Compass just over 5 octaves F–G. Ebony naturals, ivory-topped sharps. Soundhole in soundboard but rose missing. (The instrument belongs to the Henry Watson Collection.)

GUARRACINO, Honofrio [Guaracini]. Italian virginal maker. Dates ascertained, 1668–83 or 1661–92.

Surviving Virginals

(01) 1661. Berlin. Private ownership, at some time since World War II.

(02) 1661(?). Paris, M. Pierre Boyer, who bought it in Rome in 1963. Inscribed on the top key: *Onofrio Guarracino fecit 1661* [or *1667*], and on another key *Orlando Costanza* (? restorer). Rose lost. C/E–F, 4 octaves.

(03) 1667. Milan, Museo Teatrale alla Scala. The Catalogue (1940, p. 29, illustration on p. 32) calls the maker 'Fra Giovacino'. Compass 4 octaves with short octave; 45 keys, above which is the inscription: *Indocta manus noli me tangere.*

(1) 1668. In the possession of Lord Hylton. Cypress, in a painted outer case. Inscription on top key in ink: . . . [illegible] *Guarracino fecit 1668.* Compass C/E–C, 4 octaves with short octave. Keys of beech, the naturals faced with ivory (probably modern) and the sharps with ebony. The cypress soundboard, with its very fine rose, is original. Stand modern. Restored by Alec Hodsdon in 1935. Formerly the property of Miss Wilmot of Warley Place.

(2) 1678. Redhill, Dr. Mirrey. Cypress. Inscription on top key in ink: *Honofrio Guaracini fecit 1678 15 Maggio.* Compass as in 1. Rose missing from soundhole.

(3) 1683. Kings Worthy, Richard T. Boston (1957); formerly John G. Boston. Cypress; compass as in 1. Inscription on top key: *[H]onofrio Guarracino Fecit 1683.* Ivory naturals, ebony sharps. Size $57\frac{1}{2}'' \times 16''$. (Formerly the property of Noel Dilkes, Nottingham.)

(4) 1692. Rome, Collegio Romano. C–C, 4 octaves with short octave [*GL*].

(5) 1692. Rome, Museo Nazionale degli Strumenti Musicali. Polygonal virginal, inscribed: *Honofrius Guarracinus fecit 1692* [*ChamP*]. Possibly = no. 4.

GUISSIÈRE. *See*: DUBUT GUISSIÈRE.

GUNDET, Robert. Virginal maker in Westminster, 1551. [Acts Privy Council (1891), III. 306; quoted in *O.E.D.* s.v. *Virginal.*]

GUNZER, Marx. Organ builder of Stuttgart, *fl.* 1600 when he made a 'Clavier' for Prince Achilles Friedrich [*Württ. Vierteljahresschrift, 1900*].

GUSNASCHI, Lorenzo [*also* Gusnasco, Lorenzo di Pavia, Laurentius Papiensis], of Pavia. Maker of organs, harpsichords, and clavichords. Dates ascertained: 1494, he died before 1539.

He was a friend of Aldus Manutius and acquaintance of Leonardo da Vinci. His contemporaries esteemed him so highly as an organ builder that they called him *Principe.* Beatrice d'Este had a clavichord of his construction, and he made for Pope Leo X in 1514 a large harpsichord ('uno clavecimbalo grande con do registri'). (*See also below*: VINCENTIUS, probably of Florence.) A stone was erected to his memory at Mantua.

Va refers to the remains of a little organ made by him in 1494, preserved in the Correr Museum at Venice.

See further Teseo Albonesio, who has a few paragraphs on him in his *Introductio in Chaldaicam linguam*, Pavia, 1539; also Carlo dell'Acqua's *Lorenzo Gusnasco e i Lingiardi da Pavia,* Milano, 1886.

H, A. W. Two ottavino virginals in the Flemish style bearing these initials survive:

(1) 1619. Berlin Collection. Inscription: *Sic transit gloria mundi. A.W.H. Anno 1619.* Compass 3 octaves F–F. Paper rose. 48 × 26 cm. Naturals of ivory, sharps of ebony.

(2) 1623. Rome. Accademia S. Cecilia. Inscription, round the soundboard *Omnia dat dominus, non habet ergo minus, 1623* and on the nameboard *Sic transit gloria mundi. A.W.H.* Compass 3 octaves and 4 notes, F–A. Size 55 × 27 cm.

H, D. An undated polygonal virginal in the Brussels Conservatoire bears initials which appear to be *DH* (number 2924).

H, H. *See*: HILL, Henry.

H, I. A spinet owned by E. M. Ripin, New York, has its original name batten, which is blank; but the inscription *IH 1771* is roughly painted on the inside of the bottom of the spinet, which has its bent side ending in a straight tail. The names John Harris, Joseph Harris, and John Harrison occur to one as possible makers.

H, J. B. A clavichord in Copenhagen is signed *JBH*, undated. 4 octaves; fretted; black naturals. [Seen by Frank Hubbard.]

H. O. N. *See*: N, H. O.

H. V. L. *See*: L, V.

HAASE, Georg. Maker of organs and clavichords, was born, according to the church records of S. Petri, Bautzen, at Ossling near Kamenz in Saxony, in 1650, and married Dorothea Wentzel at Bautzen (for which Budissin is the old Wendish name) in 1679. He died there on 9 March 1712, a 'Vornehmer Bürger und Kunsterfahrner Orgel- und Instrumentmacher'.

A gebunden clavichord in the Heyer Collection, Leipzig, bears this inscription: *George Haas orgel / Maher* [sic] *in Bidissin* [?] *1692.* The instrument also bears the name 'Bernarda Mülnerin 1697'—presumably one of its earliest owners. 28 pairs of strings; all notes except 3 are gebunden. The names of the notes are written on the keys in an early hand. Compass 4 octaves C–C with short octave.

HAASE, Jovann Ernst. A clavichord in the Museo de Música, Barcelona, bears the maker's label which appears to read (though several words are indistinct): *Jovann Ernst Haase / Orgelmacher ŭnd erhalter / Organist zŭ Sti. Petri / in Budissin / 1728.* This maker, if the reading of his surname is correct, may well have been related to Georg Haase (above).

HABOR. *Nor* (91) refers to a clavichord by 'Habor, Ansbach'. This is a mistake (? misprint) for Huber, an alternative spelling of Hubert, the Ansbach maker. The instrument is numbered 528 in the Berlin Collection, and is described by *Sa* (p. 50) with a photograph.

HACKER, Jörg. Organ and 'instrument' maker at Steyr, Austria, in the sixteenth century. In 1587 he sold a 2-manual harpsichord; and in 1591 a pedal clavichord to Kremsmünster [*MarcP*].

HADRIANUS, *of Rome*. A 1-manual harpsichord repaired in 1971 by Michael Thomas for export to Africa, bears on the jackrail the somewhat Franciolinian inscription: *Hadrianus Roma 1753*. It has 2×8′ stops (to which Alec Hodsdon had added a 4′, removed by Michael Thomas).

HAFFENREFFER, Samuel, of Ulm, *fl.* 1540. Made according to *Va*, a 'monocordo speciale', which may have been a clavichord.

HAGAERTS [*otherwise* Haquaerts, Haghens, Hagart]. Harpsichord and virginal makers in Antwerp:

(*a*) **Cornelius.** Dates ascertained 1626/7—died 1641/2. [Books of the Guild of St. Luke, Antwerp, quoted by *St*, p. 56, where he is described as *clavesimbalmaeker* and *claversingelmaker*.]

(*b*) **Simon.** Very probably son of Cornelius. Entered the Guild 1641/2 as a harpsichord maker (*clavesimbelmaker*).

Surviving HAGAERTS Instruments

Cornelius

(1) 1641. Virginal, inscribed: *Cornelius Haquaerts* [?] *me fecit Antverpiae 1641*. Sold in the Claes sale in 1933 (no. 1479 in the catalogue, from which the inscription is quoted). Now in the Magne Collection, Cherbourg.

(2) Undated. Virginal. Brussels, M. R. Drappel. Inscription on jackrail: *Cornelius Hagaerts me fecit Antwerpiae*. Compass C/E–C. *CH* rose. Size 143×47·5 cm. Presumably = no. 15 in the Régibo sale catalogue (1897); see *St*, p. 57.

Simon

(3) Undated. Harpsichord. Brussels Conservatoire (Snoeck Collection). 2×8′, buff stops. *SH* rose. Compass 4 octaves with short octave. Size 184×73 cm.

(4) 1612. Harpsichord, 2 manuals. Paris, Comtesse de Chambure. *SH* rose, damaged, which was probably mistaken for a Ruckers rose, from which error springs the nameboard legend attributing the instrument to Ruckers. The date 1612 on the soundboard was added when the instrument was *ravalé* in the eighteenth century. Illustrated in *Jur*, p. 48.

HAGERÜF, Johann Christian. Clavichord maker at Tübingen, *fl.* 1795.

Surviving Clavichords

(1) 1795. Signed: *Joh. Christian Hagerüf / Orgel und Clavier Instru/mentmacher in Tübingen. / 1795*. Formerly in the Rück Collection; now owned by Reinhardt Menger, Abtei Arnsburg, near Giessen.

HAGHENS. *See*: HAGAERTS.

HAHN, Klaus. Maker of clavichords ('Klafficordienmacher'), presumably at Leipzig. *Fl.* 1555–65, at which dates he is recorded as having children [R. Wustman, *Musikgeschichte Leipzigs*, Vol. 1, Leipzig, 1909].

HÄHNEL, Johann Ernst [Höhnel], of Meissen. Clavichord maker and organ builder to the Court of Saxony, flourished in the first half of the eighteenth century. He is mentioned in *Adl* (II. 126) as adding certain stops to the Cembal d'amour invented by Silbermann. *Va* mentions him (s.v. Hoenel) as a maker of cembals d'amour. See *Fé* (IV. 176) who mentions 3 organs built or rebuilt by him.

HAIDEN. *See*: HAYDEN.

HAINHOFFER, Philipp, of Augsburg, born 1578. He made automatic spinets. Cf. Biderman.

HAKE, Henning, of Riga, *fl.* 1657. Stockholm Musikhistorisk Museet has a clavicytherium by him signed: *Henning Hake, Riga 1657*.

HALLEY, Robert. *See*: HATLEY, Robert.

HANCOCK, James, was alive in 1820. An organ builder [*GD*].

James and John may have been brothers, and may well have been related to Thomas. They are both mentioned in the contract for an organ at Chelmsford in 1772 [*GD*]. John Crang (q.v.) took one, or perhaps both, of them into partnership in piano making and organ building, the firm being called *Crang & Hancock*. Nine organs built by them are recorded by *Sum* (p. 173).

HANCOCK, John, died 1792. Organ builder [*GD*] and spinet maker. A spinet by him in the Benton Fletcher Collection is signed on the nameboard: *Johann Hancock Fecit London*. G–G, 5 octaves. Length 6′ 6″. Repaired by Alec Hodsdon, 1948. A 'fine toned single keyed harpsichord by Hancock', sold (for 1 guinea!) at Christie's on 21 December 1793 may have been by this maker.

HANCOCK, John Crang. John Crang Hancock was a piano maker and organ builder, living at 32 Parliament Street, Westminster, and afterwards at 82 Wych Street, St. Clement Danes. Dates ascertained, 1779–99 [*Ha*].

In patent number 1743, dated 10 May 1790, he describes himself as 'John Crang Hancock, Of Wych Street, in the Parish of Saint Clement Danes . . . Organ Builder'.

In 1794 he is recorded in J. Doane's *Musical Directory* (London, 1749) [L. G. Langwill in *Music and Letters*, London, January 1949].

He made a number of pianos in the shape of spinets. One dated 1782 is in the possession of Messrs. Broadwood. Another such, dated 1779, belonged in 1885 to A. M. Lawrence. Both were shewn at the International Inventions Exhibition, London, 1885.

HANCOCK, Thomas. Harpsichord and spinet maker, London. Dates ascertained 1700–20. A harpsichord by him dated 1720 was the property of the Earl of Darnley at Cobham Hall near Rochester until 23 July 1957, when it was sold by Sotheby's (bought by R. Russell). Now (1968) at Edinburgh University. Illustrated in *RussColl*.

Inscription: *Thomas Hancock Londini fecit 1720*. Five octaves minus 1 note, F–E; 2×8′; black naturals, skunk-tail sharps; modern stand; 7′×3′.

HANS VAN CUELEN, i.e. Hans from Cologne. This 'very important but shadowy figure', as Edwin Ripin [*RG.I*, p. 13] aptly calls him, was primarily concerned with organ building and in 1509 came to Antwerp to do some work on the organ at the O.L.V. Kerk there. But he also concerned himself with the making of stringed keyboard instruments, and it seems that we should seek in him the earliest signs of the development of the great Flemish tradition of harpsichord making which culminated in the work of the Ruckers family (q.v.).

Hans van Cuelen appears under various names, such as Hans Suys (Süss), Johan de Colonia, Meister Hans Suest von Nürnberg, Maistre Hans Blangz, Jan van Zwanenbroeck, and a number of others (if we are to believe *Vente*, though G. Pietzsch in *MGG*, vol. 12, s.v. Süss, is considerably more cautious).

At any rate, in 1512 he made a 'clavicenon' for Eleanor of Austria, the deed of payment for which is reproduced, transcribed, and translated in Ripin's paper given at the May 1970 Colloquium of the Ruckers Genootschap [*RG.I*, pp. 13–14].

Relying on *Po*, p. 28, where one reads 'Beiden (i.e. Joos Karest and Gosuin Karest) zijn zij de zoons van Hans van Ceulen [*sic*]' and on *St*, p. 67, where a quotation from an original document is given: 'Goosen Kareest, van Coelen, Janssone, schilder', I recorded Hans van Cuelen in my first edition under 'Karest (Jan)'; but more recent research has made it necessary to change this, as the name 'Jan Karest' (or a similar variant) has not—at any rate yet—been found in any relevant archives.

HANSEN, Christian. Clavichord maker at Satrup, Schleswig-Holstein, in 1799.

Surviving Clavichords

(1) 1799. Halle, Händel-Haus. Inscription: *Chr. Hansen-Satrup a. 1799.* Compass C–E, 4 octaves plus a 3rd. Bundfrei.

HANSON, J. *See*: Longman and Broderip's instrument no. 6.

HARRASS, Johann Heinrich, of Gross-Breitenbach. Harpsichord maker, died 1714. A 2-manual harpsichord by him is recorded as being in the Library of the Hofkapelle at Sondershausen [G. Kinsky, 'Zur Echtheit des Berliner Bach-Flügels', *Bach-Jahrbuch*, 1924]. He is presumably the Breitenbach maker referred to by Adlung [*Adl*, II. 110]. *See further above*: BREITENBACH.

HARRIS, Baker, of London. Maker of spinets and harpsichords, and also of organs and pianofortes. Earliest and latest dates known, 1740–80. In 1763 his name appeared in *Un.* as 'Harpsichord maker, *Denmark-street*'.

Longman and Broderip of Cheapside acted as agents for Baker Harris (see instrument 1 under Longman and Broderip) and probably also John Kemys, q.v.

A 'grand piano Forte with pedal by Baker Harris in a neat inlaid case' was sold at Christie's on 9 October 1772 for £9.

The inscription on the nameboard of no. 7 below gives the date 1766; but the third figure has been altered and would appear to have been 7 originally. On the back of the nameboard is scribbled in pencil *No. 21* [?0], the third numeral being illegible. Compass 5 octaves F to F without bottom F sharp. Ivory naturals, ebony sharps. Length 74½″.

A. J. Hipkins had a harpsichord-nameboard inscribed *Baker Harris Londini fecit 1780*. This belonged to Henry Tull, and is now owned by C. F. Colt.

See table 13 for instruments by Baker Harris.

TABLE 13. *Surviving Instruments by BAKER HARRIS*

No.	Date	Type	Kbs.	Signature	Owner/Remarks
1	1740	S	1		Lent by T. L. Southgate to Loan Exhibition 1904, London.
2	n.d. (*c.* 1750)	S	1	*Baker Harris fecit*	Boston Museum of Fine Arts. Formerly F. W. Galpin. 1×4′; C/E–G, 4½ octaves.
3	1760	S	1	*Baker Harris Londini fecit 1760*	Offered for sale by J. G. Morley in 1949. In 1965 was owned by George Vollmer, Wichita, Kans. F–F, 5 octaves.
4	1761[?]	S	1	*Baker Harris London fecit 1761*[?]	Dundee Museum, Simpson Collection. Date indistinct.
5	1763	S	1		Shewn at International Inventions Exhibition, 1885, by James Russell.
6	1763	S	1	*Baker Harris Londini fecit 1763*	Leonard Partridge, London, July 1947. 5 octaves F–F without bottom F sharp. Possibly same as no. 3 above. Owned in 1953 by L. R. Samuels of New York City.
7	1766[?]	S	1	*Baker Harris Londini fecit 1766*	Norman Anderson, Haslemere. (Bought by Messrs. Naylor at Sotheby's, June 1932.) The third digit of the date shews signs of having been altered.

TABLE 13 (*cont.*):

No.	Date	Type	Kbs.	Signature	Owner/Remarks
7a	1766	S	1	*Baker Harris Londini fecit 1766*	Bought by Roger Warner, of Burford, for £1,150 at an auction sale held in November 1969 by Knight, Frank, and Rutley at Fairway Close, Wildwood Road, Hampstead, the property of a Mr. Kidner (erroneously described as a harpsichord). [Is *not* the same instrument as no. 7, which Anderson still has.] Inscription on nameboard. 5 octaves F–F; ivory naturals. Uncertain numerals stamped on top key. *33*, *60*, and *33*; on bottom key: *33*. Original stand with unusual cabriole legs. Sold to a Chelsea dealer by Roger Warner, December 1969.
7b	1769	S	1		Richmond, Alan Rubin (acquired 1969).
8	1770	H	1		Sold at Puttick & Simpson's, London, for £26 on 22 June 1939, to Messrs. Morley. 5 octaves.
9	1770	S	1	*Baker Harris Londini fecit 1770*	London, Victoria and Albert Museum. (Bequeathed by Charles H. Laycock.) 5 octaves F–F without lowest F sharp.
10	1771	S	1	*Baker Harris London 1771*	Cleveland, Ohio, Messrs. Lorimer Brooks (1954). 5 octaves F–F without lowest F sharp. Mahogany case; ivory naturals.
10a	1772	S	1	*Baker Harris Londini fecit 1772*	D. W. Ayers, who bought it at Sotheby's on 12 March 1970 from Edgar Hunt.
11	1773	S	1	*Baker Harris Londini fecit 1773*	Toronto. Museum of Archaeology. 5 octaves F–F, without lowest F sharp.
12	1773	S	1		Shewn at Chickering Exhibition, Boston, Mass., in 1902. Now at Essex Institute, Salem, Mass.
12a	1773	S	1	*Baker Harris Londini fecit 1773*	New York, Henry Burrows. Restored 1909 by A. Dolmetsch.
12b	1774	S	1	*Baker Harris Londini fecit 1774*	Glasgow, Royal Scottish Academy of Music and Drama. Numbered *148* on top jack, key, and inside soundboard. F–F without lowest F sharp.
13	1776	S	1	*Baker Harris Londini fecit 1776*	Edinburgh Music School. Seen by Rimbault in 1858 (see *Ri*, p. 400). F–F, 5 octaves without low F sharp. Perhaps the 1776 spinet shewn at South Kensington in 1872. Almost certainly belonged to General Reid formerly.
14	1777	S	1		Advertised for sale in *The Times*, February 1939.
15(?)	1780	H	2	*Baker Harris Londini fecit 1780*	C. F. Colt, Bethersden. This may well be a conversion by Henry Tull (from whose daughter, Mrs. Stubbs, it was acquired) of a single. *BH* rose. New nameboard made by Tull.

HARRIS, John. Son of James Harris of Sherborne, Gloucestershire, was apprenticed to Stephen Keene (q.v.) in 1675 and entered the Joiners' Company in 1685. Master of John, the son of Benjamin Sison (q.v.).

HARRIS, John. Son of Joseph Harris. Spinet and harpsichord maker, Red Lion Street, Holborn (also London Wall; see instrument 1 below); later Boston, Massachusetts. Dates ascertained, 1730–69.

On 22 October 1730 John Harris took out a patent (numbered 521) for: 'A new invented Harpsichord, upon which (having only two Sets of Strings) may be performed either one or two Unisons and one Octave together, or the Forts and Pianos, or Loud or Soft, and the contrary, may be executed as quick as Thought, and also Double Basses, by touching only single Keys, whereby hard Divisions on the Bass Part may be well played in a Double Manner without the Thumb and Finger together, which could not well be executed otherwise; that besides the above-menc͠oned Advantages a great deal of time and Trouble will be saved in Quilling and Tuning the said Harpsichord, and it will keep much longer in Tune than any Harpsichords that have Octave Stops, and consequently will not be so expensive to keep the same in good Order as those Instruments which are made in the Common Way, neither can any double-key'd Harpsichord be so serviceable and useful as the Petic͠oner's new-invented Harpsichord, although the Expence is vastly greater.'

The octave and 'double-bass' stops described here cannot have been true octave and 16′ stops, since the instrument had only 2 sets of 8′ strings. They must therefore presumably have been a kind of super-octave and sub-octave coupler, the one working on one 8′ register, and the other on the second; though it is not easy to see exactly how these would have been contrived. Certainly the instrument never attracted much public attention, in spite of the long notice of it which appeared in the press (quoted by *Ri*, p. 86); and Harris's monopoly of 'making and vending the said new invented harpsichord for the term of 14 years' would seem to have been unnecessary. No example of it has survived.

The John Harris who appears in *Un* (1763) as a 'Maker of the Armonica', resident in Bloomsbury Market, may be the same person.

In 1768 Harris emigrated to Boston, Mass. The *Boston Gazette* for 18 September 1769 contains the following notice (quoted by *J*):

'It is with pleasure that we inform the Public, that a few days since was shipped for Newport, a very curious Spinnet, being the first ever made in America, the performance of the ingenious Mr. John Harris, of Boston, (Son of the late Mr. Joseph Harris of London, Harpsichord and Spinnet Maker) and in every respect does honour to that Artist.'

Surviving Instruments

(1) Spinet. Inscribed: *Joannes Harris London Wall 1796*. Messrs. Edmund C. Legg, Cirencester. Inscribed on nameboard; numbered 1796 (if authentic); 73″ wide. Sold at Puttick & Simpson's, 31 October 1929 (no. 198 in catalogue). G–G, 5 octaves; arcaded ivory naturals, skunktail sharps; walnut case. Formerly belonged to the Cadbury family.

(2) Spinet. Inscribed: *Joannes Harris fecit*. Bought by Mr. Neville at Sotheby's, 22 March 1934 (the owner anon.). Black naturals, white sharps. Size 46″ × 69″.

(3) Spinet. Made in Boston, Mass., after 1768. In 1952 this instrument was in Birmingham, Mich.

(4) Spinet. Lewes, Horace Jackson Collection. Five octaves; ebony naturals, ivory sharps. (Formerly belonged to E. J. Wheeler.)

(5) Spinet. Inscribed: *Joannes Harris fecit Londini*. Boston, Mass. Formerly owned by Elizabeth B. McIlvaine of Downington, Pa. [*MarcP*].

(6) Spinet. Inscribed: *John Harris Boston New England fecit*. Buffalo, N.Y. Mrs. Walter B. Robb Collection. Illustrated *Antiques*, Vol. 93 (1966), p. 189.

HARRIS, Joseph. Spinet and harpsichord maker, London. Dates ascertained, 1737–65.

Surviving Spinets

(1) 1750. Shewn by Kendrick Pyne at the International Inventions Exhibition in 1885. Bought by H. Boddington and still owned by his descendants living near Aberdeen. Inscribed: *Josephus Harris London fecit 1750*. G–G, 5 octaves. Mahogany case.

(2) 1751. Manchester, Boddington Collection. G–G, 5 octaves. Inscribed: *Josephus Harris Londini fecit 1751*. Walnut case with satinwood stringing.

(3) 1757. B. Coppinger Prichard in 1930. Illustrated in *J* (plate 31). It has a double buffstop. Maker's note on back of nameboard: *This is not one of my Comon instruments But the Best Ton'd I ever made*.

(4) Undated(?). London, Messrs. Moss Harris in 1937. Illustrated in the *Antique Collector*, London, 1937, p. 16. In 1953, owned by Messrs. Morley. (This seems to be the same instrument as that pictured in the *Connoisseur*, October 1937, p. xxv, in a Frank Partridge advertisement. Compass 5 octaves, G–G.) Inscribed: *Josephus Harris Londini fecit*.

(5) Undated(?). Great Waltham, Essex. J. J. Tufnell in 1964. Numbered *1716* inside the case and on some of the keys. Owned by the Tufnell family since the eighteenth century and shewn in a family conversation piece dated 1737. Inscribed: *Josephus Harris Londini fecit*.

(6) Undated. Mrs. John Nicoll, U.S.A. (1954). G–G, 5 octaves. Ivory naturals, skunktail sharps. Inscribed: *Josephus Harris Londini fecit*.

(7) Undated. Mr. Rustin, New York (1955). Top and bottom keys initialled *JJ*, presumably by a workman.

HARRIS, William. Spinet and harpsichord maker, 44 Fetter Lane, London. Earliest and latest dates known, 1765–93.

Surviving Instruments

(01) 1765. Spinet, inscribed *Gulielmus Harris London fecit 1765* on nameboard, the bottom key being also signed with the maker's name and date. Owned 1966 by Charles Angell (Antiques), Bath; earlier in private ownership in Swansea.

(1) 1766. Spinet. St. Louis Museum. Presented by L. Isaacson of New York.

(2) 1773. A spinet of this date was sold by Miss E. A. Wilmott of Warley Place, Essex, at Sotheby's on 5 April 1935 to Messrs. Oliver. Five octaves. Mahogany case. Ivory naturals.

(3) 1773. Royal Manchester College of Music. Spinet signed on nameboard: *Gulielmus Harris Londini fecit 1773*. Compass 5 octaves F to F, without bottom F sharp. Mahogany case. (Henry Watson Collection.)

(4) 1776. Spinet, owned (1970) by Mrs. K. Thompson, Moseley, Birmingham. Signed on nameboard: *Gulielmus Harris Londini fecit 1776*. Compass C–G, 4½ octaves. Mahogany case. Restored in the late 1960s by T. Beckerleg.

HARRISON, John. Harpsichord and spinet maker, living in London; dates ascertained, 1743–81. Freeman of the Joiners' Company, 12 April 1743. In 1781 his address was 8 Bell Head Court, Newgate Street. A 'fine ton'd doublekey'd harpsichord by Harrison' was sold at Christie's on 16 November 1791 for 9 guineas. Archibald Pringle (q.v.) was working for him in 1757.

Surviving Spinets

(1) 1749. Oxford, Taphouse Collection (housed in the Faculty of Music). G–G, 5 octaves. Length 6′ 2″. Mahogany case. Inscribed: *Johannes Harrison Londini fecit 1749*.

(1a) 1750. Cirencester, C. A. Legg, 1956. Inscribed: *Johannes Harrison Londini fecit 1749*, also, under the soundboard: *John Harrison London January 18th 1749–50*.

(2) 1757. Edinburgh University (formerly Raymond Russell). Repaired by Legg, Cirencester in 1954. Inscribed: *Johannes Harrison Londini fecit 1757*. Some keys and jacks signed by Archibald Pringle, q.v. Length 6′.

(3) 1764. Glasgow Museum. Inscribed: *Joannes Harrison Londini fecit 1764*.

(4) 1765. College Park, Md., Howard Serwer. Inscribed: *Joannes Harrison Londini fec^t 1765*.

Howard Serwer acquired it in February 1971 from Mrs. Ruth Rollins Stieff whose family had owned it for about 45 years. To restore the instrument he, with Scott Odell acting as his consultant, found it necessary to dismantle it and reglue most of the structural joints. Several inscriptions came to light: (1) on lowest key: *1765*; (2) on the keyboard: *7558* (possibly modern); (2) on underside of soundboard, in ink: *Arch. d Pringle / March 29th: 1765 / London*; (4) on inside of bottom, in chalk, mostly indecipherable: . . . *factor* [??] . . . *1765*. The jackrail is modern and crude. Upper and lower jack guides (not box slide).

(5) 1781. Mudeford House, Christchurch, Hants, Dr. C. Conyers Morrell. Inscribed: *Johannes Harrison Londini fecit 1781 No 8 Bull Head Court, Newgate Street*.

HARTAFFEL, Robert. Builder of organs and other keyboard instruments, 1717–82. Born 25 February 1717 at Leidek, Bingenheim (Hesse-Darmstadt). He lived near Marienborn and made a number of clavichords. In 1746 he emigrated to America, living in or near Lititz, Pa., for a time and moving thence to Lancaster, Pa., where he died on 7 November 1782 [*Armstr*, p. 14].

HARTMAN, Jean Benjamin. Harpsichord maker, *fl.* 1769 in the rue Betizy, Paris [*Pi*]. Died 7 July 1770 [*GL*].

HARTMANN, Jacob. *Fl.* 1765 at Dresden as harpsichord maker.

Surviving Instruments

(1) 1765. Eisenbach, Bach-Haus. Two-manual harpsichord signed: *Jacob Hartmann / 1765 Dreszden* [*Thoene*, p. 98 n.]. (The signature is in pencil on the underside of the soundboard. Attributed in the 1939 catalogue to Gottfried Silbermann; 1×4′, 1×8′, 1×16′. The 1964 catalogue gives the maker correctly and notes the disposition restored to the original 2×8′, 1×4′. The style suggests that Hartmann was a pupil or employee of the Gräbners.)

HARTUNG, Cornelis [Hartungh, Hartingh]. Harpsichord and organ builder in Utrecht. Dates ascertained, 1622–4; he had died by 9 February 1624 [*Curtis*, pp. 51–2].

HARTWELL, Thomas. Virginal maker in the parish of St. Giles Cripplegate, London. Dates ascertained 1589–92 [*Parish Reg.*].

HASERT, Johann. Born in 1680 at Bercka vorm Haynich. From early childhood he had music lessons, and also did a great deal of carpentry. At the age of 17 he started to make keyboard instruments. Two years later he learnt to play the trumpet, and in 1701 entered military service. He took part in 9 campaigns in Brabant, but kept up his musical studies all the time.

From 1709 onwards he was Court Trumpeter at Eisenach; and made at the same time violins, bass viols, cellos, and clavichords [*Wa*].

HASS [Hasse, Hasch]. Family of harpsichord, clavichord, and organ makers resident in Hamburg in the eighteenth century. The following members are recorded or may be deduced:

(*a*) **J. A. Hass,** *fl.* 1710, if intrument no. 1 is really dated 1710. The true date may well be much later, e.g. 1770, in which case this harpsichord would be the work of Johann Adolph Hass (maker (*c*) below).

(*b*) **Hieronymus Albrecht Hass,** born 1689; latest date ascertained 1744 [on instrument 10].

He was baptized as the son of Conrad Hass at the S. Jakobi Kirche, Hamburg, on 1 December 1689, having been born probably within the preceding week. He married on 12 October 1711 Margreta Dorotea von Höffen. On 23 March 1714 he acquired Hamburg citizenship. A daughter of his, named Maria Johanna, was baptized at S. Jakobi on 3 April 1715. [Hamburg archives.]

(*c*) **Johann Adolph Hass,** son of the preceding; *fl.* 1740–68; died by 30 January 1776. Received Hamburg citizenship 28 October 1746 as son of 'Hieronymus Albert Hasse, Klaviermacher'. Married Anna Elizabeth Tramnitz 22 November 1746 in Hamburg.

Ge (Vol. 1, 1790) says: 'Hasse, Vater und Sohn beyde Orgelmacher zu Hamburg, auch beyde nicht mehr am Leben; machten vortreffliche Flügel und Klaviere, die noch sehr gesucht werden.'

[**Dietrich Christopher Hass** *fl.* 1796 [instrument 23]. H. Schröder in his catalogue of the Hamburg Collection (p. 19) assumes that he was the restorer of instrument no. 23. He may well have been the maker, though he was not a member of the celebrated Hass family. *See table 14*.]

HASS, Dietrich Christopher. Baptized at Hamburg, 3 October 1731, the third son of Christian Hase III. Not related to the celebrated Hass family, unless very remotely [*Schultze*, from Hamburg archives].

HASSLINCK. *See*: HESSELIUS.

HASSORDE, William [Hassard, Hassett]. London virginal maker. He is mentioned in the parish registers of St. Giles Cripplegate intermittently from 1610 until his burial in May 1617.

HASTEY, Robert. A misreading of Hatley, q.v.

TABLE 14. *Surviving HASS Instruments*

No.	Date	Type	Kbs.	Signature	Owner/Remarks
1	1710[?]	H	2	*J. A. Hass Hamb. Anno 1710*	Yale University, Belle Skinner Collection (formerly Morris Steinert). Illustrated and described in the catalogue. Compass 5 octaves F–F; 1×16′, 2×8′, 1×4′, 1×2′, buff, coupler. Length 9′ 1¼″. (The true date must be much later, e.g. 1770.) It was owned by Salomon, Paris, in the 1920s [*MarcP*].
2	1721	[H]	[2]	*H. A. Hass fecit Hamburg 1721*	Gothenburg, Göteborgs Museum. Now converted into a piano; 4 octaves and a 6th, F–D.
3	1723	H	2	*Hieronymus Albrecht Hasch in Hamb. Anno 1723*	Copenhagen, Musikhistoriska Museet. See catalogue.
3a	1728	Cd	1	*H. A. Hass fecit Hamb. 1728*	Berlin Collection. Shewn at the Allgemeine Musik-Ausstellung, 1898. C–F, 4½ octaves (originally C–D, 4 octaves plus 1 tone). *Sa* gives the date wrongly as '1778'.
4	1732	H	1	*Hieronymus Albrecht Hass fecit Hamburg. Anno 1732*	Oslo, Kunstindustrimuseet (since 1895). Inscribed on soundboard. Described and pictured by H. Glahn in the *Årbok* of the Museum for 1950/8 and by N. Lunde in *Harpd*, Vol. 4, no. 4, November/January 1971/2.
5	1734	H	2	*Hieronymus Albrecht Hass fecit Hamb. Anno 1734*	Brussels Conservatoire. Restored by Fleury of Paris, 1858. Shewn London, International Inventions Exhibition, 1885. Has original 16′ stop. Illustrated in *Pag*, p. 43.
6	1740	H	3	*Hieronymus Albr. Hass in Hamb. Anno 1740*	Paris, Rafael Puyana (formerly Mme de Jouvenel). Exhibited Paris 1900, Exposition Universelle Internationale class 17; illustrated in catalogue, Paris, 1900, at which time it belonged to E. Costil. Has original 16′ stop and a 2′ stop. Illustrated *Russell 1959*.
6a	1740	Cd	1	*Hieronymus Albr. Hass in Hamb. 1740*	Stockholm, Nydahl Collection. C–D, 5 octaves and 2 notes.
7	1742	Cd	1	*Hieronym. Albr. Hass in Hambg. Anno 1742*	Hamburg Museum. 5 octaves F–F, bundfrei. Ivory naturals, tortoiseshell-faced sharps. Inside of lid painted with a musical scene on a landscape background. Presented by J. N. Bartels in 1899. Size 174×52 cm.
8	1743	Cd	1	*Hieronym. Albr. Hass In Hamb. Anno 1743*	Oxford, Taphouse Collection. Compass 5 octaves F–F; bundfrei. Probably that shewn by J. B. Cramer & Co. at International Inventions Exhibition, 1885. Ivory naturals, chequered sharps; 69×20½″. Now (1973) housed in the Music Faculty, Oxford.
9	1743	Cd	1	*Hieronymus Albr. Hass*	Copenhagen, Claudius Collection. Compass 5 octaves F–F; bundfrei. Illustrated in catalogue.
10	1744	Cd	1	*Hieronymus Albr. Hass Hambg. Anno 1744*	Brussels Conservatoire. Compass 5 octaves F–F, bundfrei. Illustrated in *Pag*, p. 68.
10a	1744	Cd	1	*Hieronymus Albr. Hass, Hamburg, Anno 1744*	Stockholm, Nydahl Collection. F–F, 5 octaves. In bass, 22 notes with additional 4′ strings.
10b	1746	Cd	1	*J. A. Hass Hamb. 1746*	Koldinghus Museum, Denmark (1970). Red lacquer and gold, richly decorated [*Nord, DAM*]. Gebunden. Inscribed on soundboard. Trichord in bass. On inside of lid, painted a crown with monogram *EMJ* underneath [*Müller*].

TABLE 14 (*cont.*):

No.	Date	Type	Kbs.	Signature	Owner/Remarks
11	1747	Cd	1	*J. A. Hass*	Oslo, Norsk Folkemuseet. Compass 5 octaves F–F; bundfrei. Octave strings on lowest 22 notes. Length 179·6 cm.
11a	1748	Cd	1	[Signed by J. A. Hass and dated 1748]	Leipzig, Heyer Collection (no. 26 in *Ks*, who thought it was anonymous). During thorough restoration about 1966 the maker's name and date were found underneath the grime on the soundboard [*Ernst*]. Compass G–D, 4 octaves and a 5th; bottom octave and a half, trichord; ivory naturals, tortoiseshell sharps.
12	1755	Cd	1	*J. A. Hass Hamb. Anno 1755*	Copenhagen, Musikhistoriska Museet. Compass 5 octaves F–F; bundfrei. Restored 1901 by Hornung & Möller. Illustrated in *Wint 1966*.
12a	1756	Cd	1	*J. A. Hass Hamb. Anno 1756*	Known to *Ernst*, 1934–6, but has now disappeared. Gebunden; C–D, 4 octaves plus 2 notes; 15 keys have a 3rd string.
13	1760	Cd	1	[Signed by *J. A. Hass*, but exact signature not known]	Hamburg, Museum für Kunst und Gewerbe. The instrument was probably destroyed in World War II. It may well have been the gebunden clavichord, dated 1760, shewn by H. Kohl of Hamburg at Allgemeine Musik-Ausstellung, Berlin, 1898. Gebunden.
13a	1761	Cd	1	*J. A. Hass Hambg Anno 1761*	Copenhagen, Musikhistoriska Museet. Gebunden; trichord in bass. Belonged to the Danish composer C. F. Weyse (1774–1842). (*Not* the same instrument as no. 14.) Later owned by the Danish singer Albert Meyer (1839–1921), whose heirs gave it to the Museum in 1926.
14	1761	Cd	1	*J. A. Hass*	Copenhagen, Claudius Collection. Compass 4 octaves C–C; gebunden.
14a	1761	Cd	1		Copenhagen, Musikhistoriska Museet. F–F, 5 octaves, gebunden; trichord in bass.
14b	1762	Cd	1	*J. A. Hass*; [on lid-painting: *1762*]	Manchester, Forsyth Collection. Compass 5 octaves C–C; bundfrei; 19 octave strings in bass; ivory naturals, ebony sharps. Soundboard decorated with flowers. Inside of lid lacquered with red *chinoiserie*, and dated 1762.
15	1763	Cd	1	*J. A. Hass Hamb. Anno 1763*	Edinburgh University. Formerly Raymond Russell; formerly (until 1956) at Wanstead, Captain Lane. Formerly belonged to Lord Dartmouth. Sold at Sotheby's 5 December 1947. Compass 5 octaves F–F, with octave strings for the lowest octave-and-a-half (F–B); bundfrei. Tortoiseshell naturals with ivory arcaded fronts; ebony sharps faced with mother-of-pearl. Interior of the case veneered in olive, apart from the lid on which is painted a river scene; exterior lacquered with *chinoiserie* in red, black, and gold. The mahogany stand with cabriole legs is not original.
16	1763	Cd	1	*J. A. Hass Hamb. Anno 1763*	Vere Pilkington, Portugal (1966); formerly Michael Thomas, Hurley (1954). Formerly belonged to Captain Lane, Hugh Gough (1945–7), and earlier to Messrs. Legg of Cirencester (bought Sotheby's 13 December 1935). Strung as no. 15; bundfrei. Case inside lacquered with *chinoiserie* in red and gold, outside painted brown. Restored by Dolmetsch, who made the present stand. Illustrated, before restoration, in *HiMI*.

TABLE 14 (*cont.*):

No.	Date	Type	Kbs.	Signature	Owner/Remarks
17	1763	Cd	1	*J. A. Hass Hamb. Anno 1763*	Sir Humphrey Noble, Bt., whose family have owned it for many years. Strung as no. 15; bundfrei. Ivory naturals with ebony arcaded fronts. Mottled painted case.
18	1764	H	1	*J. A. Hass Hamb. Anno 1764*	Edinburgh University. Formerly Raymond Russell. Formerly Stockton, Calif., Miss Mary Dunne. Formerly in the Six Collection, Amsterdam. Compass 5 octaves F–F; 2×8′, 1×4′, buff; length 7′ 8″.
19	1767	Cd	1	*J. A. Hass Hamb. Anno 1767*	London, Mrs. Maud Russell (bought by Raymond Russell in 1952). Formerly Miss Margaret Glyn and before that Sir Gervas Glyn, Bt., who owned it when it was shewn in London in 1904. Strung as no. 15. Tortoise-shell naturals; chequered sharps; inside lid painted with a landscape. Outside case painted to resemble wood.
20	1768	Cd	1	*J. A. Hass*	Leipzig, de Wit Collection (1893). Gebunden; 175×23 cm.
[21]—An error for no. 3a above, q.v.					
22	1786	Cd	1	[Signed by *Hass*, but exact signature not known]	Shewn by H. Kohl of Hamburg at the Allgemeine Musik-Ausstellung, Berlin, 1898. Gebunden.
[23]	1796	Cd	1	*Dietrich Chr. Hass Hamburg 1796*	Hamburg Museum. Bundfrei. (See Schröder's Catalogue, p. 19, where D. C. Hass is regarded as probably a restorer and the date of the instrument *c.* 1760.) This Hass did not belong to the celebrated family. *See below.*
24	n.d.	Cd	1	[None]	Ghent, the Snoeck family (1953).
[25]—An error for no. 14b above, q.v.					
26	?	Cd	1	?	Port-of-Spain, Trinidad, in private ownership (1947).
[27]	—	Cd	1	[None]	Halle, Händel-Haus. Rose with letter *H*, which leads *Sasse* (p. 21) to suggest it may be a Hass. C–D, 4 octaves plus 2 notes; bundfrei. Second half of eighteenth century. Friedrich Ernst, reviewing *Sasse* in *Die Musikforschung*, Vol. 21 (1968) regards its *Stichmass* of 47·5 cm. as making this attribution impossible, since the Hamburg makers used a *Stichmass* of at least 49 cm.
28	—	Cd	1		Hamburg, Dr. Harro Schmidt. Lacks original signature, but carries an inscription dating a repair: *J: A: Hass Hambg. Reparirt 1761*, and another dated 1934. Its style shews Hass to have been the original maker.

HATLEY, Robert. London virginal maker; *fl.* 1664, in which year he resided in the parish of St. Giles Cripplegate [*Parish Reg.*].

Surviving Virginals

(1) 1664. London, Benton Fletcher Collection. F–C (55 keys), no low F sharp. 5′ 7″×1′ 9″. Flat cover. Two small roses. Bought by Major Fletcher at Puttick & Simpson's, 2 November 1933.

(2) [? Undated.] London (? Mr. Parkyn, dealer, Cromer St., Grays Inn Rd.), 1906, when it was seen by Arthur Hill. Inscription: *Roberthus Hatley* [*GD* (1940), 5, 545]. Probably the same instrument as no. 1.

(3) Undated. Bushey, *c.* 1915, the property of a lady. Also seen by A. Hill [ibid.].

See also: TOLLEY, Robert.

HAUERT, Johannes. *See*: HOWARD, Johann.

HAUG, Friedrich, *c.* 1791, court instrument maker at Stuttgart. His harpsichords cost between 80 and 100 florins [*Ge*].

HAUK, Kasper, of Cracow, harpsichord maker in the seventeenth century [*Szulc*].

HAUSER, Johann Hermann, *fl.* 1761. German clavichord maker. A 4-octave (C–C) gebunden clavichord in the Heyer Collection Leipzig, bears this inscription along the bridge: *1761 Johannes Hermannus Hauser in Gimb.*

Whether this refers to Gimborn in the Rhineland, Gimbsheim in Hessen, or Gimbweiler in Oldenburg, it is impossible to say.

Thirty-two pairs of strings. Dimensions 131 × 38·5 cm. Formerly in the possession, throughout several generations, of the Mühlinghaus family, Wupperfeld.

HAUSLAIB, Lorenz. Maker of keyboard instruments at Nuremberg, *fl.* 1596. The Crosby Brown Collection in the Metropolitan Museum of Art, New York, has an organ-spinet inscribed: *D.G. quid posible* [sic] *apud Laurentium Hauslaib Nor*[*im*]*bergense*[*m*] *1596*. The spinet is of 4′ pitch; the organ has 4 registers. C–A, just under 4 octaves, without top G sharp. (The catalogue gives the date as '1598', but this should be *1596*.)

HAWARD [*also* Hayward]. A famous family of spinet and harpsichord makers resident in London in the seventeenth century.

(1) **Charles.** Dates ascertained, *c.* 1660–87 [*J*]. Lived in Aldgate Street.

Pepys ordered a spinet from him in April 1668:

To White Hall. Took Aldgate Street in my way, and there called upon one Haward that makes virginalls, and there did like of a little espinette, and will have him finish them for me . . . [4 April].

On 13 July in the same year he called again. The spinet was delivered at his house on the 15th, and it cost him £5.

Thomas Salmon (*Vindication of an Essay to the Advancement of Music*, 1672, p. 68) refers to a 'curious pair of Phanatical Harpsichords made by that Arch Heretick Charles Haward' which he had seen.

In 1674 Haward was paid £6. 10*s*. 'for mending the harpsichords and pedalls in the Great Hall in the Privy Lodgings and for the private musick, for 2 whole years', and next year £2 was paid to 'Mr. Haward, the virginall-maker, for mending the harpsichords' [*La*, pp. 299, 300].

Queen Anne had a virginal by him, which she was said to have prized very highly [*Ri*, p. 68]. *See table 15.*

(2) **John.** Earliest date ascertained 1622. In 1649 he resided in the parish of St. Helen Bishopsgate [*Parish Reg.*].

John Haward probably died in 1667 [*Join*]. The John and Charles Haward admitted to the Joiners' Company by patrimony in 1652 and 1660 were probably his sons, as also may have been the Thomas Howard (Haward) similarly admitted in 1657. (Yet another John Haward was admitted 1647/8.)

Thomas Mace (*Musick's monument*, 1676, pp. 235–6) has an interesting passage about a harpsichord fitted with registration pedals, invented by John Haward:

. . . the *Pedal* . . . contriv'd . . . by one Mr. *John Hayward* of *London* . . .

Concerning *This Instrument*, call'd the *Pedal* (because It is contriv'd to give *Varieties* with the *Foot*) I shall bestow a few Lines in making mention of, in regard It is not very commonly used, or known; because *Few make of Them Well*, and *Fewer* will go to the *Price of Them: Twenty Pounds* being the *Ordinary Price of One:* but the *Great Patron of Musick* in *His Time*, Sir *Robert Bolles* . . . had *Two of Them*, the one I remember at 30 l. and the other at 50 l. very *Admirable Instruments*. [N.B. This is a high price, when we recall that 8 years before Pepys had bought his spinet from Charles Haward for £5.]

This Instrument is in *Shape and Bulk* just like a *Harpsicon;* only It differs in the *Order* of *It*, Thus, *Viz.* There is made right underneath the *Keys*, near the *Ground*, a kind of *Cubbord*, or *Box*, which opens with a little *Pair* of *Doors*, in which *Box* the *Performer* sets *both his Feet*, resting them upon his *Heels*, (his *Toes* a little turning up) touching nothing, till such time as he has a *Pleasure* to employ them; which is after this manner, *viz.* There being right underneath his *Toes* 4 *little Pummels of Wood*, under *each Foot* 2, any one of *These* 4 he may *Tread* upon at his *Pleasure*; which by the *Weight of his Foot drives a Spring*, and so *Causeth the whole Instrument to Sound either Soft* or *Loud, according as he shall chuse to Tread any of them down;* (for without the *Foot* So us'd, *Nothing speaks*). The *out-side* of the *Right Foot* drives *One*, and the *In-side* of the Same *Foot* drives another; so that by treading his Foot a little awry, either outward or inward, he causeth a *Various Stop* to be heard, *at his Pleasure:* and if he claps down his Foot Flat, then he takes *Them both*, at the same time, (which is a 3d. *Variety*, and *Louder*).

Then has he ready, under his Left Foot, 2 other *Various Stops*, and by the like *Order* and *Motion* of the Foot, he can immediately give you 3 other Varieties, either *Softer* or *Louder*, as with the *Right Foot* before Mentioned, he did.

So that thus you may perceive he has several *Various Stops* at *Pleasure;* and all *Quick* and *Nimble*, by the *Ready Turn* of the Foot . . .

I caus'd one of *Them* to be made in my *House*, that has 9 several other *Varieties*, (24 in all) by reason of a *Stop* (to be *Slip'd* in with the *Hand*) which my Work-man calls the *Theorboe-Stop;* and indeed It is not much unlike It; But what It wants of a *Lute*, It has in Its own *Singular Prittiness*.

We had in those days *Choice Consorts*, fitted on purpose to suit with the *Nature of This Instrument*.

Hubb 1965, p. 147, has shewn that Mace's harpsichord was a single with 4 rows of jacks (2 unisons, a lute, and an octave—controlled by the 4 pedals—and a hand-operated buffstop).

The above paragraphs are important on several accounts. First, we are left in no doubt as to the nature of the instrument called *Pedal*, which is named freely in contemporary documents, though not described, for example, in a warrant dated 3 November 1664 'to pay John Hingeston . . . for repairing the organs, harpsichords, pedalls, and other instruments . . .' (*La*, p. 173). This is the earliest occurrence of the term I have found—twelve years before the publication of Mace, which sorts quite well with his words '*an Instrument* of a *Late Invention*'. Another warrant, dated 29 January 1668, is to 'pay John Hingeston . . . for strings for the pedals, harpsichords, and virginalls . . .' (*La*, p. 200). This leaves little doubt that they are instruments of the type described by Mace. Compare a 1671 warrant for 'strings for the base violl, pedals and harpsichords' [*La*, p. 231].

Thus it is not to be confused with the *Pedal* described by Adlung, which is a clavichord or harpsichord fitted with a pedal keyboard [*Adl*, § 596]:

Wir wandern endlich zum *Pedale*, . . . welches uns aber nicht lange aufhalten wird, weil das meiste mit dem Clavichorde, oder auch mit dem Clavicymbel, übereinkommt.

TABLE 15. *Surviving Instruments by Charles HAWARD*

No.	Date	Type	Kbs.	Signature	Owner/Remarks
1	1683	H	1	*Carolus Haward Londini 1683*	Yorkshire, Hovingham Hall, Sir William Worsley. 2×8′ stops; 4 roses. Many Italian influences.
2	1683	S	1	*Carolus Haward Fecit. 1683*	The Earl of Haddington. On loan to Victoria and Albert Museum until a few years ago. Soundboard signed underneath: *King 1886* [? workman to Taphouse who owned it then].
3	1684	S	1	*Carolus Haward 1684*	New York, Metropolitan Museum of Art. Illustrated in catalogue, 4 octaves and a 5th, G–D, with short octave. Rose. Length 4′ 6″.
4	1687	S	1	*Carolus Haward Fecit 1687*	Manchester. Former Boddington Collection. Black naturals, skunktail sharps. B–D, 4 octaves plus 3 notes.
5	1687	S	1		Leipzig. Heyer Collection. *Ks* (2, 672) lists 'Spinett von Haworth (Chas. Haward, London) 1687'.
6		S	1		Figured in *GD* (1940), s.v. *Spinet*. In Coventry 1946.
7(?)	—	V	1	[Nameboard missing]	Warrington Museum. Has keys alphabetically marked according to H's custom. G/B–F (55 keys). 5′ 9½″ × 1′ 7½″. Ebony naturals, ivory sharps. On jackrail: *Musica donum dei.*
8		S	1		Undated. Shewn at International Inventions Exhibition 1885 by the Revd. L. K. Hilton. Also shewn in Vienna 1892.
9		S	1		Manchester, Henry Watson Collection. Undated.
10		S	1	*Carolus Haward Fecit* [on nameboard]	Formerly Cirencester, C. A. Legg. G/B–C (50 keys). This instrument was lent to the Victoria and Albert Museum for some years about 1932; after which it was sold, and was later bought by Dr. W. H. Brazil. After his death it was sold at Johnson, Dymond's on 24 September 1947, and was bought by C. A. Legg of Cirencester, to whose father Edmund Legg it had once belonged. The soundboard, embellished with handsome decorations in ink, has a rose of wood and vellum. The keyboard is of pine, with ebony naturals, and ivory sharps, and the keys have fronts of embossed white paper. The bridge and nut have brass wire along the crown. The jacks are not original but date from the eighteenth century. The case is walnut, and the stand (probably original) of oak. On the wrestplank is an inscription which might be read as '1151'. The instrument is illustrated in the *Antique Collector*, London, 1937, p. 15. Length of back, 4′ 5″; greatest width, 1′ 10″; depth 7¼″. C. A. Legg sold the spinet to Howard Phillips, London about 1965.
11		S	1		Messrs. Partridge, New York, had a spinet by him in 1951.
12		S	1	[Signature on jackrail obliterated]	Location unknown. Mahogany case. G/B–F, nearly 5 octaves, lowest C sharp divided. Ebony naturals arcaded; ivory sharps. Elaborate marquetry.
13	—	S	1		Formerly property of William Dale. Depicted in *DEF*, II.
14	—	S	1	*C. H.* [but no normal signature]	Athelhampton, Dorset, R. V. Cooke (1965).

It is interesting to observe in passing that a clavichord with pedal-keyboard was known in the fifteenth century, being described by Paulus Paulirinus of Prague in his *Liber viginti artium*, *c.* 1460: 'Clavichordium . . . quo cum suo calcatorio datur magnum preambulum in studium organorum . . .'

The earliest picture of a pedal clavichord is in a MS. at Stuttgart containing Hugo von Reutlingen's *Flores musice*, which was written in 1464. The picture dates from the second half of the fifteenth century and is reproduced in *Jeans 1950*, also in *Handschin 1935*.

Mace implies that, although John Haward was the inventor of the pedal, other makers produced them (*Few make of them well*); and, to judge from references such as the above, they must have existed in considerable numbers; which makes it all the more singular that no example should have survived into modern times.

Indeed the paucity of extant English harpsichords of any kind earlier than the eighteenth century is remarkable. John Haward made the earliest certain one, dated 1622 and figured in *J* (p. 120), a handsome instrument but unfortunately only a shell; but the undated harpsichord bearing the repairer's signature Jesses Cassus (q.v.) is probably English work of about the middle of the seventeenth century.

Surviving Harpsichords by John Haward

(1) 1622. At Knole. Inscribed: *Johannes [H]a[w]ard fecit Londini MDCXXII.* (*Ri*, p. 401, misread the surname as 'Asard'.) Keyboard, jacks, and soundboard are gone. It originally had 1 keyboard and 3 sets of strings, but 2 pairs of choirs tuned to different pitches. *Hubb 1965*, pp. 140–2, describes the instrument in great detail. It is pictured at *J*, p. 120, in *Apollo* (March 1949) and *DEF* (Vol. 2, p. 375).

(3) **Thomas.** Virginal maker in London. Dates ascertained 1656–63. In 1656 he resided in Bishopsgate (*J*); in 1663 he was living in the parish of St. Giles Cripplegate (*Parish Reg.*).

He was probably the Thomas Haward or Howard who is recorded in *Join* as master of apprentices in 1650 and 1653. (He must be distinguished from the Thomas Howard (? Haward) who was admitted free of the Joiners' Company in 1657, and who may well have been a son of the well-known John Haward, q.v.)

HAXBY, Thomas. Spinet and harpsichord maker (also music seller) at The Organ, Blake Street, York. Born *c.* 1737; died 1796.

Son of Robert Haxby, a joiner. In 1756 he opened a shop in Blake Street, advertised thus in the *Yorkshire Courant*: 'Musical instruments at T. Haxby's warehouse Blake Street are made and sold.' Two years later he took up the freedom of the city of York as musical instrument maker. On 28 December 1770 he patented 'a new single harpsichord, containing all the stops of a double one, which by the use of one pedal only, produces every increase, diminution, and variation of tone that a double one is capable of performing . . . A single harpsichord of two unisons, octave, lute and harp, which by the use of one pedal only (which pedal has a connection with several sliding tumblers, springs, &c) produces ten variations of stops, also an increase and diminution of tone (either gradually or instantaneously) from the softest stop to the

TABLE 16. *Surviving Instruments by Thomas HAXBY*

No.	Date	Type	Kbs.	Signature	Owner/Remarks
1	1764	S	1	*Thomas Haxby York 1764*	London, Miss Joan Hassall. Shewn by Wm. Dale at International Inventions Exhibition 1885. Case of walnut (a thick mahogany varnish was removed in 1950). Sold at Sotheby's, 4 July 1947. Black naturals, white sharps. (Formerly owned by Raymond Barnett.)
2	1766	S	1	*Thomas Haxby York 1766*	I. N. Williams, who bought it at Sotheby's, 18 April 1968, from St. Michael's College, Tenbury. Formerly belonged to Sir F. G. Ouseley. Referred to by Hipkins in *GD* (1928), art. *spinet*. Ivory naturals; ebony sharps. Length 6′ 6″.
3	1772	H	1[?]	*Thomas Haxby York 1772*	Formerly Manchester, Boddington Collection. G–F, nearly 5 octaves, without lowest sharp. Walnut case, square legs.
4	1772	S	1		Dublin Museum.
5	1775	H	1	*Thomas Haxby York 1775*	Cleveland, Ohio, Theodore Cleveland, 1956– . Until 1956 belonged to Dr. J. Cameron Gibson, Monmouth. 2×8′, with buff added by R. Goble, Oxford, who repaired it in 1956; F–F, 5 octaves without low F sharp.
6	1777	H	1	*Thomas Haxby York 1777*	York, Castle Museum. 2×8′, 1×4′, buff, 1 pedal. F–F, 61 notes. Repaired by Robert Morley about 1962.
7		S	1		Mrs. Steinert, Beverly, Mass.

full harpsichord, or from the full harpsichord to the softest stop' [Patent no. 977].

He seems to have started advertising his patent a year later in the London press, e.g. the *St. James Chronicle or British Evening Post* and *Lloyds Evening Post and British Chronicle*, which carry notices in July 1771 to this effect:

> Harpsichords: His Majesty having granted his Royal Letters Patent to Thomas Haxby of York for his new invention of an improved single harpsichord he takes this method of acquainting the public that [here follows the same wording as the patent quoted] . . . to the softest stop. To which is added a swell in the lid. Price 35 guineas. These instruments (which have been approved by many Professors and Judges in Music) may be tried any time of the day at his Warehouse, near the Assembly Rooms, York; where may be had Chamber Organs, Upright harpsichords and all sorts of musical instruments, music, strings and every other article in the Musical Branch, Wholesale and Retale. Instruments repaired.

In 1760 and 1778 he did some work on the organ in York Minster, and, in 1767, on that in Leeds parish church. He made also violins and guitars, and later on pianos, besides selling and publishing music. Although he had a son, John, after his death his establishment in Blake Street was continued by Edward Tomlinson (brother-in law) and Thomas Tomlinson (nephew)—*not* by Samuel Knapton, who claimed to be Haxby's successor [*York Herald*, 5 November 1796]—until about 1840.

HAYDEN, Hans, *the Elder* [Heyden] of Nuremberg, *c.* 1540–1613. Organist at S. Sebald. Made clavichords, violins, etc. [*Va*].

About 1600 he invented the *Nürmbergisch Geigenwerck*, which is described in his *Commentatio de musicali instrumento* . . . (1605) and *Musicale instrumentum reformatum* (1610) [*Ge*, 1812]. He used steel and brass strings; otherwise his invention is the same as earlier *Gambenwerke*, i.e. a keyboard instrument in which the strings are not plucked but are set in vibration by bands or rotating discs.

Praetorius (p. 67) refers to it, giving much of Hayden's description, and illustrates it as Plate III of his *Theatrum instrumentorum*.

Kinsky has an account of Hayden in *ZfM*, Vol. 6, Heft 4/5, 1924.

Fé misdates his second treatise as 1620 and his death as 1623.

HÉART, Jehan, of Paris. *Fl.* 1578–1617 when he died. Organist of Saint-Jean-en-Grève and harpsichord maker [*Les*, *Verlet*].

HEERDINCK, Artus C. *See*: Gheerdinck, Artus.

HEETWOLF, Martinus. Harpsichord maker from 'Fredtborg in der Wetterau bij Frankfurt' [? Friedberg], *fl.* in Amsterdam 1635 [*Curtis*, p. 52].

HEHLEN, J. L. *See*: Hellen, J. L.

HEIJDEN, P. van der. *See*: Verheyden, P.

HEINEMANN, Johann J., of Antwerp. A blind harpsichord maker, dates ascertained, 1790–3; he also made lutes [*Gö*]. He restored a Van den Elsche (q.v.) harpsichord in 1790.

Surviving Harpsichords

(1) 1739. Brussels Conservatoire, Snoeck Collection. 2×8′ registers. Rose bears initials: *JJH*. Four octaves and 2 notes, with short octave. 180×73 cm. Inscribed: *Joannes Heinemann me fecit Ao 1793, Antverpiae*. This appears to be the latest surviving Flemish harpsichord.

HEINRICH, Johann Christoph. *Fl.* 1729 as a clavichord maker in Hamburg.

Surviving Clavichords

(1) 1729. Heimatmuseum at Stade, about 20 miles from Hamburg. Inscription on the soundboard: *Johan Christoph Heinrich / Auxit Ham: . . . 1729*. There is no sign of the instrument having been extended, as 'auxit' would suggest, so that we must interpret the word simply as 'constructed' (as we must also on Fleischer no. 1). Gebunden top 2 notes only [*Thoene*].—*see* Addenda and Corrigenda.

HELLEN, Johann Ludwig [*also* Hehlen]. Maker of harpsichords and pianos in Berne; *c.* 1716–81 [*Rindl*].

HELLER, Ambros. German clavichord maker. An inventory of 1626 records 'ein Clavicordium, so Ambr. Heller gemacht' [*Sit*, p. 47].

HEMSCH [*also* Hems *and probably* Echme]. Two harpsichord makers of this name lived in the rue Quincampoix, Paris, in the eighteenth century. They were brothers, born at Castenholz, near Cologne, and came to Paris about 1720.

I. **Henri,** or sometimes **Jean Henri.** Dates ascertained 1747–69, when he died [*MC*, pp. 109, 728, 28 September 1769]. He became *juré comptable* of the Guild of Instrument Makers in 1746 [Hardouin in *GSJ*, Vol. 13 (1960), p. 52]. From 1760 Henri worked with his nephew Jean Henri Moers (q.v.). In 1767, an ageing bachelor, he made his will; 2 years later he died.

(Jean Henri Echme (*fl.* 1759–67) from Cologne is presumably the same person. In 1759 he was expert for the inventory of Galland (q.v.), when he mentions his nephew Henri Moers who inherited his workshop [*Hubb 1965*].)

(*Pi*, p. 91, refers to a harpsichord of 1775 by J.-H. Hemsch as being shewn in Paris in 1889. He must have mistaken the date of it, as the maker had died 6 years before.)

Surviving Harpsichords

(1) 1751. Paris, Mme F. Moulinié, [*ClavHist*, where it is illustrated]. Inscribed: *Henri Hemsch Fait à Paris 1751* on the nameboard, and *Henri Hemsch* round the rose, with the initials *HH* in the rose. Two manuals; F–E, 60 notes. Still in its original state, this instrument may have been played by Rameau as Hemsch was tuner to M. de la Poplinière, whose protégé Rameau was.

(2) 1754. Paris, Claude Mercier-Ythier. Signed *Henri Hemsch* round the rose, and dated 1754 on the soundboard. Five octaves.

(3) 1756. Paris, C. Noisette de Crauzat. Signed *Henri Hemsch* round the rose, dated *1755* on the soundboard and *1756* on the bottom jack. Two manuals.

(4) 1756. Boston, Museum of Fine Arts. Inscribed: *Henri Hemsch 1756* (the 5 is not absolutely certain). Two manuals; 2×8′, 1×4′ stops; F–F, 60 notes. Rose with

initials: *HH*. Restored by Danti of Paris in 1888, which date appears on one key, and by Frank Hubbard of Waltham, Mass., in 1968. John Searles, the Boston collector who died *c.* 1921 bought it in Paris in the 1880s; his heirs lent it to the New England Conservatory of Music, which has lent it to the Museum of Fine Arts permanently. The arms of the Wittelsbach family of Bavaria carved on the stand and painted on the case point to its original owner.

(5) Date not known to me. Paris, private ownership. Restored by Tomasini in 1885 [*ClavHist*].

II. **Guillaume,** younger brother of Henri. *Fl.* 1748–76 [*GSJ*, Vol. 13 (1960), p. 52; *Pi*, p. 117]. Admitted to the Guild in 1748 and *juré comptable* of it in 1760. In 1759 he had married Marie Anne Offenheizer, daughter of a former Austrian officer.

Surviving Harpsichords

(1) Versailles, in private ownership. Two manuals; undated.

(2) 1763. Cherbourg, Magne Collection. Two manuals; 2×8′, 1×4′ stops; 5 octaves.

HENDRIKSZ, Maarten. Harpsichord maker in Amsterdam, 40 years of age in 1630 [*Curtis*, p. 52].

HENISCH. *See*: HEMSCH, of which it is a misreading.

HENNEFUS, J. L., junior, of Berlin. Clavichord maker, *fl.* 1802.

Surviving Clavichords

(1) 1802. Berlin Collection. Bundfrei, F–G, 5 octaves plus 2 notes. Inscription on nameboard: *J. L. Hennefus junior / à Berlin, 1802.*

HENOCQ, Louis. Harpsichord maker in the rue du chemin de Menilmontant, Paris. *Juré comptable* of the Guild in 1773; married, on 13 November 1783, Marie Marthe Françoise de Southieux; died 10 November 1790 [*Hardouin* in *GSJ*, Vol. 12 (1959), p. 83, where the inventory taken at his death is transcribed in full].

HENOCQ, Jacques, brother of the above. *Fl.* 1790 as 'maître luthier' [*Hubb*].

HENRICHINI, Augustin. Silesian harpsichord maker, *fl.* 1706. A harpsichord by him was exhibited in Bologna in 1888. Inscribed: *Augustinus Henrichini, Silesiensis, organifex et instrumentalis magister fecit mense Augusti anno MDCCVI.* (*Va* in his schedule, in another part of the work, wrongly gives the date in Arabic numerals as 1606.) It is now in the Musée Historique de Vandreuil, Quebec. Parchment rose.

HERMEL. *See*: ERMEL.

HERMES, Jean-Liborius. Parisian maker of harpsichords, and from 1777 onwards of pianofortes. Born at Paderborn, Westphalia. Dates ascertained, 1749–5 August 1813. In 1773 he married Thérèse-Victoire, a daughter of Jean Goermans the Elder, harpsichord maker (q.v.). He lived in the rue du Colombier from 1773 to 1783, and was living in the rue des Saints-Pères in 1788 [*Pi, Verlet*].

HERREMANS, Willem, of Antwerp. Harpsichord maker; figures in 1557 in the books of the Guild of St. Luke [*St*].

HERSTENBERG. A misreading of Gerstenberg (q.v.).

HERZ, Daniel. Organ builder of Innsbruck *fl.* 1653–78, when he died. A harpsichord made by him is recorded in an inventory of musical effects of the Arch-Duke Siegmund Franz of Austria taken in 1665: 'Ein Instrument mit unterschidlichen Registern, so der hiessige Orgelmacher Daniel Herz gemacht und auswendig grien angestrichen' [*Senn*, p. 337], also a 'spineta, darinnen zway claine spinetlin liegen'.

HESSEL. German instrument maker in St. Petersburg, 1785 [*Moos*]. May have made harpsichords.

HESSELIUS, Gustav. *Fl.* 1743 as spinet maker in Philadelphia [*ZIM*, Vol. 7, 1905–6, p. 122]. His name is given as 'Hasslinck' in *Schweiz. Musikzeitung*, Vol. 88/2, 1948, p. 48.

HEUSE, Johann Hermann, of Gimborn, near Cologne. Clavichord maker, *fl.* 1656.

Surviving Clavichords

(1) 1656. Liège, Albert van Zuylea. Inscribed on soundboard: *1656. Johannes. Hermannus. Heuse. in Gimborn.* Three octaves C–C gebunden. Top key inscribed: *J: P: Korte 1658* (first owner?). A second soundboard runs under the keys. Dimensions 129·2×37×12·6 cm. Bought in 1883 by Armand van Zuylen, of Antwerp. Badly restored by J. Bernard, Liège, in 1957 [*Nev*].

HEUSSLER, Urban. A German who made two 'Instrumente'—i.e. spinets or possibly harpsichords—in 1602 [*Monatshefte für Musik*, 1876].

HEVILEZ, Johan de. Clavichord maker in Antwerp, 1561 [*St*].

HEYDEN, Hans. *See*: HAYDEN, Hans, *the Elder*.

HEYER, Frederick. Organ builder of New York City, *fl.* 1773; also made and repaired harpsichords and spinets [*Diapason*, 1 March 1957, article by Maurer].

HICKS, Peter. English clavichord maker; *fl. c.* 1720.

Surviving Clavichords

(1) *c.* 1720. Victoria and Albert Museum, London. Gebunden. Inscription on nameboard: *Peter Hicks fecit.* C–D, 4 octaves and 2 notes. Black naturals and white sharps. Bent line of wrestpins. Mahogany case. 4′ 1″×14″. The lowest 9 tangents have leather tops which appear to be original; at any rate keys 2 to 6 and 8 have never had conventional tangents—cf. *Hirt*, p. 321 for a 5-octave clavichord with leather-topped tangents in the bass, also s.v. *Oesterlin* below. The transition from leather to brass in the Hicks is almost imperceptible tonally, and the arrangement is certainly a success. Illustrated in *J*, p. 94. (N.B. This is the only known early English clavichord extant. Some have doubted its genuineness.) Bequeathed by Dr. Lea Southgate.

HIERONYMUS, *Bononiensis*, i.e. Jerome of Bologna. Harpsichord maker, *fl.* at Rome, 1521. The references in *Cor* and *Bq* are probably to Zenti, q.v.

Surviving Instruments

(1) 1521. London, Victoria and Albert Museum. Harpsichord inscribed on nameboard *Hieronymus Bononiensis faciebat Romae MDXXI*. Length 6′ 3″, in outer case covered with finely tooled leather. Boxwood keys, arcaded. 1 manual, 2×8′ stops (originally 1×8′). The present keyboard originally belonged to another instrument and was C/E–F but was cut down to C/E–D to make it fit. A scribed line on the wrestplank ends 2 pins short of the top, suggesting that there were originally 45 notes, so that the original compass was probably C/E–C or F–F, without low F sharp and G sharp (cf. Antegnato no. 1). The slides are from another instrument, having a more angled jackline than Hieronymus, and the jacks are not original. See further, *Hubb 1965*, p. 5. Illustrated at *J*, p. 114, in *RussellV&A*, and in *Wint 1966*. The earliest surviving dated harpsichord.

HIERONYMUS DE ZENTIS. *See*: Zenti, Girolamo.

HILBERG. A harpsichord by him was offered for sale in *The World*, 27 March 1788 [*J*].

HILDEBRAND, Zacharias, of Münsterberg (Silesia), 1688–1757 [*Hirt*]. An organ builder, at one time the favourite pupil of Gottfried Silbermann. He also made (*c.* 1740) a *Lautenklavizymbel* (a gut-strung harpsichord) according to the ideas of J. S. Bach. *Adl* (II, 139) describes this instrument. It had 2×8′ registers of gut, and an octave register of brass wire; and was shorter in length than the normal harpsichord. This instrument must not be confused with the *Nürmbergisch Geigenwerck* and others of this type—e.g. the 'arched viall' mentioned by Pepys (5 October 1664), and Roger Plenius's *lyrichord*—in which the strings were not plucked but set in vibration by resined wheels. Burney in 1773 refers to one Hildebrand as 'the best harpsichord maker of Berlin'. But this may have been his son Johann Gottfried Hildebrand, organ builder, who *fl.* 1740 and died 1775 [*MarcP*]. See further 'Bach's "Lauten Werck"', by H. Ferguson, in *ML*, Vol. 48 (1967), pp. 259–64.

HILL, Henry. Spinet maker; baptized in St. Botolph without Cripplegate, London, 6 July 1715, the son of Henry Hill, weaver [*Parish Reg.*]. Apprenticed to John Ladyman 30 March 1731; free of the Joiners' Company, 2 April 1745 [*Join*].

The *H. H.* on the bottom and top keys of a spinet by Joseph Mahoon (q.v.) dated 1748 may be the initials of this maker. The Geffrye Museum, Kingsland Road, London, E.C., has a large ottavino spinet by him. The nameboard is missing, but the bottom key is signed *H. Hill 1750 Fricker 27* (the latter being presumably the workman's name and instrument number); and the top key *H. Hill 1750*. The case is of walnut. Pine keyboard, with ivory naturals with arcaded fronts, and rosewood sharps. Compass 4 octaves and 2 notes, C–D, plus 1 note in the bass presumably tuned to G.

HILLIAR, William, *fl.* 1733 in London. He worked at this time for Thomas Hitchcock the Younger (q.v.), on one of whose spinets his signature appears.

HIMMENRAET, Michele. *See*: Immenraet, Michel.

HINGSTON, John [Hingeston]. Died in Westminster near London in the year 1683. He should perhaps be mentioned here since he held the office of 'keeper and repayrer of his majesty's organs, pedalls, harpsichords and other instruments', although he may never himself have made an instrument. The Lord Chamberlain's accounts refer to him frequently. For instance on 29 May 1670 there is a warrant to pay him £56. 16*s*. 'for stringing and repairing the harpsichords . . . for strings for the . . . virginalls'. Again, 3 years later, 'for repairing and mending two harpsichords for the practise of the private musick in the Great Hall, £1–10–0. For repairing and amending two harpsichords and carrying them to the playhouse, £0–10–0' [*La*, pp. 173, 223, 229].

It is interesting to find the composer Henry Purcell in 1673, as a boy of 14, admitted as 'keeper, maker, mender, repayrer and tuner of the regalls, organs, virginalls, flutes and recorders . . . without fee . . . and assistant to John Hingston, and upon the death or other avoydance of the latter, to come in ordinary with fee'. Hingston died in 1683, and early in the following year Purcell succeeded him at a wage of £60 per annum [*La*, pp. 255, 364].

A portrait of Hingston was lent by Oxford University to the International Inventions Exhibition in 1885 [*Cat*, p. 25]. It is now in the Music Faculty.

HINRICHINI, A. *See*: Henrichini, Augustin.

HINRICHS, Johann Peter. Attained on 8 January 1796 to the citizenship of the city of Hamburg. He made harpsichords and pianofortes [*Ge*, *Lü*]. Born at Billwärder-Moorfleth 1765; died Hamburg 1848. See *Schultze 1957*.

HITCHCOCK. A family of spinet and harpsichord makers in London in the seventeenth and eighteenth centuries. Three members of the family would appear, from surviving instruments, to be known to us as makers.

(N.B. The Hitchcock makers have normally been regarded as 2—numbers 2 and 3 in the present article. Burney, writing in Rees's *Cyclopaedia* s.v. *spinet*, held this view. But spinets 1 and 2 below presuppose an elder Thomas Hitchcock. This is confirmed by *Join*.)

(1) **Thomas Hitchcock,** *the Elder*. Dates ascertained, 1660–1700. He died before February 1700 [*Join*]. He was a freeman of the Haberdashers' Company. See spinets 1–3 below.

(2) **Thomas Hitchcock,** *the Younger*. A son of the above. Born about 1685, since he was apprenticed to Benjamin Slade from 13 February 1700 for 8 years. He took up the freedom of the Haberdashers' Company by patrimony, in preference to becoming free of the Joiners' Company, in 1715 [*J*, p. 31]. Latest date ascertained, 1733.

(N.B. *J* (p. 70) gives this maker's earliest date as 1690, but does not note the evidence for it. If it is based on the style of the harpsichord in the Victoria and Albert Museum it is probably far from correct, for this harpsichord would appear to be some 20 years later than 1690.)

While still apprenticed to Slade he apparently did some work for Edward Blunt or at least used him as his retailer; for the first jack of a spinet formerly in the Taphouse Collection, ostensibly by Blunt, is inscribed: *Thos. Hitchcock No. 54—1703* [*J*, p. 65 n.].

The date of his death is not known, but it probably occurred some years later than 1733; for his spinet numbered 1425 was made in that year, and an instrument by him numbered 1547 has survived.

(3) **John Hitchcock** almost certainly son of (2). Earliest date known, 1743; he died in 1774 [*J*].

In 1750 he was admitted by patrimony to the Company of Haberdashers [*J*]. In 1761 his harpsichords and spinets are commended by John Arnold (quoted above under John Crang).

From *Un* we know that in 1763 he was living in Fetter Lane, at the corner of Dean Street. A watch-rate book gives the number of the house as 28 [*J*].

A painting *c.* 1765 by Allan Ramsay of Queen Charlotte with the Prince of Wales and the Duke of York (now in Buckingham Palace) depicts a Hitchcock spinet.

The announcement of his death on 23 November 1774, quoted by *J* [p. 31] from the *General Evening Post*, tells us that he was one of the common councilmen for Farringdon Without.

On 16 December 1774 administration of the property of 'John Hitchcock late of the parish of St. Andrew Holborn . . . was granted to Frances Hitchcock widow, relict of the said deceased' by the Prerogative Court of Canterbury.

A small-scale sketch in red crayon by Sir James Thornhill (1675–1734) of a scene shewing Apollo and the Muses (reproduced in *Russell 1959* as plate 62), formerly in the H. S. Reitlinger Collection, is at the Fitzwilliam Museum, Cambridge (Sotheby's, 26 May 1954). It is outlined in ink in the shape of a harpsichord lid, $5\frac{1}{2} \times 13\frac{1}{2}''$. Below is written in an eighteenth-century hand: 'Mr. Handel has or had the Harpsichord this design was made for.' The artist's name appears in pencil in the bottom left-hand corner: *Jas. Thornhill.*

The shape of the instrument suggests that it may have been a Hitchcock.

See table of surviving Hitchcock instruments.

TABLE 17. *Surviving HITCHCOCK Instruments*

My no.	Type	Case no.	Date	Workman's name	Past owners	Present owner	Remarks
Thomas the Elder							
1	S		1660		Capt. Beaumont		Shewn by Capt. B. at the Loan Exhibition, London, 1900.
2	S		1664				*J* (p. 65) refers to a spinet, ostensibly by Blunt but signed on the first key: *Thos. Hitchcock his make in 1664.*
	S		1700		Howard Head		Shewn by H. H. at the Loan Exhibition, London, 1900. This instrument must have been finished in January 1700, as Thomas I was dead by February [*Join*].
Thomas the Younger							
4	S		1703		Oxford, Taphouse Collection		Ostensibly by Blunt, but the first jack is signed: *Thos. Hitchcock no. 54—1703.*
	S	511	—	*J. J.* [on lowest key]		Private ownership, England (1955)	Inscribed on nameboard: *Thomas Hitchcock Londini fecit.*
5a	S	1060	—	*James is 2* [on front edge of wrestplank]		In 1966 owned by Norman Benz, Eastbourne	Inscribed on nameboard: *Thomas Hitchcock Londini fecit No. 1060.* G–G, 5 octaves. Length 5′ 10″, maximum width 2′ $2\frac{1}{2}''$. Restored by Kent. Modern stand.
5b	S	1075	n.d.	*James is 9* [on lowest key]		Formerly the property of the late Sir Eldred Hitchcock (1960) possibly a descendant of the maker. Now (1965) the property of his daughter-in-law Mrs. E. A. Hitchcock, Dulwich	G–G, 5 octaves. Skunktail sharps; bone arcaded naturals; 7′ 2″×3′ 2″; offered at Sotheby's 20 December 1957 and again 11 March 1960. Repaired by Messrs. Robt. Morley, 1965.
6	H	—	—	*James is Harpsichord* [on bottom key of both keyboards]	Mrs. Luard-Selby. (For many years at Ightham Mote, Kent)	Victoria and Albert Museum, London	2 man. Illustrated in *J*, p. 124. Exhibited 1885. Curved tail. *Hubb 1965*, pp. 154–5, describes this harpsichord in detail, but misreads the inscriptions on the lowest keys.
6a	S	1143	—			New York, French & Co. (1955)	Inscribed: *Thomas Hitchcock Londini fecit.*
7	S	1193	—		Bought by Graham Baron Ash at Christie's in 1926. Mr. Baron Ash gave Packwood House and its furniture to the National Trust 1941	Packwood House, Warwicks. (National Trust)	
8	S	1228	—			Smithsonian Institution, Washington	Inscribed on jackrail: *Acti labores sucundi* [sic].

TABLE 17 (*cont.*):

My no.	Type	Case no.	Date	Workman's name	Past owners	Present owner	Remarks
8a	S	1241	—		Goodrich Court; Raymond Russell	Edinburgh University	Illustrated in *RussColl.*
9	S	1243	—	[Inscribed: *Thomas Hitchcock, Londini fecit no 1243*]	Mrs. G. H. Potter; sold (by auction) in Edinburgh, winter 1954/5	J. Barnett, The Grotto, Tettenhall, Staffs. (1961); he bought it from a man in Harrogate	
9a	S	1279	1729	[On top key]: *Tho no 20*; [On bottom key] *Jo J fecit*	Arnold Dolmetsch in the 1890s; Mr. and Mrs. Louis Davis (*c.* 1900–70)	Graham Wilton, Watford (1970–)	Inscribed on nameboard: *Thomas Hitchcock Londini fecit No. 1279*; on back of nameboard *No. 1279* and *20* (both in pencil); on the keybed: *AD 1729* [sic], applied in black with a brush. G–G, 5 octaves. Skunktail sharps. Jacks not original (perhaps by Dolmetsch). The date is odd seeing that the number is 1279. Did Hitchcock have the instrument back for overhaul in 1729 and only then put the date on it?
9b	S	1287	—			Smithsonian Institution, Washington	Illustrated in *Wash 1969*.
10	S	1335	—	*Tho. 8.*	Arthur F. Hill	Sulgrave Manor	*Thomas Hitchcock Londini fecit*. Curved tail.
11	S	1379	1710	*Tho. 65*		Broadwood & Sons Ltd.	Exhibited 1885, 1904.
11a	S	1396	—		Sir Somerville Gurney	Given by him to King's Lynn Museum	*Thomas Hitchcock Londini fecit No. 1396*.
12	S	1425	1733	*Tho. 9*. Also *Wm. Hilliar* (signed on top key)	Wm. Barrow, Llandudno	U.S. Ambassador Middendorf, The Hague, (Sotheby's, 21. 12. 1972).	Dated 1733 on top key. Straight tail. Skunktail sharps. Offered for sale at Sotheby's, 21 December 1972.
13	S	1444	—	*James's No. 10* (appears in several places inside the instrument)	J. Southall (the pre-Raphaelite painter)	R. Newton who sold it at Sotheby's, 27 November 1969, for £1,400 to F. R. Rubens	Repaired by Arnold Dolmetsch Ltd. in 1947.
14	S	1460	—		Sterndale-Bennett; T. Case		Exhibited 1885. Probably the spinet owned in 1956 by T. G. Odling, London.
15	S	1484	—	*James No. 4*. Inscription: *Thomas Hitchcock Londini fecit 1484*		Victoria and Albert Museum. (On loan to Aberdeen Art Gallery)	
16	S	1518	—	*Emanuel No. 2*. Inscription: *Thomas Hitchcock Londini fecit No. 1518*	Drexel	New York Metropolitan Museum of Art, Crosby Brown Collection	Illustrated in catalogue.
17	S	1547	—			Dr. Black, Birmingham	The highest number yet discovered of Thomas.
18	S				Steinert Collection	Present location unknown	
19	S		—	Inscription: *Thomas Hitchcock Londini fecit*	Sir Charles Lawes-Wittewronge, Bt., Rothamsted		Sold at Christies, 14 May 1936, to Permain, perhaps acting for W. R. Hearst.
20	S	—	—	Inscription: *Thomas Hitchcock Londini fecit*		Williamson's of Guildford (1937). Advertised in *Connoisseur*, May 1937, XXIV (illus.)	5 octaves G–G.
20a	S	—	—	Inscription on nameboard: *Thomas Hitchcock Londini fecit*			Roger Warner (1969), Burford, but on loan to the Faculty of Music, Oxford. Arcaded naturals (white), skunktail sharps, 61 pinewood keys. Modern jacks; original stand. Pencilled restorer's inscription on front edge of wrestplank: *Rep. V. K. Deutsch Bern März 1954*. Previously in private ownership in Switzerland, having been bought about 1920 from Messrs. Williamson, antique dealers, Guildford.
John							
21	H			*Sam's No. 3*	Lyme Park, Cheshire; Henry Ford Museum, Dearborn, Mich., but lost in 1972		Two manuals; 2×8′, 1×4′. Repaired by Hugh Gough, 1954. ('Sam' may be Samuel Blumer, q.v.)

TABLE 17 (*cont.*):

My no.	Type	Case no.	Date	Workman's name	Past owners	Present owner	Remarks
22	S	1520				Winterthur Museum, Delaware, U.S.A.	Inscribed: *Johannes Hitchcock fecit Londini 1520*. Restored 1968 by Pro Musica, Annapolis, who found inside a label showing it had been repaired in 1892 by R. H. Breitenstein & Son, 80 Richmond St., Providence R.I.
22a	S	1570	1756 (?)	*Sam's No. 12* [back of nameboard]		Robt. E. Lee Memorial Foundation, Stratford Hall, Westmoreland Co., Va.	Inscribed: *Johannes Hitchcock me fecit Londini 1570*. Seen by Pro Musica Inst. Co., Annapolis, Md., December 1968.
23	S	1625		*No. 13* [on bottom and top keys]	O. V. Watney, Cornbury Park, Charlbury	Harold Cox, Great Missenden, bought 1967 at Christie's for £850	Mentioned by *J*, p. 124. Nameboard inscribed *Johannes Hitchcock fecit Londini 1625*.
24	S	1630		*Sam's No. 21*	W. Dale		Exhibited 1885. Illustrated in *Connoisseur*, July–December 1939, p. 93.
25	S	1676			G. F. Handel who gave it to A. G. Leahmon (Lemon); A. J. Hipkins	Royal College of Music, London. (Given by Edith Hipkins in 1903)	*Johannes Hitchcock Londini fecit 1676* [on nameboard]. G–G, 5 octaves; ivory naturals arcaded, skunktail sharps. Round tail. Illustrated in *Hi*; Exhibited 1904.
26	S	1677		*Sam 28* [. . . illegible]		Dearborn, Mich., Ford Museum	Wrestplank stamped *29*. Inscribed: *Johannes Hitchcock fecit 1677*.
27	S	2012		*Backus No. 8*	at Chipping Campden		'Highest number yet discovered' (*J*, p. 124). Shewn at the Antique Dealers' Fair, 1961. Belonged (1962) to Messrs. M. Harris, 44 New Oxford Street, London. Repaired by Robt. Morley, 1962. ('Backus' may well be Americus Backers, q.v.)
28	S				C. Claudius	Copenhagen, Musikhistoriska Museet	Illustrated in catalogue.
29	S			*Culliford No. 10*	M. Steinert	Yale University	Illustrated in catalogue (1893). Restored by Lotta van Buren in 1928.
30	S				C. T. Crewes of London in 1905		
31	S			*Culliford No. 12*	Searles, Methuen, Mass.	N. Andover, U.S.A., D. Rowland	5 octaves G–G; inscribed on nameboard: *Johannes Hitchcock Londini fecit*.
Hitchcock (not known which)							
32	S						Location unknown. About 1948 belonged to Albert Schumacher of Jackson Heights, New York.
33	S						May well be a Hitchcock instrument, but maker's name (if any) on nameboard has been covered by *c.* 1800 paintwork. The number *1007* on back of nameboard is probably within the last 100 years. Owned (1966) by Peter Davies of Enborne, Newbury.

HOENEL. *See*: HAEHNEL.

HOFFMANN. A harpsichord maker living in the rue Quincampoix, Paris, towards the end of the eighteenth century [*Verlet*].

HOFFMANN, Christian Gotthelf. Clavichord maker of Ronneburg, *fl.* 1763–84.

Surviving Clavichords

(1) 1763. Leipzig, Heyer Collection. Inscribed: . . . *Hoffmann* / . . . [*Instru*]*ment*/[*macher in Ronn*]*eburg* / . . . [*Anno*] *1763*. Compass 4 octaves. See *Ks*, p. 42.

(2) 1784. Yale University, Belle Skinner Collection. Inscribed: *S. D. G. Christian Gotthelf Hoffmann in Ronneburg. Nom: 1784*. Compass 5 octaves F–F. Former locations: Todhunter Collection, and subsequently Arnold Dolmetsch.

HOFFMANN, Johann Wilhelm. Born at Desmannsdorf near Anspach, 11 February 1764; died on 23 September 1809 at Anspach. He assisted Chr. Gottl. Hubert (q.v.) from 1789 until his death in 1793, when he took over his workshop and title of 'Hochfürstlich Anspachischer Hof-Instrumenten-Bauer' [*Ks*]. A grand pianoforte dated 1798 by him is in the Rück Collection, Germanisches Nationalmuseum, Nuremberg.

HOFMANN. Organ and instrument maker in Gotha, 1779. He built a large 'doppeltes Klavizymbel' with

2 keyboards at each end. This could be played either by a player at each end, or by one player using a keyboard-coupler. The Duke of Saxony bought the instrument [*Ko, Fé, Wa*].

HOFMANN, Ferdinand, *c.* 1756–1829. Viennese keyboard-instrument maker, chiefly known for his pianofortes.

Surviving Clavichords

(1) Undated. Historisches Museum, Vienna. A handwritten label inside the case, to the left, reads: *Ferdinand Hofmann / bürgl: Orgel- und Instru-/mentmacher, wohnt bei 3 / Hufeisen nächst dem Getreid-/markte No. 28.* The initials *JE* on an oval plaque on the nameboard are presumably those of an owner. Bundfrei; F–G, 5 octaves and 2 notes. Said to have been played by Haydn. Given by J. V. Widmann to Brahms who kept it in his house in Vienna (Karlsgasse 4). It passed to the Museum in 1914 with the greater part of Brahms's estate [*Walter*, p. 286; see also *Ks*, p. 232].

HOHLFELD, Johann. Born at Hennersdorf in Saxony in 1711 and died in 1771. Originally an assistant at lace making, he later worked as a craftsman in Berlin, where he became known on account of 3 inventions:

(1) A machine to be connected to a harpsichord and to take down the improvisations of composers. This was submitted to the Berlin Academy in 1752. But the problem was apparently not fully solved, and the Academy only praised the skilled workmanship of the individual parts of the machine [*Ko, Lü, Fé*].

A similar machine had been devised, slightly earlier, by Johann Friedrich Unger (1716–81). Indeed Adlung refers to Hohlfeld as the perfecter of Unger's invention [*AdlG*, 2nd edition, p. 691]. A workable device for this purpose is found on the harpsichord/piano by Merlin (q.v.) in the Deutsches Museum, Munich.

(2) The *Bogenflügel*, a gut-strung instrument after the fashion of Hayden's Geigenwerk. This was played to Frederick the Great in 1754. C. P. E. Bach observes: [*Versuch* . . . 2. Aufl., 1762. II. 1] 'Es ist schade, dass die schöne Erfindung des Hohlfeldischen Bogenclaviers noch nicht gemeinnützig geworden ist; man kann dahero dessen besondere Vorzüge hierinnen noch nicht genau bestimmen.' F. W. Marpurg refers to it in his *Anleitung zum Clavierspielen* (1755).

(3) A register-changing pedal for harpsichords which, according to C. P. E. Bach's *Versuch über die wahre Art das Klavier zu spielen*, II. 245, made it possible to bring on all the registers by light foot-pressure while playing.

HÖHNEL. *See*: HÄHNEL.

HOLLISTER, Thomas. Dublin harpsichord maker. Dates ascertained, 1728–75 [*Fld, J*].

HOLLISTER, William Castell. Harpsichord maker in Dublin. *Fl.* 1762–99. See *Teahan* for addresses and dates.

HONGARO. *See*: FRANCISCUS *Patavinus*.

HOPKINSON. Francis. Born Philadelphia 21 September 1737; died there 9 May 1791; composer, and signatory of the Declaration of Independence. Accounts of his experiments with the quilling of harpsichords appear in the *Transactions of the American Philosophical Society*, Philadelphia, 1786, pp. 185–94, and in his *Miscellaneous Essays* . . ., Philadelphia, 1792, pp. 286–92. Reprinted in *Russell 1959*.

Ri (p. 82) refers to a 'Franz Hopkinson' resident in Paris in 1788 and experimenting with harpsichord plectra. He was doubtless thinking of Francis Hopkinson.

HOPTON, Heming. *See*: LOCKTON, Heming.

HORN, Christian August, of Dresden. Son of Gottfried Joseph Horn; made clavichords and pianofortes [*Hirt*].

HORN, Gottfried Joseph, 1739–97 [*Hirt*]. Miller and instrument maker. Born at Nickern near Dresden; died 25 December 1797. He came into possession of the tools, plans, etc. of Schwarze, who before his death had worked for many years with Silbermann in Strasbourg. This stimulated him to take up instrument making, and in 1772 he completed his first clavichord. Between then and 1795 he made 464 clavichords which had a great reputation for silvery tone and would seem to have maintained the Silbermann tradition [*Ge*, 1812]. He was called 'Senior' to distinguish him from his younger brother, Johann Gottlob. He devoted his attention chiefly to clavichords, but made a few pianos besides. (Gerber's statement: 'Nach Privatnachrichten . . . war dieser fleissiger Mann 1796 schon nicht mehr am Leben' was mistaken.) See *Ks*, p. 232.

HORN, Johann Gottlob, 1748–96. Younger brother of the above. From his youth he shewed a great enthusiasm for instrument making; and his father had him taught joinery by Keitel in Dresden. In 1771 he went to Augsburg to work with the famous Stein, and stayed there for 2 years. Then he went on to Friederici in Gera to perfect his craftsmanship, and on his advice settled in Dresden in 1779 and began to make clavichords, harpsichords, and pianos. (He worked with Mack here for a time.) His first clavichord here was bought by Count Reuss of Koestritz, who was then in power. By 1795 he had sold 556 instruments. His prices were: clavichords, 30 thalers; pianofortes, 100; harpsichords, 200. On his death in 1796 his pupil Carl Renzsch took over his workshop [*Ge*, 1814; *Ks*, p. 232]. See table of Horn instruments (table 18).

HÖTZEL, Peter. German clavichord maker, *fl.* 1804.

Surviving Clavichords

(1) 1804. Berlin Collection. Gebunden; C–F, 4½ octaves. Zigzag bridge. Label on soundboard: *Verfertigt von Peter Hötzelbürgl. Orgel und Instrument / behaust / zu/ Steyer Gersten* [?] / *1804 März.*

HOUSTON & CO. Spinet and harpsichord makers (best known as piano makers), 54 Great Marlborough Street, London. (Their establishment here must have been rented by them, since their names do not appear in the rate-books [*RB.J*].)

TABLE 18. *Surviving Instruments by the HORN Family*

No.	Date	Type	Signature	Owner/Remarks
Gottfried Joseph Horn (1739–96)				
1	1785	Cd	*Gefertiget / Gottfried Joseph Horn senior / in Nickern b. Dresden 1785 / Das 150 te*	Leipzig University, Heyer Collection. F–G, 5 octaves and 2 notes. 2 roses 171 × 51 cm. Inscription reproduced in *Ks*.
2	1790	Cd	*Gottfried Joseph Horn Nick[ern], 1790*	Munich, Deutsches Museum. Compass 5 octaves. Bundfrei; signature on original soundboard, now replaced by a modern one. (The date has also been reported to me as 1796.)
2a		Cd		Berlin, Dr. Walter Thoene. Compass F–G, 5 octaves plus 1 note; 2 roses in soundboard identical with those in no. 5. The owner ascribes it, beyond doubt, to Gottfried Joseph Horn. Size: 170 × 53 cm.
Johann Gottlob Horn (1748–96)				
3	1775	Cd	[Horn & Mack]	Boston Museum of Fine Arts (formerly F. W. Galpin's Collection). Shewn at Music Loan Exhibition, London, 1904. Made at Dresden in collaboration with Mack.
3a	1789	Cd	*No. 292 Johan Gottlob Horn Instrumentmacher in Dresden d. 10 February 1789.*	Copenhagen. Musikhistoriska Museet. Inscription on nameboard. Compass F–G, 5 octaves plus 1 note; 2 roses, without initials. Former owner: the Danish singer Mrs. Ina Lange (1846–1930). Given to the Museum in 1930.
4	1791	Cd	*No. 380 Johan Gottlob Horn Instrumentmacher in Dresden 1791.*	Formerly Lucerne, Schumacher Collection. Probably = the 1791 Horn clavichord now (1968) owned by Louis Sauteur of Fribourg, who received it from his teacher Professor Leo Kathriner who died 1964 [*Rindl*]. Compass F–G, 5 octaves plus 1 note; size 170 × 50 × 19·5 cm.
5	1793	Cd	*No. 482 / Johann Gottlob Horn / Instrumentmacher / in Dresden 1793.*	Berlin, Dr. Walter Thoene (1965). Compass F–A, 5 octaves plus 2 notes. 2 roses in soundboard. Size: 170 × 51·3 cm.
6(?)	—	Cd		One of the 6 unsigned clavichords in the Sammlung Neuner, Munich, is very probably by Horn. It is virtually identical, in essentials, with 2 above.

Earliest and latest dates known: 1790–4. The firm is recorded in J. Doane's *Musical Directory* (London, 1794). *See* L. G. Langwill in *Music and Letters*, London, January 1949.

A small clavichord signed *Houston & Co. Londini fecit* on the nameboard, 4-octave keyboard C–C, white naturals and black sharps, 3′ 9½″ × 1′ 3½″, came up for sale at Sotheby's on 13 July 1962.

HOVEN, Lucas van. Harpsichord maker in Amsterdam, *fl.* 1616 in which year he was 'about 22 years of age'. He was a nephew of Artus Gheerdinck, q.v. [*Curtis*, p. 52].

HOWARD, Hans [*also* Hauert]. Swiss harpsichord maker; 1730–1800; elder brother of Joseph Howard [*Rindl*].

HOWARD, Johann [*also* Hauert]. Son of Hans Hauert; Swiss maker of harpsichords, etc.; born 1757 [*Rindl*].

HOWARD, Joseph. Born Wengi bei Büren (Canton Bern) 1749; died Bern 1824. Originally surnamed 'Hauert', he called himself 'Howard' from 1795 onwards.

He is known chiefly as a pianoforte maker; but in the *Berner Adressbuch* for 1810 he appears as 'Facteur de clavecins et Forté-pianos'. See further *Hirt*, p. 474.

HOWARD, Thomas. *See*: HAWARD, Thomas.

HUBERT, Christian Gottlob, [Huber], 1714–93. Born at Fraustadt (Wschowa) in Poland. *Ge* says of him:

> Orgel- und Instrumentenmacher bey der Kapelle zu Anspach, geb. zu Fraustadt in Polen 1714; kam im Jahr 1740 nach Bayreuth in Fürstl. Dienste und 1769 mit der Kapelle nach Anspach. Seine Arbeiten, sowohl selbst erfundene als verbesserte Klaviere, Flügel, und Pianoforte werden sehr gesucht, theuer bezahlt und zum Theil nach Frankreich, England und Holland versendet.

See table of his instruments (table 19).

The surviving clavichords of Hubert justify Gerber's favourable account of them. He died at Ansbach, nearly 80 years of age, in 1793. His workshop and title were taken over by Johann Wilhelm Hoffmann, 1764–1809, who had been his assistant since 1789.

J. G. Meusel has some interesting remarks to make about Hubert (*Miscellaneen artistischen Inhalts*, Heft 27, Erfurt, 1756, p. 137):

. . . He is famous far and wide not only for his good clavichords and pianofortes, durable and of the most beautiful tone . . . but also for other instruments and for his building of the organ in the Catholic *Bethaus* at Anspach. His pianofortes have already been sent as far as France, England and Holland; and although they are not as expensive as the English ones, they are very little inferior to them. A typical clavichord costs 3 Carolins. On the other hand he makes pianofortes for 20 to 25 Carolins. He is a very small man of a quiet and noble nature, though at the same time somewhat choleric and headstrong; in his work he is uncommonly accurate and exact . . .

His name is sometimes spelt 'Huber'. See further *Krautwurst*. *Va* lists him erroneously as Hubert, Christiano-Gottlob.

See table 19 for a list of Hubert instruments.

TABLE 19. *Surviving Clavichords by Christian Gottlob HUBERT*

No.	Date	Signature	Owner/Remarks
01	1761		Neuwied/Rh., private ownership. Made in Bayreuth in 1761.
02	1763	*Christian Gottlob Hubert / Hof-Orgel und Instrumentenmacher in Bayreuth fecit Ao: 1763.*	Nuremberg, Rück Collection in the Germanisches Nationalmuseum (formerly Klinkerfuss, Stuttgart). Bundfrei.
03	1765		Nuremberg, Germanisches Nationalmuseum. Destroyed in World War II. Bundfrei.
04	1771		Nuremberg. Rück Collection in the Germanisches Nationalmuseum. Bundfrei.
1	1772	*Christian Gottlob Hubert, Hochfürstl. Anspachischer Hof Orgel u. Instrumentenbauer in Bayreuth anno 1772.*	Freiburg i. Br. Univ., Musikwiss. Seminar. (Formerly Paul de Wit, Leipzig, in 1892. Illustrated in *Perlen aus der Instrumentensammlung von Paul de Wit*, 1892.) 5⅓ octaves F–A, bundfrei. 159×42 cm.
2	1776	*Chr. Gottl. Huber / fecit Ao.: 1776.*	Berlin, Collection. Gebunden, C–F, 4½ octaves. Destroyed in World War II.
3	177?	*Christian Gottlob Hubert / Hochfürstl. Anspachisch. Bayreuthischer / Hoff-Orgel und Instrumenten Bauer / fecit Ao: 177. . Anspach.*	Leipzig, Heyer Collection. F–A, 5 octaves and a 3rd, bundfrei.
4	1782	*Christian Gottlob Hubert / Hochfürstlischer Hof-/ Instrumentenmacher Fecit Ao. 1782.*	Berlin Collection. C–F, 4½ octaves, gebunden. Case and stand of pine, painted white, with yellow decoration in rococo style.
5	1782	*Christian Gottlob Huber Hochfürstl.-Anspachischer Hof-Instrumentenmacher Fecit Ao: 1782.*	New York Metropolitan Museum of Art has a gebunden clavichord dated 1782, C–G, 4½ octaves. (Their no.: X 253.6.) Inscription on a label.
6	1782	*Christian, Gottlob, Hubert. Hochfürstlischer Hof. Instrumentenmacher. Fecit. Ao. 1782.*	Basel, Historisches Museum. C–G, 4 octaves and a 5th, gebunden.
7	1782	*Christian Gottlob Hubert Hochfürstlich Anspachischer Hof-Instrumenten-Bauer fecit Ao. 1782.*	Munich, Deutsches Museum. 4½ octaves, gebunden.
8	1783	*Christian Gottlob Hubert, Hoff Instrumenten Bauer fecit, Andzbach*[?] *Ao: 1783.*	Liverpool, Rushworth and Dreaper Collection. C–G, 4½ octaves, gebunden. Illustrated *J*, p. 96.
9(?)	1783		Vienna, Kunsthistorisches Museum. Gebunden. Property of the Gesellschaft der Musikfreunde until it passed to the Sammlung A. Pfeiffer, Stuttgart. Friedrich Ernst, reviewing *Luith* in *Die Musikforschung*, Vol. 21 (1968), thinks that there are insufficient grounds for attributing this instrument to Hubert.

TABLE 19 (*cont.*):

No.	Date	Signature	Owner/Remarks
10	1784	*Christian Gottlob Hubert, Anspach bayreuthischer Hoff-Instrumenten-bauer fecit Ao: 1784.*	Halle, Händel-Haus (formerly Neupert Collection). C–G, 4 octaves and a 5th, gebunden.
10a	1784		Berlin Collection. C–G, 4½ octaves, gebunden. Illustrated. *GSJ*, Vol. 23 (1970), pl. 6.
10b	1784	*Christian Gottlob Hubert / Hochfürstl. Anspachischer Hof-/Instrumentenbauer fecit A. 1784.*	Weissenburg, Bavaria, Heimatmuseum der Stadt Weissenburg. C–G, 4½ octaves. Inscription on MS. label.
11	1784	*Christian Gottlob Huber Anspachisch u. Bäyreuthischer Hof-Orgel u. Instrumentenbauer fecit ao. 1784.*	Edinburgh, Dr. J. D. Dickson (to whom it was bequeathed by Sir Donald Tovey). Compass, 4½ octaves C–F; gebunden. Ebony naturals, ivory sharps. Length 4′ 3″. [MS. label].
11a	1784	*Christian, Gottlob, Hubert. / Hof-Orgel und Instrumentenbauer, / in Anspach. Fecit. Anno. 1784*	Berlin Collection. Bought since World War II. Gebunden. Compass C–G, 4½ octaves.
12	1787	*Christian, Gottlob, Hubert, / Hoff-Orgel und Instrumenten Bauer / in Anspach fecit Ao: 1787.*	Leipzig, Heyer Collection. A–F, 4 octaves and a 6th. Gebunden, 42 pairs of strings. *Ks*, p. 234.
12a	1787	*Christian Gottlob Hubert / Hochfürstl: Anspachisch: bayreutischer / Hof-Instrumentenbauer fecit 1787.*	Nuremberg, Neupert Collection (in the Germanisches Nationalmuseum). A–F, 4½ octaves, gebunden.
13	1789		Nuremberg, Rück Collection (in the Germanisches Nationalmuseum).
14		See above, no. 01.	Formerly Stuttgart, B. Klinkerfuss. Bundfrei [*Ks*, Vol. 2, p. 664].
15(?)	n.d.		Leipzig, Heyer Collection. Second half of eighteenth century. No maker's name but ascribed to H. [*Ks*, p. 46]; F–F, 5 octaves, bundfrei.
16(?)			Frankfurt/Main, Goethehaus. Case and stand lacquered red and gold in rococo style. C–C, 4 octaves with low C. Uninitialled rose. Formerly Paul de Wit's, from whom it passed to the Goethehaus in 1903. (De Wit ascribed the instrument to Hass.)

Note: All Hubert's surviving instruments seem to have been clavichords except 2: a 'kleiner Hammerflügel' dated 1785 illustrated in *MGG*, Vol. 6, col. 817, and described as having been 'früher Rück, früher Heyer'; and a 'spinet' dated 1791 auctioned at Parke Bernet's, New York, on 1 July 1956.

HÜBNER, Johann Christoph. Instrument maker in St. Petersburg, 1777–*c.* 1800 [*Moos*]. May have made harpsichords.

HUFFEL, Frans van [van Huffel], of Antwerp. Harpsichord maker. Dates ascertained, 1609–20. He entered the Guild of Saint Luke in 1609 [*St*]. He probably made lutes and theorboes as well [*Lü*].

Surviving Harpsichords

(1) 1620. Berlin Collection. One manual. Three stops (8′, 8′, 4′), at the side. Rose contains the initials: *FVH*. Compass C–D, 4 octaves and 2 notes. Stand missing. 186 × 76 cm. (Snoeck makes this ascription, which seems likely and is endorsed by *Sa*.)

HUFFEL, Lucas van [Uffel]. Harpsichord maker, perhaps the son of the foregoing. Dates ascertained, 1634–5. Born in Antwerp, he had moved to Amsterdam by 1634, when he accepted Nicolaes van Carpel (q.v.) as a pupil for 2 years. See further *Curtis*, p. 52.

HULSMA, Coenraad. Amsterdam harpsichord maker, died in 1649 [*Curtis*, p. 52].

HUMBERT, *priest*, of Metz, *fl.* 1521. May have made double spinets [*Va*]. *Jac* quotes: '1521, a messire Humbert, prebtre, demeurant à Metz, 38 francs pour une espinette double, que monseigneur a fait prendre de luy pour mettre en sa chambre.' However, this does not of course imply that he was a *maker*, which indeed seems unlikely.

HUNTER, David. Harpsichord maker at Waterford; died 1781 [*Teahan*].

HUYSEN, Johannes. Harpsichord maker, presumably Flemish, *fl.* 1610 [*Va*].

I. A. *See*: A, I.

I. G. *See*: GELLINGER, Israel.

I. H. *See*: H, I.

I. K. F. *See*: KILIAN, Lucas.

I. M. B. *See*: B, I. M.

I. N. C. *See*: C, I. N.

IADRA, Marco. *See*: JADRA, Marco.

ILSAAS, B, of Österdalen, Norway. A clavichord with a hand-cranked barrel-organ (? late eighteenth century) by him is at Bygdö, Oslo [*Nor*, p. 148]. It is recorded as a clavichord combined with an organ, in the catalogue of the Norsk Folkemuseums Særudstilling 1904 (p. 66). C–C, 4 octaves; black naturals, white sharps.

IMMENRAET, Michel. Son of Lucas Immenraet, born at Cologne. Harpsichord maker at Antwerp, *fl.* 1610 [*St*].

IRENA, Antonio. *Fl.* in Rome 1564 as a virginal maker. A polygonal spinet attributed to him is in the Paris Conservatoire. This instrument, which apparently was made in 1564, was given in 1581 by Henri III to Beaujoyeux.

Another polygonal spinet by him is in the Kunstgewerbe Museum, Zürich (1969): his signature, partially illegible, is on the front of the soundboard, left; 4 octaves C–C including short octave in bass; restored in Milan in 1899. Closely resembles the Paris instrument.

J. A. *See*: A, J.

J. B. H. *See*: H, J. B.

J. F. *See*: F, J.

J. J. *See*: Joseph Harris instrument no. 7, and Hitchcock instrument no. 5.

J. N. C. *See*: C, I. N.

J. W. R. *See*: R, J. W.

JACOBUS, *of Modena, fl.* 1494. Harpsichord maker [evidence from a letter of Duke Ercole d'Este, 24 July 1494, cited by *Va*, p. 249].

JACOMINO, *of Rome*. Harpsichord maker, *fl.* 1655. *Va* (p. 166) quotes from an inventory dated 1655: 'Un cimbalo a tre registri di Jacomino, coperto di veluto turchino et frinetta d'oro, con Chiodi indorati et dentro lauorato d'oro all'Arabesca et foderato di broccato con una chiave di ferro per accordare, et suoi piedi a colonne', and later: 'Cimbalo di Jacomino che fa sei toni diversi, dipinto di chiaro et scuro . . .'

JACOT & LION. A 2-manual harpsichord by these makers dated 1723 is privately owned in France [*ChamP*].

JACQUET, Jean [Jacquard]. Parisian harpsichord maker, *c.* 1575–after 1648. He was already making instruments when he married, in 1600, Françoise Dupuy who died in 1632. *Mer* (III. 159) praises his work. He also made organs, according to *Va*. *Verlet* gives further details and a family tree. She also mentions Marcel J., a son of Jean, as a harpsichord maker. This is not certain, although his apprenticeship to the organ builder Robert Despont makes it quite likely.

JACQUET, Claude. Son of Jean Jacquet. Parisian harpsichord maker; 1605–61; married in 1630 [*MC*, pp. 68, 155, 26 January 1661].

Surviving Harpsichords

(1) 1652. *Hubb 1965*, p. 101, refers to a harpsichord signed *Jacquet fecit 1652* in the Ringling Museum, Sarasota, Fla. No jacks or keys remain; 2×8′, 1×4′ registers. G/B–C, 4½ octaves. Size 7′ 3″×2′ 6½″. Hubbard, who has examined the instrument, gives further details at loc. cit. See also *Harpd*, Vol. 4 (1971), p. 22. (The instrument is more likely to have been by Claude than by his father.)

JADRA, Marco, *known as* Marco dai Cembali *or* Marco dalle Spinette. Dates ascertained, 1552–68. Italian virginal maker. (His name appears in *Va* as 'Ladra', but this is corrected in the 4th Suppl. p. 26.)

Surviving Instruments

(1) 1552. Oxford, Pitt Rivers Museum. Formerly owned by Valdrighi, then by Canon F. W. Galpin, also Alec Hodsdon (Puttick and Simpson's, August 1946). Polygonal virginal. Compass C/E–F, 4½ octaves. Inscription: *Marci Jadra MDLII.*

(2) 1565. Moscow Conservatoire, Glinka Museum. Polygonal virginal. Inscription reported to me as *Marci Jadrae fecit MDLXV*. Compass as (1). Geometric rose. Presumably the instrument advertised in *The Times*, 8 July 1858, as: 'Magnificent and historical harpsichord [*sic*] . . . the great work of Marco Sadre [*sic*]', at one time the property of the Medicis, three of whom are portrayed on its case [*Ri*, p. 399].

(3) 1568. London, Victoria and Albert Museum. Polygonal virginal. Inscribed on jackrail: *Marci Jadra MDLXVIII*, but under the sound board *Francisci* [sic] *Brixiensis fecit 1569*. Described fully under Antegnato above.

JAMES, John. English virginal maker; *fl.* 1571 [*J*]. *See* C. van den Borren, *The Sources of Keyboard Music in England*. London, Novello, 1914[?], p. 108.

JANSEN, H., *c.* 1757. A clavichord maker at Moss in Norway. Dates ascertained: 1754–63.

Surviving Clavichords

(1) 1754. Sarpsborg, Norway, Östfold Fylkesmuseum. C–C, 4 octaves; octave strings on 13 notes. Signed: *H. Jansen me fecit, Moss 1754*. Black naturals. Length 153·4 cm.

(2) 1757. Skien, Norway. [Fylkesmuseum for Telemark. F–F, 5 octaves. Signed: *H. Jansen. Hoc fecit, Moss 1757.* (Signature painted on soundboard; also *UAB* painted close to wrestpins.) Brown (? boxwood) naturals, black sharps. Octave strings in bass. Lacks 13 keys (1970). Length 178·5 cm.

JARAS. Professor Santiago Kastner has (1952) a Spanish clavichord signed: *Jaras me hizo, Año 1809, Belorado* [Burgos province]. See *Kastner 1952.*

JASPERS, Jan. Harpsichord maker, native of Coesvelt. Applied for citizenship of Antwerp *c.* 1570 [*Po*, p. 29]. *Va* notes him as a lute and harpsichord maker, *fl.* 1568.

JEHANNIS. *See*: JOANNES.

JEROME, *of Bologna. See*: HIERONYMUS *Bononiensis.*

JÉROSME. *See*: ZENTI, Girolamo.

JESSE, Johann Christoph. Organist at St. Martin's Church, Halberstadt, *fl.* 1765. A clavichord by him is in the New York Metropolitan Museum of Art (Crosby Brown Collection). It is bundfrei; dated 1765; 5 octaves F–F.

JOACHIM, of Halle. Clavichord maker; *fl.* 1785. An unknown Silesian writer signing himself *Hermes Jun.* refers to clavichords in his possession: 'eins von Friderici in Gera, eins von Horn aus Dresden, eins von Joachim aus Halle und — horchen Sie auf — ein Silbermannsches' (*Schlesische Provinzialblätter*, Vol. I, Breslau, 1785, p. 196); which would seem to imply a high degree of excellence in this obscure maker.

JOANNES, Antoni. Harpsichord maker. Member of the Guild of Saint Luke, Antwerp, in 1627 [*Bu*; *St*, p. 8]. A 'Clavecin de Jehannis' was advertised in 1757 [*Bq*, p. 10]; this is probably the same maker. *Va*, spelling him Johannes, also gives his *floruit* as 1627.

JOBERNARDI, Bartolomeo [Giobernardi]. A musician of Italian origin, was living in Madrid (at least 1634–6, probably earlier and perhaps later) as harpist to Philip IV, King of Spain. He designed a *cimbalo perfetto* or 'perfected harpsichord', which he described in an unpublished *Tratado de la musica*, dedicated on 15 October 1634 to the King and preserved in the Biblioteca Nacional, Madrid.

For a discussion of this treatise, with considerable quotation from the original text, see Santiago Kastner's paper in *Anuario musical del Inst. Español de Musicología*, Vol. VIII, Barcelona, 1953, pp. 193–209. See also *Russell 1959*, p. 116.

JOHANE ANTONIO. *See*: BONISSIMO, Giannantonio.

JOHANN, *Meister*. Organ builder at Werden, *fl.* 1437, when he is recorded as selling a 'clavecordium' [*Mos*].

JOHANNES BAPTISTA, *Bononiensis* or Giovanni Battista of Bologna. Virginal maker, *fl.* 1602. The Smithsonian Institution, Washington, has a virginal made by him in 1602 and signed: *Johannes Baptista Bononien* (which has previously been read as 'Bonomen'). C/E–F, rectangular.

JOHN, John de. Stringed keyboard instrument maker in London, *fl.* 1526–31 [*Russell 1959*, p. 65].

JOHNSTON, John. Spinet maker of Edinburgh. Perhaps *fl. c.* 1800.

Surviving Spinets

(1) Providence, R.I. Rhode Island School of Design. Signed: *Johannes Johnston, Edinburgh.* Veneered in mahogany. Two curves in bent side.

JONECK, Michael. Maker of keyboard instruments. Born at Würzburg on 14 May 1748. Entered the Oberzeller monastery, which was later dissolved, in his youth. Here he began to play the keyboard, and was driven by lack of a suitable instrument to the idea of making one himself. Soon afterwards he left the monastery and devoted himself to keyboard-instrument making. In 1812 he was still alive [*Ge*].

JONECK, Joseph. Son of Michael, likewise a maker of keyboard instruments at Würzburg. He worked at first under the direction of his father, but later had instruction from Walther in Vienna. Afterwards he returned to Würzburg to work [*Ge*].

JONES, Philip. English maker of virginals and harpsichords, born about 1643; apprenticed to John Haward for 8 years from 13 July 1658; freeman of the Joiners' Company, August 1667. In a catalogue (1714) of the sale of the music and instruments of Thomas Britton after his death, there appears 'a good harpsichord by Philip Jones' [*J*].

Surviving Instruments

(1) 1671. Virginal, belonging to Lt.-Col. Leicester Warren, Tabley Hall, Knutsford. 5′ 9″ × 1′ 10″; B–F (55 keys) short octave. Depicted in a painting by J. Fulleylove, 'A 17th century virginal', which was shewn at the Inventions Exhibition in 1885. The virginal was then the property of Lord de Tabley. It was in 1950 in a very poor state.

JØRGENSEN, Johan Jesper. Clavichord maker at Odense in Denmark; *fl.* 1777.

Surviving Clavichords

(1) 1777. Copenhagen, Musikhistoriska Museet. Bundfrei. F–F, 5 octaves. Inscription: *Johan Jesper Jörgensen. Odense. 1777.*

JOUBERT. Parisian maker of harpsichords and other instruments, 1777 [*Hubb*].

JOYCE, George, *and* **Peter East,** of London, *fl.* 1694, are sometimes misleadingly referred to as authors of a 'self-acting harpsichord'. What they patented, however, (no. 327, dated 20 October 1694) was:

> A certain instrument which being applied to clocks, organs, and any other key instrument, as harpsichords, virginalls, or the like, will cause the same to chime, or play any manner of tune, air, or notes plain or performe a consort, and is alterable to any tune or air in halfe an hour by any person, (tho noe master of musick) without changing the instrument.

JUNGCURTH, Heinrich Wilhelm. Maker of stringed keyboard instruments; born at Tüngeda, Kr. Gotha, 1743, died Hamburg 1823 [*Schultze 1957*]. Lived at Breitenbach, Thuringia, for a time; acquired Hamburg citizenship in 1782.

A clavichord by him dated 1760 was shewn at the International Inventions Exhibition by R. M. Rogers in 1885. C. P. E. Bach had a clavichord by him.

The form of his surname 'Langgath' is a misreading.

JUNGERSON, Johann Christian. *See*: Jürgensen, Johann Christian.

JÜRGENSEN, Johann Christian, of Schleswig. Pianoforte maker, born *c*. 1754. He began instrument making in 1780 and invented a 'clavecin royal' with 12 variations of tone. Died at Schleswig in 1815 [*Fé*]. *Hirt* notes him as having made clavichords.

K, V. The Heimathaus at Wasserburg am Inn, Bavaria, has a virginal signed on the keys: *V.K. 1588*. On a lower soundboard, acting as a jack-guide, the date *1588* is repeated [*VdM*].

KAISER, Martin. Harpsichord maker at Füssen (Allgäu), *fl.* 1698 [*Hirt*].

Surviving Instruments

(1) Vienna, Kunsthistorisches Museum. A clavicytherium, made about 1675 inscribed: *Martinus Kaiser Ser. Electoris Palatini Instrumentorum Opifex Et Huiusmodi Inventor*. 2×8′. (At one time the property of the Emperor Leopold I, 1658–1705.)

KALIX. Maker of keyboard instruments in Berlin, *c.* 1786 [*Ge*].

KAMP, Hubert van. *See*: Van Kamp, Hubert.

KAREST, Jan. Confused in the first edition with Hans van Cuelen, q.v.

KAREST, Joos [Josse Careest]. Maker of clavichords, spinets, and harpsichords; born in Cologne shortly before 1500, died 1559–60 [*St*, p. 66]. Son of Hans van Cuelen, q.v. In 1516–17 he became a citizen of Antwerp. He was received into the Guild of Saint Luke in 1523 as a painter and engraver ('Joos Kerrest, clavecordmaker, snyt en scildert' [*Ro*, I. 101]). Joos Karest headed the harpsichord makers who in 1557 petitioned the Guild of St. Luke for admission as instrument makers rather than as painters [*St*, p. 63].

In the Dresden Inventory (1593) there is an entry: 'ein Instrument [i.e. virginal], so ettwan Jobst Karest gemacht.' (Inuentarium Über die Instrumenta, welche . . . dem Hof-organisten Christoff Walthern in Vorwahrunge gegeben . . . zu Dressden den 2 Aprilis 1593.) Edited by M. Fürstenau in the *Mittheilungen des K. S. Alterthums-Vereins*, Dresden, 1872) [*Bu, Gö, Lü*].

Surviving Instruments

(1) 1548. Brussels Conservatoire. A virginal inscribed: *Joes Karest de Colonia*. Four octaves with short octave. Inscription round the soundboard: *Omnis spiritus laudet Dominum in cordis et organo*, and outside the case: *Laudate Dominum in cordis et organo, laudate Eum in symbalis bene sonantibus*. 147×48 cm. See further Ripin's paper in *RipKb*, p. 65.

(2?) 1550. *FrancII* contains a 'spinetta a forma d'arpa' inscribed: *Joes Karest de Colonia fecit 1550*. Its provenance arouses suspicion at once; but, if genuine, it must be the earliest surviving harp-shaped spinet. Or was *Franc* confusing it with the instrument mentioned s.v. Claes Karest?

KAREST, Gosuin *or* Goosen. Dates ascertained 1519–68. Born at Cologne, son of Hans van Cuelen. In 1519 he was the pupil of Peter Matthys [*St*, p. 67]. Entered the Guild of St. Luke in 1529 as painter and harpsichord maker. Received citizenship of Antwerp as a painter, 9 March 1536. Worked with his brother Joos Karest on harpsichords, and had a reputation as a maker of clavichords and theorboes [*Lü*]. He appears to have married twice [*St*, who quotes a number of references to him in documents].

KAREST, Claes. This is a misreading of Joos Karest.

KÄSTNER. German(?) clavichord maker, *fl.* 1748.

Surviving Clavichords

(1) 1748. Hasse, Händelhaus. Inscription: *Kästner me fecit Ao 1748*. Compass F–G, 5 octaves plus 1 note. Rose.

KEENE, Stephen. Virginal, spinet, and harpsichord maker. Born about 1640, son of Richard Keene of Sydenham, Oxon. Apprenticed to Gabriel Townsend in London for 7 years from 6 August 1655; freeman of the Joiners' Company, November 1662; Master of the Company, 1704/5. In 1693 he lived in Threadneedle Street. Among his apprentices were Blunt, Brackley, and Barton [*Join*].

Playford's *Introduction to the Skill of Music* (1672) refers to Mr. Stephen Keen as a maker of 'Harpsycons and Virginals'.

Charles Brackley was in Keene's employment in 1711, as instrument no. 8 below shows. By 1719 Brackley had been taken into partnership, as is proved by instrument no. 22 in the table, as also by a spinet-nameboard belonging formerly to A. J. Hipkins, later to Henry Tull inscribed *Stephanus Keene Carolus Brackley Londini fecerunt*, and stated to have come from an instrument dated 1719.

Keene also took Blunt into partnership (see the inscription on no. 13d).

KEEYS. Workman in an English eighteenth-century harpsichord and spinet making firm. John Paul bought at a Sussex auction sale in 1966 held by the executors of Miss Coke Richards, of Westmeston, Sussex, a spinet whose style dates it as from the late eighteenth century. On the baseboard, underneath the keyboard, is the signature: *Keeys no. 11*. (It is clear, and could not be Keene or Kemys.) Jack 41 is inscribed *Edward Peel*. Compass 5 octaves G–G; length 6′ 4″. Its finely painted satinwood case makes it unique—probably custom-built [*Paul*].

KEISER, Jean Baptiste, *called* 'L'Empereur'. A native of Haute-Alsace, he made harpsichords in Paris; master in 1736 and *juré* in 1749; died 1772 [*Verlet*]; he taught and adopted his nephew Joseph Treyer, q.v., also called 'L'Empereur' [*Hardouin 1959*].

TABLE 20. *Surviving Instruments by Stephen KEENE*

No.	Date	Type	Signature	Owner/Remarks
1	1668	V	*Stephanus Keene Londini fecit 1668*	Edinburgh University (formerly Raymond Russell). (Formerly at Goodrich Court, Ross-on-Wye) F–D, 57 keys, without lowest F sharp. Gilded paper embossed with the royal arms of the House of Stuart. Illustrated in *RussColl.*
1a	1675	V	*Stephanus Keene fecit 1675*	Cheshire, private ownership. B–F, 55 keys; 3 roses.
2	1685	S	*Stephanus Keene fecit Londini 1685*	1941, Messrs. Legg of Cirencester; probably the one formerly at Bexhill-on-Sea in private ownership. Compass B–D, 4½ octaves. Inscribed behind jackrail: *Repaired by H. Greening 1841*. Length 61″ over all. Floral design with bird inlaid on nameboard. Stand of 3 pairs of turned legs. Dated on jackrail. E. R. Hawkings, bought it *c.* 1958 from a Mr. Gerhold of Bexhill-on-Sea who moved to the U.S. at that time, having owned the spinet for only a short time.
3	1685	S		In very fine condition, on original stand. Seen by John Boston, in 1954, in private ownership near London. (Not identical with no. 2.) Nameboard has marquetry of foliage and a bird.
3a	1690	S		Messrs. Legg, Cirencester (1936) [*GL*].
4	1700	S		Messrs. Morley, 1953. Nameboard has floral marquetry with a bird, different from that on the foregoing instrument, but identical with that on no. 10 below.
5	[?1700]	S	*Stephanus Keene Londini fecit*	London, Royal College of Music, their no. 179 (formerly Sir George Grove, who shewed it in 1885). G–D, 4 octaves and a 5th; ebony naturals, skunktail sharps; inscribed on jackrail; uninitialled rose. Very obscure inscription on top key: *S*[?*K* then a numeral]. Curved tail. Length 5′ 9″.
5a	1705	S	*Stephanus Keene Londini fecit*	The bottom key, inscribed *TB/1/1705*, shews it to be the work of Thomas Barton [q.v.] an apprentice of Keene. Bought by Messrs. Legg, Cirencester, at a country sale about 1965. Entered the possession of Messrs. Barling, Mount St., London in November 1968.
5b	1706	S	*Stephanus Keene Londini fecit*	Steventon, G. N. Harding (1966). On top key and jack: *54/CB/1705/6*. CB is Keene's apprentice Charles Brackley (q.v.). (Sold at Sotheby's 19 June 1959 when the catalogue wrongly gave this inscription as '54 J.H. 1703'.) Repaired by Alec Hodsdon 1934. Jackrail new. Bought by Mr. Harding on 12 October 1965 from Phillips Son & Neale, when the catalogue described it as 'from the Geo. Parker Collection'.
6	1706	S		Shewn at International Inventions Exhibition, 1885, by E. R. Hughes.
[?7]	1708	S		London, Royal College of Music. Perhaps by Keene (cf. number 14). Nameboard bears marquetry including 2 birds, but no inscription. Top key inscribed: *1708*. G/B–D, 4½ octaves; lowest 2 sharps divided. Ebony naturals, ivory sharps. No rose. Straight tail. Length 5′ 6″.
8	1711	S	*Stephanus Keene Londini fecit*	Edgar Lister. Marquetried nameboard; ebony naturals with embossed paper fronts; ivory sharps. On the top key is inscribed in ink: *C. B. / 1711 / 18*, indicating the date, and suggesting it to be the eighteenth spinet made by Brackley in Keene's employ.

TABLE 20 (*cont.*):

No.	Date	Type	Signature	Owner/Remarks
9	—	S	*Stephanus Keene Londini fecit*	Mrs. Nathaniel Lloyd, Northiam, Sussex. Undated. G/B–D, 4½ octaves. Original stand; black naturals, ivory sharps. See note below.
10	—	S	*Stephanus Keene Londini fecit* [on nameboard]; *Gilbert Dawson* and *W. G. Steed* [on back of nameboard]	Hugh Gough, New York, (Sotheby's, 21. 12. 1972); formerly W. Barrow, Llandudno. Undated; short octave; case of walnut. B–D 4 octaves plus; black naturals, white sharps; straight tail. On nameboard (besides inscription) floral marquetry with a bird. Formerly belonged to Lord Lovat.
11	—	S		Deerfield, Mass. Much restored. Originally had split keys. Compass after restoration G/B–D, 4½ octaves.
12	—	S	*Stephanus Keene Londini fecit*	Connell Collection, National Gallery of Victoria, Melbourne.
13	—	S	*Stephanus Keene Londini*	The late Harry Simmonds, London (d. by 1954), bought it from Messrs. F. E. Anderson of Welshpool, who bought it from Messrs. E. C. Legg of Cirencester. Black naturals, solid ivory sharps. Original stand, spirally turned. Nameboard, besides inscription, has elaborate marquetry of arabesque pattern. It was probably this Keene spinet on which E. M. Ripin did some work in 1956 and which was sold to a private collector in U.S.A. by J. J. Wolff Antiques Ltd., 825 Madison Avenue, New York. Probably equals no. 19.
13a	—	S	*Stephanus Keene Londini fecit* (on nameboard)	Bristol, R. Mickleburgh, bought from R. R. Henshaw of Turleigh, Bradford-on-Avon, about 1948. Inscription on nameboard; on back of nameboard: *John Knowles 1701* and *R. Clark his spinet 1750*.
13b	—	S		Bristol, Red Lodge.
13c	—	S		Drummond Castle, Crieff, Perthshire, the Earl of Ancaster. [*Wm. Thomas.*]
13d	—	S	*Stephanus Keene Edwardus Blunt Londini Fecerunt*	Lord Bute. G/B–D, with lowest 2 sharps divided.
13e	—	S	*Stephanus Keene Londini fecit*	Searsdale, N.Y., Dr. and Mrs. Robert Rosenbaum (previously Messrs. Morley, previously private ownership in London). Inscription on front of jackrail; on top key: *S * K*. Arcaded ebony naturals; bone sharps. Marquetried foreboard with typical bird and leaf motifs.
14	—	S	*Stephanus Keene Londini fecit*	H. J. Dale of Cheltenham, 1888. Black naturals, white sharps. Besides the inscription, the nameboard bears a marquetry pattern which includes 2 birds. Straight tail. Length 5′ 6″. Illustrated in *HiMi*, p. 51.
15	—	S		Shewn by Frere at the 1900 Exhibition, London.
16	—	S	*Stephanus Keene Londini fecit*	Formerly in Boddington Collection. G/B–D, 4½ octaves. 2 lowest sharps divided.
17	—	S	*Stephanus Keene fecit Londini*	Bolton, Hall-i'-the-Wood Museum. G/B–D, 4½ octaves. 2 lowest sharps divided. Geometrical rose.
18	—	S	*Stephanus Keene Londini fecit*	Christie's, 15 November 1956. Nameboard has spray of flowers inlaid on an ebony ground. Width 4′ 11″.
19	—	S	*Stephanus Keene Londini fecit*	New York, J. J. Wolff (antique dealer), 1957. Ivory sharps, ebony naturals; usual G/B–D compass. Probably equals no. 13.

TABLE 20 (*cont.*):

No.	Date	Type	Signature	Owner/Remarks
20	—	S		Messrs. Luther, Antique Dealers, 56 George Street, W. 1, had this about 1962, but had sold it by 1965. Compass G/B–D, 54 notes; lowest C sharp and D sharp split. Repaired by Robert Morley about 1962.
21	—	S	*Stephanus Keene Londini fecit*	Dr. B. E. Juel-Jensen, Oxford (1972), who bought it from Roger Warner, Burford, in 1957. Inscription on nameboard, divided by marquetry of flowers and foliage. Keyboard not original; no initials on jacks. Repaired by Michael Thomas, Hurley. (Owner before R. Warner: Charles Thornton.)
22	—	S	*Stephanus Keene Carolus Brackley Londini fecerunt*	Sir Ilay Campbell, Coldstream, Berwickshire. Compass G–E, nearly 5 octaves without bottom G sharp and top D sharp.

KELLERMANN, C. F. A., of Nordhausen. A man of letters and of the law, also an amateur maker of keyboard instruments, in the eighteenth century [*Ge*].

KEMP, J. Spinet maker in Bristol in the eighteenth century. An undated spinet by him, 4′ 3″ long, belonging to Lady Kathleen Pilkington, was sold at Sotheby's, 5 July 1934, to Messrs. Mallett.

KEMYS, John. Spinet and harpsichord maker, Small Street (then King Street), Bristol, *fl.* 1752–9 [*J*; *Byrne*].

Surviving Instruments

(1) Undated [*c.* 1755]. Spinet. The Hon. Mrs. Ionides, Twickenham. Inscription on nameboard: *John Kemys, Bristol.* F–F without low F sharp. Pine keyboard; ivory naturals with arcaded fronts in ebony; ebony sharps. Lowest 31 notes have double bridge-pins. Gilt rose with harping King David and initials *BH* [doubtless *Baker Harris*]. Mahogany case with rectangular walnut inlays surrounded by holly stringing. Modern wrest-pins. Length 6′ 10″.

How and when a Baker Harris rose entered this soundboard is matter for speculation. Perhaps Kemys acted as an agent for Baker Harris, as Longman and Broderip did.

KERSHAW. *See*: KIRSHAW.

KETTENHOVEN, Pierre, of Lyon. 'Facteur de clavecins, épinettes, "forte è piano", harpes à pédales, tympanons, serinettes, guitares, mandolines, vielles'; dates ascertained, 1772–8.

A daughter of his was baptized at the Church of Saint-Nizier on 28 October 1775. In 1778 he did some work on the organ of the Charité [*Vallas*].

KEUSE, P. *See*: KUESE, P.

KEYSER, Paul. German seventeenth-century harpsichord maker. An inventory of 1681 records a 'Clavizimbul, Mitt 4 Registern, mitt einem Elffenbeinern Clavire, bis ins Contra G . . .' [*Drechsel*, p. 497].

KIBURTZ. *See*: KYBURZ.

KIEDOLPS, F., of Schweinfurth. Organ builder. He also made clavichords, one of which dated 1751 is in the Smithsonian Institution, Washington. It has 4½ octaves C–E, without bottom C sharp. Inscription: *F. Kiedolps, Orgelmacher, Schweinfurth 1751.*

KIEJCHER, Krzysztof. Maker of harpsichords and clavichords at Cracow in the sixteenth and seventeenth centuries [*Szulc*].

KILIAN, Lucas. A Hungarian engraver, active (? in Budapest) 1607–37, may have designed a virginal, said to have belonged to Catherine of Brandenburg, the wife of Gábor Bethlen, Prince of Transylvania, in the Hungarian National Museum, Budapest. It is inscribed: *1617 L:K:F:* and (lower down) *I:K:F:*, which has been interpreted as 'Lucas Kilian invenit; I. Kilian [his son] fecit', a possibility accepted by M. Rosenberg (*Der Goldschmiede Merkzeichen*, Vol. I, 3rd edition, Frankfurt am Main, 1922). Gábry (1959) considers it likelier that it was made by Johann Klebiller of Augsburg and brought by Catherine with her from Germany. Illustrated in *Gábry 1969*.

KING, Federico. *See*: RING, Friedrich.

KINSTRÖM, Lars. The Musikhistoriska Museet, Stockholm, has a gebunden clavichord by him dated 1752.

KINTZING, Christian, of Neuwied. Maker of keyboard instruments, *fl.* 1763. A clavichord signed *C. Kintzing in Neuwied 1763* is owned by H. G. Salloch, Sea Cliff, N.Y.; 4½ octaves C–E, black naturals; an additional set of tangents provides a pantalon stop worked by knobs in the endblocks of the keyboard. The instrument is much restored. Illustrated on p. 152 of *Michel*, who gives the date incorrectly as 1734.

Christian made pianos, as also did his son Peter.

KIRKMAN [Kirckman]. Anglicized form of the German *Kirchmann*, surname of a family of eminent harpsichord and subsequently pianoforte makers. The firm of Kirkman & Sons dated their foundation 1730. (Cf. their advertisement in the *Daily Graphic*, London, 31 July 1893 and in the first issue of the *Evening News*, 26 July 1881.)

Jacob Kirkman anglicized his name first of all as *Kirckman* (as when witnessing Tabel's will in 1738), and this form continued to be used by the firm on the nameboards of their instruments; but at least from 1755 Jacob customarily signed his name *Kirkman* in documents.

(1) **Jacob** (1710–92), an Alsatian of Swiss extraction (his great-grandfather, Conrad, lived at Burgdorf in the canton of Bern), was born at Bischweiler near Strasbourg, where the archives describe him as a 'cabinet maker'—*ébéniste*. In the early seventeen-thirties he came to England and worked for Hermann Tabel, a Flemish harpsichord maker who had brought over the traditions of the Ruckers (q.v.) family of Antwerp, and for whom there had worked during the previous decade Burkat Shudi (q.v.), who was destined to be the founder of the house of Broadwood. Only 1 harpsichord by Tabel, dated 1721, has survived; and his name would have been almost forgotten but for his distinguished pupils and for Burney's entertaining paragraph, telling us how 'Kirchmann worked with the celebrated Tabel as his foreman and finisher till the time of his death. Soon after which . . . Kirchmann married his master's widow, by which prudent measure he became possessed of all Tabel's seasoned wood, tools and stock-in-trade . . .'. This took place in 1738 (although Burney mistakenly says that Kirkman arrived in England in 1740).

On 8 May 1739 the following advertisement appeared in the *Daily Gazetteer*:

Whereas Mr. Hermann Tabel late of Swallow Street, the famous Harpsichord maker, dead, hath left several fine Harpsichords to be disposed of by Mr. Kirckman, his late Foreman; this is to acquaint the Curious, that the said Harpsichords, which are the finest he ever made, are to be seen at the said Mr. Kirckmann's the corner of Pulteney Court in Cambridge Street, over against Silver Street, near Golden Square.

From this time until at any rate the end of 1749 he rented a house in Great Pulteney Street East.

It was Kirkman who, some time in the middle seventeen-forties, introduced Fulke Greville to Burney, who became Greville's harpsichord teacher. The occasion is amusingly described by Fanny Burney, daughter of the musician (*Memoirs of Doctor Burney*, London, Moxon, 1832, Vol. I, p. 24), who refers to Kirkman as 'the first harpsichord maker of the times', and is summarized by P. A. Scholes in *The Great Doctor Burney* (London, Oxford University Press, 2 vols., 1948), Vol. I, pp. 36 ff., where he quotes that Kirkman 'came forward to announce that in the following week he [Greville] should have a new harpsichord with double keys [i.e. 2 keyboards] and a deepened bass ready for examination'. We do not know the upshot, but it is possible that Kirkman made one or two harpsichords reaching down to the C below his usual bottom F just as Shudi did.

Naturalization was granted to Kirkman on 25 April 1755 [*HuD*]. Mrs. Delany writes in the same year: 'She [Mrs. Donellan] has got a new harpsichord of Mr. Kirkman' (*Autobiography and Correspondence of Mary Glanville* (1861–2), Vol. III, p. 383).

About 1757 Kirkman constructed an enharmonic harpsichord according to a plan supplied by Robert Smith, Master of Trinity College, Cambridge, whose remarks approving the instrument are quoted below on p. 168. Like Shudi, Kirkman collaborated with Snetzler in the building of claviorgana, one of which, made in 1750, has survived. (See instrument no. 109 in the list below.)

The *Universal Director* for 1763 announces Jacob Kirkman 'Harpsichord maker to her Majesty, and to several foreign princes. Broad Street, near Golden Square'.

About 1770 a sudden fashion for the English guitar sprang up, which threatened to ruin the harpsichord makers, if we are to believe Burney's oft-repeated story. But Kirkman saved the situation by buying a few such guitars and putting them into the hands of milliner girls and street singers, which made the ladies of the *beau monde* so ashamed of themselves that they repented of their follies and returned to the harpsichord. Another aspect of his practical shrewdness is illustrated (if we can trust Burney) by his 'becoming a pawnbroker and a usurer; obliging young heirs with money as kindly, and with as much liberality, as a Hebrew'.

In 1771 or the previous year Kirkman brought an action against Robert Falkener (q.v., also spelt 'Ffalknor') for putting up for sale as by Kirkman a harpsichord made by another maker. He claimed £500 damages; but the issue of the suit is not known [*J*, p. 43 n.].

The catalogue of the International Inventions Exhibition, London, 1885, lists a portrait by Hogarth of a 'Jacob Kirckman', possibly the harpsichord maker; but considerable researches have not discovered whether it is still in existence.

It has sometimes been assumed that Kirkman was the same person as the Jacob Kirkman who was organist of St. George's, Hanover Square and published a number of musical compositions. This is a mistake; for the harpsichord maker died in 1792, while the organist lived at least until 1802, in which year he resigned from his post. Apparently the Vestry would not grant further leave of absence 'in the hope of re-establishing his health by a residence at Bath and Brighton'. But it appears the organist had been spending far too much time at Richmond, Brighton, and elsewhere for reasons not primarily connected with his health. It seems, however, almost certain that the organist is to be identified with Jacob Kirkman, *nephew* of the harpsichord maker—a supposition endorsed by the *D.N.B.* This nephew, who died in 1812, was clearly fond of music, for his will refers to '3 charges of £50 a year which I have on the Opera House', and implies tenancy of houses in London from 1797 until his death. It is probably this nephew who figures in the list of subscribers to Burney's *History of Music*, published in 1776, where 3 members of the Kirkman family appear: 'Mr. Kirkman, Mr. Abraham Kirkman, Harpsichord makers to Her Majesty' [i.e. the celebrated Jacob and his nephew Abraham, who were in partnership at this time]; and 'Mr. Jacob Kirkman'.

An anonymous print of about 1750, seen by J. G. Morley in 1954, represents a lady playing a 2-manual harpsichord on whose nameboard the signature *Thomas Kirckman* appears clearly in an oval cartouche. The instrument was probably by Jacob Kirkman, since no one in the family was, as far as I know, named Thomas.

It must have been at least as early as 1772 that Jacob, the harpsichord maker, having no children by his marrige, took his nephew, Abraham, into partnership, for a surviving harpsichord of this date is inscribed: *Jacobus & Abraham Kirckman.* About this time the piano began to be made in the Kirkman workshops, for there is record of a square piano inscribed *Jacob & Abraham Kirckman* dated 1775, and a grand piano dated 1780 also bore their names, so that the piano and harpsichord were manufactured side by side by them for some years, as also by the firm of Shudi–Broadwood. The house of Kirkman continued to make harpsichords for some years later than that of Shudi–Broadwood; for a Kirkman dated 1800 survives, and Engel states that the last harpsichord was made in their workshop in 1809: 'The late Mr. Kirkman [i.e. the Joseph who died in 1877] told me that he, with his father [i.e. the Joseph, several of whose harpsichords have come down to us], constructed the last harpsichord in 1809' ('Some account of the Clavicord . . .', in *Musical Times*, 1 July 1879).

Kirkman harpsichords retained for many years certain minor characteristics inherited from the Antwerp tradition, such as the omission of the bottom F sharp from the 5-octave keyboard, F to F; and the rose in the soundboard. Their lutestop plucks nearer the nut than that of Shudi, thus giving a more nasal tone. The invention known as the Venetian swell, patented by Shudi in 1769, was fitted in some cases to Kirkman instruments (see list of instruments below); but they were also frequently fitted with a lid-swell, whereby a small part of the lid was hinged to the rest and could be raised and lowered by means of a pedal. Burney's claim that Kirkman's instruments were more durable than Shudi's cannot now be verified. It is true that more Kirkmans (more than 150) have survived than Shudis, of which we know just over 50; but Kirkman produced many more than Shudi. It seems that Kirkman's harpsichords commanded a higher price than those of his rival, for in 1761 a 2-manual Kirkman cost 90 guineas, and a single-manual 50 guineas, whereas Shudi's prices varied from 35 guineas to 80 guineas (1770). (Burney considered the harpsichords of both these makers to be far superior to any which he came across in Germany or Flanders [*BurnG*, II. 147; I. 48].) The preface to John Arnold's *Compleat psalmodist* . . . (5th edition, London, 1761), states that 'Mr. Kirkman's are said to be the best, but are of great Price' while there are 'very good common Harpsichords to be sold at the Music-Shops for five-and-twenty Guineas each'. In 1782, according to *Der musikalische Almanach* published at Leipzig in that year, Kirkman instruments cost from £60 to £90. Another indication of Kirkman's fame having spread to the Continent is the notice, admittedly brief and inadequate, in *Ge*: 'Kirchmann: Ein Instrumentmacher zu London um 1772, ist wegen seiner schönen Flügel berühmt'.

Kirkman harpsichords maintained their value very well in the second-hand market, as is shewn from the following prices paid at Christie's during the last decade of the eighteenth century: for single-manual harpsichords—18 guineas (16 April 1792), £19. 8*s*. 6*d*. (28 September 1792); for 2-manual instruments—£21 (16 May 1791), £50 (16 April 1792), £36. 15*s*. (25 February 1793). As might be expected, fewer Shudis came up for sale, and usually fetched slightly lower prices than Kirkmans. Thus a 2-manual Shudi harpsichord was sold at Christie's on 7 May 1793 for 19 guineas.

There remain no harpsichords signed by Abraham alone; and the latest surviving one by Jacob and Abraham is dated 1790. It was in this year that Jacob Kirkman retired to a house at 'Crumshill' in the parish of Greenwich. There remain in the road called Crooms Hill today several pleasant mid-eighteenth-century houses, in one of which Jacob spent his declining years. It survives still (1972): Charles Mould has identified it as the house known as Park Hall, at the top of the hill.

Jacob Kirkman's will is dated 31 March 1792. It was proved on 13 June in the same year. In dating Kirkman's death 1778 Burney is strangely wide of the mark; and although Kirkman was a man of considerable substance, he was certainly not worth the £200,000 with which Burney credits him. He was a member of the Reformed German Church of the Savoy, which he mentions in his will as the place where he would wish to be buried. In point of fact he was buried in the parish church of St. Alfege, Greenwich, on 9 June 1792. He was succeeded by his nephew

(2) **Abraham** (1737–94), son of his half-brother Abraham Kirchmann of Bischweiler. Abraham, after being in partnership with his uncle for about 20 years, worked with his son Joseph for several more; in fact he seems to have taken Joseph into partnership in the year before Jacob's retirement, to judge from the inscription on instrument number 85, dated 1789. He died in 'the hamlet of Hammersmith in the parish of Fulham', and was buried in the parish church of St. Alfege, Greenwich, on 16 April 1794.

His wealth was a good deal greater than his uncle's, and he left property in several parts of London and elsewhere in England, and even in Wales.

He had 9 children by his wife Charlotte; and the business was carried on by his second son

(3) **Joseph,** whose name appears with his father's on at least 4 surviving harpsichords, and alone on 3 more. Joseph joined the firm in 1789 and managed it from 1794 onwards. His son

(4) **Joseph,** *the Younger*, died at the age of 87 in 1877, his second son

(5) **Henry** having died some years earlier. The showrooms were for many years in Soho Square. In 1896 the business was amalgamated with that of Collard, later taken over by Chappell, and is now extinct.

(6) **Thomas.** [See above under (1).]

[*Da*; Burney's articles in Rees's *Cyclopaedia* (1820); A. J. Hipkins's researches; wills of the Kirkman family; rate-books of parishes in Soho and near by; Alsatian archives.]

At least 3 types of Kirkman roses are known. The first (which occurs for instance in instrument no. 01 dated 1744) is a monogram in the form of a plant from whose stem spring intertwined tendrils some of which have the shape of *IK* initials, both forward and in reverse, the whole forming an elaborate pattern, in which the letters themselves are not distinguishable without scrutiny, and bordered by a wreath.

The second shews King David seated, his knees together, playing the harp, flanked by the letters *IK* in type-style, the whole encircled by broken-off Gothic architectural tracery from which a curtain hangs in the form of a swag. (See below, plate 34.)

In the third King David sits, his right leg in front of his left, playing the harp; the type-style *IK* letters flanking him are lower down in the design and smaller in proportion, and the rest of the circle is filled with instruments of various kinds, e.g. horns, recorders, oboes, lutes and viols; there are also flowers and fragments of vegetation.

This species of rose is found in instrument no. 93, dated 1798. (See below, plate 35.)

Mrs. Piozzi (not wholly accurately!) wrote on 10 July 1803: 'Mason the poet I am told was the first inventor of the Piano & Forte; They used Harpsichords till his time, about 1767 was the notion made public and perfected by Professors in Music and in Mechanism. Kirkman's Harpsichords were once so famous, people broke off ye front boards to put them on their own instrument if that was made by Tchudi—tho' a better workman; you may now buy the best Kirkman in England—for a guinea 1803' (*Thraliana*, ed. K. C. Balderston, 1942, Vol. II, p. 1036 n.).

Summary Tree of the KIRKMAN family

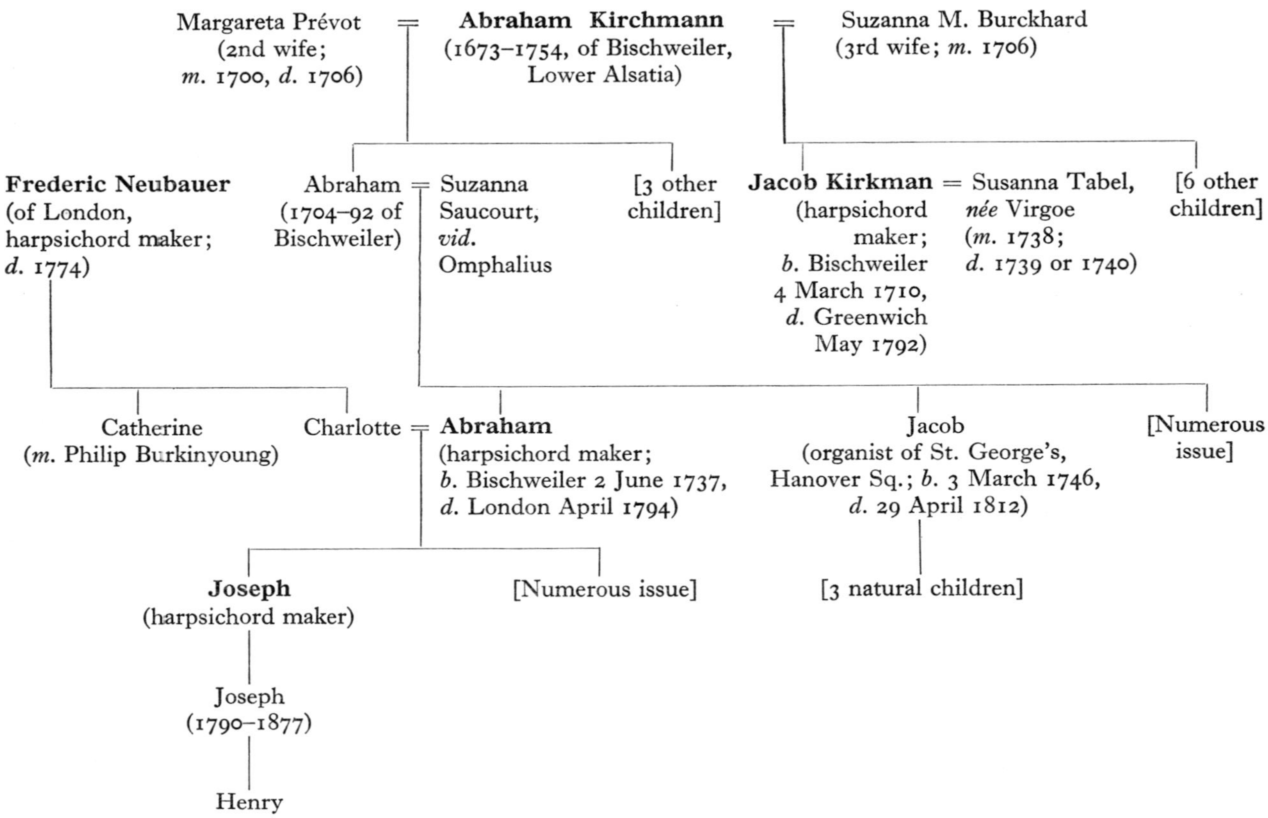

TABLE 21. *Surviving Instruments by the KIRKMAN Family*

The heading to the second column (G–D (5 edn.)) refers to *Grove's Dictionary of Music and Musicians* (5th edition, 1954).

* Key to abbreviations in the fourth column:
J = Jacobus Kirkman, J&A = Jacobus & Abraham K., A&Jo = Abraham & Josephus K., Jo = Josephus K.

No.	G–D (5 edn.) no.	Date	*Maker(s)	Kbs.	Past owners	Present or recent owner	Remarks
							A. HARPSICHORDS
		[1725					See below, no. 2]
		[1735					See below, no. 51]
01	—	1744		2		New York, private ownership	Inscribed: *Jacobus Kirckman Londini fecit 1744*; *IK* rose. Hugh Gough, who repaired it in 1961, sees no obvious reason why it should not date from 1744. This then is the earliest Kirkman known. *Hubb 1965* refers to it on p. 159. Marquetried case.
02	—	1749		1			Skelton, York, N. L. Wright (1961). Repaired by Robert Morley in 1962, the tail, which had at some time been sawn off 10 inches from the end, being replaced. 2 × 8′ stops. Typical *IK* rose with intertwined initials. (For subsequent instruments, these typical roses will not be recorded consistently.)

TABLE 21 (*cont.*):

No.	G–D (5 edn.) no.	Date	*Maker(s)	Kbs.	Past owners	Present or recent owner	Remarks
1	—	1750	J	2	England. Private ownership (1954), in which year it was acquired by Charles Fisher of Framingham, Mass.	Toronto, Michael Koerner (since about 1956)	2×8′, 1×4′, lute, with machine and buffstop added. No swell. F–F, 5 octaves, without bottom F sharp. Burr walnut with boxwood squares; marquetry round keyboards. Stand not original.
1a	—	1750	J	1	Hon. Mrs. Lucas, daughter of Baroness Pouche, to whose family it had always belonged	Bethersden, C. F. Colt	2×8′ stops and a buff added by R. Goble. Original walnut stand with 'spoon' feet.
2	1	1752	J	1	Kirkman & Son; T. G. Dyson (repairer); sold at Puttick & Simpson's, 27 June 1929, the buyer being Bolton	London, Benton Fletcher Collection, Fenton House	2×8′ stops only. F–F, 5 octaves without bottom F sharp. Rose, without initials. Case veneered in satin-wood, probably in modern times. Sold in 1934, when the catalogue misprinted the date as '1725'. Shewn at the International Inventions Exhibition, 1885.
3	2	1754	J	2	Charles Staal, Brompton Rd., S.W. 3 (1947), who bought it at Christie's; Mr. Van Zwannenberg (died about 1951); Messrs. Jetley, Bruton St., W.1 (1954)	Hampstead, Mr. Warburg (bought at Sotheby's, 11 March 1960)	An exceptionally fine instrument in appearance and tone. 2×8′, 1×4′, lute, machine; F–F, 5 octaves without lowest F sharp. Originally had lid-swell, which was unique in shape and size—probably an experiment—but is now glued up to make a solid lid; it was superseded by a Venetian swell, which has been removed since 1969. Nameboard bears silver plaque set in tortoiseshell and engraved with a trophy of instruments and (above) *O decus Phaebi* [Horace, *Odes* I. 32. 13], and (below) *Jacobus Kirckman Londini fecit 1754*. Veneered in burr walnut; case, lid and cheekpieces inlaid with boxwood squares. It was repaired by Messrs. Broadwood (1897), and T. R. C. Goff (1947).
4	3	1755	J	2	Padworth House. O. J. S. Moore; London, Raymond Russell; Mrs. Maud Russell, who sold it at Sotheby's to Edinburgh University	Edinburgh University, who bought it at Sotheby's, 22 October 1970	2×8′, 1×4′, lute. Richly marquetried, including the straight side. Illustrated in *DEF* (II. 375).
5?	4	1755	J	1	Napoleon Bonaparte (?); Simon Bates; Mrs. Wharff	Yale University (Steinert Collection)	2×8′, lute. Restored by Lotta van Buren, 1928. This instrument is probably not a Kirkman, in spite of the *IK* rose. The 2×8′ and lute would be unique on a Kirkman, but occur in harpsichords by Ferdinand Weber, who may well be the maker.
5a	—	1755	J	1	Dr. Edward Hill (1781–1830), a professor at Dublin University	Dorking, Mrs. Raymond Jennings	2 stops.
6	5	1756	J	2		G. C. Bushby (1946)	2×8′, 1×4′, lute. F–F, 5 octaves without bottom F sharp. Case richly marquetried.
7	—	1757	J	2		Trustees of Lady Burdett-Fisher. On loan to the Bristol Museum. (Formerly at Ramsbury Manor, Wilts.)	*IK* rose. 2×8′, 1×4′, lute, machine. No swell. Straight side not veneered. Elaborate marquetry including a trophy of instruments in middle of foreboard above keys. Inscription in pencil on back of nameboard: *J B R[estauravit] 1789* (? John Broadwood).
8	6	1758	J	2	Sir John J. Smith of Epping (formerly of Havering-at-Bower), who sold it by auction in London, 30 January 1959; sold at Sotheby's in 1960 to Frank Partridge, who sold it to a U.S. buyer	New York, P. Tolstoy (1965)	2×8′, 1×4′, lute. Case of burr walnut with laburnum banding. Fascia board inlaid with trophies of trumpeting angels and eagles.
9	7	1758	J	1		New York, Miss Perugina Adler	2×8′, 1×4′, 2 pedals.
9a	—	1758	J	1	Mrs. C. Cabot (1965)	Forest Hills, N.Y., E. M. Ripin	Came to light, 1924; had been fitted with a piano action and crescendo pedal by Merlin.
10	—	1759	J	2		White Post, Va., Alexander M. Smith	No rose. Used by B.B.C. about 1930.
11	8	1760	J	1	B. Rainbow; Hugh Gough; Messrs. Hubbard & Dowd, Boston	Newton, Mass., Dr. John Montgomery	2×8′, 1×4′, no pedals. Restored by A. Dolmetsch, 1897.

TABLE 21 (*cont.*):

No.	G–D (5 edn.) no.	Date	*Maker(s)	Kbs.	Past owners	Present or recent owner	Remarks
11a	—	1760	J	1		University of Western Australia, Armadale, W.A.	2×8′, 1×4′; remains of machine. No rose.
12	—	1760	J	2	Mrs. Arthur Tritton, Denford Mill, Hungerford; Mrs. G. Oldroyd, Croydon	M. Ekstein (1968)	2×8′, 1×4′, lute. Hand-stops only. Richly marquetried. Bought at Sotheby's, 12 June 1931, for £110 by Professor G. Oldroyd. Sold there by Mrs. Oldroyd, 18 April 1968, to M. Ekstein for £2,600.
13	—	1760	[J]	1	Cusworth Hall, Doncaster; Roger Warner, Burford; Michael Thomas, Hurley		2×8′, 1×4′. The inscription on nameboard: *Kirckman Londini fecit, 1760*, although unique, as far as I know, in omitting the Christian name, appears to be genuine. Usual compass, without bottom F sharp. No rose. 2×8′ hand-stops on R of nameboard, 1×4′ on L.
[14]	9	1761	J	2	Mrs. Hutton, Sevenoaks; Messrs. J. G. Morley (1946); J. S. Shelton (1947–52); Arnold Dolmetsch Ltd. (1952)	Kingswood, Surrey, Kenneth Skeaping	2×8′, 1×4′, buff, lute, machine; skunktail sharps; rose quite unlike a Kirkman rose. Not a Kirkman instrument. Behind the modern nameboard dated 1761 are the following inscriptions: *Andrew Douglas, Ewell 1951*; *Arnold Dolmetsch Ltd., 1949 Haslemere*; *Restored by J. S. Shelton, Lewisham, London, 1947–49*; *Repaired by Alec Hodsdon, Lavenham, Suffolk, 1948*. In the previous edition it was given the date 1763 in error and numbered 22.
15	10	1761	J	2	? Charlotte, Queen of George III; Arthur Hill; Major Cecil Wills (1946)	Dr. R. V. Cooke, Athelhampton Hall, Dorset (1965)	2×8′, 1×4′, lute. Richly marquetried, including the straight side. Illustrated at *J*, 130. This instrument is a claimant to the distinction of having been owned by Charlotte, Queen of George III. See also no. 14 above.
16	11	1761	J	1		Berlin Collection.	2×8′, 1×4′, buff, machine.
16a	—	1761	J	1	Robert Johnson, of Solana Beach, Calif., who passed it in 1960 to Colin Sterne, Philadelphia	Boston, Mass., Angus Whyte who bought it from Mr. Sterne in 1962	2×8′, 1×4′, machine. *IK* rose. Almost certainly the same instrument as nos. 17. and 20a below, there being a mistake in the record of the date of one of the instruments.
17	12	1762	J	1	Weald Hall, Brentwood, Essex	Mrs. Ramsay	2×8′, 1×4′, lute, buff, machine; lid-swell.
17a	—	1762(?)	J	2		Claydon House, Bucks. (1959)	
17b	—	1762	J	1		Boston, Mass., Angus White	2×8′, 1×4′ [*GL*].
17c	—	?	J	1		Pittsburgh, Pa., Colin Stone	
18	13	1762	J	2		London, Benton Fletcher Collection, Fenton House	2×8′, 1×4′, buff, lute, machine. *IK* rose.
19	14	1762	J	2		Williamsburg, Virginia	2×8′, 1×4′, lute, machine.
20	—	1762	J	2	Norman Wilkinson (until 1934)	Bought by Messrs., Morley, London, at Sotheby's, 6 July 1934	2×8′, 1×4′, lute, buff, machine. *IK* rose. Length 7′ 9″.
20a	—	1762	J	1	John Morley, London; Robert Johnson, Los Angeles; C. Sterne, Pittsburgh; A. Whyte, Boston, Mass.	Amsterdam, F. Brüggen (1972)	2×8′, 1×4′; pedal working the 4′. F–F, 5 octaves. See no. 16a above.
21	15	1763	J	1	Sir L. T. Davies	C. F. Colt, Bethersden, Kent	2×8′ only.
21a	—	1763	J	1	Stockport, Mr. Philpot; Messrs. Robert Morley (1960)	Gresford, N. Wales, Mrs. Graesser	2×8′ only.
[22]		[1763]					See above, no. 14.
23	17	1763	J	2		Stockholm, Musikhistoriska Museet	2×8′, 1×4′, buff. Exhibited at the Norsk Folkemuseet, 1904.
24	18	1763	J	2	J. S. Shedlock; Miss Eleanor Wilkinson; Miss M. Foster Evans; Lady Jordan, Sydney, N.S.W.	Sydney, N.S.W., Museum of Applied Arts and Sciences (1964–)	2×8′, 1×4′, machine. *Jacobus Kirckman Londini fecit 1763*.

TABLE 21 (*cont.*):

No.	G–D (5 edn.) no.	Date	*Maker(s)	Kbs.	Past owners	Present or recent owner	Remarks
24a	—	1763	J	1		Wahroonga, N.S.W., Timothy C. Yates	
25	—	1763	J	2		T. G. Odling (1953)	2×8′, 1×4′, lute. Rose not original.
26	—	1764	J	1	Tunbridge Wells, David Kent; London, R. Russell	Humphrey Evans	
27	19	1764	J	1		Messrs. J. G. Morley (1946); Randolph Michaelson (1971)	2×8′, 1×4′.
28	—	1764	J	1	Sir Charles Lawes-Wittewronge, Bt., of Rothamsted, Herts.		Sold at Christie's, 14 May 1936, to Messrs. J. G. Morley. Possibly same instrument as no. 27.
28a	—	1764	J	1			Reported by Robert Robinette as in the U.S.A., 1967. Walnut case; no stand. (*Not* the same instrument as no. 28.)
[29]							= no. 26 above.
29a	—	1764	J	1			2×8′ stops. Seen by Raymond Russell in 1957 at Morley's (South Kensington), who had not seen the instrument before.
29b	—	1764	J	1		Goudhurst, Kent, Messrs. Adlam and Burnett	2×8′, 1×4′, machine (later, but eighteenth century, addition). F–F, 5 octaves, without lowest F sharp. *IK* rose. Bought at Sotheby's, 1971.
30	20	1765	J	1	Mrs. F. R. Hammond, Holyoke, Mass.	Williamsburg, Virginia	2×8′ only.
30a	—	1765	J	1		Dunster Castle, Somerset, Mrs. Alys Luttrell	2×8′ stops; 'acorn' stop-knobs in brass.
30b	—	1766	J	1	Mrs. R. Sherry of Cecil House, Bentley, Essex; Messrs. Ratcliff, Kelvedon, Essex; Pro Musica Instrument Co., Annapolis, Md.	Joseph Rawley, High Point, N.C. (1967)	2×8′, 1×4′; 3 hand-stops, 1 pedal for disengaging the 4′.
31	—	1766	J	2		Amerongen, Dr. G. A. Graaf Bentinck	*IK* rose; 2 pedals; 5 stops.
32	21	1766	J	2	Sir Rowland Winn, Bt.	Nostell Priory	Richly marquetried; 2×8′, 1×4′, lute, harp, machine, lid-swell. Kirkman's original bill, preserved at Nostell, reads: 'Sir Rowland Winn, Bart. Dr to Jacob Kirkman September ye 1st 1767: An Inlaid Double Keyed Harpsichord Cover Veneerd Desk inside with machine pedals 85 guineas £89. 5. / Leather cover for D° £1. 10. –. / Packing case for D° £–. 15. –. / [Total] £91. 10. –. / For the use & Tuning of a Double Key'd Harpsichord from March 10th to June 18th 1767 £2. 14. – / Recd July the 5th 1768 the contents in full of all demand for Uncle Jacob Kirkman: £94. 4. –.'
32a	—	—	J	1		Christopher Hogwood, Cambridge	Bought at Puttick & Simpson's in 1972; 2×8′, 1×4′, buff. *IK* rose. Restored at some time by Alec Hodsdon.
33	22	1766		2	? Charlotte, Queen of George III; Warley Place, Essex; Miss E. A. Wilmot who sold it at Sotheby's, 5 April 1935	Major Robert Berkeley (at Spetchley, Worcs., 1968)	5 stops, machine, lid-swell. Very fine marquetry. The straight side is veneered with burr walnut panels, as on the bent side. According to *Burlington Magazine*, Vol. 37 (1920), p. 263, this instrument belonged to Charlotte, Queen of George III. The other claimant to this honour is no. 15 above. This instrument and no. 32 are unlike any others in that they have lid-swells and machine-stops but their stands have only 1 pedal. Apart from no. 3 above they are the earliest lid-swells we know; the lid-swells are much smaller, and may perhaps represent an experiment with a new type, the earlier having proved too cumbersome. No. 33 was restored in 1969 by Charles Mould.
34	—	1767	J	1		Leipzig University, Heyer Collection	2×8′, 1×4′ registers. Pedal for disengaging 4′; 5 octaves F–F, without bottom F sharp. Rose depicted at *Ks*, Vol. 2, p. 662.
35	23	1767	J	2	Mrs. Spencer Curwen, who sold it in 1927 to the present owners	Liverpool, Messrs. Rushworth & Dreaper	

TABLE 21 (*cont.*):

No.	G–D (5 edn.) no.	Date	*Maker(s)	Kbs.	Past owners	Present or recent owner	Remarks
36	24	1767	J	2	W. Barrow, Llandudno	U.S. Ambassador, Middendorf, The Hague (Sotheby's, 21. 12. 1972)	2×8′, 1×4′, lute. See *The Listener*, 12 January 1939. [Mr. Barrow's 'Joseph' is a mistake for 'Jacob'.] Offered for sale at Sotheby's, 21 December 1972.
37	25	1768	J	1	Sold anonymously at Puttick & Simpson's, 18 October 1934. Bought by Mr. Weather [?]		
38	26	1768	J	2	C. K. Salaman; Malcolm Salaman (1937); F. Walker who offered it for sale at Sotheby's, 6 May 1955		2×8′, 1×4′, lute, buff, machine. Venetian swell. Selected by Dr. Burney in 1768 for the tuition of Malcolm Salaman's great-grandmother. See *Antique Collector*, 1937. Exhibited in 1872.
39	27	1768	J	1		Messrs. Forty, Birmingham	
40	—	1768	J	1	Sold anonymously at Puttick & Simpsons, 27 June 1935. Bought by 'Wertheim'		
41	28	1769	J	2		M. Steinert Collection, Yale University	2×8′, 1×4′, buff, lute, machine. Restored by Lotta van Buren, 1928.
42	29	1769	J	1	Mrs. Trafford, Goodrich Court; Alan Legg; Hugh Gough; Albert Honey; Noel Dilkes; R. Bibby (bought 1 June 1961 at Christie's)	D. Graebe, Eastbourne (1967)	2×8′. Workman's signature *Cross* on top key and back of nameboard.
[42a]	—	1770	J	2	S. Gabriel, Glasgow	Glasgow University	2×8′, 1×4′, lute, doglegged 8′. Inscription on nameboard: *Jacobus Kirckman Londini fecit 1748* (probably genuine, but from an earlier instrument); but under the soundboard is inscribed: *Robt. Falkener London fecit 1770*. Restored by W. R. Thomas and J. Rhodes, 1959–60.
43	29a	1770	J	1		Rushworth and Dreaper Collection, Liverpool	2×8′ stops. Nameboard missing; date given in the owners' catalogue.
44	30	1770	J	1	Mrs. Hughes-Martin; Messrs. J. G. Morley		2×8′ only.
44a	—	1772	J	1	Hugo Worch, Washington, D.C.; Charles Fisher, Framingham, Mass.	John Fespermann, Washington, D.C. (1965–)	2×8′ stops. Was in a Baltimore antique shop in 1931.
45	31	1771	J	?	J. E. Minns, Taunton (1904)		Advertised in the *Musical Times*, August 1904.
46	31a	1771	J	2		Aberdeen University	Restored by Alec Hodsdon, 1950, and Charles Mould, 1969. Has 2×8′, 1×4′, lute, buff, machine, and lid-swell. Little of the original instrument remains.
47	—	1771	J	1	Wm. Alexander Simpson (d. 1918)	Dundee Museum (since 1918)	Walnut. *IK* rose; 2×8′ only.
48	32	1772	J	2	John Bacon, R.A., sculptor (1740–99); Dr. Slatter, priest-vicar of Exeter Cathedral; Carl Engel; Mrs. P. E. Bowman	Oxford, Ashmolean Museum	2×8′, 1×4′, buff, lute, machine. Venetian swell. Case of burr walnut inlaid with tulip wood. Cheek-pieces and nameboards marquetried, with trophy of musical instruments on the nameboard. Claw-and-ball cabriole legs. Straight side not veneered. Restored by Robert Goble, 1965.
48a	—	1772	J	2		Marquis of Bute, Cumnock, Ayr	2×8′, 1×4′, lute. On back of nameboard: *Restrung, requilled, regulated, tuned and repaired by John Denham, 1888– organist to Lord Bute* [*Thomas W*].
49	32a	1772	J&A	2	Cecilia, Countess of Strathmore; Countess of Granville; Raymond Russell	Mrs. Maud Russell, London. (On loan to Geraint Jones, 1972)	F–C, 5½ octaves. This extension upwards to C appears to be unique. On the keys above top G the colouring is reversed, the naturals being black and the sharps white. Bought at Sotheby's 5 June 1953 by Raymond Russell. 2×8′, 1×4′, buff, lute, machine, no swell. 1 pedal. Rose (harping King David, with trophy of instruments Illustrated *Russell 1959*, pl. 72.

TABLE 21 (*cont.*):

No.	G–D (5 edn.) no.	Date	*Maker(s)	Kbs.	Past owners	Present or recent owner	Remarks
50	33	1772	J	2	Lady Bray, Stanford House, Swinford; Irvin Hinchliffe (1946); at Polesden Lacey, Surrey until about 1952; Glyndebourne (bought at Sotheby's 1 August 1958)	London, Horniman Museum, 1972 (bought through Sotheby's)	Restored by R. Bagot, Kendal, 1959.
51	34	1772	?	1	Irvin Hinchliffe		Sold at Sotheby's (like no. 50) on 1 August 1958; the catalogue gave the impossible date '1735'.
51a	—	1772	?	1		Chas. F. Willis, Jr., Washington, D.C. (1967)	2×8′ [*CM*].
52	—	1773	J&A	1	Sir Chas. V. Stanford, who gave it to the present owner's grandfather	R. McEwen, Greenlaw, Berwicks. (1970)	
53	35	1773	J&A	2	Carl Engel; A. J. Hipkins	London, Royal College of Music	Lid-swell. All stops. *IK* rose. Presented to the R.C.M. by Edith Hipkins in 1903.
54	36	1773	J&A	2	J. K. Pyne		Lid-swell. Exhibited 1885. 2×8′, 1×4′, lute, buff, machine.
55	—	1773	J&A	1	Captain R. E. Huddleston, R.N., Sawston Hall, Cambridge (d. January 1970)		Bought in 1788 for £27. 2*s*. [*Country Life*, 24 June 1954, p. 2092].
[56]	67	1773	J	2	General Reid (not Sir Donald Tovey)	Edinburgh University	Not by Kirkman but by Falkener. Nameboard inscribed: *Jacobus Kirkman* [sic] *Londini fecit*, no date being given. Un-Kirkman like rose; 2×8′, 1×4′, lute, buff. Hand-stops now dummies. All stops except the buff are worked by a unique 2-pedal machine. Pencilled inscription on underside of soundboard: *Robert Falkener London fecit 1773 September.*
56a	—	1774	J&A	1	Countess of Dysart, at Stobo Castle	Sold by the Countess to an anonymous buyer at Sotheby's, 13 March 1972	F–F, 5 octaves without lowest F sharp; 2×8′, 1×4′, buff, machine. *IK* rose. Length: 7′ 3″.
57	37	1774	J&A	1	E. Croft-Murray; Hugh Gough; Mr. Lambert, Bath	E. F. Taylor, Newport, Isle of Wight (1968)	2×8′, 1×4′, buff. Originally had Kirkman machine-stop. *IK* rose. Restored by Dolmetsch, 1948.
57a	—	1775	J&A	2		Hon. Wayland H. Young	Sotheby's 27 April 1956.
57b	—	1775	J&A	2	Raymond Russell (bought 1956)	Gustav Leonhardt (1957)	2×8′, 1×4′, lute, buff, machine, lid-swell.
57c	—	1775	J&A	2		Brockenhurst Park, J. Morant	2×8′, 1×4′, lute, buff. (See *Antique Collector*, August 1954, p. 140.)
58	38	1776	J&A	1	Messrs. J. G. Morley (1946)	Nicholas Jackson, London	2×8′, 1×4′ stops.
59	39	1776	J&A	1	Steinert Collection (Chicago version of catalogue)	Washington, Smithsonian Institution	2×8′, 1×4′, Kirkman machine. Presented by Hugo Worch in 1892.
60	40	1776	J&A	1	London, Trinity College of Music; London, Victoria and Albert Museum	Dr. R. Mirrey, Redhill (1969)	2×8′, 1×4′, Kirkman machine.
60a	—	1776	J&A	2		London, Bethnal Green Museum	(See *Antique Collector*, August 1954, p. 154; also *Russell V&A*.)
60b	—	1776	J&A	1		Arbroath, Angus, The Patrick Allan Fraser of Hospitalfield House, since 1800 when it went there from Hawkesbury Hall, Warwicks., residence of the then Mrs. Fraser's father, Francis Parrott, M.D., for which it was probably originally bought	
61	—	1776	J&A	2		Balmanno Castle, Hon. James Bruce	Machine-stop; *IK* rose. Elaborate marquetry but plain straight side.

TABLE 21 (*cont.*):

No.	G–D (5 edn.) no.	Date	*Maker(s)	Kbs.	Past owners	Present or recent owner	Remarks
61a	—	1776	J&A	2		Trinity College, Dublin	Found in a farm building; repaired by Robert Morley, 1962. 2×8′, 1×4′, lute, buff, nag's-head swell. *IK* rose.
62	41	1777	J&A	2	T. R. C. Goff; Anthony Sharp	Michael Thomas (1970)	5 pedals. Lid-swell. Illustrated in *Apollo*, September/October 1943, p. 99. *IK* rose. Cross-banded mahogany case with burr walnut cheek-pieces; 2×8′, 1×4′, buff, machine. Converted by T. R. C. Goff and J. C. Cobby in 1939 to pedal action (though the brass hand-stops remain *in situ*) and inscribed by them below the lower manual: *T.R.C.G. et J.C.C. refecerunt MCMXXXIX.* Bought by M. Thomas from A. Sharp at Sotheby's, 12 March 1970.
62a	—	1777	J&A	1	Alan Steinert	Yale University	2×8′, 1×4′.
63	42	1777	J&A	2		London, Benton Fletcher Collection, Fenton House	Lid-swell. All stops. *IK* rose. Original music rest.
64	43	1777	?	1		Messrs. H. Taylor & Son, Walsall	2×8′, 1×4′.
64a	—	1777	J&A	1	Col. Jones who inherited it from a Cromwellian house in Shropshire; Mrs. Farquhar of Heswell, Cheshire	London, A. Doran (acquired about 1968)	2×8′, 1×4′; *IK* rose. Original stand.
65	44	1778	J&A	1	Miss Joyce Riddle	London, Chas. McKerrow (1961)	2×8′, 1×4′, buff, simple machine-stop.
65a	—	1778	J&A	1	Cliftonville, Mr. Kennard; R. B. Bibby of Seale, Farnham, who bought it from Mr. Kennard in 1964	David Simpson, Thorpe-le-Soken, who acquired it from R. B. Bibby in 1964	2×8′, 1×4′, simple machine-stop; nag's-head swell.
65b	—	1778	J&A	1	Mrs. Emans, Colchester	Miss Zena Tibbenham, Lower Ufford, Suffolk (1972)	2×8′, 1×4′, buff.
66	45	1779	J&A	2	Miss Rosemary Howard; Raymond Barnett, London	The Revd. James Simpson, Winchester (1965)	Bought at Sotheby's 23 June 1961 by J. G. Morley for a client. Lid-swell.
66a	—	1779	J&A	1	Mr. Burt, Dower House, Woodbridge, Suffolk	Private ownership, St. Albans (1972)	2×8′, 1×4′, Kirkman machine. Repaired by R. Morley, 1964.
66b	—	1779	J&A	1	Queens' College, Cambridge (1967)	Mrs. S. Stevens, Maxey, Peterborough (1967–)	2×8′. Restored by T. Beckerleg, Cambridge, in 1969.
66c	—	1780	J&A	2		Boston, Mass., private ownership	Originally a single-manual instrument.
67	47	178–?		1	Mrs. A. E. Southall	Mrs. Hutchinson, Hampstead	
68	48	1781	J&A	2		The Earl of Jersey. Kept at Osterley Park until the National Trust took it over in 1949.	Present whereabouts unknown.
68a	—	1781	J&A			Wellington, N.Z., Ronald B. Castle (1959)	2×8′, 1×4′, lid-swell. Bought by present owner from J. G. Morley in 1939.
68b	—	1781	J&A		Had been in the Smarden area of Kent for some time	Tunbridge Wells, David Kent (1971)	2×8′, 1×4′, buff, a unique type of machine; *IK* rose. Original stand, with 4 underslung drawers curved to follow the outline of the instrument; original music-rest. Barely changed since leaving Kirkman's workshop.
69	49	1781	J&A	1		New York, Metropolitan Museum of Art	Machine; no swell.
70	—	1781	J&A	1		Forsyth Collection, Manchester	Machine; no swell.
70a	—	1782	J&A	?		C. Pinkey, Ladyholt, Chichester	A shell, converted into a bureau.
	50	1783	J&A	2	Van Raalte College, Brownsea Island	John Ticehurst	2×8′, 1×4′, lute, buff, machine; lid-swell.

TABLE 21 (*cont.*):

No.	G–D (5 edn.) no.	Date	*Maker(s)	Kbs.	Past owners	Present or recent owner	Remarks
71a	—	1784	J&A	1		Robt. Hawkings, Salisbury (1966)	2×8′, 1×4′, buff.
71b	—	1784	J&A	1		Believed sold in Israel [*CM*, 1965]	
71c	—	1785	J&A	1	Gerrards Cross, Mrs. J. Tomlin	Augustine Ford, London	Sold at Christie's, 15 December 1955, to the present owner; 2×8′, 1×4′, buff, machine.
72	—	1785	J&A	2		C. Brackenbury, Berwick-on-Tweed	2×8′, 1×4′, lute, buff, machine; lid-swell.
73	51	1785	J&A	2	G. S. Hughes, Hitchin; R. R. Henshaw, Bradford-on-Avon	N. L. Wright, William House, Yorks.	2×8′, 1×4′, lute, buff, machine; lid-swell.
73a	—	1785	J&A	1	Robt. Johnson, Solana Beach, Calif., who bought it through John Morley *c.* 1956	Dr. Myron C. Smith, Malibu, Calif. (1969)	2×8′, 1×4′ stops.
73b	—	1785	J&A	2	David Drey (bought at Christie's	[1971 owner not ascertained]	2×8′, 1×4′, buff, machine; *IK* rose [*Falc*].
74	—	1786	J&A	2	At Robertsbridge	John Barnes, Edinburgh	2×8′, 1×4′, lute, buff, machine; lid-swell; *IK* rose. Restored in 1915 by Charles Hersant of Finsbury Park.
75	52	1786	J&A	2	Major Benton Fletcher (1934)	Eric Johnson, London	Originally single-manual with 2×8′, 1×4′ stops. Another manual and a lute stop added recently.
76	53	1787	J&A	1	H. J. Dale; Mrs. Trafford, Goodrich Court	John Ticehurst	2×8′, 1×4′, buff. Pedal to disengage second unison. Exhibited 1885.
77	54	1787		1		Birmingham (1946)	
77a	—	1787	J&A	1	Norman Wilkinson	Glasgow, Royal Scottish Academy of Music and Drama	2×8′. *IK* rose.
78	—	1787	J&A	1	Duke of Rutland	G. M. Grocott	2×8′, 1×4′, no buff. (Purchased by the present owner in 1936.)
79	55	1787	J&A	2	H. B. Noble (sold it at Sotheby's, 13 December 1935 to E. C. Legg, Cirencester); Roger Yates	Geraint Jones	2×8′, 1×4′, lute, buff, machine; lid-swell.
79a	—	1787	J&A	2	St. Albans, L. Larholt	P. Badura-Skoda	2×8′, 1×4′, lute, buff, machine; lid-swell. *IK* rose. Venetian swell added by Morley in 1965. Note on back of nameboard: *After years of silence I was made to speak by John Sebastian Morley AD 1922*, followed by an inscription by Morley's foreman: *My speach* [sic] *failed again. Restored 1964 K S Rolfe* [*CM*].
80	—	1788	J&A	2			International Inventions Exhibition 1885.
81	56	1788	J&A	2	Dr. Charles Burney; Mr. Wilson	Edward Croft-Murray, 1939–	2×8′, 1×4′, lute, buff, machine. Venetian swell.
82	—	1788	J&A	1		Forsyth Collection, Manchester	Machine; Venetian swell. 2×8′, 1×4′, lute, buff.
83	57	1789	J&A	2	J. K. Pyne		Venetian swell (originally lid-swell). Exhibited 1885. 2×8′, 1×4′, buff, lute, machine.
84	58	1789	J&A	2	Norman Wilkinson; Alec Hodsdon (Sotheby's, 6 July 1934)		Full range of stops; machine; lid-swell. *IK* rose. Length 7′.
85	—	1789	A&Jo	2	Said to have been made for Dr. Philips Hayes, organist of Magdalen College, Oxford; Miss Nellie Chaplin (until 1932)	Bought in 1932 by David McKenna, who now (1965) owns it	2×8′, 1×4′, lute, buff, machine; had at one time a lid-swell. Rose *IK* and harping figure. Restored by Charles Hersant, 1907. Was used in Nigel Playfair's production of *The Beggar's Opera*, Lyric Theatre, Hammersmith 1920–2.
85a	—	1790	A&Jo	1		Sammlung Chrysander, Hamburg (Hamburg-Bergedorfer Händel-Archiv)	See *Quick*. München, Vol. 9, no. 36, September 1956, pp. 3–4.

TABLE 21 (*cont.*):

No.	G–D (5 edn.) no.	Date	*Maker(s)	Kbs.	Past owners	Present or recent owner	Remarks
86	59	1790	J&A	1	F. Pickett; Mrs. E. M. Jones, Tunbridge Wells; Hugh Gough (1951)	Miss Philippa Saunders, Chelsea	2×8′, 1×4′; no buff; no pedals, but traces of a Kirkman-machine pedal.
87	—	1790	A&Jo	1		Taunton Castle Museum	2×8′, 1×4′, Venetian swell, machine.
88	—	1791	A&Jo	2	Miss Ellen Willmott	David McKenna (acquired in 1935)	2×8′, 1×4′, lute, buff, machine. New soundboard and wrestplank by Tull. *IK* Rose. Lid-swell.
89	60	1791	A&Jo	1	The Revd. F. N. Davey, Hampstead	Scarsdale, N.Y., Collection of Dr. and Mrs. R. M. Rosenbaum. (Bought at Sotheby's, 8 June 1971)	2×8′, 1×4′, buff; machine, lid-swell. *IK* rose. Restored by Rushworth and Dreaper.
90	61	1791	?	1	Alec Hodsdon		
91	—	1793	?	1		In private ownership in Hampstead (1950)	2×8′, 1×4′, buff
92	62	1796	?	1	Alec Hodsdon; Messrs. Arnold Dolmetsch	John Baines, London, S.W. 7 (1965)	2×8′, 1×4′.
93	63	1798	Jo	2	Canon F. W. Galpin	Boston Museum of Fine Arts	2×8′, 1×4′, buff, lute, machine, Venetian swell. Illustrated in catalogue. Inscription: *Josephus Kirckman Londini fecit 1798 / No. 19 Broad street, Soho.*
94	64	1798	Jo	2	A. Fuller-Maitland; Esther Darlington; Miss Margaret Field-Hyde	Mrs. Katherine Thirkell	2×8′, 1×4′, lute, buff, machine. Venetian swell. Stops have ivory handles.
95	65	1800	Jo	2	Capt. J. R. Lane, Wanstead	C. F. Colt	2×8′, 1×4′, lute, buff, machine. Venetian swell. Stops have ivory handles.
[—	—	1809					See above. (The last Kirkman harpsichord was made in this year)]
96	66	[? 1758]	J	1	R. Powys Lybbe; Messrs. Arnold Dolmetsch Ltd.		2×8′, lute, buff added later. Original machine-stop removed.
[—	67	n.d.	J	2	Sir Donald Tovey	Edinburgh University	See above number 56.]
97	68	n.d.	?	2	Miss Lane Poole, Oxford; Messrs. Arnold Dolmetsch Ltd.	Boston, Mass., Messrs. Fisher-Pierce (1953)	2×8′, 1×4′, buff, lute, machine. Venetian swell.
98	—	n.d.	J	2			2×8′, 1×4′, buff, lute, machine, and lid-swell. *IK* rose. In wrecked condition when it was sold by auction at 245 East 23rd Street, New York on 6 December 1949.
99	—	n.d.	?	1		Lord Sackville, Knole	Nameboard missing. *IK* rose in soundboard. Date probably *c.* 1770.
100	46	n.d.	J	2	Lady Kathleen Pilkington (until 1934)	Bought by Alec Hodsdon at Sotheby's, 6 July 1934	All stops. Lid-swell. Length 7′ 10″. In bad condition in 1934. Sotheby's catalogue dates it *c.* 1780.
101	—	n.d.	J	1	Boston Antique Shop, Mass.	Ford Museum, Dearborn, Mich., until 1972, when lost	Unsigned, but with rose. Much restored, with new keyboard and soundboard. 2×8′, 1×4′. Reported compass F–E nearly 6 octaves.
101a	—	n.d.	J	1	Lotta van Buren	Forest Hills, N.Y., private ownership (1968)	Nameboard missing; 2×8′ stops.
102	—	n.d.	J	2			[Same as no. 98 above, q.v.]
103	—	n.d.	J	2			2×8′, 1×4′, lute, buff, machine, lid-swell. Oak case with line inlay. Lot 96 at Sotheby's, 6 July 1934. Catalogue says: 'By J. Kirckman, *c.* 1780, in poor condition.' 92″ long. Perhaps the same instrument as no. 98 above.
103a	—	n.d.	?	2		Chas. Fisher, Framingham, Mass.	Nameboard missing; 2×8′, 1×4′, buff, lute, machine, lid-swell. Case and lid in burr walnut veneer. Trophy of instruments on fascia board. Found in a Bronx warehouse. An inscription inside records repairs by Wm. Knabe, March 1917.
104	—	n.d.	?			Toronto, R. Ontario Museum	No inscription, but *IK* rose says *Hirt*, p. 266; 2×8′ 1×4′; Venetian swell. Illustrated in *Alb.*

TABLE 21 (*cont.*)

No.	G–D (5 edn.) no.	Date	*Maker(s)	Kbs.	Past owners	Present or recent owner	Remarks
					B. SPINETS		
104a	—	1748	J	1			In U.S.A. in 1965 [*CM*].
105	—	1750	J	1	Mrs. Harrison Williams (U.S.A.)	Bought in New York, October 1952, by Miss N. Feldman	
106	—	? 1751	J	1	Lord Cholmondeley	Messrs. Scotney of Stamford (1953)	Said to be dated 1721, but the date has been altered. Illustrated in an advertisement in the *Collectors' Guide*, September 1953.
107	—	1755	J	1	Firm of Kirkman & Sons, who shewed it at the International Inventions Exhibition, London, 1885		
107a	—	1763	J	1	Stibbington, near Peterborough, Mrs. Christie (1958)	Stibbington, Dr. Huntsman (1969)	Mahogany case. Repaired in 1958 by Robert Morley. Lid taken from another instrument [*CM*].
108	—	?	J	1		From Peckforton Castle, Cheshire. Walnut case. Sold at Christie's, 14 May 1953 by the Trustees of the Tollemache Estates. Bought by an agent	*Jacobus Kirkman Londini fecit.*
					C. CLAVIORGANA		
109	—	1745	J	2		In private ownership in Scotland	Made by Kirkman and Snetzler. 2 manuals, of which the lower can be coupled to the organ. Harpsichord stops: 2×8′, 1×4′, lute; organ: 5 stops. Inscription on nameboard: *Jacobus Kirckman fecit Londini*, above which is a monogram *IK*, repeated in the rose. Compass 5 octaves F–F, without low F sharp. Signature on the organ: *Johan Snetzler fecit Londini 1745*. See further Peter Williams's article in *RipKb*, p. 75.

KIRSCHNIGK. *c.* 1787–90, St. Petersburg. Made fortepianos organisés [*Moos*]. May have made harpsichords.

KIRSHAW [Kershaw]. Family of harpsichord and spinet makers in Tib Lane, Manchester.

(*a*) **John**, dates ascertained, 1740–73; mentioned as a harpsichord maker in the *Manchester Directory* of 1772 (where he is spelt 'Kershaw'). *Hirt* has found him in 1740.

Surviving Instruments

(1) Tenterden, John Ticehurst. Spinet. (Formerly at Goodrich Court, Ross-on-Wye.)

(2) Morley had an undated transverse harpsichord by Kirshaw (May 1946), having 2 strings to each note. Case of walnut; ivory naturals.

(3) Liverpool, Rushworth and Dreaper Collection. Spinet. 5 octaves F–F.

(4) Paris, private ownership (1953). Spinet.

(5) Madison, Wis., Norman Paulu. Harpsichord signed: *John Kirshaw Manchester 1769*. F–F, 5 octaves; 2×8′, 1×4′, buff. *IK* rose, rather similar to a Kirkman rose. Inscribed on lowest jack: *John Kirshaw, April 19th, 1769.* Michael Thomas bought it from Alan Legg of Cirencester in 1961, and it was restored by Alfred Reeve, Maidenhead, in 1962 (illustrated in *The Guardian*, 3 April 1962). From a tin containing the jacks, in 1962, it appears to have belonged to the vicar of Snodland, Kent, early in this century.

(6) Halifax, Yorks. (1966). D. Greenwood, whose family have owned it at least from the time of his great-grandfather. Spinet, signed on nameboard: *John Kirshaw Manchester*; 61 notes; walnut-veneered case.

(7) Edgworth, Lancs., Miss M. Whitehurst. Spinet, bought from a local antique dealer about 1962. The very faint inscription on the nameboard reads something like: *Johannes Kirshaw Mancunii fecit.*

(*b*) **Joseph,** perhaps son of John, whom he joined as partner in 1773, according to the *Manchester Directory* of that year, which lists the firm as 'John and Joseph Kershaw, harpsichord makers, Tib Lane'.

KLEBILLER, Johann. Perhaps a virginal maker, *fl.* 1617 in Augsburg. *See under*: KILIAN, Lucas.

KLEIN, Joseph. A spinet *c.* 1800 (4 octaves F–F) signed *Joseph Klein Wien* is in the Nymphenburg Palace, Munich.

A gebunden South German clavichord bearing the inscription inside the bottom, under the keys, *1783 IK*, might be by him. C/E–F, 4 octaves; 33 pairs of strings; string gauges from 1 to 9 on some of the keys. Early (? original) tuning-hammer. White naturals. Rose *PMD*. Size 123×37×16 cm. Restored by Peter Kukelka in 1968. (Vienna, private ownership, 1971.)

KLEMM, J. G. *See*: CLEMM, Johann Gottlob.

KLIEM, *c.* 1800. Lived at Brüheim near Gotha. Maker of keyboard instruments. Previously he had lived at Kassel for a long period [*Ge*].

KNEIPHOF, Peter von. *See*: PETER *vom Kneiphof.*

KNOEBEL, Johann Christian. Organ builder, pupil of Oehme, *fl.* 1799; made clavichords, 'only of soft wood, it is true, but of good tone' [*Fla*, 1953 edition].

KOCH, Chr. A 2-manual harpsichord in the Musée Grévin, Paris, formerly attributed to Koch, is now known to be by Christian Kroll, q.v.

KOCH, Mathias, of Strasbourg 'wohnhaft in der Münchenstrasse'. Harpsichord and spinet maker, *fl.* 1757. In this year a description of a 3-manual harpsichord made by him appears in *Marp*. It had 3 unisons, an octave, and a double harp-stop (i.e. a divided one, which could work on either half of the keyboard, leaving the other half unaffected).

A spinet by him dated 1757 is in the Nationalmuseum, Munich [*Ks*, p. 428].

KORYCKI, Stanisław, of Warsaw. Eighteenth-century harpsichord maker [*Va*, *Szulc*].

KRAFT, Mathias Peter. Instrument maker of Stockholm. Born 14 June 1753 at Gävle; died 9 July 1807 at Stockholm. The best-known instrument maker of his time in Sweden. Son of a joiner, he learnt instrument making under Lundborg (q.v.). In 1780 he was already Instrument-maker to the Swedish Court, which office he still held in 1802, for a square piano, now in the Göteborgs Museum, bears the label: *Pet. Kraft. Kongl. Hof. Instrum. Makare, Stockholm n 276 A 1802*. (Nordiska Museet, Stockholm, has grand pianofortes by him of 1788 and 1800.) In 1788 he received the citizenship of Stockholm. For over 2 decades he confined himself to violins, lutes, and harps, but towards the end of the century he turned to clavichord making and in 1798 became a member of the Guild of Joiners in order to obtain journeymen joiners for this purpose [*Lü*; *Nor*, p. 93].

Surviving Clavichords

(1) 1806. Stockholm, Nordiska Museet; 5 octaves and 7 notes.

KRÄMER

(*a*) **Johann Paul** (1743–1819), maker of harpsichords and clavichords, was born 1743 at Jüchsen in Meiningen. He was instructed in instrument making at Grossbreitenbach in Thuringia and settled in Göttingen. His harpsichords won him a great name throughout Saxony and Hanover, and were as highly valued (according to Gerber) as the violins of Stradivari and Guarneri. Without being himself a great musician, he apparently had a very acute ear for beauty of tone.

In 1806 his sons set up on their own; but he continued alone, and died at Göttingen 9 March 1819 [*Ge*, *Ks*].

He charged from 4 to 14 *louis d'or* for his clavichords [C. Engel, *Musical Instruments*, revised edition, London, 1908, p. 122].

(*b*) **Siegmund Theodor** (1750–1828), maker of clavichords and pianofortes, perhaps the brother of (*a*). He married Elisabeth Moringer, who bore him two sons. He died at Göttingen 26 October 1828.

KRÄMER. *See also*: MERCATOR, Sir Michael.

KRETZSCHMAR, Georg. Dates ascertained, 1565–1623 [*Hirt*]; organ builder and instrument maker at Dresden *c.* 1574. In an inventory having the date 1593 there is an entry (no. 26): 'Geigeninstrument so Georg Kretschmar gemacht', also for 'ein Flügel darunter auch ein Positif', 'ein gross Positif mit einem Instrument' [probably a spinet], and (twice) 'ein Clavicordium darunter ein Flötwergk'. In 1547 he built an organ for the Schlosskirche at Annaberg, which earned him 200 florins, and in 1587 he received 250 thalers for an organ built for the Schlosskirche at Freiberg [*Lü*]. According to *Hirt* he made clavichords as well.

KREUEL, Pius. Born Zug 1629; died Einsiedeln 1696. Builder of organs and other keyboard instruments [*Hirt*, p. 477].

KRICKHOF, Frederick. Spinet maker in London in 1731, doubtless of German extraction.

Surviving Spinets

(1) 1731. Tunbridge Wells, Mrs. Cecil Burns. Inscription: *Friderick Krickhof Londini Fecit 1731*. Compass G–E, 4 octaves and a 6th. Skunktail sharps. Walnut case. Repaired by Alec Hodsdon in 1948.

KROLL, Christian. An eighteenth-century harpsichord maker of whom we know nothing except that 3 of his instruments have been preserved. *See* Addenda.

Surviving Harpsichords.

(1) 1770. Claude Mercier-Ythier, Paris. Two-manual, dated 1770.

(2) 1779. Paris, Musée Grévin. Two-manual; 2 × 8′, 1 × 4′ stops; compass, 5 octaves and 1 note, E–F.

KUESE, Pieter [? Keuse, ? Ruese]. Harpsichord maker in Haarlem in 1611, when his age was 34 [*Curtis*, p. 52].

KUNZ, Ignaz. Clavichord maker, *fl.* 1821 at Jaromer, near Königsgraz, Bohemia.

The National Museum, Prague has a bundfrei clavichord by him signed: *Ignaz Kunz Jaromer, 1821*. Black naturals, ivory sharps. Compass F–A. Size 160×48 cm.

KUPPLER, Johann Georg. Nephew and pupil of Stein (q.v.). Settled in Nuremberg as instrument maker in 1789. His work was chiefly piano making, and converting harpsichords into pianos; but he presumably made a certain number of harpsichords in his earlier years [*Ge*].

KURTZ, Johann. Organist in Tübingen, built in 1681 a keyed harp, 'eine neu erfundene Harfe, so durch ein Klavier gleich einem Spinett zu schlagen', probably a kind of gut-strung clavicytherium [*Ge*]. He presumably built normal keyboard instruments also.

TABLE 22. *KRÄMER Clavichords Extant, or until recently Extant*

No.	Date	Signature	Owner/Remarks
Johann Paul			
1	1787	*Sorte 3, Nr. 207 / Johann Paul Kraemer und Sohn, Göttingen*	Nuremberg, Germanisches Nationalmuseum. Bundfrei, 5 octaves. F–F. Destroyed in World War II.
1a	1796 Oct.	*Sorte 4, Nr. 398 / Johann Paul Kraemer & Söhne, Göttingen / Oktober 1796*	Nuremberg. Germanisches Nationalmuseum. F–A, 5⅓ octaves with octave strings in the bass. Acquired from the Neupert Collection before May 1944.
2	1797	*Johann Paul Kraemer & Söhne Göttingen 1797*	Berlin Collection. F–A, 5⅓ octaves; 4′ strings added in bass.
3	1800 Aug.	*Sorte 1, Nr. 478 / Joh. Paul Kraemer und Söhne, Göttingen / August 1800*	Nuremberg, Germanisches Nationalmuseum. Bundfrei, with pedal keyboard. Destroyed in World War II.
4	1801 Oct.	*Sorte 7, Nr. 509 / Verfertiget / von / Joh. Paul Kraemer und Söhnen / Instrumentenmacher / in / Göttingen / im Oktober 1801*	Brunswick, Stadtisches Museum. Bundfrei. F–A, 5⅓ octaves; 171 × 55 cm.
5	1803 Dec.	*Sorte 7, Nr. 580 / Johann Paul Kraemer und Söhne, Göttingen / Dezember 1803*	Nuremberg, Germanisches Nationalmuseum. Bundfrei; F–A, 5⅓ octaves. Destroyed in World War II.
5a	1803 Dec.	*Sorte 8, N. 578 / Verfertiget von Joh. Paul Kraemer und Söhnen, Instrumentenmacher in Göttingen. im Decemb: 1803*	Halle, Händel-Haus (formerly in Neupert Collection). F–A, 5⅓ octaves.
6	1803	*Sorte 4, Nr 571 / Verfertiget von Joh. Paul Kraemer und Söhnen Instrumentenmacher in Göttingen im Aug. 1803*	London, Cecil Clutton (formerly Capt. J. Lane, Wanstead; earlier T. W. Taphouse, who shewed it at the International Inventions Exhibition, 1885; earlier Carl Engel).
7	1803		Formerly in Neupert Collection.
Siegmund Theodor			
8	n.d.	*Siegmund Theodor Krämer / in Göttingen / verfertigt Claviere und Fortepiano's*	Leipzig University, Heyer Collection [*Ks*, p. 50]. Bundfrei; F–A, 5 octaves and a third. Kinsky assigns this instrument to the beginning of the nineteenth century, and illustrates it at *Ks*, p. 235.
Gebrüder Krämer			
9	n.d.	*Brüder Krämer Göttingen*	Göttingen Museum.
10	n.d.	*Gebrüder Krämer*	Göttingen, Herr Bonhoff, whose family has owned the instrument since the eighteenth century [*Schultze 1957*].

KYBURZ, Georg Adam [*also* Kiburtz], of Obererlinsbach in the canton of Solothurn. Worked 1745–1801 in Berne making harpsichords and pianofortes [*Rindl*].

KYLE, William. Organ builder and harpsichord maker at Charlemont St., Dublin, in 1790 [*Teahan*].

L.K.I. *See*: KILIAN, Lucas.

L.V. *See*: V, L.

L, H. V. The Brussels Conservatoire Collection has a 2-manual harpsichord dated 1762 on the soundboard, and inscribed: *Laudate Deum in Cymbalis et Organo.* The rose represents King David playing the harp and bears the initials: *H. V. L.*

The catalogue gives the Netherlands as its place of origin; this instrument was formerly in the private collection of V. and J. Mahillon.

LAAG, Heinrich, 1713–97. Organist at the Marienkirche at Osnabrück; he later devoted himself to making keyboard instruments, and gave music lessons.

His *Anfangsgründe zum Clavierspielen . . .* was published 1774.

Surviving Instruments

(1) 1756. Neupert Collection. Clavichord with stops. Inscribed: *Heinrich Laag Osnabrück 1756.*

LA BARRE, Pierre de Chabanceau, *Sieur de La Barre.* Harpsichordist and lutenist to Louis XIII and Anne of Austria; died 1656. About 1648 he caused to be made in Paris, according to his own design, a harpsichord with 'two manuals and triple strings with the device for shifting the keyboards for playing in all keys'.

A letter to M. Zuylychem (i.e. Constantijn Huygens) referring to this instrument, dated at Paris, 31 July 1648, in La Barre's own hand, was sold at Sotheby's on 12 October 1954. The letter, and a reply, are quoted in full in the *Revue de musicologie*, Vol. 9 (1928), pp. 7–9. More details of the La Barre family are given in the article cited above, which is devoted to a study of them.

LA BORDE, Jean-Baptiste de. Published in Paris in 1761 a description of his invention 'Le clavessin électrique, avec une nouvelle théorie du mécanisme et des phénomènes de l'électricité', which had appeared in the form of letters in the *Journal des Sçavans*, August and October 1759.

The instrument was not a harpsichord as its name implies, but consisted of bells electrically stimulated under the control of a keyboard. Forkel says of it: 'Das Clavecin Electrique ist nicht wie das Augenklavier [Castel's *Clavecin oculaire*], wo man bloss Farben untereinander mischt; es klingt wirklich . . . Da nun jede Taste mit seinem Heber und jeder Heber mit seiner Glocke in Verhältniss steht, so kann man alle Stücke auf diesem Instrument spielen, die man auf einem gewöhnlichen Clavessin oder auf einer Orgel spielen kann.'

La Borde died about 1777, pastor at the village of Colancelle in the former Département Nivernais. He had been a Jesuit until the suppression of that order in France [*Eit*].

LA COUTURE, Pierre de. *Cor* (p. 84) refers to harpsichords 'de Geronimo, de la Couture, Rozé . . .'. Of these 3 makers the first is probably Zenti (q.v.) rather than Jerome of Bologna (Hieronymus Bononiensis). P. de La Couture's earliest date is 1678 when he was received into the Guild [*Hubb 1965*, p. 90]; he had died by 1700.

LADRA, Marco. *See*: JADRA, Marco.

LADYMAN, John. Baptized at St. George-the-Martyr's, Southwark, 3 January 1693/4, son of William Ladyman. Apprenticed to Thomas Burton 1708, but not admitted free of the Joiners' Company until 1725. He died before 1745. Two spinets survive bearing this name:

(1) 1694 [falsified]. G–G, 5 octaves. Ivory naturals, with arcaded fronts in ebony. Stand and lid not original. This instrument would appear to have been made 30 or 40 years later than the date which it bears; and the style of the inscription on the nameboard is rather suspicious (*Johannes Ladyman London 1694*).

(2) 1741. Repaired by Miss S. Marcuse, New York, 1953. Bought (£410) at Sotheby's, 7 November 1968, by Mrs. I. Enthaven from Mrs. Titania Hill. In 1956 it belonged to C. F. Colt, and previously to Lady Bland.

Suspicious inscription on nameboard: *Johannes Ladyman London 1741*. G–G, 5 octaves; skunktail sharps. The name *W. Wilkinson* appears in ink on the wrestplank, back of nameboard, and on top and bottom key, with the date *1741* on the keys. (The instrument belongs now (1972) to William Goedde, New York City, formerly to Miss Lucile Hook, also of New York.)

LAESKE, C. F. Harpsichord maker in Amsterdam, *fl.* 1768.

Surviving Instruments

(1) 1768. Chicago, Laurence Libin. Harpsichord, inscribed on nameboard: *C^l. F^k. Laeske fecit Amsterdam An^o. 1768.* Single-manual; C–F, 54 notes chromatic; 2×8′, 1×4′, buff, the front 8′ and 4′ being quilled and the back 8′ leathered. The beechen registers extend through the right cheek-piece, where they are drilled for tassels. Ivory-faced naturals inscribed with 2 pairs of lines which have been painted red in the grooves, and have arcaded fronts; ebony sharps. Jack-rail missing. Soundboard, having *CFL* rose with harpist, painted with flowers and berries.

The instrument was brought from Paris to the U.S.A. many years ago by a Chicago piano maker and lay in a piano dealer's shop for several more years until it was discovered there by the present (1972) owner.

LAINE, De. Listed by the *Almanach Dauphin* (1777) as a music master and inventor of a new mechanism for the harpsichord, described in *Mercure de France*, August 1769. Address: Bureau d'Indication & Négociations Générales, rue Comtesse d'Artois, vis-à-vis celle de la Comédie Italienne [*Hubb 1965*, p. 254 n.]. Dates ascertained, 1768–85. In the *Mercure de France*, August 1769, he claimed to have invented leather plectra for jacks; and the *Encyclopédie* mentions (1785) harpsichords plucked with leather 'somewhat the same as those made today by M. de Laine and M. Pascal Taskin' [*ClP*, p. 46; *Verlet*].

LALANDE, De. A 2-manual harpsichord in the Rhode Island School of Design, Providence, R.I., is inscribed: *Fait par Mr. de Lalande a Caen 1746.* The inscription, on the front face of the wrestplank, can only be seen when the nameboard is removed; 2×8′, 1×4′ registers (the 4′ on the upper manual), push–pull coupler. Five octaves F–F. Parchment rose of Italian type. Size 6′ 7½″×2′ 10½″.

LANDI, Agostino. Florentine harpsichord maker; dates ascertained, 1694–1701. He was living near the Duomo in 1694, in which year he paid a matriculation fee to his Guild. His name appears in 1701 in the records of a lawsuit [*Pu*].

LANDI, Giovanni, of Siena. Virginal maker, *fl.* 1670.

Surviving Instruments

(1) 1670. Lisbon Conservatoire. Virginal, inscribed: *Joannes Landi fecit Sienna Anno Domini 1670.* Compass C/E–F, 4½ octaves. Geometrical rose. Marine landscape painting on lid. Size 163×55 cm. Formerly belonged to the Clementini family, whose arms are painted on it. Illustrated in catalogue.

LANGGUTH, H. W. *See*: JUNGCURTH, Heinrich Wilhelm.

LA ROUSSELIÈRE, Jean-Baptiste de. A Frenchman who invented a new kind of plectrum described in his *Traité des languettes impériales* (Paris, 1679). See *Hubb 1965*, p. 323.

LASSEN, Herlo. *Fl.* 1745 as organ and harpsichord maker in Amsterdam [*Amsterdamse Courant*, 6 May 1745, quoted by *Curtis*, p. 52].

LAURENTIUS, *Papiensis. See*: GUSNASCHI, Lorenzo.

LAUTERBORN, Joseph Gaspard. Bohemian in origin, he made harpsichords and pianos in Paris. Born *c.* 1745; died 10 February 1814. Admitted to the Guild in 1781. Died at Bougival [*Verlet*, who gives further details].

LE BRETON, Jacques. Parisian 'épinetier', born *c.* 1589; latest date ascertained, 1656. Apprenticed to Médéric Lorillart (q.v.) on 17 April 1603, at which time he was living at Villers-Cotterêts.

He became in 1624 'maître joueur et faiseur d'espinette et d'instrumens du roi', in 1627, 'maître faiseur d'espinettes du roi', and in 1656 'maître faiseur d'instrumens ordinaire du roy' [*Les*].

Mer (III. 159) praises him.

LECLERC, Nicholas. Harpsichord maker in Paris; *fl.* 1740 [*Verlet*].

LECLERC, Jean-Pierre. Harpsichord maker in Paris. Perhaps a son of the foregoing. *Fl.* 1777–89. In 1777 he entered the Guild of Instrument Makers. From 1777 to 1783 he lived in the rue Chapon; 1788–9, rue Beaubourg; *An* VIII, rue Simon-le-Franc [*Pi*, p. 134; *Verlet*].

LE CROTONE. Early seventeenth-century Italian harpsichord maker [*Hullm*].

LEE, Edmund. Harpsichord and piano maker, 2 Dame St., Dublin. 1786–1810 [*Teahan*].

LEE, John. Musical-instrument maker, 70 Dame St., Dublin. 1789–1803 [*Teahan*]. It is likely that they were related.

LEENHOUWER, A., of Leyden. Harpsichord maker and organist. Baptized 8 June 1752; died 1798.

Surviving Harpsichords

(1) 1787. The Hague. Gemeente Museum. Inscribed: *A. Leenhouwer me fecit Leyden, anno 1787.* Two manuals; 2×8′, 1×4′. Jack-slides protrude through cheek-piece for changes of registration, in the old style. Five octaves. Length 2·40 m. Formerly in the Régibo Collection, Renaix. *AHL* rose with trophy of instruments. Jackrail modern. Ivory naturals.

LEEST, Willem. Dates ascertained: 1561–9. Son of Godschalck Leest, he was a maker of clavichords and harpsichords in Antwerp, of which town he acquired citizenship as a clavichord maker in 1561 [*Bu*].

LEFAURE, Joseph, of Lyons. Harpsichord maker, *fl.* in 1779 when he is recorded among the luthiers [*Vallas*].

LEFEBVRE, Charles *and* **Jean-Baptiste.** Both sons of Nicholas Lefebvre (I), lutemaker at Rouen in 1630. They made organs, harpsichords, and flutes, and were both alive in 1725 [*Lü*].

LEFEBVRE, Nicholas (II). Organ builder and maker of spinets and harpsichords at Rouen. Dates ascertained, 1733–72 [*Vannes*].

LE GAY. French (not German) harpsichord maker, *fl.* 1763 [*SIM* 1910/11, article by C. Sachs].

LEGROS, Claude, of Metz. Organ builder, also made harpsichords. In 1714 he received from the Duke of Lorraine a sum of money for making a harpsichord. See further *Fleury*.

LEGROS, Pierre. Brother of the foregoing. Builder of organs and harpsichords at Metz. In 1713 he was awarded the title of Maker to the Prince de Vaudemont, at Commercy [*Fleury*].

LEHMANN, Gotthelf David. Dates ascertained, 1764–96. Born in 1764 at Serkewitz near Dresden. For 6 years he worked with the instrument maker Wagner. In 1790 he opened a workshop in Dresden, where he made clavichords and pianos. The former were sold for 26–30 thalers. In 1796 he completed his 50th clavichord.

LEHNER, Gottlieb, of the Hochstrasse, Pressburg (Bratislava). Clavichord maker, *fl.* 1816.

Surviving Instruments

(1) 1816. Leningrad, Institute for Scientific Research on the Theatre and Music. Clavichord. Compass F–G, 4 octaves plus 2 notes; 51 keys. Label inscribed: *Gottlieb Lehner, bürgerlicher Instrumentenmacher wohnhaft in Presburg auf der Hochstrasse den 19 Januari An. 1816.* (This instrument was formerly in the Hermitage, and is illustrated in *Muzȳka v muzee*, by S. L. Ginzburg, Leningrad, 1927.)

LEISERT, Jean. Harpsichord maker in the Cul-de-sac de l'Oratoire, Paris, *fl.* 1769 [*Pi*].

LEMAIRE, Marin. Organist and spinet maker in Paris. Born *c.* 1520; died 1587. In 1556 he was 'maistre organiste et faiseur d'instrumens'. He married twice. *See also* LEMAIRE, Claude [*Verlet*].

LEMAIRE, Jean. Parisian spinet maker. Perhaps a brother of the foregoing, he lived towards the end of the sixteenth century [*Verlet*].

LEMAIRE, Claude. Parisian spinet maker; *fl.* 1563–79. Son of Marin Lemaire by his first marriage [*Verlet*].

LEMME

(*a*) **Friedrich Carl Wilhelm** (1747–1808), born at Brunswick. He was trained to be an organist, but at the same time received instruction in instrument making from his father. About 1780 he became organist at the Church of St. Catherine and St. Magnus, in Brunswick; but he continued making instruments, and by 1787 had made 800 with his father.

Forkel says (*Musikalischer Almanach* 1782) 'His instruments rank with the best, in respect of both workmanship and tone . . . The usual price of his clavichords varies between 3 and 10, even 12, louis d'or, according to the various types.' (Seine Instrumente gehören mit zu den besten, sowohl in Betracht der Arbeit als des Tons . . . Der gewöhnliche Preis seiner Claviere ist nach der verschiedenen Sorten 3–10 auch 12 Louis d'or.)

Lemme, like other instrument makers, found himself at times (e.g. 1780, 1785) in conflict with the Guild of Joiners, who complained that some of his work came under the heading of joinery [*SB*, p. 47].

In 1802 he published at Brunswick his *Anweisung und Regeln zu einer zweckmässigen Behandlung englischer und deutscher Pianofortes und Klaviere* [i.e. clavichords] . . . This contains a list of the various types of piano and clavichord made by him:

(1) 'Large grand pianos made in the style of the great English masters', F–C, 5½ octaves, 60 and 55 gold Fredericks.

(2) Another large grand piano, F–F, 5 octaves, 36, 34, and 26 Fredericks.

(3) Square pianos. 22, 18, or 16 Fredericks, according to compass.

(4) 'Clavichords of all kinds, all of them unfretted', 14 types of varying compass and size, costing from 4–15 Fredericks.

He writes of type 14, which is represented by the clavichord in the Heyer Collection, listed below: 'A kind newly invented by myself. The outer case oval, in oldfashioned [Louis Seize] style . . . F to A [5⅓ octaves], at 15 Gold Fredericks.'

'In the last five types I use the kind of soundboard which I invented in 1772 [laminated] . . .; they give an excellent tone and are not subject to splitting and cracking.' N.B. Gerber (Vol. I, 1790) attributes this invention to Lemme's father in 1771. In any case they were working together at this time. By 1802 Lemme had probably acquired the habit of ascribing the invention to himself. According to *Fé*, its purpose was to prevent damage by the heat when the instruments were exported to India.

This invention is described by *Ge*, 1790, in a curious article recounting some supposed improvements in clavichord making effected by Lemme, in collaboration with his father:

(i) Straight keys, producing 'a lighter touch and more durable keys'. But careful workmanship could produce excellent touch and durability in reasonably crooked keys. And such a straightening could be attained only at the expense of either the string-scaling or the good position of the bridge on the soundboard.

(ii) 'in den gepressten Resonanzböden oder doppelten Böden', i.e. laminated soundboards with the grains running in opposite directions, referred to above.

(iii) 'oval-shaped clavichords, which in shape and arrangement depart completely from the old style. They combine with a pleasing shape an uncommonly beautiful and powerful tone.' As exemplified in a clavichord in the Heyer Collection (see below), this design has no particular advantage over the normal oblong shape, to the modern eye.

However, even if we cannot help being suspicious of his 'improvements', we must recognize the excellence of a maker who ranked with Hubert and Krämer, and of whom Forkel says: 'his instruments are among the best, both as regards workmanship and as regards tone' (*Musikalischer Almanach* . . . 1782) [*Ks*, *Ge*].

Surviving Clavichords

(1) 1766. Munich, Deutsches Museum. The inscription, not normally visible, is said to run: *C. W. Lemme, Braunschweig, 1766.* Compass 4½ octaves. Lowest octave, 3 strings to a note.

(2) 1787. Leipzig, Heyer Collection. Illustrated in *Ks*. Bundfrei. Rounded ends ('ovalrunde Form'). Inscription on soundboard: *Carl Lemme Organist / in Braunschweig / Anno 1787. Nro 802 Sorte 14.* F–A, 5⅓ octaves. Bottom 1¼ octaves (F–A), 3 strings to each note.

(*b*) **Carl** (1769–1832), son of (*a*), born at Brunswick. Learnt clavichord and piano making from his father. In 1799 settled in Paris and founded an instrument-making firm.

Fé calls him a good maker of the second class; and his instruments, although inferior to those of Erard and some others and cheaper in price, were exported in considerable numbers, especially to America. His *Nouvelle Méthode de musique et gamme chromatique, qui abrège le travail et l'étude de la musique; de onze douzièmes, on la réduit à un douzième* . . . was published in Paris by himself in 1829.

He died at Charenton-le-Pont in October 1832. For further details see *Fé*.

LEMOYNE, Claude. Organist and organ builder in Paris; *fl.* 1632–6. He probably made harpsichords also [*Laborde*].

L'EMPEREUR. *See*: Treyer, Joseph, *called* L'Empereur; *also* Keiser, J. B., *called* L'Empereur.

LENAERT, . . . van. Harpsichord maker in Antwerp in the sixteenth century. His name occurs in the books of the Guild of St. Luke [*St*].

LENKER, Christoph Michael, *c.* 1765. Instrument maker at Rudolstadt. He imitated Silbermann's pianos, and his clavichords were considered little inferior to those of Silbermann, q.v. [*Ge*, 1814].

LENOIR. According to *Bq* (p. 9) a 'Clavecin de Lenoir' was advertised in Paris on 1 July 1754. There is no other trace of this maker. It is conceivable that 'Lenoir' is a misreading of 'Levoir' (q.v.).

LEO, Johann Christoph (I). Born at Stettin. Settled at Augsburg as organ builder in 1685. Had a considerable reputation for keyboard instruments of all kinds—clavichords, harpsichords, spinets, and pianos [*Ge*].

LEO, Johann Christoph (II). Son of (I). Born in Augsburg. After his musical education he became 'Churf. Mainzischer und Markgr. Anspachischer Hoforgelbauer zu Augsburg', where in 1721 he built the organ at the Ulrichskirche. He also made clavichords, harpsichords, pantalons, and glockenspiels [*Ge*].

A spinet by Johann Christoph Leo (presumably the Younger) is in private ownership in Melrose; undated.

LEO, Manuel Anjos. No relation to Johann Christoph (I) or (II). Portuguese, *fl. c.* 1703 as harpsichord maker at Beja [*Gö*]. A harpsichord by him, with a partially illegible inscription on the top key, is in the Berlin Collection [no. 4; *Sa*, p. 71]. Compass C–D, 4 octaves plus; 2×8′ registers. Sachs read the maker's name as 'Miguelanjo'.

LEONI, Giovanni Paolo. Italian harpsichord maker, *fl.* 1773.

Surviving Instruments

(1) 1773. New York, Metropolitan Museum of Art. Harpsichord inscribed: *Jo. Paulus Leoni Civ. RH. F. An. D. MDCCLXXIII.* Length 5′ 8″. Rose; 2×8′ stops. Illustrated in catalogue. Should we interpret as *CIVITATIS RHEGINAE*, i.e. Reggio di Calabria? (*Hirt* assigns this maker to Rome.)

LE PRÊTRE. Italian harpsichord maker in the early seventeenth century [*Hullm*].

LE ROY, Martin. Harpsichord maker in Paris. Was apprenticed to Pierre Baillon on 26 September 1674 [*Hubb*].

Surviving Instruments

(1) 1685. Harpsichord, 2 manuals, recorded and illustrated in Savoye Collection III sale catalogue (Paris, 13 June 1924), which gives the inscription as *Le Roy pingebat* [*sic.*? for *fingebat*] *1685*.

LESCLAN, Claude. 'Faiseur d'instrumens de musique rue St. Honoré', Paris, 1624. He took Robert Baudin as apprentice in 1632 [*Hubb*].

LESCUIER, G., of Paris. *Fl.* in the sixteenth century; called himself 'maistre faiseur d'orgues et espinette' [*Les*].

LE TOURNEUR

(*a*) **Étienne,** singer, organist, and harpsichord maker at Lyons. Earliest date known, 1715, when he and Antoine Fioco succeeded Rameau as organists at the Jacobin church; he had died before the marriage of his son in 1730 [*Vallas*].

(*b*) **Joseph Brunon,** son of (*a*), and, like him, organist and harpsichord maker at Lyons. Married 9 October 1730, at Saint-Pierre, where a son of his was baptized on 24 September 1731 [*Vallas*].

See also: Treyer, Jean-Baptiste, *called* Le Tourneur.

LEUMS. *See*: Leunis.

LEUNIS, Reynier, of Antwerp. Maker of lutes and harpsichords; dates ascertained, 1620–6. He entered the Guild of St. Luke in 1610 [*VdS, Bu, St*].

LEUTIS, Gerolamo de. According to *Lü*, and *Va, fl.* at Rome in 1638. Made harpsichords, and perhaps lutes as well. But *Leutis* may be a misreading of *Zentis* (q.v.) as *Ks* points out (283 n.).

LEVERSIDGE, Adam. London virginal maker. Admitted to the Joiners' Company 1649/50 and to the Livery 1657/8 [*Join*]. Latest date ascertained, 1670.

Surviving Virginals

(1) 1666. Yale University, Belle Skinner Collection. Inscribed: *Adamus Leuersidge Londini fecit 1666* and on the back of the nameboard: *Restored by Chickering and Sons under the direction of Arnold Dolmetsch. Boston U.S.A. 1909.* Formerly owned by Messrs. Chappell, who described it as having once belonged to Nell Gwynn, and shewed it at the International Inventions Exhibition, 1885; and by T. Mackinlay, E. F. Rimbault, Arthur Hill, and Morris Steinert. Compass G/B–D, 4 octaves and a 5th. 5′ 6¼″×1′ 8″. Illustrated in catalogue.

(2) 1670. Oxford, Ashmolean Museum. Formerly the property of the late Arthur F. Hill, London. Inscription on jackrail: *Adamus Leuersidge Londini fecit 1670.* Case of oak and cypress, with stamped gilt paper. Soundboard and inside of domed lid painted, the latter representing St. James's Park. Geometrical rose. Compass G/B–F, 55 keys; 5′ 7½″×1′ 9½″. Illustrated in colour in *DEF*, III. 4.

LEVERSIDGE, William, *the Elder*. Father of Adam Leversidge and master of Thomas Makeham; *fl.* 1641/2; probably a virginal maker.

LEVIEL, Adrian. *Fl.* 1570–8 in Paris as organist of St. Barthélemy and 'faiseur d'espinettes' [*Les, Verlet*].

LEVOIR. *Fl.* in Paris 1730–55. He invented a 'bowed-harpsichord', similar to Hayden's *Geigenwerck*, which he submitted to the Paris Académie des Sciences in 1742. [The action is described at *Pi*, p. 91, and by *Verlet*].

LEWES, William, *fl.* 1518–31. He supplied virginals to Henry VIII, and probably made them also. In 1526 the Court bought five virginals from him. An entry in the King's Privy Purse Expenses runs as follows: '1530. Paied to William Lewes for ii payre of Virginalles in one coffer with iiii stoppes brought to Grenewich, iii li.' This was probably a 2-manual harpsichord with 4 stops or registers, as A. J. Hipkins, *Hi* (p. 78) suggests; in which case this is the earliest reference to a double-manual harpsichord. *Ga* (p. 127) thinks that the reference is to 2 separate instruments, packed in one trunk for transport, since the earliest surviving 2-manual harpsichords were made much later (though a 2-manual Ruckers dated 1588 was sold in the eighteenth century [*Bq*]).

But it is by no means unreasonable to suppose that this type of harpsichord had been evolved by the early years of the sixteenth century, since 2-manual organs had been known for well over a century (the famous Halberstadt organ built in 1361 had 2 manuals as well as pedals and another keyboard which could be played by either the hand or the knee [*Pr*, p. 98]). Moreover the words 'iiii stoppes' suggest strongly that only 1 instrument was in question; the clerk who made the entry would hardly add together the stops of 2 individual instruments packed in one case.

J (p. 34) favours the view that the reference is to a 2-manual harpsichord, and suggests very reasonably that the instrument derived from the Low Countries.

Another entry in the Privy Purse expenses, of the same date, records that £3 was paid to Lewes for 'ii payer of Virginalles in one coffer brought to the More' (Henry's Hertfordshire residence).

LEYDECKER, Johann. Harpsichord maker in Vienna, *fl.* 1755.

Surviving Instruments

(1) 1755. Harpsichord in Schloss Eggenberg, Graz, signed: *Johann Leydecker, Vienna 1755*.

LEYKES, Johann. *See*: Weil, Johann Wilhelm.

LIENARD, Charles. Harpsichord maker from Meaux [*Hubb*].

LINCOLN, John. Harpsichord maker, 199 High Holborn, London, *Fl.* 1793 [*J*].

LINDHOLM, Pehr, 1742–1813 [*Hirt*], of Stockholm. Maker of keyboard and other stringed instruments. In 1781 he invented a compound harpsichord, called by him a *crescendo*, which had five varieties of tone: (i) Harpsichord, (ii) Pantaleon, (iii) Harpsichord and pianoforte together, (iv) Pantaleon and pianoforte together, (v) Pianoforte [*Nor*, p. 149]. In 1791 he was received into the Guild of Joiners as a Master. *Lü* quotes a violin label dated 1780. From 1803 until 1806 he signed his instruments with Söderström, who was his son-in-law [*Hirt*].

Surviving Clavichords

(1) 1776. Åbo, Historiska Museet. Inscribed: *Förfärdigadt af Instrumentmakeren Pehr Lindholm Stockholm 1776 No. 1*[?].

(2) 1780. Stockholm [*Hirt*].

(2a) Menlo Park, Calif., Miss Joan Benson. Dated 1780; F–F, 5 octaves; lowest 22 notes trichord. May well be the same instrument as no. 2.

(3) 1782. Hälsingborg Museet [*Glar*, II. 3 (1953)].

(4) 1785. Stockholm, Nordiska Museet. F–C, 5½ octaves.

(4a) 1786. Linköping, Sweden, Östergötlands Museum, (1966) [*Nord*].

(5) 1787. Stockholm, Musikhistoriska Museet.

(5a). 1788. Bought at Sotheby's 8. 3. 1973 by Dr. and Mrs. R. M. Rosenbaum, Scarsdale, N.Y. Inscribed: *Forfärdigadt af Pehr Lindholm, Instrumentmakare Stockholm ar 1788*. F–C, 5 octaves and a fifth; trichord in bass.

(6) 1792. Åbo Academy, Sibeliusmuseum. Inscribed: *Förfärdigadt af / Pehr Lindholm / Instrumentmakare Stockholm ar 1792*. Formerly belonged to the Mannerheim family.

(7) 1797. Stockholm, Musikhistoriska Museet.

(8) 1798. Copenhagen. Carl Claudius Collection. Illustrated in catalogue. Bundfrei. 5½ octaves. Inscription: *Forfärdigadt af Pehr Lindholm Stockholm 1798*.

(9) 1803. Gothenburg. Göteborgs Museum. Compass F–C, 5½ octaves; lowest 1½ octaves F–C, trichord, the third string sounding an octave above the others; the rest, bichord. Printed label: *Forfärdigadt af Pehr Lindholm: & Söderström Instrumentmakare Stockholm ar 1803*. 207×59·8 cm.

(10) 1803. Stockholm [*Hirt*].

(11) Undated. Stockholm [*Hirt*].

Note: Another clavichord in the Åbo Academy was restored by Lindholm: *Renoveradt ett Claver af Pehr Lindholm, Stockholm 1897*.

LION, Jacoust [?]. A double harpsichord with almost illegible inscription was owned (1956) by M. Alain Vian, Paris.

L'ISLE, Blondel de. Harpsichord maker of the seventeenth or early eighteenth century, presumably French. A harpsichord by him was repaired by Blanchet [*Hardouin 1957*, p. 12].

LOCHMANN, Andrzej. Seventeenth-century harpsichord maker at Wilno [*Szulc*].

LOCKTON, Heming. Harpsichord maker in Rupert Street, St. James's, London. Dates ascertained, 1739–52 [*RB.J*]. *J* (p. 71) lists 'Heming Hopton' as a harpsichord maker in Rupert Street, his name appearing in a Westminster pollbook of 1749. This is *J*'s error for 'Lockton'.

LOERS, Marc. *See*: Moors, Marc.

LOEUVRE, Honoré de. *See*: Deloeuvre, Honoré.

LOEUVRE, Pierre de. *See*: Deloeuvre, Pierre.

LOEWE, Christopher. *See*: Löwe, Christopher.

LOGAN, James, of Edinburgh. Spinet maker; *fl.* 1774. He supplied instruments to Neil Stewart (q.v.) and perhaps others.

LONGFELLOW. A 'harpsichord with gut-strings, made by Mr. Longfellow, of Pembroke Hall, Cambridge' was in the Duke of Chandos's house in Boswell Court, London, in 1720 [*Chandos*, p. 140].

LONGMAN, James. Founded about 1767 at 26 Cheapside a firm which achieved distinction in music publishing and as dealers in keyboard and wind instruments. In 1769 he was joined by Lukey so that the firm became:

LONGMAN, LUKEY, & CO, 1769–75.

Surviving Spinets

(1) Undated. Formerly the property of Edmund C. Legg of Cirencester. Spinet, inscribed on nameboard: *Longman, Lukey and Co. Instrument makers*, G–G, 5 octaves. White naturals, black sharps.

About September 1775 they were joined by Francis Fane Broderip, making the firm:

LONGMAN, LUKEY, AND BRODERIP, 1775–6

Among their advertisements is the following:

Longman, Lukey and Broderip, No. 26 Cheapside, London. Longman, Lukey, and Broderip, having purchas'd the most valuable Part of the old Stock of Mr. Lewer, the Successor of the later Mr. Tyther, in Moorfields, (the oldest Shop in London) have it now in their Power to oblige their Friends, Customers, and the Public in general, with the greatest Choice of fine old Instruments and scarce Books, with many other Articles in the Musical Way, on much lower Terms than usual; in particular Harpsicords and Spinnets, having purchas'd all the prime Instruments of the late ingenious Mahoon, Harpsicord-maker to his Majesty, which are now ready for Sale, and will be sold Fifty per Cent. under his usual Prices.

In the above Stock are Instruments made and Books printed upwards of three Hundred Year since.

[A copy of this advertisement is bound with Langdon's *Divine Harmony* (1774) in the library of St. Michael's College, Tenbury].

In 1776 Lukey left the firm, which then became:

LONGMAN AND BRODERIP, and continued in this form in Cheapside, and from 1782 onwards at 13 Haymarket as well, until 1798 when they went bankrupt. (See further *H&S*.)

A considerable number of spinets, harpsichords, and pianofortes, as well as wind instruments, were sold bearing their name; but it appears that they were dealers rather than makers, at any rate as far as keyboard instruments were concerned. John Geib (q.v.) worked for them at one time; Culliford (q.v.) supplied them with instruments which were sold with their names on the nameboard, e.g. numbers 2, 3, 7, 9, 11, 13, 14, and 14a below; they also acted as agents for Baker Harris (q.v.).

In Kent's *Directory* for 1871 Longman and Broderip are advertised as musical-instrument makers; and the firm's name appears in J. Doane's *Musical Directory . . .* London 1794 [L. G. Langwill in *Music and Letters*, London, January 1949].

TABLE 23. *Surviving Instruments bearing the Name of LONGMAN AND BRODERIP*

No.	No. in 1956 edition	Maker's or sub-contractor's no.	Type	Date	Kbs.	Signature	Owner/Remarks
1	1		H	1775	1		Paris Conservatoire (Léon Savoye Collection). Restored by Tomasini 1883 and P. Brunold 1944; 5 octaves, F–F, 2×8′, 1×4′, lute, buff. Hand-stops labelled L. to R.: *Harp, lute, 1st Unison, Silent, 2nd Unison, Octave*. Signed by *Baker Harris*.
2	—	10	S	1779	1		An auction sale of the property of the late C. N. Fahrney held at State Armory, Pa., on 6–7 May 1966(?) included a 'rare Harpsichord Spinet [*sic*] by Longman and Broderick [*sic*] with inscription *Culliford, London 1779*' [advertisement of sale]. It actually bears Culliford's number *10* and is a spinet; rebuilt by Frank Rutkowski in 1957 [*MarcP*].
3	2	12	H	1780	1		Royal Manchester College of Music, H. Watson Collection. Inscribed on underside of soundboard: *Thomas Culliford, Maker, April 1780 No. 12* [*J*, p. 66 n.].
4	—		H	c. 1780	1		Portsmouth, N.H., Warner House Association, to whom it is (1970) on loan from Mrs. J. Templeman Coolidge; formerly owned by the daughter of Benning Wentworth, Governor of New Hampshire, 1767–75. 2×8′, 1×4′ stops.
4a	—		S	1782	1	*Longman and Broderip Musical Instrument Makers Kings Arms No. 26 Cheapside London* [on name-board]; *Culliford Maker London 1782* [under original soundboard towards tail]	San Francisco, Mrs. Alfred Koch, who bought it at the dispersal of the Cline Collection, San Francisco, 1970. 5 octaves, F–F without lowest F sharp.

TABLE 23 (*cont.*):

No.	No. in 1956 edition	Maker's or sub-contractor's no.	Type	Date	Kbs.	Signature	Owner/Remarks
4b	17	—	H	1782	1	*Longman and Broderip Musical Instrument Makers Kings Arms No. 26 Cheapside London.* On back of nameboard: *Thos Culliford Maker Fountain Court Cheapside February 1782*	Cambridge, Christopher Hogwood. Formerly belonged to Miss Grace Gurteen, Haverhill, who bought it from Alec Hodsdon in 1926. F–F without low F sharp; 2×8′, 1×4′, lute, buff, machine, swell, rose surrounded by lettering: *Longman and Broderip Cheapside.* Repaired by Alec Hodsdon in 1926 and Derek Adlam in 1972.
5	4		H	Not later than 1782	1	*Longman & Broderip, Musical Instrument Makers, Cheapside*	Shewn by J. K. Pyne at International Inventions Exhibition, 1885. Handstops labelled; 2×8′, 1×4′, lute, harp, machine; inner lid raised by pedal as swell; 5 octaves, F–F, rose.
[5a			H	1783	1		The same instrument as no. 9, q.v.
6	—	54; 277	H	1783	1	*Longman & Broderip* [on front of name-fillet]; *Thos. Culliford Maker / Fountain Court, Cheapside / No. 54 / 1783* [on back of name-fillet, also in key-well]. *J. Hanson No. 5* [pencilled signature of Culliford's workman]. *No. 277* stamped on wrest-plank	Maidenhead, Alfred Reeve (1958). Sold at Sotheby's 20 December 1957 by Mrs. Le Hunte Cooper, who had bought it at Margate *c.* 1900 for 10 shillings. Rose of harping figure against leafy background, surrounded by inscription: *Longman & Broderip Cheapside.* 5 ivory-mounted stop-knobs engraved [L. to R.): *Machine*; *harp*, *octave*, *1st unison*, *2nd unison*. 2 pedals (L, machine; R, swell). F–F, 5 octaves without lowest F sharp. Swell opens half of an inner lid; wrestplank covered by a board on which are pasted Longman and Broderip's *Directions to Purchasers.* Label in Culliford's hand on the bottom of the instrument. Size 7′ 2″×3′ 2″.
7	—	123	S	1784	1		Private ownership in Philadelphia (1972). Formerly J. K. Pyne. G–F nearly 5 octaves. Made by *T. Culliford.* Shewn at International Inventions Exhibition, 1885. (Number 9 in the Boddington–Pyne catalogue.)
8	3	129	S	—	1	*Longman & Broderip, Musical Instrument Makers, No. 26 Cheapside and No. 13 Haymarket London*	London, Messrs. Robert Morley (1966); bought from Geoffrey Harding, Steventon, who had bought it at Puttick and Simpson's, February 1965, from C. F. Colt, Bethersden, Kent. Numbered *129* on wrestplank. Originally had a swell whereby a pedal raised part of the lid.
9	14		H	1784	1	*Longman and Broderip Musical Instrument Makers No 26*	London, Benton Fletcher Collection, Fenton House. F–F, 5 octaves without low F sharp; 2×8′, buff; 1

TABLE 23 (*cont.*):

No.	No. in 1956 edition	Maker's or sub-contractor's no.	Type	Date	Kbs.	Signature	Owner/Remarks
						Cheapside and No 13 Hay Market London	pedal. Restorer's mark *L. Ward* stamped on wrestplank. Signed behind nameboard: *Thos. Culliford 1783*; dated under soundboard *1784*.
10	—	142	S	1785(?)		*Longman & Broderip, Musical Instrument Makers No. 26 Cheapside and No. 13 Haymarket, London 1785*	Bangor, Maine, Charles J. Harrington (1965). May have been made somewhat before 1785.
11	6	430	H	1785	2	*Longman & Broderip Musical Instrument Makers, No 26 Cheapside and No 13 Hay Market, London*	Lisbon Conservatoire. Compass 5 octaves F–F, 2×8′, 1×4′, buff, machine, Venetian swell. Also bears inscription: *Thos Culliford Maker Fountain Court Cheapside London, June 1785*.
11a	—		H	1785	2		Olveston, Glos., A. C. N. Mackenzie; formerly (1946) Lady Headlam. 2×8′, 1×4′, lute, buff, machine. This instrument was made by T. Culliford, q.v. Restored by Arnold Dolmetsch in 1899, the second keyboard being added then. According to *The Times Literary Supplement* of 21 December 1956, p. 766, it bears Longman and Broderip's label, has a Venetian swell, and was restored for Violet Gordon Woodhouse.
12	8	444	H	?	1	*Longman & Broderip, 26 Cheapside and 13 Haymarket*	Mrs. K. Bradshaw, who bought it at Sotheby's, 18 February 1952; formerly belonged to Dolmetsch (until *c.* 1900) and Mrs. Julia Neilson-Terry. Wrestplank branded 444. 5 hand-stops: *Buff, zymbal, octave, harp, lute*. Rose with maker's name and address.
13	—	447	H	1785			Vienna, Jörg Demus, who bought it in 1963 from Robert Morley who repaired it in 1959. Inscription on key 61: *Culliford and Co., Makers, Fountain Court, Cheapside, London, July 1785 No: 447*. 2×8′, 1×4′. Mahogany case. Original scaling marked on bridge.
14	19	463	H	1785	2	*Longman and Broderip Musical Instrument Makers No 26 Cheapside and No 13 Haymarket, London*	Florence Conservatoire (from the Casamorata bequest). Machine, Venetian swell. 6 hand-stops labelled *Harp, Lute, Octave, Silent, 1 Unison, 2 Unison*. Rose. The top key is inscribed: *Culliford & Co., Makers Fountain Court Cheapside London Sept. 1785, No. 463*.

TABLE 23 (*cont.*):

No.	No. in 1956 edition	Maker's or sub-contractor's no.	Type	Date	Kbs.	Signature	Owner/Remarks
14a	—		S	1786	1		London, Messrs. Gordon Smith, antique dealers, in 1967, in which year it was repaired by Robert Morley. Signed and dated 'inside the soundboard' (as reported to me) by Thos. Culliford. G–G, 5 octaves.
15	7		H	1787	1		Messrs. Dolmetsch (1953). Signed by *John Spielspegger* [i.e. Spielsberger]. Dolmetsch added 16′ and pedals.
16	9	600	H		1		New London, Conn., Connecticut College, on loan from Mrs. M. J. Shaw, New London. Bronze rose; 2×8′, 1×4′ stops.
17	10	721	H		2	*Longman & Broderip, Musical Instrument Makers, No. 26 Cheapside and No. 13 Haymarket, London*	Yale University, Belle Skinner Collection; *721* on wrestplank; 2×8′, 1×4′, lute, buff, machine, Venetian swell; F–F, 5 octaves, illustrated in catalogue.
18	11	735					Mount Vernon, Va. Ordered by George Washington for Nellie Curtis in 1793. 6 hand-stops of which 1 is a dummy.
19	12		H		1		Sold by Mrs. Alston at Sotheby's, 10 March 1933, to Alec Hodsdon; 2×8′, 1×4′, lute, buff, machine, swell (single cover without slats), rose. Length 7′ 2″.
20	—		H				Sold by Lady Dulverton in 1962.
21	13		S			*Longman and Broderip Musical Instrument Makers, No. 26 Cheapside, London*	London, Royal College of Music, formerly Sir Walter Parratt. Shewn at International Inventions Exhibition, 1885. Beautifully preserved. F–F, 5 octaves.
22	15		H		2		Cambridge University Music School. 2×8′, 1×4′, lute, buff; F–F, 5 octaves. Lid-swell.
23	16		H		1		Alec Hodsdon, Lavenham (1946). Hand-stops marked, L. to R.: *Harp, Lute, Octave*; *Silent, 2nd unison, 1st unison*; and on left cheek-piece: *Machine*.
24	18		H		1		Formerly R. R. Henshaw, Turleigh, Bradford on Avon.
25	20		S		1		Sold at auction at Berkhamsted, 1942.
26	21		S		1	*Longman & Broderip Musical Instrument Makers No 26, Cheapside and No 13 Haymarket London*	Southampton, Tudor House Museum. Said to be by Culliford. (Formerly owned by Charles Dibdin, 1745–1814.)

TABLE 23 (*cont.*):

No.	No. in 1956 edition	Maker's or sub-contractor's no.	Type	Date	Kbs.	Signature	Owner/Remarks
27	—	—	S		1	*Longman & Broderip Musical Instrument Makers, Kings Arms, No. 26 Cheapside, London*	Burford, Roger Warner (1969).
28	—		H		1	*Longman & Broderip Musical Instrument Makers No. 26 Cheapside & No. 13 Haymarket London*	Probably at a school in Hampstead (1970). 2×8′ stops, 2 brass hand-stops. Inscribed in pencil inside a jackslot: *Dore.* 5 octaves chromatic; 61 notes. M. Thomas had the instrument about 1961. Restrung by A. Reeve, Maidenhead.

LONGSHALL, J. of Wigan. Spinet maker in the eighteenth century.

Surviving Instruments

(1) Undated. In the possession of Mrs. Bronwen Lloyd Williams, Oswestry; repaired by Hugh Gough in 1949. Spinet in walnut case (*c.* 1760); 5 octaves. Inscription: *J. Longshall Wigan.*

LOOSEMORE, John. Organ builder and virginal maker of Exeter. Born 1613; died 1681 [*J*].

The organ in Exeter Cathedral was built by him, and some of his pipes were retained when it was rebuilt. A regal at Blair Atholl was made by him in 1650 (see *Ga*, p. 232 for description and photograph). An organ made by him for the hall at Nettlecombe Court, Somerset, is still *in situ*.

Surviving Virginals

(1) 1655. London, Victoria and Albert Museum. Inscription on jackrail: *John Loosemore Fecit 1655.* Compass C–D, 51 keys. 5′ 8¼″ × 1′ 8¼″. Two geometrical roses. Illustrated in *GD* (1928) art. *Virginal.* (Formerly belonged to Charles K. Salaman. Exhibited S. Kensington 1872.)

LORENZO, *di Pavia. See*: GUSNASCHI, Lorenzo.

LORILLART, Médéric. Sixteenth-century harpsichord maker in Paris; son of the organist Pierre Lorillart, he was over 21 years of age in 1569.

For a time he was himself an organist, but from 1579 onwards was 'faiseur d'espinettes du roi'. He set up in the rue de la Fontaine-Maubué in the parish of Saint-Nicolas-des-Champs, where he was still living in 1603 when he accepted Jacques Le Breton (q.v.) as apprentice. His daughter Anthoinette married the instrument maker Jehan Jacquet. Lorillart died before 1616 [*Les*].

Mer (p. 159) refers to him ('Mederic ou Emery') and Antoine Potin, as having been in their time the best makers in France.

LORILLART, P. Harpsichord maker; son of Médéric Lorillart; 'faiseur d'espinettes du roy'; died October 1622 [*Les*, p. 50].

LOTH, J. Harpsichord maker, later than Johann Loth. An undated single-manual harpsichord by him survives [*GL*].

LOTH, Johann. Born in Cologne; harpsichord and spinet maker, *fl.* 1647 (*ZI* 1900–1, p. 730).

On 3 February 1766 there was advertised for sale in Paris 'un clavier de Jean Loth, de Cologne', the price being 1,200 louis [*Bq. Clavier* here probably means *harpsichord*, for it is applied to a harpsichord by Kirkman elsewhere in *Bq*].

A harpsichord by Loth dated Cologne 1648 was sold at Saint Paul en Vence in 1957 or 1958; 1×8′, 1×4′, restored in Leipzig in 1900 and later in 1956 [*Nord*].

A harpsichord which was formerly in de Wit's Collection bore the inscription on the soundboard round the rose: *Johann Loth Coloniae me fecit Anno Dmi. MDCXXXXVII.* It had 2×8′ registers [*VdMBei*, p. 104]. The instrument appeared in an antique-dealer's shop in Vence (Alpes Maritimes) about 1959 but has disappeared again since.

LÖWE, Christopher, of Augsburg. Son of a silversmith, *fl.* 1632. A spinet by him dated 1632 is in the Collection André Meyer, Paris. Illustrated in *Hin* (pl. 33); 4 octaves E/C–C.

LUCA, Tommaso de. *See*: TOMMASO de Luca.

LUCKSTADT. *Fl.* 1793 as instrument maker in Berlin. His clavichords were said to be good [*Ge* (1812), who refers to *Berl. Mus. Zeit.* 1793, p. 175].

LUDOVIC, of Avignon. In a deed of 1503 he is alluded to as making harpsichords with a double case, bone naturals and black sharps [*GL*].

LUGT, Dirk van der, of Amsterdam. *Fl.* 1770–89, harpsichord maker. He married in 1771 and again in 1789 [*GL*].

Surviving Instruments

(1) 1770. Berlin Collection. Harpsichord; 1 manual, 2×8′, 1×4′; C–F. Inscription on the soundbo rd: *Dirk*

van der Lugt fecit Amsterdam 1770. Rose in shape of angel with harp and the initials *DVL*. Size 79 × 181 cm. (Lost in World War II.)

LUKEY. *See*: Longman and Lukey.

LUNDBORG, Pehr, of Stockholm. Dates ascertained 1772–96, maker of clavichords and other keyboard instruments. Also made lutes and harps [*Lü*].

Surviving Instruments

(1) 1772. Organized clavichord. Stockholm, Musikhistoriska Museet.

(2) 1787. Clavichord. Stockholm, Musikhistoriska Museet. Bundfrei. F–A, 5 octaves and a 3rd. Size 193 × 60 cm.

(3) 1794. Clavichord. Stockholm, Nordiska Museet. F–A, 5 octaves and a 3rd.

(4) 1796. Clavichord. Ibid. F–A, 5 octaves and a 3rd.

(5) Undated. Clavichord. Nydahl Collection, Stockholm. Size 166·8 × 50·6 cm.

LUSSER, Joseph. Organ builder and clavichord maker at Brixen (Bressanone), Austria, at the turn of the eighteenth and nineteenth centuries.

Surviving Clavichords

(1) Nuremberg, Germanisches Nationalmuseum (Rück Collection). Signed: *Joseph Lusser, Orgel-/macher zu Brixen*. The instrument is assigned to *c*. 1810 by *VdM*.

LUXTON, Richard. Maker of virginals 'of St. Ethelborrowe's' London; *fl*. 1611 [*J*].

LYEN, Pieter de. Clavichord maker of Antwerp, *fl*. 1543 [*St*].

M. R. *See*: Richard, Marius.

M . . . . ., Joseph. A clavichord in the Berlin Collection bears upon the soundboard the inscription: *Dn. Josef M . .* [rest illegible] / *Madrid ano . . . .* (The *M* is uncertain and may be *N*[*otto*].)

It is gebunden, and Sachs ascribes it to the end of the eighteenth century.

MAAG, J. C. Born 1744 at Oberglatt in the canton of Zürich; died 1822 in Zürich. Described himself as 'faiseur des orgues et des clavecins' [*Rindl*].

M'DONNELL. Dublin harpsichord maker. *See*: Pemberton.

MACDONELL, Daniel. Harpsichord and piano maker, Dublin: 26 Fleet Street, 1793–1800; 28 Fleet Street, 1801–3; 12 Anglesea Street, 1804–15 [*Teahan*]. Made a harpsichord as late as 1804 [*Fld*].

MACDONNELL, James and Alexander. Harpsichord, piano, and guitar makers in Dublin: 34 Anglesea Street, 1787–8; 2 Church Lane, 1790–1800; 12 Anglesea Street, 1801–5; 2 Church Lane, 1806–10 [*Teahan*].

MACHY, Pierre de, of rue de Prêtre, parish of St. Paul, Paris. Born about 1675; married 1698; died 1726 [*MC*, Vol. 62, p. 340, 26 April 1726]. Related by marriage to the Denis family [*Verlet*]. Apparently more a dealer than a maker towards the end of his life [*Hubb 1965*].

MACHY, Pierre Antoine. French harpsichord maker of the eighteenth century. A 'Clavecin de Machy, 1713–74' advertised for sale, is quoted by *Bq*. Probably related to the preceding maker.

MACK, Heinrich Rudolph. Clavichord maker at Dresden in the eighteenth century; died 1807. Worked for a time with J. G. Horn, q.v. Set up on his own in 1799 [*Hirt*].

MACKHAM, Thomas. *See*: Makeham, Thomas.

MADDEY, John. Harpsichord maker in Custom House Lane, Queen Square, Bristol, *c*. 1785 [*J*]. He tuned and repaired the organ in St. James's Church, Bath, during 1792–3 [*Falc*].

MAGNELLI, Giovanni Battista. Italian harpsichord maker, probably of the seventeenth century. A polygonal virginal, undated, by him was in the collection of Prince Ferdinand of Tuscany in 1700 [*Gai*, p. 12].

MAGNIAI, Lorenzo, of Florence. Harpsichord maker; *fl*. 1689.

Surviving Instruments

(1) 1689. Leipzig, Heyer Collection. Harpsichord, inscribed on back of nameboard: *Lorenzo Magniai 1689. / A Firenze*. 2 × 8′ stops. C–C, 4 octaves with short octave. 196 × 78 cm. Illustrated in *Ks*, p. 92; inscription illustrated in *Ks*, p. 241.

MAGONA, Pietro de, of Ferrara. Harpsichord maker, *fl*. 1494 [*Va*].

MAHIEU, Jérôme, of Brussels. Harpsichord maker. Earliest date ascertained, 1732; died 1737 [*Cl*, p. 39]. Had several Ruckers harpsichords [*St*, p. 93].

He made harpsichords of:

2	manuals	3	registers	58	keys	
1	,,	3	,,	58	,,	
1	,,	3	,,	61	,,	
1	,,	2	,,	58	,,	(1 × 8′, 1 × 4′).

A 1-manual harpsichord by him dated 1732 was sold by Legouix of Paris in 1948. An instrument, possibly the same as the above, inscribed *Hieronymus Mahieu me fecit Bruxellis A. 1732* was for sale early in 1952 at Jacob, 19 rue Cambon, Paris. 5 octaves, D–D chromatic.

A 'double-key'd harpsichord by Maihu of Brussels, and later in the possession of Joseph Kelway Esq.' was sold at Christie's on 7 February 1791. (Vendor, the Revd. Mr. Fountain; buyer, Higins; price, £16. 5*s*. 6*d*.)

MAHOON, Joseph. Spinet and harpsichord maker, living in York Buildings, and 'King's Arms, North side of Golden Square', London. Dates ascertained, 1735–73.

A harpsichord by him is illustrated in Hogarth's *Rake's Progress* (2nd plate; the painting was done in 1735).

'Joseph Mahoon, harpsichord maker' is recorded in

LC 3/64, 24 June 1729. In the *Evening Post*, London, 8 July 1729, we read that 'on Wednesday last Mr. Moon [*sic*] in York buildings was appointed harpsichord maker to His Majesty', a post which he held in 1739 according to the list of subscribers in Roseingrave's edition of *XLII suites de pièces pour le clavecin* . . . by Scarlatti. In 1763 he is described as 'Harpsichord maker to his Majesty, and resident in Marybone' [*Un*].

He died in London on 17 November 1773 [*Gentleman's magazine*].

A 2-manual harpsichord by him was sold at Christie's, 18 December 1772, for £24.

TABLE 24. *Surviving Instruments by Joseph MAHOON*

No.	Date	Type	Kbs.	Signature	Owner/Remarks
1	1738	H	2	*Joseph Mahoon, London*	Bethersden, C. F. Colt; 2×8′, 1×4′ and lute. Burr walnut case. Dated 1738 on upper keyboard; on lower, 1742, in which year some alteration was probably carried out. One of the keys is signed: *Broom Smith 1738* [*Hubb 1965*, p. 158 n.].
2	1742	H	1		Put up for sale at Sotheby's, 13 July 1963 by A. S. Beazley of Bethersden, Kent. Illustrated in *Country Life*, 13 October 1950, p. 1205. Black naturals, ivory sharps; 2×8′ stops; rounded tail; length 6′. This may be the instrument seen in a Paris dealer's shop by *GL* in 1963.
2a	1742	S	1	*Joseph Mahoon, London*	Sold anonymously at Sotheby's, 28 May 1970, and bought by C. F. Colt. Compass F–G, 5 octaves and a tone; skunktail sharps, arcaded ivory naturals. Workman's signature *J. Burr* on bottom and top keys. Length 6′ 2″.
3	1745	S			Walnut case. 6′ 2″ long. Sold by H. Lambert at Sotheby's, 4 March 1932. Bought by Messrs. Hooper.
[4]		S	1		See 4b below.
4a	1748	S	1	*Joseph Mahoon, London*	London, Messrs. Morley (1956). On bottom key: *HH 1748 no. 12* . . . ('HH' perhaps = H. Hill, q.v.) A 1748 Mahoon spinet was advertised for sale in the personal column of the *Sunday Times*, summer 1958.
4b	1753	S	1		Washington, Smithsonian Institution. Of unusual polygonal shape, 5 octaves G–G. This may be the instrument which Hipkins knew as belonging to W. H. Cumming.
5	1771	S	1	*Joseph Mahoon, London*	London, Victoria and Albert Museum. Inscription *1771—no. 45* on first key is workman's number. Ivory naturals, skunk-tail sharps. Walnut case, varnished to look like mahogany (*pace RussellV&A*, p. 54) [*AdlP*]. On loan to the Horniman Museum (1970–).
6		S	1	*Joseph Mahoon, London*	Parham Park, Sussex. Formerly belonged to Mrs. Sigismund Goetze; bought at Sotheby's, 25 May 1951, by Messrs. Gooden and Fox, London. Beech and walnut case; 5 octaves with arcaded ivory naturals and ebony sharps inlaid with ivory. First key bears illegible date, and last key illegible signature (conceivably *Buntebart*). 6′ 1″×4′ 9″.
7	—	S	1		5 octaves G–G. Skunktail sharps. Walnut case. On sale at Partridge, New York, June 1951.
8	—	S	1	*Joseph Mahoon, London*	5 octaves G–G. Inlaid walnut. Owned (1966) by Mrs. P. Harding, Birling Manor, near Eastbourne. Length 6′ 3″.
9	—	S	1	*Joseph Mahoon, London*	Langleys, Great Waltham, Mr. Tufnell. The original bill of sale is with the instrument.

MAHR, Johann Andreas. A craftsman at the court of the Duke of Nassau at Wiesbaden. From about 1788 onwards he had a wide reputation for his keyboard instruments. He worked with his brother; and besides the normal keyboard instruments he made 'Klavi-Mandors' [*Ge*, 1814].

MAIHU, J. *See*: MAHIEU, Joseph.

MAIR, Sixt, of Stuttgart. Maker of organs and other keyboard instruments, *fl.* 1584–92 [*Württ. Vierteljahrsschrift*, 1900, article by Bossert].

MAKEHAM, Thomas, *also* Mackham, Mekehum, of London. Virginal maker. Born *c.* 1626. Apprenticed to William Leversidge (q.v.) in 1641/2; admitted free of the Joiners' Company 1649/50. John Crosse was apprenticed to him, May 1656 [*Join*]. In 1652 he resided in the parish of St. Michael Bassishaw, and for several years up to 1661 his name appears in the parish registers of St. Giles Cripplegate.

MALADE, Jean Jacques. Harpsichord maker, living in the rue Bourbon-Villeneuve, Paris, from 1773 to 1779. Married 1769, and again in 1774; died 1781. Son of M. Barthélémy, citizen of Mainz. Master harpsichord maker in Paris, 1768 [*Hardouin 1759*; *Verlet*].

MALARME. One of the jacks in Ruckers no. 4 is signed: *Fait par Malarme et* [*d*]*Anton . . . 1790*.

MALER, Sigismondo. The Smithsonian Institution, Washington, has a clavicytherium (given by the Cooper Union) inscribed: *Sicismondo Maler faciebat Anno Domini MDXXV Venetiae*. However, it should be remembered that the nameboard bearing the signature does not belong to the instrument. Compass B–E, 3½ octaves. White naturals; black inlaid sharps; 3 roses; a small instrument. One row (originally two) of jacks.

MANUEL, M. Harpsichord maker, of Lugo near Ravenna. Dates ascertained 1821–7 [*Va*].

MANUELANJO. *See*: LEO, Manuel Anjos.

MARBACH, Conrad. Clavichord maker at Kirchfembach near Langenzenn, *fl.* 1781. A gebunden clavichord of that year is in private ownership at Erlangen [*VdM*].

MARCHAL, N., of Nancy. Organist, and maker of clavichords, harpsichords, and organs—chiefly organ builder. Dates ascertained: 1724–63 [*Jac, Va*].

MARCHIONUS, Franciscus. Harpsichord maker, born in Florence, *fl.* in Rome in 1666.

Surviving Instruments

(1) 1666. Boston, Mass. Arthur Kohlenburg. A harpsichord, having 2×8′ stops, and inscribed: *Franciscus Marchionus Florentinus Fecit Romae 1666*. On the wrestplank the carved legend: *FMFFR 1666*. Compass, C–C, 4 octaves including short octave. Repaired by Messrs. Hubbard and Dowd, Boston, in 1949. Originally all the accidentals were split.

MARCO DAI CEMBALI, MARCO DALLE SPINETTE. *See*: JADRA, Marco.

MARCUS SICULUS. *See*: SICULUS, Marcus.

MARIUS, Jean, of Paris. Harpsichord maker; *fl.* 1700–15. He invented the *clavecin brisé*, a harpsichord which folds up by means of hinges and so becomes more easily portable; in 1700 he received a royal privilege of 20 years for his invention. (His *cachet* is depicted on *Jur*, p. 60.)

Like Schröter in Germany, Marius was working independently of Bartolommeo Cristofori, in the second decade of the eighteenth century, on the mechanism which became the foundation of the modern piano. He also

TABLE 25. *Surviving folding Harpsichords by Jean MARIUS*

No.	Date	Signature	Owner/Remarks
1	1700		Paris Conservatoire. Illustrated in *Jur*, pp. 60, 63.
2	1709	*Marius 1709*	Brussels Conservatoire. Formerly in the Tolbecque Collection, Paris.
3	1709		Auctioned in London, July 1901. (*ZIM* II. 409.)
4	1713	*Marius* [on wrestplank]; *1713* [on soundboard]	Leipzig University, Heyer Collection. 2×8′, 1×4′. G–E, 4 octaves and a 6th with short octave. Illustrated in *Ks*, p. 98; inscription in *Ks*, p. 242. (Formerly in Kraus Collection, Florence.)
5	1715		Paris, Comtesse de Chambure. (Formerly owned by Mm. M. and A. Salomon.) Illustrated in *J*, p. 126.
6	—	*Exclusif privilege du Roy / Marius* [maker's cachet on soundboard]	Berlin Collection. Belonged to Frederick the Great. Shewn at International Inventions Exhibition, 1885; 2×8′, 1×4′.

A folding harpsichord in the Gemeente-Museum, The Hague, attributed to Marius, is not by him but is a later instrument.

In the Medici Collection directed by Cristofori (q.v.) from 1716 to 1731 there was a *clavecin brisé* ('un' cimbalo da ripiegare, lavoro fatto in Francia, con il fondo dipinto a rateschi, con tastatura d'avorio, et ebano in tre pezzi, con invenzione per poterlo accordare di uno Strumento d'ottone'). This may have been one of Marius's instruments.

A spinet attributed to Marius was shewn at the International Inventions Exhibition in 1885 (Catalogue, p. 34).

Br records a 'clavecin de Marius' for sale in 1755, and *clavecins brisés* by him for sale in 1757 and 1765.

According to *GD*, suppl. 1945 (p. 512), Marius was the first to make upright pianofortes.

designed a hybrid which he called 'clavecin à maillets et à sautereaux', of which no example has survived [*Fé*]. *Pu* (pp. 111 ff.) quotes from *Recueil des machines approuvées par l'Académie Royale des Sciences*, 1716 onwards, regarding various 'clavecins à maillets' by Marius, with illustrations.

MARSAM, Andrew. Virginal maker at Leicester 1579–80; dead by October 1601. The Leicester Chamberlain's Accounts for 1579–80 record: 'Andrewe Marsam virgynall maker for his fredom. 10*s*.' [*Records of the Borough of Leicester*, by Mary Bateson. Vol. 3, p. 184. Cambridge University Press, 1905. The name might easily be misread as 'Marsani'.]

The Coventry Chamberlain's Accounts note the payment in October 1601 of ¾*d*. 'to Widdoe Massam [*sic*] the virginal makers wife to bring her to Basing stoke'.

MARSANI, Andrew. *See*: MARSAM, Andrew.

MARSCIANI. Italian firm of instrument makers, *fl.* 1771. They restored in May 1771 a harpsichord made by Bombini (q.v.).

MARSH, George, of London. Virginal maker, resident 1604–5 to 1608 in the parish of St. Giles Cripplegate [*Parish Reg.*].

MARTEL. *See*: BAS, L.

MARTIN, of Cracow, *fl.* 1609. Clavichord maker [*Va*].

MARTINELLI, *called* 'il Gobbo'. Instrument maker at Modena in the seventeenth century. Besides bass-viols and violins he made keyboard instruments [*Lü*]. In assigning him to the nineteenth century *Va* must be confusing him with another of the same name—a pianoforte maker.

MARTINI, of Friedrichstadt near Dresden. Maker of harpsichords and organs, *fl.* 1740 [*Fé*].

MARTINUS. Harpsichord maker in Leyden in 1623. The little we know of him consists largely of frauds and swindles. See *Curtis*, p. 53.

MASSAM, Andrew. *See*: MARSAM, Andrew.

MATHEUS, Johannes Franciscus, of Aerschot. Harpsichord maker. Dates ascertained 1770–83 [*Gö*; *VdS*, VII. 288].

The nameboard from a harpsichord by him is preserved in the Brussels Conservatoire; inscribed: *Joannes Franciscus Matheus, Aerschot anno 1783*.

MATTHIAS, *of Ghent*. Eighteenth-century harpsichord maker who went to Rome and set up his workshop there. He was considered to be the equal of the best Italian makers [*VdS*, VI. 514]. *Va* lists him, under *Gand*.

MATTHYS, Peter, of Antwerp. Gosuin Karest became his pupil in 1519. Matthys was probably only a painter, not an instrument maker.

MAYER. Instrument maker at Görlitz in the eighteenth century, made 'Bogenflügel' like Hohlfeld, etc. He presumably made at any rate some harpsichords [*Ko*].

MAYER, Johann. Maker of organs and other keyboard instruments at Salzburg; *fl.* 1619.

The Museum Carolino-Augusteum at Salzburg has a harpsichord by him signed: *Johann / Mayer Orgel / Und Instrum[en]t/macher In Slbg / 1619 gmacht* [sic]. Single-manual; 2×8′, buff, lute (i.e. 3 rows of jacks); geometrical rose; the compass, strange but original, is B flat to C, 4 octaves and 1 note. The instrument is described in detail and illustrated in *VdMSalzb*.

MAYWALDT, Johann Christof, of Weigandsthal. Clavichord maker, *fl.* 1729.

Surviving Clavichords

(1) 1729. Poznań, Muzeum Wielkopolskie, formerly in the Muzeum Narodowe. Formerly Breslau, Schlesisches Museum. Gebunden clavichord, C/E to C, 4 octaves with the label: *Johann Christof Maywaldt / in Weigendsthal / Anno 1729* [Catalogue by Epstein and Scheyer, 1932; *Szulc*].

MAZŁOWSKI, of Poznań, in Poland. *Fl.* 1805, harpsichord maker [*Va*].

MECK. The *Gazette de Moscou*, no. 17 of 1795, mentions a concert given by Hässler on 'deux clavecins et pédalier' made by Meck, probably not a Russian maker [*Moos*, II. 626].

MEDARO, Antonio, of Florence, and later Nancy. Clavichord maker, *fl.* 1616 [*Va*].

MEDERIC. *See*: LORILLART, Médéric.

MEDIOLANENSIS, Annibalis. *See*: ROSSI, Annibale dei.

MEER, Albrecht van. A native of Niel, near Julich, lived in Antwerp as clavichord and harpsichord maker; dates ascertained, 1542–60. He received the citizenship of Antwerp in 1542, in which year and in 1553 he is referred to as a clavichord maker; in 1560 he is called harpsichord maker [sources quoted by *St*]. He is presumably the Aelbrechts van Neere who was the fourth signatory to the petition headed by Joos Karest in 1557 [*St*, p. 63].

MEEUWSZ. Harpsichord maker in the Low Countries; *fl.* 1629 [*Curtis*, p. 54].

MEIDTING, Anton, of Augsburg. Instrument maker, *fl.* 1587. A spinet-regal, in the form of a chessboard, by him is in the Kunsthistorisches Museum, Vienna (illustrated in Schlosser's catalogue). It is inscribed: *Anthonius Meidting Augustanus fecit anno dom. 1587 mensae* [sic] *Decembrij*.

MEKEHUM, Thomas. *See*: MAKEHAM, Thomas.

MELA, Domenico del, of Gagliano in central Sicily. *Fl.* 1739, maker of keyboard instruments. (*Hirt* gives his dates as: born 1683, died between 1751 and 1752.)

The late Canon Galpin saw at Pistoia an upright piano by this maker dated 1739. This instrument is now in the Florence Conservatoire. Inscription: *P. Dominicus del Mela de Gagliano invenit et fecit anno MDCCXXXIX.* Rose without monogram.

MELLY. Harpsichord and pianoforte maker in London, late eighteenth or early nineteenth century. A square piano belonging (1969) to Mrs. Edith Chudley of Leigh, Surrey, contained a card inscribed *Melly, Harpsichord and Pianoforte maker, No. 40 Fleet Street . . .* [*CM*, 1969].

MENDINI, Giuseppe, *also* Mondini, of Florence. Probably a native of Imola; dates ascertained, 1631–46. He made harpsichords and portative organs [*Ch*]. Amongst the instruments of Ferdinand de' Medici entrusted in 1716 to the care of Cristofori was a *spinetta a due registri* by Mendini [*Pu*], while the inventory of the Prince's Collection made in 1700 records also 2 harpsichords by him dated 1687 and 1678, the signatures being *Joseph Mondini Imolensis* with the date [*Gai*, p. 11]. A large harpsichord of 3 registers by him was amongst the instruments of Cardinal Pietro Ottoboni, 1610–91, who became Pope Alexander VIII [*Kirk*, p. 360]. *See* Addenda.

Surviving Instruments

(1) 1631. Alec Hodsdon (1943). Polygonal virginal. Date on jackrail. Shewn by J. A. Fuller-Maitland at Music Loan Exhibition, London, 1904 (Catalogue p. 170).

(2) 1646. At Rochester, N.Y. Harpsichord (information from F. Hubbard).

(3?) 1660. *Francl* lists a 'spinetta' inscribed: *Joseph Mondini 1660.*

MENEGONI, Giovanni Andrea, of Venice. Maker of harpsichords and virginals. Dates ascertained, 1690–1715. In 1707 a double harpsichord of his was sold to the Conservatorio, Naples, for 70 ducats [*MarcP*].

Surviving Instruments

(1) 1690. Smithsonian Institution, Washington. Harpsichord. Four octaves with short octave; 1×8′. Boxwood naturals. Very large rose. Inscription: *Giovanni Andrea Menegoni Venetus fecit 1690.* Nameboard spurious.

(1a) 1692. Milan, Museo Civico. Polygonal virginal inscribed: *Ioannis Andreae Menegoni Veneti MDCLXXXXII.* Forty-five keys. Size 73×44 cm. Illustrated in *Gall*, pl. 128.

(2) 1696. Basel, Historisches Museum. Harpsichord. C/E–C, 4 octaves. 2×8′. Rose.

(3) 1715. M. and Mme Roesgen-Champion (1927, when it was shewn by Sautier et Jaeger of Geneva at the Exposition Internationale de Musique). Polygonal virginal.

(4) 1715. Mlle Laurence Boulay, Paris (1969) [*ClavHist*]. Perhaps equals no. 3.

MENSEN, Hendrik [Mensz]. Born *c.* 1590; *fl.* 1625 as harpsichord maker in Amsterdam; died 1647. See further *Curtis*, p. 54.

MERCATOR, *Sir* **Michael,** *vulgo* Krämer, of Venloo, 1491–1544. Maker of virginals to Floris Count of Egmont, to Cardinal Wolsey, and to King Henry VIII. A medal struck in his honour (perhaps by Hagenauer) in 1539 is reproduced in A. J. Hipkins's *Musical Instruments, Historic, Rare, and Unique*, p. v.

There is no evidence of his being connected with the cartographer Gerardus Mercator (1512–94, born at Rupelmonde in Flanders).

MERCIA. According to the appendix in *Ge* (1792), Mercia 'improved' the harpsichord in 1783 'durch Nachahmung des Trompeten und Paukentons'(!).

MERLIN, John Joseph. Harpsichord maker and inventor, 1735–1804. He was born at Huys, near Liège, on 17 September 1735. After 6 years in Paris he came to England in 1760 in the suite of the Spanish ambassador, Count de Guentes, with whom he resided for some time in Soho Square.

In 1774 he took out a patent (no. 1081) for a 'compound harpsichord' which was a combination of a single-manual harpsichord—with 2 unison registers and an octave—and a pianoforte with a down-striking action. The patent specification shews a 5-octave keyboard without the bottom F sharp. It has 2 pedals: the left-hand pedal brings on the pianoforte action working on the unison registers; the right-hand pedal brings on the unison and octave registers one after the other (with a mechanism completely different from the machine-stop), thereby producing the effect of a swell. Merlin's description of the instrument runs: 'A new kind of compound harpsichord, in which, besides the jacks with quills, a set of hammers of the nature of those used in the kind of harpsichords called Piano Forte, are introduced in such manner that either may be played seperately [*sic*] or both together at the pleasure of the performer, and for adding the aforesaid hammers to an harpsichord of the common kind already made, so as to render it such compound harpsichord.'

Dr. Charles Burney bought a piano from him in 1777 and had the compass extended in both directions. He bequeathed it to his daughter Esther ('My large Piano Forte with additional keys at the top and bottom originally made by Merlin with a compass of six octaves the first that was ever constructed expressly at my desire for duets a quatre mains in 1777').

The following curious scene is described in Busby's *Concert Room Anecdotes*, II. 137:

> During the latter part of the eighteenth century, that ingenious mechanic and musical instrument maker gratified the curious and tasteful by the public exhibition of his organ, pianoforte, and other inventions, at his Museum in Princes Street, Hanover Square. Merlin's mind was adequate to the embracing the whole compass of mechanical science and execution; at least, in the articles connected with elegant and domestic amusement. One of his ingenious novelties was a *pair of skaites*, contrived to run on wheels. Supplied with a pair of these and a violin, he mixed in the motley group of one of the celebrated Mrs. Corneily's masquerades at Carlisle House, Soho Square; when, not having provided the means of retarding his velocity, or commanding its direction, he impelled himself against a mirror of more than five hundred pounds value, dashed it to atoms, broke his instrument to pieces and wounded himself most severely.

Among his many inventions, some useful, some diverting, Merlin's invalid chair is still sold under this name today. For further details about Merlin's life and inventions see

P. A. Scholes, *The Great Doctor Burney* (Oxford University Press, 1948), II. 202 ff.

An instrument by Merlin (either a harpsichord or a grand pianoforte) is depicted in a portrait, now in Buckingham Palace, by Gainsborough of Johann Christian Fischer (1733–1800), the oboeist, who married the painter's daughter Mary. Gainsborough also painted a portrait of Merlin himself. Some instruments in Merlin's possession at the time of his death were sold by auction in 1837; the advertisement is quoted by *Ri* (p. 93).

Surviving Instruments

(1) 1780. Munich. Deutsches Museum. A 5-octave compound harpsichord inscribed: *Josephus Merlin, Privilegiarius Novi Fortepiano Nr. 80, Londini, 1780.* 1×16′, 2×8′, 1×4′ registers. Three rows of jacks. Four hand-stops labelled: (on the left) Nr. 1 OCTAVE, Nr. 2 VNISON, (on the right) Nr. 1 CELESTIAL HARPE, Nr. 2 WELSH HARP. The 'Celestial Harpe' stop lifts one set of 8′ jacks off the strings, which are then free to vibrate sympathetically. The Welsh harp is a buffstop. The pianoforte action is brought on by one pedal and the 16′ by another. A copying-machine was attached to the instrument, which was formerly in the Bayerisches Nationalmuseum, Munich.

According to the Deutsches Museum this instrument came from Russia. May it have been the 'English harpsichord' of Catherine the Great?

(2?) *Nor* (p. 149) describes, as existing in Munich, a compound harpsichord having 1×16′, 2×8′, 1×4′ registers, and a hammer action brought into play by a pedal. According to him it is dated 1774, and is fitted with a copying-machine and a clock. It seems likely that he has mistaken the date and that this instrument is identical with 1 above.

MESCHITA, Joseph. A Carmelite monk, probably Spanish. On 23 June 1730 he finished the restoration of a 2-manual clavicytherium dating from the first half of the sixteenth century. In the course of the work it was extended ('mis en ravalement') [*Ks*, p. 81 n.].

MESNAGER, Yves. Parisian harpsichord maker and organist, who lived, with his wife Catherine Foulon, in the rue des Arcis; died 1556. He also made clavichords, for in an inventory of goods in his house, made after his death and dated 2 June 1556, there appears: 'Item le boys d'un manicordion non parfaict . . .' [*Les*, *Verlet*].

MESSAN, Vincent. Was apprenticed to Claude Jacquet on 7 May 1653 [*Hubb*].

MEUNIER, Jacques. Parisian harpsichord maker; *fl.* 1674–1705 [*Verlet*].

MEYER. Clavichord maker in Lübeck, *fl.* 1781. See below, WINTHER AND MEYER.

MEYER, Daniel. Organ builder at Göttingen. In 1575 he built an organ with 'geduppelten Saittenwerk'.

MIDDELBURG, Johann. Organ and clavichord builder at Hamburg, where he received citizenship on 15 January 1692. By 23 August 1694 he was married to Sophia Margaretha Fleischer (*née* Zaego), formerly wife of Hans Christoph Fleischer, q.v.

Mattheson writes in 1713:

'Middelburg reussirt in Clavicordiis vor allen, wiewol die Fleischer [i.e. the brothers Johann Christoph and Carl Conrad] es ihm ziemlich gleich thun; deren einer die kostbarste und sauberste Arbeit von der Welt machet, der andere seinen Wercken einen besonders starcken und hellen Resonanz zu geben weiss' [*MatNO*].

MIETCKE, Michael. Instrument maker in Charlottenburg, Berlin; dates ascertained: 1680–1719, the latter being the year of his death [*Wa*]. *Wa* thought well of his harpsichords ('schöne Clavicymbel'). From 1697 he was 'Hofinstrumentenbauer'. In 1719 J. S. Bach went from Cöthen to Berlin to buy a harpsichord by him—'das gross Flügel mit 2 Clavituren, von Michael Mietcke in Berlin, 1719' [*Bach-Dokumente*, II. 74 (Kassel, 1969)]. *Ge* refers to his harpsichords.

MIGLIAI, Antonio [Antonius de Migliais] of Florence. Son of Michelagnolo Migliai. Dates ascertained: 1682–1704.

He made harpsichords, harps, and probably lutes as well. His address in 1684 when he paid a matriculation fee to his Guild, was 'Da' Gesuiti'. In 1704 he was involved in a lawsuit [*Pu*].

Surviving Harpsichords

(1) 1682. Paris, Savoye Collection (auctioned 1882). Number of keyboards not known.

(2) 1696. Berlin Collection. 3×8′ stops; F–C, 4½ octaves. Inscription: *Antonius de Migliais Florentinus fecit anno MDCLXXXXVI.*

(3) 1702. Leipzig University, Heyer Collection. Compass F–C, 4½ octaves; 2×8′; lowest key split, giving F and G; no bottom G sharp; 263×97 cm. Inscription: *Antonius di Migliais Florentinus F. A. MDCCII* (reproduced at *Ks*, p. 247). *FrancI* lists a harpsichord inscribed: *Antonius Migliai Florentinus 1617.*

The Musikhistorisk Museum, Copenhagen, has a clavicytherium with spurious inscription on the jackrail: *Angiolus Migliai Florentinus fecit anno 1590*; 4′ pitch; 2 uninitialled roses; jacks and parts of the case are nineteenth- and twentieth-century replacements. Bought by the Museum in 1912 from Rodolfo Subert, Milan.

MIGUELANJO. *See*: LEO, Manuel Anjos.

MILCHMEYER, Peter Johann *also* Milchmaier. Son of a clockmaker, born at Frankfurt am Main, 1750. Although lame in both feet he became in 1798 attached to the Court and the Electoral chapel at Munich. His treatise *Über die wahre Art das Pianoforte zu spielen* was published in 1797 at Dresden, where he may have been living at the time. In 1803 he became a teacher of the piano at Strasbourg, and in this capacity attained a considerable reputation. He died there on 15 March 1813, at the age of 63 years [*Fé*, *Eit*].

He invented *c.* 1780:

einen neuen mechanischen Flügel mit 3 Klavieren [sc. manuals] und 250 Veränderungen [!], der doch nicht viel grösser als ein gewöhnlicher Flügel [harpsichord] war. Das untere Klavier lässt sich herausschrauben, wenn zwei Personen zugleich auf diesem Instrument spielen wollen. Das Steigen und Fallen der Töne soll auf diesem Instrument sehr gut ausgedrückt werden können. Die Veränderungen imitieren die Flöte, das Fagott, die Clarinette und die Harfe u.s.w. [*Magazin der Musik* ('Cramers Magazin'), Hamburg, 1783].

MIRABAL, Francisco Perez. Harpsichord maker in Seville in 1745. A fine lacquered harpsichord, apparently 2-manual, inscribed *Me fecit Francisco Perez Mirabal en Sevilla 1745*, belonged to Gonzalo Bilbao, who left his collection to the state. The harpsichord is now probably somewhere in Madrid [R. Robinette]. An illustration of it in *Spanish Interiors and Furniture*, by Arthur Byne and Mildred Stapely (New York, Helburn, 1922, pl. 192) shews a resemblance to a large Hass harpsichord, and suggests that it may have 2 manuals, 2×8′, 1×4′, and possibly 1×2′ registers. The case is elaborately lacquered *à la chinoise*.

MOENS, Simon. *See*: Moyns, Simon.

MOERMANS, Hans *or* **Jan.** It appears that there were 2 harpsichord makers of this name in Antwerp, perhaps father and son: *The Elder, fl.* 1570–1610, entered the Guild of St. Luke as a harpsichord maker in 1570; resident 'op de Cathelijnevest, Int gulden Serpent' in 1584; was singing bass in the choir of O.L. Vrouwe Kerk in 1610 [*St*]. *The Younger, fl.* 1642, made instrument no. 1 below.

Surviving Harpsichords

(01) 1584. Waltham, Mass., Frank Hubbard (1963). One manual. Inscribed: *Hans Moermans Antwerpiae 1584*. Rose with initials *HM*. 1×8′, 1×4′ stops; G/B–F, nearly 5 octaves. Formerly belonged to Alphonse von Neste.

(1) 1642. Redhill, Dr. R. Mirrey, who bought it at Sotheby's on 13 March 1972 from William Post Ross of Boston, Mass., who had bought it from Pastoor H. Lippens of Ghent, who had acquired it in 1922. (It was formerly in the Régibo Collection, sold in 1897.) Two manuals. Inscription on the jackrail: *Hans Mœrmans me fecit Antwerpiæ 1642*. Rose with initials *HM*. 2×8′, 1×4′, dogleg. Never altered in range or disposition. Length 7′ 9″ (232·5 cm.).

(2) Two-manual harpsichord formerly in the Régibo Collection. Five octaves, 3 registers. Length 245 cm.

(3) Single harpsichord, formerly Régibo's. Length 225 cm.

(4) Single harpsichord, formerly Régibo's. Three registers. Length 215 cm.

MOERS, Anton. *See*: Moors, Antonius.

MOERS, Jean Henri. Parisian harpsichord maker; *fl.* 1754–93 [*Verlet*]. Nephew and pupil of Jean Henri Hemsch, q.v. He came to Paris from Castenholz near Cologne and was naturalized in 1760. Ten years later he was *juré comptable* of the Guild of Instrument Makers. In 1791 he was called in as expert after the death of Louis Henocq.

MOFERREZ. Known as the 'Moor of Saragossa', he was, in the fifteenth century, a maker of harpsichords and claviorgana in Spain [*Russell 1959*, p. 115].

MÖLLER, H. P. Eighteenth-century maker of clavichords, pianofortes, and other instruments in Copenhagen. He patented an instrument called the 'Cylinder Lyre', an example of which survives in the Claudius Museum, Copenhagen; it bears the inscription: *H. P. Möller i Kiöbenhavn, forfaerdiger Pianoforter og Cylinderlyrer*, and is illustrated in the catalogue.

He was an ancestor of the firm of Hornung and Möller, piano makers, who are now once again making clavichords.

MONDINI. *See*: Mendini, Giuseppe.

MONGUET, François, of Lyons. Harpsichord maker, *fl.* 1779 when he is recorded among the *luthiers* [Lyons archives].

MONSUTTO, Antonino, of Udine. Harpsichord maker *fl.* 1574. A quint virginal signed *Antonino Monsutto Vdiniae 1674* is in the Rück Collection in the Germanisches Nationalmuseum, Nuremberg.

MONTAZEAU, Jean. French harpsichord maker, *fl.* 1632. A spinet inscribed by him on the jackrail was in the Tolbecque Collection in 1922 [*MarcP*].

MONTECUCCHI, Vincenzo. An Italian harpsichord privately owned at Englewood, Florida, bears a partially legible inscription on the nameboard: *Vincenzo Montecucchi fecit* [?] *Ancone . . . 1768*. Single-manual, 2×8′ stops; C/E–C, 4 octaves. Its general appearance, and the inscription, call Franciolini to mind as having handled it, though this maker does not figure in those of his catalogues that I know.

MOOR OF SARAGOSSA. *See*: Moferrez.

MOORS, Antonius, *also* Mors, Moers. Celebrated maker of keyboard instruments (including organs) in Antwerp, member of a family of organ builders (*St*, p. 77 gives a tree). Earliest date known, 1514; he died before August 1562. In 1516 he received from Eleanor of Austria (1498–1558) 15 livres for a clavichord ('. . . que madicte dame Lyenor d'Austria a fait prendre et acheter de luy').

St (pp. 79–82) quotes a number of references to Moors from various archives. See also *VdS*, VII. 206 ff.; *Vente*, p. 26.

MOORS, Marc, of Lierre, Low Countries. Related to Jacob Moors of the family of organists, *fl.* 1508, made clavichords. In August 1508 he received 31 livres 5 sous for 'ung manicor que Monsieur [the archduke Charles, later Charles V, who had taken refuge at Lierre from the plague] a fait acheter de lui pour son desduit et passe temps' [*St*, p. 780; *Va*; *Fé* who misnames him Loers].

MOOSER, Jean Pierre Joseph Aloys. *See*: Moser, Jean Pierre Joseph Aloys.

MOREL. Parisian harpsichord maker. Earliest date ascertained, 1772 [*Verlet*]. Entered the Guild of Instrument Makers between 1776 and 1778. *Hirt* gives 1783 as a date ascertained.

MORELLATI, Paolo, of Vicenza. Made a harpsichord for the singer Farinelli (1705–82) who presented it to the Duke of Parma [*Sac*, p. 48, cited by *Kirk*].

MORELLI, Pietro Paolo. Italian maker of stringed keyboard instruments, *fl.* before 1681, in which year a Dresden inventory includes an 'Instrument, welches einfach bezogen und Eckicht daran da fördere Breth sambt dem Schlosse mangelt' made by him [*Drechsel*, p. 496].

MORLAND. Harpsichord maker in Dublin; *fl.* last decade of the eighteenth century [*Fld*].

MORS, Antoine. *See*: MOORS, Antonius.

MORS, Henry, of Lierre, Low Countries. According to *Cl* (p. 20) an organ and 'manicordion' maker in the sixteenth century.

MOSER, Joseph Anton, of Niederhelfenschwil in the canton of St. Gall, lived 1731–92 in Fribourg as an organ builder. He also made harpsichords (advertisement of 1773). Father of the next maker [*Rindl*].

MOSER, Jean Pierre Joseph Aloys. Known as Aloys Moser (after 1791 'Mooser'); born Fribourg 1770; died there 19 December 1839. Known chiefly as an organ builder, he also made pianofortes and apparently harpsichords [*Hirt*, p. 478, q.v. for further details].

MOSHACK, Moritz Georg, of Copenhagen. Organ and instrument maker. Born 1730; licensed 1761; had died by 1772.

Surviving Instruments

(1) 1768. Oslo. Norsk Folkemuseum. Clavichord. 5 octaves, F–F. Signed: *Moritz Georg Moshack in Copenhagen, Ao 1768.* 173×50 cm. Octave strings for lowest 22 notes.

(2) 1770. Copenhagen. Musikhistorisk Museum. Clavichord, signed: *Moritz Georg Moshack in Copenhagen Ao. 1770.* Bundfrei. F–F, 5 octaves, partially trichord in bass. Bought by the Museum in 1922 from A. Madsen, Copenhagen.

(3) 1770. Falsters Minder Museum, Nykøbing Falster, Denmark. Harpsichord; 1 manual, 2×8′ and buffstop; compass F–F, 5 octaves. Signed: *Moritz Georg Moshack Copenhagen Ao. 1770* (on the soundboard). Dimensions 234·5×97×25 cm.

MOUCHERELLE, Christophe, of Toul (Meurthe/Moselle) and Metz. Maker of organs and harpsichords. Dates ascertained, 1686–1761.

While in Rodez in 1734 he wrote a *Mémoire instructive pour faire les devis, desseins, plans, marchés et réception des orgues*, in which he describes himself as 'architecte, machiniste facteur de clavessins et de toutes sortes d'instrumens à vent'. While in Trévous he built a harpsichord [*Jac*]. See further *Fleury*.

MOULLE, Pierre. *See*: ALLIAMET, F.

MOYNS, Simon, *also* Moens. Harpsichord maker in Antwerp. Dates ascertained, 1552–7 [*Bu, Lü*].

MOYSE, Johann. Viennese instrument maker, *fl.* 1765. The Kunsthistorisches Museum, Vienna, has an ottavino clavichord by him in the form of a book entitled *Ditionario armonico.* The barely legible inscription runs: *Joannes Moyse 17. Vienna. 65* [*Luith*, p. 5]. In 1781, when he was 'K.-K.-Nationaltheater Instrumentenmacher und Stimmer' he repaired 3 spinets for the Esterházy court [*Walter*, p. 258].

MUELEVOETS, Johannes. Harpsichord maker of Antwerp, *fl.* 1584 [*Va*].

MÜLLER, Hans, of Leipzig. Harpsichord and clavichord maker. Dates ascertained, 1537–43 [*Cerv*; *Kü*, p. 19].

Surviving Instruments

(1) 1537. Rome, Raccolta Statale di Strumenti Musicali (formerly in the Evan Gorga Collection). Harpsichord; inscription stamped on gilded paper on the nameboard: *Gottes Wort bleibt ewick beistan den armen als den reichen. Durch Hans Muller cu Leipcik im 1537*; 2×8′ strings, 3 rows of jacks; geometrical rose. The keyboard originally could be shifted sideways for transposing. The oldest surviving German harpsichord. For a discussion of it see *Cerv.*

MÜLLER, Hartwich. Organ and instrument maker in Copenhagen, 1716–93.

Surviving Clavichords

(1) 1769. Musikhistorisk Museum, Copenhagen. Clavichord signed: *Hartwich Müller i Copenhagen 1769.* Gebunden; 4 octaves C–F. Brutally rebuilt by the piano maker Søren Jensen in 1917, the case being a copy of the Hubert instrument no. 1. Bought by the Museum in 1950 from Mr. Nielsen.

MULLER, Michael, of Marburg. Clavichord and piano maker; born 1758 [*Hirt*].

MUNIER. Parisian harpsichord maker, probably eighteenth century. A 'Clavecin de Munier' was advertised 12 December 1754 [*Bq*, p. 9; *Pi*, p. 91].

MURDOCK. Organ builder and harpsichord maker in Dublin in 1785 [*Teahan*].

MURER, Bernhard, called 'Der Deutsche'. Was organist at St. Mark's, Venice. He is said to have invented *c.* 1445 a pedal mechanism for change of registration on the clavichord and harpsichord [C. F. Weitzmann, *Geschichte des Clavierspiels* . . . 2. Aufl., 1879, p. 253].

MUSCH, Johann. An ottavino or spinet signed with this name and dated 1684 is in private ownership in New Haven, Conn. Its authenticity is reported to me as dubious. The signature is a printed label, genuine, but does not belong to the instrument [*MarcP*].

MUSSARD, Henry. Maker of virginals in the parish of St. Andrew's, Holborn, about 1621.

N., H. O. The Museum Carolino-Augusteum at Salzburg has an ottavino, unsigned except for the letters *HON* on the 5th key lever. *VdMSalzb*, who gives a detailed account of the instrument, regards it as German but shewing strong Italian influence.

N . . ., Josef. *See*: M . . ., Josef.

N, N. *See*: Bonafinis, Francesco.

NADREAU. According to *Br* a French eighteenth-century harpsichord maker.

NASH, Stephen. Harpsichord and piano maker at 106 Capel Street, Dublin, 1799–1803 [*Teahan*].

NAUBAUER. *See*: Neubauer.

NAULOT, Jean. Parisian harpsichord maker. Dates ascertained, 1777–83. Entered the Guild of Instrument Makers in 1777, at which time he was living in the rue Gaillon. In 1783 he lived in the rue du Bac [*Pi*]. *Verlet* gives more details.

NEERE, Albrecht van. *See*: Meer, Albrecht van.

NEPRIDI, *pseudonym. See*: Pedrini, Theodoric.

NERI, Francesco, of Rimini. Harpsichord maker, *fl.* 1695.

Surviving Instruments

(1) 1695. Salzburg, Museum Carolino-Augusteum. Harpsichord, single manual, E/C–C, 4¼ octaves; 2×8′ stops. Rose. Inscribed on the back of the nameboard: *D. Francisci Nerii Ariminensis MDCVC.* Illustrated in catalogue.

(2) Prague. City Museum. Harpsichord. Illustrated in *Buchner 1956*.

NESLE, J.-J. French, *fl.* 1780. M. Coffinières de Nordeck exhibited in 1889 an Italian harpsichord inscribed: *fait à Milan pour sonner à la quinte; refait pour sonner au ton, par J.-J. Nesle. 1780* [*Pi*].

NEUBAUER, Frederick. Dates ascertained: 1763–died 1774. Harpsichord maker of Compton Street, Soho, London. He appears in *Un* (1763) as 'Maker of double-basset and treble-key'd Harpsichords, with six stops, and of Pianofortes, Lyrichords, Classichords, etc., living in Compton Street, St. Anne's, Soho'.

On 11 February 1772 there were announced

> to be sold by auction by Mr. Christie, at his Great Room, late the Royal Academy, in Pall Mall . . . Fifteen fine ton'd Harpsichords, with double and single keys, several of which with double and single bass pedals, and being the stock in trade of Frederick Naubauer [*sic*], Harpsichord maker, together with a Lyrichord a capital melodious instrument made by the famous Rutgerus Plenius . . .

He had 2 daughters, one of whom, Charlotte, married Abraham Kirkman the harpsichord maker.

He died in 1774, and on 22 November in that year 'administration of the goods . . . of Frederick Neubauer late of the parish of St. Ann Westminster . . . widower deceased was granted to Catherine Burkinyoung wife of Philip Burkinyoung, and Charlotte Kirkman wife of Abraham Kirkman, the natural and lawful daughters of the said deceased . . .' [*Un*; *Mor*; *Ri*, p. 88; Admon. Acts of P.C.C. 1774].

The notice quoted from *Un* above is interesting on several counts. The reference in Neubauer's stock in trade to harpsichords with a pedal keyboard is the only indication that such instruments were known in this country. The 'double-basset' harpsichord was presumably an instrument with a 16-foot register, and the 'treble-key'd' one a harpsichord with the range extended in the treble.

NÈVE, Godefroi de. According to *Cl* (p. 32), he was a seventeenth-century clavichord maker in Antwerp.

NEWBANE. Harpsichord maker, *fl.* 1773. Lived in Greek Street, Soho, London. He is mentioned in an advertisement in the *Morning Post*, 26 July 1773 [*J*].

NIEBUHR, Henning, of Brunswick, *fl.* 1662. Made clavichords, harpsichords, etc. *SB* (p. 49) quotes the following ruling relative to Niebuhr:

> 2 December 1662. 'Henning Niebuhr darf Clavichordia, Clavicymbal, Harpfen und andere musikalischen Instrumenta . . . ungehindert verfertigen und verkaufen. Das ihm bei der jungsten 'Besuchung' von den Tischlern abgenommene Clavichordium und Werkzeug wird ihm ohne Entgeld zurückgegeben . . .

NIGETTI, Francesco (called also 'Cestinetti' by *Va*), composer and performer, organist at the Cathedral in Florence, *fl. c.* 1660, died in 1682.

To him is ascribed the invention of a harpsichord without sharps ('senza tasti neri') to facilitate transposing [*Eit*]. A. M. Salvini (*Della perfetta poesia italiana*) refers to a harpsichord with quarter-tones, constructed by Nigetti and called *strumento onnisono*; it was also called a *Proteus* and had, according to C. Sachs, *Reallexicon . . .*, p. 306, 5 manuals.

G. B. Doni, writing *c.* 1640 (*Trattato sopra gl'instrumenti di tasti*, in *Lyra barberina*, 1763, Vol. I, p. 327), refers to 'un Clavicembalo fatto ultimamente raccomodare qui in Firenze dal virtuosissimo Sig. Francesco Nigetti'. The 1665 Innsbruck inventory of Siegmund Franz, Archduke of Austria, records (according to the transcription in *Wald*): '. . . ein anderes Instrument mit vielen [? vieren] Claviaturen von weissem helfenbein, worauf die Florentinische Wappen und in der Mitte des *Auctoris Francesci* Nigetti namen, und einem von Schwarzen Leder überzochenen Futerall.'

NIXON, Thomas. Eighteenth-century harpsichord maker in the parish of St. James, Piccadilly, *fl.* 1767, before which he had at some time worked for Shudi for about 2 years. He figures in an affidavit sworn on 12 January 1767 concerning the work of Shudi's nephew, Joshua, q.v.

NOBILI, Antonio Francesco, of Florence and Rome. Son of Piero Nobili. Dates ascertained, 1693 [*Va*]–1695. He made instruments, including harpsichords and guitars. A harpsichord in the collection of Professor Fritz Neumeyer, Freiburg in Breisgau, bears the inscription: *Francesco Nobili in Roma fec. 1695.* 2×8′ stops, buff; 146×102 cm. (formerly lent to the Museum für Hamburgische Geschichte).

NOBILI, Tommaso, of Rome. Harpsichord maker, *fl.* 1684 [*Va*]. Possibly brother of the preceding.

NOESSLER. *See*: Nössler.

NOLCK, Joachim Friedrich, of Lübeck. Dates ascertained 1799–1802. Maker of organs and other keyboard instruments. On 19 June 1802 he advertised in the Lübeck *Anzeiger*: '. . . zugleich empfehle ich mich mit Verfertigen aller anderen Arten von Orgeln und Saiteninstrumenten wie auch Stimmen derselben' [*Lü*].

NONA, Francesco della, of Rome. Harpsichord maker. Dates ascertained, 1610–12 [*Va*].

NONNEMACKER, Christian, *fl.* 1757. German instrument maker. Imitated Marius's *clavecin brisé* in 1757 [*Cl*, p. 76]. A folding harpsichord by him is in the Metropolitan Museum of Art, New York, inscribed: *Christianus Nonnemacker Anno 1757*. Illustrated in *Wint 1961*.

NORDQUIST, Carl Jac., of Stockholm, *fl.* 1818. A clavichord signed: *Carl Jac. Nordquist Stockholm 1818* is in the Historical Museum at Åbo (Turku). Another, signed: *Carl Jacob Nordquist 1818* is in the Nydahl Collection at Stockholm; 6 octaves C–C.

NORGATE, Edward. Dates ascertained, 1629–32. Repairer of organs and virginals to Charles I.

An entry in State Papers (Domestic) Vol. 229, no. 67, reads:

> A list of the Hon. Lord Chamberlain's Warrants payd Anno Domini 1632 . . .
>
> Edw. Norgate of the Organs, Virginalls etc. 042 0 0 . . .

Norgate may have been only a repairer or tuner; but he was probably a maker as well.

(Quoted in *MA*, III. 238 (1911–12). See also *La*, pp. 68, 79, where he is paid for repairing organs and virginals.)

NORTON, William, of London. Virginal maker, held a shop in Bishopsgate Street in the parish of St. Ethelburga before 1594 [Chanc. Inq. p.m. ser. II, vol. 238, no. 92].

NÖSSLER, Johann Georg Kaspar. Clavichord maker at Rothenburg, *fl.* 1785. Son-in-law of Gessinger (q.v.).

Surviving Clavichords

(1) 1785. Formerly in the Rück Collection. A clavichord which, according to Rück's notes, originally had a label (lost during a restoration) ascribing the instrument to Johann Georg Nössler, Rothenburg ob der Tauber, 1785. The clavichord, similar in style to Gessinger's instruments, now belongs to Reinhardt Menger, Abtei Arnsburg, near Giessen.

NOTTLE, Bonifazius. The account-books of Paul Behaim of Nuremberg for the year 1568 contain this entry: 'A di den 12 jenner zalt dem Bonifazius Nottle für ein Clafficordia darauf mein Paulus lernen soll cost 2 fl.' ('On 12 Jan. paid 2 florins to Bonifazius Nottle for a clavichord for my Paul to learn on'). [*Ki*, p. 96].

This would presumably be a hiring fee; and Nottle may or may not have been a *maker* of clavichords.

OBERNDORFER. Schoolmaster at Jugenheim 'besass besondere mechanische Geschicklichkeit in Verfertigung der Klaviere und Fortepianos. Seine Instr. waren ums Jahr 1782 so geschätzt, dass man davor 100 Thaler bis 200 Gulden bezahlete. Auch sogar ausser Deutschland fanden sie häufigen Abgang' [*Ge* (1792), II. 38].

OBERT. Harpsichord maker of Boulogne, *fl.* 1753. A letter in the *London Chronicle*, 17–19 May 1753, refers to his upright harpsichords, 6′ 3″ high, 3′ wide, 15″ deep, costing 21 guineas. Two were then in England and two on order [*Hubb*].

OBICI, Bartolomeo, of Verona. Spinet maker, *fl.* 1683. The polygonal virginal by him, C/E–C, 4 octaves, with label inside: *Bortolam̃io Obici in Verona* [printed] *1683* [MS.], now (1970) in the George F. Harding Museum, Chicago, was presumably the 1683 polygonal virginal owned by de Bricqueville in 1895.

OEHME. Maker of organs and other keyboard instruments at Freiberg (Saxony), 1795; pupil of Gottfried Silbermann [*Ge*, 1812].

Hirt gives an Adolf Gottfried Oehme, 1718–died 25 November 1789, pupil of G. Silbermann; maker of organs and keyboard instruments at Freiburg. (A Freiburg organ builder and maker of stringed instruments, Adam Gottfried Oehme, a guitar by whom is dated 1831 [*Vannes*], was presumably related). A clavichord by A. G. Oehme is (1966) in the Gemeentemuseum, The Hague. Gebunden; 2 rose-holes; walnut case.

OESTERLIN, Johann Christoph. Dates ascertained, 1773–94. Lived in Berlin. *Ge* (1814) writes: '. . . besonders verbreitet waren seine Flügel mit den neuerfundenen ledernen Tangenten.' This probably refers to leather plectra, already reintroduced by Taskin in France; though it might imply an instrument similar to Späth's *Tangentenflügel*, but having the tangents covered with leather.

It is probably to this maker that *ClP* (p. 46) is referring when he writes 'J. K. Osterlein, in Berlin, employed the *buffle* after 1773'.

Fe (VI. 352) records a C. H. Oesterlein, piano maker in Berlin, who died in 1792, particularly renowned for his grand pianofortes.

ONDEO. Perhaps a Venetian maker of stringed keyboard instruments. *Wald* quotes: 'Ein einfaches Spinetl Thiorbata, so in Venedig von dem *Ondeo* gemacht worden, so ohne Anstrich' (inventory of 1665). If the inventory is mistaken in the maker's habitat, this maker might be identifiable with Donatus Undeus (q.v.) of Bergamo.

ONDERHOST, Deetlef. Organ and harpsichord builder in Amsterdam (1749) and The Hague (1763) [*Curtis*, p. 54].

ONGARO. *See*: FRANCISCUS, *Patavinus.*

OORT, Daniel van der. Amsterdam harpsichord maker; died in or before 1627. See further *Curtis*, p. 55. Sweelinck chose an instrument by him in 1599 to be given by the town of Amsterdam to the Danish King (*GL*).

OOSTERLINGH, Joannes. Harpsichord maker born in Kassel 1637 or 1638; married in Amsterdam, 1675 [*Curtis*, p. 55].

OPPERMANN, J. Bartholomäus. Maker of *cembals d'amour* in Hamburg in the eighteenth century [*AdlG*, II. 123 ff.).

OPPELT. 'Orgelbauer and Instrumentenmacher', at Regensburg; born 1578. At the age of 26 he went to Italy and in 1604 built an organ in the church of St. George at Verona [*AdlG*, *Ge* (1814)].

ORLANDUS, Petrus Michael. Italian virginal maker, *fl.* 1702–10. The surname occurs also as 'Orlando').

Surviving Instruments

(1) 1702. Haslemere, Dolmetsch Collection. Polygonal virginal, signed: *Petrus Michael Orlando 1702*. Decorated soundboard with parchment geometrical rose. In outer case.

(2) 1710. Edinburgh University (formerly Raymond Russell, who bought it in 1956). Ottavino virginal. C–C with short octave. Projecting keyboard. Parchment rose. The nameboard bears on the front an ink inscription in an early hand: *Dū Vixi Tacvi Mortva Dvlce Cano*. On the back of it Arnold Dolmetsch, who restored the instrument, has written *Petrus Michael Orlandus anno 1710*, copied no doubt from some other part, possibly the jackrail, which he replaced with one of his own making. Illustrated in *RussColl*. The whole instrument is in cypress, and is painted dark green.

OSSA, Sebastiano, of Bologna. Organ and harpsichord maker, *fl.* 1687. He was apparently connected with the house of Este [*Va*].

OSTERLEIN, J. K. *See*: OESTERLIN, Johann Christoph.

OTS, Jan. Harpsichord maker in Amsterdam in 1631 [*Curtis*, p. 55].

P.B. [?], of Modena, *fl.* 1802. Made virginals [*Va*].

P.W. *See*: W, P.

PADOVANO, Bortolo. *See*: CRISTOFORI, Bartolommeo.

PAGNINI of Pistoia. Organ and virginal maker in the eighteenth century [*Va*].

PALAZZI, Nicola. Clavichord maker of Rome, *fl.* 1776. A clavichord by him is at the Royal Academy of Music, London. Its compass is 4 octaves and 2 notes, C–D. The keyboard is of pine, the naturals being faced with ebony and the sharps with ivory; the fronts of the keys are in ivory, arcaded. The case is of cypress and it is now housed in an outer case of walnut.

An inscription on the palmulae runs: *Nicola Palazzi Romano fece 1776*.

PALIARINO. *See*: CRICCA.

PAMPES, *also* Pampet, of Paris. Organ, harpsichord, and spinet maker. *Fl.* 1671, in which year he supplied Louis XIV with an organ, a spinet, and a harpsichord.

('1671 — 11 Janvier — A Pampes, faiseur d'orgues et de clavessins pour une orgue, une espinette et un clavessin qu'il a fait pour le roi: 7500 l.'—quoted by *Loub*, p. 164). See further *Verlet*.

PAMPRES, Peter. *See*: PAMPUS, Pieter.

PAMPUS, Pieter. Harpsichord maker who came to Amsterdam from Elberfeld in Germany. Dates ascertained, 1623–8. On 18 February 1626 he patented a type of automatic organ and automatic harpsichord. In 1627 he sued William Deacons (q.v.) for infringement of his patent.

In 1628 he accepted 'Coenradus Gijsen' from Elberfeld as a pupil in the construction of these instruments.

Thurston Dart [*ML* 1960, p. 58, in a review of *Russell 1959*] suggested that Pampus may be the same man as Pampes (q.v.); but this is unlikely.

PARADIJS, Andries. Maker of organs and harpsichords from Oosterenburg who settled in Amsterdam. Dates ascertained, 1757–77. See further *Curtis*, p. 56.

PARRINI, Serafino. Harpsichord maker of Perugia, *fl.* 1627 [*Va*].

PARRONCHI, Adriano. *FrancII* records an ottavino inscribed as restored by someone of this name in Prato, 1841.

PARTICI, Giovanni da. *See*: PERTICI, Giovanni.

PASI, Alessandro, [Pasio] of Modena. Organ and harpsichord maker. Maker of what purports to be the earliest known Italian polygonal virginal, dated 1493, formerly in the Museum at Perugia. Inscription: *ALEXANDRI / PASII MUTIN/ENSIS OPUS M / CCCCL / XXXX / III*. The genuineness of this instrument is widely doubted, and its present whereabouts unknown to me.

Va (p. 254) quotes a letter of 1513: '. . . Alessandro de Modena esibitore presente viene a Ferrara dove dee fare un organo e un clavicembalo . . .'

See also *GD* (1910) s.v. 'spinet'.

PASTIN, Antoine. *See*: POTIN, Antoine.

PATAVINUS, Antonius. *See*: ANTONIUS, *Patavinus*.

PATAVINUS, Franciscus. *See*: FRANCISCUS, *Patavinus*.

PATAVINUS, Johannes. *See under*: FRANCISCUS, *Patavinus*.

PATIN, Antoine. *See*: POTIN, Antoine.

PATRY, Pierre. Parisian spinet maker, mid sixteenth century, living in the parish of St. Merri [*Verlet*].

PAUL. Instrument maker at Gotha. He built clavichords of a compass F–A, 5¼ octaves [*Ge*, 1814].

PAULUS, Petrus de. *FrancI* lists a clavicytherium with the astonishing inscription: *Petrus de Paulus, 1587*.

PEBORGH, Jan *or* **Hans van.** Harpsichord maker in Antwerp in 1557, in which year he was received as a master in the guild of Saint Luke [*St*].

PEDRINI, Theodoric [Nepridi, *pseud.*]. 1670–1745. A Lazarist priest sent to China to succeed the Jesuit Father Pereira as court musician to the Ch'ing emperor K'ang Hsi (1662–1723). Pedrini left Rome in 1702, but did not reach Peking until 1711, after which he spent the rest of his life in the emperor's service.

As well as teaching the princes, he made several harpsichords and 2 organs, one of which was automatic.

Eight sonatas for violin and figured bass written by him under the pseudonym of 'Nepridi' were preserved (1937) in MS. in the National Library of Peking (*Échos de l'École César Franck*, April 1937. See also *Musical Times*, May 1937).

PELLE, Christiaan, of Antwerp. Harpsichord maker. Received into the Guild of Saint Luke, 1658–9 [*St*].

PEMBERTON & M'DONNELL. Harpsichord and piano makers at 26 Fleet Street, Dublin, 1789–92 [*Teahan*] *Fl.* 1790 [*Fld*].

PENTORISI. Keyboard-instrument maker at Murano in 1590. The Gallini Collection in Milan has a spinet (bent side) by him, without a stand, signed on the bottom key by Pentorisi and giving the place and date as 'Murano, 1590' [*Gall*, p. 236; pl. 119].

PENTOTIUS, D. Bartholomaeus. On a polygonal ottavino formerly in the Ford Museum, Dearborn, Mich., but recently destroyed by fire was the barely legible inscription: *D. Bartholom. Pentotij Murane Neap. 1694.* Compass 4 octaves C–C with short octave. Projecting keyboard. Built into its outer case. Its authenticity was reported to me as doubtful.

Another ottavino by him, bearing on the lowest key the same inscription with the clear date *1694*, belongs to the antique dealer William P. Firth of Oswego, Ill.; restored in 1971 by Bjarne Dahl of Sunnyvale, Calif., who does not consider it spurious, although work has been done on it since it was first made.

PERES, Valerius, of Rome. Harpsichord and virginal maker. Dates ascertained, 1625–31.

Surviving Instruments

(1) 1625. Yale University, Belle Skinner Collection. Harpsichord, inscribed: *Valerius Peres faciebat anno Jubilei MDCXXV.* 1×8′ register. 4 octaves C–C, with short octave. Length 6′ 10″. Illustrated in Catalogue. Formerly in Steinert Collection.

(2) 1631. Leipzig, Heyer Collection. Ottavino virginal, in the form of a sewing-box. Inscription: *Valerius Perius Romanus / fecit anno Domini M.D.C.XXXI* (on bottom key), followed by *Core d'amore che mi ai robato tu* ('Heart full of love, which you have stolen from me') with a heart pierced by 2 arrows. On the outside of the fall, a miniature of a woman, over which is inscribed *Non bene da vn solo* ('It is not good to be alone'). Compass G–E, 2 octaves and a 6th, without bottom G sharp and top D sharp. Dimensions 38×20×13 cm. Both the instrument and the first inscription are pictured in *Ks*.

PÉRONARD, François-Balthazard, of Paris. Maker of harpsichords, spinets, and pianos. Dates ascertained, 1760–89. A harpsichord by him dated 1777 is listed in *Br* (p. 105); and another, dated 1760, ibid. 207. A spinet made by him in 1763 was advertised 20 February 1777 [*Bq*]. About 1780 he fitted a pedal keyboard to harpsichords [*Pi*, p. 118]. He is mentioned favourably in *EncMéth.*

PEROUARD according to *Ch*, quoted by *Gö*, flourished at the beginning of the eighteenth century as a maker of harpsichords. Probably a mistake for Péronard, q.v.

PERRINI, Giovanni. *See*: FERRINI, Giovanni.

PERROT, Jehan. Curt Sachs [*SaHMI*, p. 336] mentions the Frenchman Perrot as the maker of an échiquier given by Edward III in 1360 to his prisoner King John of France. Perrot may have made clavichords as well.

PERTICI, Giovanni da, *otherwise* Johannes de Perticis, of Florence. Son of Piero da Pertici. Harpsichord and virginal maker. Earliest and latest dates known, 1665–90. His grandfather's name was Bartolomeo [*Ks*, p. 250]. *Pu* (p. 80) lists him as 'Buonaccordaio' (i.e. tuner) 1665.

FrancI lists (nos. 10 and 11) a 'spinetta' signed *Ioannes di Perticis fecit anno Domini 1672. Florentinus* and a 'cimbalone' signed *Ioannes di Perticis fecit anno Domini 1672. Florentinus.*

Surviving Instruments

(1) 1672. The Hague, Gemeente-Museum. Harpsichord. Inscribed on nameboard: *Joannes de Particis* [sic] *Florentinus fecit Anno Domini 1672.* C/E–F, 4½ octaves. Rose missing. Acquired 1939.

(2) 1680. Harpsichord. Offered for sale anonymously in France in 1953. Inscribed: *Ioannes de Perticis Florentinus fecit MDCLXXX.*

(3) 1683. Harpsichord. Leipzig University, Heyer Collection. Much restored. Undoubtedly originally 2×8′, 1×4′. Now 1×4′ (upper kb.), 1×8′ and 1×16′ (lower kb.). C–E, 4⅓ octaves.

(4) 1684. Polygonal virginal. London. Private ownership. *Ioannes de Perticis Florentinus Faciebat Anno MDCLXXXIV.*

PESSETTI, Giovanni Battista, of Mantua. *Fl.* 1674 as joiner, lute, and harpsichord maker [*Vannes*].

PETER vom Kneiphof, of Königsberg. Organ builder who also made virginals and spinets, *fl.* 1542 [Federmann, *Musik und Musikpflege zur Zeit Herzog Albrechts*, 1932].

PETHER, George. Maker of harpsichords (also of pianos, see *Ha*, pp. 59, 263; *Ks*). 61 Oxford Street; 16 John Street, Oxford Street, London. Earliest and latest dates known, 1775–94 [*J*, *Ha*]. The inscription *From Mr. Kirkman's* on a square piano by him (quoted by *J*, p. 74) indicates that he worked at one time for Kirkman.

PETHER, William. English harpsichord and spinet maker, *fl.* 1763–5. Perhaps related to the foregoing. He appears in *Un* (1763) as 'Organ-builder and Harpsichord maker, *Brownlow-street, Drury-lane*'.

A spinet by him was in the Steinert Collection, New Haven, Conn. 5 octaves; inscribed '*Sollicitae jucunda oblivio vitae*'. A 'single-keyed harpsichord by William Pether, mahogany case', was sold at Christie's on 30 March 1793.

Surviving Instruments

(1) 1775. A single-manual harpsichord by him was restored by Michael Thomas in 1961–2 and sold by him to Norman Paulu of Madison, Wis., from whom it passed to Dr. Ray T. Dufford of Evansville, Ind., who still (1971) possesses it. Inscribed on nameboard: *Guglielmus Pether Londini Fecit 1775*; 2×8′ and buffstops; 5 octaves, presumably F–F.

PIAZOLI, Antonio, of Modena. Harpsichord maker, *fl.* 1723 [*Va*, pp. 70, 288].

PIAZZA, Carlo. Restorer and presumably maker of harpsichords etc., *fl.* 1749, perhaps in Verona. Instrument no. 3 of Bruneti delli Organi bears an inscription on the front-board: *Fu restaurato da me Carlo Piaža / Año 1749*.

PICCHI, Gaetano, of Florence. Son of Severo Picchi; *fl.* 1716, harpsichord maker [*Va*].

PICINANI, Francesca di. An early owner, not a maker. Christopher Hogwood of Cambridge has a Florentine harpsichord, probably seventeenth century, with her name painted on the front board. Length 5′ 9″; no rose; 2×8′ stops; A–F, 4 octaves and 8 notes. He acquired it in 1972 from Colin Tilney, who had bought it about 1962 from Michael Thomas.

PIECHBECK. *See*: PINCHBECK, Christopher.

PIER FRANCESCO, *of Udine*
PIER GIOVANNI, *of Udine* } Harpsichord makers in Venice, *fl.* 1473 [*Va*].

PIETRO JACOPO [surname unknown] of Ferrara, harpsichord maker at the turn of the sixteenth and seventeenth centuries [*Va*].

PILZNA, Michael de, of Rzeszów. Made clavichords at Cracow in the fifteenth century [*Szulc*].

PINI, Bartolomeo. Florentine harpsichord maker. In 1664, when he paid a matriculation fee to his Guild, he was working for Antonio Bolcioni (q.v.) in the Via dei Servi. His father's name was likewise Bartolomeo [*Pu*].

PINCHBECK, Christopher [Piechbeck, Pinchelbeck]. Clockmaker in London; 1670(?)–1732. Born about 1670, probably in Clerkenwell, London; died 18 November 1732. His inventive disposition was shewn in a wide variety of ways besides the copper and zinc alloy which perpetuates his name. For instance, according to the appendix to *Ge* he 'improved' the harpsichord in 1724 'durch Zuthun von Flöten, Trompeten und Pauken'!

PISAURENSIS, Dominicus. *See*: DOMINICUS, *Pisaurensis*.

PLAYER, John. Spinet, virginal, and harpsichord maker in London. Born about 1634, son of Giles Player, shepherd, of Longborough, Glos. Apprenticed to Gabriel Townsend for 7 years from 24 June 1650; freeman of the Joiners' Company, June 1658; master, 1684/8 [*Join*, which suggests that he died or retired between 1705 and 1708. *J*'s latest date for him seems purely conjectural]. Ambrose Warren (*Tonometer*, 1725, p. 7) mentions Player as having made spinets with quarter tones.

We read in a letter from Thomas Day to Edward Hanford of Woollas, dated 10 June 1712: 'I have been this morning to see another harpsichord: it is of Player's making, with split or quarternotes . . .' [MS. quoted in *Apollo*, March 1950].

PLENIUS, John. Harpsichord and spinet maker, 89 Holborn, London. Earliest and latest dates known, 1765–93 [*J*].

Surviving Instruments

(1) A spinet dated 1765 was shewn by Rosamond Horsley at the International Inventions Exhibition in 1885.

(2) A spinet of 1768, formerly the property of W. A. Simpson (d. 1918), is in Dundee Museum. Inscription: *Johannes Plenius Londini fecit, 1768*.

PLENIUS, Roger [Rutger Pleunis]. Born in 1696 at Orsoy; died 1774 in London. While still young, his parents having died, he went to live in Amsterdam with his uncle of the same name. In 1720 he married Catharina de Harder, but none of their children survived infancy and she died in 1733.

In 1734 he married Maria Stam, and in the following year advertised a type of harpsichord of his own invention 'zijnde een staertstuk, met 2 sangbodemen, 2 clavieren, 4 registers, en 2 halve registers van 16 voet, spielende onzienbar'—perhaps (as *Leonh* suggests) a 16′ stop similar to the one in the Swanen (q.v.) instrument of 1786, using the bottom of the instrument as a soundboard, the jacks working upside down.

By 1741 he was living in South Audley Street, London, and on 30 December took out a patent (numbered 581) for various devices to be applied to the harpsichord (see *Pat*, pp. 3 ff.) which included a machine of weights and swivels for keeping harpsichords in tune; ivory and tortoiseshell plectra, and regulating screws behind the tongues; metal jack-slides; hollow keys, made of four laths, to prevent warping and to 'make their motion more true and accurate'; also 'octave strings are kept in tune full as long as the unison strings by means of iron or other metall pegs or screws which are fixed in the body of the harpsichord, and appear through the belly thereof, and to which the said octave strings at the end are fastned to the tops of the said pegs or screws'.

Four years later, on 10 July, he patented (number 613) a 'stop which imitates the Welch harp', i.e. a buffstop; keys bushed by leather underneath and by 'a little frame' mortised and 'lined on each side with silk twist', which is stuck on top of the key. The keys have front-bushing, also with silk twist. He describes further how he takes steps 'to prevent the tongues sticking to the sides of the jacks by closing the tops of the jacks, making them thereby more firm and solid, so that their sides can never touch the tongues, though squeezed ever so hard . . .'. Damping-cloth is glued in the jacks, in notches on either side of the tongue; and 'bits of vellum glewed behind the tops of the jacks to prevent their tongues from flying too far back when the quills on playing return under the strings'; and double bridge-pinning is used, 'so that the strings having

TABLE 26. *Surviving Instruments by John PLAYER*

No.	Date	Type	Signature	Owner/Remarks
1	1664	V	*Johannes Player Londini Me Fecit 1664*	Formerly R. Russell, London; formerly Wanstead, Captain J. Lane. 2 roses; soundboard adorned with flowers. Signature on jackrail. Domed lid. Paintings inside badly restored in recent times; gilt-embossed paper now painted over.
2	n.d.	S	*Johannes Player fecit*	London, Victoria and Albert Museum. Inscription on nameboard. Compass G–C, 4 octaves plus a 4th with short octave. Bottom 2 sharps split. Length 4′ 10″. Details and picture at *J*, p. 109.
3	n.d.	S	*Johannes Player fecit*	York, Castle Museum.
4	n.d.	S	*Johannes Player Londini fecit*	Dr. Fenyre (Sotheby's, 21 December 1972); formerly Llandudno, Barrow Collection. Inscription on nameboard. Compass A–D, 4½ octaves with short octave. Bottom 2 sharps split. Ebony naturals, solid ivory sharps. Walnut case. Perhaps the Player spinet shewn by Messrs. Kirkman at the 1872 and 1885 exhibitions, London.
5	n.d.	S	*Johannes Player fecit*	Washington, Smithsonian Institution. Compass 4 octaves plus, the lowest note being C; lowest C sharp and D sharp split. Black naturals, white sharps.
6	n.d.	S		Helmingham Hall, Suffolk. [*Country Life*, 4 October 1956, p. 714.]
7	n.d.	S	*Johannes Player fecit*	Mrs. Priston, Ryde House, Ripley (October 1957). B–C, 4 octaves plus 1 note, black naturals. Perhaps equals no. 6.
8	n.d.	S	*Johannes Player fecit*	Sold at Sotheby's 4 July 1966, by Miss E. Stone to T. Ord. Signed on jackrail. Nameboard inlaid with tulips and carnations issuing from foliate cornucopias. G–F, 5 octaves, lacking bottom G sharp and A sharp in bottom octave but having split C sharp and D sharp in octave above; arcaded naturals; walnut case. Length 4′ 11½″.

no pressure downwards, the belly is at full liberty to vibrate more equally than the belly of other instruments'.

Unfortunately no instrument by Roger Plenius has survived to give us examples of these innovations, nor of his 'lyrichord, which imitates the violin, violincello, double bass, and organ, by catgut strings alone . . .'. Eric Halfpenny [*GSJ*, Vol. 3, 1950, pp. 46–7] quotes 'A description of the nature and construction of the lyrichord', which appeared in *The General Magazine of Arts and Sciences*, August 1755, and reproduces 'A perspective view of the lyrichord' which accompanied the description.

In 1756 Plenius became bankrupt. However, there survives a letter from George Washington to John Didsbury of London, dated at Mount Vernon 12 October 1761, and containing a request for '1 Very good Spinit, to be made by Mr. Plinius, Harpsichord Maker in South Audley Street Grosvenor Square. // Note it is beg'd as a favour, that Mr. Cary [the shipper] would bespeak this instrument as for himself or a friend, and not let it be known that it is intended for Exportation. Send a good assortment of spare strings to it' (*The Definitive Writings of George Washington*, Vol. II, Washington, D.C., 1931, pp. 369–70). Presumably Washington had not heard of Plenius's bankruptcy. Or perhaps Plenius had already started up again, for a notice of a Plenius without Christian name appears in *Un* (1763) as resident in Catherine Street, Strand. (Washington must have had Roger, and not John, Plenius in mind, as he gives Roger's address.) See further *Curtis*, pp. 56–60.

The burial register of St. Mary-le-Strand, London, records under 9 January 1774: Rutgerius Plenius.

PLEYEL. (For detailed information see *GD*.)

(1) **Ignaz Joseph,** 1757–1831, may have made, or supervised the making of, a few harpsichords.

(2) **Camille,** his son, 1788–1855. The firm of Pleyel has made a number of harpsichords since the revival.

POGGIO, Francesco, *called* Crinetus. Virginal maker in Florence; dates ascertained, 1586–1634, the latter being the year of his death. The epithet 'Crinetus' may perhaps allude to birth at Krinetz in Bohemia.

The matriculation records of the Guild of Instrument Makers in Florence, where his residence was in the Via dei

Servi, note his death, without heirs, in 1634, giving his surname as 'Poggi'. His father's Christian name was Piero.

Surviving Polygonal Virginals

(1) 1586. Stuttgart, Württembergisches Landesgewerbemuseum. Inscribed: *Franciscus Poggio Crinetus 1586.* Compass 4 octaves C–C with short octave. On the inside of the lid are painted 3 medallions, the central one containing a ship. Illustrated on p. 13 of Josten's catalogue. (Presented by Georg Steingräber.)

(2) 1620. Providence, R.I., Rhode Island School of Design. Inscribed: . . . [*forename illegible*; ? Franc.] *Poggio 1620.* Compass 4½ octaves C–F, with short octave. In fine condition with original plush-covered outer case. [*Hubb*]

POHLMAN, Johann. London maker of pianofortes, in Compton Street, Soho, and later at 113 Gt. Russell Street, Bloomsbury. Dates ascertained 1767–93. He also made harpsichords, as is shewn by an entry in a London directory of 1790 [*Byrne*], and the following entries in Christie's sale catalogues:

14 January 1793. Number 36 in the catalogue:

A fine toned double keyed harpsichord, with 5 stops, by Pohlmann [Vendor anonymous; buyer Mr. Price; price £9. 2*s*. 6*d*.].

3 November 1794. Number 63 in the catalogue:

A fine toned single-keyed harpsichord by Pohlman in a neat inlaid mahogany case [Vendor anonymous; buyer Maxton; price 18½ guineas].

POINT. '1 Dec. 1551. Paid to Point for the mending and tuning of any virginals, 13*s*. 4*d*.' [Private accounts of Sir Thomas Chaloner (1521–65); B.M. Lansdowne MS. 824. See *Woodf*, p. 255.]

POLIZZINO, Giovanni Pietro. Harpsichord maker, presumably of Florence. G. B. Doni, writing *c.* 1640, praises him as the highly skilled maker of an enharmonic harpsichord according to the design of Pietro della Valle (1586–1625):

. . . un Cembalo . . . fatto da Gio: Pietro Polizzino peritissimo, ed ingegnosissimo artefice di questa sorta d'instrumenti per l'Illmo. Sig. Pietro della Valle con due ordini di corde sulla tavola, de quali il più alto comprende quelle dell'Armonia Frigia, ed il più basso quelle della Doria, e dell'Ipolidia . . . [*Trattato sopra gi'instrumenti di tasti*, in *Lyra barberina*, 1763, I. 330].

POLLASTRIS, Cesare de, of Ferrara. Made a 2-manual harpsichord on which the sharps were split throughout. Recorded in an Innsbruck inventory of 1665 [*Wald*].

PONCELET. French harpsichord maker; dates not recorded [*Va*].

PONTANA. A misreading of Fontana, q.v.

PORTALUPI, Francesco de', of Verona. Maker of virginals *fl.* 1523. *VdS* (I. 288) quotes Pontécoulant on the instrument listed below (no. 1); Pontécoulant gives the maker's name as *Portalesqué.*

Surviving Instruments

(1) 1523. Paris Conservatoire. Polygonal virginal; inscribed: *Francisci de Portalupis Veronen. opus MDXXIII.* (Formerly in the Clapisson Collection.)

PORTIN, Jean. *See*: Potin, Jean.

POTIN, Antoine. Son of Robert Potin, *fl.* 1548–58; Parisian organist who worked as a harpsichord maker from 1548 onwards [*Les*]. *Mer* praises him highly.

POTIN, Jean, of Paris. Probably youngest son of Robert, he lived in the rue de la Verrerie.

POTIN, Pierre. Parisian maker of spinets and other instruments; *fl.* 1540–50 [*Laborde*]. Possibly a younger brother of Robert [*Verlet*].

POTIN, Robert. Parisian mid-sixteenth-century organist who towards the end of his life took to making spinets. He lived in the parish of St. Merri [*Verlet*].

POULLEAU. Harpsichord maker in Moscow *c.* 1795 [*Russell 1959*, p. 114].

PRATO, Vincenzo da. *See*: Vincentius, *Pratensis.*

PREIBLAN [?], Giuseppe, of Senigallia. Harpsichord maker, *fl.* 1774. A photograph owned by John Challis, Detroit (1953), of a harpsichord formerly in private ownership in California, says it is inscribed *Giuseppe Preiblan Sinigaglia* and dated 1774. 29″ × 79″. Two *putti* seated on stand.

PRENO. A priest, *fl.* Italy sixteenth century, when he made a harpsichord, formerly in Savoye Collection II, which was repaired in 1610 by Vincentius Pratensis. Inscriptions: *Fra Preno nelli angli*; and on back of nameboard: *Vincentius Pratensis 1610 restauro* [*Ks*, p. 278].

PRÊTRE, Le. *See* Le Prêtre.

PREUSS, Joachim Bernard. Clavichord maker, *fl.* 1773; pupil of Barthold Fritz of Brunswick. He is referred to in the German edition of Dr. Burney's Musical Journeys [*Tagebuch seiner mus. Reisen*, 1773]. Preuss may have worked in Hamburg [*Schultz 1957*].

PRINGLE, Archibald, of Budge Row, near St. Paul's Cathedral, London. Made spinets and perhaps pianofortes; from 1757 until 1765 (at least) he was working for John Harrison, q.v.

Surviving Instruments

(1) 1765. Annapolis, Md., Pro Musica Instrument Co. (1971). Spinet. Inscribed on nameboard: *Archibald Pringle Londini fecit 1765*, the same legend being scribbled in ink on the back. 5 octaves G–G. Top and bottom keys have workman's signature *Jon Bondbough.* Bottom jack stamped *A-P.*

In 1953 it was owned by Messrs. Morley, London, who sold it in 1954 to Professor Harry John Brown of the Music Department, State University of New York at Fredonia.

In 1970/1 Pro Musica, in the course of complete restoration, removed the soundboard, on the underside of which was inscribed: *Arch. Pringle Budge / Row, London / September 27th, 1765.*

The Thomas Pringle whose name appears on the action of a Longman and Broderip square piano of about 1785 may be related to this maker; and either Archibald or Thomas is probably the pianoforte maker Pringle recorded by *J* (without Christian name) as flourishing in 1792.

PROSPERI, Pietro, of Siena. *Prof.* (p. 292, as usual without giving sources) relates that in 1700 he invented a kind of machine-stop for the harpsichord, which by means of a pedal shut off one or more registers, leaving only one on. A 1716 spinet by him was formerly in the Kraus Collection [Kraus, A., in *SIM*, vol. 13 (1911)].

PRUDENT, of Paris. *Fl.* in the latter half of the eighteenth century; probably made harpsichords. The following advertisement appeared on 30 December 1782: 'Clavecin à rav. peint en gris, à filets d'or. 30 louis. Prudent facteur d'instruments, rue Dauphine, chez un pâtissier' [*Bq*].

PUCCINI, of Florence, *fl.* 1696. Harpsichord maker. Later one of Cristofori's assistants in pianoforte making [*Va*].

PRZEWORSKI, Bernard, of Cracow. Harpsichord maker, died 1620 [*Szulc*].

PUCHERT, Johann Samuel, 1741–94. Born 10 October 1741 at Adlersruh, near Rudelstadt in Silesia. His father Siegmund Puchert (1719–68) made organs and other instruments, and married Anna Renata Hauptmann (1704–74). After his father's death Johann Samuel carried on the business, moving to Rudelstadt; but in his later years he returned to his birthplace, and died there 11 September 1794 [*Ks*].

Surviving Clavichords

(1) 1783. Leipzig University, Heyer Collection. Gebunden, C–F, 4 octaves and a 4th; 37 pairs of strings. Inscribed on the side of a key: *Joh. Samuel Puchert, orgel / u. Instrumentmacher in Rudelstadt / 1783.* Dimensions 129×41 cm. Inscription reproduced at *Ks*, p. 252.

PURCELL, Henry. Composer, born in London (probably in 1659) and died there in 1695. In 1673 was appointed 'Keeper, maker, mender, repayrer and tuner of the regalls, organs, virginals, flutes and recorders . . . (*without fee*) . . . and assistant to John Hingston, and upon the death or other avoidance of the latter, to come in ordinary with fee' [*La*, p. 255]. On Hingston's death in 1683 Purcell succeeded him in the following year at a fee of £60 a year.

QUEBON, Juan Baptista, of Madrid. Probably a harpsichord maker, *fl.* 1583. An inventory of the Archduke Albert of Spain, taken in 1583, records 'Un clavicordio grande con dos juegos que se compro de Juan Baptista Quebon' [quoted by *VdS*, II. 311].

QUERCI, Pasquino. Maker of harpsichords, spinets, and polygonal virginals in Florence; *fl.* 1610–25. Instruments 4 and 6 below are listed in Franciolini catalogues; and nos. 2 and 5 probably passed through his hands.

Surviving Instruments by, or ostensibly by, him

(1) 1610. Chicago, George F. Harding Museum. Polygonal virginal inscribed: *Pasquinus Quercius Florentinus fecit AD. MDCX.* Restored by Berceau Royal, 1927.

(2) 1613. Smithsonian Institution, Washington, Harpsichord inscribed: *Pasquino Querci Florentino fecit 1613 In Cijmbalis* [sic] *Bene Sonantibus Laudate Domine* [sic] *Ac Semper Amen.* 2×8′ stops; $4\frac{1}{2}$ octaves with short octave. The inscription seems to be by two different hands, and the second line, at least, invites suspicions connected with Franciolini.

(3) 1614. Berlin Collection. Harpsichord, inscribed: *Pasquinus Quercius Florentinus F. a.d. MDCXIV. / El Napoleo Dominicus Borrius Castroflorentini emit A.S. MDCCCXXVIII.* 2×8′ stops. C–C, 4 octaves with short octave. Rose. Size 190×84 cm. (Lost in World War II.)

(4) 1615. New York, Metropolitan Museum of Art (given in 1911 by B. Boekelman). A sixteenth- or early-seventeenth-century German ottavino inscribed on nameboard: *Paspuino* [sic] *Querci fiorentino fece 1615 / La sua presenza e la sua abilità / Bona estortio cvm ieivnio et elemosina.* The Latin phrase is corrupt; and the preceding Italian one obviously incomplete. Franciolini's work is apparent throughout. See *RipQ*, where an ultra-violet photo shews a first attempt at the spurious inscription, the other way up, underneath the one at present visible.

(5) 1624. Aix-en-Provence, William Dobson (in 1966, *GL*). Polygonal virginal, inscribed: *Pasquino Querci Fiorentino fece 1624. La sua presenza, la sua abilità.*

(6) 1625. New York, Metropolitan Museum of Art, Crosby Brown Collection. Ottavino. Signed on back of nameboard: *pasquino querci fiorentino f 1625* and, below, the incomplete and almost illegible phrase: . . . *sua presenza e la sua abilità.*

The outer case bears, inside the lid, a painting illustrating events from the Book of Tobit in the Apocrypha, below which appears the motto: *Bona est oratio cum ieivnio et eleemosina*—perfectly good Latin likewise from the Book of Tobit (12: 8). See *RipQ* for an excellent illustrated discussion of this instrument and the spurious no. 4 above.

QUERCI, Vincenzio. Son of Pasquino (see above), *fl.* 1634. Harpsichord maker in the Via dei Servi, Florence, in 1634, when his name appears on the matriculation books of his Guild.

QUERNBACH, Edmund Ignatz, *fl.* 1780. Maker of keyboard instruments in Mainz. A piano by him in the Neupert Collection, signed *Edmund Ignatz Quernbach, Klavierinstrumentenmacher in Mainz* and dated 1780, is the only surviving instrument I know. But he very probably made clavichords as well as pianos.

QUINTILIUS. *See*: BORTOLUS.

QUOCO, Nicolaus de. Two Florentine harpsichord

makers bearing the same name and spanning between them the years 1615–94. (*Hirt* gives 1612 as the earliest known date.)

Surviving Instruments.

(01) 1612. Copenhagen, Musikhistorisk Museum. Harpsichord signed on nameboard: *Nicolaus de Quoco fecit anno Domini 1612.* 2×8′ stops; C/E–C, 4 octaves. Rose without initials. Buffstop added later, and side stops moved to the front. Previously owned by J. G. Steingraeber, from whom the Museum bought it in 1932. The instrument is genuine, but there are suspicions that the inscription was put on by Franciolini.

(1) 1615. Copenhagen, Claudius Collection. Harpsichord signed: *Nicolaus de Quoco Fecit. Ao 1615.* Four octaves C–C with short octave. 2×8′ registers. 177×78×25 cm. Illustrated in catalogue.

(2) 1690. Lisbon Conservatoire. Two-manual harpsichord. Inscription: *Nicolaus de Quoco Fecit Anno MDCLXXXX.* Apparent compass, B–A just under 4 octaves. Rose without monogram. Lid painted with landscape including a castle and huntsmen. Length 212 cm.

(3) 1694. Brussels Conservatoire. Harpsichord signed: *Nicolaus de Quoco fecit anno 1694.* Another signature inside, *Giuseppe Solfanelli fece 1730 Pisa*, presumably refers to its restorer. F–C, 4½ octaves. 260×93 cm.

(4) 1694. Washington, Smithsonian Institution. Harpsichord. Inscription (on front of the wrestplank, hidden by a removable nameboard): *Nicolaus de Quoco fecit anno MDCLXXXXIIII.* 2×8′, 1×4′ registers. Boxwood naturals; black sharps inlaid with boxwood.

R. *See*: RICHARD.

R, A. *See*: ROCHEAD, Andrew, & Son.

R, C. Two virginals, having identical *CR* roses, though clearly by different builders, are known today:

(1) New York, Metropolitan Museum of Art. Much altered, probably in the nineteenth century, although original parts of the instrument appear to date from the sixteenth century. Keyboard to the right (originally C–A lacking lowest C sharp and highest G sharp, but now C/E–E lacking highest D sharp). Size 3′ 8″×1′ 5″. Former owners: A. Régibo, Renaix; A. Pley, Brussels.

(2) Namur, Musée de Croix. Seventeenth century in style; 'sea-horse' paper still of the earlier kind, which seems to have gone out of use about 1645. Keyboard to the right; C/E–D chromatic, appears to have been enlarged possibly from G–B. Size 4′ 2¾″×1′ 6½″. Formerly in the Château de Rieudotte.

These two instruments used to be attributed to Christoffel Ruckers (q.v.), who was assumed to be a member of the celebrated family of instrument makers. But the attribution is not now tenable nor the assumption justified.

R, J. W. An undated virginal in the Norsk Folkemuseum, Bygdøy, Oslo, has the initials *JWR* written on the soundboard. C–C, 4 octaves including short octave. Brown naturals fronted with white *putti* heads; black sharps. Painted on the nameboard the elegiac couplet: *Ignis fatalem patientur cuncta ruinam: | In coelum verbum et musica diva volat.* Width 133·5 cm.

RABUS, Johann Georg. Organ and instrument maker of Memmingen, Bavaria, where he was born 1 January 1762 and died 4 December 1826. Son of Georg Rabus, cabinet maker, and Anna Catharina *née* Abrell. A 5-octave clavichord by him, undated, is (1968) in the Museum at Frauenfeld, Switzerland; trichord bass octave [*Rindl*].

RACCERIS, Filippus. An ottavino in the form of a book, in the collection of Lord Howard de Walden, Dean Castle, Kilmarnock, bears the inscription: *Filippus Racceris Fecit Mantuae 1535.* Compass E–F, 2 octaves plus 1 note; jacks about 1″ long. Boxwood naturals, ebony sharps. Oil-painting inside lid.

The form of the surname, *Racceris*, is very strange.

R...CINI, J. Antonio. A small harpsichord in the Musikhistorisk Museum, Copenhagen (4 octaves, 2×8′ registers, rose in the soundboard) bears the inscription on the underside of the soundboard: *Sia come il nome di Dio e della Madona e tutti i Santi del Paradis. Jo Antonio R...cini 1723. Parma.*

RACKWITZ, George Christoffer, of Stockholm. Clavichord and pianoforte maker, *fl.* 1796.

A 5½-octave compass (F to C) clavichord, length 79½″, formerly in Canon Galpin's Collection at Kew, bears a label on the soundboard: *No. 22 | af | G. C. Rackwitz | i | Stockholm | 1796.* With octave strings, bottom F to tenor C (1½ octaves). Now (1972) property of the Galpin Society; housed formerly at Fenton House, Hampstead, then in the Music Faculty at Oxford, now (1968) in the Faculty of Music at Edinburgh.

RAFA, Antonio. A 1580 'spinet' said to be by this maker was owned by Marcel Salomon, Paris. May be a misreading of Baffo, and be the pseudo-Baffo ostensibly of 1580 in the Heyer Collection.

RAISIN, *called* l'Aîné [Rayzin]. Organist at Troyes and spinet maker, *fl.* 1661, 1662. He invented a special kind of spinet (see *Pi*, p. 68). According to *Va* he made spinets with 3 keyboards, whatever that may mean! (The date '1561' in Suppl. 5 to *Va*, under Rayzin, is a mistake for 1661.)

RAMERINI, Jacopo. Florentine harpsichord maker of the late sixteenth and early seventeenth centuries. He is mentioned by Giovanni Battista Doni (*Compendio del trattato de' generi e de' modi della musica*, Rome, Andrea Fei, 1635, p. 70) as having devised a transposing harpsichord. *Kircher 1650* (I. 461) gives a full description of the instrument, (giving Nicolaus as his forename).

Ramerini is also alluded to by *Wa* and *AdlG* (2nd edition, p. 664). See further *Hubb 1965*, p. 34.

RAMUCINO, Giacomo. Italian harpsichord maker, probably in the seventeenth century. The composer Luigi Rossi had a harpsichord by him in 1622 [*MarcP*].

RAND, John. Virginal maker in Threadneedle Street, London, in 1663 [*Join*].

RANGSTRÖM, Anders. Stockholm clavichord maker. A 1778 clavichord by him (5 octaves plus 4 notes) is in Nordiska Museet there.

RASORI, Luigi. Italian harpsichord maker of the eighteenth century. The catalogue of the Museo Teatrale alla Scala (1940) records a 'Cembalo in noce. Opera di Luigi Rasori. Sec. XVIII'.

RASTOIN, Honoré. Parisian harpsichord, spinet, and organ maker; dates ascertained 1687–1721, when he died. In 1687 he made a 'buffet d'orgues' and in 1692 became a *juré comptable* of the Guild of Instrument Makers. A 'clavecin de Rastoin' was advertised for sale 13 November 1760 [*Bq*]. *Cor* (p. 84) mentions him in passing.

Surviving Instruments

(1) 1689. Spinet signed: *H. Rastoin à Paris 1689*. C–C, 4 octaves, black naturals, white sharps. (Location unknown; photograph formerly in the possession of Raymond Russell.)

RASTOIN, Jacques. Son of Honoré. *Hubb 1965* quotes a harpsichord 'par Rastoin le père' from an inventory of 1744.

RAYZIN. *See*: RAISIN.

REDOLFI, Giacomo. *See*: RIDOLFI, Giacomo.

REDPATH & CO. Eighteenth-century pianoforte makers, presumably English. They also made harpsichords, as is shewn by Christie's sale of 18 March 1790:

Item 91. A fine toned double key'd harpsichord by Redpath & Co. in a mahogany case. [Vendor anonymous; buyer and price not given.]

J (p. 74) records Redpath and Davidson as pianoforte makers.

REGNAULT, Jacques. Parisian instrument maker who made harpsichords; *fl.* 1658–1701 [*Verlet*, pp. 62, 67].

REINECKE. German keyboard-instrument maker of the eighteenth century, to whom the maker Tölleke was at one time apprenticed [*SB*, p. 48].

REINHART, Andreas, of Schneeberg [Reinhardus Nivemontanus]. Organist and notary. *Fl.* 1604; had died by 1614. Not really a maker, he designed a clavichord with a view to experimenting with purity of intonation, described in his book *Monochordum Andreae Reinhardi* (Leipzig, J. Rosius, 1604) [Abraham Bartolus, *Musica mathematica* . . . Leipzig, 1614, pp. 147–8, 167–8. *AdlG*, p. 279].

RELFE, John. English spinet maker, *c.* 1740.

Surviving Spinets

(1) Norwich, Nugent Monck. No date or number. Skunktail sharps.

(2) A spinet signed *Joannes Relfe London*, of eighteenth-century style, was offered for sale at Messrs. Phillips, London, on 10 May 1983. Perhaps the same instrument as no. 1.

REMOTI, Simone. A 3-manual harpsichord in the Stuttgart Württemberg Museum bears the inscription: *Simone Remoti fecit Ao 1602. Cimbalis bene sonantibus.* Josten in his catalogue of the collection suspects this signature, a suspicion echoed by *Nor* (p. 131) and shared by us when we find the instrument in a sale catalogue of L. Franciolini. Illustrated in Josten, p. 23. Presented by Georg Steingräber.

REMUS, John. A misreading of Kemys, John, q.v.

RENAUD. A native of Orléans, lived in Paris, spinet maker. *fl.* 1745. He invented a 'bowed spinet' (*épinette à archet*) in 1745 (*Pi*, p. 91).

RENAULT, Jean [*also* Renaud], from Lorraine. Organ builder, also made harpsichords and spinets; dates ascertained, 1708–10. In 1708 he repaired harpsichords and provided 2 spinets for the opera *Vénus*, given at Lunéville, in the service of Duke Leopold. In 1710 he received money for furnishing harpsichords to the Court [*Jac*].

RENTSCH, Salomon. Organ and instrument maker at Schwarzenberg in the latter part of the eighteenth century [*Ge*].

RENZSCH, Carl Ernst Fürchtegott. Assistant in Dresden to J. G. Horn, on whose death in 1796 he took over the workshop; but in 1797 he set up on his own. He made clavichords and pianos [*Ks*, p. 232; *Hirt*].

RESPINI, Zaccaria, of Brescia, *fl.* 1818. Messrs. de Gaal and Walker, New York, had (November 1954) a virginal signed: *Zaccaria Respini e figlio Brescia 1818*; walnut case. In shape it closely resembles a square pianoforte. Is it a conversion?

REWALLIN, Charles. Maker of virginals in St. Sidwell's parish, Exeter. Dates ascertained: 1657–97, the latter being the year of his death.

On 23 September 1657 he married Hester Gosticke of Laurance in Exeter Cathedral. He died in 1697, and letters of administration of his property were granted on 5 July of that year. His wife would appear to have died before him.

Surviving Virginals

(1) 1675. Taunton, Castle Museum. Formerly the property of Arthur Hull of Chard. Inscription on jackrail: *Charles Rewallin made it [E]xon: 75*. Case, with convex lid, painted, 5′ 4½″ × 1′ 9″. The soundboard has 2 roses. Boxwood naturals, walnut(?) sharps. Compass B–D, 52 notes. (See *The Connoisseur*, London, October 1916, for an illustrated article on it by H. S. G. Gray.)

(2) 1679. Exeter Museum. Inscription on jackrail: *Charles Rewallin made it in [E]xon: 1679*. Two geometrical roses.

RICE, John. Maker of harpsichords, *fl.* 1790 in Dublin [*Fld*].

RICEVUTI, Aurelio. Florentine harpsichord maker, *fl.* 1650, in which year his name appears in the matriculation books of his Guild as apprenticed to Stefano Talvini, a tuner. His father's name was Appollonio Ricevuti [*Pu*].

TABLE 27. *Surviving RICHARD Instruments*

No.	Maker's Forename	Date	Type	Kbs.	Signature	Owner/Remarks
1						See no. 4a below.
?2	[Unknown]	—	H		*R* rose [?Richard]	Musée des Arts Décoratifs, Paris (1948); now (1954) no longer there.
3	?Michel	1672	Ot. V	1	*Richard me fecit 1672* [on jack-rail]	Berlin Collection.
3a	Michel	1688	H	2	*Faict par Michel Richard à Parice Rue du Paon 1688*	Providence, R.I. See under Ruckers instrument no. 18.
4	?Michel	1690	S	1	*Faict à Paris par Richard, rue du Pan praes St. Nicolas du Chardonnet 1690* [on jack-rail]	Montreal. Private ownership. Illustrated in *Russell 1959*.
4a	[?Michel]	1693	S	1	*Fait par Richard, à Paris, rue du Paon, près Saint-Nicolas-du-Chardonnet, 1693.*	Paris, Conservatoire.
5		1752	H	2	*M.R.* [on rose]	Paris, Cons. Nat. Arts et Métiers. 2×8′, 1×4′ stops; 4 rows of jacks; pedals. There is no authority for attributing this harpsichord to a 'Marius Richard', writes *Hubb* after a detailed examination.
6	Jean		H	2		Paris, Musée Grévin.

RICHARD of Paris. Several harpsichord and spinet makers with this surname, some of them related, worked in in the seventeenth and eighteenth centuries:

RICHARD, Jean. The Musée Grévin, Paris, has (1956) a 2-manual harpsichord by him. Otherwise he is unknown.

RICHARD, Michel. Earliest date known, 1659 (in *MC*), made harpsichords and spinets. He took Des Ruisseaux as apprentice in 1670. Hullmandel praises him in *Enc. méth.* [I. 286]. He probably made the harpsichord purporting to be the work of Hans Ruckers of 1613 and listed as Ruckers number [18] below, signing the underside of the soundboard. *Faict par Michel Richard 1688.*

RICHARD, Robert. *Fl.* 1753–8 in Paris primarily as an organ builder but also as a maker of harpsichords. Son-in-law of Galland, q.v. He was *juré comptable* of the Guild of Instrument Makers in 1758/9 [*Loub*].

RICHARDSON, Abraham. Apprenticed to Stephen Keene (q.v.), February 1664; free of the Joiners' Company 1671 [*Join*].

RIDOLFI, Giacomo. Italian harpsichord maker; according to the doubtful inscription on instrument no. 2 he was a pupil of Girolamo Zenti (q.v.). Dates ascertained, 1650–82. His name appears as Ridolfi, Redolfi, and Rodolphus.

Surviving Harpsichords

(1) 1650. New York, Jock Newman. Inscription: *Jacobus Rodolphus de Zentis Fecit Anno Domini 1650.* Formerly owned by Salomon, Paris.

(1a) 1662. Nuremberg, Germanisches Nationalmuseum, Rück Collection. Signed: *Jacobus Redolfi* [sic] *fecit anno 1662.* Two of the keys are signed *Jacomo Ridolfi* [sic], one of them with the date 1662 added [*VdM*].

(2) 1665. Smithsonian Institution. Compass 4 octaves with short octave; 2×8′; painted case supported by 3 gilt kneeling *putti.* Inscription: *Jacobus Rodolphus Hieronymi de Zentis discipulus MDCLXV facieba*[*t*]. (Ex-Franciolini).

(3) 1682. Providence, R.I., School of Design. Inscription: *Jacobus Ridolfi fecit anno Domini MDCLXXXII.* Compass 4 octaves C/E–C; 2×8′; Boxwood keys arcaded; 75″×27¾″; in painted outer case. Fine workmanship well preserved.

RIEDLEN, Gottlieb Friedrich. Born at 1749 at Tuttlingen (Württemberg); went to Bonn in 1782 and became craftsman and instrument maker. He made harpsichords in the ordinary style, but also some quilled with steel instead of feathers; also pianos, and gut-stringed keyboard instruments imitating the tone of 2 violins, a viola, a cello, a double-bass, and flutes. Further he devised an instrument on which whatever the player played was taken down in score [*Ge*, 1794].

RIESCH, Georg Matthias, of Ilmenau, Thuringia,

where he was born *c.* 1710. Built a *Gambenwerck* [*Ks*, vol. 2, quoting *Ge*], which he played in public in 1752 [*Fé*].

RIGAULT, Jean-Baptiste. Parisian harpsichord maker; *c.* 1670–between June 1723 and April 1724. He was received into the Guild in 1691. A 'Clavecin de Rigault' was advertised on 4 March 1756 [*Bq*], and he is mentioned in passing by *Cor* (p. 84). See also *Verlet.*

RIGOLI, of Florence. Instrument maker, *fl.* 1620. *Gö* (p. 108, probably relying on Chouquet) wrongly attributes to him the invention of the clavicytherium, which was known well before his time. *Va* gives the name as *Rigali.*

RIGUNINI, Cristoforo, of Florence. Harpsichord maker, *fl.* 1602.

Surviving Harpsichords

(1) Michigan University. Compass 4 octaves C–C with short octave. Signed: *Cristoforus Rigunini. Firenze, A.D. 1602.* 178×72 cm.

RIJKERS. Virginal maker at The Hague *c.* 1630? The Herzog-Anton-Ulrich-Museum at Brunswick has an unsigned ottavino (2½ octaves), presented in 1876 by Th. Steinweg, who attributed it to Rijkers, 'having seen at the Paris Exhibition instruments by this maker which were in exactly the same style'. Are we concerned with a Ruckers here, 'The Hague' being a mistake?

RING, Friedrich [Rinck], of Strasbourg. Harpsichord maker; born 1667 or 1668; died at Strasbourg on 16 March 1701 at the age of 34 [Strasbourg city archives, quoted in Werner Müller's *Auf den Spuren Gottfried Silbermanns,* 1968, p. 47].

When Andreas Silbermann, q.v., came to Alsace in 1699 he worked for a time for 'Friedrich Rinck', who had been concerned with organs at Weissenburg and Hagenau [*Schweizer Musikzeitung,* vol. 94 (1954)].

A 2-manual harpsichord by Ring (2×8′, 1×4′) was shewn at the International Inventions Exhibition, 1885, by Klinkerfuss of Stuttgart (Catalogue, p. 50).

Va (5th supplement, 1894) records a maker 'Federico King Argentinensis', mistaking the form of the surname.

RITMULLER, Gottlieb Wilhelm, 1772–1829. Born at Göttingen, where he set up in 1798 as an instrument maker. First of all he made lutes, harps, and guitars; but later also clavichords and pianos. In 1800 he married Dorothea Schenke, and had several sons, of whom Johann Wilhelm (born 1802) and Johann Martin (born 1803) carried on the pianoforte business; which still existed, as probably the oldest in Germany, in 1910 [*Ge* (1814); *Gö*].

RIVA, Alessandro. Born at Villa d'Adda, 5 February 1803; died at Bergamo, 21 December 1868; maker of keyboard instruments. He married Romilda Claudi. The spinet number below marks him as the last maker in the old tradition [*Ks*].

Surviving Instruments

(01) 1836. Gallini Collection, Milan. Spinet, inscribed on nameboard: *Alessandro Riva in Bergamo—A. 1836.* Compass 4½ octaves.

(1) 1839. Leipzig University, Heyer Collection. A spinet, inscribed on nameboard: *Alessandro Riva / in Bergamo 1839.* Compass C–A, 4 octaves and a 6th. 127×55 cm. Inscription reproduced at *Ks,* p. 255.

RIVA, Giuseppe. Father of the foregoing. Joiner and maker of harpsichords. Married Rosa Villa [*Ks*].

ROCHEAD, Andrew, & Son. Pianoforte maker at Greenside Place, Leith Walk, Edinburgh; dates ascertained, 1793–1854 [*J*]. They made spinets too; the inscription *A.R. for N.S.* on a 1784/5 spinet by Neil Stewart(q.v). may refer to them. *See* Addenda.

ROCK, William. Harpsichord maker in Parliament Street, Westminster, in 1780 [*Byrne*].

RODILLY, Loys. Organ builder of Nancy; *fl.* 1511, in which year he constructed for Antoine Duke of Lorraine an instrument comprising chekker, organ, spinet, and flutes [*Jac*; see further *Fleury*].

RODOLFI. *See*: Ridolfi, Giacomo.

RODOLPHUS, Jacobus. *See*: Ridolfi, Giacomo.

ROMA, Hadrianus. *See*: Hadrianus, Roma.

ROMANO, Nicola Palazzi. *See*: Palazzi, Nicola.

ROMARINI, Nicolas. *See*: Ramarinus, Nicolaus.

RÖMER, Anton. Born at Brünn (Brno) 1724; died at Graz 1779. Clavichord maker, probably in Austria.

Surviving Instruments

(1) 1774. Clavichord. Owned (1971) by Herr Schuster, the violin maker in Graz [*GL*].

ROMITO, Giulio, of Ferrara. Clavichord maker, *fl.* 1572 [*Va*].

ROSENAU, Gottlieb, of Stockholm. Harpsichord maker; dates ascertained, 1757–86 [*Hirt*].

Surviving Instruments

(1) 1786. Copenhagen, Claudius Collection. Harpsichord, signed: *Forfärdigat af Gottlieb Rosenau, Instrumentmakare i Stockholm. 1786.* 2 manuals; 5 octaves; 2×8′, 1×4′, lute. Dimensions 276×105·5 cm. Illustrated in *Russell 1959* (*Hubb 1965,* p. 176, gives 1785 as the date).

ROSSI, Annibale dei, otherwise *de Roxis* and *Rosso.* Virginal maker of Milan. Earliest date known, 1542 He died between 1577 and 1595 [*J*]. He 'was the first to introduce virginals in the modern shape, as we now see them' [P. Morigi, *La nobiltà di Milano,* 1595, p. 289. See *J*, p. 100].

ROSSI, Ferrante dei, *or* Ferandus de Rosis. Virginal maker of Milan, son of Annibale dei Rossi. Dates ascertained, 1580–95. Morigi (loc. cit.) praises him as maintaining his father's high standard of workmanship and making valuable innovations; but this is hardly borne out by the surviving instruments.

TABLE 28. *Surviving Instruments by A. and F. ROSSI*

No.	Date	Type	Kbs.	Signature	Owner/Remarks
Annibale					
01	1542	Pol. V	1	*Opus / Hannibalis Medio/lanensis 1542*	Monroe, Conn., Laurence Witten. Rose; C/F–C, 4 octaves. Size 135×47 cm.
1	1550	Pol. V	1		Hipkins (*GD*, 1910, s.v. Spinet) refers to a Rossi spinet, belonging to Miss Marie Decca. I suspect that this is the instrument referred to by *Ks* (p. 56) under the mistaken date 1520.
2	1555	Pol. V	1	*Opus Anibalis Mediolanensis MDLV*	London, Victoria and Albert Museum. 4½ octaves C–F with short octave. Pinewood; inlaid sharps, ivory naturals, rose. Cypress; ivory studs.
3	1569	Pol. V	1	*Opus Annibalis Mediolanensis MDLXVIIII*	New York, Juillard School of Music (1955). Compass as in 2. Boxwood naturals; Gothic rose. Covered in red velvet; no outer case. Shewn at the Allg. Musik-Ausstellung, Berlin, 1898, and mentioned by *Hi*. Formerly owned by Sam Grimson, New York.
4	1569	Pol. V *or* V	1	*Opus Annibalis Mediolanensis MDLXVIIII*	Hamburg, Museum für Kunst und Gewerbe. Acquired in 1904. Sent away, during World War II, to a part of Germany now in the German Democratic Republic, and now (1970) housed in the Museum für Kunsthandwerk, Dresden.
5	1577	Pol. V	1	*Anniballis de Roxis Mediolanensis MDLXXVII*	London, Victoria and Albert Museum. 4 octaves and a 5th with short octave. Case heavily bejewelled. Made for a member of the Trivulzio family. See *J.* 100, where it is illustrated. Large rose.
5a		Pol. V	1		Milan, Gallini Collection.
Ferrante					
6	1580	Pol. V	1	*Ferandi de Rosis, Mediolanensis, M.D.LXXX*	Michigan University.
6a	1597	Pol. V	1	*Ferandi de Rossis Mediolanensis MDXCVII*	Monroe, Conn., Laurence Witten. No outer case; C/F–F, 4½ octaves. Rose. Arcaded box naturals; ebonized accidentals; size 148×52 cm.
7	—	Pol. V	1		Turin, Museo Civico. Illustrated in catalogue.

ROSSI, Toma, of Viterbo. Harpsichord maker; *fl.* 1759.

Surviving Harpsichords

(1) 1759. Yale University, Belle Skinner Collection. 2×8′ stops, one of them fixed. Inscribed: *Toma Rossi Viterbese fece anno 1759*. Compass apparently 4 octaves minus 2 semitones, D–C; but presumably the bottom octave is 'short', making the full 4 octaves. 6′ 7″×2′ 7″. Restored by W. Ruhenbeck, Arlington, N. J. Illustrated in catalogue. Probably a spurious instrument.

ROSE, of Berlin. Harpsichord maker, *fl.* 1760 [*Ge*].

ROST, Johann. *Ge* records a harpsichord maker Rost (without forename) who flourished in Berlin in 1760. In other sources we find references to a harpsichord ('Flügel') 'anno 1706 von dem berühmten Rost gemacht', and learn that a Johann Rost was paid by the Queen of Prussia for a 'Flügel' on 26 February 1720. (*See* W. Stengel, *Alte Wohnkultur* (Berlin, 1958), pp. 75–6.) Perhaps *Ge*'s Rost was Johann's son?

ROTH, Johann. Organ builder at Ödenburg (Sopron), Hungary, repaired 2 harpsichords at the Esterházy court in 1775 [*Walter*, p. 258].

ROTHER, Henry. Maker of harpsichords, spinets, and other instruments in Dublin; *fl.* 1762–74.

Surviving Instruments

(1) 1774. Dublin, National Museum. Upright harpsichord.

ROTHER, Henry William. Organ and harpsichord maker in Dublin; dates ascertained, 1770–82: Great Booter Lane 1770–4; 9 Great Booter Lane 1775; 9 Bishop Street 1776–82 [*Teahan*].

ROUSSELIÈRE, Jean-Baptiste de la. *See*: LA ROUSSELIÈRE, Jean-Baptiste de.

ROVERIO, Vittore de, of Rome, *fl.* 1696. Virginal maker [*Va*].

ROXIS, Annibale de. *See*: ROSSI, Annibale dei.

ROZÉ. Eighteenth-century Parisian harpsichord maker. The inventory of J. H. Hemsch's goods (28 September 1769) records: 'un clavecin de Rozé . . . 120 livres' [*MC*, pp. 109, 728; *Hardouin 1960*]. *Cor* (p. 84) refers to him.

ROZET. Seventeenth-century French spinet maker. A spinet by him dated 1680 is in the Musées de Besançon [*ChamP*].

RUBINO, Domenico. Perhaps a harpsichord maker at Castro, in Lombardy, 1743.

On 16 March 1971 there was sold at Sotheby's a single-manual harpsichord, described in the catalogue as 'a rare Spanish . . . harpsichord inscribed on the key shafts *Dominicus Rubino fecit 1743 a Castro nit . . .?*'. Vendor: Robin Langdon; buyer: S. E. Towers. In Michael Thomas's workshop, November 1971.

Although Rubino does not figure in either of the Franciolini catalogues, the instrument is dubious or, to say the least, much altered. The lid bears a painting in the Spanish style but is not native to the instrument, which is of Italian origin. There are 2×8′ stops.

RUCKERS [*also* Ruckaerts, Rickers, Ruykers, etc.]. The most famous name in the history of harpsichord making, belonging to a family, perhaps of German extraction, resident in Antwerp in the sixteenth and seventeenth centuries. *St* sets out many of the sources for their history, and later J. Lambrechts-Douillez found some more information about them in the Antwerp city archives. The 6th edition of *GD* gives a full account of them by Lambrechts-Douillez, so that only a summary is necessary here.

The best-known members of the family are:

(*a*) **Hans,** *the Elder*, born *c.* 1550 at Malines (Mechelen) the son of Frans Ruckers, died between 5 July 1597 and December 1599 (probably some time in 1598). Married Naenken (Adriana) Knaeps at the Cathedral Church of Our Lady, Antwerp, 25 June 1575, and was admitted to the Guild of St. Luke in 1579 as 'Claversinbalmakerre' [*Ro*]. The earliest surviving instrument definitely from his hand is dated 1581 (the harpsichord dated 1573, no. 1, being spurious). *HR* roses normally have a diameter of about 65 mm., and the harpist looks to her right. A few instruments, however, have 85-mm. roses with the harpist looking to her left. There is no doubt that a number of harpsichords with *HR* roses were not made by Hans Ruckers but by later makers who sought to increase the value of their instruments by inserting *HR* roses and passing them off as coming from the Ruckers workshop.

(*b*) **Hans,** *the Younger, frequently called* 'Jean'. Eldest son of (*a*), baptized 15 January 1578. Married Maria Waelrant at Antwerp Cathedral in 1604. Entered the Guild in 1611. From 1615 until his death about 24 April 1643 he was honorary 'orgel en clavesimbelmaker van de cappelle', i.e. the Royal Chapel at Brussels [*VdB*].

An indication of the esteem in which Jean Ruckers was held is given by the documents quoted by Stellfeld in *VdB*. In 1623 his name appears together with Rubens, Jan Breughel, Hans van Mildert, and Abraham Verhoeven, in a list of citizens exempted from Civic Guard duties.

The roses in Jean Ruckers instruments are of 2 sizes: the larger measures about 85 mm. across and has the figure turning to its left (type 2 in *GD* 5th edition); the smaller measures about 65 mm. and has the figure turning to its right (type 1 in *GD*).

(*c*) **Andreas,** *the Elder*, second son of (*a*), baptized 20 August 1579. Married Catharina de Vries 25 January 1605. Earliest harpsichord recorded, 1601 (sold 1760, *Bq*); earliest surviving, 1608. Probably shortly before 1608 he entered the Guild. Latest date ascertained: 1644, on a document [*Po*, p. 32; *GD*] and on an instrument [no. 112].

In 1643 and 1644 Andreas the Elder, then 64 years old, signed himself *Andreas Ruckers den Oudere* (or *den Ouden*) on certain instruments (no. 112 in the list, and at least 1 harpsichord in the Seelhof sale, 1759, quoted by *St*, p. 95); presumably, therefore, instruments from these and later years signed simply *Andreas Ruckers* are to be attributed to Andreas the Younger.

(*d*) **Andreas,** *the Younger*, second child of (*c*), baptized 31 March 1607. Entered the Guild in 1637 or shortly before. Married *c.* 1637 Johanna Hex (*GD* 1954 and *Po* give the name as Heeght). Latest date ascertained, 1667 (on a harpsichord reported by Fétis in 1865). Latest date on a surviving instrument, 1651 [*Po* says that Andreas II died in 1659].

He may have worked with his father for a few years after his entry into the Guild; but at any rate by 1643 he was working independently, since an instrument of this date is recorded as signed explicitly by Andreas the Elder [*St*, p. 95].

GD refers to 'undoubted instruments' by Andreas the Younger (my numbers 120–3 and 125). On what grounds did Régibo assign them to this maker? Clearly not on account of date, since 125 is undated. Presumably, then, by reason of their roses; but the distinction between the *AR I* and *AR II* roses, if it exists at all, is not as clear as the cuts in *GD* suggest, and in any case number 118, made in 1651 and therefore almost inevitably by Andreas the Younger, has a rose of the pattern assigned by *GD* to Andreas the Elder.

A firm line of demarcation between the instruments of Andreas the Elder and those of Andreas the Younger has yet to be discovered.

The roses in Andreas Ruckers instruments measure about 65 mm. across.

(*e*) **Christoffel.** Organist at Termonde (Dendermonde) in 1594 and later, to whom the virginals having a *CR* rose were formerly ascribed. His relationship, if any, with the other Ruckerses is not known, and there is no evidence that he made instruments.

Whether the Ruckers workshops produced examples of

all the different sizes of harpsichords and virginals built in seventeenth-century Flanders is not known. Examples survive of single-manual harpsichords of 2 different sizes, of 2-manual harpsichords of 2 different compasses, of rectangular virginals of 5 different sizes, some with the keyboard at the right (called *muselaars* by *Dou*) and some with the keyboard at the left (called *spinetts* by *Dou*) and double virginals consisting of an 8′ virginal and another octave virginal contained in a single box. In addition, there survive a single polygonal virginal and 3 rectangular instruments consisting of a harpsichord with an octave virginal built into the space next to the bent side.

Tree of the RUCKERS family

Frans Ruckers
(of Malines)

HANS, the Elder = Adriana (Naenken)
(born *c.* 1550; died *c.* 1598) Knaeps, 1575

JOANNES Ruckers = Maria Waelrant, 1604
[Hans, *the Younger*, Jean]
1578–1643

ANDREAS, *the Elder* = Catharina de Vries, 1605
(born 1579; still living 1644)

[Numerous issue]

[CRISTOFFEL Ruckers, date and relationship not known]

ANDREAS, *the Younger* = Johanna Hex, *c.* 1637
(born 1607; still living 1667)

[issue]

TABLE 29. *List of Instruments by (or ostensibly by) the RUCKERS Family, Surviving into Modern Times*

It is noteworthy that although Hans Ruckers (strictly Joannes the Elder) died probably in 1598, *HR* roses continued to be used by his eldest son Joannes (Hans the Younger) until 1612—a year after his entry into the Guild of St. Luke—when he adopted his own *IR* rose. (In this check-list all, including undated, instruments with an *HR* rose are placed before the instruments having an *IR* rose.) On the other hand, Hans's second son, Andreas I, used his own *AR* rose from at least 1608 although he did not enter the Guild until 1610/11. There is a great deal that we do not yet know about procedure in the Ruckers workshops. It is quite probable that many apparently genuine Ruckers instruments were in fact the work of other makers but had Ruckers roses fitted later to increase their value.

The mottoes and proverbs with which the Ruckers habitually adorned their instruments such as 'Musica donum Dei', 'Sic transit gloria mundi', 'Musica laetitiae comes medicina dolorum' (with its irritating omission of *et* from the fourth foot, perpetuated, it is sad to see, in at least one fine-toned harpsichord of recent make) are omitted except on the rare occasions when they contain important evidence about the instrument, such as the date.

Raymond Russell, in his list in *GD*5, gave Hans, Joannes, Andreas I, etc. the letters A, B, C, etc., and used these when giving the instrument numbers employed in earlier editions of *Grove*. In quoting the *Grove* numbers given by Russell in the 5th edition I have thought it clearer to preface the number with 'H' for Hans, 'J' for Joannes, 'A(I)' for Andreas the Elder, and 'A(II)' for Andreas the Younger. Furthermore, the unnumbered instruments in Russell's list are so numerous that, in order to make it easier for readers to find his detailed descriptions, I have given references to them such as e.g. [J3b], [A(I)31a].

In preparing this list I have leaned heavily on information and advice from E. M. Ripin, on J. H. van der Meer's 'Beiträge zum Cembalo-Bau der Familie Ruckers' (*Jahrbuch des Staatlichen Instituts für Musikforschung*, Berlin, 1971), as also on Russell's list in *GD*5.

No.	No. in *GD* 5th edn.	No. in *GD* 4th edn.	Date	Type	No. of Kbs.	Remarks	Former owners	Present or recent owner
Hans the Elder, *c.* 1550–*c.* 1598								
[1]	H1	—	1573	H	1	*HR* rose with *Anno 1573* in an uncharacteristic position, flanking it. Inscription on jackrail: *Hans Ruckers me fecit Antverpiae 1573*; 2×8′, 1×4′; side stops; 4 octaves. This instrument is probably a pure fake, of unknown origin. Hans Ruckers entered Guild of St. Luke in 1579.		Munich, Deutsches Museum.

No.	No. in *GD* 5th edn.	No. in *GD* 4th edn.	Date	Type	No. of Kbs.	Remarks	Former owners	Present or recent owner
2	H2	1	1581	V/Ot	2	*HR* rose. Double virginal, the ottavino to the left, removable. Illustrated in *Connoisseur*, 1916 and *Wint 1966*. Monogram on tool-box. Inscription on front of ottavino jackrail: *Hans Ruekers me fecit 1581*. Geometrical roses. Compass of both instruments 4 octaves C–C with bass short octave. Large virginal has divided arpichordum stop. Size 5′ 9″ × 1′ 7″.	Marquis of Oropeza, Cuzco, Peru; B. H. Homan, who gave it in 1929 to the Metropolitan Museum of Art.	New York, Metropolitan Museum of Art.
2a	(Suppl.) H2a	AR43	1583	V	1	*HR* rose. C–A, 3¾ octaves, chromatic. Keyboard to left. Date on soundboard. Restored by H. Bédard. Illustrated in *Hin* (pl. 32). Size 3′ 8″ × 1′ 4″. A valuable example of the early Ruckers style.	Paris, Collection Strauss.	Paris, André Meyer.
[3]	H3	2	1590	H	2	*HR* rose; date on soundboard. Compass G–E, 4 octaves plus, chromatic; 2 × 8′, 1 × 4′ stops, the 4′ on the upper manual, manual, without dogleg jacks; push-pull coupler. Size 7′ 4″ × 2′ 9″ (widened during *ravalement*) Not a genuine Ruckers, though it may be Flemish. See further *VdMCemRuck*.	Renaix, Abel Régibo in 1897.	Brussels, M. Hanlet.
[4]	H4	3	1590	H	2	*HR* rose; date on soundboard. Not by Ruckers. In the 1960s when it was opened up for restoration, the real maker's name—*Jean-Claude Goujon*—was found inside the case. It was repaired in 1784 by *Swanen*, who signed the lower 8′ row of jacks. Stops 2 × 8′, 1 × 4′, *peau de buffle*, with 5 genouillères. F–F, 5 octaves. Inscribed (eighteenth century) above the keys: *Hans Ruckers me fecit Antwerpiae*. Size 7′ 9″ × 2′ 10″.	Château de Pau, France.	Paris Conservatoire.
5	H5	4	1591	Pol. V	1	Only extant Ruckers polygonal virginal (6-sided). Inset keyboard to the left. C/E to C 4 octaves. Inscribed on jackrail: *Hans Ruckers me fecit Antverpiae*; and inside lid: *Scientia non habet inimicum nisi ignorantem / 1591*. Restored in 1959 by H. Maillefer, Renens (Switzerland). Illustrated in *Russell 1959*.	T. J. Cannel, Ghent.	Bruges, Museum Gruuthuuse.
6	H18	18	1591	V/Ot	2	*HR* roses. Date 1591 is in painting on lid. Ottavino on the left. Present compass C–C, 4 octaves. Inscribed on both instruments: *Ioannes Ruquers me fecit*. Original compass of the ottavino was C/E to C. The much altered main virginal's original compass cannot be determined for certain. See further *VdMCemRuck*. Size 5′ 7″ × 1′ 5½″.	Chappell; Sir George Donaldson; M. Steinert.	Yale University, Belle Skinner Collection.
7	H6	5	1594	H/Ot	2	Single harpsichord with ottavino in the bent side. *HR* rose (geometrical rose in the ottavino). Inscribed *Hans Ruckers me fecit Antverpiae 1594*. Harpsichord compass C–C, 4 octaves (possibly originally C/E–C); 2 × 8′, 1 × 4′ stops (probably 1 × 8′, 1 × 4′ originally). Compass of the ottavino, as originally, C/E–A, 3 octaves plus, without top G sharp. Size 5′ 11″ × 2′ 6″.	The Kings of Prussia.	East Berlin, Staatliche Kunstsammlungen Displayed in the Kunstgewerbemuseum in Schloss Köpenick.
[7a]	—	—	1595	V	1	Unauthentic.		Cincinnati Museum of Art.

No.	No. in *GD* 5th edn.	No. in *GD* 4th edn.	Date	Type	No. of Kbs.	Remarks	Former owners	Present or recent owner
8	H7	6	1598	V	1	*HR* rose. Inscribed on jackrail: *Iohannes Ruckers me fecit Antverpiae.* Date *1598* inside lid. Original compass C/E to C, 4 octaves, present compass G/B–C, 4½ octaves, received during the repair recorded on the nameboard: *Francois Chapelle a reparé cette espinette et luy a donné de l'armonie 1739*, at Soissons. Keyboard to the left. The only completely undoubted Ruckers of this kind. Size 5′5½″ × 1′ 7″.	Paris, Jeanne Lyon.	Paris, Comtesse de Chambure.

Hans the Younger, otherwise **Joannes** (II), 1578–1643. (*It seems likely that the division comes here, even though the instruments continue to have* HR *roses. See text*)

No.	No. in *GD* 5th edn.	No. in *GD* 4th edn.	Date	Type	No. of Kbs.	Remarks	Former owners	Present or recent owner
9	H8	—	1599	H	2	*HR* rose. Date painted, and also scratched, on the soundboard. The jackrail (not original) bears the name *Hans Ruckers* and the date *1599*. It now has a compass of 5 octaves F–F, with 1 × 8′ and 1 × 4′ stops on the lower manual and 1 × 8′ on the upper. Has always had 2 manuals—in fact, the earliest undoubted Ruckers 2-manual harpsichord—but has been much altered. See *VdMCemRuck*.	Nuremberg, Neupert Collection.	Halle, Händelhaus.
[10]	—	—	1600			A 'ghost' instrument, the same as [137] below.		
11	H9	7	1604(?)	V	1	*HR* rose. Inscribed on jackrail (which, though authentic, does not belong to the instrument): *Ioannes et Andreas Ruckers fecerunt.* No date now visible; Mahillon gave '1604'. C/E–C, 4 octaves; keyboard to the right.	Abel Régibo; César Snoeck, Ghent.	Brussels Conservatoire (no. M. 2927).
12	H10	8	1610	V/Ot	2	*HR* rose. Double virginal. Signature of Hans Ruckers and *HR* roses in both instruments. Signature above nameboard in main instrument is not original. Present compass of both: C–F, 4½ octaves. Original compass of the ottavino was C/E–C, 4 octaves. Main instrument also much altered, but original compass probably the same. At present the ottavino stands on top of the main virginal to which it is coupled. Originally the ottavino could be stored within the main virginal to the left of its keyboard. On main instrument, keyboard to the right; on the smaller it is central. Illustrated in *Russell 1959*. Size 5′ 7″ × 1′ 9″ and 2′ 8½″ × 1′ 4¼″.	Fétis.	Brussels Conservatoire (no. M. 275).
[12a]	H unnumbered	9	1620 (*not* 1610)			See below, no. 23a.		
13	H unnumbered	10	1610	V	1		A. Sol, Tournai; J. Hel, Lille (1927).	
14	H11	—	1610	V	1	*HR* rose. Much altered in eighteenth century so that original compass is uncertain. Present compass: C–F, 4½ octaves with bass short octave. Keyboard to the right. The case *may* be by Ruckers, but the rest of the instrument (except the soundboard) cannot be earlier than an eighteenth-century *ravalement*. Size 4′ 5″ × 1′ 7″.	Nuremberg, Neupert Collection.	Halle, Händelhaus.
[15]	—	11	1611	V	1	*AR* rose. Wrongly ascribed to Hans. Equals instrument no. 75 below.		

No.	No. in *GD* 5th edn.	No. in *GD* 4th edn.	Date	Type	No. of Kbs.	Remarks	Former owners	Present or recent owner
16	H12	12	1612	H	2	*HR* rose, but inscribed on front-board: *Ioannes Ruckers*, etc. Modern keyboards G–F, nearly 5 octaves without lowest G sharp. Instrument much altered. Size 7′ 6″ × 2′ 11″.		H.M. Queen Elizabeth II. At Fenton House, Hampstead, in care of the National Trust.
17	H13	13	1612	H	2	*HR* rose, but a French eighteenth-century instrument. Inscribed: *Mis à ravalement par Pascal Taskin à Paris 1774* and *Restauré par Tomasini à Paris 1905*. Compass F–F, 5 octaves; 2 × 8′, 1 × 4′, push-pull coupler. Date on soundboard 1612. Seems to have been built round a Flemish virginal soundboard. Illustrated in *Pag*, p. 37. Size 7′ 6″ × 3′ 0″.	M. de la Chevardière, Paris (1777); Torlini, Rome (1842); Viscount Powerscourt; Edgar Speyer, New York; Major Bowes; Sibyl Marcuse, New York.	Brussels Conservatoire (acquired 1960), no. M. 3848.
17a	—	—	1612	H	2	'Petit ravalement' 1733; 52 notes; 1 × 8′ and 1 × 4′ on each keyboard.		Amiens, Musée d'Histoire Locale [*ChamP*].
[18]	H un-numbered	14	1613	H	2	*HR* rose. Ostensibly by Hans Ruckers but probably by Richard, who signed it under the soundboard: *Faict par Michel Richard 1688*. Compass 4½ octaves G/B–C; 2 × 8′, 1 × 4′ stops. Date on soundboard. Size 6′ 4½″ × 2′ 8½″.	Planchet, Paris; Albert Steinert, Providence, U.S.A.	Providence, R.I., School of Design. (On loan to Yale University.)
19	H14	15	1614(?)	V	1	*HR* rose. Date no longer visible; not given by Mahillon or Snoeck. C/E–C, 4 octaves. White naturals. Keys to the right. Size 5′ 5½″ × 1′ 7½″.	C. Snoeck, Ghent.	Brussels Conservatoire (no. M. 2930).
20	H15	16	1614	H	2	*HR* rose and date 1614. Compass F–G, 5 octaves plus 1 note, not original. White naturals; 2 × 8′, 1 × 4′ strings; 3 × 8′, 1 × 4′ stops, 2 × 8′ stops using the same strings. Size 7′ 4½″ × 3′ 3″.	C. Snoeck, Ghent; Berlin Collection.	(Lost in World War II.)
21	—	—	1615	H	2	*HR* rose and name of Hans Ruckers. Compass F–F, 5 octaves; 1 × 8′, 1 × 4′ choirs and *peau de buffle*; push-pull coupler. Date on soundboard; lowest jack dated *1732*. Name-board not original, nor keyboards, which date from *c.* 1860.	Vogüé family, Château de Peseau; Mme de Bousquet, great-grandmother of the present owner.	Paris, Maurice Le Roux (1970).
22	H16	17	1616	H	2	*HR* rose. Date on wrestplank and jackrail. Present compass 4½ octaves F–B without top B flat. Modern keyboards; 4 rows of jacks, 1 × 8′ and 1 × 4, for each keyboard, controlled by extensions of the slides passing through the case at the side. Size 7′ 4″ × 2′ 6″.	Paris, M. E. Costil.	Paris, M. Mirouet.
[22a]	H un-numbered	—	1617	V	1	Probably German. Not by Ruckers.		Paris Conservatoire.
23	H17	—	1620	V/Ot	2	*HR* rose. The ottavino is missing, the space for it being to the left. Compass 4 octaves C–C, bass short octave. Main keyboard to the right. Inscribed on jackrail: *Hans Ruckers me fecit Antwerpiae anno 1620*.		Lisbon, Conservatório.
[23a]	[H23e]	9	1620	Ot	1	German work, not Ruckers.	Jules Audéoud.	Paris Conservatoire.
23b	—	—	1644 [false]	H	2			Lausanne, private ownership [*GL*].

No.	No. in *GD* 5th edn.	No. in *GD* 4th edn.	Date	Type	No. of Kbs.	Remarks	Former owners	Present or recent owner
24	H10	—	1658 [false]	H	2	*HR* rose, and jackrail signed *Hans Ruckers*, but date *1658* painted on soundboard. The instrument was rebuilt in the eighteenth century, but all the original parts are Ruckers in style. A puzzle—see *VdMCemRuck*, also *RG.I*, p. 67. Present compass C–C, 4 octaves; 2×8′, 1×4, lute.	Hanns Neupert.	Nuremberg, Germanisches Nationalmuseum.
25	H20	19	n.d.	H		*HR* rose. Compass C/E–A, 4¾ octaves; 1×16′, 1×8′, 1×4′, and lute stops. Lengthened to house longer soundboard for 16′ stop. Stop-handles at side. Much restored by Charles de Vestibule, Brussels, in 1899. Shews evidence of having originally been a transposing instrument. See *VdMCemRuck*. Size 9′ 4″×2′ 9½″.		Brussels Conservatoire (no. M. 2510).
26	H21	20	n.d.	H	2	No rose or signature, but probably by Joannes Ruckers. Present compass C–F, 4½ octaves on both keyboards; 2×8′, 1×4′ stops. Originally a transposing instrument, but there is no space for a fourth row of jacks. Size 7′ 4″×2′ 7″.	A. Régibo; C. Snoeck.	Brussels Conservatoire (no. M. 2934).
[26a]	[H23a]	21	n.d.	Ot	1	Probably German. Not by Ruckers.		Leipzig University, Heyer Collection.
[26b]	[H23b]	22	n.d.	Ot	1	Probably German. Not by Ruckers. (Either this or 26a was lost in World War II.)		Leipzig University, Heyer Collection.
—	—	23	1628	H		Converted into a piano by Zeitter; attributed by Hipkins to Ruckers; = no. 95 below.		
27	—	—	n.d.	V		*HR* rose; 5 octaves [*Po*, p. 44].	Hanns Neupert.	
28	H22 and [J1a]	24	n.d.	H	2	*HR* rose. F–F, 5 octaves; 5 stops. Size 7′ 10″×3′ 9″.	Pilette, Brussels (1878). Later bought by A. Dolmetsch at the Hôtel Drouôt; Mrs. H. E. Crawley, London; sold 1951 in the W. R. Hearst estate.	Said to be in South America (1971).
[29]	H23	—	n.d.	H	1	*HR* rose. G–E, 4¾ octaves; 2×8′, 1×4′ stops. Inscribed on jack-rail *Hans Ruckers me fecit Antwerpiae 1637* and over the keys *Hans Ruckers me fecit 1637*. But it is not a genuine Ruckers instrument.	C. Snoeck; Mme Pereira, Ghent.	Brussels Conservatoire (no. M. 4276).
[30]	[H23f]	—	—	H	1	*HR* rose, modern, and *AR* in design; 1×8′, 1×4′ stops. Inscribed on nameboard: *Terrae reddo quod a caelo accepi*. Not a Ruckers instrument.	Cooper Union, New York (formerly on loan to Yale University).	Washington, Smithsonian Institution (given by the Cooper Union).
30a	H unnumbered	—	—	V	1	*HR* rose. Inscribed in box to the left of the instrument: *Iohannes Ruckers me fecit Antverpiae*; executed in the nineteenth century [*BruxPar*]. C–C 4 octaves including bass short octave. Soundboard and case painted in the nineteenth century. Only the case, keyboard, soundboard, and wrestpins are original according to *BruxPar*. It is difficult to decide to which maker this instrument should be attributed. (No. 2930 in *Mah*, no. 415 in the Snoeck 1903 Catalogue.)	C. Snoeck.	Brussels Conservatoire.

No.	No. in *GD* 5th edn.	No. in *GD* 4th edn.	Date	Type	No. of Kbs.	Remarks	Former owners	Present or recent owner
30b	—	—	1644	H	1	*HR* rose. Date on soundboard. Not a Ruckers, but probably a French instrument of the late seventeenth century. Originally 2 manuals, but the upper now lost.		Stockholm, Nydahl Collection.
30c	—	—	1612	H	2	*IR* rose. Originally a transposing instrument but keyboards aligned in France after 1730 leaving them both G/B–D. 4½ octaves. Still has 4 jack-slides with side-stops. See *RG.I.* p. 78.		Amiens, Musée d'Histoire Locale.
31	J1	24	1612	H	2	*IR* rose; date on soundboard. Present compass F–F, 5 octaves and stops 2 × 8′, 1 × 4′. *Ravalé* in eighteenth century and so much altered that the original form cannot be guessed.	Said to have belonged to Elisabeth, Queen of Philip IV of Spain, given her by Maria de Medici and kept first in the Escorial and later in Mme de Maintenon's rooms at Versailles. Later, L. Clapisson, Paris.	Paris Conservatoire.
[32]	Suppl.					Equals no. 28 above.		
33	J1a	43	1617	H	2	English eighteenth-century casework and jacks. Size 7′ 6″ × 3′ 0″.	Alexander Steinert, Providence, R.I. (formerly at his wife's house at Beverly, Mass.); Los Angeles, Robert Haas.	Los Angeles, Robert Johnson.
34	J2	2	1618	Ot	1	*IR* rose. The 'child' of a 'mother-and-child' double virginal. Compass C/E–C. Date on soundboard. Inscribed on jack-rail: *Ioannes Ruckers me fecit.* Patterned paper on inside and outside of case. Size 2′ 8½″ × 1′ 3½″.	Paris, A. Colin.	Paris Conservatoire.
35	Suppl. J2a	—	1618(?)	H	2	*IR* rose; signed on nameboard: *Ioannes Ruckers fecit 1618*(?); 52 keys; white naturals. Reported to me as dated 1618; but *VdMCemRuck* could find no date. Present compass G/B–D, 4½ octaves. Present stops 2 × 8′, 1 × 4′. Some jacks carry a restoration-date *1854*. Space for 4 rows of jacks. Possibly a transposing instrument originally.		Schloss Cappenberg bei Lünen, displayed on loan from the Museum für Kunst- und Kulturgeschichte, Dortmund.
35a	—	—	1618(?)	H	2	Signed on nameboard: *Iohannes Ruckers me fecit Antwerpiae Anno 1618* [? or *1619*—last digit not clear]. *Johan Christoph Fleischer auxit et restituit Hamburgi Anno 1724* Next to the *IR* a canopy has been painted.	Queen Louisa Ulrica of Sweden (1720–82), daughter of King Friedrich Wilhelm of Prussia	Lund University (deposited at Kulturhistoriska Museet, Lund).
[36]						Equals no. 37.		
37	J3	32	1619	H/Ot	3	*IR* roses (that in the harpsichord differing from that in the ottavino) in both harpsichord and ottavino, which is built into the bent side of the harpsicord. Compass on both keyboards of main instrument G/C–C, 4½ octaves; the ottavino has original compass C/E–C (1971). Present sets of strings on the harpsichord 2 × 8′, 1 × 4′; but 4 jack-slides. The main keyframes are old and suggest that the instrument was originally a transposer. The main jackrail is old, but its inscription *Ioannes Ruckers me fecit Antwerpiae 1619* was suspected by Russell.	A. Régibo; C. Snoeck.	Brussels Conservatoire (no. M. 2935).

No.	No. in *GD* 5th edn.	No. in *GD* 4th edn.	Date	Type	No. of Kbs.	Remarks	Former owners	Present or recent owner
						The instrument has been almost entirely rebuilt by Charles de Vestibule of Brussels, partially supervised by E. Closson. The patterned paper was specially reprinted. Wrestplanks, soundboards, bridges, jacks, and nearly all the casework are modern. Size 7′ 3″ × 2′ 8″.		
38	[J3b]	4	1619	V	1	*IR* rose. C–C, bass short octave; white naturals. See *Frankf. 1927*.	A. Régibo.	?
39	J4	4b	1620	V	1	*IR* rose. C–F, 4½ octaves at present, but may originally have been C/E–C, 4 octaves, as the instrument has been much restored and the compass increased. Inscribed on jackrail: *Iohannes Ruckers fecit Antwerpiae 1620*. Keyboard to the right. Restored by A. Dolmetsch. Size 5′ 7″ × 1′ 6½″.	Boston, Mass., Messrs. Chickering.	Boston, Mass., New England Conservatory of Music.
40	J5	5	1622	V	1	*IR* rose. Keyboard to right, C–F, 4½ octaves. Originally C/E to C. Date in ink on soundboard *Anno 1622*. Size 5′ 7″ × 17½″.	Brussels, V. Mahillon.	New York, Metropolitan Museum of Art.
41	J6	6	1623	V/Ot	2	*IR* roses. The ottavino to the left, removable. C–C, 4 octaves, bass short octave. Inscribed: *Joannes Ruckers me fecit*. Date on soundboard. Size 5′ 8″ × 1′ 8″. Illustrated in *Russell 1959*.	Paris, Salomon; Chicago, Col. Harding.	Chicago, Harding Museum.
42	[J6a]	7	1626	V	1	Size 4′ 3″ × 1′ 7″. Inscribed: *Joannes Ruckers fecit Antverpiae 1626*.	Brussels, Pley Collection (dispersed 1906).	?
43	J7	8	1627	H		*IR* rose. Inscribed: *Joannes Ruckers fecit Antverpiae*. Present compass C–E, 4¼ octaves (originally C/E–C, 4 octaves). Date on soundboard. Not known when the instrument was enlarged. Illustrated and described by Friedrich Ernst in *GSJ*, vol. 20 (1967) and by A. Berner in *RG.I*, p. 60. Size 6′ 0″ × 2′ 7½″.	E. van der Straeten; C. Snoeck.	Berlin Collection.
44	J8	9	1627(?)	H	2	*IR* rose. Inscribed on jackrail: *Joannes Ruckers me fecit Antverpiae 1627* (the last digit mutilated but probably 7). Above the keys: *H. Rukkers* [sic] *Antverpiae* and below *Refait par Blanchet facteur du Roi à Paris 1756*. Restored by A. Dolmetsch, 1908. Present compass F–E, nearly 5 octaves. Size 7′ 8″ × 3′ 0″.	A French family since Louis XIV; Miss Belle Skinner.	Yale University, Belle Skinner Collection.
44a	—	—	1627	H	2	*IR* rose. Date on soundboard. Extended and newly encased in 1753.	Paris, Mme Bailly (1967).	Paris, Claude Mercier-Ythier (1970).
44b	—	—	1627	H	2	*IR* rose; 4 octaves.	Bought by Sully (1559–1641), minister of Henri IV, for the Château de Villebon. Sold in 1904, and again *c.* 1920 to Salomon, Paris. Bought in 1927 by the present owner for the Château.	P. de La Raudière, Château de Villebon (Eure-et-Loir).

No.	No. in *GD* 5th edn.	No. in *GD* 4th edn.	Date	Type	No. of Kbs.	Remarks	Former owners	Present or recent owner
45	J9	10	1628?	V	1	*IR* rose; 4½ octaves C–F, no low C sharp. Keyboard to the right. Date 1628 on soundboard is not old. Modern case marqueteried. There has been a buffstop worked by genouillère. Much altered and restored. Exhibited at Brussels Exhibition, 1850. Size 5′ 7¼″ × 1′ 8½″.	Brussels, L. Jouret; Ghent, C. Snoeck.	Brussels Conservatoire (no. M. 2926).
46	—	—	1628	H	2	A–C, 4 octaves plus 3 notes; coupler; 2 × 8′, 1 × 4′.	Sold at Christie's in 1953, by an anonymous vendor, to Raymond Russell.	Colares, Portugal, C. Vere Pilkington.
47	J10	—	1628	H	2	*IR* rose. G–D, 4½ octaves. Black naturals; push-pull coupler. Date 1628 on soundboard. Painted case in Louis XIV style. Restored by Marcel Asseman of Saint Denis, 1952. Illustrated in *HMP*. Size 7′ 5½″ × 2′ 9″.	Musée de Cluny, Paris.	Palace of Versailles.
47a	Suppl. J10a	—	1628	H	?	*IR* rose; 4½ octaves A–D. Black naturals. Date *1628* on soundboard has at some time been altered to 1728. Inscription above keys is modern as is the rose. Size 7′ 4″ × 2′ 7″.	?	
48	[J10a]	11	1629	H	2		Louvain, G. de Prins.	?
49	J11	12	1629	V	1	*IR* rose. C/E–D 4 octaves and 1 tone; keyboard to left; date on jackrail.		Brussels Conservatoire (no. M. 2511).
[50]	J12	29	1629	H	1	*IR* rose; 59 wrestpins suggesting an F–D compass, 4¾ octaves, though this was not the original one; 1 × 8′, 1 × 4′, but at one time altered to 2 × 8′. Date 1629 on soundboard. Lid missing. Not a Ruckers [*Barnes*]. Size 7′ 3″ × 2′ 11″.	Antwerp, Musée du Steen.	Antwerp, Vleeshuis.
51	[J12a]	13	1630	H	2	Illustrated in *Po*. Size 4′ 10½″ × 2′ 10″.	Paris, F. Pigeory; Paris, Baroness J. de Rothschild.	?
52	[J12b]	14	1632	H	2	*IR* rose. F–G 5 octaves plus 2 notes. Size 8′ 2″ × 3′ 3″.	Snoeck.	
52a	—	—	1632	H	2	Original rose missing; 2 × 8′, 1 × 4′, buff. Inscribed on nameboard: *Jean Ruckers fecit Antwerpiae 1632*. Date also on soundboard. F–F, 5 octaves. Bottom keyboard made in France in 1757. *Ravalé* in the eighteenth century. Dimensions 6′ 1″ × 2′ 8″.	Marquis de Boisgelin, Paris, and his family during the twentieth century. History before 1900 not known.	J. Martinod, Paris.
52b	—	—	1632	H	2	*IR* rose.		Ghent, private ownership (1972) [*EMR*].
[52c]	[J12c]	[15]	1632	H	2	Rose is that of Hagaerts (q.v.), damaged; probably mistaken for a Ruckers rose, hence the inscription *Joannes Ruckers* . . . added later. Size 7′ 9″ × 2′ 0″.	de Breyne, Ypres.	Comtesse de Chambure, Paris.
53	J25	—	[1632?]	H	2	No rose. Signed: *Johannes Ruckers me fecit Antwerpiae*. F–E, nearly 5 octaves; 2 × 8′, 1 × 4′, push-pull coupler. No date visible [*MarcP*].	Said to have been Marie Antoinette's and taken to Switzerland by refugees from the French Revolution.	Neuchâtel, Musée d'Histoire et d'Archéologie.
[54]	J13	16	1634	H	2	*IR* rose. On lid: *Acta virum probant, 1634*. Compass G–E, 4½ octaves; 2 × 8′, 1 × 4′. Sea-horse paper with reversed colours (i.e. white on black). Not a genuine Ruckers: mostly made in England in the eighteenth century. Illustrated in *V&A*, *MIWA*, and *Russell V&A*. Size 7′ 3″ × 3′ 2″.	Earl of Dysart; Sir Lyonel Tollemache, Bt.	London, Victoria and Albert Museum, but deposited at Ham House, near Richmond.

No.	No. in *GD* 5th edn.	No. in *GD* 4th edn.	Date	Type	No. of Kbs.	Remarks	Former owners	Present or recent owner
[55]	J14	—	1636	H	2	*IR* rose; F–G, 5 octaves plus 2 notes; 2×8′, 1×4′. Worked by genouillères. Date on soundboard. Date *1766* on bottom and top keys.	C. Snoeck, Ghent; Mme Planchard, Paris, who sold it *c.* 1925 to Mlle Berthe Vaucher, Geneva.	Geneva, Mme Isabelle Nef (1970).
55a	—	—	1636	V	1	*IR* rose. See *MGG*, vol. 11 (1963), s.v. 'Ruckers'. Restored by Frank Hubbard. 5′ 7″×1 ′6″. Keyboard to the right.		Harvard University.
56	[J14a]	17	1636	V	1	Inscribed: *Ioannes Ruckers fecit Antverpiae, 1636.* Size 5′ 9″×1′ 8″.	Pley Collection, Brussels.	?
57	J15	17b	1636	H	2	*IR* rose; F–F, 5 octaves (originally E–F); 2×8′, 1×4′ stops. Not a Ruckers but an eighteenth-century instrument. The hinges and certain other small details suggest that it was made in England, where the jacks, slides, and keys were made. Size 8′ 0″×3′ 2″.	Sir Douglas Seton-Stewart, Bt., Stirling.	Edinburgh, Palace of Holyroodhouse.
58	J16	18	1637	V	1	*IR* rose. C–C, 4 octaves with bass short octave. Keyboard to right. Illustrated in Snoeck's Catalogue, 1894. Size 5′ 7″×1′ 8″.	C. Snoeck.	Berlin Collection until destroyed in World War II.
59	J17	19	1637	H	1	*IR* rose. Date on soundboard. A–F, 57 notes. *Ravalé* in England in the eighteenth century; 2×8′, 1×4′. Restored by Hugh Gough in 1952 and by John Barnes in 1972. Size 6′ 1″×2′ 9½″.(See *RG.I*, p. 36, article by Barnes.)	J. C. Horsley, R.A., Hugh Gough; Raymond Russell.	Edinburgh University.
59a	J24	—	1637	H	2	Geometrical rose replacing the original. On small nameboard: *Ioannes Ruckers fecit Antverpiae.* Date 1637 on soundboard; 2×8′, 1×4′ stops. Originally a transposing instrument with 1×8′, 1×4′, and now (1972) restored to transposing form by John Barnes, thus being at present the only playable transposing Ruckers.	Commendatore Evan Gorga, Rome.	Rome, Museo di Strumenti Musicali.
60	J18	20	1638	V	1	*IR* rose. C–D, 4 octaves plus 2 notes. Keyboard to the right. Much altered (e.g. new soundboard and bridges). Traces of its original compass having been C/E–C. Size 5′ 7¼″×1′ 7″.	C. Snoeck.	Brussels Conservatoire (no. M. 2933).
61	J19	21	1638	H	2	Geometrical rose. Date on soundboard. The only substantially unaltered example of a transposing harpsichord, unaltered except for the rose and some minor details: the jack-slides (whose ends have been cut flush with the cheek-piece), and the removal of the 6 metal plates carrying the extra strings, also patching up of the relevant wrestplank bridges. Illustrated in *Russell 1959*, pls. 33–5 (showing the crossing-over of the keys). Size 7′ 4½″×2′ 6″.	E. Spence, Florence (before 1896); Sir B. Samuelson, sold 1915; Mrs. Lotta van Buren Bizallion, who lent it to Yale University; Raymond Russell.	Edinburgh University.
62	J20	22	1639	H	1	*IR* rose. Date on soundboard. Lacks keyboard; 2×8′, 1×4′. Original compass C/E–C; 55 notes. Illustrated in *Russell V&A*. Size 5′ 9″×2′ 7″.	King George III; Messrs. Kirkman, London.	London, Victoria and Albert Museum.

No.	No. in *GD* 5th edn.	No. in *GD* 4th edn.	Date	Type	No. of Kbs.	Remarks	Former owners	Present or recent owner
63	—	—	1640	H	2	*IR* rose. Date on soundboard; 2×8′, 1×4′ stringing; 3×8′, 1×4′, buff stops. Restored by Otto Marx of Messrs. Wilhelm Rück, Nuremberg, 1954.	Acquired from the maker in 1640 by Alexander Reichsgraf von Velen, Freiherr von Raesfeld, in whose family's possession it remained for many years, the owner in the 1950s being Dieter Graf Landsberg-Velen, Schloss Ahaus, Westphalia.	Present location unknown.
63a	—	—	1642	V	1	*MGG*, vol. 11 (1963) s.v. Ruckers. C–C, 4 octaves; signed on jackrail: *Ioanes Ruckers fecit Antwerpiae.* Keyboard to the right. Originally 4 octaves including short octave; *ravalé* so as to become 4 octaves, chromatic. Keyboard to right.		Stockholm, Musikhistoriska Museet.
64	J21	23	1642	H	2	*IR* rose; 2×8′, 1×4′. G–D, 4½ octaves with short octave; 4 stops with the remarkable arrangement of 1×8′ and 1×4′ on lower manual, 1×dogleg 8′ worked by both manuals, and 1×4′ on upper manual. The key-frame (original) shews it to have been made as a transposing instrument. Illustrated in *Musical Times*, July 1904. Restored by Dolmetsch, 1896. Size 7′ 4½″×2′ 8″.	Cornelius Winkelaar, Zaandam; F. R. Leyland; Countess of Dudley; Richard Newton, who sold it at Sotheby's, 27 November 1969, to the present owner.	New York, Hugh Gough
65	—	—	1642	H	1	2×8′, 1×4′; slides project right. Lid does not fold back.	Wanda Landowska.	
65a	—	25	n.d.	H	1	Italian work; not by Ruckers. Size 7′ 0″×2′ 7″.		Paris, Hôtel de Cluny.
66	—	26	n.d.	H	1	C–F, 4½ octaves. Size 5′ 11″×2′ 7½″.	Snoeck.	?
67	—	27	n.d.	H	1	*IR* rose; 3 stops. Size 6′ 0″×2′ 7″.	Régibo.	?
68	—	28	n.d.	H	1	*IR* rose cut in hardwood.	Régibo.	?
[69]	J22	30	n.d.	V	1	*IR* rose. Keyboard to the right. Size 4′ 4″×1′ 4½″. F–G, 5 octaves plus 1 tone. Almost certainly spurious, and regarded as such by Sachs in his 1922 catalogue.	Snoeck.	Formerly Berlin Collection; lost in 1945 [*GSJ*, 1967, p. 75].
70	J23	31	n.d.	H/Ot	2	*IR* roses. A 1-manual harpsichord with an ottavino in the hollow of the bent side. Compass of both instruments 4 octaves C–C with bass short octave. Main keyboard with 2 stops. Illustrated in the Berlin 1922 catalogue. See Friedrich Ernst in *GSJ*, Vol. 20 (1967) and A. Berner in *RG.I*, pp. 61–2. Size 5′ 11″×2′ 5½″.		Berlin Collection.
70a	—	—	n.d.	V/Ot	2	*HR* roses (2). The only surviving Ruckers double virginal with the ottavino to the right. Inscribed on jackrail: *Ioannes Ruquers fecit.* Illustrated in *Gall.*, pl. 125.		Milan, Gallini Collection. Illustrated.
71						See above, no. 59a.		
[71a]	[J25a]					*IR* rose in a fragment of a decorated soundboard.		Paris Conservatoire.

No.	No. in *GD* 5th edn.	No. in *GD* 4th edn.	Date	Type	No. of Kbs.	Remarks	Former owners	Present or recent owner
Andreas the Elder; born 1579, latest date ascertained: 1644								
72	A(I)1	45 add. [Suppl.]	1608	H	2	*AR* rose. Originally a transposing instrument. Lower keyboard original, upper modern. Present compass G–C. Converted into a grand pianoforte in the eighteenth century with compass C–D. Converted back in 1928 into a 2-manual harpsichord with compass C–D. In 1953 again restored, and now 2×8′, 1×4′ on lower manual, the further 8′ with *peau de buffle*, and 8′ on upper manual with coupler. Illustrated in *Russell 1959*. See Barnes in *RG.I*, p. 38. Size 7′ 4″×2′ 7½″.	C. van Raalte; Sir A. Wheeler, Brownsea Island; Miss D. L. Smith, Wickhambrook, Suffolk; Raymond Russell.	Edinburgh University.
73	A(I)2	1 [Suppl.]	1609	H	1	*AR* rose. C–D, 4 octaves plus 1 tone. Date on soundboard. Black naturals; 2×8′, 1×4′; operable by knobs on the foreboard or by 3 pedals added by Lambert. The case was extended and veneered in England in the eighteenth century. The present wrestplank, bottom, keys, jack-slides, and jacks are by Dolmetsch, but the keyframe and the 8′ wrestplank bridge, transferred to the new wrestplank by Dolmetsch, are eighteenth-century. Decorative paper round the inside of the case above the soundboard, patched by Lambert but probably mostly original. Illustrated in *Apollo*, September/October 1943, p. 99. Size 6′ 0″×2′ 7″.	Arnold Dolmetsch; Herbert Lambert, Bath.	Peter Williams, Edinburgh (1967).
74	A(I)3	2	1610	V	1	*AR* rose. C–C, 4 octaves, bass short octave. White naturals. Keyboard to the right. Date on soundboard; has arpichordum stop. Illustrated in 1941 Boston Catalogue. Size 4′ 3″×1′ 6″.	Canon F. W. Galpin.	Boston, Mass., Museum of Fine Arts.
75	A(I)4	44	1611	V	1	*AR* rose and date on soundboard. An inscription on the (ill-fitting and presumably not original) jackrail *Ioannes Ruckers Fecit Antwerpiae* caused it to be recorded also under Hans the Elder. (See above, no. 15.) C/E–C, 4 octaves; keyboard to the right. Illustrated in *Russell 1959*. Size 5′ 7½″×1′ 2¼″.	A. Jacob-Wens, Antwerp; Antwerp, Rubens-Huis.	Antwerp, Vleeshuis (given to Antwerp before 1876 by A. Jacob-Wens.)
76	A(I)5		1613	V	1	*AR* rose. C–C, 4 octaves, bass short octave. White naturals. Keyboard to the left. Date on soundboard. Patterned paper (modern reproduction). Crudely repaired in 1930. Size 3′ 8¾″×1′ 4¾″.	Matthias van der Gheyn, 1740; Chev. X. van Elevyck, Louvain.	Brussels Conservatoire (no. M. 274).
77	A(I)6	3	1613	V	1	*AR* rose. C–C, 4 octaves, bass short octave. White naturals. Keyboard to the left. Date on soundboard. Size 3′ 8½″×1′ 5½″.	M. Haveaux, Rebecq-Rognon; C. Snoeck.	Brussels Conservatoire (no. M. 2928).
78	A(I)7	4	1614	H	2	*AR* rose. A–E, 4½ octaves. White naturals; 2×8′, 1×4′, but 4 registers. Much altered in England in the eighteenth century, and again restored in 1949. Illustrated Boddington Catalogue (no. 12). Size 7′ 5″×2′ 8″.	Dr. Blow, Bath; the Revd. J. Bower, Bath; Gen. Hopkinson; J. K. Pyne; Boddington College, Manchester; Howard Head, London; W. C. Priestley and Messrs. Angell, Bath.	Leonard Elmhirst, Dartington Hall.

No.	No. in *GD* 5th edn.	No. in *GD* 4th edn.	Date	Type	No. of Kbs.	Remarks	Former owners	Present or recent owner
79	A(I)8	32	1615	H	1	Rose missing and no maker's inscription. Attributed to A(I) by Russell on structural grounds (*GD5*). 2 keyframes; keys missing. Originally a transposing instrument. Pivot-pins for lower keyboard rearranged. Compass of upper keyboard was C–C, 4 octaves, bass short octave, 45 notes; of the lower, C–F, bass short octaves, 50 notes. 1 × 8′, 1 × 4′, 4 rows of jacks. Iron plates guiding the extra strings on the wrestplank bridges. Date 1615 on soundboard. Buffstop. Probably came from church of St. Jacques. Size 7′ 6″ × 2′ 7″. Probably = no. 80.	Musée du Steen, Antwerp.	Antwerp, Vleeshuis (given anonymously before 1876).
[80]	[A(I)8a]	5	1615	H	2	Regarded by Russell (*GD5*) as same instrument as no. 79. Probably had 2 keyboards originally.	Antwerp, Church of St. James.	
81	A(I)9	—	1617	H	2	*HR* [*sic*] rose, signed *Andreas Ruckers* on the jackrail; 2 × 8′, 1 × 4′. *VdM* regards it as probably a southern-French instrument of the eighteenth century.	Dr. Hanns Neupert.	Nuremberg, Germanisches Nationalmuseum.
82	[Suppl.] A(I)9a	—	1617	V	1	*AR* rose, and *Andreas Ruckers* inscribed on jackrail and above keys. Present compass C–F, 4½ octaves. Keyboard to the left. One of the only 2 full-size Ruckers-signed instruments of this type.		Munich, Deutsches Museum.
83	A(I)10	6	1618	H	1	*AR* rose, 2 stops. Size 7′ 4″ × 2′ 10″. See Friedrich Ernst in *GSJ*, Vol. 20 (1967) and A. Berner in *RG.I*, pp. 53–6.		Berlin Collection.
[83a]	—	7	1619	H	2	Sculptured rose. Attributed to Andreas.	Régibo.	
[83b]	—	—	1619	—	—	Nameboard only, inscribed: *Andreas Ruckers me fecit Antwerpiae 1619*.		Brussels Conservatoire.
84	A(I)11	8	1620	H	2	*AR* rose. G–F nearly 5 octaves with bass short octave. Date on soundboard; 2 × 8′, 1 × 4′ strings, but 4 registers so that two 8′ rows of jacks pluck the same 8′ strings. Originally a transposing instrument. (See Friedrich Ernst in *GSJ*, Vol. 20 (1967) and A. Berner in *RG.I*, pp. 56–60.) Size 5′ 10″ × 2′ 8″.		
85	A(I)12	9	1620	V	1	*AR* rose. C–C, 4 octaves with bass short octave. White naturals. Keyboard to the left. Illustrated in Steinert Collection catalogue (1893) and in *Wash 1969*. Size 3′ 7″ × 1′ 5″.	Morris Steinert, New Haven, Conn.; Hugo Worch, Washington.	Washington, Smithsonian Institution.
86	A(I)13	10	1620	V		*AR* rose. C–C, 4 octaves, chromatic. White naturals. Keyboard to right. Modern reprint of patterned paper. Date on soundboard. Much restored. Signs that the original compass was C/E–C, 4 octaves. Illustrated in *J*, pl. 25.	V. and J. Mahillon, Brussels.	Brussels Conservatoire (no. 1597).
87	[A(I)13a]	11	1620	V	1	C–C, 4 octaves, bass short octave. White naturals. Exhibited Brussels 1880. Possibly = no. 88.	Campo, Brussels.	

No.	No. in *GD* 5th edn.	No. in *GD* 4th edn.	Date	Type	No. of Kbs.	Remarks	Former owners	Present or recent owner
88	— —		1620(?)	V	1	Inscribed on jackrail: *Andreas Ruckers me fecit Antverpiae.* Rose with *AR*. The present owner has found no date visible on the instrument. She suggests that C. Mercier-Ythier, who restored it, may have found the date inside.	Henri Prunières, who bought it in Belgium *c.* 1920.	Gif-sur-Yvette, Mme F. Labeyrie (daughter of M. Prunières).
88a	—	—	1621	H	2	2 × 8′, 1 × 4′; 4 rows of jacks. Lid painted by L. J. Vernet.		Sinaia (Romania), Palace Museum (formerly tne palace of the Hohenzollern King Carol I).
[89]	—	—	1622	H	2	*AR* rose and *Andreas Ruckers* . . . inscription on the nameboard, but actually by a member of the Blanchet family (my Blanchet no. 1), q.v. [*VdMCemRuck*, p. 10].		Frankfurt am Main, Museum für Kunsthandwerk.
90	[A(I)13b]	12	1623	V	1		Mahillon.	?
91	A(I)14	13	1623	H	2	*AR* rose. F–F, 5 octaves. Rebuilt and case veneered in England in the eighteenth century—in fact perhaps English. Size 7′ 9″ × 3′ 1″.	John Hillah, London; Mrs. J. Cyriax, London; Capt. J. Lane, Wanstead.	Rickmansworth, E. W. Clark (in 1956).
92	(AI 15)	14	1624	H	1	*AR* rose. Originally a 2-manual, as the depth of the case shews, and almost certainly a transposer. *Ravalé* to 5 octaves (F–F) in the eighteenth century. Inscription on inside of lid: *1624 Musica laetitiae | comes ⟨et⟩ medicina dolorum.* Date also on soundboard. The right cheekpiece (presumably the original one cut off at the back) shews where the space for a 4th jackslide was filled in. Moreover, the lengthened jackrail is 3¾″ wide. Thus there can be little doubt that it was originally a transposing instrument. The original compass would then have been C/E–F, 4½ octaves on the lower manual. The present registration is 2 × 8′, 1 × 4′, with a buff worked by a genouillère. See further E. M. Ripin in *GSJ*, Vol. 21 (1968). Size at present 7′ 0″ × 3′ 1″.		Bruges, Museum Gruuthuuse.
93	—	15	1626	V	1	3½ octaves plus 2 notes; compass extended in the eighteenth century.	E. van der Straeten.	
94	(AI 16)	—	1627	H	1	*AR* rose. Originally a 'quint' harpsichord with 1 × 8′, 1 × 4′ stops and compass C/E–C. For a detailed and illustrated account see van der Meer in *GSJ*, Vol. 18 (1965), with a postscript in *GSJ*, Vol. 21 (1968), p. 209. Size 4′ 0½″ × 2′ 3¼″.	D. F. Scheurleer, The Hague.	The Hague, Gemeentemuseum.
95	HR unnumbered & A(I)17 & [H23d]	16 & 17 and HR23	1628	H	2	*AR* rose. Converted into a grand pianoforte by Zeitter; converted back again to a harpsichord by Hugh Gough. Date on soundboard. Illustrated in *Old furniture*, September 1927. Originally a French instrument with a soundboard made up of pieces of old virginal soundboards, probably Flemish and possibly Ruckers. Size 7′ 7″ × 3′ 0″.	Balbastre, Paris; James Goding; Earl of Lonsdale (sold 1887); W. H. Burns and Capt. Hall; Viscountess Harcourt; Raymond Russell, who sold it at Sotheby's 9 May 1958 to the present owner.	Dr. J. R. Mirrey, Redhill.
96	—	—	1630	V	1	*AR* rose. Sold at Puttick and Simpson's, 14 December 1910.	Prince de Caraman de Chimay.	?

No.	No. in *GD* 5th edn.	No. in *GD* 4th edn.	Date	Type	No. of Kbs.	Remarks	Former owners	Present or recent owner
97	[A(I)17a]	18	1632(?)	V	1	*AR* rose. Date almost illegible. C–F, 4½ octaves. Handwritten on back of nameboard: *F. D. Graeve . . . orgenist*[?] *. . . in . . . seghem. Wonartig*[?] *bij den . . . digen pastoor*; and *Dit is mijn*, in the eighteenth or early nineteenth century. Keyboard to the right. Size 5′ 8″ × 1′ 7½.″	A. Régibo, Renaix; Wanda Landowska.	Brussels Conservatoire (no. 4600). (Acquired 1972.)
98	A(I)29	34	1632(?)	V	1	*AR* rose. C–F, 4½ octaves, chromatic. Keyboard to the left. Patterned paper. Scratched on the wrestplank is: *A 1632*. There are traces of the keyboard having been lengthened at both ends; original compass C/E–C. Size 3′ 8¾″ × 1′ 5⅝″.		Brussels Conservatoire (no. 1593).
99	[A(I)17b]	19	1633	Ot	1	*AR* rose. C–F, 4½ octaves. Hardwood jacks of double thickness. Keyboard to the left. Size 2′ 1½″ × 1′ 6″.	Régibo.	?
100	A(I)18	20	1633	H	1	*AR* rose. C/E–F, 4½ octaves. Inscribed: *Andreas Ruckers in Antverpen, anno 1633*. Illustrated in P. de Wit's *Perlen . . .* (1892). Now 1 × 8′, 1 × 4′, but may at one time have been 2 × 8′, 1 × 4′. The depth of the case shews that there must originally have been 2 manuals. Originally a transposing instrument. The wrestplank and jackslides are not original so that we cannot determine whether there were originally 4 rows of jacks. Size 7′ 0″ × 2′ 3″.	Paul de Wit, Leipzig.	Leipzig, Heyer Collection.
[101]	Suppl. 18a	—	1633	H	2	*AR* rose. Date on soundboard. Black naturals; 2 × 8′, 1 × 4′. Size 240 × 95 cm. A spurious instrument.	Duca Ernesto del Balzo.	Naples Conservatoire.
102	—	21	1634	V	1	*AR* rose; 4 octaves.	E. de Bricqueville.	
102a	—	—	1634	Ot	1	Many alterations. *Ravalé* in 1763.		Paris, Comtesse de Chambure.
103	—	22	1636	H	2		M. Girard, Paris(?).	May well be the instrument which, at one time in Dijon, now (1971) belongs to Dr. Stefanovitch, Menton [*Chambure*].
[104]	A(I)19	23	1636	H	2	*AR* rose. Inscribed above the keys: *Andre Rukuers, annee 1636*. Not by Ruckers. See below: Taskin, instrument no. 3b.		
105	A(I)21	—	1637	H	1	*AR* rose. C–C, 4 octaves with bass short octave. White naturals. Patterned paper. Date on soundboard. 1 × 8′, 1 × 4′. The rose is a modern facsimile; otherwise the instrument is little changed from its original condition. Numbered *23* on the bottom and top keys, but *24* on the jackslides. Illustrated in *Schott*.	Dr. U. Rück, Nuremberg.	Nuremberg, Germanisches Nationalmuseum (Rück Collection).
106	—	—	1639	H	1	*AR* rose. C–B, nearly 4 octaves, originally C/E–C. Date on soundboard; 2 × 8′ (originally 1 × 8′, 1 × 4′). Jackrail with typical Andreas Ruckers inscription probably a replacement. Much altered.	Musée Charlier, Brussels.	Brussels Conservatoire (no. 3908).
107	A(I)22	31	1639	Ot	1	*AR* rose. Originally part of a double virginal (i.e. the 'child' of a 'mother and child'). Former compass C–C, 4 octaves. Restored in 1961 with original compass C/E–C.	Régibo.	The Hague, Gemeentemuseum.

No.	No. in *GD* 5th edn.	No. in *GD* 4th edn.	Date	Type	No. of Kbs.	Remarks	Former owners	Present or recent owner
108	A(I)20 (and 31)	24 (and 41)	1639	H	1	*AR* rose. Date on soundboard. Converted into a 2-manual instrument in the late eighteenth century, probably in England. Converted back to a single, with 2×8′ and 1×4′ (its original layout), under the direction of J. H. van der Meer in 1962, as described by him in detail in *GSJ*, Vol. 17 (1964), pp. 5–15.	J. K. Pyne; Boddington; Howard Head; E. Dodd Cramp, Byfield; J. Morley; D. F. Scheurleer, The Hague.	The Hague, Gemeentemuseum.
109	A(I)23	25	1640	H	1	*AR* rose. The present foreboard with *Andreas Ruckers 1640* in Gothic lettering is nineteenth-century, but the original small nameboard with *Andreas Ruckers me fecit Antverpiae* remains, though lengthened at both ends when the instrument was extended. Present compass C–D, 4 octaves plus 1 tone; originally C/E–C. White naturals; 1×8′, 1×4′ stops. The 8′ wrestpins were moved back and the original ones, numbering 45, stopped up. The 2 bridges were somewhat lengthened, concealing some of the painted decoration. Date on soundboard. Restored by F. Hubbard, 1971. Illustrated in Belle-Skinner Catalogue. Size 6′ 0″ × 2′ 5½″.	Given by Chas. Burney to the Revd. Thomas Twining, Colchester, *d.* 1804; Miss Twining, Twickenham, who bequeathed it to her niece, Mrs. A. B. Donaldson of Hampstead in 1889; Miss Belle Skinner, Holyoke, Mass.	Yale University.
109a	—	—	1640	H	2	*AR* rose. Date on soundboard. Originally a transposing instrument. Nameboard and keyboards have disappeared. 4 jackslides and divided buffstop. Upper keyboard shews the expected C/E–C, 4 octave compass, but the lower has been re-pinned for G/B–C, 4½ octaves. Although the keyboards were brought into alignment the second 8′ was not added. Traces of sea-horse paper in key-well.	Came from the Château de Francwaret. Was given to the Namur Museum by Comte Vizard de Bocarmé.	Namur, Musée de Croix.
109b	[A(I)31b]	—	1640	V	1	Geometrical rose. C–C, 4 octaves, chromatic. Keyboard to the right. Patterned paper.		Amsterdam, Rijksmuseum.
[110]						Mistaken entry in 1956 edition.		
111?	—	—	1643	V	1	No rose. Date on soundboard. 4 octaves C–C, chromatic; keyboard to the right. No inscription, except date *1643*. Probably a Ruckers.		Amsterdam, Rijksmuseum.
112	A(I)25	40	1644	H	1	*AR* rose. Date on soundboard. C–C, 4 octaves (originally C/E–C). White naturals; 2×8′, but originally 1×8′, 1×4′. Inscription on nameboard: *Andreas Ruckers den Ouden me fecit Antverpiae*. Patterned paper (sea-horses, but white on black). Size 6′ 0″ × 2′ 5″.		

Andreas the Younger, born 1607; latest date ascertained: 1651; he had died by 14 July 1667. (*It seems probable that the division between Andreas I and Andreas II should come here.*)

No.	No. in *GD* 5th edn.	No. in *GD* 4th edn.	Date	Type	No. of Kbs.	Remarks	Former owners	Present or recent owner
113	A(I)24	26	1644	V	2	*AR* rose. Double virginal, the octave instrument being modern and to the left; 4 octaves C–C lacking bottom C sharp. Originally C/E–C. Date on soundboard. Patterned paper. Illustrated in *Po*.	Prince de Caraman de Chimay.	Leipzig University, Heyer Collection.
114	[A(I)25a]	27	1644	V	1	Inscribed *Andreas Ruckers anno 1644*. C–C, 4 octaves. Size 5′ 8″ × 1′ 8″.	Mahillon.	

No.	No. in GD 5th edn.	No. in GD 4th edn.	Date	Type	No. of Kbs.	Remarks	Former owners	Present or recent owner
115	[A(I)26a]	28	1646	H	2	*AR* rose. Inscribed on wrest-plank: *Refait par Pascal Taskin, Paris 1780*; printed label inside the bent side: '*remis à ravalement . . .*'. Keyboards probably Blanchet's work. 2×8′, 1×4′ (all dated 1756), *peau de buffle* (dated 1780). Restored by H. Bédard. Genouillère action illustrated in *RipExpr*. Size 7′ 5″×3′ 0″.	At the Paul Eudel sale of 1898 bought by Mme Adrien Allez, from whose daughters' heirs it was acquired in 1962 by the present owner.	Mme de Chambure (but on exhibition at Paris Conservatoire).
115a	—	—	1646	H	1	Originally 1×8′, 1×4′, C/E–C, 4 octaves. Extended in Flanders in the eighteenth century to C–F, 4½ octaves, another 8′ stop being added. The full drawing of the enlargement was found on the inside of the bottom, with notes in Flemish.	Brussels, Alphonse Van Neste.	Boston, Mass., William Post Ross.
116?	26	—	1646	H	1	*AR* rose. F–E, nearly 5 octaves, without lowest F sharp. Perhaps an English eighteenth-century instrument.		Lord Tollemache, Helmingham Hall, Ipswich.
117	—	29	1648	H	1	*AR* rose. Restored in 1965 by Frank Hubbard, who made the rose; 2×8′, 1×4′ stops.	New York, Otto van Koppenhagen; Amsterdam, Professor G. Leonhardt.	Copenhagen, Musikhistorisk Museum (bought 1968).
118	A(I)27	30	1651	H	2	*AR* rose. Date on soundboard. Said to have belonged to Handel. G–F without bottom G sharp. Originally 1 manual only with the normal 4-octave compass. [See *Russell 1959*, p. 166; also *GSJ*, 1968, p. 38.] Illustrated in *RussellV&A*. Size 6′ 7″×2′ 11¼″.	Christopher Smith; Lady Rivers; Mr. Wickham; Canon Hawtrey; Dr. Chard; Mr. Hooper; Messrs. Broadwood (1852).	London, Victoria and Albert Museum.
118a	—	—	1651	H	1	*AR* rose. Inscribed on name-board: *Andreas Ruckers And: F[ilius] me fecit Antwerpiae.* Date on soundboard; 2×8′, 1×4′ stops. Keywell lined with sea-horse paper. Compass C–D, 4 octaves plus 2 notes; but various internal evidence points to an original compass of C/E–D.		P. Maxwell-Stuart, Traquair House, Peebles, where it has probably been since it was first imported.
119	A(I)28	—	1654(?)	H	2	*AR* rose. Inscribed on jackrail, which, however, is not original but probably eighteenth-century: *Andrea Ruckers me fecit Antverpiae anno 1654*. Originally 1-manual, with compass C/E–C. Second manual added, probably in the Low Countries in the eighteenth century and compass extended to C–E. A 3rd extension produced the present compass of G/B–F. 2×8′, 1×4′ stops.	Dr. Hanns Neupert.	Nuremberg, Germanisches Nationalmuseum.
120	A(II)1	1	1655	H	?		M. Lavigné (from the Château de Perceau, near Cosne).	
121	A(II)2	2	1656	H	1	*AR* rose. C–D, 4 octaves plus 1 tone; white naturals. Size 5′ 4½″×2′ 2½″.	Régibo.	?
122	A(II)3	3	1659	H	1	*AR* rose. C–C, 4 octaves; white naturals. Size 5′ 10″×2′ 4″.	Régibo.	?
123	A(II)4	4	1667			'Un beau clavecin' reported by Fétis in 1865.		?
—	—	—	1672	H	2	Frankfurt am Main. See above, no. 89.		?

No.	No. in *GD* 5th edn.	No. in *GD* 4th edn.	Date	Type	No. of Kbs.	Remarks	Former owners	Present or recent owner
Undated instruments by either ***Andreas I*** or ***Andreas II***								
124	A(II)5	5	n.d.	V	1	*AR* rose. Keyboard to the left. D–E, 4 octaves plus 1 tone. White naturals.	Régibo.	?
125	[A(I)28a]	33	n.d.	H	2	F–F, 5 octaves. Black naturals. Extended 1758 (date on a jack). Exhibited Brussels, 1880. Size 7′ 3″×2′ 11″.	Baron de Goer, Château de Velu, Pas de Calais (in 1883).	?
126	[A(I)29a]	35	n.d.	H	2	No rose. G–F, nearly 5 octaves with bass short octave. White naturals. Size 6′ 6″×2′ 8″.	Snoeck.	?
127	[A(I)29b]	36	—	V	1	*AR* rose. C–C, 4 octaves with bass short octave. Size 3′ 8″×1′ 4″.	Snoeck.	?
128	[A(I)29c]	37	—	H	1	*AR* rose. C–C, 4 octaves without bottom C sharp. White naturals. Hunting scene on lid. Size 6′ 1″×2′ 10″.	Gérard de Prins, Louvain.	?
129	[A(I)29d]	38	—	Ot	1	*AR* rose. Keyboard projects 4″. C–D, 4 octaves plus 2 notes, bass short octave. Patterned paper; eighteenth-century mahogany case. Size 2′ 8″×1′ 0½″.	W. H. Hammond Jones, Witley, Godalming.	?
130	(AI)30	—	—	H	1	*AR* rose. No keys, but originally 47; 1×8′, 1×4′, but at one time 2×8′. Red marbled case.	Musée du Steen(?).	Antwerp, Vleeshuis.
—	(AI)31 (and 20)	41 (and 24)	—	H	2	Same as no. 108 above, q.v.		
[130a]	—	—	—	H	2	*AR* rose. Stamped on the wrest-plank: *Fait par Pascal Taskin à Paris 1780*. See below under 'Taskin', instrument no. 3a.		Milan, Museo Civico di Antichi Strumenti Musicali.
[131]	[A(I)31a]	42	—	H	2	Crude *AR* rose glued on top of soundboard. Black naturals; E–F, 5 octaves plus 1 note; 62 keys. No signs of *ravalement*, and so cannot have left, in its present state, the Ruckers workshop. Probably a French eighteenth-century instrument. Jacks and wrestplank modern.	Albert Steinert, Providence, R.I.	Providence, R. I., School of Design.
132	[A(I)31b]	43	—	H	2	*AR* rose. Date illegible. G–F, nearly 4 octaves. White naturals. Size 5′ 6″×3′ 0″.	Mrs. Alex Steinert of Boston, Mass., and Beverly, Mass.	(The Steinert family had no knowledge of this instrument in 1954.)
133	Suppl.	—	—	Ot	1	*AR* rose. The 'child' of a 'mother and child' double virginal. Signature on jackrail: *Andreas Ruckers fecit Antwerpiae.*		Cincinnati Museum of Art.
[134]	—	—	n.d.	H	2	*AR* rose. F–D, 4 octaves plus a 6th; 2×8′, 1×4′ (originally 1×8′, 1×4′), front row of jacks doglegged; black naturals, sloping ivory sharps; projecting slides. Jackrail (not original) reads: *Andrea Ruckers me fecit Antwerpiae.* Lid in one piece (i.e. does not fold back). Inside lid a painting of Flemish village dancing. This was originally a single-manual instrument (see *GSJ*, 1968, p. 38). It is illustrated in *MGG*, Vol. 11 (1963), pl. 58. It is probably early eighteenth-century French.	Brussels, Galerie Giroux (July 1954).	Brussels, Knud Kaufmann.
Christoffel [Christopher]								
135						*See above*: R, C.		
136						*See above*: R, C.		

No.	No. in GD 5th edn.	No. in GD 4th edn.	Date	Type	No. of Kbs.	Remarks	Former owners	Present or recent owner
Ruckers (not known which)								
136a	—	—	—	H	2	*Ravalé* by Dubois in 1780.		Paris, Y. Le Gaillard [*ChamP*].
Attributed formerly to a member of the **Ruckers** *family*								
[137]	—	—	1770	H	2	F–F, 5 octaves; 2×8′, buff, coupler. Illustrated by *J* (p. 127) who attributed it to the Ruckers family without giving his evidence. This instrument is actually by Taskin and is recorded below as his no. 2a, q.v.	S. Grimson, New York.	Yale University.
Possibly by a member of the **Ruckers** *family*								
138?	—	—	—	H	1	Rose resembles a crude *IR* rose lacking the *I*; the instrument was badly damaged by fire before its latest rebuilding. Inscribed on underside of soundboard: *refait par pierre dubois sis a Paris 1730 rue St honoré vis a vis Les ecurÿ du roÿ.* Repaired in 1971 by C. Mercier-Ythier, who considers the case 'undoubtedly a Ruckers'.		Paris, private ownership (1971).
139?	—	—	—	H	2	Patterned rose. Not inscribed. Extended in bass *c.* 1700, making the length 3 metres. Resembles very closely the Paris instrument of 1612 (no. 17a above). Michael Thomas considers it a Ruckers instrument.		Michael Thomas, Hurley (November 1971).

RUDLOFF, Rudolph Friedrich Leopold, of Brunswick, *fl.* 1795. He was a journeyman joiner, and obtained a concession on 21 April 1795 to make keyboard instruments, including organs, in spite of the opposition of the Joiners' Guild [*SB*, p. 50].

RUELLE, Pierre. Harpsichord maker in Paris, *c.* 1700–after 1754. In 1753 he became *juré comptable* of the Guild of Instrument Makers.

RUELLE, Joachim. Second son of Pierre (the elder by his second marriage). Harpsichord maker in Paris; *c.* 1732–after 1789. Master in 1755.

RUESE. *See*: KUESE, P.

RUETSCHI, Fridolin, of Bütschurl in the canton of St. Gall. Lived in Lucerne 1742–1822. In 1784 an advertisement announced that he made 'Flügel mit Federnwerk'—presumably harpsichords [*Rindl*].

RUIVE. Harpsichord maker at Liverpool, probably in the eighteenth century. On 11 January 1790 there was sold at Christie's:

> Item 36. A fine toned single keyed harpsichord with 4 stops by Ruive of Liverpool. [Vendor anon.; buyer Yeatman; price £1. 10*s*.]

RUNGELL, Mattheus. Instrument maker at Augsburg. Born 1565; still alive in 1622. An automatic claviorganum (organ plus spinet) by him is preserved in the Mathematisch-Physikalischer Salon at Dresden. Signed on a metal plate: *Mattheus Rungell, Augspurg* [*VdMBei*, pp. 125–6].

RYDER, Charles. Harpsichord maker at 88 Marlborough Street, Dublin, 1800–6 [*Teahan*].

S, C. *See*: SLADE, Charles.

S, G. The Deutsches Museum, Munich, has a harpsichord inscribed *G.S. a.D. 1729* on the top and bottom keys, which suggests perhaps either Giuseppe Solfanelli or Giuseppe Si as the maker. Its compass is $4\frac{1}{2}$ octaves; 2×8′, 1×4′, buff. Another harpsichord by G.S., dated 1722, is cited by *Hubb 1965* without a note of its location.

S, I. H. An eighteenth-century Italian harpsichord offered for sale at Sotheby's on 21 December 1972 bears on the top key the initials *IHS* with a cross. C–F, $4\frac{1}{2}$ octaves. Length 7′ $5\frac{1}{2}$″. The vendor was H. C. Robbins Landon. The inscription presumably stands for *Iesus hominum salvator*, not for the maker's name.

S, N. V. An Italian ottavino spinet in the Berlin Collection bears an inscription including *N.V.S. A. 1757*, whose authenticity is regarded by *Sa* (p. 62) as open to question.

SABBATINI, Galeazzo. Composer and theoretician, was born at Pesaro towards the end of the sixteenth century. [See further *Fé, Eit.*] He is said to have invented a harpsichord with enharmonic tuning [A. Kircher, *Musurgia universalis* . . . (1610), I. 460].

SABERINO, P. Gasparro. Italian harpsichord maker, *fl.* 1612. A harpsichord of this date (with outer case, C–C, 4 octaves, 2×8′ stops) was offered for sale in 1971 by the Parisian dealer René Denis [*GL*, who considers the instrument genuine].

SADRE, Marco. *See*: JADRA, Marco.

SALETZ, Nicolaus. Possibly a harpsichord maker in southern Germany (? Stuttgart) in the sixteenth century, to judge from an entry in a 1589 inventory of the instruments at the court of Eberhard III [*WVS*, Vol. 21 (1912), pp. 133–7].

SALODIENSIS. Three makers have this final name, which one would expect to be formed from a place-name (? Salò near Brescia):

(1) **Alberto**, *fl.* 1573. A collection of instruments offered for sale anonymously in France (1953) contains a virginal which is said to be inscribed *Alberti Salodiensis* [?*O*]*PVS* and dated 1573.

(2) **Baptista Carenonus,** *fl.* 1689. The same collection has a harpsichord dated 1689, decorated in black and gold chinoiserie, with a rose, apparently inscribed *Baptista Carenonus Sali*[*o* ?]*diensis MDCLXXXIX.*

(3) **Joseph,** *fl.* 1559–74. Vienna Kunsthistorisches Museum has a harpsichord inscribed *Joseph Salodiensis fecit Anno Dni MDLIX.* 2×8′ registers. C/E–C, 4 octaves. See further *Luith*, pp. 12–13.

The Boston Museum of Fine Arts has (1970) on loan from Mrs. Ada MacArthur of Scituate, Mass., a polygonal virginal inscribed on the nameboard: *Joseph Salodiensis F . . . MDLXIIII.* Compass C/E–F, 3½ octaves. Rose.

SANTINI, A. Spinet maker of Arezzo, *fl.* 1570 [*Va*].

Surviving Instruments

(1) 1570. Brussels Conservatoire. Polygonal virginal, inscribed: *A. Santinius in Arezzo, 1570.* Rose. 176×56 cm.

(2?) *Francl* lists a 'spinetta' inscribed: *A. Santinus 1571.*

SARAISSAC, François, of Lyons. Clavichord maker, *fl.* 1670 [*Va*].

SASSADIAS, Johann Sigismund. In 1740, organist at the parish church in Brieg. Mattheson praises his skill not only as an organist but also as a craftsman. He made harpsichords and clavichords [*Ge, Fé, Va*].

SAUMET, Nicholas Joseph. Harpsichord maker in Versailles. A native of Besançon [*Verlet*].

SAUMLIN, Anton. *See*: SOUMLIN, Anton.

SAVEUR, Joseph. Maker of clavichords ('monocordi') at 'La Flèche' in 1653 [*Va*].

SCAPPA, Petrus, of Milan. *Francl* lists a 'spinetta' signed: *Petrus Scappa Mediolani 1670.*

SCHAAR, Timotheus, of Lübeck. Dates ascertained: 1647–50. He lived in M. Andreas Poeleke's house in the Kurze Königsstrasse. He was a schoolmaster, but also made viols and other instruments, probably including keyboard instruments [*Lü*].

SCHANTZ, Johann. Lived in Vienna. Dates ascertained, 1780–90. He called himself 'Bürgerl. Orgel und Instrument Macher', which probably includes harpsichords and clavichords. He probably made harps, guitars, and violins as well [*Lü*].

SCHAUTZ, Mathieu. Maker of clavichords, harpsichords, and pianos at Augsburg, 1755–1831.

A 5-octave (F–F) clavichord by him in the Neupert Collection, Germanisches Nationalmuseum, Nuremberg, is inscribed: *Mathieu Schautz, faisseur de Clavecin et de Fortepiano 1793 à Augsbourg.*

SCHEIBE, Johann, of Leipzig. Organ and clavichord maker. Born 1710; still alive 1765 [*Kü*].

SCHENK, Johann Georg. Pupil of J. A. Stein; born at Ostheim, 1766; maker of clavichords and pianofortes at Weimar, where he was Hof-Instrumentenmacher in 1817. He died about 1830.

Ks (II. 665) quotes an advertisement in *Musikalische Real-Zeitung* (Speyer, 1788) of pianofortes (grand and square) and clavichords: 'Simple bundfreie Klaviere mit einem hellen singenden Ton, und sehr fleissig und fein gearbeitet von Nussbaumen Holz 8 Karolin.' A square by Schenk dated 1817, formerly in the possession of the Lortzings family, is in the Bach-Haus at Eisenach; a MS. note by Obrist on the maker's label gives Schenk's date of birth as 1766 and the fact that he was a pupil of Stein.

SCHERI, Fortunato Maria. Son of Adamo Scheri; of Benedello, virginal maker. Dates unknown [*Va*].

SCHERZER, *c.* 1780. Organist at the cathedral of Merseburg. He appears to have been a maker of clavichords as well [*Eit*].

SCHETZ, Carolus J.—the spelling of the surname is not certain—of Bratislava. Repaired, in March 1767, a number of instruments at the Esterházy court, including 2 spinets and a harpsichord [*Walter*, p. 258].

SCHETZ, Edmonde. Stringed-keyboard-instrument maker in London, *fl.* 1587–1601 [*Russell 1959*, p. 65].

SCHIEDMAYER. The house of Schiedmayer, like that of Broadwood, originating in the eighteenth century as makers of clavichords or harpsichords and later of pianofortes, has continued to the present day. A full account of the family, with a list of instruments surviving from the early times, is given by *Rupprecht*. Only 4 members concern us here:

(1) **Balthasar,** born at Erlangen 1711, died there 1781. Son of a baker, he worked for some time as a joiner and then turned to instrument making ('Orgel- und Claviermacher', 1775). No instruments from his hand are known today, although an early catalogue of the 'Pianofortefabrik Schiedmayer' at Stuttgart recorded a clavichord made by Balthasar in 1735.

Of his 5 children 3 were sons, all of whom were instrument makers:

(2) **Johann Christoph Georg**, born at Erlangen 1740, died Neustadt an der Aisch 1820; eldest son of Balthasar. Several clavichords from his workshop have survived. If he made any pianofortes, none are known today.

(3) **Adam Achatius**, born at Erlangen 1745, died there 1817; second son of Balthasar, whose workshop he carried on. *Ge* calls him 'Instrumentenmacher'. Only 1 instrument from his hand has survived, a grand pianoforte (now in the Rück Collection, Germanisches Nationalmuseum, Nuremberg), whose label on the soundboard reads: *Adam Achatius Schiedmayer Instrumentenmacher in Erlangen 1797*. Although it is not certain that he made clavichords, it is likely that a few came from his workshop in his early years.

(4) **Johann David**, born at Erlangen 1753, died at Nuremberg 1805; third son of Balthasar, by whom he was sent in 1778 as a pupil to Johann Andreas Stein in Augsburg. From then until his death Johann David kept a workshop book recording details of each of his instruments. Most unfortunately this book was destroyed when the premises of Schiedmayer were bombed in 1943, although a few passages from it had been transcribed by *Eisenmann*.

On the death of his father in 1781, Johann David returned to Erlangen, where he set up his own workshop, being awarded, at some time before 1781, the title *Hochfürstl. Hofinstrumentenmacher Erlangen*. By this time he was making mostly pianofortes, but that he still made some clavichords is proved by the bundfrei instrument of 1791 formerly preserved by the firm of Schiedmayer in their Stuttgart factory but destroyed by bombing in 1943.

Johann David never had more than one assistant in his workshop—indeed he often worked alone—although later his sons helped him. His conscientious craftsmanship is emphasized by *Ge*: '. . . auch die kleinsten zur Mechanik gehörigen Partikelchen durch seine eigenen Hände gehen könnten. Dafür sind aber auch seine Instrumente von innen und von aussen, fürs Auge und fürs Ohr, das Non plus ultra in ihrer Art.' Other contemporary accounts of Johann David, cited by *Rupp*, pp. 52 ff., make it clear that by the 1790s he had reached the front rank of instrument makers.

In 1797 he moved to Nuremberg, where he was joined by a former apprentice of his, Georg Kohlmann, and where he died on 20 March 1805.

Johann David married 3 times. A son of his first marriage, Johann Lorenz (1786–1860), carried on for a few months the workshop in Nuremberg: 'Den 30. September [1805] habe den Resonanzboden eingeleimbt an dem ersten Pianoforte, das ich nach dem Tode meines Vaters gemacht habe . . .' [quoted by *Eisenmann*]. But within a year he had left Nuremberg for Vienna, where he made friends with Carl Dieudonné, who was working for Nanette Streicher. In 1809 the two moved to Stuttgart, where they founded the house of Schiedmayer, which still flourishes today.

A portrait of Johann David, owned by the firm of Schiedmayer, is reproduced in *Rupp*.

Tree of SCHIEDMAYER

JOHANN SCHIEDMAYER
of Erlangen, baker, *m.* 1710

- **Balthasar** (*b.* Erlangen 1711; *d.* there 1781)
  - **Johann Christoph Georg** (*b.* Erlangen 1740; *d.* Neustadt a.d. Aisch 1820)
  - **Adam Achatius** (*b.* Erlangen 1745; *d.* there 1817)
    - Johann Erhardt (*b.* Erlangen 1787; *d.* there 1821)
      - [2 daughters]
      - Johann Lorenz (*b.* Erlangen 1814; *d.* there 1895)
      - Georg (*b.* Erlangen 1817; *d.* there 1884)
  - **Johann David** (*b.* Erlangen 1753; *d.* Nuremberg 1805). Married twice; a son by his 1st wife was:
    - Johann Lorenz (*b.* Erlangen 1786; *d.* Stuttgart 1860) His partnership with Carl Dieudonné was the origin of the modern:
      - ⋮ House of Schiedmayer, Stuttgart
  - [2 daughters]

Note: All the members in this tree (except the original Johann S.) made pianofortes. Those in bold type made clavichords also. (Although no clavichord by Adam Achatius has survived, it may be taken as certain that he made a few clavichords in his early years.)

TABLE 30. *SCHIEDMAYER Clavichords*

. B = Balthasar; JCG = Johann Christoph Georg; JD = Johann David.

(*Note*: Many of the Schiedmayer instruments surviving from the classical period are listed in *Rupp*.)

No.	Old no.	Maker	Date	Signature	Owner/Remarks
1	—	B	1735		Recorded in an early catalogue of the firm of Schiedmayer; now lost.
2	—	JCG	?1770		Formerly the property of the firm of Schiedmayer, but destroyed in World War II. Described and illustrated in *Eisenmann*.
3	—	?	1776	*Jean Ether* [?] *G. Schiedmayer 1776*	Mrs. Carl Parrish, U.S.A. Compass: F–A, 5 octaves and 4 notes. Inscription on inside; visible through the rose in the soundboard. Repaired by J. C. Neupert, Nuremberg, in 1936.
4	1	JCG	1782	. . . *mayer, Neustadt an der Aisch*	Stuttgart, Württembergisches Landesgewerbemuseum, Baden-Württemberg. Bundfrei. Josten's catalogue (1928) gives no date. *Ks*, Vol. 2 (1912) refers to a bundfrei clavichord in Stuttgart Museum dated 1728, which is presumably this instrument. *Rupp* (p. 102) says that no date appears on the instrument, but the Museum catalogue gives 1782. C–A, 4 octaves and a 6th.
5	—	JCG	1787		Formerly in Neupert Collection. Sold to Professor Becking at Erlangen, 1930. Present location unknown; possibly = 6 or 7.
6	—	?	1787		Owned by Messrs. Hubbard & Dowd in 1953.
7	2	JCG	1787	*Verfertigt von Johann Christoph Georg Schiedmayer in Neustadt an der Aisch 1787*	Formerly in Neupert Collection. Destroyed in World War II; 5 octaves F–F.
8	3	?	1789	*Verfertiget / Schiedmäyer / in Neustadt an der Aisch / 1789*	Formerly in the Steinert Collection. Illustrated in 1892 Catalogue. F–G, 5 octaves plus 2 notes. Listed in 1912 Catalogue. Not at Yale University, 1954. Probably the clavichord by J. C. G. Schiedmayer owned by Eric Herz, Boston, Mass., 1966, which is signed on the underside of the soundboard; inscription on paper label.
9	—	JD	1791	*Johann David Schiedmayer, Hochfürstlich Anspachischer Instrumentenmacher in Erlangen 1791*	Stuttgart, firm of Schiedmayer. Bundfrei; 5 octaves and a 2nd F–G. Black naturals, white sharps. Illustrated in *Rupp*. Destroyed in World War II.
10	—	JCG	1792	*Johann . . . Schiedmayer Orgel- und Instrumentenmacher in Neustadt an der Aisch 1792*	Stuttgart, firm of Schiedmayer. Bundfrei; 4 octaves and a 4th C–F. Black naturals, white sharps. Illustrated in *Rupp*. Destroyed in World War II.
11	—	JCG	1793		Würzburg, E. Müller-Schiedmayer (1971) [*VdM*].
12	5	JCG	1796	*Johann Christoff Georg / Schiedmäyer / in Neustadt an der Aisch / 1796* [This date was formerly misread as 1790]	Forest Hills, N.Y., E. M. Ripin. (Formerly Princeton University, Arthur Mendel (1954); formerly owned by Mrs. Alexander Steinert.) Underside of soundboard signed: *Schiedmäyer / in Neustadt an der Aisch / 1795*.

SCHIFFENSTEIN. Keyboard-instrument maker, *fl.* at Dresden in 1618 [*Fla*, p. 220 n.].

SCHIRMER, Johann Georg. Was born at Hauröden in the principality of Schwarzburg-Sondershausen. He was a pupil of Friederici in Gera for a considerable time, and later rivalled his teacher in the quality of his instruments. From 1782 onwards he lived at Sondershausen, where he built all manner of keyboard instruments, but especially clavichords and pianos.

The biographer Gerber possessed a large grand piano made by him.

Schirmer became court instrument maker of Schwarzburg. He died in 1790 [*Ge*, 1794].

SCHLEGEL, Elias (I) of Altenburg in Saxony, *fl.* 1730. Made lutes, harps, and keyboard instruments [*Lü*]. (Contemporaneously a Christian Schlegel, perhaps his brother, made wind instruments and harps at Basel [*Vannes*].)

SCHLEGEL, Elias (II) of Altenburg. In 1794 (according to *Nor*, p. 149, who refers to the *Hamburgischer Correspondent* for 1794, no. 10) he constructed a combined harpsichord and pianoforte.

SCHLEGEL, Jeremias, of Basel. Maker of keyboard instruments; *Hirt* gives him the surprisingly prolonged *floruit* of 1730–92. *Va* records a Schlegel, of Swiss nationality, resident in Basel as a harpsichord maker in 1794.

But there appears to be some confusion amongst makers bearing the name Schlegel.

SCHMAHL. Family of German instrument makers, divided chiefly between Heilbronn, Ulm, and Regensburg. The following concern us here:

(1) **Friedrich,** *fl.* 1692 at Regensburg. Maker of clavichords and other instruments. His relationship to the other members of the family is not known.

A clavichord dated 1692, 5 octaves in compass, and shaped like a harpsichord, is recorded by Bierdimpfl in his catalogue of the instruments in the Bayerisches Nationalmuseum, Munich, 1883. This instrument has disappeared. Hanns Neupert considered that it was a small clavichord in a wing-shaped case, similar to one in the Neupert Collection.

(2) **Georg Friedrich,** *the Elder*, 1700–73, of Heilbronn and Ulm. Born at Heilbronn; 1723 in Augsburg; 1729 moved to Ulm. Pupil of his father. Maker of organs (he built 43) and other instruments. A surviving guitar by him inscribed *Georg Friedrich Schmahl, Orgel- und Instrumentmacher in Ulm, 1757*, is figured at *Herrm*, p. 36.

(3) **Carl Friedrich,** *fl.* 1790 at Regensburg [*VdM*]. See instrument 1a and 1b.

(4) **Johann Matthäus,** 1734–93, of Ulm. Made organs, clavichords, pianofortes, and violins. About 1770 he made a small number of harp-shaped square pianos ('Hammerklaviere in Harfenform'), examples of which survive in the Württembergisches Landesgewerbemuseum, Stuttgart (pictured in Josten's catalogue, p. 34), in the Rück Collection in the Germanisches Nationalmuseum, Nuremberg, in the Mozarteum at Salzburg, in the collection of Dr. Fritz Ernst, Sierne, Geneva, and in the possession of C. F. Colt of Bethersden, Kent.

Tree of the SCHMAHL Family, Shewing the Ulm and Regensburg branches

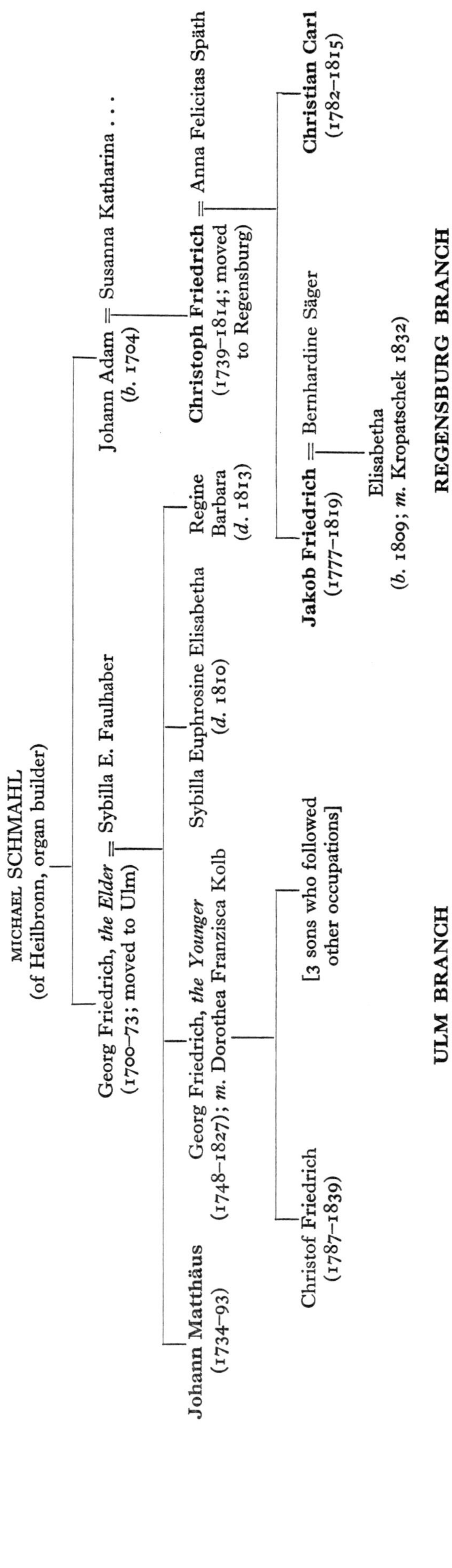

TABLE 31. *Surviving Stringed Keyboard Instruments by the SCHMAHL Family*

No.	Date	Maker	Type	Kbs.	Signature	Owner/Remarks
1	1692	Friedrich	Cd	1		Munich, Bayerisches Nationalmuseum, 1883; now disappeared.
1a	1790	Carl Friedrich	Cd	1	*C. Friedr. Schmahl in Regensburg 1790*	Munich, Bayerisches Nationalmuseum.
1b	1790	Carl Friedrich	Cd	1	*C. Fr. Schmahl, Regensburg, 1790* [on soundboard]	Regensburg Museum. Previously owned by Adolf Boehm, Munich.
2	1794	Christoph Friedrich	Cd	1	*C. Friedr. Schmahl Regensburg 1794*	Salzburg, Museum Carolino-Augusteum. F–F, 5 octaves, gebunden.
3	1[?8]07	Georg Friedrich *the Younger*	Cd	1	*Georg Friedrich Schmahl Orgel und Instrumentenmacher in Ulm Ao 1[?8]07 No. 44* [label on soundboard]	Mudeford House, Dr. C. Conyers Morrell. C–F, 4½ octaves; top 3 octaves gebunden. 4′ 6″ × 1′ 4″. Keys of limewood, the naturals faced with stained beech, the sharps with stained pear. Case of coarse pine unpainted. The engraved label is not earlier than the eighteenth century in style; the second numeral of the date has been tampered with.
4	1812	Christoph Friedrich	Cd	1	*C. Friedr. Schmahl und Söhne in Regensburg 1812*	Berlin Collection. F–A, 5⅓ octaves, gebunden. Illustrated in *Herrm*, p. 79.
5	[?Between 1812 and 1815]	Jakob Friedrich *and* Christian Carl	Cd	1	*Gebrüder Schmahl in Regensburg*	Munich, Deutsches Museum. F–C, 5½ octaves, bundfrei. Illustrated in *Herrm*, p. 80.
6(?)	[Between *c.* 1805 and 1815]	Christian Carl	Cd	1	*Carl Schmahl, Regensburg*	Freiburg im Breisgau, Professor Fritz Neumeyer. Bundfrei, 5 octaves plus 2 notes, F–G. No rose. Oak case, inlaid. Black naturals, white sharps. The inscription was said to have been found under the soundboard by the late Adolf Hartmann (restorer at the Berlin Collection). But a Basel restorer said (1970) that it is not signed and not by Schmahl.
7	n.d.	?	Cd	1		Freiburg im Breisgau, was owned by Willibald Gurlitt.
8	n.d.	Christoph Friedrich	Cd	1		Munich, Bayerisches Nationalmuseum. Gebunden; F–F, 5 octaves.

(5) **Georg Friedrich,** *the Younger,* 1748–1827, of Ulm. Pupil of his father. Maker of organs and other instruments, including clavichords.

(6) **Christoph Friedrich,** 1739–1814, of Heilbronn and Regensburg. Married Anna Felicitas Späth, the eldest daughter of Franz Jakob Späth, inventor of the 'Tangentenflügel'. See further *Herrm*. His 2 sons were:

(7) **Jakob Friedrich,** born at Regensburg 1777, died there 1819; and

(8) **Christian Carl,** 1782–1815.

SCHMID, Michel, of Stuttgart, *fl.* 1752. Organ builder and maker of stringed keyboard instruments [Bossert in *Württembergische Vierteljahrsschrift für Musik*, 1900].

SCHMIDT, Johann. Born at Strühlingen or Stichlingen in the Black Forest. He learnt carpentry, and later organ building from Samuel Öxle of Schönberg. Later he worked for Stein at Augsburg. In 1785 he became court organ builder at Salzburg on the recommendation of Leopold Mozart. *Ge* (1814; IV. 86) pays great tribute to his mechanical genius.

He also made pianos and clavichords which apparently were highly thought of [*Fé*, VII. 477].

SCHMIDT, Tobias. According to *ClP* (p. 71 n. 2) a German maker and player of the harpsichord who settled in Paris by 1785 and took the oath of entry into the Corporation of *Tabletiers-luthiers*. He is said to have devised or recommended, with Dr. Guillotin, the guillotine ordered by the Assembly in 1789, and to have charged 824 livres (the price of a good harpsichord) [*Verlet*].

SCHMUZ, Conrad. Goldsmith and harpsichord maker, born 12 November 1721 at Zürich, died there 8 April 1771. Son of Leonhardt below (though he also had a brother Leonhardt, 1719–78) [*Rindl*].

Surviving Instruments

(1) Prestegg, Altstätten, Switzerland, Historisches Museum. Harpsichord inscribed: *Conrad Schmuz fecit A° 1761*. 2×8′ stops.

SCHMUZ, Leonhard. Harpsichord maker, Kapellmeister in Zürich; born there 1681, the son of Caspar and Dorothea Schmuz; married on 21 June 1716. A. Magdalena Häussli; died on 19 February 1769; father of Conrad above [*Rindl*].

Surviving Instruments

(1) An ottavino virginal. Inscribed: *Leonhard Schmutz* [sic] *fecit anno 1733*. Illustrated in catalogue of Savoye Collection III, which was auctioned in Paris, 13 June 1924. Compass 4 octaves plus 1 note.

SCHNELL, Johann Jakob. Dates ascertained, 1740–1809. Born at Vaihingen an der Enz (Württemberg) in 1740. He was trained as a cabinet maker and then worked for the instrument maker Geissinger of Rothenburg, and later for other makers also; finally for J. D. Dülcken in Brussels for 6 years. In 1777 he settled in Paris and made harpsichords, receiving the title of court instrument maker to the Comtesse d'Artois and the position of citizen-craftsman of Paris; in 1780 he was living in the rue Saint-Hyacinthe [*Bq*, p. 13]. He invented the *anémocorde*, in which the keys opened little doors, which admitted a pressure of wind, causing the strings to sound (1789). He shewed this instrument in Vienna (1799), and sold it in 1803 to the physicist Robertson, who brought it to London [*Ge*, *Fé*]. He was still alive in 1809 [*Me*].

He is not to be confused with the composer of the same name who was 'hochfürstlicher Bamberger Kammer- und Hofmusikus' *c.* 1736; but he is probably identical with the Schneller listed below.

SCHNELLER. Harpsichord maker in Paris in the eighteenth century. On 10 January 1782 there was offered for sale: 'Clavier de Rukers à grand rav. avec 4 registres, jeu de buffles et mécanique pour les crescendo et les diminuendo chez le Sieur Schneller, facteur de clavecin, Marché des Enfants Rouges' [*Bq*]. Probably identical with Johann Jakob Schnell.

SCHOBERT. *Ri* (p. 81) calls him 'an ingenious mechanic and an elegant composer of music, the inventor of a harpsichord with double bottom, in which was placed, above the first sounding-board, a range of strings of two octaves, of considerable size and length, to strengthen the bass. These strings were sounded by a piece of mechanism brought into action by a range of pedals'.

SCHÖNE, Georg Daniel [Schoene], 1760–1807. Son of Johann Christian Schöne (1713–83) who came from Torgau, Saxony, to Norway in 1750. Georg Daniel was admitted to the Joiners' Guild in Oslo on 10 August 1787. Meanwhile he had spent time in London, where in 1783 he was working for Christian Shean (q.v.). *Hirt* finds him in Oslo again in 1793 and he is recorded as an instrument maker there in 1801. He died 22 November 1807. Probably related to Schoene, the London pianoforte maker, successor to Zumpe.

SCHONNAT, Johann Wolfgang. German seventeenth-century organ builder who also made stringed keyboard instruments [*Mainfränkisches Jahrbuch f. Geschichte und Kunst*, Vol. 19 (1967), p. 99]. A rectangular virginal by him dated 1645 is in the Gemeentemuseum, The Hague. Hugh Gough, however, strongly suspects the authenticity of this instrument, though it may incorporate some remains of an old one.

SCHORSE, *fl.* 1780. Journeyman instrument maker working for the celebrated Lemme in Brunswick. He had earlier worked in Strasbourg and Osnabrück [*SB*, p. 47].

SCHRAMM, Tobias. Born 1701 at Schandau; latest date ascertained, 1750. Organ and harpsichord maker; pupil of Gottfried Silbermann. In 1742 he obtained the citizenship of Dresden. The date of his latest known organ is 1749.

Of his sons, Johann August was a tuner, Johann Jakob (not to be confused with the organ builder Joh. Jak. Schramm, 1724–1808) was an instrument maker in Berlin, and Johann Christian was a well-known maker of harpsichords, etc. [*Fla*, *Fé*].

SCHRAMM, Johann Christian. Son of Tobias, born in Dresden, lived in Berlin as a maker of harpsichords and clavichords. Dates ascertained, 1768–73. *Fla* says he 'wurde 1768 Nachfolger Ph. Em. Bachs in Berlin', and had a wide reputation as a maker of very fine harpsichords and clavichords.

Burney refers to him as 'the son, from Dresden', who 'resides in Berlin and makes very good harpsichords and clavichords'.

SCHROETER, Christoph Gottlieb [Amadeus] of Hohenstein and Dresden, 1699–1782. An organist. One of the claimants to the invention of the pianoforte. In his boyhood he learned to quill and tune harpsichords, but it is unlikely that he made any clavichords or harpsichords. For further details of his life, see *GD*, *Fé*, *Eit*, *Herrm*.

SCHUBERT, David. An organ and instrument maker, whose clavichords had a high reputation. He learnt his craft from Gottfried Silbermann in Freiberg, and later settled in Dresden, where he built the organ in the French church (1765) and that in the Dresden Josephinenstift (1767). He was also responsible for organs at Herzogswalde and Haynichen.

He died at Dresden in 1767 (*Va* says 1769) [*Ge* (1814); *Fé*].

SCHÜLLER, Friedrich. Repaired a clavichord at the Esterházy court in 1761 and 1764 [*Walter*, p. 257].

SCHULZE, F. G., of Leipzig. *Fl.* 1794 as a maker of 'Klaviere [probably clavichords] and pianofortes' [*Kü*].

SCHURRIG, Johann Andreas Christian. Maker of harpsichords, clavichords, etc. His father was a court sculptor. He worked with J. H. Silbermann at Strasbourg from 1776 to 1780. On 25 July 1780 he applied for permission to settle in Brunswick and make 'musikalische Stuben-Instrumente, als Claviere [= clavichords], Clavecins, Pantalons, Fortepiano' [*SB*, p. 50].

SCHWANDTNER, Carl. Clavichord maker, probably Austrian, *fl.* 1782. A clavichord of this date is in the Schloss Eggenberg at Graz.

SCHWARZE. Organ and instrument maker at Dresden, who worked for many years with [? Andreas] Silbermann at Strasbourg. Towards the end of his life he moved to Friedrichstadt near Dresden (1748), where he made clavichords which won a high reputation [*Ge*, 1814].

SCHWEINEFLEISCH, Johann Christian Immanuel. German maker of organs and clavichords in Leipzig, where he was *Universitäts-Orgelbauer*. Dates ascertained: 1731–92. From 1731 to 1739 he was a pupil of his uncle the organ builder Gottfr. Heinr. Trost of Altenburg. In 1740 he worked with Joh. Gottfr. Hildebrand on the renovation of the organ at St. Wenzeslaw, Naumburg, and from 1755 onwards independently as an organ builder in Leipzig. In 1768 he built the organ of the Reformed Church there, and in 1772 that of the Thomaskirche, which was dismantled in 1887 [Forkel's *Musikal. Almanach*, 1782].

SCHWEINS, Johann, of Darmstadt, *fl. c.* 1800. Made guitars, lutes, harpsichords, clavichords, and pianos [*Lü*, *Gö*].

SCHWINGSTEIN, Johann Michael. Keyboard-instrument maker in Heutingsheim (Swabia), *c.* 1799. At first he worked for the cabinet maker Röntgen at Neuwied, but his interest in instrument making led him to Stein's workshops, where his skill was such that he was entrusted with the making of whole instruments from start to finish [*Ge*, 1814].

SCOTTI, Antonio. Harpsichord maker of Milan, *fl.* 1753. A single-manual harpsichord by him dated 1753 (C–F, 4½ octaves, 54 keys) in the Gallini Collection, Milan, is described and illustrated in *Gall.* It is inscribed on jackrail: *Antonio Scotti in Milano 1753*, and was given to Mozart by Count Firmian, Governor of Lombardy, on the occasion of Mozart's first visit to Milan.

SCOULER, James, *the Elder*. Maker of spinets and harpsichords in London. Dates ascertained: 1762–82, the latter being the year of his death. *J* (p. 75) gives the dates ascertained as 1762–88; but on 11 December 1782 letters of administration of the goods and chattels of James Scouler 'of St. George's Bloomsbury, widower, deceased' were granted to his son, also called James Scouler, who [*J*, p. 75] was a painter of miniatures.

From 1762 to 1765 he lived in Great Newport Street [*RB.A*]; and in *Un* (1763) his name appears as a harpsichord maker. Whether he was connected, or identical, with the music publisher J. Scouler who flourished in 1759 in Duke's Court [*H&S*], I do not know. In the Shudi account-books there is an entry against 5 March 1772: 'Sold Mr. Hullmandel a harpsichord made by Scouler for 25 guineas' [*Da*, p. 73].

Scouler also made combined instruments. There was sold at Christie's on 9 October 1792:

> A capital fine toned harpsichord with piano Forte containing 2 complete distinct stops with set of keys to each, and pedal, by Jacob Scouler, in a neat mahogany case [Vendor anon.; buyer Sir Archibald Murray; price 9½ gns.].

Surviving Spinets

(1) Undated. Sold at Sotheby's 21 June 1946. White naturals, black sharps; 5 octaves; walnut case. Length 6′ 2″. Soundboard modern. Poor condition. Inscription: *Jacobus Scouler Londini fecit.*

(2) Undated. Sold by Messrs. Moss Harris to a member of the Lyons family, summer 1954. Good condition; original stand.

(3) 1763. Inscription: *Jacobus Scouler Londini fecit 1763*. Sold by Messrs. Legg of Cirencester in 1964 to Mrs. W. Talbot of that town.

(4) Undated. Messrs. H. M. Luther, London (1972). Inscription: *Jacobus Scouler Londini Fecit.* On back of nameboard: *No. 2.*

SEAT, Christoph. A misreading of *Fecit* in *Christoph Fecit . . . See*: CHRISTOPH.

SECRET, Jean de [? Segret]. Organist and maker of instruments, probably including harpsichords. He lived in the parish of Saint-Jacques-de-la-Boucherie, Paris, towards the end of the eighteenth century [*Verlet*, based on *Les*]. *Laborde* gives 'Segret'.

SEEDE, Bruce. Harpsichord maker. Lewin's Mead, Bristol. Dates ascertained: 1753–72 [*J*]. He is better known as an organ builder [*Sum*].

SEGAER, Passchier [Segar, Segaert, Chegaer]. Harpsichord maker, born about 1573, who moved in 1595 from Bondues near Lille to Leiden, where he became a citizen on 16 February 1609. See further *Curtis*, p. 60.

SELLIER, Jean. Born *c.* 1597; died after 1676. In 1611 he was apprenticed to Pol Belamy II (q.v.). In 1662 Nicolas Dubuc, who had been apprenticed to Jacques Regnault (q.v.), transferred to Sellier (q.v.). There can be no doubt that he made harpsichords [*Verlet*].

SELLIER, Louis. Born *c.* 1625, a much younger half-brother of Jean. Maker of instruments, probably including harpsichords, in Paris [*Verlet*].

SELLIER, Nicolas. Born before 1630; died after 1701. Harpsichord maker in Paris, a relative of Jean and Nicolas. In 1674 he became a member of the Guild [*Verlet*].

SELLS. Harpsichord maker, *fl. c.* 1750, London. 'Mr. Sells, Harpsichord-maker' appears among the subscribers to John Travers's *Eighteen canzonets* (London, *c.* 1745; another edition *c.* 1750).

SEMLIN, Anton. *See*: SOUMLIN, Anton.

SENFT, Ignace Joseph. Eighteenth-century maker of organs, pianofortes, and harpsichords at Augsburg. *Sa* (p. 81) records a square pianoforte with the following inscription (of uncertain grammar): *Ignace Joseph Senft / faiseur d'Orgues de Clavecins de forte-piano / grands et petites et de forte-piano Vis à Vis / à Augsbourg.*

SENTIS, Gerolamo de. *See*: ZENTIS, Girolamo de.

SERMANNI. *See*: FERMANNI.

SEXTUS, Mutinensis. *See*: TANTINI, Sesto.

SHEAN, Christian. Harpsichord and spinet maker, of London until about 1760 and thereafter of Edinburgh.

Shean is recorded at New Street, Canongate, Edinburgh, from 1775 to 1794. Born 1711 or 1712; died in Edinburgh on 14 September 1794, aged 82 years.

In 1777 he is recorded [*Williamson's Directory of Edinburgh*] as 'harpsichord and spinnet maker' and in 1784 as 'harpsichord maker'. He figures also in 1776 in Shudi's account-books: 'Mrs. Battman of Hampstead bought and received a single keyboard harpsichord made by Sheene' (*ShJl*, 9 August 1776).

Surviving Spinets

(1) 1769. Signed: *Christian Shean from London.* Messrs. Legg, Cirencester, 1953 (formerly Dr. J. M. Bryan; before that Miss A. Liddell Grainger). G–G, 5 octaves. Date on a key. 6′ 2″ × 4′ 0″.

(2) 1779. Rebuilt by Hugh Gough in 1950, when it belonged to R. R. Henshaw.

(3) 1783. Signed: *Christian Shean from London R. C.* (Sotheby's 25 May 1951). Spanish Embassy, London.

(4) A. Cross, London.

(5) Signed: *Christian Shean from London.* Edinburgh, Royal Scottish Museum (since 1908). F–F, 5 octaves.

John Reid (*New Lights on Old Edinburgh*, 1894, p. 165) refers to a 'musical instrument maker, Christian Shean, "lately arrived from London", advertising in 1761 (*Edinburgh Courant*) that she "made and sold all sorts of harpsichords and spinets, etc."'. If there is any other evidence suggesting that Shean was a woman, I have not found it. Reid seems to be in error in his reference, for no such advertisement appears to be in the volume of the *Edinburgh Courant* for 1761.

SHEDE, Benjamin. *See*: SLADE, Benjamin.

SHEENE, Christian. *See*: SHEAN, Christian.

SHUDI. The anglicized form of the Swiss-German Tschudi; surname of a family of harpsichord makers.

(1) **Burkat,** *the Elder* (1702–73). Famous harpsichord maker and founder of the house of Broadwood, pianoforte makers. His instruments are inscribed *Burkat Shudi*, but his name was originally Burkhardt Tschudi, the Tschudis being a noble family of the canton of Glarus. William Dale (who did much valuable research on Shudi's life, and whose monograph on Shudi should be consulted for further details) tells us that Shudi's father, Joshua Tschudi, wool-merchant and surgeon, was a councillor of Schwanden, Glarus, where Shudi was born, and that his mother belonged to the Elmer family.

Shudi came to England in 1718 as a journeyman joiner, having been taught this trade by his uncle, whose name was also Joshua. Within a short time he took to harpsichord making, and worked for Hermann Tabel (q.v.), who lived in Oxendon Street off Piccadilly—a Fleming who, according to J. S. Broadwood's notes (1838), had derived his style from the Ruckers tradition, which, transplanted here, was to enjoy a second flowering in the great English school of harpsichord making, represented chiefly by Kirkman and Shudi. It seems likely that by 1723, when Tabel announced his intention to retire, Shudi had already been working for him for some time. When Shudi left Tabel and set up on his own account we do not know, but he had certainly taken this step by 1729, for a harpsichord made in that year and bearing Shudi's signature survives. This harpsichord is particularly interesting, for it bears on the back of the nameboard the inscription: *Questo cimbalo è del^{a} Sig^{ra} Anna Strada, 1731 London,* and might possibly have been given to that celebrated singer by Handel, who was a friend of Shudi's.

The earliest business record of Shudi occurs in the diary of John Hervey, 1st Earl of Bristol (1688–1742), under the date 11 April, 1733: 'Paid B. Shudi for tuning the harpsichord, 17/6', which may well have been for 7 tunings during the previous year.

Some time between 1728 and 1732 Shudi married Catherine, daughter of Hans Jakob and Salome Wild, natives of Schwanden, who had already settled in London by the time he arrived there. (Catherine Wild, 1704–*c.* 1758, was descended from Anna Zwingli, sister of the Protestant reformer.) It seems likely that the marriage took place about 1728 or 1729, for at this time Shudi had set up on his own, and it is reasonable to suppose that this step had been made possible by some financial help from Jakob Wild, who was a prosperous merchant.

In 1739 (as the rate-books of the parish of St. Anne's, Soho, tell us) Shudi took up his residence in 'Meards Street', off Dean Street. The number of the house is not known, but it was one in the handsome row on the southern side of Meard Street, photographed in *Dale*. Handel, whose friendship must have been of great value to Shudi, was a frequent guest at his table, and owned a harpsichord by him—perhaps one of the very few eighteenth-century harpsichords in England, or for that matter anywhere, to possess a 16′ stop—though it might well have been simply one of his C–F, 5½-octave instruments, which could have been regarded by an organist as equivalent to a harpsichord with a 16′ stop (cf. the harpsichord with a 'deepened bass' which Kirkman (q.v.) undertook to provide for Fulke Greville). Unhappily this instrument has not survived into our time, though it was mentioned in a notice in the *Morning Herald*, London, in 1788 (quoted by *J*, p. 42): 'Handel's Harpsichord, at Mr. Cross's opposite the Town Hall, Oxford. On Thurs. the 26th June 1788, at two o'clock in the afternoon. A capital double Key'd HARPSICHORD by BUREAT [*sic*] SCHUDI, made for the Immortal Handel and used by him till his death, at the different Concerts in London. It consists of four stops, which are as follows: two unisons, an upper and lower octave, has a powerful tone and is well calculated for Concerts.'

Shudi remained in Meard Street until 1742, when according to the *Daily Advertiser* (5 October) he 'removed from Meard's Street in Dean Street Soho to Great Pulteney Street, Golden Square', where his house was occupied by his descendants the Broadwoods until 1904. About 2 years after this removal the portrait of Shudi and his family, which is still in the possession of Messrs. Broadwood and is reproduced as a frontispiece to *Dale*, was painted, perhaps by Philip Mercier, who shortly afterwards executed his fine portrait of Handel. Shudi is represented tuning a large harpsichord of his own make, while his wife Catherine is taking her tea and their 2 sons Joshua and Burkat stand near by with the cat.

Shudi took for his sign at 33 Great Pulteney Street the Plume of Feathers, a reflection of the patronage of Frederick Prince of Wales; while the house in Broad Street, Carnaby Market, of Jacob Kirkman, who in earlier years had worked with Shudi under Tabel, bore the sign of the King's Arms—an echo of the unfriendly relations between George II and his eldest son. The 2-manual harpsichord made by Shudi for Prince Frederick in 1740 still survives, and may be seen in Kew Palace. Its compass is 5 octaves F–F; but like many of Kirkman's instruments (though unlike Shudi's later ones) it lacks the lowest F sharp.

An entry in Leopold Mozart's diary of his visit to London with Wolfgang, apparently July 1765, reads:

> Mr Tschudi Claviermacher in Pulteney Street near Brewer Street. [Reproduced in Leopold Mozart's *Reise-Aufzeichnungen 1763–71*, edited by A. Schurig, Dresden 1920.]

On this occasion the nine-year old Mozart played the 2-manual harpsichord of 5½ octaves compass (numbered 496), which Shudi presented to Frederick the Great the following year. Frederick must have been well pleased with this gift for later in the same year he commissioned 2 more such harpsichords from Shudi, which, numbered 511 and 512, were housed at Potsdam.[1] These last 2 were (perhaps the earliest to be) fitted with the machine-stop. When this is engaged, by means of a knob inside the left cheek-piece, the lower keyboard gives the 8′ and the 4′ stop. By pressing the left pedal the player takes these 2 off and exchanges the ordinary 8′ on the top keyboard for the lute stop. This pedal appears to have been added to permit the playing of crescendos and decrescendos (see *RipExpr*). None of these instruments had the Venetian swell.

This device, which received its apt name later, was patented by Shudi on 18 December 1769. (The Dublin maker F. Weber was fitting a similar but inferior mechanism to his harpsichords at about the same time.) It consists of a kind of inner lid to the harpsichord, covering the whole soundboard area, and made up of slats which could be raised and lowered by means of a pedal, thus increasing or diminishing the volume, and incidentally altering the timbre. Ten guineas was the price for its attachment to a harpsichord; it soon became popular, and was later transferred to the organ—to which instrument it was in fact better suited.

In 1761, nearly 20 years after Shudi's removal to Great Pulteney Street, the young Scottish cabinet maker John Broadwood began to work for him. This craftsman followed the traditional course of marrying (in 1769) his employer's daughter Barbara (bapt. 1748, d. 1776), and later in the same year was taken into partnership by his father-in-law. Thenceforward the firm's harpsichords normally bore the inscription *Burkat Shudi et Johannes Broadwood*, though a few (such as number 639 dated 1771) were sent out bearing Shudi's name alone.

In March 1771 Shudi retired to a house in Charlotte Street, not far away, where he died on 19 August 1773. In his will John Keble, the organist of St. George's, Hanover

[1] According to a deposition sworn before G. Wrighte, Middlesex, 12 January 1767 [*ShAf*], Shudi supplied altogether *four* harpsichords to Frederick the Great. The Breslau harpsichord is reported missing since the end of World War II.

Tree of the SHU

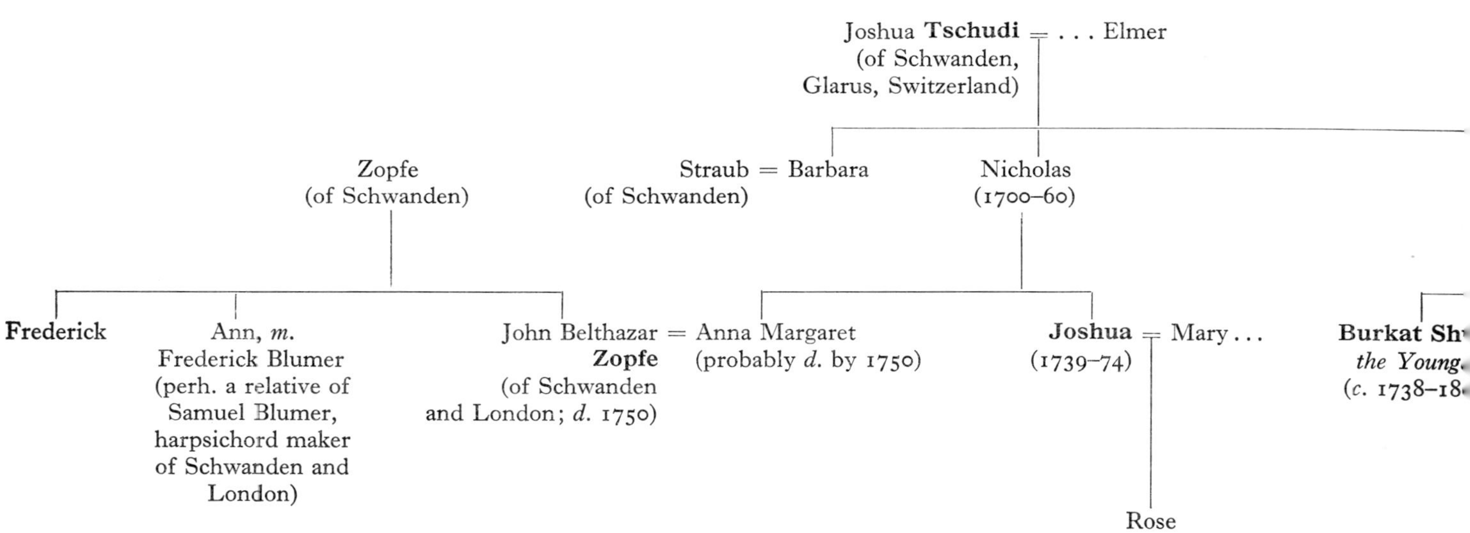

Square, in succession to Thomas Roseingrave, is named as one of the beneficiaries. On the day after his death the harpsichord made for the Empress Maria Theresa and numbered 691 was sent on board ship for Vienna. Two years later another was sent to the same city for Joseph Haydn.

After Shudi's death his son Burkat took his father's place in the partnership (Broadwood being now the controlling partner) until about 1792 (*pace* Hipkins, who places the withdrawal of the younger Shudi about 1782). During the second half of the century Shudi's fame spread to the Continent, so that we find Gerber making brief mention of him in his *Hist. biog. Lexicon d. Tonkünstler* (1790–2): 'Schudi: Instrumentenmacher zu London, ums Jahr 1772, ist vorzüglich wegen seiner Flügeln berühmt.'

Since all the extant Shudi harpsichords except one are both numbered and dated, we are able to witness the expansion of his business. It is interesting that the number of harpsichords built each year by the firm increased steadily right up to the time—in the middle seventeen-nineties—when the harpsichord was ousted by the pianoforte. Thus during the decade 1740–9 the average yearly output of harpsichords was 13; from 1750 to 1769 it was 15; 1770 to 1779, 23; and 1780 to 1789, 25. The average yearly output over the whole half-century 1740–90 was 20 harpsichords.

A contemporary printed label, observed by Frank Hubbard on one of the keyboards of the Shudi harpsichord numbered 955, may record one of Shudi's sources for ivory. It reads: 'William Drane / Comb maker / (no. 25) Aldgate Street / makes and sells all sorts of Ivory, tortoiseshell, horn and Boxcombs, wholesale and retail sells also Ivory, Bone and Hard-wood-Turn'—[*the rest wanting*]. It may even be a label for the keyboard. Hubbard notices, in this connection, that Messrs. Pratt-Reed, the largest American keyboard manufacturers today, started as ivory comb makers early in the nineteenth century.

The price, about the year 1770, of a single manual Shudi harpsichord with two 8′ stops was 35 guineas; with a 4′ stop, 40 guineas; with swell also, 50 guineas; a 2-manual harpsichord with swell was 80 guineas, though of course special models were sometimes made at a greater price, such as that made for Haydn, which cost £110. The last harpsichord made at Pulteney Street, in March 1793, for Henry de la Maine (Shudi's agent in Cork), cost £84.

Burney states that Shudi's harpsichords were more durable than those of his rival Kirkman—a statement which it is now impossible to verify. The fact that more than 100 Kirkmans survive against merely 50 bearing the name of Shudi affords no indication, since the house of Kirkman was much bigger and produced many more instruments. The 2 makers used very similar principles of construction, so that the differences were largely superficial: Kirkman retained the rose and omitted the bottom F sharp for many years, arranged his stops differently, and used a different type of swell. The most important difference was in the lute-stop, which in the Kirkmans has a more characteristic nasal tone, the string being plucked nearer to the nut-bridge. Burney preferred the Shudi tone; but the modern ear finds little to choose between them.

Several account-books of Shudi and later Broadwood have survived, affording interesting sidelights on their work and workshop. Thus, they had 2 Ruckers harpsichords which they used to hire out in addition to their own instruments. They also dealt in harpsichords by other makers, e.g. Scouler (5 March 1772, 20 March 1777), Tabel (18 March 1777), and Kirkman (13 November 1783, 16 May 1775). One harpsichord—no. 750—which was sold on 10 August 1775 to Lady Stavordale, of Redlinch, Somerset, is still in the possession of her descendants. On 9 October 1773 Shudi sold some 'brass wire for a clafcord', gauges 3, 4, 5, 6, 7, 8, 9, 10, 03. Familiar names such as Hullmandel, Gainsborough, Reynolds, Avison, Morland, occur. The firm sold individual parts of harpsichords, e.g. 6 soundboards (21 October 1782), crow and raven quills (28 June 1784), flannel for dampers (26 August 1784), keys, jacks and 'sockets', tongues, machine-stops, and bridges, also such tools as pliers for making

udi) family

Hans Jakob Wild = Salome Kubli
(of Schwanden and London; 1674–1741)

Burkat Shudi (Burckhardt Tschudi, 02–73, of Schwanden and London) = (i) Catherine Wild (1704–?; *m. c.* 1728; *d.* before 1759) = (ii) Elizabeth Meier (*m.* by 1759; *d.* Dec. 1802 or Jan. 1803)

Jacob

Joshua (1736–54)

John Broadwood (1732–1812) = (i) Barbara (*bapt.* 1748; *m.* 1769; *d.* 1776) (ii) A second wife

Margaret (*d.* 1778)

Elizabeth (who was under 21 in 1773) = The Revd. Peter Will

James Shudi Broadwood (1772–1851)

Thomas

The House of Broadwood today

loops (28 June 1784) and tuning forks (of which a set was sold on 26 August 1784) and even other instruments altogether, e.g. guitars (13 January 1776).

Harpsichords were also frequently hired for concerts and for longer periods, and payments for tuning harpsichords are recorded.

Besides harpsichords, Shudi made claviorgana (organized harpsichords). On 11 June 1800 there was sold at Christie's: 'an organized double keyed harpsichord by Shudi' [Vendor the Duke of Leeds; buyer Smith; price 13 gns.].

In addition to the 3 children already mentioned, Shudi had by Catherine Wild a daughter Margaret, who died in 1778. Soon after Catherine's death he married an Elizabeth Meier, who bore him a daughter, also named Elizabeth, and survived him by 30 years.

(2) **Burkat,** *the Younger* (*c.* 1738–1803), younger son of Burkat the elder. After his father's death in 1773 he took his place in the partnership with John Broadwood, though as junior partner. Exactly how long this partnership continued is uncertain. Hipkins places its dissolution about 1782, but it was probably about 1792 that Burkat the younger withdrew, for a harpsichord dated 1791 bears the names of both of them, while a solitary harpsichord signed by Broadwood alone is dated 1793.

(3) **Joshua** (1739–74), a nephew of Burkat the elder, being the son of Shudi's elder brother, Nicholas (born 1700, of Schwanden, and later London, when he stayed with Burkat, then Holland and finally America, where he died in 1760). Joshua apparently spent a short time at sea and then came to work for Shudi in 1761. His work, however, was not satisfactory, and an affidavit sworn on 12 January 1767 by John Broadwood and 2 other men who had at one time worked for Shudi states that Joshua 'during the whole time he lived with the said Burkat Shudi never did begin and finish any one harpsichord' [*ShAf*]. Shortly before this, probably towards the end of 1766, Joshua had set up on his own in Silver Street, Golden Square, at the sign of the Golden Guitar, relations having become strained between his uncle and himself.

On the same day as the above affidavit was sworn he put a notice of some length in *The Gazetteer* defending himself and inviting the nobility and gentry to his apartments where they could see 'harpsichords of my own making'. See further *Da*, pp. 51 ff.

In 1775 his widow, Mary Shudi (by whom he had one daughter, Rose) announced in the *Public Advertiser* her intention of carrying on the business, which she did in Joshua's name. Only 2 harpsichords bearing his name, dated 1773 and 1776, have survived into modern times. A 'double-key'd harpsichord by Joshua Shudi' was sold at Christie's on 16 April 1792 for £10. 12*s*.

Joshua's sister Anna Margaret married the harpsichord maker Zopfe of Schwanden and London.

(4) **Bernard** (*fl.* 1769). The only evidence of the existence of this maker is a harpsichord in the possession of Edgar Lister. The nameboard bears the legend *Bernardus Shudi Londini Fecit 1769*, and on the back is the signature *Bernardus Shudi 1769*.

In style the instrument is very similar to those of Burkat, except that it has a gilt rose in the soundboard giving the initials *BS* and a harping angel. There are the usual 2×8′, 1×4′, lute-, and machine-stops, with inlaid mahogany case and 1 pedal to work the machine. But there is no music rest and no accommodation for one. The 2 keyboards, without the bottom F sharp, are of ivory and ebony, the natural fronts being of arcaded ivory. The stand is modern except for the cross strut. Length, just over 8′.

The instrument was restored by Dove of Pimlico. The hitchpin rail is new, and the excessive side-draught between the bridge and hitchpins is obviously not original.

That Bernard was related to Burkat Shudi is beyond doubt; but the relationship remains a mystery; and it is strange that Burkat makes no mention of him in his will (proved 3 September 1773), unless Bernard had predeceased him, or the two had not been on friendly terms [*Da*; Shudi's will; *RB*].

TABLE 32. *Surviving harpsichords by the SHUDI Family*

* *Key to abbreviations in the third column*

S = Burkat Shudi, SB = Burkat Shudi and J(ohannes) Broadwood, Be = Bernardus Shudi, J = Joshua Shudi, B = Johannes Broadwood

Shudi's no.	Date	Signature*	Kbs.	Former owners	Present or recent owner	Remarks
—	1729	S	2	First owner was Anna Strada del Pò, to whom it was presumably given by Handel. Its subsequent history is unknown until about 1905 when it was bought by Paul de Wit in Rome.	Copenhagen, Carl J. Michaelsen, who bought it from Paul de Wit.	2×8′, 1×4′, lute. Closely similar to the only surviving Tabel harpsichord. Lettering in upper-case Roman, after the Flemish style: *Burckat Tschudi Londini fecit 1729*. On the back of the nameboard: *Questo cimbalo è del*[a] *Sig*[ra] *Anna Strada 1731, London.* The instrument was presumably given by Handel to Anna Strada, one of the singers he chose in Italy in 1729 to perform in his operas. See *Da*, pp. 32 ff., where the harpsichord and its nameboard are illustrated. The instrument has been re-veneered; keys and action new.

Shudi's no.	Date	Signature*	Kbs.	Former owners	Present or recent owner	remarks
94	1740	S	2	Frederick Prince of Wales, son of George II.	H.M. The Queen. (Kept at Kew Palace, formerly in Windsor Castle.)	2×8′, 1×4′, lute. 5 octaves, F–F without bottom F sharp. Keyboards faced with bone instead of ivory, not original. Case in burr walnut crossbanded with plain walnut.
103	1740	S			Mrs. Delany.	
120	1742	S	1		Lt.-Col. Myddleton, Chirk Castle, Denbigh.	Marquetry round the keyboard.
144	[*c.* 1743]	S	2	Steinert Collection.	Smithsonian Institution (formerly at Yale).	F–F, 5 octaves without bottom F sharp. The lower nameboard, giving the date 1747, is not native to the instrument. Illustrated in *Nash 1969*.
160	1744	S	1		The Hague, Gemeentemuseum.	2×8′ only. Numbered on bottom keys as well as on the nameboard.
190	1747	S	2	Hugo Worch.	Washington, Smithsonian Institution.	Presented by Hugo Worch in 1920.
229	1749	S	2	Mr. Warre (? William Ware, Shudi's agent in Belfast—cf. *ShJl*, 15 August 1785).	Cambridge, Mrs. Mary Potts.	5½ octaves C–F; 2×8′, 1×4′, lute, buff, machine, Venetian swell. Original nameboard missing. Music-rest numbered 95.
260 (264)	1751	S	1	F. Fairley, Newcastle, Myles Archibald, Ulverston. Purchased from Messrs. Legg, Cirencester, 1930.	Cambridge, Robin Orr (bequeathed by M. Archibald).	F–F, 5 octaves; 2×8′ stops. Underside of soundboard has signature, date 1751, and number 264 [*sic*].
407 (405)	1760	S	2	H. J. Dale.	Messrs. Broadwood.	Venetian swell added at a later date. The underside of the soundboard is signed by Shudi as *405 (1760)*.
423	1761	S	1	Miss Fanny Davies, pupil of Clara Schumann. (Sold it 23 June 1932.)	London, Benton Fletcher Collection at Fenton House.	2×8′, 1×4′, lute. Sold at Puttick and Simpson's 23 June 1932. Burr walnut case. Illustrated in *Apollo* September/October 1943. p. 98.
427	1761	S	1			Shudi's autograph under soundboard (reproduced at *Da*, p. 40); *Burckat Tsudi No. 427 Stuck 1761 London.*
428	1761	S				
496	1765	S	2	Frederick the Great; Schloss Breslau.	Breslau, Schlossmuseum, until World War II when it disappeared [*Russell 1959*, p. 163].	Compass C–F, 5½ octaves; 2×8′, 1×4′, lute, buff, machine (but no swell). The 9-year-old Mozart played it in London, 13 May 1765, before its dispatch to the Emperor.
499	1765	S	2	Milan Conservatoire.	Milan, Museo Teatrale alla Scala.	Original stand lost. No machine, swell, or music-rest; 5 stops.

Shudi's no.	Date	Signa-ture*	Kbs.	Former owners	Present or recent owner	Remarks
511 } 512 }	1766	S	2	Frederick the Great.	Potsdam (but see next column).	2×8′, 1×4′, buff, lute, machine, but no swell. 511 bears Shudi's explanation of the stop mechanism (MS. in German, illustrated at *Da*, p. 48); 512 disappeared after the Allied capture of Berlin 4195, and is now (1972) in the Mikhail Glinka Museum for Musical Culture, Moscow.
529	1766	S	2	Harry Hodge, Edinburgh.	W. R. Thomas, Burntisland, Fife.	Bears J. Longman's, Joshua Shudi's, and A. Dolmetsch's autographs under the soundboard. Venetian swell, possibly fitted later (according to Hipkins). 5 octave F–F, without lowest F sharp.
540	1767	S	1	Col. Dove, The Old Manse, Stansted (sold 1967).	M. A. Sigal, Newtonville, Mass. (1969).	1×8′, 1×4′. (*Note*: This instrument was sold by auction by Edw. Watson & Sons at Bishops Stortford, November 1967, for £1,000; bought by Messrs. Wearn, dealers, of Wenders Ambo near Saffron Walden, and sold by them almost at once to Messrs. Ratcliff, of Kelvedon. By December 1969 it was owned by M. A. Sigal.)
—	1769	Be	2		Edgar Lister.	See text s.v. Bernard Shudi.
625	1770	SB	2	Dr. David Hartley; W. Dale; Gerald Cooper.	London, Benton Fletcher Collection. (Major Benton Fletcher bought it from Gerald Cooper at Puttick and Simpson's, 20 February 1936.)	2×8′, 1×4′, lute, buff, machine, Venetian swell. C–F, 5½ octaves.
?	1770	J	1		New York, private ownership (1968).	Empty case only. Inscription: *Joshua Shudi Londini fecit 1770*.
639	1771	S	2		Messrs. Broadwood.	Played on by Ernst Pauer, Moscheles, and Hipkins in their historical performances; 5½ octaves.
652	1771	SB	2	J. Connell, Melbourne, Victoria	National Gallery of Victoria, Melbourne (Connell Collection).	2×8′, 1×4′, lute, buff, machine, Venetian swell.
671	1772	SB	2	Originally sold to a Mr. Atkinson of Newcastle on 24 November 1772 [*ShJl*]; later owned by Margaret Glyn; Alec Hodsdon, Lavenham, who sold it (1959) to Raymond Russell, from whom it was acquired in the same year by Durham University, where it was cared for by Professor [of Music] Arthur Hutchings, who moved to Exeter in 1968. Sold in same year to Michael Thomas, who sold it to E. M. Ripin.	E. M. Ripin, Forest Hills, N.Y. (1969).	F–F, 5 octaves; 2×8′, 1×4′, lute, buff, machine, Venetian swell. (The entry under the date 24 November 1772 reads: 'Sent a Double Harp^{d} No. 671 to Newcastle'. The fact that it was for a 'Mr. Atkinson' Russell must have derived from another source.)

Shudi's no.	Date	Signature*	Kbs.	Former owners	Present or recent owner	Remarks
686	1773	SB	2	T. W. Taphouse; Messrs. Broadwood.	St. Michael's College, Tenbury.	All stops. Compass 5½ octaves C–F.
691	1773	SB	2	Empress Maria Theresa; V. Mahillon.	Brussels Conservatoire.	All stops. Compass 5½ octaves C–F. Length 8′ 10″. Illustrated by *J*, p. 132.
—	1773	J	2	Mrs. E. B. Wimbush, Triscombe House, West Bagborough, Taunton, who sold it by auction through Messrs. Greenslade, Taunton, 1–4 November 1954, to O. R. Bagot.	O. R. Bagot, Levens Hall, Kendal.	Inscribed: *Joshua Shudi Fecit Londini 1773*. 6 stops; 2 pedals. Length 7′ 11″. Compass 5 octaves F–F. No provision for music-desk. Restored by A. Dolmetsch (1895) and J. C. Cobby (1954/5).
708	1774	SB(?)	?	First owner, Gainsborough. The entry in *ShJl* under 5 March 1774 reads: 'Mr. Dashwood and Gardine [i.e. the violinist Felice de Giardini] bought a harp[d], No. 708, for Mr. Gainsborough, painter in the Circle Bath.'	?	Mentioned by *Da*, pp. 67–8.
736	1774	SB	1	Made for Charles Avison [*ShJl*].	Liverpool, Rushworth and Dreaper Collection.	2×8′ stops.
750	1775	SB	2	*ShJl* (10 August 1775) records that it was made for Lady Stavordale (of Redlynch, Bruton); Messrs. Price & Sons, Craven, Somersbury Manor; George Malcolm.	Miss Leni van der Lee, Utrecht.	Beautifully preserved, with original leather wool-lined cover. 2×8′, 1×4′, lute, buff, machine, Venetian swell. The entry in *ShJl* (10 August 1775) reads: 'Lady Stovorddales [*sic*] Harpsichord was Packed and sent to Redlinch near Bruton Sommerset [*sic*] No. 750.'
762	1775	SB	2	Joseph Haydn; J. Herbeck.	Vienna, Gesellschaft der Musikfreunde (on permanent loan to the Kunsthistorisches Museum, Vienna).	2×8′, 1×4′, lute, buff, machine, Venetian swell. Compass 5½ octaves. Illustrated in *Hin* (pl. 41).
787	1776					(Only date and number known.)
789	1776	SB		J. Kendrick Pyne.		Shewn at the International Inventions Exhibition, 1885.
—	1776	J				*Da* (p. 57) refers to a harpsichord by Joshua Shudi of 1776 as the only instrument by him known. It has since disappeared; but see under the years 1770 and 1773.
837	1778(?)	SB(?)	2		Oslo, Norsk Folkemuseum (since 1898).	F–F, 5 octaves. Nameboards missing, but lowest key on each manual stamped *837*.

Shudi's no.	Date	Signa-ture*	Kbs.	Former owners	Present or recent owners	Remarks
842	1778	SB	1	Harry C. Johnson.	Mrs. R. La Cosse, Glencoe, Ill.	Venetian swell; originally 2×8′, 1×4′. Restored by John Challis, who substituted a 16′ stop for one of the 8′s.
862	1779	SB	1	John Francis; A. W. Sodon, Hampstead; D. H. Crompton, Thriplow.	A. B. Cross, 1953– .	2×8′, 1×4′, buff, machine, Venetian swell. Advertised by Mr. Crompton in *The Times*, 18 February 1953, the date being wrongly given as 1770. Sold by him at Sotheby's, 5 June 1953.
899	1781[1]	SB	2	Miss Anson, Sudbury, Derby; T. W. Taphouse.	Mrs. K. F. Hammitt, New York.	2×8′, 1×4′, lute, buff, machine. Venetian swell. Shewn at the International Inventions Exhibition, 1885.
902	1781	SB	2	Sir Hubert Parry; C. H. Lloyd, Gloucester.	Messrs. Taphouse, Oxford, on loan to the Faculty of Music, Oxford University.	Shewn at the International Inventions Exhibition, 1885. Destroyed in a fire, 1970(?).
919	1782	SB	2	The Wrottesley family, S. Stratton, Birmingham; Charles H. Laycock.	Victoria and Albert Museum.	2×8′, 1×4′, buff, lute, machine, Venetian swell. Compass C–F, $5\frac{1}{2}$ octaves. Exhibited 1885. Illustrated in *Russell V&A* and *Russell 1959*.
938	1782	SB	2		The Duke of Devonshire, Chatsworth House (1965).	2×8′, 1×4′, buff, lute, half-shift on the lower-manual 8′, machine, Venetian swell. Had original strings when repaired by Hugh Gough, 1947. Illustrated in *DEF* (II. 375). Compass $5\frac{1}{2}$ octaves.
955	1789					*Da*, p. 75.
?	1789			Charles Carroll of Carrollton, U.S.A., for whom it was made; Messrs. Knabe & Co., Baltimore; Mrs. Fanny Reed Hammond.	Groton School, Groton, Mass., to whom it was given by Mrs. Hammond	
1015	1785	SB	2	Sir Edward Burne-Jones, Bt., Mrs. J. W. Mackail.	Miss Mary Phipps (on long loan to Christopher Wood, 1954).	2×8′, 1×4′, buff, lute, machine, Venetian swell. Repaired by Arnold Dolmetsch in the eighteen-nineties.
1070	1787	SB	SB	2	Bought by Capt. Evelyn Broadwood at Puttick & Simpsons on 27 October 1938. The catalogue does not record the vendor.	
1124	1789	SB	1	Mrs. Maud Osborn; Miss Elizabeth Needham.	G. Braithwaite.	2×8′, 1×4′, buff, machine, Venetian swell. Repaired by Goble in 1952.
1137	1790	SB	2		Messrs. Broadwood.	
1145	1790	SB	1		Manchester, Forsyth Collection.	2×8′, 1×4′, buff, lute, machine, Venetian swell.
1148	1791	SB	1	Dr. Henry Watson, Manchester.	Manchester Central Library.	2×8′, 1×4′, buff, lute, Venetian swell.

[1] After 1780 Broadwood's Latinized Christian name was written out in full: *Johannes*.

Shudi's no.	Date	Signa-ture*	Kbs.	Former owners	Present or recent owners	Remarks
1155	1793	B	1	Raymond Russell.	Edinburgh University.	Noted without further details by *Da.* Signed: *Johannes Broadwood London Fecit 1793.* 2×8′, 1×4′, lute, buff, machine, swell. Formerly (1953) housed in Messrs. Blüthner's Perivale workshops. The only surviving harpsichord signed by Broadwood alone. See *Russell 1959*, p. 81.

SI . . ., Giuseppe. A clavichord in the Heyer Collection, Leipzig, formerly in the Kraus Collection, Florence, bears the legend on the top key: *1721 Ge* [= Giuseppe] *Si.* Si may be only the beginning of the surname—presumably that of an amateur. Compass C–C, 4 octaves with short octave; 28 pairs of strings; mostly gebunden.

See also above: S, G.

SICULO, Marco. Sixteenth-century virginal maker, presumably Italian though perhaps of Sicilian origin.

Surviving Polygonal Virginals

(1) 1540. Signed: *Marcus Siculus faciebat MDXXXX.* Benton Fletcher Collection, Fenton House, Hampstead, before which it belonged to Sir Charles Lawes-Wittewronge, 2nd Bt., of Rothamsted, Herts. Compass C/E–F, 4½ octaves. Elaborate geometric rose in 2 tiers. Width 51″. Inscription on jackrail. Repaired by Hugh Gough in 1936.

(2) 1570(?). Signed: *Marcus Siculo faciebat Anns* [sic] *1670* [sic]. W. A. Marshall, Cuxton, Kent. Compass C/E–F, 4½ octaves. Inscription above the keyboard. Exhibited at the Crystal Palace, 1900 (no. 50). Sold by Alfred du Cros at Sotheby's to Messrs. Morley, 11 February 1938.

(3?) Messrs. Morley had (February 1954) an unsigned polygonal virginal whose decoration and rose are so similar to those of no. 1 above that it seems likely that the instrument came from the same workshop.

SIEGMULLER, Heinrich Adam. Maker of keyboard instruments in Berlin, *c.* 1793 [*Ge*]. May have made clavichords.

SIERCKS, Martin, of Lübeck. Dates ascertained 1712–14. Maker of keyboard instruments [*Lh*].

SILBERMANN. A name famous in the history of the organ and other keyboard instruments. Two members of the family concern us particularly here:

(1) **Gottfried,** 1683–1753, outstanding member of the Silbermann family, builder of organs, harpsichords, clavichords, and pianofortes, was born at Klein-Bobritzsch in Saxony on 14 January 1683. He was a pupil from 1702 until 1709 in the workshop of his brother Andreas at Strasbourg, deputizing for him 1704–6 during his absence in Paris. In 1710 he settled at Freiburg in Saxony.

He paid great attention to his store of old and mature wood. The *Schlesische Provinzialblätter* (Vol. 2, 1785, p. 439 n.) tell us that 'as he travelled from village to village mending the pews in the churches for the peasants, he took away their old pews, which were then over 100 years old, instead of payment'.

C. P. E. Bach had a Silbermann clavichord, and his rondo *Abschied von meinem Silbermann'schen Clavier* (1781) depicts his sorrow at parting with it. A celebrated passage in Burney (*Present State of Music in Germany . . .*, 2nd edition, 1775, I. 269) describes C. P. E. Bach playing it in 1772. (Welcker von Gontershausen's *Neu-eröffnetes Magazin . . . musikalische Tonwerkzeuge*, 1855, p. 107, seems to be the authority for the statement in *GD* (1940) that the clavichord particularly prized by C. P. E. Bach was by *Gottfried* Silbermann. He writes: 'Capellmeister Bach in Hamburg hatte fast 50 Jahre lang ein Clavier von [Gottfrieds] Arbeit . . .'.)

Silbermann clavichords were praised by C. F. D. Schubarth (*Ideen zu einer Ästhetik der Tonkunst*, 1806, p. 168): 'Rosetti's Compositionen wirken auf bekieltem Flügel schlecht; auf Stein's Fortepiano stark; am meisten auf einem Silbermann'schen Clavichord, denn in seinen Compositionen ist etwas Leichtes, Lichtvolles, Honigsüsses . . .'

In 1736 Silbermann completed 2 pianofortes, closely modelled on Cristofori's, and shewed one of them to J. S. Bach, who played it but considered its tone too weak in the treble and the instrument 'zu schwer zu spielen'. Some time afterwards, however, when Silbermann had made some improvements, Bach (we are told in *Adl.* II. 117) tried one again and gave it his full approval—though he never forsook the clavichord and harpsichord for the instrument destined to oust them. (According to *Ernst 1961*, the 3 grand pianofortes of Frederick the Great at Sanssouci (Potsdam) were undoubtedly made by Gottfried Silbermann. One of these instruments was destroyed in World War II.) A verbal statement by Adolf Hartmann (the restorer of the Berlin Collection, who died in 1943) recorded that one of them bore on the underside of the soundboard the signature: *G.S. 1746, Freiburg in Meissen.*)

Silbermann was granted, in 1736, the title of court organ builder ('Kgl. Poln. und Churfürstl. Sächs. Hof- und Landorgelbauer').

Fifteen years earlier he had invented an instrument which was given the inappropriate name of *Cembal d'amour*—on account of its blending so well with the viola d'amore, we are told in the earliest description of it, by Johann Ulrich König (*Breslauische Gedrückte Sammlungen*, 1721). Actually it had nothing in common with the harpsichord ('Cembal') at all, but was a variant of the clavichord.

A description of it was given later on in the century by

Gerber, who was at pains to make it clear that Silbermann was the sole inventor of the *Cembal d'amour*. He goes on to describe it:

> It has keys and tangents exactly the same as those in the clavichord, to which it is somewhat similar in shape. But the strings are twice as long as in the clavichord, for they are struck in the middle by the tangent and must give a note of the same pitch on both sides of it. For the same reason there is a bridge and a soundboard on either side of the tangent. In the middle the string rests on a rail covered with cloth and slotted [after the fashion of a jack-slide], and through these slots the tangents strike the string, which is thereby lifted up from the cloth and gives a double note, from both sides of the tangent . . .

Gerber remarks on the greater danger of sharpening the note on account of the double length of the string, and commends this problem to the attention of a 'geschickter Künstler' (a tangent-rail being of course impracticable since the string has to sound on both sides of the striking point). The advantages of this instrument over the ordinary clavichord are (he says) threefold: (1) a strong tone, (2) a longer duration of tone, (3) a wider range of loudness and softness.

E. van der Straeten contributed an interesting article on the *Cembal d'amour* to the *Musical Times* of 1 January 1924. He came across some notes on the instrument by Johann Mattheson (1681–1764) in the Hamburg Library. These contain a very good drawing of it, which is reproduced (Adlung's diagram, at *Adl*, II. 125, is only sketchy), and an interesting note, perhaps in Mattheson's hand, calling it 'Clavir d'amour oder ein doppelt Clavir', which is a more sensible name.

The instrument never became popular, and unfortunately no example of it seems to have survived from classical times. Hugh Gough, however, made one in 1954.

Silbermann was unmarried, and left a considerable sum of money when he died in 1753. His nephew Johann Daniel Silbermann carried on the business, and likewise attained the title of court organ builder.

(2) **Johann Heinrich** [Jean Henri], 1727–99, maker of clavichords, harpsichords, spinets, and pianofortes; also an organist and composer. The youngest son of Andreas Silbermann, he was born at Strasbourg on 24 September 1727. Apart from making harpsichords, etc., he carried on the pianoforte tradition of his uncle Gottfried, in whose workshop at Freiberg (Saxony) he studied the making of keyboard instruments in 1742–3. Forkel says, in his *Musikalischer Almanach* (1782): 'His instruments are so well known in the musical world that there is no need to say anything in praise of them. Both his harpsichords and pianofortes, as well as the other instruments with keyboards, and pedals, partly invented by him, are outstanding for their fine workmanship and beautiful tone. . . . His pianofortes cost usually 300 talers each.'

In the *Strassburger Gelehrte Nachrichten* for 1783 (p. 255) we read that his work consists of 'all kinds of keyboard instruments, some of which have been brought by him to a high pitch of excellence through careful thought and long practice, while others have been quite recently designed, of which three deserve special notice: (1) an unusually large harpsichord at 16-foot pitch, (2) a *forté-piano en pédals*, (3) a *forté-piano manuel*. These instruments of his have, as is well known, earned such widespread praise that they have been sent not only to France, Switzerland, and Germany, but also to Lettonia, Russia, Sweden, England, etc., and even to India, and are still on order from such places.' *Ge* (1790) says that his pianos had widespread fame, especially in France.

He married Katharina Margarethe Mosseder about

Tree of the SILBERMANN Family
based on Ks (*p. 367*)

- Michael **Silbermann** (born *c.* 1650; carpenter at Klein-Bobritzsch = Anna Maria Preussler of Grossaltersdorf, 1676)
  - Andreas (1678 Klein-Bobritzsch–1734 Strasbourg) = Anna Maria Schmid
    - Johann Andreas (1712 Strasbourg–1783 ibid.) = 1. Anna Salome Mannberger, 1742 2. Eliz. Schatz, 1772, without issue)
      - Johann Josias (Strasbourg, 1765–86)
      - Johann Andreas (merchant) = Anna Maria Karth
        - Johann Andreas
        - Friedrich Theodor (cellist, *d.* 1816)
    - Johann Daniel (*b.* Strasbourg 1717) = Elisabeth Bär,
      - Ludwig (*d.* young)
      - Johann Friedrich (1762–[?]1805)
    - Johann Gottfried (Strasbourg, 1722–62)
  - **Gottfried** (1683–1753; instrument maker, friend of J. S. Bach

1760, and had 2 sons, of whom the elder, Johann Friedrich (1762–1805) became a builder of organs and maker of keyboard instruments.

He died at Strasbourg on 15 January 1799.

SIMONNEAU, Pierre-Charles. Harpsichord tuner and perhaps maker who lived in the rue Saint-Landry, Paris. Dates ascertained, 1775–9. He provided harpsichords for the *Opéra* [*Pi*, p. 134].

SIMPSON, James & John, of London. Music publishers and perhaps makers of musical instruments (flutes, harpsichords)—though they may have been only dealers. Dates ascertained, 1770–1800. They seem to have been descendants of the music publisher John Simpson, whose premises they were occupying in 1770 and in 1800.

Surviving Keyboard Instruments

(1) Undated. Akron, Ohio, F. A. Seiberling. Harpsichord, 2 manuals. Compass 5 octaves [? F–F] without bottom F sharp; 4 rows of jacks; 5 handstops; no pedals. (Formerly the property of Sir Edward Barry, Ockwells Manor, Bray, Berks. [*Ladies Field*, 6 March 1909]. Said to have belonged to Handel.)

SISON, Benjamin [Sisson, Sissons]. London spinet maker, *c.* 1658–1710. The son of Henry Sissons, he was apprenticed to John Needler, joiner, on 10 October 1673 for 7 years. He was, we presume, chiefly a furniture maker and had numerous apprentices. His son John was apprenticed to John Harris, son of James H. of Sherborne, Oxon.

Benjamin Sisson and Anne his wife were living in the parish of St. Michael's, Cornhill, in 1695 (*Lo*, 1695), in Birchin Lane.

The registers of St. Michael's, Cornhill, record that Sison was buried on 12 November 1710.

Surviving Spinets

(1) Port Sunlight, Cheshire, Lady Lever Art Gallery. Inscription on jackrail: *Benjamin Sison Birchin Lane London Fecit.* Compass A–D, 54 notes.

(2) London, Miss Margaret Hornby. Inscription as on (1), but on nameboard. Compass G/B–D, $4\frac{1}{2}$ octaves. Inscription on front of wrestplank: *WH* 5[?]7.

SKEENE. English harpsichord maker, *fl.* 1779 [*J*]. Or possibly a misreading of Sheene (= Shean, q.v.)

SLADE, Benjamin. Maker of spinets and harpsichords. Born about 1669. Apprenticed to James Aland in September 1684, he was turned over to George Castleman. Freeman of the Joiners' Company, March 1698. Among his apprentices was Thomas Hitchcock the Younger. A 'Benjamin Shede' is referred to in the appendix to R. Seymour's *Survey of the Cities of London and Westminster* (1933–5) as harpsichord maker to the royal household. This is probably a misreading of Slade, for 'Benjamin Slade harpsichord maker in ordinary' is recorded in *LC*, 3/64, 21 August 1727.

SLADE, Charles. Charles Wilson, of King of Prussia, Pa., has (1972) a spinet formerly (1970) owned by E. M. Ripin of Forest Hills, N.Y. It is in walnut, $4\frac{1}{2}$ octaves, and was made in 1734. On the nameboard is the inscription *Carolus Slade Londini fecit 1734*, and the bottom key is marked *C.S. 1734*. No *Charles* Slade is recorded in *Join* or at the Public Record Office.

This spinet was sold by a private collector in New Jersey on 8 March 1952 by Parke–Bernet, New York. It came up there again in 1969 when it was bought by E. M. Ripin.

SLAGH MEULEN, Pieter van der. An ottavino in the Raccolta Statale di Strumenti Musicali, Fondo Evan Gorga, Rome, bears on the nameboard an ink signature: *Pieter van der Slagh / Meulen tot Antwerpen 1600.* The instrument is highly dubious. See *VdMBei*, p. 121.

SMID, Bernhard, of Peissenberg, Bavaria. Maker of clavichords and harpsichords, *fl.* 1433 [*Hirt*].

SMIT, Jan Christoffel. *Fl.* as organ and harpsichord builder in Amsterdam 1736–54. The *Amsterdamse Courant* for 12 June 1736 and again for 29 June 1743 advertised 3-manual harpsichords by him. See further *Curtis*, pp. 60–1.

SMITH, John, *of Bristol.* Maker of spinets and harpsichords, *fl.* 1775 at 20 Bridge Street, Bristol [*J*].

SMITH, John, *of Edinburgh.* Maker of spinets, *c.* 1760 College Wynd, Edinburgh [*J*].

SMITH, Joseph. Harpsichord maker, London. *Fl.* 1799 [*J*].

Abraham
(died young)

Johann Heinrich = Katharina Margarethe
Strasbourg, 1727–99, Mosseder (*c.* 1760)
(instrument maker)

Johann Heinrich
(Writer; took over the publishing-house of his parents-in-law)

Friederike Magdalena
(*m.* Strohl; dead by 1840)

Gustav
Inherited his father's business; printed Mooser's *Silbermann-Festschrift* in 1861)

TABLE 33. *Surviving Stringed Keyboard Instruments by or attributed to the SILBERMANN Family*

No.	Type	Date	Kbs.	Signature	Owner/Remarks
A. Gottfried Silbermann					
[1]	S	1723	1	*G. Silbermann 1723*	Göteborgs Museum. G–F, 4 octaves and a 7th. 175 × 67 cm. Walnut case. Signature unauthentic; *not* by Silbermann [*Ernst*].
2	Cd	1723	1	*Gebauet v. Gottfried Silbermann 1723* [on vellum attached to the balance-rail]	Markneukirchen, Städtisches Gewerbemuseum. C–E, 4 octaves and a 3rd. Ebony naturals, ivory sharps. 140 × 45 cm. Rose. Repaired by Merzdorf. See *Wö*, p. 21.
The following have been attributed to, or may be by, G.S.:					
[3]	H		2	*GS* [on music-desk, which is modern]	Eisenach, Bach-Haus. Not by Silbermann but by Jacob Hartmann (q.v.).
4	H	1776	2		Berlin Collection; 2 mls. F–F, 5 octaves. 2 × 8′, 1 × 4′, coupler. Attributed by Sachs to 'Gottfried(?) Silbermann'; *S* rose.
5	Cd	—	1		Formerly Boddington Collection, Manchester. C–F, 4½ octaves, bundfrei. 2 stops, one silencing one of the unison strings, the other damping.
6	Cd	—	1		Formerly in Steinert Collection. 5½ octaves.
[6a]	H	1774	2		Leipzig, Heyer Collection. 1 × 4′, 1 × 8′, 1 × 16′. 8′ and 16′ on lower keyboard; 4′ on upper; coupler. Attributed by *Ks* to Silbermann in 1910; later discovered to be by J. H. Gräbner, q.v.
B. Johann Heinrich Silbermann					
7	S	1767	1	*Jean Henry Silbermann / Faiseur de Fortépiano & / de Clavecins 1767 / à Strasbourg*	Neupert Collection (Germanisches Nationalmuseum, Nuremberg). 5 octaves F–F. Silbermann rose of intertwined *Ss*. Illustrated in Hanns Neupert, *Das Cembalo* (Kassel, 1933), p. 23 (2nd edition, 1951, p. 24), and *Russell 1959*.
8	S	(1767?)	1		Erlangen University. Date not visible, given by *Brun*. Presented in 1923 by Dr. Reinhold Neupert [*VdM*].
9	S		1	[Signature as above, without date]	Leipzig, Heyer Collection (formerly de Wit). F–F, 5 octaves. 195 × 115 cm. Illustrated at *Ks*, p. 78.
10	S		1		Basel, Historisches Museum.
11	S		1	*Jean Henry Silbermann / Faiseur de Forté-Piano & / de Clavecins / a Strasbourg* [label]	Eisenach, Bach-Haus. Walnut case. Parchment rose. Dimensions 115·5 × 193·5 cm.
12	S		1		Ibid. similar to the foregoing.
13?	S		1		The Hague, Gemeentemuseum, has a spinet strongly resembling the J. H. Silbermann in the Bach-haus at Eisenach (1964 catalogue, no. 71), no. 11 above, the compass, dimensions, and legs being identical. Its rose, combining 3 *S*'s in a triangle, is the same as that in no. 7 above. It can, I think, safely be attributed to J. H. Silbermann.

No.	Type	Date	Kbs.	Signature	Owner/Remarks
13a?	S		1	[Unsigned]	Zürich, Landesmuseum. F–F, 5 octaves. Walnut case. Restored 1968 by *Rindl*, who attributes it to Silbermann.
13b	Cd	[*c*. 1775]	1		Nuremberg, Germanisches Nationalmuseum, Rück Collection. Has the typical Silbermann rose.
14?	Cd	[*c*. 1776]	1		Berlin Collection (formerly P. Spitta's). F–F, 5 octaves. Parchment rose. 138×50·5 cm. Key length 10·5 cm. Undoubtedly by J. H. S., say *Sa* and *Zö* (*Sa*, no. 913).
15	Cd		1		Ibid. Also given by Spitta (*Sa*, no. 914).
16	Cd		1		Formerly J. Joachim [*Sa*, p. 53].
17	Cd		1		Formerly Zelter, then Karl Lütge in Berlin [*Sa*, p. 53].
18	Cd		1		Went *c*. 1920 to Russia.
18a?	Cd		1		Vienna, Kunsthistorisches Museum. Ascribed to J. H. S. by Friedrich Ernst. Bundfrei, F–F, 5 octaves. Rose [*Luith*, p. 7]. Gesellschaft der Musikfreunde, no. 521.
18b?	Cd		1		Paris Conservatoire. Perhaps = no. 14?

TABLE 34. *Surviving Instruments by Benjamin SLADE*

No.	Type	Date	Kbs.	Signature	Owner/Remarks
01	S	1690	1		Messrs. Dolmetsch, who bought it from Leslie Spacie, of Yatton, Somerset.
1	S	1700	1	*Benjamin Slade faciebat 1700* [on jackrail]	Illustrated at *J*, p. 110. G–D, 4 octaves and a 5th. Apparent compass B–D; 2 lowest sharps split. Skunk-tail sharps. Richly marquetried.
2	S	n.d.	1	*Benjamin Slade Londini fecit* [on marquetried name-board]	Bristol Museum (Red Lodge). Keyboard as in 1, but ivory sharps. Plain walnut case. Apparent compass B–D, 4 octaves plus; bottom C sharp and D sharp divided.
3	S	n.d.	1	*Benjamin Slade Londini fecit*	Restored by Messrs. Morley in 1924, and by Alec Hodsdon in 1948. Seen by C. F. Colt, 1949. G–E, 4 octaves plus, without low G sharp. Ivory sharps, ebony naturals; walnut case.
4	H		1		Owned by Dr. J. R. Mirrey, Redhill, 1963. G–G, 5 octaves; 2×8′ stops; length 6′ 7″. Rose with harping figure and *BS*. Bought at auction at Braboeuf Manor, Guildford, 10 June 1963.
5	S	n.d.	1		Sold in 1951 at Salem, Mass. 4 octaves.
6	S	n.d.	1		Stockholm, Nordiska Museet.
7	S	n.d.	1	*Benjamin Slade Londini fecit*	Owned, 1968, by an English lady living in Zug, Switzerland.

Surviving Harpsichords

(1) Undated. Formerly in the Boddington Collection, Manchester. Two manuals, 5 octaves (F–F), 3 stops. No pedals. Length 5′ only. Oak case with brass fittings. Inscribed: *Josephus Smith Londini fecit.*

SMITH, Robert, 1689–1768. Plumian Professor of Astronomy, and Master of Trinity College, Cambridge, from 1742, was interested in temperament; and although we may regard it as certain that he never made an instrument himself, he should be recorded here on account of the enharmonic harpsichord which he designed.

To the second edition (London, 1759) of his *Harmonics, or the philosophy of musical sounds* he added a *Postscript . . . upon the changeable harpsichord: which being supplied with all the useful flat and sharp sounds and tuned in the best manner, is made as harmonious as possible: and yet the execution of music upon this perfect instrument is the same as upon the common harpsichord* (1762). On page 8 of this he writes:

About five years ago Mr. [Jacob] Kirkman made me a changeable harpsichord, which is much admired by the best judges for the delicacy and distinctness of the harmony; owing not only to a more copious scale and a better tuning than usual, but also to the single strings; which when the pens are as strong as they ought to be, throw out clearer and distincter sounds than unisons, and loud enough for very large rooms, especially in playing *Sostenuto*, as on the organ . . .

The *Postscript* gives complete details of the means whereby this harpsichord allowed the performer to change from one tuning to another using hand-stops.

SMITH, William. *Fl.* as harpsichord maker in London about 1700–20.

Surviving Harpsichords

(1) Oxford, in private ownership; 2×8′ stops. Inscription on nameboard: *Gulielmus Smith Londini Fecit.* The instrument clearly dates from about the first quarter of the eighteenth century.

SNETZLER, John. Born Schaffhausen 6 April 1710, died in London 28 September 1785, organ builder. (The error giving Passau as his birthplace seems to have been due to Burney. See further *Sum*, p. 156.) Having come to England about 1740, he opened in 1747 (not 1755) a workshop in Soho, where besides his normal organ-building he collaborated with Kirkman, in making claviorgana. He is recorded in *Un* in 1763 (without forename) as 'organbuilder, Oxford-road' [i.e. Oxford Street]. Shudi bequeathed the ring given him by Frederick the Great to Snetzler, who was one of Shudi's 3 executors.

SOCHER, Johann, *fl.* 1742. Maker of keyboard instruments at Sonthofen, Allgäu. Although no clavichord from his workshop survives, it may be accounted certain that he made them.

A square piano (the oldest extant) by him is in the Neupert Collection, Germanisches Nationalmuseum, Nuremberg. It is inscribed: *Joh. Socher im Obern Sonthofen, Allgau 1742*, and is illustrated in the catalogue, as also in *Ha.*

SÖDERSTRÖM, H. J. Clavichord maker in Stockholm; dates ascertained, 1803–16. From 1803 to 1806 he signed his instruments with Lindholm (q.v.), who was his father-in-law.

Surviving Clavichords

(1) 1803. Göteborgs Museum. [In collaboration with Lindholm, q.v. for details.]

(2) 1816. Stockholm, Nordiska Museet. [By Söderström alone.] Compass 5½ octaves.

SODI, Vincenzio. Harpsichord maker in Florence; *fl.* 1779–92.

SOLFANELLI, Giuseppe, of Pisa, *fl.* 1730. *See*: QUOCO.

SOMER, Nicolas. Harpsichord maker and perhaps organ builder in Paris. *Fl.* 1769–74 [*Verlet*].

SOMIGLIANA, Carlo Antonio. Born at Como; *maestro di cappella* there in 1737. Besides composing he made harpsichords and other musical instruments [*Ge*, 1794].

SONDERMAN, Marcus Gabriel. Clavichord maker at Rendsburg, near Kiel, *fl.* 1796.

Surviving Clavichords

(1) 1796. Copenhagen, Musikhistorisk Museum. Bundfrei. F to F, 5 octaves. Inscription: *Marcus Gabriel Sondermann, Rendsburg Ao 1796.* This instrument was restored in 1908 by Hornung & Møller.

SONNEMANN

(1) **Anton.**

(2) **Peter,** probably related to each other. Both were clavichord makers living in Cologne in 1797, according to a directory for that year [*Ks*].

SOUMLIN, Anton, of Basel and Freiburg im Breisgau. Organ builder and clavichord maker; dates ascertained 1490/1–1506 [*Hirt*].

SOUTHWELL, John. Recorded as harpsichord and piano maker at 34 Marlborough Street, Dublin, in 1815 and at 9 in the same street in 1822. He is recorded as piano maker at three Dublin addresses between 1824 and 1844.

SOUTHWELL, William, of Dublin. Harpsichord maker, 1756–1842. Became apprenticed to Ferdinand Weber (q.v.) in 1772, and stayed with him for 10 years. In 1782 he opened shop at 26 Fleet St., Dublin, and this address is given for him until 1786 [*Teahan*]. In 1786 he turned his attention particularly to the piano, and in 1787 he succeeded Weber's son in Marlborough Street. In 1793 he moved to Lad Lane, London, where Haydn visited him. He returned to Dublin in 1836, died at Rathmines, and was buried at Glasnevin [*Fld*].

William Southwell & Co., harpsichord and piano makers, are recorded at 34 Marlborough Street, 1804–14 [*Teahan*].

Several pianos in the shape of a semicircular table survive; one, with a Venetian swell, was in 1955 in the possession of Mrs. Basil Ionides, of Buxted Park, Kent (see also *J*, pl. lix); and Messrs. J. G. Morley, London, had (1947) an upright cabinet grand piano by the same maker. Dundee Museum has an upright piano by him dated 1798.

TABLE 35. *Surviving instruments by Vincenzio SODI*

No.	Type	Date	Kbs.	Signature	Remarks
01(?)	H	1778	1	*Vincetius Sodi Florentinus fecit Anno Domini 1778*	Listed in *FrancI.*
1	H	(?1779)	1	*Vincenzo Sodi me fecit 1739* [?1779] *Firenze.* (Signature also on G sharp above middle C)	New York, Albert Augustine. 2×8′, 4½ octaves. C–F.
[2]	H	1779	3		New York. Metropolitan Museum of Art. A spurious instrument made from an eighteenth-century German or Austrian piano-forte. 2×8′, 1×4′.
3	H	1780	1	*Vincentius Sodi Florentinus Fecit Anno Domini 1780*	Detroit Institute of Arts. Earlier owners: Homer Wickline, Pittsburgh; Robert Johnson, Los Angeles; Craig Ely, Westtown, Pa. Registers 2×8′, 2 rows of jacks, each jack having 2 tongues, one facing each way. This type of jack is depicted in *Cemb. Ang.* (1775). Plates 4 and 5.
4	H	1782	1	*Vincentius Sodi Florentinus Fecit anno Domini 1782*	Exeter Museum. G–G, 5 octaves; 2×8′ stops.
5	H	1792	1	*No. 95. Vincenzio Sodi Fece / Firenze 1792*	Leipzig, Heyer Collection. 2×8′. F–F, 5 octaves. 2 genouillères, one working on *Fagott-Zug* [paper pressed against strings], the other a buffstop. Boxwood naturals. Latest known Italian harpsichord.
6	H	—	1	*No. 93. Vincentius Sodi Florentinus fecit anno 1792.*	Bologna, L. F. Tagliavini. C–F 4½ octaves; 2×8′ stops. Lowest key dated 1791.
7?	H	—	1		Helen Hewitt, North Texas State College, has a harpsichord one of whose jacks bears the initials *VS.*

For details of Southwell's pianoforte patents see *Ha.*
A James and a Marcus Southwell are recorded as piano makers in Dublin from 1822 to 1844 [*Teahan*].

SPÄTH

(1) **Franz Jacob,** *the Elder* [Spath]. Died 4 January 1760. Two years before, he had built the organ in the Church of the Holy Trinity, Regensburg. He may have been the father of:

(2) **Franz Jacob,** *the Younger.* 1714–86 [*Hirt*]; maker of clavichords, organs, etc. and inventor of the *Tangentenflügel,* in which wooden tangents, covered with leather and held in guides like the jacks of a harpsichord, are thrown against the strings when the keys are struck (see *Ks,* pp. 197 ff.). *Ge* says, in his 1814 edition: 'In 1751 he provided the Elector at Bonn with a *Tangentenflügel* with 30 varieties of tone, and had by 1770 through his industry produced an instrument with 50 varieties of tone. He died about 1796.' He married Johanna Rosina Schlessinger and had 7 children, of whom Anna Felicitas was the eldest. Forkel's *Musikalischer Almanach . . .* 1782 praises his instruments.
Anna Felicitas was married to Christoph Friedrich Schmahl (q.v.) on 28 September 1772. This Schmahl later became a partner in Späth's business.
See further *Herrm.*

(3) **Johann Adam,** 1742–94. Cantor at Anspach, neither an instrument maker nor connected with the Regensburg Späths. It seems, as Eitner says (IX. 214), that *Ge* has confused him with number (2) above. *Herrm,* whom see further (p. 27), agrees with this conclusion.

SPATZ. *Schub* (p. 288) mentions a 'Spatz' together with Fritz and Stein as an outstanding clavichord maker. This is a misprint for 'Späth' (q.v.).

SPECKEN, Philip Jacob. Dates ascertained, 1737–42; maker of clavichords and harpsichords who learnt his art in Dresden, and moved to Stockholm, where he is known to have also made *cembals d'amour* (*Nor,* p. 96).

Surviving Instruments

(1) 1737. Harpsichord, 2 manuals; signed *Philip Jac. Specken, Stockholm, 1737*; 5 octaves.

(2) 1742. Clavichord, signed: *Jacob Specken, Stockholm 1742.* C–D, 4 octaves and 2 notes.
Both are in Nordiska Museet, Stockholm.

(3) Undated(?). Clavichord. Östergötlands Museum, Linköping, Sweden.

SPEER, Christian Ferdinand. Emigrated from Silesia to Denmark and obtained his maker's licence in Copenhagen in 1761 (organs, harps, and stringed keyboard instruments) [*Müller*]. The Rosenborg Castle Museum, Denmark, has a virginal by him dated 1762: C–C, 4 octaves; 40·5×87·7 cm. Inscribed on soundboard: *Christian Ferdinand Speer in Coppenhagen 1762*. Rose. The instrument is said to have been in Gottorp Castle, where Princess Louise, daughter of King Frederik V of Denmark and wife of Prince Karl of Hessen, lived from 1768 to 1836. Given to Rosenborg in 1875/6 by F. S. Bang, who had bought it in Flensborg.

SPEISSEGGER, Johann Konrad. Organ builder in Schaffhausen during the eighteenth century. Also made harpsichords and spinets [*RindlKlav*, p. 254].

SPEISSEGGER, Alexander. Born 19 January 1727 at Schaffhausen; died 16 July 1772. Son of the well-known organ builder Johann Konrad Speissegger. Organist and organ builder at Neuchâtel. In 1760 he was commissioned to make a large 2-manual harpsichord for the Academy of Music there. See further *Hirt*, p. 480.

SPIGHI, Francesco, of Florence, *fl.* 1790. Made pianofortes; may have made harpsichords [*Ge*].

SPINETTI, Giovanni, of Venice, *fl.* 1503. Maker of virginals. According to Banchieri (*Conclusione nel suono dell'organo*, Bologna, 1608) the term *spinet* is derived from this maker's name. Others have derived it from *spina* = thorn, supposedly referring to the plectrum held in the jack-tongue.

SPINETUS, Johannes. *See*: SPINETTI, Giovanni.

STECKLER, N., of Metz, maker of harpsichords and pianofortes (? eighteenth century). An instrument [? harpsichord] by him was in the Château de Lunéville in 1910 [*Jac*].

STEEVENS, Gerrit. Dutch eighteenth-century instrument maker. Born at Tongeren *c.* 1710, he was registered at Leiden University as 'musicorum instrumentorum artifex' in 1741. In 1750 he moved from Overmaren to The Hague. There is evidence of his having made viols, harpsichords, and organs. Latest date ascertained, 1765 [*Vlam*].

STEFANO DI BIAGIO. *See*: BONISSIMO, Stefano.

STEFANO DI GIANNANTONIO. *See*: BONISSIMO, Stefano.

STEFANO DI GIOVANNI. *See*: BONISSIMO, Stefano.

STEFANO DI MODENA. *See*: STEPHANUS MUTINENSIS.

STEHLIN, Benoist, *also called* Stellé. Born before 1732 at Jettingen in Upper Alsatia, he became an organ builder and harpsichord maker in Paris; a son of Georg Stehlin, a joiner in Oltingen in Upper Alsatia; married 1753; died 11 July 1774. *Bq* quotes a 'clavecin de Stella, 1714' which must be a mistake. See *Verlet* for further details.

Surviving Harpsichords

(1) 1750. St. Quentin, France, Musée Antoine Lecuyer. Two manuals; 2×8′, 1×4′, buff, coupler; 5 octaves F–F. Given to the Museum by Bernard Jumentier (1749–1829), composer and *maître de chapelle* at St. Quentin Cathedral. Restored in 1913.

(2) 1760. Smithsonian Institution, Washington. Two manuals. Inscribed on bottom 4′ jack: *Benoist Stelle* and dated 1760 on the soundboard. *BS* rose; 2×8′, 1×4′, buff, push-pull coupler; 5 octaves F–F. Illustrated in *Smithsonian Journal of History*, Vol. 1, no. 3 (1966). The instrument was previously in Florida, and a packer's label on the stand below the keyboard shews that at one time it passed through Salomon's hands. Restored by J. Scott Odell, Smithsonian Institution, 1968–70.

STEIBELT, Carl Ludwig. Dates ascertained 1797/8 [*Hirt*]; made clavichords and pianos in Berlin. According to Gerber (1814) he collaborated with his son in the work.

STEIN, Johann Andreas, 1728–92. Organ builder and inventor of the 'Viennese' or 'German' pianoforte action; was born at Heidelsheim in Baden. From August 1748 until June in the following year he was a pupil of the organ builder J. A. Silbermann in Strasbourg. During 1749 and 1750 he spent a good deal of time at Augsburg, and settled there from 1751 onwards. A few years later he built the organ at the Barfüsserkirche there, and became organist in 1757.

From October 1758 until the following January he was in Paris. After his return to Augsburg, pianoforte making supplanted organ building as his chief interest. It is true that he had made pianofortes before this time [*Hertz*, p. 44]—indeed, from the beginning of his working life he had shewn an interest in the new instrument—but from 1759 onwards his inventive disposition concentrated on the pianoforte. He was also much exercised by the problem of making a stringed keyboard instrument capable of 'expression' and *sostenuto* tone. In the pursuit of this aim he invented 4 instruments:

1. His *polytoni-clavichordium*, described in the *Augsburger Intelligenzblatt* of 5 October 1769, was perhaps suggested by Marius's pianoforte/harpsichord of 1716 in Paris (though in Marius's instrument 1 set of strings served for both the hammers and the jack action). The *PC* consisted of 2 instruments, one above the other: on top a harpsichord with 3×8′ and 1×16′ stops and 2 keyboards; underneath, a pianoforte with 1 manual.

2. His *melodika*, completed in 1772 after 15 years of experiment, consisted of a small organ with pipes arranged horizontally in a wing-shaped case, designed to be laid upon another keyboard instrument. Its compass reached down only to G below middle C, since it was meant to supply the 'melody' only; volume could be varied by means of touch. The instrument is described in Stein's *Beschreibung meiner Melodika, eines neuerfundenen Clavierinstruments* (Augsburg, 1772).

3. The *vis-à-vis*, a long rectangular instrument with a pianoforte (its keyboards at both ends) and a harpsichord with its keyboards at one end, could be played either by

Tree of STEIN, shewing their connection with VOIT. (Based on Hertz)

. . . **Stein**, of Helmsheim

- Johann Georg Stein (1697–1754; organ builder at Heidelsheim)
  - **Johann** (Georg) **Andreas Stein** (1728–92; instrument maker at Augsburg)
    - Anna Maria Stein (Nanette, 1768–1833) = J. A. Streicher (1761–1833; piano maker, Vienna)
      - Joh. Baptiste Streicher (1796–1871; K. K. Hofpianofabrik, Vienna)
        - Emil Streicher (1836–1916; piano maker Vienna)
    - Math. Andr. Stein (1776–1842; piano maker, Vienna)
      - Karl Andreas Stein (1797–1863; Pianist and K. K. court instrument maker at Vienna)
  - Joh. Heinrich Stein (1735–67; organ builder, Durlach)
- Andreas Stein (1711–77; tailor, Heidelsheim)
  - Georg Markus Stein (173–894; organ builder, Durlach)
    - Kath. Friederike Stein (1772–1813) = Joh. V. Voit (1772–1806; organ builder, Durlach
      - Ludwig Voit (1802–83; organ builder in Durlach)
        - Heinrich Voit (1834–80; organ builder, Durlach)
          - Siegfried Voit, (born 1870, organ builder in Durlach, proprietor of the Firm of H. Voit & Söhne)
    - Christ. Friedr. Stein (1782–1823; court instrument maker at Karlsruhe)
  - Joh. Andr. Stein (1752–1821; organ builder, Wolmar and Pernau)

TABLE 36. *Relevant Surviving Instruments by STEIN*

No.	Date	Type	Kbs.	Signature	Owner/Remarks
				Joh. Andr. Stein Orgel u. Claviermacher in Augsburg 1762	Budapest, Hungarian National Museum (bought 1965). Formerly Mozart's (probably the instrument referred to above in the text) and later Hummel's. C–F, 4 octaves, gebunden. Black naturals, white sharps. Size 99×35×11 cm. Shewn at the Vienna Weltausstellung, 1873, and the Internationale Ausstellung für Musik- und Theaterwesen, Vienna, 1892. See G. Gábry's illustrated article 'Das Reiseklavichord W. A. Mozarts' in *Studia musicologica*, Budapest, Vol. 10 (1968), pp. 153–62.
[2]	1770	Piano-organ	2		Göteborgs Museum. Upper manual: pianoforte; lower manual: organ.
[?]3	[*c.* 1770]	Cd	1	. . . *o* . . . *a Augsburg* [on torn label]	Berlin Collection, no. 1279. Attributed to Stein by *Wö.*
4	1777	*Vis-à-vis*	3+1		Verona, Museo Civico (formerly, according to *Hertz*, belonged to the Società Filarmonica, Verona). A combined grand pianoforte and 2-keyboard harpsichord. The instrument is a rectangle 9′ 5″×3′ 4″ on 6 legs. Keyboards at each end. The harpsichord has 4 stops; 1×16′, 2×8′. 1×4′; 2 hand-stops. Illustrated in *Russell 1959*.
5	1783	*Vis-à-vis*	2+1	*Jean André Stein, faiseur d'Orgues, des Clavicins et Organiste a l'Eglise des Minorittes a Augsbourg 1783*	Naples Conservatoire (formerly belonged to the the Duke Ernesto del Balzo). A combined grand pianoforte and 2-keyboard harpsichord. The harpsichord has 3 stops, presumably 2×8′, 1×4′. Compass 5 octaves F–F. Ebony naturals, ivory sharps; 2 genouillères. The instrument was presented in 1784 by the Emperor Joseph II of Austria after he was entertained at Naples by King Ferdinand (1751–1825).

1 person alone or by 2 simultaneously. Two surviving examples of this type of instrument are recorded below.

4. In 1783 Stein brought out his *Saitenharmonika* (described in the *Musikalische Realzeitung*, Speyer, 1789), which consisted of a bichord pianoforte, to which a third set of strings, set in motion by a 'sehr elastische Materie' was added. This stop was called by Stein 'ein uraltes deutsches Spinettchen', and could be played either alone or in conjunction with the pianoforte.

In the anonymous work *Die vornehmsten Merkwürdigkeiten der Reich-Stadt Augsburg* [by P. von Stetten, 1772] is an advertisement: 'Hr J. A. Stein, Orgelmacher, verfertigt Orgeln, Clavicembel, Claviere, die von ihm erfundene Melodica. Man sieht auch dermalen bey ihme ein Clavicembel von besonderer Zusammensetzung u. Wirkung.'

Stein paid great attention to the clavichord, building a large number of instruments which spread throughout Germany, France, and the Low Countries. Mozart paid a tribute to Stein's clavichords in a letter dated at Augsburg, 14 October 1777: . . . Ich hatte oben die Ehre . . . so beylaüfig ¾ Stunde auf einem guten Clavichord von Stein zu spiellen'; and in a letter written 3 days later he gives a detailed account of Stein's treatment of soundboards. He also owned a Stein clavichord, which Leopold Mozart had bought for him when he was 7 years old. Leopold wrote to Leopold Hagenauer on 20 August 1763: '. . . Ich habe ein artiges Clavierl vom H. Stein in Augspurg gekauft, welches uns wegen dem Exercitio auf der Reise grosse Dienste thut . . .'. This instrument still survives.

Schub (p. 216) calls Stein 'einen vorzüglichen musikalischen Kopf' who 'kennt alles Grosse, besonders was Klavier- und Orgelspiel betrifft; als Mechaniker hat er schwerlich seines Gleichen in Europa. Seine Orgeln, Flügel, Fortepianos und Clavikorde sind die besten, die man kennt. Stärke mit Zartheit, Tiefsinn mit Schönheit gepaart'.

In 1770 Stein made for a Swedish client a claviorganum, of which the upper keyboard worked on a pianoforte and the lower on an organ. This instrument is preserved in the Museum at Göteborg.

His son Andreas and daughter Nanette supervised his business during the last years of his life. He died at Augsburg at the age of 64. For further details see *GD* and *Hertz*.

STEINERT, Michael. Organist at Leipzig in the eighteenth century; made a *Geigenwerk* [*AdlG*].

STEINICHE. *See*: STEINICHT, Paul.

STEINICHT, Paul, of Danzig, *fl.* 1657–61. Virginal maker.

Instruments Surviving up to World War II

(1) Berlin Collection. Ottavino virginal. Inscribed: *Paulus Steinicht me fecit anno MDCLVII.* Four octaves with short octave. Rose. 65×39 cm. (Formerly belonged to M. Snoeck, Belgium. Shewn at the Special Exhibition of Ancient Musical Instruments, S. Kensington Museum, 1872.)

(2) 1661. Ibid. Another ottavino, similar. Inscribed on the jackrail: *Paulus Steinicht / me fecit Gedani / Anno 1661.* 65×38 cm. Rose.

STELLA. *Bq.* mentions a 'clavecin de Stella, 1714'. This would seem to be an erroneous reference to Benoist Stehlin, q.v.

STELLE, Benoît. Eighteenth-century Parisian harpsichord maker. *See*: STEHLIN, Benoist.

STEPHANINI, Bartolommeo. Italian harpsichord maker, *fl.* 1694.

A harpsichord by him is preserved in the Historisches Museum, Frankfurt a/M., inscribed: *Anno MDCXCIV / Bartholomaeus / Stephanini / faciebat.* 2×8′, side-stops. Compass G–D, without G sharp. Boxwood naturals, ebony[?] sharps. 100×245 cm.

FrancI lists a harpsichord signed: *Bartolomeo Stephanini 1646.*

STEPHANUS MUTINENSIS. Virginal maker of Modena, *fl.* 1537.

A beautifully preserved polygonal ottavino by him is in the possession of Edgar Lister of Westwood, Wilts. The nameboard is inscribed *Stephanus Mutinensis MDXXXVII.* The compass is 3 octaves and 4 notes. The case is inlaid with ivory, and the cypress soundboard has a fine rose. Repaired by Ian Harwood in 1959.

STERNEMANN, Jacob. *See*: STIRNEMANN, Jacob.

STEWART, Neil. Music seller and publisher, also dealer in spinets and pianofortes, of Edinburgh; earliest date ascertained, *c.* 1759–60. Logan, and perhaps Andrew Rochead, made spinets for him. In 1787 his sons Neil and Malcolm entered the firm, which carried on as Neil Stewart & Co., or N. and M. Stewart, until about 1805. For their various addresses in Edinburgh see *H & S.*

Surviving Spinets

(1) 1774. Mr. C. A. Legg, Cirencester (1954). F–F, 5 octaves, without bottom F sharp; white naturals, ebony sharps. The nameboard is signed: *Neil Stewart Edinburgh fecit MDCCLXXIV.* But during repairs Mr. Legg found an ink inscription on the inside surface of the bottom: *James Logan Edinburgh fecit no. 104, for N. Stewart No. 12.* The date *1774* is stamped on the lowest key.

(2) Edinburgh University, formerly Raymond Russell (formerly at Goodrich Court, Ross-on-Wye).

White naturals, black sharps. Inscription: *Neil Stewart Edinburgh fecit*; on the back of the nameboard: *A. R. for N. S. 21* [? Andrew Rochead for Neil Stewart]. Bottom key stamped *1784.* F–F, 5 octaves; 61 keys. Long side 6′ 2″. (Sotheby's, 25 November 1955.) See *RussColl.*

(3?) A spinet with an uninscribed name-panel inlaid in the nameboard and very closely resembling no. 1 above, except that it has 2×8′ stops, may perhaps be a Logan/Stewart. Owned in 1958 by M. Thomas, who had apparently found it in Scotland. Restored by Alfred Reeve in that year. A pedal engages the proximal jacks. The double stringing is accomplished by bridges of double height, half the strings passing through holes. Bought and taken home by an Australian. Now (1973) owned by Miss Mary McMillan.

Shudi's books record the sale of pianos to Neil Stewart.

STIRNEMANN, Jacob [Sternemann]. Organ builder at Lyons; also made harpsichords. Dates ascertained, 1777–89 [*Vallas*]. A 'piano organisé' signed *Stirnemann à Lyon 1783* was shewn at the 1889 exhibition, Lyons.

Surviving Instruments

(1) 1777. Geneva, private ownership (1968), a 2-manual harpsichord, 2×8′, 1×4′; rose painted on soundboard (not cut); 5 octaves. Signed by *Jacob Stirnimann, Lyon, 1777* [*Rindl*].

STODART, Robert. Dates ascertained: 1775–96, became a pupil of John Broadwood in the making of keyboard instruments. During 1775 he did some tuning for customers, according to Broadwood's books [*GD*]. While working for Broadwood he joined with his employer in helping Backers (q.v.) in the design of the 'English' pianoforte action.

In 1776 he moved into a house on the west side of Wardour Street; and in the following year he was granted a patent (number 1172) for: 'A new sort of instrument, or grand forte piano, with an octave swell, and to produce various tones together or separate [*sic*], and which instrument will be more durable, and produce finer and more variable tones, than any yet made.'

No. 1 pedal brings on the harpsichord action and switches off the piano action in one movement.

No. 2 pedal operates the swell.

In addition to the piano action, there are 2 rows of jacks, which act on the 8′ and 4′ string respectively.

In 1788 Stodart took over the adjacent house from William Rigg, and his name appears against both houses in the rate-books until 1796, when Thomas Sheraton took over one of them. In 1797 Stodart's name disappears altogether from the Poor-Rate book. William Frecker, the pianoforte maker who later lived at 21 Rathbone Place, lived 2 doors away from Stodart in Wardour Street from 1787 to 1800 [*RB*].

A combined pianoforte and harpsichord preserved in the Smithsonian Institution, Washington, has 2 manuals. Inscriptions: (*a*) on upper board: *Combined harpsichord and grand piano. Upper bank Piano; lower, harpsichord.* (*b*) On lower board: *Robertus Stodart. Londini fecit 1777.* But the nameboards do not look genuine; and the instrument is unlike the drawing in Stodart's patent, but corresponds very closely with the 2-manual instrument illustrated in James Davies's patent of 1792—moreover the divided bridge makes the earlier date highly unlikely.

Stodart founded the firm of pianoforte makers bearing his name, which endured until 1861. A certain number of his pianos are still in existence, notably a fine grand pianoforte dated 1779 owned (1938) by Arnold Dolmetsch, and another of 1784, which even at that late date had a bridge of harpsichord profile and a single bridge-pin for each string. A grand pianoforte in Göteborgs Museum is signed *Mattheus et Gulielmus Stodart Londini fecerunt 1798. Wardour Street, Soho.*

There was sold at Christie's on 30 June 1790: 'Item 40. A capital full toned harpsichord by Stodart in a neat mahogany inlaid case and leather cover' [Vendor Robert Sanderson; buyer Dorset; price £43. 1*s*.].

STOPPACIO, *Priest.* A harpsichord at Vassar College, Poughkeepsie, N.Y. (1 ml., C/E–E, 4 octaves, 2×8′) is inscribed on the back of the nameboard: *Fatto dal Padre Stoppacio del carmine nell'Anno 1554*; also *Vincentius Pratensis 1610.*

STOYTE, Richard. Harpsichord and spinet maker in Golden Lane, Dublin, in 1745 [*Teahan*].

STRÄHLE, David. Clavichord maker, *fl.* at Stockholm in 1738.

Surviving Clavichords

(1) 1738. Stockholm, Nordiska Museet; 4 octaves and 2 notes.

STRANGE, Adrian. *See*: STRONG, Adrian.

STRAUBE, Johann Augustin, 1725–1802. Born at Alt-Brandenburg, 15 May 1725. Moved to Berlin as 'musikalischer Instrumentenmacher', and acquired citizenship on 28 August 1764. Forkel praises his harpsichords (*Musikalischer Almanach*, 1782, p. 202) and his square pianos, which cost 60 talers. Gerber also mentions his high reputation as a pianoforte maker [*Ks*].

Straube was assisted in designing his instruments by the theorist and composer J. P. Kirnberger (1721–83), according to a footnote in C. F. Reichardt's *Briefe eines aufmerksamen Reisenden* (Part 2, 1776): 'Besonders gewinnt der letzte [i.e. Straube] durch die Hülfe des Herrn Kirnbergers, der ihn mit seinen theoretischen Kenntnissen des Instrumentbaues unterstützt . . .' He also made and repaired violins [*Lü*]. He died in his Berlin house, Leipzigerstrasse 17, on 18 April 1802 [*Ks*].

(01) 1783. Clavichord. The Hague, Gemeentemuseum. Bundfrei; rose; soundboard extended to cover keyboard, the tangents coming up through a slit.

(1) 1786. Clavichord. Berlin Collection. *Johann Augustin Straube, Musikalischer Instrumentenmacher / Fecit à Berlin Anno 1786.* Bundfrei F–F, 5 octaves. Lost in 1945.

(2) 1787. Clavichord. Leipzig University, Heyer Collection. Bundfrei F–F, 5 octaves. See *Ks*, p. 49. *Johann Augustin Straube, Musikalischer Instrumentenmacher / Fecit à Berlin, Anno 1787.*

(3) Date not ascertained. Clavichord. East Berlin, Märkisches Museum.

STRONG, Adrian. Maker of virginals, *fl.* 1639–55, Dublin. He married Mary Meade, 19 August 1651, and was appointed Master of the Dublin House of Correction in the same year [*Fld*].

STUMPFF, J. G. Clavichord maker at Ruhla bei Eisenach, *fl.* 1816. A clavichord of this date survives in Germany. Compass F–C, 5½ octaves, bundfrei [*Berner*]. His brother Johann Andreas made harps and pianos.

STUPAN, Jakob. Probably the early owner (1722) of a seventeenth-century ottavino in the Zürich Landesmuseum. See further *RindlKlav*, p. 224.

SÜSS, Hans. *See*: HANS VAN CUELEN.

SWANEN, Jacques Joachim. Harpsichord maker in Paris; *fl.* 1783–1816. Presumably of German origin, he was living in 1783 in the rue du Faubourg-Saint-Germain, in 1786 in the rue des Fossés-Monsieur-le-Prince (called rue de la Liberté after the Revolution). His apprenticeship was served probably for the most part not in France [*Verlet*].

Surviving Instruments

(1) 1786. Paris. Conservatoire des Arts et Métiers. *JS* rose. Two manuals (E–A, 5½ octaves) and a pedal keyboard (E–E, 2 octaves) with piano action; 2×8′, 1×4′ stops, with a 16′ worked by the pedals (besides the piano action). Inscribed: *Joachim Swanen Facteur à Paris 1786 rue des Fossés Mr. le Prince au no. 106.* Five pedals (? original) for changing the registers. Restored by Tomasini in 1883.

Swanen signed one of the rows of jacks in the harpsichord ostensibly by Ruckers (actually by Goujon), no. 4 in the Ruckers list: *Fait par Joachim Swann*[?], *rue des fosses* [sic] *Mr le Prince, 1784* [*GSJ*, p. 13 (1960), p. 58, note 15].

SWART, Willem [Swert]. Dutch composer; born in Arnhem, by 1602 he was living in Amsterdam. He holds the distinction, unique as far as I know, of having made a harpsichord of porcelain, after 13 years' work on the considerable problems of resonance involved. (He even extracted 20 florins from the States General for his achievement.) See further *Curtis*, p. 61.

SYMELIN, Anton. *See*: SOUMLIN, Anton.

T. A. *See*: A, T.

TABEL, Hermann [Tabell; Table]. Harpsichord maker. Dates ascertained, 1716/17–1738 (year of death).

He was born in the Low Countries. J. Shudi Broadwood [*Broad*, p. 4] related the important fact that Tabel learnt harpsichord making from the successors to the Ruckers in Antwerp (i.e. the Couchets).

He settled in London, probably about 1700. From the rate-books of St. Martin-in-the-Fields we learn that he took up his residence in Oxendon Street in 1716 or 1717.

It is not certain whether Burkat Shudi (q.v.), who had come over from Switzerland in 1718, had begun working for Tabel by 1723, when the latter put the following announcement (quoted by *J*, p. 41 n.) in the *Evening Post* (30 May): 'Mr. Tabel, the famous Harpsichord maker, has 3 Harpsichords to dispose of, which are and will be the last of his making, since he intends to leave off Business. At his house in Oxendon Street over against the Black Horse in Piccadilly . . .' Tabel appears to have changed his mind and to have continued his work; for 10 years later in *The St. James's Evening Post* (no. 2774, 22–4 February 1733) we read: 'Whereas it has been reported, that Mr. TABEL, the famous Musical Instrument maker, was dead, and that he hath learn'd his Art to one of his Men, to make that fine Tone in Harpsichords, all which is false and foundless, he lives still at his House in Swallow-street, over-against Haddon-Court, near Golden Square.'

By this time Shudi had set up on his own, and Jacob Kirkman (q.v.) had probably come over from Alsace and started working for Tabel. At any rate, soon after this Kirkman became Tabel's most trusted assistant, for in his will, dated 28 July 1738, Tabel nominates Kirkman one of his trustees and bequeaths him £5 for mourning. In 1724 (as we learn from the rate-books of St. James's, Piccadilly) Tabel moved to Swallow Street, St. James's, where he died in 1738.

Tabel married twice. His second wife was Susanna Virgoe, who was probably the mother of his 2 daughters Gertrud and Catherine who in 1738 were living in Amsterdam, possibly in the home of Tabel's brother Barnard.

The story related by Burney in Rees's *Cyclopaedia*, how Kirkman proposed to Tabel's widow, Susanna, at breakfast and married her the same morning, is quoted by Dale (p. 26) and is fairly familiar. It has some foundation in fact, for Kirkman did marry Tabel's widow in 1738; but the marriage did not last long, for by October 1740 Susanna had died.

On 8 May 1739 the *Daily Gazetteer* contained the notice: 'Whereas Mr. Hermann Tabel late of Swallow Street, the famous Harpsichord maker, dead, hath left several fine Harpsichords to be disposed of by Mr. Kirckmann, his late Foreman; this is to acquaint the Curious that the said Harpsichords, which are the finest he ever made, are to be seen at the said Mr. Kirckmann's, the corner of Pulteney Court in Cambridge Street, over against Silver Street, near Golden Square.'

On 18 March 1777 Lady Howe 'bought a second-hand harpsichord by Table' [*sic*]. There was in 1720 a 2-manual harpsichord by *Hermanus Table* at Cannons, the residence of the Duke of Chandos [*Chandos*, p. 139].

Tabel's chief importance lies in his transplanting the Ruckers tradition to England, so that the instruments of the great English school of the eighteenth century led by Shudi and Kirkman are in a direct line of descent from the famous Antwerp workshops.

We have very little idea how many harpsichords Tabel made; but instruments by him appear not infrequently in the sale room during the second half of the eighteenth century, e.g. at Christie's:

15 March 1793. Item 54. An excellent fine toned harpsichord by Tabel [Vendor Richard Brickendon; buyer and price not given].

11 June 1793. Item 76. A fine toned harpsichord with 4 stops by Tabel [Vendor Mrs. Bacon; buyer Rixon; price 5 gns.].

One Harpsichord with a Tabel Inscription survives

1721. Warwick, County Museum (formerly Mrs. Edmonds, Chackmore, sold at Sotheby's, 2 July 1965). Inscribed *Hermanus Tabel fecit Londini 1721* and signed and numbered *43* by Tabel on the top key of the lower manual. 2 manuals F–F; 2×8′, 1×4′, lute stop. Case veneered in walnut with cross-banding; inside, sycamore with walnut stringing. Finely chased brass hinges. Gilt rose including a viscount's coronet. Restored by Broadwoods in 1900. In 1913 it belonged to Helen, Countess of Radnor, from whom it passed to Mrs. Pleydell-Bouverie of Godalming. From Captain James Lane of Wanstead it was bought, after World War II, by Raymond Russell, who sold it at Sotheby's on 25 May 1951 to Miss Baldwin (Mrs. Edmonds). Shudi's earliest surviving harpsichord (1729) is similar in many points to this instrument by Tabel. A detailed account by C. Mould of this instrument is given in *RipKb*, pp. 57–64.

TABLE. *See*: TABEL, Hermann.

TACANI. Florentine harpsichord maker mentioned in *ClP* (p. 71).

TAEGHS, Vincentius de. A virginal by this maker was in the Savoye Collection, Paris. The sale catalogue of Savoye Collection III (13 June 1924) assigns it to the seventeenth century, giving the name as *Vincentius de Taegis*.

TAMITIUS, Andreas. Born *c.* 1730 at Dohlen near Dresden; died *c.* 1770. 'Churfürstlich Sächsischer Hof-orgelbauer' at Dresden; also made clavichords [*Hirt*].

TAMITIUS, Johann Gottlieb, *the Elder*. Son of Andreas T.; born at Dresden, moved to Zittau; maker of organs and stringed keyboard instruments, including clavichords.

TAMITIUS, Johann Gottlieb, *the Younger*, son of Joh. Gottl. the Elder, whose work he continued, also making pianofortes, until *c.* 1840 [*Fla* (1953); *Hirt*].

TANNENBERG, David. Born 1728 at Berthelsdorf, near Herrnhut in Saxony. Emigrated to Bethlehem, Pa., in 1749, and was apprenticed there in 1757 or 1758 to Johann Gottlob Clemm (Klemm), an organ builder who was also an *émigré* from Europe. On his master's death in 1762, Tannenberg set up as an organ builder on his own, moving in 1765 to Lititz, Pa., where he remained until his death in 1804, having achieved a considerable reputation.

He occasionally made other instruments, e.g. a harpsichord for the Single Sisters' House in Salem, N.C., and at least 2 pianos. A design by him for a clavichord (4 octaves C–C, 4′ long), sent with instructions for building it to Salem, N.C., is reproduced in *Antiques*, July 1965, and on pl. 6 of *Armstr*, who should be consulted for full details of his life and of the organs made by him.

TANTINI

(1) **Sesto,** clavichord and harpsichord maker in Modena. Dates ascertained 1461–90 [*Va*]. He asks the Duke Borso d'Este for payment for a 'clavicinbalo' in a letter dated 15 November 1461 (*Va*, p. 243). This is the earliest reference to the harpsichord in Italian.

(2) **Costantino** his brother, also a maker. Dates ascertained 1419–81.

Va quotes from a letter of Duke Ercole d'Este dated 19 July 1481: 'Vos factores generales dari faciatis Costantino Tantinis Flor: quattuor auri et in auro pro pretio unius Manachordi facti per eum ad usum Illme. D. Isabelle Estensis . . .' [*Va*, p. 248].

(3) **Giovanni,** son of (2); *fl.* at Modena 1475. Pupil of his father, and therefore presumably a maker of keyboard instruments [*Lü*].

TASKIN. Family of harpsichord makers and musicians in the eighteenth century. Originally from the province of Liège in the Low Countries, they worked in Paris in the latter half of the century.

TASKIN, Pascal. (Strictly Pascal-Joseph *the Elder*, but now universally called simply Pascal Taskin); 1723–9 February 1793. Son of Jean Taskin and his wife Jeanne *née* Rivier, he was born at Theux, near Verviers in the province of Liège, whence he migrated in early manhood to Paris to work under the celebrated harpsichord maker François-Étienne Blanchet the Younger. A few months after his master's death (27 April 1766) Taskin married his widow, having meanwhile been accepted into the Guild. Until at any rate 1770 he was in the habit of signing himself *élève de Blanchet*. He was also harpsichord maker to the King and gave numerous details about himself on a card which he stuck on some of his instruments (the full text is given under his instrument no. 2).

In 1768 he began to include among his plectra some made of buffalo hide (*peau de buffle*), a soft woolly leather ('imitant la flûte') to be distinguished from the hard leather that may sometimes have been used by other makers as an alternative to quill. His new device was widely approved. It 'ne pince plus, mais il caresse la corde' wrote J. B. de Laborde in his *Essai sur la musique* . . . (1780; Vol. I, p. 346).

It was in 1772 that he was offered by Louis XV the position of Court Instrument Maker and Keeper of the King's Instruments, in succession to Chiquelier (q.v.). He did not in fact take over from Chiquelier until 1774; and then, not wishing to make the move to Versailles, he contrived to have part of his work for the Court done by his nephew Pascal-Joseph II. Mme du Barry had at Versailles a harpsichord by him costing 3,000 livres.

He also made pianos, four of which survive, and according to Chouquet constructed the first grand pianoforte made in France, for the Princesse Victoire.

He continued, however, to make harpsichords, assisted in his workshop by his 2 nephews Henry and Lambert Taskin and his stepson Armand-François-Nicolas Blanchet, and was not above following the practice of some of his contemporaries in making fake Ruckers instruments (see above, Ruckers instrument no. 104), apart from the common French eighteenth-century practice of extending the compass of Ruckers instruments.

For a detailed examination of Taskin's methods of harpsichord construction see *Hubb 1965*, pp. 116–25. Taskin's practice was to date the lowest jack of each register.

In 1784 he ordered 4 pianos from Shudi [*Da*, p. 74], the result (apparently) of Clementi's taking a Shudi harpsichord and square piano with him on his visit to Paris in 1781.

At the outbreak of the Revolution, while his rival Sébastien Érard withdrew to London to await the out-

TABLE 37. *Surviving Instruments by Pascal TASKIN the Elder*

No.	Date	Type	Kbs.	Signature	Owner/Remarks
01	1764	H	2		Edinburgh University. (It was bought by Raymond Russell from Mrs. George Crawley, Wentworth, Virginia Water in 1959 and delivered to him in 1962.) Dated *1764* on soundboard. 2 × 8′, 1 × 4′, and buff registers. Inscribed also: *Refait par Pascal Taskin 1784–5*. Rose with initials *IC* (i.e. Joannes Couchet, q.v.). Careful study in 1971 by John Barnes and W. R. Thomas revealed interesting points: the parts dating from 1764 would seem to be the soundboard, case, stand, and probably the keys; those from 1784–5 4 jackslides narrower than the original 3 and occupying the same space, *chinoiserie* decoration similar to that in no. 4, genouillères (replaced by pedals by Arnold Dolmetsch, who owned the instrument in 1903 and made new jacks: see *Week-end Review*, London, 12 July 1930), and parts of the bridges on the soundboard and wrestplank. The *IC* rose was inserted, doubtless to increase the value, probably by Taskin. (Plugged holes in the wrestplank point to the presence originally of 2 stop-levers like those in no. 1.)

No.	Date	Type	Kbs.	Signature	Owner/Remarks
1	1769	H	2	*Pascal Taskin Elève de Blanchet* [round the rose]	Remained in the possession of the Taskin family until 1952 when it became the property of Raymond Russell. *PT* rose. Now at Edinburgh University. See *RussColl.* (illustrated).
2	1769	H	2	*Pascal Taskin Facteur de clavessins du Roi, élève et successeur de M. Blanchet, demeure même maison Rue de le Verrerie vis-à-vis la petite porte de St. Merry à Paris*	Paris, Mlle Guerville. No lid. Taskin's card is stuck on the instrument and reads as given in the Signature column.
2a	1770	H	2	[Signed round rose]: *Pascal Taskin élève de Blanchet.* [Date on soundboard]: *1770.* [Nameboard (irremovable) inscribed]: *Refait par Pascal Taskin 1770. PT* initials interlaced decorate each cheek-piece (*J*, p. 127), who had not been able to see the instrument and thought it was a Ruckers)	Yale Collection (1957). Given by Mrs. Samuel Grimson, widow of former owner. Repaired 1905 by Tomasini. Elaborate decorations. Left panel inside lid shews the Château de Cirey, residence of Marquise du Chatelet (Voltaire's mistress). Sibyl Marcuse thinks *Refait . . .* inscription put on by a dealer. 3 rows of jacks, 2×9′, 1×4′, buff. Very fine keyboards. Push-pull coupler. Illustrated in *The Consort*, no. 20 (July 1963), p. 174.
2b	1774	H	2		Formerly owned by the Marquis de Laborde, now untraceable.
3	1778	S	1	*Fait par Pascal Taskin à Paris 1778*	Yale University, Belle Skinner Collection. Illustrated in Catalogue. Said to have belonged to Marie-Antoinette. Compass 5 octaves and 1 semitone.
3a	1780	H	2	*Fait par Pascal Taskin à Paris 1780* [stamped on the wrest-plank]	Milan, Museo Civico, Gallini Collection. E–F, 5 octaves and 1 note. There is an *AR* (Andreas Ruckers) rose of gilded wood in the soundboard. This was probably inserted by Taskin, and this instrument may be a much-rebuilt Ruckers. Size of instrument: 231×94×27·2 cm.
3b	1782	H	2	*André Rukers année 1636* [above the keys]; *Fait par Pascal Taskin à Paris, 1782* [near the wrest-pins]	Colares, Portugal, Marchesa Olga di Cadaval. Former owners: Queen Marie-Clotilde of France, wife of King Emmanuel IV of Sardinia; Museo Civico, Turin. E–F, 5 octaves and 1 note; 2×8′, 1×4′, *peau de buffle*, genouillères, push-pull coupler. *AR* rose, probably already in the virginal soundboard around which the soundboard was constructed. Size 7′ 8″×3′ 1″.
4	1786	H	1	[On nameboard]: *Fait par Pascal Taskin à Paris 1786.* [Round the rose]: *Pascal Taskin 1786*	London. Victoria and Albert Museum. 5 octaves and 1 note; 2×8′, buff. Inscribed in ink on back of nameboard: *Refait par Charles Fleury facteur de pianos à Paris an 1856 fleury.* Illustrated in *J*, p. 134, and in *V&A*, *MIWA*, also in *Russell V&A and Russell 1959*.

come, Taskin, as his letters shew, looked with favour upon the cause of the rebels and even worked for it.

In April 1791 Taskin appears as a tuner in the list of the École Royale de Chant, from which the Paris Conservatoire is descended.

Br quotes (p. 67) from an inventory dated 1795: 'Un clavecin noir, à bandes dorés, par Pascal Taskin, élève de Blanchet, en 1770, no. 15'. *Ge* remarks on the mathematical exactness of Taskin's instrument design, and also on his discernment in the choice of woods.

An anonymous portrait, probably of Taskin, painted in 1762 is reproduced in *Cl.*

E Closson's article in *SIM*, vol. 12 (1910–11), pp. 234–67, publishes a number of Taskin's letters, which are, however, of disappointingly small musical interest.

TASKIN, Henry. *Fl.* as harpsichord maker in Paris in 1793, at which time he was living in the rue du Mouton. He was Pascal Taskin's nephew and was invited by him to Paris to work in his workshop.

TASKIN, Pascal-Joseph (II). Harpsichord maker in Paris; born at Theux (Liège), 20 November 1750, died at Versailles 5 February 1829. He lived with his uncle Pascal until 1777 when he moved to Versailles. His father Henry, like Pascal Taskin's father, was a manufacturer at Theux (Liège); but Pascal-Joseph chose to join his uncle in Paris in 1763 to learn the craft. He took over part of his uncle's responsibilities as harpsichord maker to Louis XV.

TASKIN, Lambert. Harpsichord maker in Paris, *fl.* 1793, when, like his brother Henry, he helped in Pascal's workshop. Nothing is known of his later life.

TEEUS. *See*: THEEUWES.

TENBE, Geronimo di. Mahillon's Catalogue (Vol. 3, 1600) says of a small harpsichord in the Brussels Conservatoire 'Attribué à Jeronimus de Tenbe, à Rome (vers 1656)'. This is probably a mistake for Girolamo Zenti, q.v.

TERMANINI

Pietro, of Modena, violin maker. Dates ascertained: 1738–73. Also made lutes and harpsichords [*Va, Lü*].

Surviving Harpsichords

(1) 1741. Modena, Museo Civico. Single. Inscription on nameboard: *Opus Petri Termanini Mutinensis de anno MDCCXLI.* A label inside the case reads: *Petru[s Termaninus fec]it Mutinae Anno 1738.* A small pedal-keyboard operates on the lowest 8 notes also.

Giuseppe, probably his brother, likewise a violin maker [*Lü*]. Dates ascertained 1755–73. It is not known whether he made any harpsichords.

The name has sometimes been read 'Ternianini'.

TERNIANINI. *See*: TERMANINI.

TESTA, Andrea. 'Harpsicall maker' to King Charles II [*La*, p. 208]. *Fl.* 1668. In this year he petitioned the king for a pension, as granted to his predecessor, Girolamo Zenti, q.v. [*La*, p. 465].

THAMER, of Peterborough. Organ builder, *fl.* 1648. He also did some harpsichord work, for he was paid £7 in 1648 for 'repairing and setting in order both the Orgaines and Harpsicale' at Haddon Hall, near Bakewell, Derbyshire [quoted by *J*, p. 37 n.].

He built the organ for Framlingham Church, Suffolk.

THEEUWES

(1) **Jacob,** harpsichord and lute maker at Antwerp; dates ascertained, 1533–57 [*St*, who quotes detailed information from sources; *Lü*].

(2) **Lodewijk** (I), harpsichord maker in Antwerp, *fl.* 1557, in which year his name appears as the last signatory of the petition by Joos Karest [*St*, p. 63]. Possibly brother of Jacob Theeuwes.

(3) **Lodewijk** (II) [Lodewyke Tyves, Teeus], son of Jacob; harpsichord maker in Antwerp and afterwards in London. Dates ascertained, 1561–79.

In 1561 [*Hubb*] he was admitted to the Guild of St. Luke, as the son of a master [*Bu, St*]. Ten years later he is recorded as living in the parish of St. Martin-le-Grand, London ('Lodewyke Tyves, virginall maker, a Dutchman . . .') [*J*, p. 29]; and 11 years after this he made a claviorganum which is now in the Victoria and Albert Museum, London. It bears the inscription: *Lodowicus Theewes me fesit* [sic] *1579* and is illustrated at *J*, p. 116, where the arms of the houses of Hoby and Carey are to be seen painted on the case. These arms were cleaned off in 1947, revealing those of a branch of the Roper family, repeated 4 times in different places on the case. Illustrated in *Russell 1959*.

The harpsichord part of this instrument is especially interesting as being the earliest surviving English harpsichord, and also as having a 4′ stop as well as 2×8′ stops. Registration was effected by means of the moveable lower jack-guide (whereas in most harpsichords it is the upper jack-guide or 'slide' that is moved). Only 1 key now remains, and only 1 pipe in the organ part. For a detailed description of the instrument see Frank Hubbard, *Two Early English Harpsichords* (*GSJ*, III (1950), 2–115).

THEIDEL, of Breslau. Clavichord maker. In 1786 he lived in 'Junkern-Gasse zum goldnen Apfel'. Of his clavichords J. T. Hermes writes: '. . . dass sie weder so gros sind, als die Göttingschen, noch auch irgend etwas von Härte haben: sie halten genau nur das Maas der Fridericischen und Hornschen . . .' [*Schlesische Provinzialblätter*, Breslau, Vol. 3 (1786), p. 562].

THEVENARD. Harpsichord maker at Bordeaux in the eighteenth century [*Cor*].

In 1727 he submitted to the Académie des Sciences, Paris, a design for a single-string harpsichord with brass plectra. It is not known whether it was ever constructed [*Pi*, p. 91, *see also* E. Gregoir, *Bibliothèque musicale*, Vol. 3 (1879), p. 163].

THIBAUT, Vincent. *See*: TIBAUT, Vincent.

THIELEN, Jan. Clavichord maker of Antwerp; dates ascertained, 1533–9 [*St*].

THOANER. English harpsichord maker, *fl.* 1772.

Br, p. 97 reads: 'Un clavecin anglais de Thoaner, année 1772, estimé 2,000 fr.' (inventory from the year 1795). The name, however, appears corrupt.

THOMPSON, Charles, Samuel, Ann, Peter, etc. Makers of spinets and harpsichords. Dates ascertained 1764–1802. London: 75 St. Paul's Churchyard; 8 Lombard Street [*J*].

THOMPSON, Wardhaugh. Patented on 15 January 1787 'a perfect and compleat machine . . . for . . . tuning of harpsichords, pianofortes, spinnets . . .'. Patent no. 1583 [*Pat*]. Perhaps related to the preceding.

THÜRIG, Johann Ludwig. *See*: TÜRIG, Johann Ludwig.

TIBAUT, Vincent. Harpsichord maker at Toulouse, *fl.* 1679–81.

Surviving Harpsichords

(1) 1679. Brussels, Conservatoire: 2 manuals, 2×8′, 1×4′. Inscribed in marquetry: *Fait par moy Vincent Tibaut à Tolose, 1679.* Formerly belonged to A. Tolbecque of Paris. Illustrated in *Russell 1959.*

(2) 1681. Paris, M. Yannick Guillou; 2 manuals. Inscribed: *Fait par Vincent Tibaut à Tolose 1681.* (Recorded on Erato/STU/70640, played by L. Boulay.)

(3) 1681. Paris, privately owned. (Mercier-Ythier worked on it, 1970.) Two manuals. Inscribed: *Vincent Tibaut à Tolose, 1681.*

TIEFFENBRUN, Otto Joachim. Clavichord maker. Born about 1737 in Germany, he emigrated to Denmark and was married in Copenhagen in 1769. He was licensed as a maker in 1784 and died some time after 1801. His workshop perished in the 1795 fire, but he started up again.

Surviving Clavichords

(1) 1793. Bundfrei; signed on soundboard: *Otto Joachim Tieffenbrunn Kiøbenhaven 1793.* Belonged to the Danish priest H. C. W. Find (1784–1872) and stayed in his family till 1963 when Ole Find sold it to the Musikhistorisk Museum, Copenhagen. F–G, 5 octaves plus 2 notes; rose without initials; dimensions 52·2×170·7×17 cm.

(2) 1801. Signed: *Otto Joachim Tieffenbrunn. Kiöbenhavn Ao 1801.* First owned by the Norwegian composer O. A. Lindeman, who probably bought it when he left for Trondheim in 1802 after 10 years' study in Copenhagen. It is still (1970) in his family, owned by the architect Wilhelm Swensen, great-grandson of O. A. Lindeman. F–G, 5 octaves plus 2 notes; rose without initials.

TIM^O^, D. Repairer's signature, dated 1690, on a clavichord signed *AD/1562* in the Heyer Collection, Leipzig.

TISSERAN, Joseph. Harpsichord maker in London, *fl.* 1710. Possibly a Huguenot, though his name does not appear in the publications of the Huguenot Society, London.

A fine harpsichord of 1710 by him has survived, with the inscription: *Josephus Tisseran faciebat Londinij.* It has 2 manuals, 2×8′ and 1×4′ registers worked by 3 brass hand-stops, compass of 4½ octaves, split keys in the bass. The naturals are ebony and the sharps ivory. The soundboard is decorated with flowers, birds, and butterflies and has a rose representing Apollo and his lyre. The exterior of the case is painted. Dimensions, 2′ 10″×7′ 7″. The stand and front board are modern.

When the instrument was restored by Henry Tull in 1939 he misread a date he found inside it, on which some glue had dropped, as '1700'.

From 1712 until 1949 it was at Woollas Hall, Pershore. Two letters dated 1712 dealing with the instrument were sold with it on 16 December 1949 at Sotheby's. It now belongs to Tom Burn, Rous Lench Court, Evesham.

It was repaired by Alfred Reeve, of Maidenhead, in 1960, and I shall do best to quote verbatim some observations by him on it:

A number of misconceptions have grown up around this splendid instrument. These centre, in the first place, on the misreading of the date by Tull and, secondly, on the determination of two distinguished authorities, for whatever reason, to see this instrument as falling outside the English tradition of the period.

I had this harpsichord at my house for some months in 1960 in order to clean and re-touch the outside of the case and the keyboard panels. M. Thomas, who had borrowed it from Mr. Burn for a broadcast, asked me to re-string it and repair a jack guide at the same time. I took the opportunity to examine it closely, to have it photographed and to record its measurements.

The first thing I discovered was the vigorous *pen* inscription on the *inside of the bottom, under the keys*:

Opus Josephi Tisseran Londini 1710.

There was a blob of varnish between the third and fourth digits of the date making it very easy to read '1700', but, looking closer, one sees that the flourish of the writing leaves no space for a double '00' and the linking stroke between the '1' and '0' is quite plain. Percy Watts took some very good photographs and these (and he!) will confirm this. Certainly the date makes sense with the correspondence of 1712 because it is not unreasonable to suppose that the harpsichord was painted after Tisseran had signed it. Indeed, the man who painted it has actually written in gold paint on the front edge of the wrest plank *Joseph Tissern* [sic] *Londini.*

Under the elaborate decoration of the soundboard one finds the grain of the wood angled at about 23 degrees to the long side just like a number of other English instruments of that time. The three sound bars are parallel to each other and disposed at the usual angle of the main cut-off bar, and there is a normal hitch-pin bar. The bracing is all parallel with lower U-shaped members glued to sides and bottom, alternating with small rectangular-section upper braces from liner to liner. Add to this the notable thinness of the bent side (about ⅜″) and the rounded top to all sides and one has the general construction of an English spinet of the period with the keyboard turned through 45 degrees and enlarged into a harpsichord. It is clear from Hitchcock's and Haward's instruments, as Hubbard points out, that all this was standard practice at the time—even the substantial T-shaped belly-rail is the same.

But both Hubbard and Russell do less than justice to this instrument. *Russell 1959* (p. 92) 'has never seen an original painted English harpsichord, unless the Tisseran at Woollas be so considered'. But why not? What is so extraordinary about painted furniture in England at that period? We were painting cabinets enough and the English virginals were always painted. Rather should we say that here we are fortunate in having preserved for us one example of perhaps many that have been lost. At least one nearly-contemporary picture tells us it was fashionable to paint English harpsichords. Presumably, if the instrument had been quietly veneered in walnut it would have passed without question.

Hubbard (who cannot get the name right) is more outspoken, hence makes the bigger mistake. For him it 'was made by a Frenchman resident in London and therefore is not very pertinent to the history of English harpsichord making' [*Hubb 1965*, p. 153]. What then, of Tabel, Shudi, Kirkman, Snetzler, Zumpe? Are they not English either?

Curiously enough, the one feature of this instrument which might be thought foreign is never mentioned. The wrest pins do not follow a single straight line but are staggered into naturals and sharps. This may well reflect Tisseran's background but, nevertheless, I see no reason to call this other than a very characteristic English example of its period.

TODINI, Michele. Born at Saluzzo, Piedmont, in 1625; ascertained in Rome until 1681 when he was 'Decano degli Musici di Campidoglio'. Made organs, harpsichords, clavichords, and, furthermore, lutes. His ingenuity found expression in designing fantastic instruments such as an organ combined with a harpsichord and several spinets. His book *Dichiaratione della galleria armonica . . .* was published by Tirroni, Rome, 1676 (see *Monatshefte f. Musikgesch.*, 1905, Beilage 3, p. 43). He later moved to France, where he died. See further *Fé*, *GD* (suppl. 1945, p. 599), *Hirt*, *Vannes*, and pl. 33 in F. Bonanni's *Gabinetto Armonico* (1722).

Todini once owned, and perhaps made, the unsigned 'Golden Harpsichord' in the New York Metropolitan Museum of Art—see his *Dichiaratione* . . . ch. 3 and *Wint 1956*.

TODINI, Pietro, of Rome. Harpsichord maker, *fl.* 1675; probably the son of the foregoing maker. The Gallini Collection, Milan, has a 2-manual harpsichord by him signed: *Petrus Todinus fecit Anno Domini 1675 / Roma.* Illustrated in *Gall*, pl. 120, and in *Pag*, p. 46.

TÖLLEKE, Karl. In 1755 Tölleke is said to have been the only instrument maker in Brunswick apart from Fritz (q.v.). He had been apprenticed to Reinecke [*SB*, p. 48].

TOLLENARI, Joannes, *fl.* 1670. A Flemish harpsichord maker who moved to Italy and set up his workshop in a city whose name we do not know 'at the sign of the Eagle' (*nell' Aquila*).

A harpsichord in the Stuttgart collection is inscribed: *Joannes Tollenari Fiammengo Nell' Aquila 1670.* C–C, 4 octaves; 2×8′. It was presented by Carl A. Pfeiffer of Stuttgart.

TOLLEY, Robert. A spinet signed *Robertus Tolley* and dated 1661 is reported to me as having been seen in England in 1947. It has been suggested that this might be a misreading of *Hatley*, q.v.

TOMASINI, Louis. *Nor* (p. 130) mentions a 5-register harpsichord by Tomasini dated 1775 as being in Paris. This appears to be an error arising from the fact that the Longman and Broderip harpsichord in the Paris Conservatoire was repaired by Tomasini, about 1883 according to *Va*. (A 5-octave (F–F) harpsichord by Tomasini dated 1889 was offered for sale in Paris in 1952.) Tomasini was an Italian repairer working in Paris in the late nineteenth century.

TOMASO, *de Luca*. Italian virginal maker from Lucca, *fl.* 1711 [*Va*].

TOMLINSON, Thomas. *See*: HAXBY, Thomas, *ad fin.*

TONOLI, of Brescia. Nineteenth-century harpsichord and organ maker [*Va*].

TOSI, Onesto. Genoese clavichord maker. Dates ascertained, 1568 [?].

Surviving Clavichords

(1) 1568 [?]. Boston Museum of Fine Arts (formerly in Canon F. W. Galpin's collection). Compass C–C, 4 octaves with short octave; 45 keys. Painting inside lid includes Orpheus and Eurydice. 117×29 cm. Illustrated in Bessaraboff's catalogue of the instruments in the Boston Museum (1941), p. 336, and in *Ga*. The signature is now extremely indistinct, and was presumably little better 50 years ago when the *Catalogue of the Music Loan Exhibition* (Worshipful Company of Musicians) recorded it on p. 170 as: *Onesto Tosi di Genova fece, 1605.* Canon Galpin [*Ga*, 1910] did not transcribe the signature, but gave the date as 1568. The clavichord is very little altered from its original condition; but according to a reliable authority the inscription is not genuine [HG, letter of 12 July, 1965].

TOURNAN, Bertrand, of Lyons, where the Archives describe him as 'facteur de clavecins'. Dates ascertained, 1772–9.

In 1772 he rented, in partnership with Pierre Bontan, a joiner, a shop in the Place de la Charité, Lyons, for 9 years. He is recorded among the *luthiers* in 1779.

A handsome square piano by him, inscribed *Tournan a Lyon 1777,* is preserved in the Musée Historique at Lyons (F–F, 5 octaves, 2 knee-levers).

LE TOURNEUR. *See*: TREYER, Jean-Baptiste, *called* Le Tourneur.

TOUROUDE, Jacques. Harpsichord maker in the rue Vieille-du-Temple, Paris; *fl.* 1769 [*Pi*].

TOUSSAINT, Jean. Acquired the citizenship of Hamburg as 'Instrumentenmacher' on 21 February 1716 [*Lü*]. It is not certain that he made keyboard instruments.

TOWNSEND, Gabriel. English virginal maker, born about 1604. Freeman of the Joiners' Company, London, 1624/5, and Master in 1657/8. Player and Keene were among his apprentices.

Townsend had probably died by 1662, since in that year Keene, his apprentice, was admitted free of the Joiners' Company on the relation of John Player.

Surviving Virginals

(1) 1641. Brussels Conservatoire, inscribed *Gabriell Townsend fecit 1641.* Rose. C–E, 4 octaves and a 3rd; 176×54 cm. Bears the Plantagenet royal arms. Formerly belonged to Elizabeth Stuart, Queen of Bohemia, daughter of James I. Illustrated in *DEF*, II. 374.

TRAERI, Domenico. Harpsichord maker from Brescia working in Bologna in 1700. Probably a relative of the following maker.

Surviving Instruments

(1) 1700. Milan, Gallini Collection. Harpsichord, 4 octaves plus 1 note. Inscription: *Domenico Traeri detto il Bresciano fece in Bologna l'anno MDCC.* Size 220×79 cm.

(2) Bologna, Museo Davia Bargellini (but belonging to the town of Bologna). 4 octaves with bass short octave and D/F sharp and E/G sharp divided keys.

TRAERI, Ugo Annibale. Clavichord maker at Modena in 1726.

Surviving Clavichords

(1) 1726. Maidstone Museum. Inscribed: *Vgo Annibale Traeri, Vulgo Brixianus Bononienses* [sic] / *Fecit Mutinae anno MDCCXXVI.* Compass C/E–C, 4 octaves; $32\frac{1}{2}\times 10\frac{3}{4}\times 3\frac{1}{2}''$. A MS. label inside the lid reads: 'This Clavichord belonged to Handel, who used it in composition,

when travelling; it subsequently came into the possession of my Father, George James Cholmondeley Esq[re], who died in 1830 . . . Frances Sophia Buchanan Riddell, Harrietsham Rectory, Maidstone.'

TRASORI, Alexandro. Italian harpsichord maker, *fl.* 1733. A painting in private ownership in England, done by Sebastiano Lazari in 1733, depicts a harpsichord (single-manual) signed: *Alexandro* [-?*a*] *Trasori MDCCXXXIII.*

TRASUNTINO. The surname of several Italian harpsichord and clavichord makers, perhaps related:

(*a*) **Alessandro,** of Venice; dates ascertained, 1531–8, although one instrument bearing his name is reported as dated 1604.

Surviving Instruments

(1) 1531. London, Royal College of Music. Harpsichord; 2×8′; G–C, 4 octaves plus a 4th, with short octave, originally probably C/E–F; the keyboard is a replacement but old. Three roses. Length 7′ 8″. Inscription *Opus Alexandri Trasuntini MDXXXI.* Pedals controlling a buffstop were added in the eighteenth century. In an outer case.

(2) 1537. New York, Metropolitan Museum of Art. Clavichord. A forgery, made in Florence in the late nineteenth century. (See Dolmetsch in *Week-end Review*, London, 12 July 1930, p. 57.) Inscription: *Alex. Trasontini . . . hoc opus 1537.*

(3) 1537. Copenhagen, Claudius Collection. Clavichord. Likewise a forgery, though the keys are better. Inscription as in (2).

(4) 1538. Brussels Conservatoire. Harpsichord; 1×4′, 1×8′; 4 octaves. D–D; 222×81 cm. Inscription: *Intonuit nunquam melius quod Tartara flexit | Quod delphin grato pondere vexit opus. | Alexandri Trasontini opus MDXXXVIII.*

(5) 1604. Halle, Händelhaus. Polygonal virginal. Painted inscription: *Alessandro Trasuntini 1604*, on the frame; later [*Sasse*, p. 29] inscription branded on nameboard: *Alessandro Trasontini MDCIIII.* C/E–F, 4 octaves. Rose.

(? 6) 1604. *FrancI* lists (as no. 13) a 'spinetta' signed: *Allesandro Trasantini* [sic] *fecit an. 1604, Milese restaurò 1820.*

(*b*) **Giovanni Francesco** of Naples, at the sign of the Two Roses, maker of polygonal virginals, *fl.* 1532.

Surviving Instruments

(1) 1532. Leningrad, Scientific Institute for the Theatre and Music. Polygonal virginal. C/E–F, 4½ octaves, 50 keys; geometrical rose. Several inscriptions on it are reported to me as follows: (i) near the rose: *Gio Francesco Januar Trazentinus all insegna dell due Rose Napoli*; (ii) on the soundboard: *Tibi nome di Dio e de San Josepo questo e ante . . . per un Spi*[*net*]*to del Fogiolo che con un poco letizia ed anche per . . . gr . . . fara un pocho cantare alcun . . . sara mezo al mese di Ottubrio de anno 153 . . . Io Brunetto maistro su dita opera ff. In Dei nomine speravi*; (iii) on the jack-slide: *Adi 7 novembrio 1532 fato in Brunetto* [?*d*]*a*[?*lli Or*]*gani in . . .* [?*Vero*]*nese.* (*See above*: Bruneto dalli Organi.)

(*c*) **Giulio,** sixteenth-century maker of harpsichords and clavichords, of Venice, *fl.* 1588.

Thomas Garzoni (*Piazza universale di tutte le professioni del mondo*, Discorso 136, Venetia, 1585) speaks of a Messer Giulio Trasuntino, who had a singular skill in the making of harpsichords and clavichords: 'Degli instrumenti da penna c'hanno le corde di ferro, d'acciaio, et d'ottone come sono arpicordi, manocordi [i.e. clavichords], clavicembali et cithere nella compositione de quali è stato eccellente Messer Giulio Trasuntino.'

It may be this Trasontino to whom Count Giordano Riccati refers as the maker of a harpsichord in the year 1559 [*Delle corde ovvero fibre elastiche schediasmi fisico-matematici*, Bologna, 1767).

Prof (p. 292) says that he worked at Venice.

(*d*) **Guido** *or* **Vido** [Vitus de Trasuntinis], *fl.* 1560–1606, instrument maker at Venice. In 1606 he built an *archicembalo* (on the prescription of the inventor Nicola Vicentino, who describes it in his *L'antica musica . . .* 1555) for Camillo Gonzaga, Count of Novellara; this instrument passed later into the possession of the papal maestro di cappella, Baini, and is now in the Museo Civico at Bologna. Designed to achieve purity of intonation, its compass was 4 octaves, each octave having 31 keys. It was inscribed: *Solus | Camillus Gonzaga Novellariae comes || Clavemusicum omnitonum | Modulis diatonicis, chromaticis et enharmonicis || A docta manu tactum | Insigne | Vito de Trasuntinis veneto auctore | MDCVI.* It is illustrated in *Russell 1959.*

Leonardo Fioravanti (*Dello specchio di scientia universale*, Venetia, 1564, f. 273) has high praise for Guido, who 'nell' arte d'arpicordi, clavicembali, organi, et regali, è huomo di tanta et dottrina et esperientia, che il mondo si maraviglia in udire de suoi instrumenti: percioche di melodia et armonia passano tutti gli altri: et quelli che da altri sono fatti senza armonia egli si acconcia, et gli fatti divini et rari, como bene in Venetia si vede in diversi luoghi'.

Surviving Instruments

(1) ? 1560. Berlin Collection. Harpsichord, 1 manual, C–F with short octave. Inscribed: *Viti de Transvntinis MDL*[*X*], and, on the jackrail, *Vt frenvm eqvis*, and by the keyboard *Rendo lieti in vn tempo gli occhi el core.* The original 8′ and 4′ stops were changed to 2×8′. Rose 80×190 cm. (Sachs gives no explanation of his interpretation of the date.)

(1a) 1571. Milan, Gallini Collection. Harpsichord, 1 manual, 4 octaves, and 1 note, inscribed *Vidus Trasuntinus F—MDLXXI.* Illustrated *Pag*, p. 35.

(? 1b) 1591. *FrancII* records a harpsichord, *Viti de Trasuntinis MDXCI.*

(2) 1596. A harpsichord inscribed *Viti de Trasuntinis MDXCVI* was sold by Alfred du Cros at Sotheby's 11 February 1938. Two strings to a note. 2′ 9″×6′ 0″. Restored by Messrs. Morley. It was shewn at the Crystal Palace in 1900.

[(? 3) Bologna, Museo Civico. The *archicembalo* described above.]

(? 4) 1601. *FrancI* records a 'spinetta' signed: *Viti* [sic] *de Trasuntinus* [sic] *fecit anno Domini 1601.* Perhaps the one now (1972) owned by the Comtesse de Chambure.

(5) *c.* 1600. Harpsichord inscribed: *Viti de Trasuntinis*

MDLII, but last 3 letters of the date have been tampered with. Owner Mrs. Eva Rosenfelt, London, who bought it from Michael Thomas. Described to me by Dr. J. R. Mirrey, Redhill, 1963, and John Barnes, 1966. Compass now C–C, 4 octaves, chromatic—formerly G/B–C, but originally C/E–F as is proved by alterations to keys and keybed.

TRAZENTINUS, Giovanni Francesco. *See*: TRASONTINO, Giovanni Francesco.

TREASORER, William. Maker of virginals and regals in London. Dates ascertained 1521–76. He most probably died in 1584. Described in documents as 'borne in Germany', as 'a German', and as a 'Doucheman', he settled in England, the original form of his name being unknown. In *HuR* he is described as 'maker and tuner of the Queen Majestyes instruments'. He made regals for Edward VI and musical instruments for many.

From 1547 onwards he lived in the parish of Christchurch, Newgate [*MA*, III (1911–12), 103 ff.].

La (p. 14) quotes a warrant of 28 May 1560 to deliver to William Treasorer 'maker of our instruments five yards of crimson velvett, to cover one payre of regalls, and one yard of purple satin to line the same. Item for the iron work of a case for a paire of virginalls aforesaid, covered with crimson velvett'.

TREMAINE. Harpsichord maker in New York; *fl.* 1759 [*Hirt*].

TRENTIN, Gregorio, *Abbé*. Born 1768 at Conselve near Padua; died at Padua in 1854. Made guitars, harps, lutes, and pianos, and devised a *sostinente* harpsichord after the fashion of Hayden's *Geigenwerk* [*Vannes*]. Presumably to be identified with *Va*'s Trentini (*fl.* 1828 as harpsichord and violin maker).

TREYER

(1) **Joseph,** called L'Empereur. A Swiss. Came to Paris and was taught and adopted by his uncle Jean Keiser, who was likewise called L'Empereur. He was a native of the canton of Solothurn, Switzerland. He was admitted as Master in Paris in 1757, and married in 1764. Died 1788. [*Verlet*].

Br (p. 77) refers to a harpsichord 'fait par Joseph Treyer, surnommé Lempereur, à Paris, 1770'; and one of his harpsichords was advertised for sale, 8 March 1756 [*Bq*].

(2) **Jean-Baptiste,** *called* Le Tourneur, maker of harpsichords and bowed instruments in the rue Percée-Saint-Séverin, Paris; dates ascertained 1750–79 [*Pi*].

In 1750 he became *juré-comptable* of the Guild of Luthiers.

TRONCO, Giovanni Francesco. Italian maker of harpsichords, flourished 1757 [*Gö*]. An instrument of this date was formerly in the de Wit Collection; 4½ octaves, 3 sets of strings; 175 × 85 cm.

TRUCHADO, Raymundo, *Spanish priest*. Made in 1625 a bowed 'harpsichord', on the lines of Hayden's *Geigenwerck*, preserved in the Brussels Conservatoire. It is illustrated and described by F. J. de Hen in *RipKb*, pp. 17–26.

TRUSKA, Simon Joseph, 1734–1809. Born at Roudnic, Bohemia, on 5 April 1734. On 8 December 1758 he entered the Premonstratensian house of Strahov near Prague, and was ordained priest on 1 January 1761. A musician and composer, he also made various instruments, such as clavichords, violins, and viols [*Lü*].

TRUTE, Charles. Maker of harpsichords and pianofortes. Earliest date ascertained, 1760 (on a square piano); died 1807–8. From 1782 until 1789 he resided at 7 Broad Street North, Golden Square, London [*RB*]. Not long after this he emigrated to America, and we find him in 1794 in partnership with a certain Wiedberg at 25 Filbert Street, Philadelphia. From there they moved to Wilmington, Delaware, where before long Wiedberg died. Trute afterwards forsook harpsichord making for innkeeping, and died in Wilmington in 1807 or 1808.

Surviving Harpsichords

(1) 1794. Private ownership, U.S.A. Inscription (faded): *Trute & Wiedberg Makers, Filbert Street, Philadelphia, 1794*. According to John Challis, Detroit, this was originally a 2-manual harpsichord, which had been turned into a pianoforte in the nineteenth century, the front being cut off and lower keyboard destroyed, while the 4′ bridge was removed, leaving its mark on the soundboard. The case and framing are of Honduras mahogany veneered with San Dominico mahogany. The instrument was turned back into a single, and later a double, harpsichord by John Challis.

The Henry Ford Museum at Greenfield has a square pianoforte dated 1780 made by Trute during his London period; another signed *Carolus Trute Londini fecit 1784* was at Messrs. Legg, Cirencester, in 1954. A square made by him in the Wilmington period is owned by Mrs. George Cappella.

Harpsichords by Trute appear in the sale room from time to time at the end of the eighteenth century, e.g. at Christie's:

28 January 1792. A harpsichord by Trute [vendor, Sir Thomas Rumbold; buyer, Boileau; price £30. 9*s*.].

11 November 1793. A single key'd harpsichord by Trute in a neat inlaid mahogany case [vendor, Hon. Mr. St. John; buyer, Boileau; price not given].

TSCHUDI. *See*: SHUDI.

TUNONI, Giuseppe. An Italian harpsichord by *Josep Tunonus* is reported to me as offered for sale in London in 1925. 2 × 8′ stops; dated 1637. This is presumably the harpsichord in *FrancI* with the remarkable inscription: *Joseph Tunonus fecit Bononia in Platea Pavaglionis anno Domini 1637*.

TÜRIG, Johann Ludwig. An instrument maker at Wyl in Switzerland *c.* 1680. In 1910 one of his clavichords was in the collection of Heinrich Schumacher of Lucerne [*Gö*, p. 123; *Hirt*, p. 481].

TURNER, Bernard. Harpsichord maker in Cambridge in the eighteenth century.

TYVES. *See*: THEEUWES.

UBERMANN, Ludwig, of Stuttgart. Organ builder. *Fl.* 1618 when he made a stringed keyboard instrument for the 'fürstliches Frauenzimmer' for 20 florins [*MarcP*].

UDINE, Pier Francesco da. *See*: PIER FRANCESCO, *of Udine.*

UDINE, Pier Giovanni da. *See*: PIER GIOVANNI, *of Udine.*

UFFEL, Frans van. *See*: HUFFEL, Frans van.

UNDERWOOD, Thomas, of Bath. Earliest date ascertained, 1746; died in October 1777 (?). *J* (p. 78) records him as a maker or seller of spinets and harpsichords. In 1746 he had a shop 'next door to the Spread Eagle and Crown' on Belvedere Hill, in the parish of Walcot, near Bath. Later he moved to the Market Place. He seems to have been mainly a dealer in musical instruments of many kinds, although he calls himself 'musical instrument maker' in an advertisement in the *Bath Journal* of 18 November 1754 'at the sign of the Bass Violin in Stall-Street, near the White Hart Tavern: sells or lets by the week violins, basses, tenors, German flutes, English flutes, flagelets, bassoon reeds, hautboy reeds etc. etc. Likewise sells harpsichord wires . . .'. Nor does he confine himself to musical goods, for lower down we read: 'To be sold at the above place: fine pickled mushrooms at four shillings per quart. . . .'

In 1765 he subscribed to a set of harpsichord concerti by Thomas Chilcot [*Byrne, Falc*].

The Bath Abbey burial records contain an entry for a Thomas Underwood under 1 November 1777.

UNDEUS, Donatus, *Bergomensis,* [Donatus de Undeis] of Bergamo. Harpsichord maker, *fl.* 1592–1623. *See also*: GIOVANNI CELESTINI, *and* ONDEO.

Surviving Instruments

(01) 1590. Nuremberg. Polygonal virginal in Germanisches Nationalmuseum, Rück Collection. Inscribed: *Donatus de Undeis Bergomensis MDXC.*

(1) 1592. Copenhagen. Musikhistorisk Museum. Harpsichord, 2 × 8′ registers C–C, 4 octaves with short octave. Signed: *Donatvs de Vndeis Bergomensis MDXCII.* Rose of parchment.

(1a) 1597. Zurich, private ownership. Polygonal virginal.

(2) 1623. Brussels. Conservatoire. An arci-spineta, i.e. a virginal with elongated soundboard inscribed: *Donatus Undeus, Bergomensis, MDCXXIII.*

UNDEUS, Hieronymus. Son of Donatus Undeus, harpsichord maker, *fl.* 1632. The Instrumentenkammer at Innsbruck had a single-manual harpsichord by him signed: *Hieronymus Undeus, Donati Filius, Anno 1632* [*Senn*, p. 340].

UNGARO, Franco. *See*: FRANCISCUS Patavinus.

V. K. *See*: K, V.

V, L. A harpsichord in the Heyer Collection, Leipzig, has a rose containing the initials *L. V.* The top key bears the legend *Ao. 1766*; and the lowest, *Amsterd[am]*. It is a product of the Flemish school. (2 × 8′, 1 × 4′ stops. Three register-knobs outside the case at the right-hand end. Compass B–F, 4½ octaves. Ivory naturals, ebony sharps. 191 × 88 cm.)

VAILLANT, Denis. Parisian harpsichord maker in 1737 [*Hubb*].

VALLE, Pietro della. *See*: POLIZZINO, Giovanni Pietro.

VALTER, Antoine. *See*: VATER, Antoine.

VAN CASTEEL. *See*: CASTEEL.

VAN DEN ELSCHE, J. *See*: ELSCHE, Jakob van den.

VAN DER BIEST, M. *See*: BIEST, Marten van der.

VAN DER SLAGH, P. *See*: SLAGH, Pieter van der.

VANDERVELDE, P. *See*: DEFIELD.

VAN DIEREN, Willem. *See*: DIEREN, Willem van.

VAN DORT, C. *See*: DORT, Cornelis van.

VAN HOVEN, L. *See*: HOVEN, Lucas van.

VANINI, Francesco. Spinet maker, *fl.* at Bologna, 1673 [*Va*].

VAN KAMP, Hubert [Vankemp] of London. Spinet maker. Dates ascertained: 1751–64; he probably died by 1766. In 1751 he moved into a house on the north side of Eagle Street, Holborn, where he remained until 1754 [*RB.GM*]. His children John and Hannah were baptized at the church of St. George the Martyr, Queen Square, Holborn, in 1752 and 1754. From 1754 until 1764 he lived in Lee Street (now northern part of Dane Street), Holborn [*RB* 1765–6 wanting].

Surviving Spinets

(1) 1762. London, Geffrye Museum (Kingsland Road, Shoreditch). Inscribed: *Hubert Van Kamp Londini fecit 1762.* Five octaves F–F, without lowest F sharp. Mahogany case, pine keyboard with ivory naturals and ebony sharps; oaken stand, apparently not original. Interior workmanship poor, but tone quite good.

VAN KAMP, William Hubert, of London. Organ builder and maker of other instruments. Perhaps son of Hubert. Dates ascertained: 1767–72, when he lived in Lee Street, Holborn, in Hubert's house.

He placed the following notice in nos. 155 and 156 of the *Liverpool General Advertiser* (9 and 16 December 1768):

MUSIC, WILLIAM HUBERT VAN KAMP, Organ-builder, At the Dial in Lee-street, the second Door from Red Lion Square, Holborn, LONDON, Makes and Repairs all Sorts of Barrel Organs, for Minuets, Country Dances, &c. also New-invented Concerto Organs that play whole Concertos, Songs of any Kind, by the Fingers or Windles. Likewise great Choice of Organs performed by Clock-Work, fit for Palaces, Halls, &c. finished for Sale at Reasonable Rates.

My instruments from the smallest to the largest are not only Ornamental and Harmonious but will keep in order in any Climate.

N.B. Harpsichords and Spinnets made &c.

VAN MEER, Albert. *See*: MEER, Albert van.

VASTI. Italian harpsichord maker, sixteenth (?) century. A harpsichord by him was in Modena in 1598 [*MarcP*].

VASTI, Prospero, of Reggio nell'Emilia. Organ, harpsichord, and virginal maker, *fl.* 1676–9 [*Va*].

VATER, Antoine [Watter]. Born 1689, died after 1759. A harpsichord maker born in Hanover who settled in Paris in 1715. *Juré* of the Guild there in 1737. Harpsichords by him dated 1725, 1724, and 1755 are referred to by *Br* (pp. 49, 67, 85), though he reads the name as Valter (*Antonius Valter, Lutetiae Parisiorum 1755*). This might lead to his being confused with the Viennese piano maker (Gabriel) Anton Walter who was married about 1785, and therefore perhaps born about 1760—particularly as the Crosby Brown Catalogue (New York) gives Walter's name as Vatter. [Gabriel Anton Walter (the pianoforte maker) was born at Neuhausen, 5 February 1752; he married in Vienna, on 27 January 1780, Anna Elisabeth *née* Reisinger, a widow, and died in Vienna 11 April 1826. Some of the surviving pianos from his hand are noted (and a fine grand pianoforte of 1787 in private ownership in Amsterdam (1971) illustrated) in *HaasBM*, whom see also for new light on other instrument makers associated with Mozart, especially Christian Baumann of Zweibrücken (1746–1816).].

Cor (1753, p. 90) gives some measurements taken from 'un clavecin d'Antoine Vater', and refers to him again on p. 84.

Bq mentions a number of harpsichords by a maker variously spelt Watters and Vaters, whose Christian name was Antoine. This must have been Antoine Vater. 'Un Clavecin à grand ravallement . . . avec Tuorbe [*sic*] et flageolet'. 'Clavecin à 4 rangs de sautereaux et 5 jeux.'

Surviving Harpsichords

(01) 1732. South of France, private ownership (1970). Two manuals; 2×8′, 1×4′; F–E, nearly 5 octaves. Signed *Antoine Vater* round the rose and dated 1732 [*GL*].

(1) Undated (Russell was mistaken in giving 1737). Newbury, Mrs. Hue-Williams (who was formerly Mrs. Lilley). *AV* rose, with inscription painted on the soundboard round it: *Antoine Vater*; 2×8′, 1×4′, lute; 2 manuals with push-pull coupler. Three hand-stops through foreboard controlling the 4′, the lute-stop, and one of the 8′ stops. Arcading on keyfronts, perhaps modern. Compass E–F, 5 octaves and 1 note. The instrument bears a label: *Restauré dans les ateliers / de Berceau Royal d' / Instruments de musique anciens / M & A. Salomon / 14 rue Boissy d'Anglas / à Paris le Octobre 1923.* (It is of course possible, though unlikely, that the date 1737 disappeared during this restoration, but it can never have followed the maker's name round the rose.) Size 237·5×88·7×95 cm. (This harpsichord was carefully examined in 1971 by Peter A. Kjeldsberg.)

(2) 1737 (?). The Ringve Museum, Trondheim, bought in 1953 from the family of Paul Brunold (1875–1948) a 2-manual harpsichord, 2×8′, 1×4′, lute, F–F, 5 octaves. On the nameboard are 2 handwritten rectangular plates; on the first only the name *Fissot* (? *Tissot*) can be read; on the second is inscribed: *Albert Ferney / restituit anno MDCCCCIX.* The jackrail bears a piece of vellum on which is written (presumably by Brunold): *Clavecin à grand ravalement / facture d'Ant^e Watters (1737) / réparé par Fissot (1762) / provient du Château d'O. (Oron) / (Collection Paul Brunold).* Did Brunold get this information from evidence inside the instrument laid bare by Ferney in 1909? If so, the evidence must have been removed by 1970, for when the Uppsala restorer Felix Wolff opened the instrument up in that year he found only one inscription which told of its repair by Ferney in 1909. The rose is patterned (sun with rays) and is clumsily fixed in place by means of a block of wood attached to the underside of the soundboard.

This feature and various others incline one not to attribute this instrument to Vater: other features are the completely different profile of the 8′ hitch-pin rail, the different curve to the 4′ hitch-pin rail, the curving of the bass end of the 8′ bridge, and the different scaling.

(3) 1737. In private ownership in France [*GL, Verlet*].

VAUDRY, Jean Antoine. Instrument maker in Paris. Born about 1680; died 1750 [*Verlet*]. That he must have made harpsichords is proved by 2 references to a 'clavecin fait par Vaudry' in the inventory taken after J. Bourdet's death [*MC*, XCI. 758; 1737, 2 March].

VELTMAN, Andries. Maker of organs, harpsichords, and mathematical instruments. Born 1730 or 1731 at Amsterdam; died there, aged 65, on 5 January 1796. See further *Curtis*, pp. 61–2. It is possible that Weltman, noted below, is the same man.

VENETUS, Domenicus. *See*: DOMENICO, Giovanni, *of Venice*.

VENTURA, Aloysius. Two instruments survive bearing this name. The inscriptions, which are identical in both, are more than suspicious, and one can have little confidence in either instrument.

(1) 1533. Clavichord. Signature: *Opus hoc fecit Aloysius Ventura, Venetia, qui novatur* [? moratur] *in loco nuncupato, 1533.* Snowshill Manor, Worcs. (Formerly the property of Margaret Glyn; formerly in the Van Raalte Collection, Brownsea Island, which was sold by auction in 1927.) Bundfrei; ebony naturals, ivory sharps. In a leather-covered case $32\frac{1}{2} \times 14\frac{1}{2}''$. A faked instrument.

(2) 1533. Ottavino. Signature as on no. 1. The Hague, Gemeentemuseum. Likewise a fake.

VENZKY

(1) **Carl Rudolf August,** born 1767 at Langenhennersdorf near Pirna. Learnt organ building 1780–5 from J. F. Treubluth (1739–1821) and worked with him until 1787 in Dresden. After 3 years he returned to him (1790). Next year he received the title of 'Churfürstl. Sächs. Hoforgelmacher-Adjunctus'. According to *Me* he made, besides organs, square and grand pianos, and clavichords, with or without organs attached ('Flötenwerke').

A 5-octave clavichord by this maker, dated Wien 1804,

is preserved in the Musikwissenschaftliches Seminar at Erlangen University [*Brun*, p. 21].

The Heyer Collection at Leipzig has a portative organ by him dated 1807 [*Ks*].

(2) **Ernst Christian Gotthold,** brother of the above, set up in Birkenfeld as organ and instrument maker [*Ks*].

VERBIEST, Marten, of Antwerp. Harpsichord maker, *fl.* 1580 [*St*]. Surely identical with Marten van der Biest, q.v.

VERHEYDEN, Peter, of Antwerp. Harpsichord maker. Dates ascertained 1643–55.

On 16 February 1655 he married Anna van Thienen [*St*].

VERINI, Giovanni. *See*: FERRINI, Giovanni.

VERJURE. *See*: FERCHUR, Jean.

VESEY, Richard. Spinet maker in York, *c.* 1800. The Pro Musica Co., Annapolis Md., have (1969) a spinet inscribed on the nameboard: *Richardus Vesey Ebor. Fecit.* Single bend in bent side and straight tail-end. Broken octave in bass.

VICENTINO, Nicola. Born at Vicenza in 1511, died at Milan 1575 or 1576; became a priest and studied music under Adrian Willaert; later *maestro di cappella* at the court of Ferrara, where he taught the prince and princess of the family d'Este the harpsichord. Moving to Rome in the train of the Cardinal Hippolyte of Ferrara, he devoted much study to the music of the ancient Greeks. In 1546 he published some 5-part madrigals entitled: *Dell unico Adriano Villaert discipulo D. Nicola Vicento Madrigali a 5 voci per teorica e per pratica da lui composti al nuovo modo del celeberrimo suo maestro retrovati lib I.*, designed to restore the Greek modes; to which end also he designed an *archicembalo*, having two keyboards capable of enharmonic scales, and published his theoretical work *L'antica musica ridotta alla moderna prattica* . . . at Rome in 1555. Two of these *archicembali* were constructed under his supervision, one in Rome for the Cardinal of Ferrara and one in Milan in the year before his death of the plague which swept through Italy in 1575–6. See H. Bottrigari's *Il desiderio, overo de' concerti di varij strumenti musicali* (Bologna, 1599; facsimile reprint, Berlin, 1924), pp. 40–1; also H. W. Kaufman, 'More on the tuning of the archicembalo', *Journal of the American Musicological Society*, Vol. 23, part 1 (1970), pp. 84–94; and Paul R. Brink, *The archicembalo of Nicola Vicentino.* (Ohio State University dissertation, 1966). Ann Arbor, Mich., University Microfilms, 67–2420.

Vicentino also achieved eminence as a performer on keyboard instruments.

VICENTINUS, Hieronymus Clarellus. *See*: CLARELLI, Geronimo.

VICENTIUS. In Siena there is a harpsichord signed *Vicentius* and dated *1516*. Apparently the nameboard, though genuine, does not belong to this harpsichord [*Hubb 1965*, p. 3 n. 8; based on Gough].

VI . . . IES. These syllables, which might possibly abbreviate the maker's name, are above the nameboard of a Venetian polygonal virginal, dated 1540, acquired in 1953 by the New York Metropolitan Museum of Art. On the nameboard, besides an Italian motto, is: *MDXL. Venetiis.* On the back of the nameboard is: *Ordinato e fatto per sua eccelenza la Sig.ra Duchessa D'Urbino L'anno di nostra salute 1540 è pagata* [2 words illegible] *scudi Romani No. 50.* Front of case richly inlaid. *See* E. Winternitz in *MMA journal.* New York. Vol. 1, pp. 95–108, where, however, these syllables are not discussed.

VIERERIGEL, Johannes. Of Pressburg (Bratislava), clavichord maker, *fl.* 1744.

Surviving Instruments

(1) 1744. Leningrad, Institute for Scientific Research on the Theatre and Music. Clavichord; compass C–C, 4 octaves; 47 keys. Inscription on label reported to me as: *Johannes Viererigel. Presburg, 1744.* The form of the surname seems dubious.

VIMERCATI, Petrus. *FrancI* excels itself by recording a 'spinetta' by this maker dated 1190: *Petrus Vimercati fecit Brixiai anno Domini MCXC* [sic].

VINCENTIUS, *probably of Florence.* Harpsichord maker, *fl.* 1516, at which time he enjoyed the patronage of Leo X (Giovanni de' Medici), who was Pope from 1513 to 1521.

Count Chigi Saracini has in his musical collection at Siena a handsome single-manual harpsichord which came, according to information kindly given me by the owner, from the Palazzo Tempi (formerly Bargagli) in the Piazza S. Maria sopr'Arno, Florence. It has an apparent compass of 4 octaves and 2 notes, C–D, with 2×8′ registers; the keys, of which one is missing, have arcaded fronts. The instrument, which measures 218×83 cm., is enclosed in a painted outer case, bearing a coat of arms which would seem to be that of the Tempi family of Florence. The compass and registration of the instrument, which invites comparison with the Baffo harpsichord of 1574 in the Victoria and Albert Museum, London, assign it to the latter part of the sixteenth century.

The nameboard, however, at present in the instrument bears the following inscription: *Leo Papa X / Vincenti hoc opus est ex se rude. Deme Leonis | Nomen*[,] *erit mutum*[;] *nominis omnis honos. / MVCXVI.XF.* The elegiac couplet is presumably to be translated: 'This is the work of Vincentius, rude in itself. Take away the name of Leo [and] it will be dumb; all [its] honour is in [his] name'; and the date to be read as '10 February 1516'. This nameboard appears to have been cut away along the bottom edge (for the cartouche enclosing the inscription lacks one side), and would seem to have been added to this instrument from elsewhere. There is no cause to doubt the genuineness of the lettering, which is a handsome Renaissance Roman; and the nameboard itself looks as though it belonged at one time to a harpsichord, which, if it had survived, would be the oldest dated harpsichord in existence—earlier by 5 years than that by Hieronymus of Bologna which at present holds this distinction.

Gusnaschi (q.v.) is also known to have made a harpsichord for Leo X.

VINCENTIUS *Pratensis*. Harpsichord maker of Prato, near Florence; *fl.* 1610–12. Also made lutes [*Lü*].

Surviving Instruments

(1) 1610. Leipzig, Heyer Collection. Ottavino. Inscribed on back of nameboard: *Vincentius Pratesis 1610*. Rose. Compass, C–C, 4 octaves, with short octave. Ivory naturals, ebony sharps. 80·5 cm. wide by 40 cm. deep. Inscription reproduced at *Ks*, p. 275.

(2) 1612. Ibid. Harpsichord. Inscribed on back of nameboard: *Vincenzius Pratensis 1612*. 2×8′ strings. C–C, 4 octaves, with short octave. Boxwood naturals, black sharps. 187×69 cm. Illustrated in *Ks*, p. 86.

(? 2a) 1613. *Francl* lists a harpsichord signed: *Vincentius Pratensis 1613*.

(? 3) Undated. Ibid. Harpsichord. Anon., perhaps by VP. 2×8′. C–C, 4 octaves with short octave. Ebony naturals and sharps (ornamented). On nameboard: *Laudate Dominum in cymbalis bene sonantibus*. 190×79 cm.

(? 4) Undated. Paris Conservatoire. Clavicytherium Anon., perhaps by VP. Formerly Kraus. See *Ch* (p. 84).

(? 5) Undated. An unsigned harpsichord in the Rück Collection in the German Nationalmuseum was attributed by Dr. Rück to Vincentius Pratensis. It resembles no. 1 in many respects and may well be by this maker [*VdM*].

Note: The René Savoye Collection, Paris, had (1910) a sixteenth-century harpsichord by Preno (q.v.), inscribed on the back of the nameboard: *Vincentius Pratensis 1610 restaurò* [*Ks*, p. 278]. *See also* Stoppacio, a harpsichord by whom may likewise have been restored by Vincentius in 1610.

VIRBÈS, de [Verbès]. Teacher of music in Paris, *fl.* 1768–76 [Forkel, *Mus. Krit. Bibl.* I. 298]. He was also organist of St. Germain-l'Auxerrois, and 'marchand de clavecins, rue des Belles-Étuves' [*Bq*, p. 18]. About 1771 he invented a *clavecin acoustique* which imitated 18 different instruments [*Ge*]. Three years before, he had built a harpsichord with 10 different stops [*Bq*]; and *Ko* records another built in 1777, which was called *clavecin harmonieux et céleste*, and on which his son performed in a concert in 1786, but this was a pianoforte. The exact nature of his inventions is not clear.

Six sonatas for the harpsichord, by either the father or the son, were published without date in Paris; some trios also appeared in 1785, likewise of doubtful authorship.

Ri (p. 80) quotes a handbill 'about the middle of the 18th century' [*sic*] announcing that 'the Sieur Virbes, Professor of Music, and Teacher of the Harpsichord, from Paris' would exhibit 'a most extraordinary harpsichord' at 40 Suffolk Street, Charing Cross.

Verlet cites documentary evidence that he made 'clavecins' (p. 76).

VIRY, A. A 'grande épinette de *A. Viry*, à volute' was item 478 in the Lery sale of 1910 in Paris.

VLADIMIROV. *See*: Batov, I. A.

VOGEL, Hanns. Sixteenth-century keyboard instrument makers, father and son, in Nuremberg. A Stuttgart inventory of 1589 records a keyboard instrument by him. See further *VdMDen*, p. 106.

VOIGT, of Hamburg. Maker of keyboard instruments, *fl.* 1792 [*Ge*, 1812; *Musikalischer Almanach*].

VOIT, Johann Michael, of Schweinfurt, Bavaria. Dates ascertained, 1804–12. Organ builder who made pianofortes and clavichords in considerable numbers. Probably related to the Voits who were connected by marriage to the Stein family (q.v.). By 1811 he had taken his son into partnership, although his name appears alone on an instrument of 1812.

Surviving Clavichords

(1) 1811. Yale University, Steinert Collection; was shewn at the Vienna Music Exhibition, 1892; signed *Verfertiget von Joh. Michael Voit & Sohn, Orgelmacher in Schweinfurt No. 399 Anno 1811* on paper in a box at bass end. F–A, 5 octaves plus. Stamped *no. 399*.

(2) 1812. Washington, Smithsonian Institution. Inscribed: *Verfertiget von Joh. Michael Voit—Orgelmacher in Schweinfurth. Nro. 420. Anno 1812*. Compass F–A, 5 octaves and a 3rd. ? Formerly in the Steinert Collection.

Note: The Neupert Collection in the Germanisches Nationalmuseum, Nuremberg has a piano inscribed; *Verfertiget von Joh. Michael Voit, Orgelmacher in Schweinfurt. Nr. 325 1804*.

VOLBER, Jean. Parisian harpsichord maker. Dates ascertained: 1788–98 or 1799. He entered Guild of Instrument Makers in 1784, from which time till an VII (1798–9) he lived in the rue d'Argenteuil [*Pi*, *Verlet*].

VORENBERCH, Pieter [Vornenburch]. Maker of clavichords and harpsichords, dates ascertained: 1542–52. Born at Cologne, he received the citizenship of Antwerp on 23 June 1542 as a clavichord maker, and entered the Guild of St. Luke in 1552 as harpsichord maker [*St*]. He seems to have made lutes also [*Lü*].

Probably father of Pieter van Voornenburch, the painter, who entered the Guild in 1582.

VORNENBURCH, Pieter van. *See*: Vorenberch, Pieter.

VRIES, Dirck de, of Antwerp. Harpsichord maker; died 1628–9. Probably related to Catherina de Vriese, wife of Andreas Ruckers the Elder [*St*].

VRIESE, Frans de, of Malines. Harpsichord maker; *fl.* before 1557 [*Cl*]; *Hirt* gives his ascertained dates as 1550–70.

W., P. The letters *P.W.* on a spinet formerly in the Germanisches Nationalmuseum, Nuremberg, but lost in World War II, may be a signature. The instrument has split E flat keys throughout [Wilh. Dupont, *Geschichte der musikal. Temperatur*, Nördlingen, Beck, 1935].

A 2-manual harpsichord, unsigned and undated was sold anonymously at Sotheby's on 5 December 1966; it was bought by R. Bibby. Its gilt rose includes the initials *PW* (*P* above, *W* below). Soundboard painted somewhat in Flemish style. Compass F–F, 5 octaves. Three brass hand-stops, not in an English style either in casting or in their arrangement. The top manual has 2 knobs, presumably for a shift coupler. Ebony naturals, ivory-topped sharps. The ornamentally gilded stand with cabriole legs looks French. General impression: French eighteenth century.

WAGNER

(1, 2) **Michael** and **Johann,** brothers who worked together as makers of organs and other instruments at Schmiedefeld. In 1764 they made a harpsichord combined with a flute-stop, says *Ge*, i.e. a claviorganum. In 1770 they built a 3-manual organ in the church at Arnhem. Their stringed keyboard instruments were also well thought of [*Ge*, *Fé*].

(3) **Johann Gottlob** [Jean Theophile], born *c.* 1750 at Medingen near Dresden; became a pupil in the Silbermann workshops [*Hirt*]. Harpsichord, clavichord, and organ maker at Dresden, where in 1774 he invented a piano with 6 variations in tone, obtained through pedals: lute-tone, damped lute, harpsichord, harp, and pantalon. It was called a *clavecin royal* and sold for 28 to 36 ducats [*Ge*, *Ko*]. Died 1789. The Bachhaus at Eisenach has a piano by him [*Ks*, p. 280].

(4) **Christian Salomon,** *his younger brother*, born at Medingen near Dresden in 1754. He was taken into partnership by his brother in 1773, and assisted him in the invention of the *clavecin royal.* After his brother's death C. S. W. continued making keyboard instruments until his death between 1812 and 1816. In 1796 he produced a method of quilling harpsichords which claimed to render the replacement of quills unnecessary. His most expensive harpsichord commanded a price of 600 talers [*Ge*, *Fé*].

WAGNER, John Christian. Recorded as 'single and double harpsichord and spinet maker' in Moore Street, Dublin, in 1765 [*Teahan*].

WAGSTAFFE, Jane, *early owner, not maker.* Noted here because her name identifies an English spinet sold by Mrs. Joyce Wilson at Sotheby's on 22 October 1970 to John S. P. Morley. The instrument has a mahogany case, the inside of the lid decorated with 3 marquetry panels ['probably a later addition' says the Catalogue, which includes a photograph]; G–G, 5 octaves; arcaded ivory naturals, ebony sharps; later stand in oak. The fore-edge of the jackrail is inscribed *Jane Wagstaffe 1742*, and she may have been the first owner. Walnut nameboard; oaken stand (later).

WAHL. German builder of *Claviergamben*, seventeenth century [*Wa*].

WAKEFIELD, Richard. Patented on 2 May 1771 'a new method of tuning and keeping in tune all kind of harpsichords, spinnets, forte pianos etc. . . .' Patent no. 989 [*Pat*].

WALHAUPTER, David. Harpsichord maker in New York; *fl.* 1773 [*Hirt*].

WALKER

(1) **Adam,** (2) **D.,** and (3) **J.** Earliest and latest dates known, 1772–81. Harpsichord makers at 8 Great Pulteney Street, Golden Square, London.

They invented a stop called the 'celestina', which aimed at a sostenuto by means of a continuous bow operated by a 'weight, spring, or traddle'. It is described in patent 1020 and referred to by Jefferson in his correspondence with Francis Hopkinson [*Russell 1959*, pp. 179–80].

WALKER, Henry. Apprenticed to the London virginal maker Nicholas Farnaby (q.v.). Free of the Joiners Company in 1628 [*Join*].

WALTER, Anton, of Vienna, 1752–1826. Best known as a pianoforte maker, also built organs and concerned himself with harpsichords, etc. According to an invoice of his dated 3 March 1781 he spent 12 days at the Esterházy court 'an denen zu verbesserenden Clavier und Flügel Instrumenten' [*Walter*, p. 258].

WALTHER, Anton. *See*: VATER, Antoine.

WARN, Thomas, of Gloucester. Maker of spinets and harpsichords; *fl.* 1740 [*J*].

WARTH, Philipp Jakob. Amateur maker of keyboard instruments (chiefly pianos, but probably clavichords too) at Untertürkheim, Württemberg, where he was born. Dates ascertained, 1788–1800 [*Hirt*]. He was a schoolmaster by profession. See further *Ge* (1812) and the *Speiersche Mus. Real-Zeitung*, 1788.

WATSON, John, of York. A spinet in private ownership near London (Sotheby's, 2 February 1956) is inscribed: *Johannes Watson Eboraci fecit 1762.* Black naturals, white sharps. Length 6′ 4″.

WATSON, Thomas. Appears in the list of members of the Guild of St. Luke, Antwerp, in 1658–9 as harpsichord maker and tuner [*Bu*]. He was also organist of the St. Joris-kerk, Antwerp [*St*].

WATTERS, Antoine. *See*: VATER, Antoine.

WATTS, Charles. Primarily a pianoforte maker, first in London and then from 1788 in Charleston, S.C. where he advertised himself in the *City Gazette* as also a repairer of harpsichords and spinets [Rita Benton in *Hin* (p. 181)].

WATTS, Thomas. *See*: BRADSHAW, Albion.

WE . . . An early eighteenth-century 2-manual harpsichord in the Muz. Narodowe, Poznán, bears an almost illegible label, on which the last word, perhaps the maker's surname, seems to begin *We* . . . The instrument was converted later into a pianoforte of very simple action.

WEBBER, Rachel. Recorded as a harpsichord maker at 71 Marlborough Street, Dublin, in 1706 and at number 75 from 1777 to 1778 [*Teahan*]. Probably related to the Webers below.

WEBER, Ferdinand. Organ and harpsichord maker, Werburgh Street, Dublin, 1715–84. Born at Borstendorf; died at Dublin. Learned organ building under J. E. Hähnel of Meissen, 1728–35. Came to Dublin in 1739.

TABLE 38. *Surviving Instruments by Ferdinand WEBER*

No.	Date	Type	Kbs.	Signature	Owner/Remarks
1	1746	H	1	*Ferdinandus Weber 2 fecit Londini 1746*	Sotheby's, 16 March 1956; 2×8′, lute, buff; 3 pedals. Now (1970) P. J. Watts, Maidenhead.
1a	1751	H	1	*Ferdinandus* [?] *Weber fecit Dublin 1751*	Brussels Conservatoire. 5 octaves F–F without lowest F sharp. 2×8′ stops.
2	[?1768 or 1769]	H	1		Dublin. National Museum. 5 octaves, 4 registers, 2 genouillères, Venetian swell (Weber type); 2×8′, 1×4′, lute, buff, machine. Illustrated in *Fld.*
3	[*c.* 1770]	H	1	*Ferdinand Weber Fecit*	Formerly at Limavady, Co. Derry. Similar to no. 2. (See note below); 1956–67, Margaret Lyle, Newcastle upon Tyne, who bequeathed it to the Royal College of Music.
4	—	S	1		Dublin. National Museum. G–G, 5 octaves.
5	1764	Cc	1		Dublin. National Museum. Sotheby's, 29 June 1956; 2×8′, 1×4′, harp. Date 1764 pencilled on back of soundboard during restoration in the early 1960s [*CM*]. Illustrated in *Russell 1959*, where the date is given as 1775.

When Handel came to Dublin in November 1741 he visited Weber's House in Werburgh Street frequently. Weber moved to Marlborough Street in 1750 and married in 1755; in 1784 his address was 71 Marlborough Street [*Dubl. 1784*]. In 1756 his son Thomas Ferdinand was baptized. In 1752 he made a harpsichord for Thomas Roseingrave.

On Weber's death the business passed into the hands of his son Thomas Ferdinand, 'who however' says *Fld*, 'did not long keep it owing to his convivial habits'. His recorded dates are 1787–90 [*Teahan*].

E. Halfpenny's article 'Shudi and the Venetian swell' (*Music and Letters*, July 1946) draws attention to the fact that if *Fld*'s dating for number 2 is correct, the Venetian swell may have been in use in Ireland by Weber before Shudi patented it in England (1769). Weber's and Shudi's swells are the same in principle, though different in detail.

Note on no. 3 above. This beautifully preserved instrument has remained in the possession of the same family since it was made, the present owner, Miss Margaret Hanna, being a descendant of Miss Elizabeth Orr who was the first person to possess it.

Mahogany case with satinwood stringing and crossbanding. Four hand-stops: to the left of the nameboard, Buff, lute; to the right 1st Unison, 2nd Unison. Left genouillère works a machine-stop; right, the Venetian swell. Geometrical rose of ivory.

WEGNER, Friedrich. Organ builder and maker of stringed keyboard instruments at Wels, Austria, in 1598 [*MarcP*].

WEIDNER, David Jacob. Maker of organs and clavichords in Augsburg, *fl.* 1697.

Surviving Instruments

(1) 1697. Zürich, Schweizerisches Landesmuseum. Clavichord, inscribed: *David Jakob Weidner, Orgelmacher in Augsburg, 1697*. Gebunden. Compass, 3 octaves and a 6th; 5 lowest sharps split. Formerly at the Nunnery of St. Anna, Lucerne, and in the Schumacher Collection.

WEIDTMAN, Peter. *Fl.* 1724 as a clavichord maker at Ratingen, near Düsseldorf. A clavichord by him survives, signed in red pencil on the underside of the soundboard: *Peter Weidt / man Rating / 10 9bris / 1724*. C–C, 4 octaves without bottom C sharp; gebunden. Restored in 1965 by Martin Scholz, who removed the original soundboard (with rose) which is preserved by Frau Katharina Karhausen at Aachen. The instrument is described in detail and illustrated in *Thoene*.

WEIKHART, of Halle. Eighteenth-century maker of quilled keyboard instruments—a 'berühmter Instrumentenmacher' according to J. S. Petri (*Anleitung zur practischen Musik*, 2nd edition, 1782, p. 369). He quilled his instruments with turkey quills.

WEIL, Johann Wilhelm, of Neuwied, near Coblenz. Instrument maker, *fl.* 1793.

The Bayerisches Nationalmuseum at Munich had (until World War II, when the instrument collection was almost entirely destroyed) a mechanical claviorganum, consisting of a clavichord and small organ, driven by clockwork. The clavichord was bichord and embraced 2½ octaves, the organ 1½ octaves. The bellows were inscribed: *Jean Guillaume Weil de Neuwied, fait a Wied Runckel proche Limburg sur Lahn le 3 Decemb. 1793. Nr. 37*. The mechanism was made by *Joh. Leykes in Creyfeld.*

WEISS, Johann. Clavichord maker on the Continent, *fl.* 1702.

Surviving Instruments

(1) 1702. Munich, Deutsches Museum. A clavichord bears the signature *Ano 1702 Johann Weiss* [*Thoene*]. Compass 4 octaves.

WEISSLAND, Georg, of Kassel, *fl.* 1597. Court organ builder and maker of keyboard instruments to the Landgraf Moritz of Hesse. Two spinets by him appear in the Kassel inventory of 1613 [*MarcP*].

WELCKER. German clavichord maker who was building up to the year 1820 [Blüthner and Gretschel, *Der Pianofortebau*].

WELMAN, Stephen. English spinet maker, *fl.* 1680. A spinet of this date belongs to Messrs. Robert Morley, London (1964). Compass B–C, 4 octaves and 1 note. 4′ 8″×1′ 7″×5″. Walnut case. Ebony naturals and bone sharps. Externally similar to the John Player no. 2. I could not trace Welman in *Join*.

WELTMAN. Presented in 1759 to the Académie des Sciences in Paris a method of changing registers and producing a *crescendo* by means of genouillères [*RipExpr*, p. 69]. *See above*: VELTMAN, Andries.

WESSBERG, Eric. Clavichord maker, *fl.* at Stockholm 1821.

Surviving Clavichords

(1) 1821. Stockholm, Nordiska Museet, 5 octaves plus 7 notes. The latest dated clavichord known to me from the classical period.

WEYENBERG, Josse van, of Brussels, seventeenth century, calls himself 'accordeur d'espinettes'. He was probably a maker [*Cl*, p. 77].

WHITE

(*a*) **Thomas** (I). Almost certainly a virginal maker. Master of Gabriel Townsend and father of:

(*b*) **Thomas** (II). Virginal maker. Admitted free of the Joiners' Company in 1621. Lived in Old Jewry, London. He was buried on 5 January 1660. His widow Mary died of the plague in 1665 and was buried on 2 September.
Father of James White and of:

(*c*) **Thomas** (III). Admitted free of the Joiners' Company in 1669 on the relation of Adam Leversidge and another person.

(*d*) **James.** Son of Thomas (II). Dates ascertained, 1656–70. Admitted free of the Joiners' Company by patrimony, 1 December 1656. Mentioned as virginal maker in Old Jewry, 1664. He may be the organ builder James White who subscribed to Mace's *Musicks Monument* (1676). *See table 39.*

WICLEF, Johan Christoph, [Wiegleb] of Ansbach. Dates ascertained, 1724–40. Maker of organs and other instruments. He devised a plucking mechanism for the harpsichord which used brass plectra instead of quills. (This was, of course, a rediscovery, brass having been used for this purpose in early times) [*Adl*, II. 107].

WIEDBERG. *See*: TRUTE, Charles.

WIEGLEB. *See*: WICLEF.

WIERLING, Hendrik. Baptized 14 December 1721 in Leyden. In 1747 he is described as a 'clavecimbaelmaker'. By the following year, however, he had become an innkeeper. See further *Curtis*, p. 62.

WILBROOK, John. Harpsichord and spinet maker in London in the eighteenth century. That he worked for Tabel (q.v.) is shown by instrument 2 below.

Surviving Instruments

(1) Undated. Parham Park, Sussex. Spinet. Inscribed: *Johannes Wilbrook of London.* Oak case, nameboard in walnut with boxwood inlay. Compass, just under 5 octaves. 6′ 5″×3′ 7″. Sold by Mrs. John Micklem, at Sotheby's, 25 May 1951; bought by Messrs. Gooden & Fox, London.

(2) 1730. Redhill, Dr. R. Mirrey. Formerly owned by Lady Margaret Fortescue, Castle Hill, Filleigh, N. Devon. Harpsichord inscribed on the nameboard: *Johannes Wilbrook Londini 1730*, and on the underside of the soundboard *Johannes Wilbrook Londini fecit Tabel's man.* Two manuals, 2×8′, 1×4′, lute; skunktail sharps; rose; otherwise similar to a Kirkman in general design. Bought by Dr. Mirrey at Christie's, 21 May 1970.

WILHELMI, of Kassel. Clavichord and harpsichord maker, *fl.* 1784. He charged from 20 to 50 thalers apiece for his clavichords [C. Engel, *Musical Instruments*, rev. edn., London, 1908; p. 122]. He also made pianos [*Hirt*].

WILKINSON, W., English spinet maker, *fl.* 1741. *See*: LADYMAN.

WILLENBROCK, Hermann. Maker of clavichords and harpsichords at Hanover. He made in 1712 a claviorganum for the Crown-prince Georg, afterwards King George I of England. This instrument was formerly in the Boddington Collection, Manchester, but is now in the Crosby-Brown Collection, Metropolitan Museum of Art, New York. The harpsichord part of the instrument had been turned into a pianoforte. Inscribed on the front of the batten between the keyboards: *Hermans Willen Brock Orgel und Instrumend* [sic] *Macher zu Hannover. Aō, 1712.*
His work is praised by a contemporary as 'durchgehends gut' [*MatNo*, p. 263].

WINTHER. *Fl.* 1781 in Lübeck, where he made clavichords in partnership with Meyer.

Surviving Instruments

(1) 1781. Copenhagen, Musikhistorisk Museum. Clavichord signed on the soundboard: *Winther und Meyer in Lübeck. Fecerunt 1781.* F–A, 5 octaves and 3 notes. Soundhole without rose. Bundfrei, with octaves strings in the bass.

WITTMAN. There was advertised in Paris on 11 December 1758: 'Clavecin neuf et très curieux de la composition

TABLE 39. *Surviving Instruments by James and Thomas WHITE*

No.	Date	Type	Signature	Owner/Remarks
James				
1	1656	V	[On jackrail] *Jacobus White fecit 1656*	The Revd. W. Temple Bourne, C/F–B/C, 50 keys. 5′ 7″ × 1′ 9½″. Gilt embossed paper shewing the Plantagenet royal arms. Geometrical rose. Shewn at International Inventions Exhibition, London, 1885. At present in the care of Major A. T. Bourne-Arton.
2	1661	V	*Jacobus White London 1661*	Sold at Christie's, 24 January 1946. Oak case; inside lid painted with Orpheus in a landscape. Width 5′ 6″.
Thomas				
2a	1638	Ot		Paris, private ownership [*ChamP*].
3	1642	V	[On jackrail] *Thomas White fecit 1642*	London, Victoria and Albert Museum. C–C, 4 octaves. 5′ 6″ × 1′ 8″. Boxwood naturals, black sharps. Decorated with embossed gilt paper (not armorial). Rose. Domed lid. Gift of Mrs. Ada Deacon, 1933.
4	1651	V	*Thomas White fecit 1651*	York, Castle Museum. B–D, 52 keys. 5′ 6″ × 1′ 8″. Lid painted with scenes from the life of Christ. Exhibited at International Inventions Exhibition of 1885. Illustrated in *Ga*.
5	1653	V	*Thomas White fecit 1653*	The Duke of Devonshire. The nameboard bears the name of a former owner, *Mary Byard*. Case of oak, except the bottom, which is pine. Dimensions 66 × 20½″. An oaken front-board, extending the whole length of the instrument, comes away. The lid is decorated inside with a contemporary painting, depicting *inter alia* Orpheus charming the beasts with his lyre. The interior is fitted with pear-wood mouldings, and is painted and faced in parts with embossed paper, gilded. The keyboard is of lime, with boxwood naturals, and walnut sharps inlaid with ivory, ebony, and boxwood. Keyfronts are of embossed paper, gilded, some of them being modern additions. Some of the keys bear traces of their names in MS. Compass C–C, 4 octaves. Soundboard decorated with paintings of birds and flowers. A rose of parchment and fretted wood. On the soundboard-support behind the nameboard are scratched the letters *T* [? homas] *W* [? hite], and *MM*, the latter perhaps the initials of a workman. This virginal was shewn at South Kensington in 1872 by S. H. Gill of Nottingham.
6	1654	V	*Thomas White fecit 1654*	Cardiff, Welsh Folk-Museum, previously the property of the Hon. F. G. Wynn of Llanwnda; previously Boddington College, Manchester; previously the Musgrave family of Cumberland. B–F (55 keys). 5′ 6″ × 1′ 9½″. 2 uninitialled roses. The date now reads 1664, but this is an alteration from the original 1654.

du Sr. Wittman, lequel donne, par le moyen d'un caisse de mécanisme, diverses modulations aux sons depuis le pianissimo jusqu'au fortissimo. Prix: 600 livres . . .' [*Bq*].

WOFFINGTON. Makers of harpsichords and other instruments in Dublin.

(1) **Robert**, maker of the organ, harpsichord, and pianoforte. Dates ascertained: 1773[?]–1823 [*Teahan*], the latter being the year of his death. In 1774 he was taken into partnership by William Gibson (q.v.). In 1778 this partnership was dissolved, and Woffington continued on his own account at 9 William Street 'where he has for sale several of these Instruments [mentioned above], and entreats the Commands of the Nobility and Gentry . . .'. An upright

piano by him belonged to the Duchess of Connaught in 1912; and a single-manual harpsichord by a Woffington—probably this one—passed through the hands of Messrs. Moss Harris & Son, London, about 1944 [*MA, Fld*]. Colin Tilney has (1965) a single harpsichord by Robert Woffington: 2×8′, 1×4′, buff, 2 knee-levers working a machine-stop and a Venetian swell. Acquired by him in 1954.

Inscription on nameboard: *Robertus Woffington Fect.*; on back of nameboard: (1) *Restored by John Sebastian Morley, 56 Old Brompton Rd., S.W. 7. A.D. 1945* and (2) *Fully restored by Alan McKirdy October 1954 10 Balmore St. London N. 19.* A chamber organ by Woffington was in the possession of Roger Warner of Burford in 1952.

The National Museum of Ireland, Dublin, has (1970) an upright claviorganum signed *Robertus Woffington fecit* on the nameboard. Compass F–F, 5 octaves without lowest F sharp. The instrument has one keyboard, and the organ part 2 stops—a diapason and a flute. Restored by Michael Thomas.

(2) **John**, son of the foregoing, *fl.* 1816, made harpsichords and pianos [*MA*].

Note. J (p. 79) gives 1728–1836 as the earliest and latest dates known of the firm of Woffington, instrument makers. *The above two Woffingtons should be distinguished from*:

(3) **Robert,** *fl.* 1720–49 (year of his death). Vicar-choral of St. Patrick's. Probably took part in the original performance of Handel's *Messiah* in 1742.

(4) **John**, son of no. 3; *fl.* 1750.

(5) **John**, *fl.* 1723–59, organist of Armagh Cathedral [*MA*].

WOGA, Werner, of Danzig. Maker of harpsichords. About 1740 his reputation was considerable [*Ge*, 1812].

WOLF, C. H. Maker of organs and other keyboard instruments at Leipzig in the late eighteenth century [*Ge*, 1812].

WOLFAERT, Eewout [Edward]. Belonged to the Guild of St. Luke, Antwerp, in 1589 as harpsichord maker [*St*].

WOLTKERSSON, Gustav Gabriel. Swedish clavichord maker, *fl.* 1759.

Surviving Instruments

(1) 1759. Gothenburg. Göteborgs Museum. Signed: *Gust: Gab: Woltkersson Fecit, anno 1759.* Compass, C–C, 4 octaves. Dimensions 151×48 cm.

WOOLFINDEN, John. English spinet maker, *c.* 1725 [*J*]. There is a spinet, undated, signed *John Woolfinden* at Colonial Williamsburg. Restored by Hugh Gough about 1964.

WORCKEN, Georg, of Germany. Clavichord maker; *fl.* 1636 [*Va*].

WORMS, Lodewijck. Probably a harpsichord maker, at The Hague. Baptized 1658; died 1776 [*Curtis*, p. 62].

WOYTZIG, George. Clavichord maker, *fl.* 1688, probably in Sweden.

Surviving Instruments

(1) 1688. Clavichord. Musikhistorisk Museet, Stockholm. Gebunden. C–C, 4 octaves with short octave and 2 split sharps in the bass.

YKENS, Melsen *or* **Melchior.** *See*: Britsen, Joris I.

Z, G. A harpsichord owned by Michael Thomas, Hurley, Berks., bears the inscription *GZ 1672* on a key. This inscription (if genuine) cannot refer to Girolamo Zenti, who died in 1668.

ZABEL, Gottfried Wilhelm. Dates ascertained, 1792–1803; organ and instrument maker at Tangermünde near Stendal in 1792. He was a pupil of Hildebrand of Dresden. His clavichords had a high reputation. In 1803 he was paid a fee of 620 thalers for repairing the organ in Stendal Cathedral.

ZANETTI. Early seventeenth-century Italian harpsichord maker [*ClP* (71), *Prof* (272), *Hullm*]. *ClP* domiciles him in Florence. (*Ri* (p. 79) calls him a 'Venetian priest').

ZEISS, Valentin. Builder of organs and other instruments in Linz, *fl.* 1639–46. On 17 August 1639 he was appointed court instrument maker to the Emperor Ferdinand III of Austria. See further *VdMSalzb* and *VdMZeiss*.

Surviving Instruments

(1) 1639. Salzburg, Museum Carolino-Augusteum (earlier in the Leprosenhauskirche at Mülln near Salzburg). Claviorganum; single-manual; compass C/E–C, 4 octaves, the pedal (C/E–G, 2 octaves) being coupled to the keyboard; 2×8′ stops on the harpsichord, whose soundboard has a geometrical rose and bears the inscription: *Valentinuss* [sic] *Zeiss / Orgelb: In Lüntz / 1639.*

(2) 1646. In private ownership at Schloss Aistersheim in Upper Austria. Claviorganum; single-manual, without pedal; 2×8′ stops, one of which is a lute-stop. Inscription on wrestplank: *Vil Eher Wirth Einem sein Kunst Veracht / Als Nach Oder Besser gemacht. / Valentin Zeiss Kays. Orgelmacher. lintz 1646.*

ZELL, Christian [Zelle]. Harpsichord maker at the Gänsemarkt, Hamburg, where he acquired citizenship on 14 August 1722. He married Florentina, widow of Carl Conrad Fleischer (q.v.) at the S. Petri church there on 1 September 1722. Three children were baptized at S. Petri: Christian (18 June 1723), Anna Maria (2 July 1725), and Elisabeth (11 March 1729). Among the godparents was Gabriel Tielcke (son of Joachim, the lute maker, and Catharina Fleischer) [*Hbg*].

Surviving Harpsichords

(1) 1728. Hamburg. Museum für Kunst und Gewerbe. Two manuals; 2×8′, 1×4′, buff coupler. Inscribed on a label stuck to the back of the nameboard: *Christian Zell, fecit Ao. 1728 a Hamburg.* F–D, just under 5 octaves. Ivory naturals, tortoiseshell sharps. No rose. Lacquered case. Auctioned at Marseilles about 1966 and then sold by a dealer to the Museum. See further *Conr*. Shewn at the Paris Exhibition in 1900, when A. Thibout was the owner [*Par. 1900*, p. 52; illustrated fig. 32 (as also in *Conr*)].

(2) 1737. Barcelona. Conservatorio. One manual. Inscription on back of the nameboard: *Christian Zell Hamburg 1737*. C–D, 4 octaves plus 2 notes [*Rip*].

(3) 1741. Aurich. Museum Ostfriesische Landschaft. One manual; 2×8′, 1×4′. Inscribed on label stuck on back of nameboard: *Christian Zell in Hamburg 1741*. C–D, 4 octaves plus 1 tone. Said to have been owned originally by the noble East-Friesian family Cirksena which died out in 1744. An inscription on the case *P. v. Colomb 17..6* (?) indicates the subsequent ownership of Peter von Colomb (1719–97), War Minister and afterwards President of the Royal Prussian 'Kriegs- und Domänenkammer' at Aurich. His heirs sold it in 1810, and it was owned later by the Pottere family whose last member Johann de Pottere left it to the Ostfriesische Landschaft in 1950.

ZENTI, Girolamo [Hieronymus de Zentis, Hieronymus de Zentis Viterbiensis]. Maker of harpsichords, spinets, and organs, was born probably at Viterbo north-west of Rome.

This craftsman was at the court of Queen Christina in Stockholm in 1653, and after returning to Italy contracted to build an organ for Prince Camillo Pamphilij, nephew of Pope Innocent X, in March 1660. Before this project could be completed he went to Paris, probably staying there until February 1662. We find him next in England in 1664 as the 'King's virginal maker' but he returned to Rome in that year, being succeeded by Andrea Testa (q.v.), and in or after 1666 went to Paris where he died 'in the French King's service' in 1668. See *RipZ* for details.

He may well have worked at some time for the Medici family at Florence, for an inventory made in 1700 of Prince Ferdinando's instruments records 6 made by Zenti [*Gai*, p. 6], at least 4 of which were still there when the collection was entrusted to the care of Cristofori [*Pu*].

He is mentioned by Giovanni Buontempi (*Historia musica*, Perugia, 1695, p. 47): 'I più moderni [clavicembali] sono stati ritrouati di Girolamo Zenti, fatti in figura di Triangolo non giustamente equicrure . . . per hauer tre lati ineguali, con due tastature . . . e con tre registri.' *Hubb 1965* and *RipZ* interpret this passage as referring

TABLE 40. *Surviving Instruments by Girolamo ZENTI*

No.	Date	Type	Kbs.	Signature	Owner/Remarks
[1?]	1633	H		*Hieronimus de Zentis Viterbiensis faciebat 1633*	Shewn by Alexandre Mottu at the Exposition Internationale de Musique, Geneva, 1927. This instrument is most probably *FrancI*'s no. 32 and as such must be regarded as suspect. Whereabouts unknown (1972).
2	1637	S	1	*Hieronymus de Zentis Viterbiensis faciebat 1637*	Brussels Conservatoire. 4 octaves. C–C with short octave. Size 125×44 cm. The date 1637 on the keyboard confirms Mahillon's reading of the date on the nameboard.
[3]	1658	H	1	*Hieronymus de Zentis Viterbiensis F. Romae Anno Dom. MDCLVIII*	New York, Metropolitan Museum of Art. C–F, 4 octaves and a 4th; 2×8′. Rose. Length 6′ 6″. Acquired in 1886. Illustrated in catalogue and in *Wint 1966*. Doubtful according to *RipZ*.
4	1666	H	1	*Hieronymus Zenti Fecit Romae A.S. MDCLXVI*	Ibid. 2×8′. Rose. 7′ $9\frac{1}{2}$″×3′ 0″. Restorer's inscription, 1755: *Joannes Ferrini* [q.v.] *Florentinus Restauravit MDCCLV*. This instrument may well be by Zenti.
[5]	1676	Ot.	1	*Girolano Zenti 1676*	Recorded in *FrancII*, who says it was restored by Iacopo Anichini of Cortona in 1849, and was owned by Luigi Miniati in 1851. Whereabouts (1972) unknown. Since Zenti died in 1668 the inscription cannot be authentic.
[6]	?	H	1	*K. Girolamo Zenti di Olmia A : 1683* [sic]	Leipzig University, Heyer Collection. 2×8′ stops; D–C, 3 octaves and a 7th. 209×80 cm. The date 1683 in this instrument is clearly spurious (see *Ks*, p. 282); and the ascription to Zenti is doubtful according to *RipZ*.
6a	n.d.	Ot	1	G^o Z^i [on top and bottom keys]	New York, Metropolitan Museum of Art. Attributed to Zenti by *RipZ*, citing similarities to numbers 2 and 4, and to one of the instruments by Zeriti in the Medici inventory of 1700.
[7]	n.d.	H	1		Brussels Conservatoire. C–E, 4 octaves and a 3rd; 2×8′. Attributed by *Mah* (vol. 3, 1600) to 'Jeronimus de Tenbe, à Rome, (vers 1656)' on no ground now apparent.

to the invention of the bentside spinet, of which instrument no. 2 is the earliest known example. *Lü* mentioned him as a lute maker.

Giacomo Ridolfi (q.v.) may have been a pupil of Girolamo Zenti.

There was advertised for sale in Paris on 26 February 1753 a 'clavecin à ravallement de Gerolamo de Sentis. L'enlèvement des Sabines est peint en dehors et de grands morceaux d'architecture ornent le dedans . . .' [*Bq*].

He is probably the 'Geronimo' referred to by *Cor* (p. 84) (*not* Hieronymus Bononiensis), and also the Jérosme in *Bq*'s 'clavecin de Jérosme' advertised in Paris on 5 February 1767—also the Jérosme whose harpsichord was in Treyer's possession in 1779 [*Hubb*].

Zl, Go. *See*: Zenti, Girolamo.

ZIEGLER, Johann Andrea. 1658–1737. Born at Weimar in 1658 and remained there as a maker of keyboard instruments. *Wa* speaks of the durability and good tone of his harpsichords, clavichords, and clavicytheria. In his youth he worked for his father as a cabinet maker, and assisted in the construction of the cathedral organ at Erfurt and the organ at Weimar, where he died on 20 September 1737 [*Ge*].

ZIMMERMAN. Harpsichord maker in the rue Trainée, Paris; *fl.* 1786–8 [*Verlet*].

ZIRENGAST, Joseph. Organ builder at Wiener Neustadt; dates ascertained, 1761–7, when he worked on harpsichords (among other instruments) at the Esterházy court [*Walter*].

ZOANE-MARCO. *See*: Giovan-Marco, *di Ferrara*.

ZOLFANELLI, Giuseppe, of Florence. Son of Francesco Z. Dates ascertained: 1690–1709. He made musical instruments of many kinds, including keyboard, but did not achieve distinction in any field [*Ge, Lü*].

His name appears in the matriculation books of his Guild for 1690 and 1697, when he resided 'behind the church of S. Michele Visdomini'. From 1709 onwards he was at Bologna [*Pu*].

ZOPFE, John Belthazar [Hans B. Zopfi]. Maker of harpsichords and clavichords. Dates ascertained, 1747–50, the latter being the year of his death.

Like Shudi, whose niece Anna Margarett he married [*Da*, p. 52], Zopfe was born at Schwanden, in the canton of Glarus, Switzerland, in the chronicles of which town he is referred to as Hans B. Zopfi 'claviercordmacher' [*Da*, p. 31].

RB.J. shew that Zopfi owned a house in King Street, Golden Square, from 1747 until 1749. The *RB* for 1750 is missing, but we are to presume that Zopfe was still a resident there when he died. *J* (p. 79) quotes a notice from the *London Gazette*, 23 February 1750, addressed to 'all persons indebted to the estate of Mr. John Belthazar Zopffee . . . harpsichord maker deceased', who had died between the 12th and the 17th of the previous month.

In his will, dated 12 January 1750, Zopfe describes himself as 'of the parish of Saint James, Westminster . . . harpsichord maker', and desires that his stock in trade and household effects be sold up. No mention is made of his wife Anna Margarett, who must presumably have died before him, nor of any children: the beneficiaries being the children of his late brother Frederick, the children of his sister Ann, wife of Frederick Bloomer [i.e. Blumer] of Switzerland—probably a relative of Samuel Blumer, who was also a Schwanden man—and finally 'Sarah Wood now living with me'. Samuel Tschudi of Glarus, no doubt a member of Burkat Shudi's family, is the trustee; and the organ builder John Snetzler is one of the witnesses. The will was proved on 17 January 1750.

Surviving Plucked Instruments

(1) *N.d.* Spinet, inscribed: *Johannes Balthasar Zopfe.* In private ownership in Virginia, 1960. Formerly owned by an aunt of President Tyler of the U.S.A.

ZUCCHERO, Federigo, of the nineteenth century. Maker of harpsichords [*Lü, Ge*].

ZUMPE, Johann Christoph. A German craftsman who, after being employed in the Silbermann workshops, came to England some time in the 1750s and worked for a time for the harpsichord maker Shudi.[1]

By 1761 he had started up on his own, at 7 Princes Street, Hanover Square [*RB.G.*] and had turned, or was about to turn, from harpsichord work to the making of the square pianos[2] which were destined to become so popular. He was in partnership from 1769 to 1778 with Buntebart,[3] and afterwards (*pace Ri*, p. 132) with Meyer.

Laurence Sterne wrote to Mrs. Daniel Draper in March 1767: 'I have been with Zumps [*sic*]; and first your piano forte must be tuned from the brass middle string of your guittar, which is C.—I have got you a hammer too, and a pair of plyers to twist your wire with . . .' (First published in *Letters from Yorick to Eliza*, 1773). And Gray the poet refers to a Zumpe piano in a letter to William Mason [*J*, p. 137].

In 1780 he moved to Princes Street, Cavendish Square, where he remained until 1784 [*RB*], in which year he returned to Germany, having acquired a considerable fortune, and leaving Schoene & Co. as his successors (see *J* and *Ha* for the history of Zumpe's piano making, which does not concern us here).

It is interesting that even during the period when he was selling square pianos as fast as he could make them, he found time to turn his hand to a completely different type of instrument. The late Canon F. W. Galpin noted that there is in Frankfurt Museum a lute-shaped cittern by *John Zumpe in Princes Street Hanover Square at the sign of the Golden Guitar*. The address dates it between 1761 and 1780.

[1] [Burney's article on the harpsichord in Rees's *Cyclopaedia*.] This article states that when Zumpe began making his squares he 'had long worked under Shudi', which would imply that he had come to England in the early 1750s at the latest. But Burney's chronology tends to be very unreliable. *J* dates the arrival of Zumpe in this country about 1760.

[2] The earliest surviving instrument by him is, however, not a pianoforte but a mandora of 1764 (in Glasgow), as Eric Halfpenny points out. His earliest extant pianoforte (in the Broadwood Collection), which is also the earliest English-made pianoforte, dates from 1766.

[3] The Conservatoire des Arts et Métiers, Paris, has a claviorganum, combining a piano and an organ, signed: *Johannes Zumpe et Buntebart Londini fecerunt 1778, Princes Street Hanover Square.* A square piano signed: *Iohannes Zumpe and Buntebart, London, 1769* was sold at Sotheby's on 17 December 1954.

GEOGRAPHICAL AND CHRONOLOGICAL CONSPECTUS OF MAKERS

Note. I have used the following rough method of arranging the makers chronologically: the date given is (in the few cases where this is known) the year in which the maker set up his workshop; otherwise normally the year in which he reached the age of 30 years, or (where the date of birth is not known) the earliest date ascertained.

AMERICA

BETHLEHEM, PA.
1760 Antes, J.

BOSTON, MASS.
1768 Harris, John

LITITZ, PA.
1746 Hartaffel, R.
1765 Tannenberg, D.

MILTON, MASS.
c. 1819 Crehore, B.

NEW YORK
1745 Clemm, J. G.
1759 Tremaine
Walhaupter, D.
1773 Heyer, F.
1785 Dobbs, T.

PHILADELPHIA
1739 Clemm, J. G.
1743 Hesselius, G.
1760 Feyring, P.
1794 Trute, C.
Wiedberg

SALEM, MASS.
1774 BLYTH, S.

WILMINGTON, DELAWARE
1795 Trute, C.
Wiedberg

AUSTRIA

See also: **Bohemia, Moravia**

TOWN UNKNOWN
1761 Schüller, F.
1782 Schwandtner, C.

BOZEN (BOLZANO)
1683 Baumgartner, J.

BRIXEN
c. 1810 Lusser, J.

GRAZ (?)
1754 Römer, A.

INNSBRUCK
1550 Frelich, F.
1653 Herz, D.
1781 Fuchss, J. A.

LINZ
1639 Zeiss, V.

SALZBURG
1609 Mayer, J.
1785 Schmidt, J.

STEYR
1587 Hacker, J.

VIENNA
1755 Leydecker, J.
1765 Moyse, J.
1780 Schantz, J.
1782 Walter, A.
1785 Bohak, J.
1786 Hofmann, F.
c. 1800 Klein, J.
1804 Bock, C.

WELS
1598 Wegner, F.

WIENER NEUSTADT
1761 Zirengast, J.

BELGIUM

See: **Low Countries**

BOHEMIA

See also: **Moravia**

JAROMER
1821 Kunz, I.

PRAGUE
17— Zelenka, J.
1764 Truska, S. J.

CHINA

PEKING
1711 Pedrini, T.

DENMARK

TOWN UNKNOWN
c. 1700 [?] Claudius, C.
1778 Feigenser, J. C.

COPENHAGEN
17— Möller, H. P.
1759 Christensen, M.
1761 Moshack, M. G.
Speer, C. F.
1781 Tieffenbrunn, O. J.

FLENSBURG
c. 1750 Jansen, H.

ODENSE
1777 Jørgensen, J. J.

SATRUP
1799 Hansen, C.

ENGLAND

See also: **Scotland**

TOWN UNKNOWN
1571 James, J.
1664 Blunt, E.
c. 1700 Deeley, W.
Fenton
c. 1720 Hicks, P.
c. 1725 Woolfinden, J.
c. 1740 Relfe, J.
1741 Wilkinson, W.
1760 Welman, S.
1771 H, I.
Wakefield, R.
1772 Thoaner [?]
1775 Gerber, W.
1779 Skeene
1793 Donner
Fairn, A.
c. 1795 Keeys

BATH
1746 Underwood, T.

BRISTOL
17— Kemp, J.
1752 Kemys, J.
1753 Seede, B.
1775 Smith, J.
1780 Chew
c. 1785 Maddey

CAMBRIDGE
1508 Browne, T.
17— Turner, B.
c. 1720 Longfellow
1789 Argent, H.

CHESTER
c. 1560 Goodman, W.

EXETER
1643 Loosemore, J.
1657 Rewallin, C.

GLOUCESTER
1740 Warn, T.

LEICESTER

1579/80 Marsam, A.

LIVERPOOL

17—[?] Ruive

LONDON

1521 Mercator, *Sir* M.
Treasorer, W.
1526 Estamproy, G.
John, J. de
c. 1530 Cowtes
1530 Lewes, W.
1538 Betton, W.
1566 Blanckart, J.
1568 Defield
1579 Tyves, L.
1587 Farnaby, N., [*Father & son*]
Schetz, E.
1589 Hartwell, T.
1594 Blunte, T.
Norton, W.
1604/5 Marsh, G.
1610 Hassorde, W.
1611 Luxton, R.
c. 1621 Mussard, H.
1621 White, T.
1622 Haward, J.
1623 Cloys, B.
1624/5 Townsend, G.
1628 Walker, H.
1629 Norgate, E.
1638 Vernam, T.
1641 Gill, G.
1649/50 Leversidge, A.
1656 Makeham, T.
Body, T.
Cooly, J.
Haward, T.
White, Jas.
1658 Testa, A.
1660 Haward, C.
Hitchcock, T., *the Elder*
Zenti, G.
1662 Keene, S.
1663 Rand, J.
1664 Everratt, H.
Hatley, R.
Player, J.
1667 Jones, P.
1670 Hill, T.
Hingston, J.
1671 Richardson, A.
1685 Sison, B.
1689 Purcell, H.
1698 Slade, B.
c. 1700 Coston, F.
Pinchbeck
1700 Blunt, E.
Hancock, T.
17— Bates & Co.
Celson, E.
Dawson, G.
1701 Wilson, J.
1705 Aston, C.
1706 Barton, T.
1708 Hitchcock, T., *the Younger*
1710 Tisseran, J.
1711 Brackley, C.
1712 Bradshaw, A.
1716 Tabel, H.
1723 Baudin, J.
1725 Ladyman, J.
c. 1727 Shudi, Burkat, *the Elder*
1729 Mahoon, J.
1730 Barton, W.
Harris, John
Willbrook, J.
1731 Krickhof, F.
1733 Hilliar, W.
1738/9 Kirkman, Jacob
1739 Lockton, H.
1740 Harris, B.
Snetzler, J.
1741 Plenius, R.
1743 Hitchcock, J.
1744 Blasser, T.
1745 Crang, John
1747 Zopfe, J. B.
1749 Blumer
Child, F.
Harrison, J.
c. 1750 Sells
1750 Culliford, T.
Harris, Joseph
Hill, H.
1753 Bridge, R.
1757 Pringle, A.
1758 Clark, A.
1760 Falkener, R.
1761 Zumpe, J. C.
1762 Broadwood, J.
Kamp, H. van
Scouler, J.
1763 Backers, A.
Burr, H.
Downing, G.
England, G.
Neubauer, F.
Pether, W.
1764 Thompson, C., etc.
1765 Merlin, J. J.
Nixon, T.
Plenius, J.
1766 Harris, W.
1766/7 Shudi, Joshua
1767 Longman (& Lukey & Broderip)
Pohlmann, J.
1769 Cross
Gillespy, S.
Shudi, Bernard
c. 1770 Hancock, John
1770 Garbutt, T.
Simpson, Jas. & John
1772 Burckard, C.
Kirkman, A.
Walker, A., D., & J.
1773 Newbane
Shudi, Burkat, *the Younger*
1774 Ganer, C.
Hancock, James
c. 1775 Geib, J.
1775 Pether, G.
Stodart, R.
1779 Hancock, John Crang
Shean, C.
1782 Trute, C.
1783 Schöne, G. D.
1789 Kirkman, Joseph Christoph (?)
1790 Elwick, J.
Houston
1793 Gray, R. & W.
Lincoln, J.
1799 Smith, Joseph
c. 1800 Clementi, M.
Melly

MANCHESTER

1746 Kirshaw, John
1773 Kirshaw, Joseph

OXFORD

1785 Bunce, F.

PETERBOROUGH

1648 Thamer

SALISBURY

1768 Banks, B.

WESTMINSTER

1551 Gundet, R.
1749 Glanville, G.

WIGAN

17— Longshall, J.

WORCESTER

1769 Crew

YORK

c. 1710 Vesey, R.
1762 Watson, J.
1770 Haxby, T.

FLANDERS

See: **Low Countries**

FRANCE

TOWN UNKNOWN

Undated Baillon
La Couture, De
Lenoir
Poncelet
Viry
1360 Perrot, J.
1535 Bugnon, A.
? 16— Rigault
16— Dastenet
1626 Ferchur
1632 Montazeau, J.
1677 Faby
La Rousselière, J. B. de
1679 Regnault, J.

1680	Rozet
17—	Desruisseaux, G.
	Desruisseaux, L.
	Goujon
	Machy
	Nadreau
	Wittmann
1708	Cuisinier
1723	Jacot et Lion
1742	Levoir
1759	Weltman
1762	Fissot
1780	Nesle, J. J.

AMIENS

1784	Dallery, T. C. A.

AVIGNON

1503	Ludovic
1665	Bonnot, J.
1768	Cordelier

BORDEAUX

1727	Thévenard

BOULOGNE

1753	Obert

CAEN

1746	Lalande, de

CARPENTRAS

1699	Claude . . .

DIJON

c. 1440	Henri Arnault of Zwolle

GRENOBLE

1749	Berger, J. A.
1770	Barberini, J.
1779	Deterpigny, J.

LORRAINE

1708	Renault, J.

LYONS

1506	Bontemps, N.
1523	Deloeuvre, H.
1551	Deloeuvre, P.
1670	Saraissac, F.
1674	Du Four, C.
1691	Donzelague, P.
c. 1700	Blanches, F.
d. 1709	Gondard
1715	Le Tourneur, E.
1723	Grou, D.
1730	Le Tourneur, J. B.
1739	Collesse, Joseph
1746	Collesse, Jacques
1763	Collesse, *l'Aîné*
1769	Charron, *Sieur*
1772	Bontan, P.
	Kettenhoven, P.
	Tournan, B.
1775	Franky, J.
1777	Stirnemann, J.
1779	Lefaure, J.
	Stirnemann, J.
1786	Bas

MARSEILLES

1737	Bas, J.
1778	Bas, L.

METZ

1506	'Fra Giovanni'
1521	Humbert
1686	Moucherelle, C.
1713	Legros, P.
1714	Legros, C.

NANCY

1511	Rodilly, L.
1726	Marchal, N.

NANTES

1737	Gairaud

ORLEANS

1756	Rozé [?]

PARIS

15—	Dugué, P.
1530	Denis, R. (I)
	Lemaire, M.
1532	Follon, N.
1548	Potin, A.
c. 1550	Dargillières, A.
	Daulphin, J. (I)
	Patry
	Potin, R.
1553	Daulphin, J. (II)
d. 1556	Mesnager, Y.
1561	Potin, J.
1563	Dargillières, J.
	Lemaire, C.
c. 1570	Daulphin, M.
	Potin, P.
1570	Leviel, A.
1571	Belamy, P.
1573	Despont, R.
1574	Denis, C.
c. 1575	Lemaire, J.
1578	Brissart, J.
	Héart, J.
	Leviel, A.
1579	Denis, J. (I)
	Lorillart, M.
c. 1580	Denis, R. (II)
	Gai
d. 1589	Denis, Robert
1594	Lescuier, G.
1600	Denis, J. (II)
	Jacquet, J.
1603	Despont, A.
	Le Breton, J.
c. 1615	Sellier, J.
1615	Denis, T.
d. 1622	Lorillart, P.
1623	Richard, Michel
1627	Bouton, J.
1630	Jacquet, C.
1632	Denis, P. (I)
	Lemoyne, C.
c. 1635	Denis, J. (III)
1636	Denis, J. [*later at* Nancy]
1637	Denis, Ph.
c. 1648	La Barre, P. C. de
1650	Fiteler, J.
1658	Regnault
1659	Richard, M.
1661	Douvé, M.
1663	Denis, P.
1665	Denis, L.
	Sellier, L.
1671	Dubuc, N.
	Pampes
1674	Meunier, J.
	Sellier, N.
1675	Bellot, R. (I)
1680	Dumont, N.
1687	Rastoin, H.
c. 1690	Rastoin, J.
1690	Blanchet, N.
c. 1700	Leclair
?17—	Munier
17—	Chiquelier
	Dumont, J.
	Hoffmann
	Prudent
	Schneller
1700	Marius
1702	Denis, L.
1705	Denis, P. (II)
1706	Boussu, J.
c. 1710	Vaudry, J. A.
1713	Bourdet, J. G.
1717	Bellot, L. C.
1719	Vater, A.
1723	Delavigne, P.
c. 1725	Baudin, F.
1725	Blanchet, F. E. (I)
	Vater, A.
1729	Bellot, L.
c. 1730	Jacquart, J.
1730	Blanchet, N.
	Levoir
1734	Ducastel, A. H.
1736	Bourdet, J.
	Keiser, J. B.
1740	Leclerc, N.
1743	Goermans, Jean (I)
1744	Galland, J.
1745	Renaud
1747	Bellot, P. (II)
	Garnier, S.
	Hemsch, J. H.
1749	Hermès, J. L.
1750	Bourdet, J.
	Treyer, J. B.
1752	Richard, ? Marius
1753	Richard, Robert
	Stehlin, B.
	Taskin, P. (I)
1754	Ruelle, P.
1755	Ruelle, J.
1756	Treyer, Joseph
1757	Treyer, J. B.
1760	Blanchet, F. E. (II)
	Péronard, F. B.

1761 Hemsch, G.
Hemsch, J.
Laborde, J. B. de
1768 Virbès, de
1769 Delavigne, P.
Gérard, J.
Hartman, J.
Leisert, J.
Malade
Moers, J. H.
Somer, N.
Touroude, J.
1770 Cassineau
1771 Virbés, de
1772 Taskin, P. (II)
1774 Dedeban, J. M.
1775 Goermans, Jacques
Malade
Ruelle, J.
Simonneau, P. C.
1776 Benard
Morel
1777 Leclair, J. P.
Leclerc, J. P.
Naulot, J.
Schnell, J. J.
1778 Dubois, P.
Grenot, P.
1779 Monguet, F.
c. 1780 Dulcken, J. L. [*later* Munich]
Schmidt, Tobias
Secret, J. de
1781 Lauterborn, J. G.
1782 Erard, S.
1783 Barberini, J.
Gateaux, P.
Godelart, P. J.
Henocq, L.
Swanen, J.
1785 Schmidt, T.
1786 Zimmerman
1787 Pleyel, I. J.
1788 Lauterbon
Volber, J.
1789 Freudenthaler, W.
1793 Blanchet, A. F. N.
1795 Schmidt, Tobie
1799 Lemme, C.

ROUEN
c. 1700 Lefebvre, C. & J. B.
1733 Lefebvre, N.

SOISSONS
1739 Chappelle, F.

STRASBOURG
1679 Erhart, A. F.
1699 Ring, F.
1757 Koch, M.
Silbermann, J. H.
1783 Edelmann, G. L.

TOULOUSE
1679 Thibaut, V.

TROYES
1661 Raisin

VAL D'AJOL
17— Fleurot

VERSAILLES
c. 1780 Saumet, N. J.

GERMANY

TOWN UNKNOWN
Undated Leo, J. C., I & II
Forchheim, J. W.
Füssel, J.
?15— Gansen, W.
Saletz, N.
?*c.* 1600 Heller, A.
1602 Heussler, U.
1636 Worcken, G.
1645 Schonat, J. W.
1681 Kurtz, J.
1684 Musch, J.
17— Gottheimer, C. G.
Keyser, P.
Reinecke
Wahl
1748 Kästner
1757 Nonnemaker
1761 Hauser, J. H.
1763 Le Gray
1773 Preuss, J. B.
1778 Feigenser, J. C.
1783 Mercia
1799 Knoebel, J. C.
1804 Hötzel, P.
1820 Welcker

ALT-BRANDENBURG
1776 Grüneberg, J. W.

ALTENBURG
1730 Schlegel, E. (I)
1794 Schlegel, E. (II)

ANSBACH
1724 Wiclef, J. C.
1769 Hubert, C. G.
1794 Hoffmann, J. W.

AUGSBURG
1570 Bidermann, S. (I)
1587 Meidling, A.
1608 Hainhofer, P.
c. 1610 Biderman, S. (II)
Biderman, D.
1685 Leo, J. C., *the Elder*
1697 Weidner, D. J.
17— Senft, I. J.
1721 Leo, J. C., *the Younger*
1758 Stein, J. A.
1793 Schautz, M.

BAUTZEN
1680 Haase, G.
1792 Augustin, J. G.

BERLIN
17— Conrad
1731 Schramm, T.
1741 Hohlfeld, J.
1755 Straube, J. A.
1760 Rost
1768 Bauer
Schramm, J. C.
1773 Oesterlein, J. C.
c. 1786 Kalix
1793 Luckstädt
Siegmuller, H. A.
1797 Steibelt, C. L.
1798 Bode, J. F.
1802 Hennefus, J. L.

BONN
1782 Riedlen, G. F.

BREITENBACH
See under: **Germany, Gross-Breitenbach**

BRESLAU
1713 Gebel, G.
1786 Theidel

BRIEG
1740 Sassadias, J. S.

BRÜHEIM, NR. GOTHA
c. 1800 Kliem

BRUNSWICK
1635 Dohmsen, C.
1662 Niebuhr, H.
1727 Fritz, B.
1755 Tölleke, K.
1777 Lemme, F. C. W.
1780 Schorse
Schurrig, J. A. C.
1795 Rudloff, R. F. L.
1804 Blume

CHARLOTTENBURG
1680 Mietcke, M.

COLOGNE
1550 Karest, C.
1647 Loth, J.
1797 Bartels, J. H.
Bruck, M.
Sonneman, A. & P.

CRAILSHEIM
1725 Faber, D.

DARMSTADT
c. 1800 Schweins, J.

DÖHLEN, NR. DRESDEN
c. 1760 Tamitius, A.

DRESDEN
1565 Kretschmar, G.
1653 Casparini, E.
1692 Gräbner, J. C.
1713 Bohr, C. H.
1722 Gräbner, J. H. (I)
1730 Schroeter, C. G.
1748 Schwarze
1765 Schubert, D.
1766 Gräbner, J. G.

1767 Gräbner, J. W.
1769 Horn, G. J.
1774 Gräbner, J. H. (II)
Wagner, J. G.
1779 Gräbner, K. A.
Horn, J. G.
1784 Wagner, C. S.
1790 Lehmann, G. D.
1794 Fessel, J. H. E.
1797 Renzsch, C. E. F.
c. 1799 Horn, C. A.
1799 Mack, H. L.

EISENACH
1709 Hasert, J.

ERFURT
1729 Adlung, J.

FRANKFURT A/M
1639 Gellinger, I.

FRAUENAURACH
1741 Schiedmayer, B.

FREIBURG (SAXONY)
1713 Silbermann, G.
1795 Oehme, A. G.

FRIEDBERG
Undated Glück

FRIEDRICHSTADT, NR. DRESDEN
1740 Martini

FUSSEN
1698 Kaiser, M.

GEHREN
1678 Bach, J. M.

GERA
1739 Friderici, C. E.
1744 Friderici, C. Gottfr.
1780 Friderici, C. Gottl.
[1812 Friderici, C. E. W.]

GERINGSWALDE
1746 Gerstenberg, J. D.

GÖRLITZ
17— Mayer

GOTHA
1779 Hofmann
?*c.* 1800 Paul

GÖTTINGEN
1575 Meyer, D.
1773 Krämer, J. P.
1780 Krämer, S. T.
1798 Ritmuller, G. W.

GROSS-BREITENBACH
1700 Harrass, J. H.
1760 Langguth, H. W.
1802 Deckert, J. N.

HALBRESTADT
1765 Jesse, J. C.

HALLE
17— Weikhart
1785 Joachim

HAMBURG
1668 Fleischer, H. C.
1692 Middelburg, S. C.
17— Oppelmann
1706 Fleischer, J. C.
1710 Driel, A. von
Fleischer, C. C.
[1716 Toussaint, J.?]
1719 Hass, Hieron. Albr.
1728 Zell, C.
1740 Hass, Johann Adolf
1744 Gerlach, J. C.
1778 Hass, H. A. (?)
1782 Jungcurth, H. W.
c. 1793 Voigt
1796 Hass, D. C. (?)
Hinrichs, J. P.

HANOVER
1712 Brock, H. W.
1799 Baethmann, W. H.

HEUTINGSHEIM
c. 1799 Schwingstein, J. M.

ILMENAU
1717 Gleichmann, J. G.
1752 Riesch, G. M.

JENA
1699 Bach, J. N.

JUGENHEIM
1782 Obendörfer

KASSEL
1784 Wilhelmi

KÖNIGSBERG
c. 1580 Gabrecht

LEIPZIG
1535 Frey, M.
1543 Müller, H.
1555 Hahn, K.
17— Steinert, M.
17— Wolf, C. H.
1700 Donat, J. J.
1731 Schweinfleisch, J. C. (I)
1740 Scheibe, J.

LÜBECK
1647 Schaar, T.
1712 Siercks, M.
1724 Franck, L.
1781 Winther & Meyer
1799 Nölck, J. F.

MAINZ
1780 Quernbach, I.

MARBURG
1788 Muller, M.

MEISSEN
c. 1730 Hähnel, J. E.

MEMEL
c. 1757 Bertin, D.

MERSEBURG
c. 1780 Scherzer

MUNICH
c. 1560 Faber, W.
1753 Glonner, J.
1798 Milchmeyer, P. J.

MÜNSTERBERG
1718 Hildebrand, Z.

NEUSTADT/AISCH
1770 Schiedmayer, J. C. G.

NEUWIED
1763 Kintzinger, ? F.
1793 Weil, J. W.

NORDHAUSEN
17— Kellermann, C. F. A.

NUREMBERG
1568 Nottle, B.
c. 1580 Vogel, H.
1600 Hayden, H.
17— Bodechtel, J. J.
1737 Gliss, J.
1789 Kuppler, J. G.

OSNABRÜCK
1746 Laag, H.

PALATINATE
17— Kaiser, M.

PEISSENBERG
1433 Smid, B.

REGENSBURG
1692 Schmahl, Fr.
1751 Späth, F. J., *the Younger*
1770 Schmahl, C. F.
c. 1810 Schmahl, J. F. & C. C.

RENDSBURG
1796 Sondermann, M. G.

RONNEBURG
1763 Hoffmann, C. G.

RUDOLSTADT
c. 1765 Lenker, C. M.
1771 Puchert, J. S.

SATRUP
1799 Hansen, C.

SCHLESWIG
1780 Jungersen, J. C.

SCHMIEDEFELD
1764 Wagner, M. & J.

SCHNEEBERG
1604 Reinhart, A.

SCHWARZENBERG
?*c.* 1770 Rentsch, S.

SCHWEINFURT
1751 Kiedolps, F.
1804 Voit, J. M.

SILESIA
1706 Henrichini, A.

SONDERSHAUSEN
1728 Gerber, H. N.
1782 Schirmer, J. G.

? SONNENBURG
17— Berchthold, J. von

SONTHOFEN
1742 Socher, J.

? SPEYER
1788 Schenk, J. G.

STELZEN NR. HILDBURGHAUSEN
1715 Gleichmann, J. G.

STRASSBURG
See: **France, Strasbourg**

STUTTGART
1791 Haug, F.

TANGERMÜNDE
1792 Zabel, G. W.

ULM
1540 Haffenreffer, S.
1764 Schmahl, J. M.

UNTERTÜRKHEIM
17— Warth, P. J.

VAIHINGEN/ENZ
c. 1791 Bühler, J. M.

WEIGANDSTAL
1729 Maywaldt, J. C.

WEIMAR
1688 Ziegler, J. A.
1731 Eylenstein, J. F.
1796 Schenk, J. G.

WERDEN
1437 Johann, *Meister*

WETZLAR
1783 Greiner, J. K.

WIESBADEN
c. 1788 Mahr, J. A.

WÜRZBURG
1778 Joneck, M.
c. 1800 Joneck, J.

ZITTAU
1754 Tamitius, J. G., I ; II

HOLLAND

See: **Low Countries**

HUNGARY

PRESSBURG
1744 Viererigel, J.
1816 Lehner, G.

IRELAND

DUBLIN
1639 Strong, A.
1728 Hollister, T.
1745 Weber, F.
1764 Gibson, W.
1766 Hollister, W. C.
?1773 Woffington, Robt.
1782 Southwell, W.
c. 1790 Lee, J. & E.
1790 M'Donnell
Pemberton
Rice, J.
179– Morland
c. 1795 MacDonell, Jas. & Alex.
1804 MacDonell, Daniel
1816 Woffington, J.

ITALY

TOWN UNKNOWN
Undated Tunoni, G.
15— Preno, *priest*
Zucchero, F.
1522(?) Giuseppe d'Organe
1531 Bonetti, P.
1540 Siculus, M.
1544 Brisciani, G. F.
1552 Jadra, M.
1554 Stoppacio (?)
1559 Salodiensis, J.
1570 Danis, J.
1573 Salodiensis, A.
1585 Bonafinis, J.
16— Bortolus
Zaffermi, S. & O.
1602 Bonomen, J. B.
Remoti, S.
1628 Giannini, G.
1635 Fani [?]
1650 Ridolfi, G.
1667 Giovacino, *priest*
1668 Guarracino, H.
1670 Tollenari, J.
1689 Salodiensis, B. C.
1694 Stephanini, B.
17— B., C.
Rasori, L.
1703 Bordegatus, A.
1710 Orlandus, P. M.
1725 Gozzini, J. M.
1736 Gregorio, A.
1750 Fermanni, P.
1757 S., N. V.
1757 Tronco, G. F.
1758 Barbi, M.
1762 Gasparrini, F. A.
1771 Marsciani
1773 Leoni, G. P.
1798 Brunelli, A.
1808 Argano, P.

ANCONA
1768 Montecucchi, V.

AREZZO
1570 Santini, A.
c. 1691 Bati, A.

BENEDELLO
Undated Scheri, F. M.

BERGAMO
1592 Undeus, D.
1802 Riva, G.
1833 Riva, A.

BOLOGNA
1592 Brenzi, Antonius
1635 Colonna, A.
1657 Coninus, J. M.
1687 Ossa, S.
1772 Bressano, C.

BRESCIA
1533 Antegnati, F.
1564 Francesco da Brescia
1610 Benti, M.
18— Tonoli
1818 Respini, Z.

COMO
1737 Somigliana, C. A.

CORTONA
1617 Boni, G. B.

EMPOLI
1686 Dotti, L.

FAZZANO
17— Asioli, Q.

FERRARA
Undated Pollastris, C. de
1494 Magona, P. de
1522 Giovan-Marco di Ferrara
1549 Aldigerio
1572 Romito, G.
1591 Cricca, A.
1598 Cricca, H.
c. 1600 Gherla
Pietro Jacopo

FLORENCE
Undated Doppo
Tacani
Zanetti
1490 Cellini, G.
1516 Vincentius
1586 Poggio, F.
[?16— Albani, A.]
[16— Polizzino, G. P.]
1602 Rigunini, C.
1610 Querci, P.
1615 Quoco, N. de
1616 Medaro, A.
c. 1620 Farini
1620 Rigoli
1627 Bolcioni, S.
1631 Mendini, G.
1634 Querci, V.
1650 Ricevuti, A.
1660 Buonfigliuoli, P.
c. 1660 Nigetti, F.
1663 Bolcioni, A.
1664 Pini, B.
1665 Pertici, G. da
1669 Cigulari, A.
1675 Casini, G.
1680 Feroci, M.
1682 Migliai, A.
1685 Cristofori, B.
1688 Carcassi, G.
1689 Falconi, G.

1689 Magniai, L.
1690 Zolfanelli, G.
1694 Landi, A.
1695 Bassilichi, L.
1696 Berti, N.
Puccini
1699 Ferrini, G.
1705 Feroci, A.
1716 Picchi, G.
1765 Falconi
1779 Sodi, V.
1790 Spighi, F.

GENOA
Undated 'Il Genovese'
1568 Tosi, O.

LEGHORN
1778 Cresci, R. & I.

LUCCA
1613 Bagninius, J.
1667 Giusti, G. B.
1711 Tommaso de Luca [?]
1781 Crudeli, G.

MANTUA
1535 Racceris, F.
1540 Alessandro dagli Organi
1545 Capiluto, G.
c. 1674 Pessetti, G. B.

MESSINA
1697 Grimaldi, C.

MILAN
1472 Argiropoulos, I.
1550 Rossi, A. dei
1580 Rossi, F. dei
1735 F. B. F.
1746 Berger, G. D.
1753 Scotti, A.

MODENA
1419 Tantini, C.
1461 Tantini, S.
1475 Tantini, G.
1485 Bonissimo, G.
1493 Pasi, A.
1494 Jacobus of Modena
1537 Stephanus Mutinensis
1571 Gessa
16— Martinelli
1686 Bombini
1723 Piazoli, A.
1726 Traeri, U. A.
1733 Trasori, A.
1755 Termanini, P. & G.
18— Barbieri
1802 B., P.

NAPLES
1532 Trasontino, G. F.
c. 1610 Colonna, F.
1612 Buca, I.
?1644 Pentotius, D. B.
1717 Boccalari, G. N.

PADUA
1527 Franciscus Patavinus
1550 Antonius Patavinus
1595 Alsise, G.
1798 Trentin, G.

PARMA
1723 R . . . cini, J. A.
1823 Gherardi, A.
? Gherardi, Giamb.
? Gherardi, C.
? Gherardi, Gius.

PAVIA
1494 Gusnascho, L.
1522 Belisonius, P.

PERUGIA
1627 Parrini, S.

PESARO
1554 Bertarini, G.
c. 1690 Sabbatini, G.

PIEDMONT
1786 Carretti, G. D.

PISA
Undated Creschi, A.
1730 Solfanelli, G.

PISTOIA
17— Pagnini

PRATO
1610 Vincentius Pratensis

REGGIO NELL'EMILIA
1571 Fontana, N.
1655 Cagnolati, F.
1676 Vasti, P.

RIMINI
1695 Neri

ROME
1521 Hieronymus Bononiensis
1543 Vicentino, N.
1564 Irena, A.
1610 Gigli, G.
Nona, F. della
1624 Buscorni, N.
Florano, G.
1625 Peres, V.
1626 Bottisango, G. C.
1628 Albana, O.
1631 Zenti, G.
1638 ? Leutis, G. de
1655 Annibale, of Rome
Girolamo, of Rome
Jacomino, of Rome
Todini, M.
1666 Marchionus, F.
1678 Debbonis, F.
1683 Nobili, T.
1693 Nobili, A. F.
1696 Roverio, V. de
17— Cicerone, G.
Matthias of Ghent
1700 Alari, G.
1732 Assalone, G.
1753 Hadrianus
1776 Palazzi, N.

SENIGALLIA
1631 Faber, Fr.
1774 ? Preiblan, G.

SIENA
1670 Landi, G.
1700 Prosperi, G.

TRENTO
1594 Berneri, G.
1745 Berera, J. A.

TREVISO
1570 Danis, J.

TURIN
1657 Adam, Abel
1757 Franco, G. F.

UDINE
1473 Giovanni da Udine

VENICE
Undated ? Ondeo
c. 1445 Murer, B.
1473 Pier Francesco da Udine
Pier Giovanni da Udine
15— Ungaro, F.
1503 Spinetti, G.
1506 Stefano di Giovanni
1513 Bonissimo, S.
1523 Baffo, G. A.
1531 Trasontino, A.
1533 Dominicus Pisaurensis
Ventura, A.
1556 Domenico, G.
1560 Trasontino, Guido
1568 Floriano, B.
1579 ? Albani, N.
1583 Celestini, G.
1585 Bertolotti, A.
Trasontino, Giulio
16— Giannantonio, *called* Il Veneto
1674 Monsuto, A.
1690 Menegoni, G. A.
1711 Centamin, P.
1724 Albani, M.
1748 Barbi, M.
1766 Chianei, G.

VERONA
c. 1500 Bastiano
1523 Portalupi, F. de'
1556 Bruneto
1683 Obici, F.

VICENZA
1695 Clarelli, G.
?*c.* 1760 Morellati, P.

VITERBO
1759 Rossi, T.

LATVIA

RIGA
1657 Hake, H.

LOW COUNTRIES

TOWN UNKNOWN
16— G., C.
1605 Gheerdinck, A.
1610 Huysen, J.
1619 H., A. W.
1720 Zelau

AERSCHOT
1770 Matheus, J. F.

AMSTERDAM
1766 V., L.
1768 Laeske, C. F.
1770 Lugt, D. van der

ANTWERP
15— Lenaert
1514 Moors, A.
1516 Karest, Josse
1519 Karest, G.
Matthys, P.
1533 Thielen, J.
1535 Blomsteen, M.
1542 Aelbrechts, J.
Meer, A. van
Vorenberch, P.
1543 Bos, H.
Lyen, P. de
1550 Blomsteen, C.
1552 Moyns, S.
1557 Biest, M. van der
Bogaerde, G. van den
Dierckx, J.
Herremans, W.
Peborgh
1558 Diepenrijck, L. van
1560 Gompaerts, W.
1561 Hevilez, J. de
Leest, W.
c. 1570 Jaspers, J.
1570 Moermans, H.
1576 Elst, A. van der
1579 Grauwels, J.
1580 Verbiest, M.
1581 Hans Ruckers, *the Elder*
1583 Eesbroeck, J. van
1584 Muelevoets, J.
1588 Aelbrechts, L.
1589 Wolfaert, E.
16— Nève, G. de
1600 Bader, P.
Grouwels, L.
1608 Ruckers, Andreas, *the Elder*
1609 Uffel, F. van
1610 Immenraet, M.
Leunis, R.
1611 Ruckers, Hans, *the Younger* [Jean Ruckers]
1613 Britsen, Joris (I)
1614 Léonard
1620 Carpel, N. van
1626 Hagaerts, C.
1627 Joannes, A.
1628 Vries, D. de
1631 Colyns, M.
1637/8 Ruckers, Andreas, *the Younger*
1641 Hagaerts, S.
1642 Couchet, Jan
1643 Verheyden, P.
1655 Britsen, Joris (II)
Couchet, Peter E. Jan
1655/6 Everbroek, G. v.
1658 Britsen, Joris (III)
Pelle, C.
1659 Watson, T.
1666 Couchet, Abraham
Couchet, Joseph
1710 Elsche, J. van den
1717 Britsen, A.
1741 Dulcken, J. D. [*later* Brussels]
1772 Bull, J. P.
1790 Heinemann, J. J.
1793 Bul, N.

BRUSSELS
16— Weyenberg, J. van
17— Bremers, M.
c. 1730 Dulcken, A.
1732 Mahieu, J.
1763 Henrique van Casteel

HAARLEM
c. 1637 Ban, J. A.

THE HAGUE
c. 1630 Rijkers?
17— Bruydegom, J.

LEYDEN
1787 Leenhouwer, A.

LIÈGE
1508 Moors, M.

LIERRE
15— Mors, H.

MALINES
155– Vriese, F. de
1773 Dagoneau

MONS
1780 Ermel, E.
Ermel, J. J.

ROERMOND
1735 Coenen, J. J.

TOURNAI
1750 Delin, A.

TZUM
1699 Douwes, K.

UTRECHT
1627 Deckens, W.

MORAVIA

See also: **Bohemia**

ZNOJMO (ZNAIM)
1726 Diviss, P.

NETHERLANDS

See: **Low Countries**

NORWAY

KRISTIANIA (OSLO)
1793 Schoene, G. D.

MOSS
1757 Jansen, H.

POLAND

CRACOW
14— Pilzna, M. de
16— Hauk, K.
1609 Martin
d. 1620 Przeworski, B.
c. 1700 Kiejcher, K.

DANZIG
1657 Steinicht, P.
1740 Woga, W.
1765 Delitz

POZNAN
1805 Mazlowski

WARSAW
Undated [? Buchholz, F. J.]
17— Korycki, S.

WILNO
16— Lochmann, A.

PORTUGAL

TOWN UNKNOWN
1758 Antunes, J. J.

BEJA
c. 1703 Leo, M. A.

LISBON
1783 Ferreira, J.

OPORTO
1796 Carmo, M. de S.

RUSSIA

ST. PETERSBURG
1777 Hübner, J. C.
1785 Hessel
c. 1787 Kirschnigk
c. 1790 Batov, I. A.

SCOTLAND

TOWN UNKNOWN
1652 Davidson, J.
1659 Adam, Alex.
1793 Gilchrist, D.

EDINBURGH
Undated Johnston, J.
c. 1760 Smith, J.
1761 Stewart, N.
1774 Logan, J.

SICILY

GAGLIANO
1739 Mela, D. del

SPAIN

TOWN UNKNOWN
1625 Truchado, R.

BELORADO
1809 Jaras

MADRID
15— Quebon
1567 Brebos
1634 Jobernardi, B.
17— M . . ., J.
c. 1750 Fernandez, D.

MESSINA
1697 Grimaldi, C.

SARAGOSA
14— 'The Moor of Çaragoça'

TARAZONA
17— Grabalos, J.

SWEDEN

TOWN UNKNOWN
1688 Woytzig, G.
1759 Woltkersson, G. G.

STOCKHOLM
1736 German, E.
1737 Specken, P. J.
1738 Strähle, D
1750 Broman, J.
1757 Rosenau, G.
1772 Lundborg, P.
1776 Lindholm, P.
1778 Rangström, A.
1783 Kraft, M. P.
1796 Rackwitz, G. C.
1803 Söderström
1818 Nordquist, C. J.
1821 Wessberg, E.

VOLSTADT
1720 Brelin, N.

SWITZERLAND

BASEL
1490 Soumlin, A.
1745 Brosy, P. F.
1775 Brosy, J. J.
1794 Schlegel, J.

BERNE
c. 1740 Hellen, J. L.
1755 Bossart, E.
1756 Baumgarther, A.
1777 Howard, Joh.
1779 Howard, Joseph
1810 Gleiniger, T. G.
Wyss, C.

EINSIEDELN
c. 1660 Kreuel, P.

FRIBOURG
1766 Mooser, A. (I)
c. 1792 Mooser, A. (II)
1800 Mooser, J. P. J. A.

NEUCHÂTEL
1760 Speissegger, A.

SCHAFFHAUSEN
Date unknown Speissegger, J. C.

WIL (ST. GALL)
c. 1680 Türig, J. L.

ZÜRICH
1711 Schmuz, L.
1751 Schmuz, C.

SURVIVING ENGLISH VIRGINALS

Note. The term *virginal* is used here, as generally nowadays, to describe the rectangular instrument made in great quantities in Flanders and Italy and to a lesser extent in England. It should be borne in mind, however, that in Elizabethan and early Stuart times the term was generic, comprehending all jack instruments including the harpsichord (as was the French *épinette* in the sixteenth century).

Further details of each of the virginals are given above under the maker's name. The list of virginals has been omitted from the 5th edition of *GD* (1954).

No.	No. in *GD* (1940)	Signed by	Date	Owner
1	1	*Gabriel Townsend*	1641	Brussels Conservatoire
2	1b	*Thomas White*	1642	London, Victoria and Albert Museum
3	2	*Thomas White*	1651	York, Castle Museum
4	3	*Thomas White*	1653	Duke of Devonshire, at Hardwick Hall
5	6	*Thomas White*	1654	Cardiff Museum. (The date is not 1664, as used to be thought)
6	4	*John Loosemore*	1655	London, Victoria and Albert Museum
7	5	*James White*	1656	The Revd. W. Temple Bourne
8	—	*James White*	1661	Sold at Christie's, 24 January 1946
8a	—	*Thomas Body*	1662	Roger Warner, Burford (1969)
9	6b	*Robert Hatley*	1664	London, Fenton House
10	—	*John Player*	1664	Edinburgh University
11	7	*Adam Leversidge*	1666	New Haven, Conn., Yale University
12	8	*Stephen Keene*	1668	Edinburgh University
13	9	*Adam Leversidge*	1670	Oxford, Ashmolean Museum [formerly Arthur F. Hill]
14	10	*Philip Jones*	1671	Tabley Hall, Knutsford
15	11	*Charles Rewallin*	1675	Taunton, Castle Museum
16	—	*Stephen Keene*	1675	Cheshire, private ownership
17	—	*Charles Rewallin*	1679	Exeter Museum
18	12	[? *Charles Haward*]	—	Warrington Museum

SURVIVING THREE-MANUAL HARPSICHORDS

For further details see above under the maker's name.

No.	Date	Signature	Owner
1	1602	*Simone Remoti*	Stuttgart Museum. (Authenticity of signature doubtful)
2	1627	*Stefano Bolcioni*	Edinburgh University. (Illustrated in *J*, p. 125.) Doubtful
3	1702	*Bartolomeo Cristofori*	Munich, Deutsches Museum; 3rd keyboard added by Steingräber
4	1703	*Bartolomeo Cristofori*	Neupert Collection (Germanisches Nationalmuseum, Nuremberg). Doubtful
5	1740	*H. A. Hass*	Mme de Jouvenel, Paris
[6	*c.* 1757	*Mathias Koch*	*Mar*; has disappeared]
7	1779	*Vincenzio Sodi*	New York, Metropolitan Museum of Art. Considered doubtful
[8	*c.* 1780	*Peter Johann Milchmeyer*	*Magazin der Musik*, Hamburg, 1783; has disappeared]
[9	—	—	Michigan University. (Attributed by Hipkins to Cristofori, but not authentic)]
10	?	?	Leningrad. Formerly in the Hermitage Palace; now, apparently, in the Institute for Research on the Theatre and Music. (This instrument, which is illustrated in *Ginz*, seems to be of modern construction)
[11	1909	*H. Seyffarth, Leipzig*	Heyer Collection. (Illustrated in *Ks*, p. 113)]

SOME LONDON APPRENTICES 1622–1758

This list gives the names of a number of apprentices to London harpsichord makers between the years 1622 and 1758, as preserved in the records of the Joiners' Company, London. Just under half of the apprentices became freemen of the Company, and it may well be that instruments from many of their workshops still exist and will eventually come to light. The greater part of the information embodied in this list was kindly given to me by the late John L. Boston.

Apprentice	Year of binding	Year of admission as freeman	Master
Avery, Henry	1652	1672[1]	John Haward[2]
Bancks, John	1709		Edward Blunt
Barfoot, William	1651	1659	John Haward
Barres, Corney	1658	1667	'John Haward the Elder'
Bate, John	1641/2		John Haward
Becher, Edward	1638/9		Thomas White[3]
Brome, Hugh	1650		Thomas Haward
Collet, John	1712		Albion Bradshaw
Cooke, John		1624/5	John Haward
Cooly, John	1647	1656	Gabriel Townsend
Crosse, John	1656	1663	Thomas Makeham; *turned over to* Thomas Howard (Haward)
Dawson, Benjamin	1627	1634/5	John Haward
Dermore, John	1629	1637/8	Thomas White
Draper, Zachariah	1711	1718	Thomas Barton
Dutton, Leonard	1682		Stephen Keene
Dutton, William		1623/4	John Haward
Edwardes, Orlando	1622		John Haward
Elliot, Peter	1653	1660	Thomas Haward
Forcer, Thomas	1628/9		John Haward
Frawlins, Benjamin	1661		John Haward
Green, Thomas	1648	1655	John Haward
Greetham, Daniel	1645		Gabriel Townsend
Harris, John	1675	1685	Stephen Keene
Haslupp, John	1626/72		Nicholas Farnaby
Hawkins, Furley	1714	1725	Thomas Barton
Hedger, John	1645		Gabriel Townsend
Higgins, Thomas	1705	1711	John Player, *and later* C. Aston
Hill, Henry	1731	1745	John Ladyman
Hill, Robert	1658	1668	Adam Leversidge
Hill, Thomas	1662	1670	John Player
Hudson, John	1631		John Haward
Leigh, Roger	1653	1663	John Haward
Mitchell, Nicholas	1704		Edward Blunt
Moore, Jarvis	1669		John Player
Moseley, Richard	1751	1758	Joseph Harris
Norton, Arthur	1630	1639/40	John Haward
Osborne, John	1721	1735	Thomas Barton
Pelly, Gabriel	1702		John Player

[1] This interval of 20 years between binding and admission is exceptional; the usual period was 7 years.

[2] At least 3 John Hawards (Hayward, Howard) are mentioned in the records. It is rarely possible to say which apprentices were bound to which.

[3] Thomas White (I), master of Gabriel Townsend, was the father of Thomas White (II), who was the father of Thomas White (III). Most of their apprentices cannot be assigned definitely to father, son, or grandson.

Apprentice	Year of binding	Year of admission as freeman	Master
Pelly, Gabriel	1708		Cawton Aston
Poole, Edward	1632	1641/2	John Haward
Purchas, Thomas	1640/1		Gabriel Townsend
Riall, John	1692		John Player
Richardson, Abraham	1664	1671	Stephen Keene
Robinson, John	1670		Charles Haward
Rogers, Josiah	1677		John Player
Rowley, Henry	1637		Gabriel Townsend
Russell, Thomas	1629		Gabriel Townsend
Saintcleer, Abraham	1707		Edward Blunt
Sandles, Joseph	1680	1689	Thomas Hill, *and later* Charles Haward
Sison, John (son of Benjamin S.)			John Harris, son of James Harris
Small, Thomas	1671		Philip Jones
Smith, Robert	1670		Stephen Keene
Smith, William	1709		Benjamin Slade
Sowley, John		1624/5	Thomas White
Standly, Robert	1645		Thomas White
Stanley, Thomas (brother of the above)	1643		Thomas White
Stephens, Henry	1633		Gabriel Townsend
Stevens, Henry	1635?		Gabriel Townsend
Stevenson, Thomas		1628/9	Thomas White
Thorne, Thomas	1652		John Haward
Trippett, Samuel	1635		Thomas White
Vernam, Thomas	1630	1637/8	Gabriel Townsend
Vesey, Richard	1687		Stephen Keene
Welman, Richard	1651		Thomas White
Welsborne, James	1684		John Player
Wilson, John	1693	1701	John Player

GLOSSARY OF TECHNICAL TERMS

ENGLISH—FRENCH—GERMAN—ITALIAN

English	French	German	Italian
balance rail	balancier	Waagbalken	lista centrale
beech	hêtre	Buchenholz	faggio
bent side	éclisse courbe	Hohlwand	parete curva, fascia curva
bottom	fond	Unterboden	fondo
boxwood	buis	Buchsbaum	bosso
brass	cuivre jaune	Messing	ottone
bridge	chevalet	Resonanzbodensteg	ponticello posteriore
bridge-pin	pointe de chevalet	Stegstift	punta sul ponticello posteriore
buffstop (i.e. harp-stop)	jeu de luth	Lautenzug	sordino, liuto
bundfrei (*see*: gebunden)			
case	caisse	Gehaüse	cassa
cedar	cèdre	Zeder	cedro
cheek-pieces (that part of the case of a harpsichord on either side of the keyboard)	joues	Klavierbacken, Klavierwangen	ceppi laterali
compass	étendue, ambitus	Umfang	estensione, ambito
coupler	accouplement	Koppel	unione
covered strings	cordes filées	umsponnene Saiten	corde filate
cypress	cyprès	Zypresse	cipresso
damper	étouffoir	Dämpfer	smorzo
date	date	Jahreszahl	data
dogleg jacks (jacks cut away half-way up so as to be operated by either the upper or the lower keyboard)	sautereaux à marche	getreppte Docken, abgesetzte Docken	salterelli den ati
fretfree, fretted (*see*: gebunden)			
ebony	ébène	Ebenholz	ebano
gebunden (a German term, widely used of a clavichord in which 2 or more notes are produced from single pairs of strings; the opposite term, used of clavichords in which each note has its own pair of strings, is *bundfrei*)	lié	gebunden	legato
	non lié, indépendant	bundfrei	libero, sciolto

English	French	German	Italian
handstops	tirettes	(through the fore-board) Frontzüge (through the short side) Flankenzüge	registri a mano, a tiro
harp-stop (*see*: buffstop)			
hitch-pin	pointe d'accroche	Anhängestift	punta d'attacco delle corde
hitch-pin rail	tringle (barre) d'accroche	Anhängeleiste	cornice d'attacco
holly	houx	Stechpalme	agrifoglio
initials	initiales	Anfangsbuchstaben, Initialen	iniziali
inscription	inscription	Inschrift	iscrizione
ivory	ivoire	Elfenbein	avorio
jack	sautereau	Springer, Docke	salterello
rows of jacks	rangs de sautereaux	Springerreihen, Dockenreihen	file di salterelli
jackrail	chapiteau	Dockenleiste	striscia lignea sopra*i* salterelli
jack-slide	guide coulissant	(Docken-)Rechen	lista-guida
jack-tongue	languette, bascule	Zunge	linguetta
key	touche	Taste	tasto
keyboard	clavier	Tastatur, Manual, Klaviatur	tastiera, manuale, tastatura
keyboard-coupler (*see*: coupler)			
keyfront	fronton; (*arcaded*: arcature)	Stirnkante	frontalino
knee-lever	genouillère	Kniehebel	ginocchiere
keyframe		Klavierrahmen	telaio
key-top	placage des touches	Tastenbelag	ricopertura dei tasti
lid	couvercle	Deckel	coperchio
lime	tilleul	Lindenholz	tiglio
lute-stop	jeu nasal	Oboenzug, Nasalregister	registro di oboe, registro nasale
manual (*see*: keyboard)			
nameboard	barre d'adresse	Vorsatzbrett	listello sopra la tastiera
naturals	touches diatoniques	Untertasten	tasti diatonici
n.d. (no date)	sans date	o.J.	senza data

English	French	German	Italian
note	note	Ton	nota
nut-bridge (i.e. the bridge nearest the wrestpins on a harpsichord)	sillet	Stimmstocksteg	ponticello anteriore
oak	chêne	Eichenholz	quercia
outer case	caisse extérieure	äußerer Kasten	cassa involucro
pear	poire	Birnbaumholz	pero
pin	pointe	Stift	perno, pernio
pine	pin	Tannenholz	pino
plucking-point	point d'attaque	Anreißstelle, Zupfstelle	punto di pizzico
quill	plectre	Kiel	(becco di) penna
registers (*see*: stops)			
rose (soundhole)	rose	Rosette	rosetta
scaling (of strings)	dimensions des cordes	Mensur (der Saiten)	lunghezza delle corde
sharps	dièses, feintes	Obertasten	tasti cromatici
short octave	octave courte	kurze Oktave	ottava corta
side	éclisse	Wand(ung)	fascia, parete
signature	signature	Signatur	firma
skunktail sharps (sharps of ebony along the middle of which runs a thin strip of ivory, or vice versa)	dièses au décor de queues de scons	eingelegte Obertasten	tasti cromatici intarsiati
slide (*see*: jackslide)			
soundboard	table	Resonanzboden	tavola armonica
soundboard bar	barre de la table	Rippe	catena
soundhole	ouïe	Schalloch	foro di risonanza
split keys	touches brisées	gebrochene Tasten	tasti spezzati
spruce	sapin	Fichte(nholz)	abete
stand	piètement	Gestell	sostegno
steel	acier	Stahl	acciaio
stops	registres	Register	registri
string-gauge	diamètre des cordes	Saitendurchmesser	misura delle corde
string-tension	tension des cordes	Saitenspannung	tensione delle corde
strings	cordes	Saiten	corde
tangent	tangent	Tangente	tangente

8161239 P

English	French	German	Italian
tongue (*see*: jack-tongue)			
touch	toucher	Anschlag	tocco
venetian swell	persienne, jalousie	Jalousie	persiana
walnut	noyer	Nußbaum	noce
wrestpin	cheville d'accord	Wirbel	bischero, caviglia
wrestplank	sommier	Stimmstock	somiere

SELECTIVE BIBLIOGRAPHY AND SOURCES OF INFORMATION

ActaMus	*Acta Musicologica* (Internationale Gesellschaft für Musikwissenschaft). Leipzig, 1928– .
Adl	ADLUNG, Jakob. *Musica mechanica organoedi . . .* 2 vols. Berlin, F. W. Birnstiel, 1768. (Facsimile reprint, Kassel, Bärenreiter Verlag, 1931.)
AdlG	ADLUNG, Jakob. *Anleitung zur musikalischen Gelährtheit . . .* Erfurt, Jungnicol, 1758 (2 Aufl. 1783). (Reprint edited by Hans J. Mooser, Kassel, Bärenreiter-Verlag, 1958.)
AdlP	ADLAM, Derek. Private communication.
Alb	ALBARDA, Jan H. *Wood, wire and quill: an introduction to the harpsichord.* Toronto, Coach House Press, 1968.
AlmDauph	*Almanach Dauphin, ou Tablettes royales du vrai mérite des artistes célèbres et d'indication générale des principaux marchands, banquiers, négocians, artistes et fabricans des six-corps, arts et métiers de la ville . . . de Paris & autres villes commerçantes du royaume . . . Presenté & dédié à Monseigneur le Dauphin, pour la première fois, en 1772.* Paris, 1777.
AntVle	ANTWERP. Oudheidkundige Musea Vleeshuis. *Catalogus,* V and V *bis*: *Muziekinstrumenten.* Antwerpen, 1956, 1967.
ArchfM	*Archiv für Musikforschung.* Berlin, 1936–43. (Cont. of *ZfM.*)
Armstr	ARMSTRONG, William H. *Organs for America: the life and work of David Tannenberg.* Philadelphia, University of Pennsylvania Press, 1967.
Barnes	BARNES, John. Private communication.
Bed	BEDBROOK, Gerald S. *Keyboard music from the Middle Ages to the beginnings of the Baroque.* London, Macmillan, 1949.
BédardP	BÉDARD, M. Hubert. Boulogne-sur-Seine. Private communication.
Bem	BEMETZRIEDER, Anton. *Leçons de clavecin, et principes d'harmonie.* Paris, 1771 (p. 13 gives a summary account of the gradual increase in the range of Ruckers harpsichords).
Ber	BERNER, Alfred. *Die Berliner Musikinstrumenten-Sammlung. Einführung mit historischen und technischen Erläuterungen.* Berlin, 1952.
Bess	BESSARABOFF, N. *Ancient European musical instruments. An organological study of . . . the L. Lindsey Mason Collection at the Museum of Fine Arts, Boston.* New York, October House Inc., 1941.
Biehle	BIEHLE, Herbert. *Musikgeschichte von Bautzen.* 1924.
BJ	*Bach Jahrbuch.* Leipzig, 1904– .
Bl	BLANKENBURG, Quirin van. *Elementa musica . . .* 's-Gravenhage, Laurens Berkoske, 1739.
Bos	BOSTON, John. 'An early virginal maker in Chester, and his tools'. *GSJ,* Vol. 7, 1954.
Bouv	BOUVET, Charles. *Une Dynastie de musiciens français: les Couperin . . .* Paris, Delagrave, 1919.
Box	BOXALL, Maria. 'English keyboard technique up to the death of Henry Purcell'. (Thesis, Trinity College of Music, London; typescript, 1971.)
Bq	BRICQUEVILLE, Eugène de. *Les Ventes des instruments de musique au* XVIII*e siècle.* Paris, Fischbacher, 1908 [being excerpts from the Parisian *Affiches, annonces et avis divers* from their foundation in 1786]. (Not a reliable source.)
Br	BRUNI, A. *Un Inventaire sous la Terreur . . .* Paris, Chamerot, 1890.
Brag 1967	BRAGARD, Roger, and DE HEN, F. J. *Musical instruments in art and history.* London, Barrie & Rockliff, 1968. (Translation of *Les Instruments de musique dans l'art et l'histoire.* Rhode-St.-Genèse, Belgium, 1967.)
Broad	BROADWOOD, James S. *Some notes made . . . in 1838 with observations and elucidations by H. P. Broadwood.* London, 1862.

Brun	BRUNNER, H. *Das Klavierklangideal Mozarts und die Klaviere seiner Zeit.* Augsburg, 1933.
BruxPar	*Exposition des instruments de musique des* XVIème et XVIIème *siècles, organisée par le Musée Instrumental de Bruxelles en l'Hôtel de Sully à Paris, Juin, 1969.* Bruxelles, 1969.
Bu	BURBURE, Léon de. *Recherches sur les facteurs de clavecins . . . d'Anvers.* Bruxelles, Hayez, 1863. (Reprinted from: *Bulletin de l'Académie Royale de Belgique.* 2me série. Tome 15, no. 2, 1863, pp. 348–75.)
Buchner 1956	BUCHNER, Alexander. *Musical instruments through the ages.* London, Spring Books [1956 or 1957].
BurnG	BURNEY, Charles. *The present state of music in Germany.* 2nd edition, London, T. Becket, 1775.
Byrne	BYRNE, Maurice. Private communications.
Cemb.Ang.	*Lettera dell'autore del nuovo Cembalo Angelico inventato in Roma nell'anno MDCCLXXV. che serve d'Istruzione per costruire lo stesso Cembalo . . .* In Roma nella stamperia di Giovanni Zempel, [1775]. pp. 38, 1 pl.
Cerv	CERVELLI, L., and VAN DER MEER, J. H. *Conservato a Roma il più antico clavicembalo tedesco.* Roma, Edizioni Palatino, 1967.
Ch	CHOUQUET, Gustave. *Le Musée du Conservatoire National de Musique. Catalogue descriptif et raisonné.* Paris, Didot, 1884.
ChamP	CHAMBURE, Thibault de, *Comtesse.* Private communication.
ChamR	CHAMBURE, Thibault de, *Comtesse.* 'The restoration of harpsichords at the Paris "Musée Instrumental du Conservatoire National Supérieur de Musique" '. (Paper given at Nuremberg, May 1969.)
Chandos	BAKER, C. H. C. and M. I. *The life and circumstances of James Brydges, First Duke of Chandos.* Oxford, Clarendon Press, 1949.
Chig	*Chigiana; rassegna annuale di studi musicologichi.* Firenze, [1939– ; Nos. 1–20 entitled: *Accadèmia musicale Chigiana*].
Cl	CLOSSON, Ernest. *La Facture des instruments de musique en Belgique.* Bruxelles, Huy, 1935.
ClavHist	*Le Clavecin et son histoire* [illustrated booklet accompanying a gramophone record of the same title (Erato STU 70513)]. Paris, 1969.
Clem	CLEMENCIC, René. *Old musical instruments. Translated* [from the German] *by David Hermges.* London, Weidenfeld & Nicholson, 1968.
ClP	CLOSSON, Ernest. *History of the piano. Translated by Delano Ames.* London, Paul Elek, 1947. (To be used with considerable caution.)
ClPap	CLOSSON, Ernest. 'L'Ornementation en papier imprimé des clavecins anversois'. *Revue belge d'archéologie et d'histoire de l'art,* Vol. 2, Bruxelles, 1932, pp. 105 ff.
CM	MOULD, Charles. Private communication.
CollHistMus	*Collectanea historiae musicae.* 1– . Firenze, 1953– .
Conr	CONRADT, Armin. 'Illustrated account of the Zell 1728 harpsichord'. *Stiftung zur Förderung der Hamburgischen Kunstsammlungen, Erwerbungen 1962,* pp. 42–7.
Cor	CORRETTE, Michel. *Le Maître de clavecin . . .* Paris, chez l'auteur, 1753.
	Country life dictionary of English furniture. See *DEF.*
Cou	COUTAGNE, Henri. *Gaspard Duiffoproucard et les luthiers lyonnais du 16e siècle.* Paris, Fischbacher, 1893.
Cuc	CUCUEL, G. *La Pouplinière et la musique de chambre au* XVIIIe *siècle.* Paris, 1913.
Curtis	CURTIS, Alan. 'Dutch harpsichord makers'. *TVNM,* Vol. 19, 1960–1, pp. 44–66.
Da	DALE, William. *Tschudi the harpsichord maker.* London, Constable, 1913.
DAM	*Dansk Aarbog for musikforskning* (1964/5), pp. 133–6.
DEF	*Dictionary of English furniture,* by Macquoid and Edwards. Revised and enlarged by Ralph Edwards. London, Country Life, 1954. (Article on 'Musical Instruments' in Vol. 2 by F. W. Galpin, little, if at all, changed from the original edition of 1924–7.)

Den — DENIS, Jean. *Traité de l'accord de l'espinette* . . . 2nd edition, Paris, Robert Ballard, 1650 [facsimile reprint edited by Alan Curtis. New York, Da Capo Press, 1969]. (The 1st edition had appeared in 1643.)

DNB — *Dictionary of national biography*. London, 1885– .

Dod — *Clavicordios portugueses do século dezoito. Portugiesische Klavichorde des 18. Jahrhunderts.* [Lisbon], Fundação Calouste Gulbenkian, [1971].

Dou — DOUWES, Klaas. *Grondig ondersoek van de toonen der musijk . . . Met een tweede deel, handelende van verscheidene musijkinstrumenten* . . . Franeker, A. Heins, 1699.

Drechsel — DRECHSEL, F. A. 'Alte Dresdener Instrumenten Inventare'. *ZfM*, Vol. 10, 1927–8, pp. 495–9.

Dubl 1794 — *Wilson's Dublin directory for 1794.*

Duf/Ben — DUFOURCQ, Norbert, et BENOIT, Marcelle. *Dix années à la Chapelle Royale de Musique . . . 1718–1728.* Paris, Picard, 1957.

DufClav — DUFOURCQ, Norbert. *Le Clavecin* (Que sais-je? series). Paris, 1948; 2nd edition, 1967.

DufDen — 'Une Dynastie française: les Denis'. *Revue de musicologie*, Vol. 38, 1956, pp. 151–6.

DufRic — 'Notes sur les Richard, musiciens français du XVIIe siecle'. *Revue de musicologie*, Vol. 36, 1954, pp. 116–33.

Dufourcq 1954 — DUFOURCQ, Norbert. *La Vie musicale en France au siècle de Louis XIV: Nicolas Lebègue (1631–1702) . . . Étude biographique* . . . Paris, Picard, 1954.

Eisenmann — EISENMANN, Alexander. *Schiedmayer & Söhne, Hof-Pianofortefabrik Stuttgart: Vorgeschichte, Gründung und fernere Entwicklung der Firma, 1809–1909.* Stuttgart, 1909.

Eit — EITNER, Robert. *Biographisch-bibliographisches Quellen-lexicon der Musiker und Musikgelehrten* . . . 10 vols. Leipzig, Breitkopf & Härtel, 1900–4. (Photolithographed reprint: New York, Musurgia, 1946?)

Enc(Did) — *Encyclopédie raisonnée des arts, sciences et métiers* . . . Edited by Diderot and d'Alembert. Paris, 1751–65.

EncMéth — *Encyclopédie méthodique*, [section on] *Musique.* Edited by Nicolas-Étienne Framéry and Pierre-Louis de Ginguené. 2 vols. Paris, 1791, 1818. (Hullmandel wrote the article on 'clavecin' to which a concluding note by Framéry is added. Vol. 2, pp. 285–9.)

ErnstP — ERNST, Friedrich. Private communication.

Ernst 1955 — ERNST, Friedrich. *Der Flügel Johann Sebastian Bachs* . . . Frankfurt, C. F. Peters, 1955, p. 86.

Ernst 1961 — ERNST, Friedrich. 'Bach und das Pianoforte'. *Bach-Jahrbuch*, Vol. 48, 1961.

Fab — FABBRI, Mario. 'Il primo "pianoforte" di Bartolomeo Cristofori'. *Chigiana: rassegna annuale di studi musicologichi.* N.S. Vol. 21, no. 1, 1964, pp. 162–72.

Falc — FALCONER, David. Private communication.

Fé — FÉTIS, Franz Joseph. *Biographie universelle des musiciens* . . . 2e edition. 8 vols. Paris, Firmin Didot, 1860–5. (*Supplément* . . ., 2 vols. Paris, Firmin Didot, 1878–81.)

Ferg — FERGUSON, Howard. 'Bach's "Lauten Werck" '. *Music & Letters*, Vol. 48, 1967, pp. 259–64.

Fi — FISCHHOF, Joseph. *Versuch einer Geschichte des Clavierbaues* . . . Wien, 1853.

Fla — FLADE, Ernst. *Der Orgelbauer Gottfried Silbermann* . . . (Veröffentlichungen des F. Institutes f. Musikwissenschaftliche Forschung zu Bückeburg, Reihe 5, Band 3). Leipzig, 1926. (A 2nd edition revised and enlarged, entitled: *Gottfried Silbermann. Ein Beitrag zur Geschichte des deutschen Orgel- und Klavierbaus* . . . Leipzig, Breitkopf & Härtel, 1953.)

Fld — FLOOD, W. H. Grattan-. 'Dublin harpsichord and pianoforte makers'. *Journal of the Royal Society of Antiquaries of Ireland*, Vol. 39, 1909.

Fleury — FLEURY, Paul de. *Dictionnaire des facteurs d'orgues nés ou ayant travaillé en France.* Paris, Office Général de la Musique, 1926.

FrancI	FRANCIOLINI, Leopoldo. *Catalogo con prezzi degli strumenti musicali antichi* (Firenze, Piazza S.M. Novella, 6) . . ., Stab. Tipo-Litog. G. Fratini, [? *c.* 1900]. A copy is in the Brussels Conservatoire.
FrancII	FRANCIOLINI, Leopoldo. *Catalogo dei rezzi correnti* . . . (Via de' Benci 14, Firenze). About 1895. (A copy is owned by John Morley, London. *Russell 1959*, pp. 143–4, lists the keyboard instruments from both catalogues.)
FrancIII	FRANCIOLINI, Leopoldo. *Catalogo di strumenti musicali antichi in vendita* (Via de' Benci 14, Firenze). Firenze, V. Ceccherini, 1890.
Frankf 1927	*Katalog der internationalen Ausstellung: Musik im Leben der Völker.* Von Kathi Meyer. Frankfurt am Main, 1927.
Ga	GALPIN, Francis W. *Old English instruments of music.* London, Methuen, 1910; 2nd edition, 1921; 3rd edition, revised, 1932; 4th edition, revised by Thurston Dart, 1965.
Gábry 1959	GÁBRY, G. 'Brandenburgi Katlin virginálja'. *Folia archaeologica.* Vol. 11, Budapest, 1959, pp. 179–85.
Gábry 1969	GÁBRY, G. *Old musical instruments* [in Hungarian National Museum]. Budapest, Corvina, 1969.
Gai	GAI, Vinicio. *Gli strumenti musicali della corte Medicea e il museo del Conservatorio 'Luigi Cherubini' di Firenze. Cenni storici e catalogo discrittivo* . . . Firenze, Licosa, 1969.
Gall	GALLINI, Natale and Franco. *Museo degli strumenti musicali* (*Comune di Milano*)*: catalogo.* [Milan], Castello Sforzesco, 1963.
GD	*Grove's dictionary of music and musicians.* London, Macmillan. 1st edition, 4 vols. plus index vol., 1879–90; 2nd edition [ed. Fuller-Maitland], 5 vols., 1904–10; 3rd edition [ed. H. C. Colles], 5 vols., 1927–8; 4th edition [ed. Colles], 5 vols. plus suppl. vol., 1940 [suppl. vol. reprinted 1945]; 5th edition [ed. E. Blom], 9 vols., 1954 [suppl. vol., 1961]. Sixth edition in preparation (1973).
Ge	GERBER, Ernst Ludwig. *Historisch-biographisches Lexicon der Tonkünstler* . . . 2 vols. Leipzig, J. G. Breitkopf, 1790–2; 2nd edition, 1812–14. (Facsimile reprint: Graz, Akademischer Druck 1966– . [Vols. 2, 3, and 4 issued by 1971; Vol. 1 not yet (1971) out.])
Ginz	GINZBURG, S. L. *Muzȳka v Muzee* [at the Hermitage Palace]. Leningrad, 1934.
GL	LEONHARDT, Gustav. Private communication.
Glar	*Glareana. Nachrichten der Gesellschaft der Freunde alter Musikinstrumente.* Freienbach, 1951– .
Gleich	GLEICH, Dr. C. von. Private communication.
Gö	GÖHLINGER, Franz August. 'Geschichte des Klavichords'. Basel, Birkhäuser, 1910. (Dissertation.)
GS	GERBERT, Martin. *Scriptores ecclesiastici de musica sacra* . . . Typis San-Blasianis, 1784. (Facsimile reprint, Milano, 1931.)
GSJ	*Galpin Society journal.* Cambridge, 1948– .
Ha	HARDING, Rosamond E. M. *The Piano-Forte* . . . Cambridge, University Press, 1933.
HaasBM	HAAS, Robert. *Bach und Mozart in Wien.* Wien, Paul Kaltschmid, 1951.
Halle 1764	HALLE, Johann Samuel. *Werkstätte der heusigen Künste.* Brandenburg and Leipzig, 1764. Vol. 3, pp. 358 ff., s.v. 'Der Flugelmacher'.
H&S	HUMPHRIES, Charles, and SMITH, William C. *Music publishing in the British Isles* . . . London, 1954.
Handschin 1935	HANDSCHIN, Jacques. 'Das Pedalklavier'. *ZfM*, Vol. 17, 1935, pp. 418–25.
Hardouin	HARDOUIN, Pierre. 'Harpsichord making in Paris'. Parts I, II, III eighteenth century. *GSJ*, Vol. 10, 1957, pp. 10–29; Vol. 12, 1959, pp. 73–85; Vol. 13, 1960, pp. 52–8.
Harpd	*Harpsichord. International Society of Harpsichord Builders.* Denver. Vol. 1, nos. 1– (April 1968–).
Hbg	Hamburg city archives; information communicated by Karl Egbert Schultze.
Herrm	HERRMANN, Heinrich. *Die Regensburger Klavierbauer Späth und Schmahl und ihr Tangentenflügel.* Erlangen, Döres, 1928.

Hertz — HERTZ, Eva. *J. A. Stein: ein Beitrag zur Geschichte des Klavierbaues.* Wolfenbüttel and Berlin, Kallmeyer, 1937.

Hi — HIPKINS, Alfred James. *A description and history of the pianoforte and of the older keyboard stringed instruments.* Revised edition. London, Novello [n.d.; 1916 or later]. (Originally published in 1896.)

Hil — HILLER, Johann Adam. *Lebensbeschreibungen berühmter Musikgelehrten und Tonkünstler* . . . Leipzig, Dykische Buchhandlung, 1784.

HiMi — HIPKINS, Alfred James. *Musical instruments, historic, rare and unique* . . . Plates . . . by William Gibb. London, A. and C. Black, 1888. (Reissued 1921.)

Hin — *Music libraries and instruments* (Hinrichsen 11th music book). London, 1961.

Hirt — HIRT, Franz Josef. *Meisterwerke des Klavierbaus.* Olten, URS Graf-Verlag, 1955.

HMP — KINSKY, Georg. *History of music in pictures.* London, J. M. Dent, 1930.

Hof — HOFMAN, Shlomo. *L'Œuvre de clavecin de François Couperin* . . . Paris, Picard, 1961.

Hopk — HOPKINSON, Francis. 'An improved method of quilling the harpsichord'. *Transactions of the American Philosophical Society.* Philadelphia, 1786, pp. 185–94.

Hubb — HUBBARD, Frank. Private communication.

HubbRR — HUBBARD, Frank. *Harpsichord regulating and repairing.* Boston, Tuner's Supply Inc., 1963.

Hubb 1965 — HUBBARD, Frank. *Three centuries of harpsichord making.* Cambridge, Mass., Harvard University Press, 1965.

HuD — HUGUENOT SOCIETY, London. *Letters of denization and acts of naturalization for aliens in England and Ireland, 1603–1700, 1701–1800.* (Publications of the Huguenot Society of London, vols. 18 and 27.) London, Huguenot Society, 1911, 1923.

Hullm — HULLMANDEL, N. Article on 'Clavecin' in the *Encyclopédie méthodique*, vols. entitled 'Musique' (1791 and 1818). (Translated *in extenso* by *Hubb 1965*, pp. 255–60.)

HuR — HUGUENOT SOCIETY, London. *Returns of aliens dwelling in the city and suburbs of London . . . from the reign of Henry VIII to that of James I.* (Publications of the Huguenot Society of London, Vol. 10, parts 1–3 and index.) London, Huguenot Society, 1900–8.

J — JAMES, Philip. *Early keyboard instruments.* London, Peter Davies, 1930. (Reprint, London, Tabard Press, 1970.)

Jac — JACQUOT, Albert. *Essai de répertoire des artistes lorrains. Les facteurs d'orgues et de clavecins lorrains.* Paris, Plon, 1910.

Jeans 1950 — JEANS, Susi. 'The pedal clavichord and other practice instruments of organists'. *Proceedings of the Royal Musical Association*, Vol. 77, 1950.

Jobern — JOBERNARDI, Bartolomeo. 'Tratado de la musica' [dedication dated 1934], MS. in the Biblioteca Nacional, Madrid. *See*: 'Le "clavecin parfait" de Bartolomeo Jobernardi', by Santiago Kastner. *Anuario musical del Instituto Español de musicologia*, Vol. 8, Barcelona, 1953, pp. 193–209.

Join — Records of the Joiners' Company: Registers of apprentice bindings and of freedom admissions. London, 1622–1758. MS. in Guildhall Library, London.

Jur — JURAMIE, Ghislaine. *Histoire du piano.* Paris, Editions Prisma, [1948].

Kastner 1952 — KASTNER, Macario Santiago. 'Portugiesische und spanische Clavichorde des 18. Jahrhunderts'. *Acta musicologica*, Vol. 24, 1952, pp. 52–61.

Ki — KINKELDEY, Otto. *Orgel und Klavier in der Musik des 18. Jahrhunderts* . . . Leipzig, Breitkopf & Härtel, 1910.

Kircher — KIRCHER, Athanasius. *Musica universalis* . . . Romae, 1650.

Kirk — KIRKPATRICK, Ralph. *Domenico Scarlatti.* Princeton University Press, 1953.

Ko — KOCH, Heinrich Christoph. *Musikalisches Lexicon* . . . Frankfurt am Main, bey August Hermann dem Jüngern, 1802.

Kraus KRAUS, Alexander, *the Younger*. *Catalogo della collezione etnografico-musicale Kraus in Firenze. Sezione istrumenti musicali*. Firenze, S. Landi, 1901.

Krautw KRAUTWURST, Franz. 'Hubert, Christian Gottlob'. *Die Musik in Geschichte und Gegenwart*, Vol. 6, 1957, cols. 816–19.

Ks KINSKY, Georg. *Musikhistorisches Museum von Wilhelm Heyer. Katalog. Erster Band, Besaitete Tasteninstrumente*. Cöln, Wilhelm Heyer, 1910.

Kü KÜPPERS, Paul. *Ein Beitrag zur Geschichte des Musik-Instrumentenmacher-Gewerbes mit besonderer Rücksicht auf Leipzig. Inaugural-Dissertation* . . . Leipzig, 1886.

La LAFONTAINE, Henry C. de. *The King's musick* [a transcript from the Lord Chamberlain's accounts relating to music and musicians, 1460–1700]. London, Macmillan, [1909].

Laborde LABORDE, Léon de, *marquis*. *Musiciens de Paris 1535–1792. Actes d'état civil d'après le fichier Laborde* . . . Publiés par Yolande de Brossard. Paris, Picard, 1965. (*Vie musicale en France sous les rois Bourbon: 1ère série, Études*, no. 11.)

Lambr-DP LAMBRECHTS-DOUILLEZ, Jeannine. Private communication.

Lambr-D 1970 LAMBRECHTS-DOUILLEZ, Jeannine. *Antwerpse klavecimbels in het Museum Vleeshuis*. Antwerp, Ruckers Genootschap, 1970.

Lan LANFRANCO, Giovan Maria. *Scintille di musica* . . . Brescia, Britannico, 1533.

Land LANDOWSKA, Wanda. *La Musique ancienne*. Paris, 1909; 4th edition, Paris, Senart, 1921. (Translated into English, in a condensed and revised version, in *Rest*.)

LC Lord Chamberlain Appointment Books. (Public Record Office, London. In volumes LC 3/64 and LC 3/67.)

Leonh LEONHARDT, Gustav. Private communication.

Les LESURE, François. 'La Facture instrumentale à Paris au seizième siècle.' *GSJ*, Vol. 7, 1954.

Lo 1695 'The inhabitants of London, 1695. A complete list of the population, both within and without the walls, compiled for purposes of taxation "for carrying on the warr against France with vigour"'. (Typescript index to the list in 4 volumes. London, Guildhall Library, n.d.)

Loub LOUBET DE SCEAURY, Paul. *Musiciens et facteurs d'instruments de musique sous l'Ancien Régime: statuts corporatifs*. Paris, Pedone, 1949.

Lü LÜTGENDORFF-LEINBURG, Willibald Leo von. *Die Geigen- und Lautenmacher vom Mittelalter bis zur Gegenwart*. 6. Ausgabe. Frankfurt am Main, 1922.

Luith LUITHLEN, Victor. *Katalog der Sammlung alter Musikinstrumente. I. Teil: Saitenklaviere*. Wien, Kunsthistorisches Museum, 1966.

Lun LUNELLI, Renato. *Strumenti musicali nel Trentino*. Trento, Edizione V.D.T.T., 1968.

LunCas LUNELLI, Renato. 'Eugen Casparini, un organaro italiano per i tedeschi e tedesco per i italiani'. *L'Organo*, Vol. 1, no. 1, Bologna, 1960.

MA *The musical antiquary*. [Quarterly.] Oxford, 1909–13.

Macq MACQUOID, Percy, and EDWARDS, R. *Dictionary of English furniture*. See: *DEF*.

Mah MAHILLON, Victor Charles. *Catalogue descriptif et analytique du Musée Instrumental du Conservatoire Royal de Musique de Bruxelles*. 2e édition. Gand, 1893–1922 (4 volumes).

Marc MARCUSE, Sibyl. 'Transposing keyboards on extant Flemish harpsichords'. *Musical quarterly*, New York, July 1952, pp. 414–25.

MarcP MARCUSE, Sibyl. Private communication.

MarcY MARCUSE, Sibyl. *Check-list of Western instruments in the collection of musical instruments* (*Yale University School of Music*). *Part I: Keyboard instruments*. New Haven, Yale University, 1958.

Marp MARPURG, Friedrich Wilhelm. *Historisch-kritische Beyträge zur Aufnahme der Musik*. Berlin, 1755–60 (5 volumes).

MatCM MATTHESON, Johann. *Critica musica* . . . Hamburg, auf Unkosten des Autoris, 1722–5.

MatGE — MATTHESON, Johann. *Grundlage einer Ehrenpforte.* In Verlegung des Verfassers, 1740.

MatNO — MATTHESON, Johann. *Das neu-eröffnete Orchestre* . . . Hamburg, auf Unkosten des Autoris, 1713.

MC — Minutier Central des Archives Nationales, Paris. (Information gathered either from ***Hardouin*** or ***Hubb***; or from *Documents du Minutier Central concernant l'histoire de la musique* . . ., Vols. 1– . Paris, S.E.V.P.E.N., 1970 (?)– .)

Me — MEUSEL, Johann Georg. *Teutsches Künstlerlexicon oder Verzeichnis der jetztlebenden teutschen Künstler* . . . Lemgo, Mayer, 1778–89 (2 volumes).

MeeùsCouch — MEEÙS, Nicolas. 'Le clavecin de Johannes Couchet, Anvers, 1646'. *Bulletin van het Instrumentenmuseum van Brussel*, no. 1, 1970, pp. 1–17.

MeeùsOct — MEEÙS, Nicolas. 'La Naissance de l'octave courte et ses différentes formes au 16e siècle . . .' [Dissertation, Université Catholique de Louvain, 1971.]

Mer — MERSENNE, Marin. *Harmonie universelle* . . . Paris, Pierre Ballard, 1636–7. (Facsimile reprint, Paris, Éditions du Centre National de Recherche Scientifique, 1965.) (English translation of Vol. 3 by Roger E. Chapman. The Hague, Nijhof, 1957.) It is Vol. 3 of Mersenne's work which treats of instruments.

MF — *Mercure de France.* Paris, 1672–1820.

MGG — *Musik in Geschichte und Gegenwart* . . . Kassel & Basel, Bärenreiter-Verlag, 1949/51–1968 (14 volumes); Supplement, 1969– .

Michel — MICHEL, N. E. *Historical pianos and clavichords.* Pico Rivera, the Author, 1963.

ML — *Music and letters.* London, [1920–].

Moos — MOOSER, R. A. *Annales de la musique . . . en Russie au* XVIII*e siècle.* Genève, 1950–5 (3 volumes).

Mos — MOSER, H. J. *Paul Hofhaimer.* Stuttgart, 1929.

Mould — MOULD, Charles. 'English harpsichord makers, with special reference to the Kirckman family'. (Thesis, Oxford University Faculty of Music; in preparation, 1974.)

MQ — *Musical quarterly.* New York, [1915–].

Müller — MÜLLER, Mette. Copenhagen. Private communication.

Munich 1951 — *Ausstellung Alte Musik: Instrumente, Noten und Dokumente aus drei Jahrhunderten. Katalog* [by Alfons Ott]. München, Max Hieber, 1951.

NeupCemb — NEUPERT, Hanns. *Das Cembalo.* Kassel, Bärenreiter, 1933; 2. Aufl., 1951. (English translation of the 4th edition by F. E. Kirby; *Harpsichord manual*: 2nd edition. Kassel, etc., Bärenreiter, 1968.)

NeupKlav — NEUPERT, Hanns. *Das Klavichord.* Kassel, Bärenreiter, 1948. (English translation of the 2nd edition by Ann Feldberg: *The Clavichord.* Kassel, Bärenreiter, 1965.)

Nev — NEVEN, Armand. Private communication.

Nor — NORLIND, Tobias. *Systematik der Saiteninstrumente* (*Musikhistorisches Museum, Stockholm*). *2. Geschichte des Klaviers.* Hannover, Albert Küster, 1939.

Nord — NORDSTROM, Kaj. Private communication.

OrgYb — *Organ yearbook. Journal for the players and historians of keyboard instruments*, Vols. 1– . Amsterdam, Knuf, 1970– .

Otto — OTTO, Irmgard. *Musikinstrumentenmuseum Berlin: Ausstellungsverzeichnis* . . . Berlin, 1965.

Pa — PAUL, Oscar. *Geschichte des Klaviers* . . . Leipzig, 1868.

Pag — PAGANELLI, Sergio. *Musical instruments from the Renaissance to the 19th century. Translated by Anthony Rhodes from the Italian original* '*Gli strumenti musicali nell'arte*'. London, Hamlyn, 1970.

Par 1900 — PARIS. Exposition Universelle Internationale. *Musée rétrospectif de la Classe 17, Instruments de musique* . . . Paris, 1900.

Pat — *Patents for inventions. Abridgements of specifications relating to music and musical instruments* A.D. *1694–1866.* 2nd edition. London, Printed by . . . Eyre and . . . Spottiswoode . . . Published at the office of the Commissioners of patents for inventions, 1871.

Paul — PAUL, John. Private communication.

Pi	PIERRE, Constant. *Les Facteurs d'instruments de musique, les luthiers, et la facture instrumentale: précis historique.* Paris, Sagot, 1893.
Pir	PIRRO, André. *Les Clavecinistes.* Paris, Laurens, [1924].
Po	POLS, André M. *De Ruckers en de klavierbouw en Vlaanderen.* Antwerpen, de Nederlandse Boekhandel, 1942.
Pr	PRAETORIUS, Michael. *Syntagmatis musici . . . tomus secundus de organographia . . .* Wolfenbüttel, Elias Holwein, 1619. (Facsimile reprint: Kassel, Bärenreiter-Verlag, 1929; another: Kassel, Bärenreiter-Verlag, 1958–9 (issued as Vols. 14, 15, and 22 of *Documenta musicologica*)).
Prof	PROFETA, Rosario. *Storia e letteratura degli strumenti musicali.* Firenze, Marzocco, [1924].
Pu	PULITI, Leto. *Cenni storici della vita del . . . Ferdinando dei Medici . . . e della origine del pianoforte.* (Extracted from: *Atti dell'Accadèmia del Real Istituto Musicale di Firenze*, 1874.)
RB	Rate-books.
RB.A	Rate-books of the parish of St. Anne, Soho, London.
RB.G	Rate-books of the parish of St. George, Hanover Square, London.
RB.GM	Rate-books of the parish of St. George the Martyr, Queen Square, Holborn.
RB.J	Rate-books of the parish of St. James, Piccadilly, London.
Rest	RESTOUT, Denise. *Landowska on music.* London, Secker & Warburg, 1965. See also *Land.*
Reynv	REYNVAAN, Joos Verschuere. *Muzykaal Kunst-woordenboek . . .* Amsterdam, W. Brave, 1795. [The second volume covering N to Z was never published.]
RG.I	RUCKERS GENOOTSCHAP. *Colloquium: Restauratieproblemen van Antwerpse klavecimbels, Museum Vleeshuis 10 tot 12 mei 1970.* [Ed. J. Lambrechts-Douillez.] Antwerpen, Ruckers Genootschap, 1971.
Ri	RIMBAULT, Edward Francis. *The pianoforte . . . with some account of the clavichord, the virginal, the spinet, the harpsichord.* London, R. Cocks, 1860.
Rindl	RINDLISBACHER, Otto. Private communication.
RindlKlav	RINDLISBACHER, Otto. *Das Klavier in der Schweiz . . .* Bern, München, Francke Verlag, 1972.
Rip	RIPIN, Edwin M. New York. Private communication.
RipCouch	RIPIN, Edwin M. 'The Couchet harpsichord in the Crosby Brown Collection'. *Metropolitan Museum of Art journal*, New York. Vol. 2 (1969), 169–78.
RipExpr	RIPIN, Edwin M. 'Expressive devices applied to the eighteenth-century harpsichord'. *Organ yearbook.* Vol. 1. Edinburgh (1970), pp. 65–80.
RipKb	RIPIN, Edwin M., editor. *Keyboard instruments.* Edinburgh University Press, 1971.
RipScot	RIPIN, Edwin M. A Scottish encyclopedist and the piano forte. *Musical quarterly*, Vol 55 no. 4 (October 1969), pp. 487–99.
Rip Z	RIPIN, Edwin M. 'The surviving oeuvre of Girolamo Zenti'. *Metropolitan Museum of Art journal*, New York. Vol. 7 (1973).
Ro	ROMBOUTS, T., and LERIUS, T. van. *De liggeren en andere historische Archieven der Antwerpsche St. Lucasgilde.* Antwerpen, 1864–72.
RR	RUSSELL, Raymond. Private communication.
Rouss	ROUSSELIÈRE, Jean Baptiste Charles de. *Traité des languettes impériales.* Paris, 1679, pp. 149.
Rupp	RUPPRECHT, Margarete. *Die Klavierbauerfamilie Schiedmayer . . .* [Dissertation.] Erlangen, 1955.
RussColl	NEWMAN, Sydney, and WILLIAMS, Peter. *The Russell Collection of early keyboard instruments in St. Cecilia's Hall, Edinburgh.* Edinburgh University Press, 1968.
Russell 1956	RUSSELL, Raymond. 'The harpsichord since 1800'. *Proceedings of the Royal Musical Association*, Vol. 82 (1955–6), 61–74.
Russell 1959	RUSSELL, Raymond. *The harpsichord and clavichord.* London, Faber, 1959; 2nd edition, Faber, 1965.
RussellV&A	RUSSELL, Raymond. *Catalogue of musical instruments, Victoria and Albert Museum: Vol. 1. Keyboard instruments*, London, HMSO, 1968.

Sa — SACHS, Curt. *Sammlung alter Musikinstrumente bei der Staatlichen Hochschule für Musik zu Berlin. Beschreibender Katalog* . . . Berlin, Julius Bard, 1922.

Sac — SACCHI, Giovenale. *Vita del Cav. Don Carlo Broschi* [i.e. Farinelli]. (Raccolta Ferrarese di opuscoli . . ., Vol. 15). Vinegia, Coleti, 1784.

SaHMI — SACHS, Curt. *The history of musical instruments.* London, J. M. Dent, 1942. (First published in U.S.A., 1940.)

Sasse — SASSE, Konrad. *Katalog zu den Sammlungen des Händel-Hauses in Halle, 5. Teil: Musikinstrumentensammlung: Besaitete Tasteninstrumente.* Halle an der Saale, 1966.

SB — SCHRÖDER, Hans. *Verzeichnis der Sammlung alter Musikinstrumente im . . . Museum Braunschweig.* Braunschweig, Appelhans, 1928.

Scher — SCHERING, Arnold. *Musikgeschichte Leipzigs.* [Being Vols. 2 and 3 of Rudolf Wustman's *Johann Sebastian Bach und die Musikgeschichte Leipzigs im 18ten Jahrhundert.*] Leipzig, Berlin, 1909–41.

Scheurl — SCHEURLEER, D. F. L. *Over het ornament en de autenticiteit van bedrukte papierstrooken in twee clavierinstrumenten.* Mededeelingen van de Dienst van Kunsten en Wetenschappen der Gemeente 's-Gravenhage, VI. 1. The Hague, 1939, pp. 45–9.

Schott — SCHOTT, Howard. *Playing the harpsichord.* London, Faber & Faber, 1971.

Schub — SCHUBARTH, C. F. D. *Ideen zu einer Ästhetik der Tonkunst.* Vienna, Degen, 1806.

Schultze 1957 — SCHULTZE, Karl Egbert. '850 Instrumentenmacher'. *Zeitschrift für Niedersächsische Familienkunde,* Vol. 32 (1957), pp. 44–6.

Schulze 1954 — SCHULZE, Richard. *How to build a baroque concert harpsichord.* New York, Pageant Press, 1954.

Senn — SENN, Walter. *Musik und Theater am Hof zu Innsbruck.* 1954.

ShAf — Affidavit sworn on 12 January 1767 by 3 of Shudi's apprentices, Clark, Nixon and Broadwood, before G. Wrighte, Mddx. (MS. among Broadwood papers. Cited *in extenso* by *Russell 1959,* p. 169.)

ShBa — Barbara Broadwood (*née* Shudi): book of household and business accounts together with general notes, covering the years 1769 (when she married) to 1776 (when she died), after which the book continued to be used for accounts until 1791. MS. 32×8 cm. (Bodleian MSS. Eng. misc. c.529).

ShJl — General account book of Burkat Shudi and John Broadwood covering 1771 to 1785. MS. bound in modern vellum, lettered on the spine: 'Journal 1771–1785'; 39×10 cm. (Bodleian MSS. Eng. misc. b.107.)

Sh2: 4 — General account book of Burkat Shudi and John Broadwood covering 1771–1812 and relating not only to instruments but also to rents from property and to loans of cash. MS. bound in original eighteenth-century vellum; the lettering on the spine, partially illegible, includes '2: 4'; dimensions 19·5×16 cm. (Bodleian MSS. Eng. misc. e.663.)

Shortridge — SHORTRIDGE, John D. *Italian harpsichord building in the 16th and 17th centuries.* Washington D.C., 1960 (U.S. National Museum bulletin, 225, pp. 93–108.)

SIM — *Sammelbände der Internationalen Musikgesellschaft,* Vols. 1–15. Leipzig, 1899–1914.

Sit — SITTARD, J. *Zur Geschichte der Musik . . . am Württembergischen Hofe.* Stuttgart, 1890–1.

SmithM — SMITH, M. A., of the Pro Musica Instrument Co., Annapolis, Md. Private communication.

Sprengel — SPRENGEL, Peter N. *Handwerke und Künste in Tabellen.* 2te Auflage. Berlin, 1778–95. (11te Sammlung, pp. 240–67, has articles on the construction of the clavichord and harpsichord.)

St — STELLFELD, J. A. 'Bronnen tot de geschiedenis der Antwerpsche clavecimbel- en orgelbouwers in de XVIe en XVIIe eeuwen'. *Vlaamsch jaarboek voor muziekgeschiedenis,* Vol. 4, Antwerp, 1942, pp. 3–110.

Stock — STOCKBAUER, J. *Die Kunstbestrebungen am Bayerischen Hofe* . . . Wien, 1874.

Sum — SUMNER, William L. *The organ* . . . 2nd edition, London, Macdonald, 1955.

Szulc	SZULC, Zdzislaw. *Muzeum Wielkopolskie: Katalog instrumentón muzycznych.* Poznań, 1949. (A work on the history of keyboard instruments in Poland, Poznań, announced for 1955 was apparently never published. His *Slownik lutników polskich* appeared in 1953.)
Teahan	TEAHAN, John. 'A list of Irish instrument makers'. *GSJ*, Vol. 16, 1963.
Thoene	THOENE, Walter. 'Das Clavichord von Peter Weidtman d. J, 1724'. *Beiträge zur Geschichte Ratingens*, Vol. 4, Ratingen bei Düsseldorf, A. Hinn Verlag, 1966, pp. 96–119.
ThomasW	THOMAS, Wm. R. of Burntisland, Fife. Private communication.
Todini	TODINI, Michael. *Dichiaratione della galleria armonica . . .* Roma, Tirrone, 1676.
Türk 1802	TÜRK, Daniel Gottlob. *Klavierschule.* 2. Auflage. Leipzig and Halle, 1802. (First published in 1789.)
TVNM	*Tijdschrift van de Vereniging voor Nederlandse Muziekgeschiedenis.* Amsterdam, 1882– .
Un	*Universal director . . .* London, J. Coote, 1763.
Va	VALDRIGHI, Luigi Francesco. *Nomocheliurgografia antica e moderna, ossia elenco di fabbricatori di strumenti armonici . . .* [with 5 supplements]. Modena, Società Tipografica, 1884, etc. (Extracted from: *Memorie della Reale Accàdemia di Scienze, Lettere ed Arti di Modena, Sezione d'Arti*, Vol. 2, series 2.)
Vallas	VALLAS, Léon. *Un Siècle de musique et de théâtre à Lyon, 1688–1789.* Lyon, P. Manson, 1932.
V&A, MIWA	VICTORIA AND ALBERT MUSEUM. *Musical instruments as works of art.* London, HMSO, 1968.
Vannes	VANNES, René. *Dictionnaire universel des luthiers.* 2ᵉ édition. Bruxelles, Les Amis de la Musique, 1951. (Not of much use for keyboard instrument makers.)
VdB	*Hommage à Charles van den Borren.* Anvers, 1945.
VdM	VAN DER MEER, John Henry. Private communication.
VdMCemRuck	VAN DER MEER, John Henry. 'Beiträge zum Cembalo-Bau der Familie Ruckers'. *Jahrbuch des Staatlichen Instituts für Musikforschung*, 1971.
VdMDeu	VAN DER MEER, John Henry. 'Beiträge zum Cembalobau im deutschen Sprachgebiet bis 1700'. *Anzeiger des Germanischen Nationalmuseums*, Nürnberg, 1966, pp. 103–33.
VdMFläm	VAN DER MEER, John Henry. 'Flämische Cembali in italienischem Besitz'. *Studien zur italienisch-deutschen Musikgeschichte*, Vol. 3, 1966 [= *Analecta musicologica.* Köln, Graz, Böhlau-Verlag, Vol. 3, 1966], pp. 114–21.
VdMNeup	VAN DER MEER, John Henry. *Die Klavierhistorische Sammlung Neupert.* (Check-list. Nürnberg, ?1969.)
VdMPer	VAN DER MEER, John Henry. 'Per ogni sorte di strumenti da tasti'. *Tijdschrift van de Vereniging voor Nederlandse Muziekgeschiedenis*, Vol. 19, Amsterdam, 1961, pp. 67–79.
VdMRuck	VAN DER MEER, John Henry. 'Ruckers'. (Article from: *Musik in Geschichte und Gegenwart*, Vol. 11, cols. 1049–56.)
VdMSalzb	VAN DER MEER, John Henry. 'Die Kielklaviere in Salzburger Museum Carolino-Augusteum'. *Jahresschrift. Salzburger Museum Carolino-Augusteum*, Vols. 12/13, 1966/7, pp. 38–96.
VdMZeiss	VAN DER MEER, John Henry. 'Die Orgelklaviere von Valentin Zeiss, Linz'. *Kunstjahrbuch der Stadt Linz*, 1967, pp. 154–63.
VdS	STRAETEN, Edmond van der. *La Musique aux Pays Bas avant le 19ᵉ siècle.* Bruxelles, 1867–88. (8 volumes.) (Facsimile reprint: 8 vols in 4. New York, Dover Publications, 1969.)
Vente	VENTE, Maarten A. *Die Brabanter Orgel: zur Geschichte der Orgelkunst in Belgien und Holland . . .* Amsterdam, H. J. Paris, 1963.
Verhandeling	*Verhandeling over de muziek . . . als mede hoe men de klavier instrumenten tot volkommenheit kan brengen.* In's Gravenhage, bij Jan Abraham Bouvink, Boekverkooper op de Plaets, 1772. (Especially pp. 158–272.)
Verlet	SAMOYAULT-VERLET, Colombe. *Les Facteurs de clavecins parisiens: notices biographiques et documents (1550–1793).* Paris, Société Française de Musicologie, 1966.

Vlam VLAM, C. C. 'Leidse viool- en klavecimbelmakers in de 17. en 18. eeuw'. *Jaarboekje voor geschiedenis en oudheidkunde van Leiden en omstreken*, Vol. 60, Leiden, 1968.

VM *Vierteljahrsschrift für Musikwissenschaft*. Leipzig, [1885–94].

Wa WALTHER, Johann Gottfried. *Musikalisches Lexicon* . . . Leipzig. Wolffgang Deer, 1732. [Facsimile reprint: Kassel, Bärenreiter-Verlag, 1953 (*Documenta musicologica*, Ser. 1, no. 3).]

Wald WALDNER, Franz. 'Zwei Inventarien aus dem 16. und 17. Jahrhundert . . .' *Studien zur Musikwissenschaft*, Heft 4 (Gesellschaft zur Herausgebung von Denkmälern der Tonkunst in Oesterreich). Vienna, 1916. (The second inventory, dated 10 September 1665, records the musical effects of Siegmund Franz, Arch-Duke of Austria, who died in that year.)

Walter WALTER, Horst. 'Haydns Klaviere'. *Haydn-Studien*, Vol. 2, no. 4, Köln, 1970, pp. 256–88.

Wash 1927 DENSMORE, Frances. *Handbook of the collection of musical instruments in the U.S. National Museum* (Smithsonian Institution bulletin 136). Washington, 1927.

Wash 1967 SMITHSONIAN INSTITUTION. *A checklist of keyboard instruments* . . . Washington, 1967.

Wash 1969 HOOVER, Cynthia A. *Harpsichords and clavichords*. Washington, Smithsonian Institution Press, 1969.

Weck WECKERLIN, J. B. T. *Nouveau musiciana*. Paris, Garnier, 1890.

Wint 1956 WINTERNITZ, Emanuel. 'The Golden Harpsichord and Todini's Galleria Armonica'. *Metropolitan Museum of Art bulletin*, Vol. 15, no. 5, New York, February 1956, pp. 149–56.

Wint 1961 WINTERNITZ, Emanuel. *Keyboard instruments in the Metropolitan Museum of Art: a picture book*. New York, Metropolitan Museum of Art, 1961.

Wö WÖRSCHING, Joseph. *Die historischen Saitenklaviere und der moderne Clavichord- und Cembalo-Bau*. Mainz, Rheingold-Verlag, 1946.

Woodf WOODFILL, Walter L. *Musicians in English society from Elizabeth to Charles I*. Princeton University Press, 1953.

WVS *Württembergische Vierteljahrshefte für Landesgeschichte*. Stuttgart, 1878–1936. (Cont. as: *Zeitschrift für Württembergische Landesgeschichte*, 1937– .)

ZFM *Zeitschrift für Musikwissenschaft*. Leipzig, 1918–35. (Cont. as: *Archiv für Musikforschung*, 1936– .)

ZI *Zeitschrift für Instrumentenbau*. Leipzig, 1880– .

ZIM *Zeitschrift der Internationalen Musikgesellschaft*. Leipzig, 1900–14.

Zuck ZUCKERMANN, Wallace. Private communication.

Zuck 1969 ZUCKERMANN, Wolfgang Joachim [i.e. Wallace Zuckermann]. *The modern harpsichord: twentieth-century instruments and their makers*. New York, October House Inc., 1969; London, Peter Owen, 1970.

ADDENDA

A, F. The harpsichord recorded above, signed with these initials and dated 1677, is now (1973) owned by Stuart Gilbert, U.S.A.

CORTONA. This maker, recorded above, had Giuseppe as his Christian name. He worked for Cardinal Benedetto Pamphili (1653–1730).

CRISTOFORI, Bartolomeo. An unsigned *cembalo traverso*, i.e. large double-strung spinet, at the Smithsonian Institution, Washington, is now tentatively attributed to this maker.

FLEISCHER, Johann Christoph. The surname of the signature on the clavichord of 1729 recorded above under *Heinrich* is a misreading of *Fleischer* [*Thoene*]. The instrument therefore becomes Fleischer number 4.

GIUSTI, Giovanni Battista. His harpsichord recorded above as number 9a is inscribed on the nameboard *Io: Bapta: Iustus Lucen: Ferrar: MDCLXXIX*. Compass G–C without low G sharp. [*VdM*].

GUARRACINO, Honofrio. A rectangular virginal by him dated 1663 is owned by Professor L. F. Tagliavini at Bologna. Its compass is C–C with bass short octave. [*VdM*]. It becomes number O2a among the Guarracino instruments.

HAXBY, Thomas. *See below*: Tomlinson & Son.

Instrument number 2 now belongs to Thomas R. Byrd of Baltimore. Attached to the underside of the case is an envelope containing this statement: *May 3, 1855. Instrument number 23. Parlour harpsichord with stand. Maker Thomas Haxby, York 1766. Formerly belonged to Dr. Thomas Arne. Presented to me by Horatio Arne Reynolds, Esq. aged 81, a great nephew. Frederick Gore Ousely.*

HEINRICH, Johann Christoph. Heinrich is a misreading of Fleischer (q.v. above in these addenda). He, therefore, did not exist.

HEYER, Daniel. *Fl. c.* 1570–92 at Kassel. Organ builder who also made harpsichords [*Peter Williams* in *ML* vol. 52 (1971), p. 277].

KIRKMAN, Jakob. An unsigned but probably early Kirkman two-manual harpsichord is owned in Vienna by Jörg Demus, who acquired it from Wayland Dobson of Aix-en-Provence about 1967. It has 2×8′, 1×4′, lute and machine stops, and becomes Kirkman instrument number 105 [*Demus*].

A Kirkman spinet dated 1755 belongs (1973) to the Morristown National Historic Park, New Jersey, to whom it was given by the Colonial Dames of America in 1948. It becomes Kirkman instrument number 106a.

KROLL, Christian. A Kroll harpsichord dated 1774 was acquired in Lyons in 1973 by Michael Thomas for his collection at the Harpsichord Centre in London.

LINDHOLM, Pehr. Instrument 5a was bought on 8 March 1973 for Dr. and Mrs. Robert M. Rosenbaum, Scarsdale, N.Y.

MENDINI, Giuseppe. This maker, recorded above, worked for Cardinal Benedetto Pamphili (1653–1730).

PERTICI, Giovanni da. Instrument 2a is a harpsichord dated 1681 and belonging to Barbara Lambert of Boston, Mass. The nameboard (now missing) is reported to have been inscribed: *Ioannes de Perticis Florentinus Faciebat Anno MDCLXXXI*. But it may be the same instrument as number 2.

ROCHEAD, Andrew. A spinet by this maker, who is recorded above, is owned by Charles Wilson of King of Prussia, Penna. It is undated, but bears both on the front and on the back of the nameboard the inscription: *Andrew Rochead Edinburgh fecit*, in which the form of the surname suggests a dating of 1795 (see further *RussColl* p. 68, where several forms are quoted from the early issues of the *Edinburgh Post Office directory*).

This instrument was previously owned by a Mrs. Hubbard, of Albany, N.Y., who died in the early 1970s.

ROSENAU, Gottlieb. Michael Thomas obtained in 1973 for his collection a single-manual harpsichord dated (apparently) 1765 by this maker, who is recorded above.

TOMLINSON & SON. Edward, brother-in-law of Haxby, and Thomas, Haxby's nephew, succeeded to his business in York upon his death in 1796 (in spite of S. Knapton's claims). They had been assistants in his workshop for some time before, and carried on the business of making and selling a variety of instruments including the harpsichord.

Edward was born in 1738, married Elizabeth, daughter of Thomas Haxby, and died in 1813; Thomas, son of Edward, was born on 5 October 1768 and died on 7 May 1846.

INDEX

1. Signature of Louis Bellot on a harpsichord

2a. Name-batten on Tabel harpsichord

2b. Signature on key, Tabel harpsichord

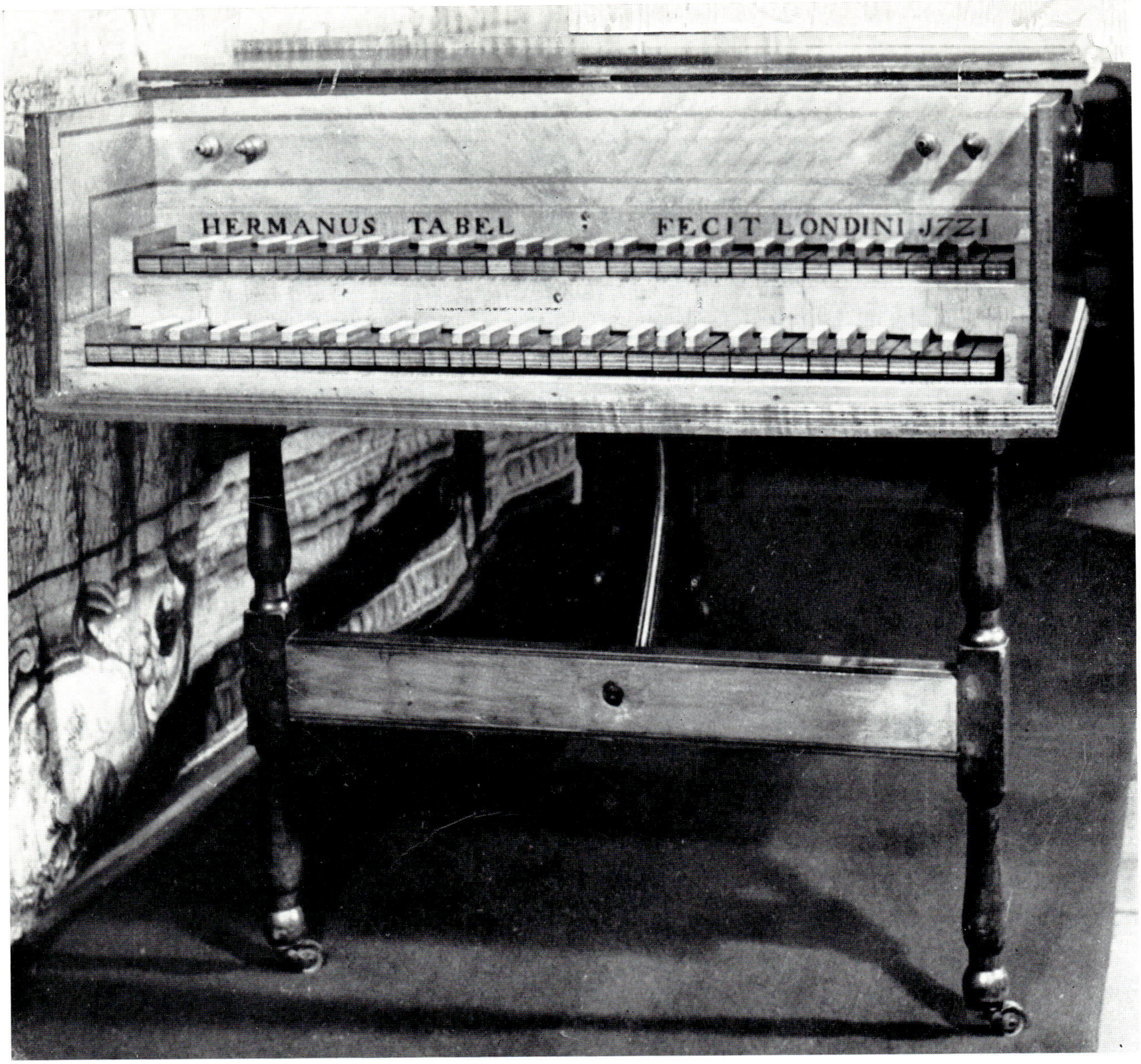

3. Tabel harpsichord, shewing name-batten

4. Nameboard of harpsichord by William Smith, London

5. Harpsichord by Jacob Kirkman, fitted with piano action by Merlin: Inscriptions

6. Nagshead swell on Kirkman harpsichord

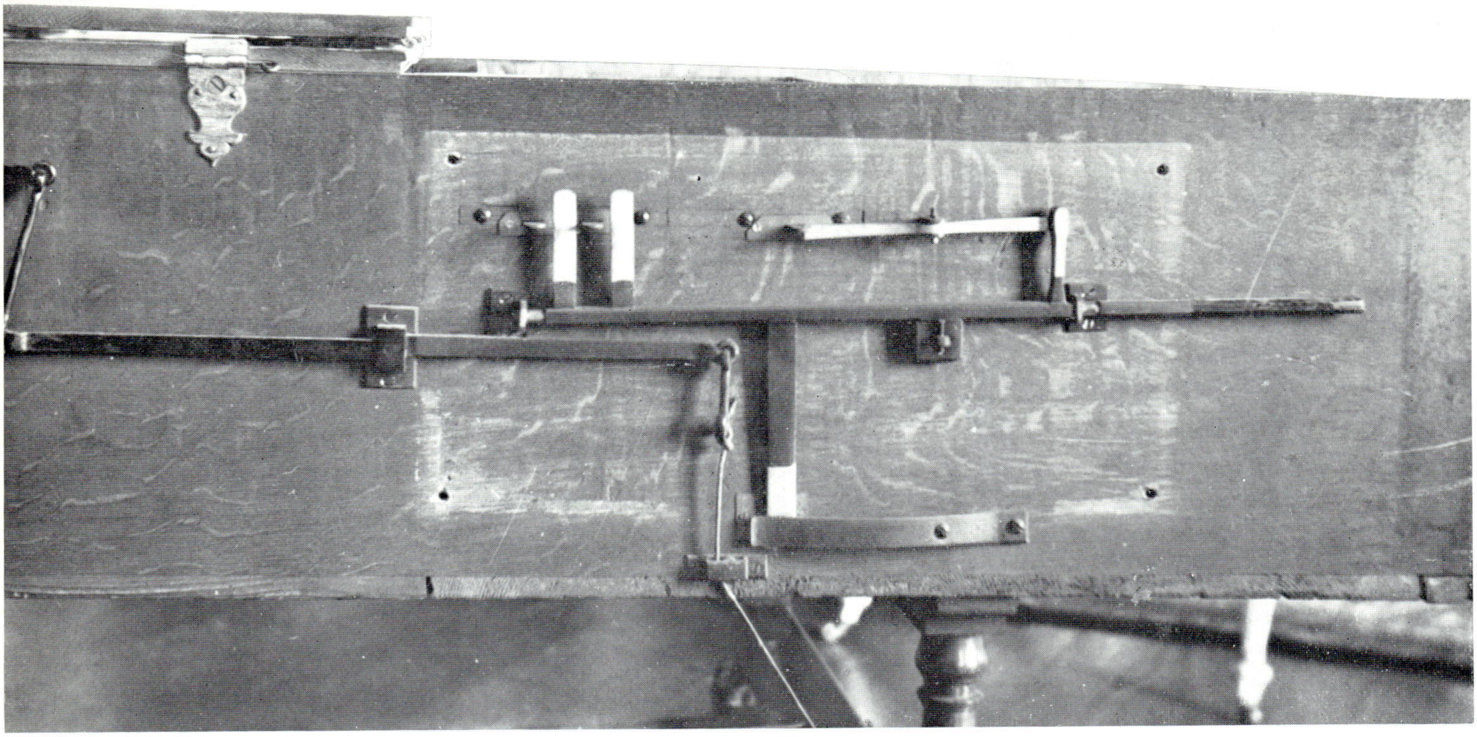

7. Machine stop on Kirkman harpsichord

8. Inscription on wrestplank of Thomas Barton spinet

9. Painting by Oswald Birley, dated 1913, showing Mrs. G. Crawley playing a harpsichord (Taskin no. 01)

10. Nameboard with the name of Vincentius, in a harpsichord

11*a*. Virginal by Body

11*b*. Jackrail of the above virginal

12. Nameboard of William Harris spinet

13. Inscription on combined harpsichord and piano by Robert Stodart, 1777

14*a*. Maker's signature on Kintzing clavichord

14*b*. Signatures, on documents, of Hans Ruckers and Jan Couchet

15*a*. Nameboard on spinet by Richard Vesey

15*b*. Nameboard on spinet by Thomas Hitchcock

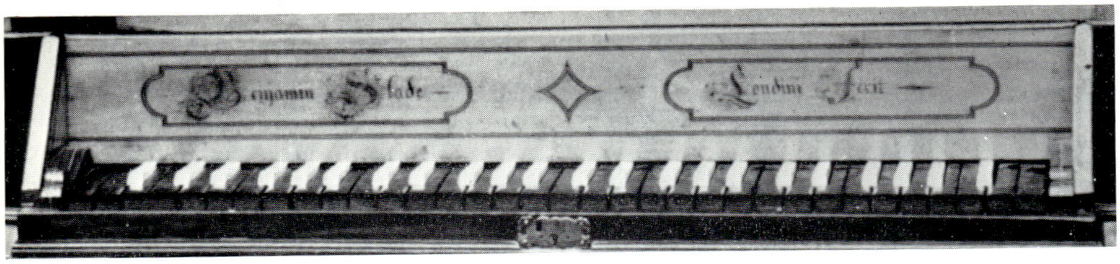

16*a*. Nameboard on spinet by Benjamin Slade

16*b*. Nameboard on spinet by John Harrison

17*a*. Nameboard on J. and A. Kirkman harpsichord

17*b*. Nameboard on Jacob Kirkman harpsichord

18*a*. Signature of Burkat Shudi the Elder, on the underside of the soundboard of harpsichord

18*b*. Restorer's signature of J. C. Fleischer on a Ruckers harpsichord

19. Zenti's name on two harpsichords

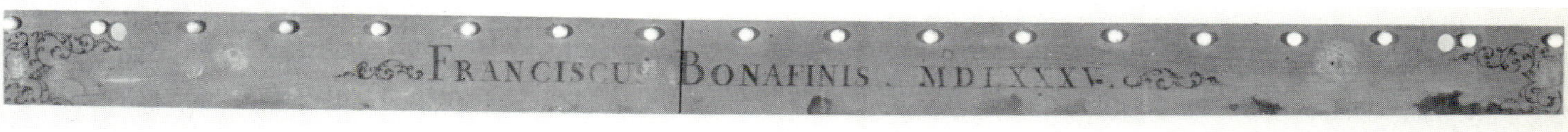

20. Name-batten on polygonal virginal by F. Bonafinis

21. Inscription on back of the name-batten above

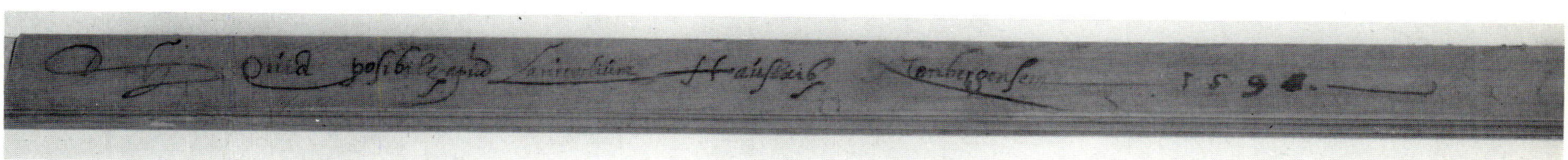

22. Inscribed jackrail of ottavino by Hauslaib

23. Maker's label on Hubert Clavichord

24. Maker's initials C. A. (Cawton Aston?) on key of a spinet

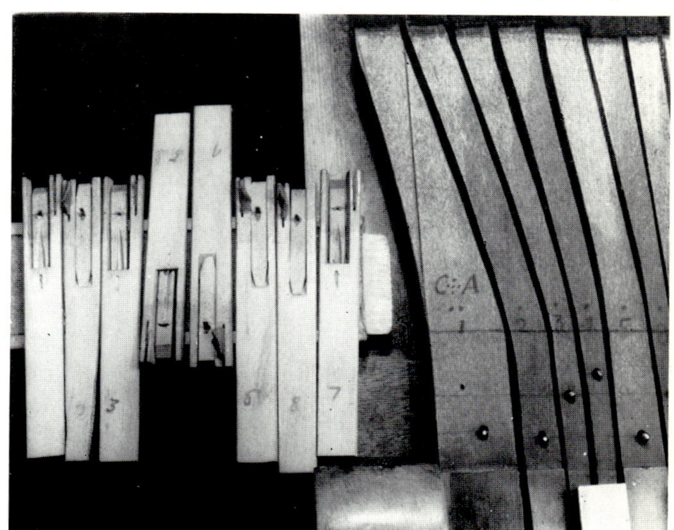

25. Maker's inscription on jackrail of virginal by Bos

26. Another inscription on the Bos virginal

27

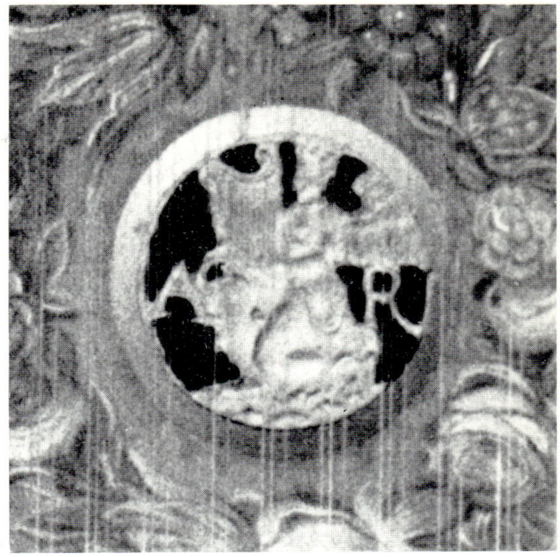

28

27. Rose in Hans Ruckers harpsichord
28. Rose in harpsichord by Andreas Ruckers the Younger
29. Rose with CR in a virginal, formerly attributed to Christoffel Ruckers, in Namur Museum
30. HB rose in Bos virginal
31. Rose in harpsichord by B. Stehlin, 1760

29

30

31

32

32. Rose with inscription in Louis Bellot harpsichord

33

33. Rose in double virginal by L. Grouwels

34

34. Rose in Kirkman harpsichord of 1761

35

35. Rose in Kirkman harpsichord

36

36. Rose in Tibaut harpsichord

37

37. Rose in Tabel harpsichord